THE MARK TWAIN PAPERS

THE MARK TWAIN PAPERS

The following volumes in this edition of
Mark Twain's previously unpublished works
have been issued to date:

MARK TWAIN'S
NOTEBOOKS
& JOURNALS

Frederick Anderson, General Editor

VOLUME III
(1883–1891)

Edited by Robert Pack Browning
Michael B. Frank
and Lin Salamo

UNIVERSITY OF CALIFORNIA PRESS
Berkeley, Los Angeles, London   1979

CENTER FOR EDITIONS OF
AMERICAN AUTHORS

AN APPROVED TEXT

MODERN LANGUAGE
ASSOCIATION OF AMERICA

®

Editorial expenses for this volume have been in large part
supported by grants from the National Endowment for the Humanities
of the National Foundation on the Arts and Humanities
administered through the Center for Editions of
American Authors of the Modern Language Association.

University of California Press
Berkeley and Los Angeles, California

University of California Press, Ltd.
London, England

© 1979 The Mark Twain Company
Library of Congress Catalog Card Number: 76–87199
ISBN: 0–520–03383–3

Designed by Adrian Wilson
in collaboration with James Mennick

Manufactured in the United States of America

49

Contents

Preface

VOLUME 3 of *Mark Twain's Notebooks & Journals* provides a continuous record of Samuel Clemens' activities in the years from 1883 to 1891. The first notebook in the volume picks up that record where the final notebook in volume 2 left off. Headnotes to the individual notebooks offer detailed summaries of the period.

The texts for the nine notebooks included in this volume have been prepared from the original documents in the Mark Twain Papers in The Bancroft Library at the University of California in Berkeley. A calendar of the forty-nine Mark Twain notebooks known to exist, with their dates, begins on page xix.

In order to avoid editorial misrepresentation and to preserve the texture of autograph documents, Clemens' entries are presented in their original, often unfinished, form with most of their irregularities, inconsistencies, errors, and cancellations unchanged. Clemens' cancellations are included in the text enclosed in angle brackets: ⟨word⟩; editorially-supplied conjectural readings are in square brackets: [word]; hyphens within square brackets stand for unreadable letters: [- -]; and editorial remarks are italicized and enclosed in square brackets: [*blank page*]. A slash separates alternative readings which Clemens left unresolved: word/word. The separation of entries is indicated on the printed page by extra space between lines; when the end of a manuscript entry coincides with the end of a page of the printed text, the symbol [#] follows the entry. The Textual Introduction, which accompanies the Textual Apparatus at the end of the volume (p. 651), provides a full discussion of textual procedures. When unusual situations warrant, specific textual problems are explained in headnotes or footnotes.

A series of documents encompassing Samuel Clemens' adult life, a life which ranged from Missouri villages to European capitals, must contain many references so obscure they cannot be annotated and many so well known their explanation would be redundant. Every effort has been made to recover the obscure and to anticipate the reader's need for information not available in standard books of reference. Much of the information in the notes has been assembled from unpublished sources or from sources not easily accessible. The list of abbreviations (pp. xv–xvii) serves as a bibliography of frequently cited publications.

The headnotes provide a general discussion of published material that Mark Twain derived from each notebook, but no attempt has been made to collate notebook entries with their development in literary form except when such reference is necessary for an understanding of an entry. Literary themes or topics which are not readily identifiable are annotated when it seems likely they might otherwise escape the reader's notice. But even these are treated selectively, with no attempt to identify each instance in which ideas for characters or episodes are reworked in the various phases of the author's writing. What appear to be tag lines for jokes persist throughout the notebooks. Variant repetitions when assembled sometimes provide the substance of the anecdote, but since the form and language of these stories were doubtless adjusted for the raconteur's audience, their full versions have been left to each reader's imagination.

A number of entries in this volume are in German. The footnotes provide translations of these entries in accord with Clemens' expressed view: "I have a prejudice against people who print things in a foreign language and add no translation. When I am the reader, and the author considers me able to do the translating myself, he pays me quite a nice compliment,—but if he would do the translating for me I would try to get along without the compliment" (*A Tramp Abroad,* chapter 16). The context of some of the short German entries—like that of the more elusive shorter entries in English—is lost, and without this context the German can sometimes yield several equally plausible readings. No effort has been made to present all the possible interpretations of ambiguous passages. The intention here has been to provide functional translations, more literal than literary.

When annotation can offer no useful information to document a troublesome entry, there is no statement of editorial failure. On one occasion Clemens himself remarked: "One often finds notes in his book which no longer convey a meaning—they were texts, but you forget what you were going to say under them" (*N&J2*, p. 259). Later editors can seldom be more successful than the original inscriber in recovering the intention behind such entries.

Acknowledgments

Among the researchers and editors employed in the Mark Twain Papers, Victor Fischer, Alan Gribben, John McBrearty, Paul Machlis, Robert Nordlie, Harriet Elinor Smith, and Bernard L. Stein made important contributions toward establishing the text and developing the annotation of this volume. Carolyn Duffy and Marie Herold patiently typed the various stages of text, apparatus, footnotes, and headnotes.

Aija Kanbergs carefully reviewed and revised the German translations.

Diana Royce of the Nook Farm Research Library in Hartford generously provided information and materials upon request.

The staff of the Photographic Service of the University of California Library took pains to produce the clearest possible illustrations from sometimes obscure originals.

The Hinman collator used in checking and rechecking the final stages of proof was made available through the generosity of William P. Barlow, Jr.

As he had for the two preceding volumes of Mark Twain's notebooks, Don L. Cook offered valuable observations and suggestions while examining this volume for the seal of the Center for Editions of American Authors.

The project has been supported by the financial aid of the University of California and of the Samuel Charles Webster Memorial Fund, made available through the generous bequest of Mrs. Webster. The National Endowment for the Humanities, through the Center for Editions of American Authors under the directorship of Matthew J. Bruccoli, has supplied necessary grants in support of the preparation of the text for this volume.

Abbreviations

THE FOLLOWING abbreviations have been used for citations in this volume. Unless otherwise indicated, all materials quoted in the documentation are transcribed from originals in the Mark Twain Papers, The Bancroft Library, University of California, Berkeley.

Berg   Henry W. and Albert A. Berg Collection, New York Public Library.

CLW   Charles L. Webster

Doheny   Edward L. Doheny Memorial Library, Saint John's Seminary, Camarillo, Calif.

DV   Prefix designating literary manuscripts in the Mark Twain Papers.

MS   Manuscript

MTM   Mark Twain Memorial, Hartford, Conn.

MTP   Mark Twain Papers, The Bancroft Library, University of California, Berkeley.

OLC   Olivia Langdon Clemens

PH   Photocopy

SLC   Samuel L. Clemens

TS   Typescript

Yale   Collection of American Literature, Beinecke Rare Book
                and Manuscript Library, Yale University, New Haven,
                Conn.

Published Works Cited

Geer's   *Geer's Hartford City Directory* (Hartford: Hartford
                Printing Co.). Published annually.

HH&T   *Mark Twain's Hannibal, Huck & Tom*, ed. Walter
                Blair (Berkeley and Los Angeles: University of Cali-
                fornia Press, 1969).

LLMT   *The Love Letters of Mark Twain*, ed. Dixon Wecter
                (New York: Harper & Brothers, 1949).

MTA   *Mark Twain's Autobiography*, ed. Albert Bigelow Paine,
                2 vols. (New York: Harper & Brothers, 1924).

MTB   Albert Bigelow Paine, *Mark Twain: A Biography* (New
                York: Harper & Brothers, 1912).

MTBus   *Mark Twain, Business Man*, ed. Samuel C. Webster
                (Boston: Little, Brown and Co., 1946).

MTE   *Mark Twain in Eruption*, ed. Bernard DeVoto (New
                York: Harper & Brothers, 1940).

MT&GWC   Arlin Turner, *Mark Twain and G. W. Cable* (East
                Lansing: Michigan State University Press, 1960).

MTHL   *Mark Twain-Howells Letters*, ed. Henry Nash Smith
                and William M. Gibson (Cambridge: Harvard Univer-
                sity Press, Belknap Press, 1960).

MTL   *Mark Twain's Letters*, ed. Albert Bigelow Paine (New
                York: Harper & Brothers, 1917).

MTLP   *Mark Twain's Letters to His Publishers*, ed. Hamlin
                Hill (Berkeley and Los Angeles: University of Cali-
                fornia Press, 1967).

MTMF   *Mark Twain to Mrs. Fairbanks*, ed. Dixon Wecter (San
                Marino, Calif.: Huntington Library, 1949).

MTS(1910) *Mark Twain's Speeches,* ed. Albert Bigelow Paine (New York: Harper & Brothers, 1910).

MTS(1923) *Mark Twain's Speeches,* ed. Albert Bigelow Paine (New York: Harper & Brothers, 1923).

N&J1 *Mark Twain's Notebooks & Journals, Volume I (1855–1873),* ed. Frederick Anderson, Michael B. Frank, and Kenneth M. Sanderson (Berkeley, Los Angeles, and London: University of California Press, 1975).

N&J2 *Mark Twain's Notebooks & Journals, Volume II (1877–1883),* ed. Frederick Anderson, Lin Salamo, and Bernard L. Stein (Berkeley, Los Angeles, and London: University of California Press, 1975).

S&MT Edith Colgate Salsbury, *Susy and Mark Twain* (New York: Harper & Row, 1965).

WWD *Mark Twain's Which Was the Dream? and Other Symbolic Writings of the Later Years,* ed. John S. Tuckey (Berkeley and Los Angeles: University of California Press, 1966).

Calendar

IN AN EFFORT to clarify the numbering of the notebooks, a new sequence has been substituted for that originally used for the typescripts in the files of the Mark Twain Papers. Since the typescript numbers have been frequently cited in print, this calendar lists both the previous and the present numbering systems.

The calendar gives the inclusive dates for each of the notebooks published in this and the two previous volumes and provisional dates, in brackets, for notebooks to be published in forthcoming volumes. The dating comes from references made by Clemens and from internal evidence when there is no specific notation of a beginning or a terminal date. The exact days when Clemens started or finished many of the notebooks have been determined, but many others can be dated only by month or season. A notebook's dates are listed here only by month, when known, and year. The headnotes discuss in more detail the period of each notebook's use.

Notebooks in Volume I

No.	FORMER No.	DATE	LOCATION
1	1A	June–July 1855	Missouri, Iowa
2	1	April–July 1857	Mississippi River
3	2	November 1860–March 1861	Mississippi River
4	3	January–February 1865	California
5	4	March, June–September 1866	San Francisco, Sandwich Islands

6	5	March–April 1866	San Francisco, Sandwich Islands
7	6	December 1866–January 1867	San Francisco to New York City
8	7	May–June 1867	New York City, *Quaker City*
9	8	August–October 1867	*Quaker City*
10	9	August–December 1867	*Quaker City*, Washington, D.C.
11	10	July 1868	San Francisco to New York City
12	10A	June–July 1873	England, Belgium

Notebooks in Volume II

No.	FORMER No.	DATE	LOCATION
13	11	May–July 1877	New York City, Bermuda
14	12	November 1877–July 1878	Germany
15	12A	July–August 1878	Switzerland
16	12B	August–October 1878	Switzerland, Italy
17	13	October 1878–February 1879	Italy, Munich
18	14	February–September 1879	Paris, Belgium, Holland, England
19	15	July 1880–January 1882	Hartford, Canada
20	16	January 1882–February 1883	Hartford, Mississippi River, Elmira
21	16A	April–May 1882	Mississippi River

Notebooks in Volume III

No.	FORMER No.	DATE	LOCATION
22	17	Spring 1883–September 1884	Hartford
23	18	September 1884–April 1885	Hartford, Lecture Circuit

24	19	April–August 1885	Hartford
25	20	August 1885–March 1886	Hartford
26	21	March 1886–June 1887	Hartford
27	22	August 1887–July 1888	Hartford
28	23	July 1888–May 1889	Hartford
29	24	May 1889–August 1890	Hartford
30	25	August 1890–June 1891	Hartford

Forthcoming Notebooks

No.	FORMER No.	DATE
31	26	[August 1891–July 1892]
32	26A	[May 1892–January 1893]
33	27	[March 1893–July 1894]
34	28	[March–December 1895]
35	28A	[May–October 1895]
36	28B	[December 1895–March 1896]
37	29	[January–April 1896]
38	30	[May–July 1896]
39	31	[September 1896–January 1897]
40	32	[January 1897–July 1899]
41	32A	[January–July 1897]
42	32B	[June 1897–March 1900]
43	33	[1900]
44	34	[1901]
45	35	[1902]
46	36	[1903–1904]
47	37	[1904]
48	38	[1905–1908]
49	39	[1910]

XXII

"I Must Speculate in Something"

(Spring 1883–September 1884)

A NUMBER of entries at the beginning of Notebook 22—addresses, notes on
stock investments, and business memoranda—cannot be precisely dated, but
it seems likely that Clemens began using this notebook in the spring of 1883.
He continued to use it until September 1884.

During the period of the notebook's use Clemens was involved in a great
number of literary and business projects, the majority of which were not
markedly successful. Many of the literary projects survived only as isolated
entries in the notebook; others were begun and then abandoned. Still other
story ideas would not be fully developed for many years. During this period
Clemens was constantly being distracted from his writing by investment
schemes and speculations. As he explained to Howells: "I must speculate
in something, such being my nature" (22 August 1883, *MTHL*, p. 439). Thus
in 1883 and 1884 he committed himself more and more to the Paige typesetter, lost thousands of dollars in marginal stock transactions, and wasted
weeks of effort on his abortive inventions—the history game, a perpetual calendar, and an improved bed clamp. In addition he involved Charles L. Webster, as his business agent, in endless investigations of investment possibilities.
These included a scheme presented to him by William Dean Howells for the

1

manufacture of some patent grape shears invented by Howells' father and, from a California group, a scheme to profit from the burgeoning California wine industry by underwriting a new vineyard.

Clemens' money-making ambitions did not limit themselves to purely business matters; with Howells, he embarked on a kind of literary speculation as well, returning to his earlier dream of making a fortune in the theater. Howells, a moderately successful playwright, was as enthusiastic as Clemens, predicting that if they let themselves "loose on the drama" they could "write a pile of plays" (Howells to SLC, 9 January 1884, *MTHL*, p. 463). Howells' tactfulness and good nature made him an easier collaborator than Bret Harte, whose friendship with Clemens had ended acrimoniously as a result of their collaboration on *Ah Sin* in 1877. In 1883 and 1884 Clemens and Howells discussed some half-dozen play possibilities. By the end of 1883 they had written one complete script, *Colonel Sellers as a Scientist*. After months of negotiating with producers and actors, Clemens and Howells shelved the preposterous farce. "Never mind about the play," Howells wrote to Clemens, "we had fun writing it, anyway" (15 September 1884, *MTHL*, p. 507).

While Notebook 22 touches on many literary involvements, the two major projects of this period—the publication of *Life on the Mississippi* and the completion of *Huckleberry Finn*—are scarcely mentioned.

Early in 1883 Clemens completed *Life on the Mississippi*. The book was scheduled for publication in May 1883, the sale to be by subscription through James R. Osgood & Company. Because of Osgood's lack of experience in the subscription field Clemens took a strong role in publication decisions: he installed Charles L. Webster as New York agent for subscription sales, and Webster found himself in the uncomfortable position of having to relay Clemens' commands to Osgood. "Charley, if there are any instructions to be given, you may give them," Clemens had written on 3 January 1883. "I will not interest myself in *any*thing connected with this wretched God-damned book" (*MTBus*, p. 207). But Clemens soon forgot this resolution and intervened directly concerning what he considered a crucial issue—the importance of advance sales, a subject on which Osgood was politely skeptical. "The big sale is always before the issue," Clemens wrote Osgood on 17 April, "after issue, the agents immediately load up the bookstores and canvassing ceases. . . . *The orders that come in after the ISSUE of a subscription book don't amount to a damn*—just write that up amongst your moral maxims; for it is truer than nearly anything in the Bible" (*MTLP*, pp. 162–163).

In the second week of May 1883 Clemens and Osgood went to Canada to establish Canadian copyright on the new book, which was issued on 12 May in

England by Chatto & Windus; it appeared in the United States about 17 May. Clemens hurried back to Canada alone in the last week of May for a visit with the marquis of Lorne and Princess Louise at Rideau Hall in Ottawa. Two weeks later Clemens and his family were settled at Quarry Farm for the summer and Clemens was soon immersed in a welter of projects, among them the completion of *Huckleberry Finn*.

Clemens had begun *Huckleberry Finn* in 1876 and worked on it intermittently until the summer of 1883 when he began the final chapters. He wrote to his mother and family on 21 July 1883 from Quarry Farm: "I haven't had such booming working-days for many years. I am piling up manuscript in a really astonishing way. I believe I shall complete, in two months, a book which I have been fooling over for 7 years. This summer it is no more trouble to me to write than it is to lie" (*MTL*, p. 434). At the end of the summer Clemens wrote to Howells with satisfaction: "I'm done work, for this season. . . . I've done two seasons' work in one, & haven't anything left to do, now, but revise. I've written eight or nine hundred MS pages in such a brief space of time that I mustn't name the number of days" (22 August 1883, *MTHL*, p. 438). Not all of the productions of that busy summer were as notable as *Huckleberry Finn*: he gave equal time to one of his dullest burlesques, the "1,002^{d} Arabian Night," and to the invention of his history game.

Meanwhile, *Life on the Mississippi* had drawn mixed reactions. Two of the early reviews present the extremes of critical opinion. Lafcadio Hearn in the New Orleans *Times-Democrat* of 30 May 1883 was enthusiastic, praising Mark Twain's graphic recreation of bygone and fast-dying Mississippi River life and hailing it as the "most solid book that Mark Twain has written" (*Mark Twain: The Critical Heritage*, ed. Frederick Anderson [New York: Barnes & Noble, 1971], p. 110). An unsigned review of the English edition in the *Athenaeum* of 2 June 1883 was less kind: the book is labeled a "disappointment," its binding "vulgar," the new chapters (chapters four through seventeen were substantially composed of Mark Twain's 1875 *Atlantic Monthly* series, "Old Times on the Mississippi") are "mere reporting" padded out with "superfluous" statistics (*Critical Heritage*, pp. 113, 114, 116).

Of more concern to Clemens than the disagreement of the critics was the sluggish sale of the book. The advance sales had been minimal despite Clemens' admonitions. By the end of 1883 only about 30,000 copies had been sold and Clemens was keenly disappointed. He wrote to Osgood on 21 December 1883: "The Prince and Pauper [also issued by Osgood] and the Mississippi are the only books of mine which have ever failed. The first failure was not unbearable—but this second one is so nearly so that it is not a calming subject for me to talk upon. . . . I have never for a moment doubted that you did the very best you knew how . . . but there were things about the publishing of *my* books which you did not understand. You understand them now, but it is I who have paid the costs of the apprenticeship" (*MTLP*, pp. 164–165).

For once Clemens was charitable in his assessment of a business associate. His letters to Osgood in the winter of 1883/1884 were unusually restrained and the friendship survived the rupture of business relations. Clemens later recalled: "Osgood was one of the dearest and sweetest and loveliest human beings to be found on the planet anywhere, but he knew nothing about subscription publishing and he made a mighty botch of it" (*MTE*, p. 157).

Clemens' dissatisfaction with Osgood's management of *Life on the Mississippi* left him temporarily undecided about the publication of *Huckleberry Finn*. He briefly considered returning to the American Publishing Company with the book. Early in 1884 the connection with James R. Osgood & Company was severed and the issue was decided: Clemens would publish the book himself. The foundation was laid for the establishment of Clemens' own publishing house, Charles L. Webster & Company.

At the beginning of 1884 Clemens was immersed in a new project—the writing of a novel laid in the Sandwich Islands. He wrote to Howells on 7 January: "My billiard table is stacked up with books relating to the Sandwich Islands; the walls are upholstered with scraps of paper penciled with notes drawn from them. I have saturated myself with knowledge of that unimaginably beautiful land & that most strange & fascinating people. And I have begun a story" (*MTHL*, p. 460). Clemens wrote to Mrs. Fairbanks on 24 January that he had finished the "book" and was revising it (*MTMF*, p. 255), a statement which is hardly credible: he could scarcely have accumulated such a mass of manuscript in slightly more than two weeks. In any event little trace of the Sandwich Islands novel remains. Clemens seems to have abandoned it by the end of January and turned to other projects. On 13 February he informed Howells: "I believe this is my first idle day in 4 weeks. In that time I have written one 4-act play, & 2½ acts of another" (*MTHL*, p. 471), referring to his dramatizations of *Tom Sawyer* (published in *HH&T*, pp. 258–324) and *The Prince and the Pauper*, neither of which was ever produced. The aborted Sandwich Islands novel and the two undistinguished plays were followed in May by a humorous piece, "Taming the

Bicycle," which Clemens found so unsatisfactory that he pigeonholed it indefinitely. In July he started on a new book, the adventures of "Huck Finn & Tom Sawyer among the Indians 40 or 50 years ago" (SLC to Howells, 15 July 1884, *MTHL*, p. 496); it was never completed (published in *HH&T*, pp. 92–140). The "booming working-days" of the previous summer were not repeated. On 1 September Clemens wrote to Charles L. Webster ruefully: "This is the first summer which I have lost. I haven't a paragraph to show for my 3-months' working-season" (*MTBus*, p. 274).

Clemens' literary failure in 1884 was due at least in part to a series of illnesses, and the demands of business and social matters. At the beginning of the year George Washington Cable came to Hartford for a one-day reading engagement and remained at the Clemens house for almost three weeks suffering from what appears to have been mumps. The disease then attacked the Clemens children. In March Clemens was struck down by "an unspeakable cold in the head" (SLC to Howells, 13 March 1884, *MTHL*, p. 478), followed in April by an attack of gout (SLC to Howells, 8 April 1884, *MTHL*, p. 483). Part of the summer was spent "in the dental chair" having his teeth "gouged out & stuffed" (SLC to Howells, 15 July 1884, *MTHL*, pp. 495–496) and "several more weeks" of the summer were occupied by daily trips to the doctor, Clemens told Twichell later, "to be treated for catarrh & have my palate burnt off" (16 September 1884, Yale).

Another nagging concern during this period was the future of Clemens' protégé, the sculptor Karl Gerhardt. Clemens had been supporting Gerhardt and his wife since February 1881. Their original agreement had been that Clemens would underwrite a five-year course of study in Paris at an expense of three thousand dollars. The high prices in Paris and the birth of a daughter, Olivia, in March 1883 made the Gerhardts' expenses considerably exceed the original estimates. Even with Clemens' addition of fifteen hundred dollars to the first sum, Gerhardt's Paris stay had to be shortened to three and a half years. By the beginning of 1884, with his return to America just a few months away, Gerhardt was despondent: the commissions he had counted on getting in Paris had not materialized and he was no closer to repaying Clemens and supporting his own family.

Meanwhile Clemens was also distracted by business matters. The dissolution of relations with James R. Osgood & Company and the establishment of a publishing house under the management of Charles L. Webster required months of discussion and maneuvering. Clemens was further preoccupied with plans for his 1884/1885 winter lecture tour with George Washington

Cable, a tour which would take them through New England and the Midwest. By September 1884 Clemens was harried and irritable. On 1 September he responded to Charles Webster's queries on business matters: "It is not my function to help arrive at conclusions in business matters. The thing should not be submitted to me except in a completed and determined form—then my function comes in: and it is merely and solely to *approve* or *disapprove*. . . . I have no diplomacy in my own nature," he explained, "and you don't suggest any to me. Try to remember that I fly off the handle altogether too easily, and that you want to think twice before you send me irritating news" (*MTLP*, p. 179).

All nine notebooks presented in this volume are of the type designed by Clemens and custom-made for him with a small tab projecting from the upper outside corner of each leaf. The tabs were meant to be torn off one at a time as each pair of facing pages was filled, so that by grasping the remaining tabs when opening the notebook the user could turn automatically to the next fresh page. Between 1878 and 1896 Clemens used at least twenty notebooks of this type, and he is known to have given at least one blank notebook away (see p. 85, note 58). Clemens had the notebooks made up in batches. Notebooks 22 through 28 are from one such batch, and Notebooks 29 through 36 are from another.

Notebook 22 originally contained ninety-two leaves of unlined white wove paper watermarked "WESTON'S LINEN RECORD 1883" and tinted red on the edges. The leaves measure 6½ by 3¾ inches (16.5 by 9.5 centimeters) exclusive of the tabs, which measure 2¹⁄₁₆ by ¼ inches (2.7 by .6 centimeters). The endpapers and outer sides of the flyleaves are marbled red, blue, cream, orange, and green, with the colors combed horizontally, while the inner sides of the flyleaves are lined with the same paper used in the body of the notebook. The covers are pliable reddish brown leather with blind-tooled borders, and their upper outside corners project to conform to the shape of the tabbed leaves. The front cover is stamped in gold, "MARK TWAIN, Hartford, Conn."

The notebook now contains 166 pages, twenty-five of them blank. Nine leaves and portions of three others have been torn out and are missing. Two leaves whose conjugate halves have been torn out are detached from the binding but remain in place. Except for several pages and scattered entries in blue and grayish blue ink, and a few notes in brownish black ink, the notebook is inscribed in black pencil. Use marks in black pencil, probably made by Paine, appear throughout but have not been reproduced. A short newspaper clipping of a humorous anecdote is pasted in the notebook at 30.14–18. Another short clipping accompanying the notebook is discussed in note 126 (p. 57).

302 Beacon st.[1]

		Pays[2]	
Bk Note	cost 105—	8 p.c	Am. Bk. Note Co.[3] certif. 1701, 20 shs ($1000) . . . . $1000. Ditto 1740 (80 shs) 4,000
N.Y. Cent.	″ 130½	8 ″	N.Y. Central 50 shs (A31929) 5,000
⟨Ad's Ex	″ 142	8 ″⟩	⟨Adams Express (9261) 50 shs . . . . 5,000⟩
Norfolk	″ 105	7 ″	Norfolk & Western Bds, 325,–6,–7, 1618–19, ... 5,000

[1] William Dean Howells wrote Clemens on 10 August 1884: "I've got a mighty pretty house here on the water side of Beacon St." (*MTHL*, p. 499). Howells had purchased the Boston house in July and had it renovated. He did not supply Clemens with his exact address until 15 September 1884 (*MTHL*, p. 507). This entry and the following entries through "Old China . . . Fulton" (11.9) were written on the initial pages of the notebook at various times during the period of the notebook's use.

[2] Clemens' list of stock investments is written in two sections on facing pages. The left side of the list (all the items below and to the left of *"Pays"*) is on left-hand pages and is written in pencil. The right side of the list (beginning "Am. Bk. Note Co.") is on right-hand pages and is written in blue ink with some pencil revisions. The section on the right was probably copied from an almost identical list in Notebook 20 (*N&J2*, p. 491), and the items on the left were probably added later.

[3] Clemens invested in American Bank Note stock and in the American Exchange in Europe at the suggestion of his Hartford banker and broker George P. Bissell. In February 1885 Clemens received an anxious inquiry from a clergyman who had been persuaded by

		Pays	
Little Rck	cost 105	7 p.c	Little Rock M R & T.
			Bds 1530–1–2–3–4 5,000
			N Y. Vaporizing Co
			(worthless) 5,000
⟨H. Eng. Co.	" 150⟩		⟨Hartford Engineering
			Co, 145 shs ⟨1,4500⟩14,500⟩
Am Ex in E	" 100—	6 "	Am. Ex in Europe 500
			shs 24001 to 24500 . . . 5,000
Conn. Fire	" 142,	10 "	Conn. Fire Ins. 12 shs
			(No 1515) . . . . 1,200.
Jewell—	" 100—	6 "	Jewell Pin Co 15ˢʰ
			(No 19) 1,500
			⟨Farnham Type-Setter
			Co⁴ 120 shs
			(No. 6) . . . . ⟨3⟩5,000⟩
Crown Pt.	" 106—	10 "	Crown Pt Iron Co (No.
			339), 100 shs 10,000
			Hartford Sanitary
			Plumbing Co, 40. shs 1,000
			⟨Ind. Watch Co.
			Howard Bros. Note in
			J L & Co hands due
			Sept 1883 . . . . 3,600⟩⁵

Bissell to buy the Bank Note Company stock on the premise that a stock subscribed to by such a "shrewd" investor as Clemens must be profitable (J. Chipchase to SLC, 23 February 1885). Clemens' reply was characteristic: "Bissell was premature in calling me a 'shrewd man.' I wasn't one at that time, but am one now—that is, I am at least too shrewd to ever again invest in anything put on the market by George P. Bissell & Co., of Hartford, Conn. I know nothing whatever about the Bank Note Co., & never did know anything about it. . . . [Bissell] sold me $10,000 worth of another rose-tinted stock [the American Exchange in Europe stock] about the same time. I have got that yet, also. I judge that a peculiarity of Bissell's stocks is that they are of the staying kind" (SLC to J. Chipchase, 2 March 1885).

⁴ The Farnham Type-Setter Manufacturing Company of Hartford was sponsoring James W. Paige's development of his delicate and complicated typesetter, later to become a major Clemens investment.

⁵ In the spring of 1881 Charles L. Webster had traveled to Hartford and persuaded Clemens to buy stock in the Howard brothers' Fredonia, New York, watchmaking company. The watch company proved to be a swindle and in September 1882 Webster forced

Pays

St. Paul R M Co.	110—	10 p.c.	St Paul Roller Mill stk	5,000
			New stk Am Ex in Europe (⟨½⟩ all paid up)	5,000
Metford	cost 125—	8	Metford (100 shs) (cost)	3,125
Burr—	" 100		Burr Index Co.	2,500
			200 shs Beech Creek Clearfield & S. W. RR Co	$10,000
			(part paid up.	

⟨Engineering Co note for $10,000.⟩
300 Western Union Tel—7 (cost $18,000.
⟨200 Union Pacif (7) cost 39¼ ($8,000)⟩

15 Grande rue Grande
   Montrouge
      France[6]

R. G. Brooks[7]
80 Broadway

All the Amer. Ex. in Europe stock was "put up" as security with Geo. P. Bissell & Co in May '84.

Gustav ⟨St[o]⟩Stechert   German books
B'way bet 8 & 9[th.] [#]

---

the Howards to sign a note, with a one-year due date, for the amount of Clemens' investment. Clemens wrote Webster on 19 September 1882: "You did miraculously with the Watch thieves. . . . I have put the note & the accompanying paper in J L & Co's safe [J. Langdon & Company, the coal firm founded by Livy's father]" (*MTBus*, p. 199). Clemens' cancellation of this notebook entry probably indicates that the note was paid as promised.

[6] Because of the serious illness of their infant daughter Olivia, the Karl Gerhardts had moved temporarily to this address, "a cheap lodging just out of the [Paris] city gates where the air is pure" (Karl Gerhardt to SLC, 24 February 1884).

[7] Clemens asked Charles L. Webster to send a copy of *The Prince and the Pauper* to "Mrs. H. G. Brooks, care of Remsen Brooks, 80 Broadway" (SLC to CLW, 24 May 1884, *MTBus*, p. 256). Mrs. Brooks and her son Remsen were old friends of the Langdon family (*MTBus*, p. 104).

Schwarz, 42 E 14[8]

Dean Sage 142 Pearl out of Wall

East India House, WH Davis & Co[9]
    56 Summer st Boston

Hutton, 229 W 34[th][10]

Addresses.

CL. Webster, 418 W. 57th & 658 B'way.[11]

No. 603 Safe Dep. box.

($\langle$S$\rangle$Century, \$33.[50] per page, 13½ p. \$450.[12] [#]

---

[8] The Clemens family often made purchases at F. A. O. Schwarz, the New York importers of toys and specialties.

[9] "Old china & things" (11.9), interlined above "Parke 186 Front st" on the next page of the notebook, stands directly opposite "W H Davis & Co" across the notebook's hinge and may have been meant to describe the merchandise of both firms.

[10] Clemens' introduction to critic and essayist Laurence Hutton was probably recent, perhaps a consequence of Hutton's friendship with James R. Osgood. Beginning in 1883 the two authors met fairly often, sharing a large circle of New York friends and associations. Clemens was a guest at Hutton's home at least once in 1883: in March, the Kinsmen, an informal club restricted to actors, artists, and writers, met at the house for dinner, Clemens attending as a new member and as Hutton's guest (*Talks in a Library with Laurence Hutton*, recorded by Isabel Moore [New York: G. P. Putnam's Sons, 1909], p. 326).

[11] Clemens notes Charles L. Webster's home address and his new business address. Webster's move to the Broadway office in the winter of 1882/1883 marked a new stage in his career with Clemens, for in addition to his duties as Clemens' personal business agent he now became "General Agent for Mark Twain's Books." Clemens had written to Osgood, who was preparing for the publication of *Life on the Mississippi*, on 18 October 1882: "I would like [Webster] to take pretty full charge of the matter of running the book, if this will disadvantage you in no way" (*MTLP*, p. 158). Osgood, who had had little experience in subscription publishing, gladly endorsed Webster as the New York agent for subscription sales.

[12] Clemens entered the same information on the *Century's* rates of payment in Notebook 20 (*N&J2*, p. 437). He did not publish anything in the magazine between November 1881 and December 1884 when the first of three selections from the forthcoming *Huckleberry Finn* appeared. Richard Watson Gilder, editor of the *Century*, responded to Clemens' query about payment for the *Huckleberry Finn* excerpts on 11 October 1884, suggesting a "lump price \$400—or \$30 a page," the same payment which Clemens had received for his first sketch in the *Century*, "A Curious Experience," published in November 1881.

Karl Gerhardt, 11 rue Boissonade[13]

Osgood, 30 St James Avenue.[14]

D^r. Geo. MacDonald,
 % A P Watt, 34 Paternoster Row[15]

Dean Sage, New No.
 839 St. Mark's ave.

214 W. 125. (Webster.)[16]

Gen Grant, 3, E. 66th.[17]

Old china & things   Parke 186 Front st, ⟨w⟩ sw of Fulton

J H Carter, Post Dispatch, St L[18]
Mrs. Jno. Ford, Campbell (?) N.Y.
Geo. MacDonald,

---

[13] The rue Boissonade atelier had been the Gerhardts' Paris mailing address since August 1882. The couple usually lived in the studio-apartment but occasionally rented temporary quarters elsewhere (see note 6).

[14] This is probably the address in London where Osgood spent the summer of 1883.

[15] Scottish clergyman and author George MacDonald, acquainted with Clemens and his family since 1873 (see N&J1, pp. 564, 570), had written to Clemens on 16 February 1883 with a literary scheme: he proposed that Clemens should write some small sections into his current book, *Donal Grant*, and that both authors' names should appear on the title page, thereby insuring MacDonald's American copyright. In his reply of 9 March Clemens tactfully declined the collaboration, tempering his refusal with the statement that were it not for the press of his own work and his uncertainty about the success of collaborative efforts, he would certainly enjoy writing "the Great Scottish-American novel" with MacDonald, "each doing his full half." In the same letter Clemens promised to send MacDonald a copy of *Life on the Mississippi* in care of MacDonald's literary agent, A. P. Watt.

[16] Charles L. Webster and his family moved from 418 West 57th Street in New York City to this address sometime in 1883 or 1884. The earliest known record of the new home address is on Clemens' will of 11 April 1884.

[17] General Grant had been living in his handsome house in New York City just off Fifth Avenue since August 1881, having at last secured what appeared to be a substantial income from his investments in the Wall Street firm of Grant & Ward.

[18] This list of people to whom Clemens meant to send complimentary copies of his books closely resembles the list in Notebook 20 (N&J2, pp. 512–514). The present list includes: John Henton Carter, river editor of the Saint Louis *Post-Dispatch*; Mrs. John Ford, a Langdon family connection; Mrs. Frances Antoinette Cox, widowed sister of

Gerhardt. 11 Boissonade
Geo. MacDonal % A. P. Watt,
   34 Paternoster Row.
Mrs. Cox & Cable, 229 8[th.]
Dean Sage
Joe Goodman.
Orion
Ma
Pamela.
Mother. Sue Crane 5.
Uncle Remus
Aldrich.
Mother Fairbanks, Weddell House
Jno Bellows. Gloucester, Eng.

4. 3 *in.* width of ⟨bed⟩ mattrass 6. [2 or 3] *in* length

Social Evening Society—Bonanza gets it "Evil"—makes drunken
speech to its members (⟨women⟩ ladies),—thinks *they* are the S E's
"Why 'on't you re*form?* (ic!)[19]

B. plays himself for deaf & dumb, & two gentlemen talk some
horribly critical truths—till at last the expression "this old fool"
brings out his angry "You're another."

B. complains too many pre-historic toads in his coal!
⟨"Here's another⟩ Pedlar *brought* him an Old Silurian toad,
found in a cake of limestone ten feet thick." By it for
⟨bricabrac⟨c⟩⟩bricabrack. Add it to the collection.

George Washington Cable; Albany businessman Dean Sage; Joseph Goodman, now raising grapes in California; and John Bellows, author of the pocket French dictionary which
Clemens had found so useful during his 1878/1879 trip abroad. Weddell House, a leading
Cleveland hotel, had been Mrs. Fairbanks address since about 1879 when the Fairbanks'
financial reverses forced them to rent their own house and move to the hotel. Clemens
sent copies of *Life on the Mississippi* and, in some cases, *A Tramp Abroad.*

[19] This is the first of a number of notes for a projected book or play about a western
mining millionaire named Bonanza. Three pages of typed notes in the Mark Twain Papers
(DV 79) contain other ideas for the story. Further on in Notebook 22 Clemens suggests
that Bonanza is to be based on railroad magnate Henry Villard (p. 45). Clemens is not
known to have attempted the projected book.

Bought an echo.

⟨H[is]⟩ B's little brother was long at foot of class but thought he was at head. Said the last potato in the pile was on top—so he thought *he* was.

Pretends to be deaf & dumb & hears a conversation of ladies.

Turn Statue of Liberty Enlightening the World into Adam.[20]

N. C. Goodwin, admirable young burlesque actor played grave-digger at Cincinnati dramatic festival.[21]

Man's delight upon reaching an enchanted country where the rivers were all wines & liquors, & *water* was sold & drank as a costly

---

[20] Excavation for the foundation which would support the pedestal of Bartholdi's colossal statue of "Liberty Enlightening the World" was begun in May 1883 on Bedloe's Island in New York Harbor. For several months previously the newspapers had carried frequent reports of the success of the subscription committee in raising funds for the statue's pedestal. Clemens was invited to contribute an autograph letter to be raffled off at the Bartholdi Pedestal Fund Art Loan Exhibition. His response, which appeared in the New York *Times* on 4 December 1883, elaborated the idea recorded in this notebook entry. "What do we care for a statue of liberty when we've got the thing itself in its wildest sublimity?" Clemens asked. "What you want of a monument is to keep you in mind of something you haven't got—something you've lost. Very well; we haven't lost liberty; we've lost Adam. . . . What have we done for Adam? Nothing. What has Adam done for us? Everything. He gave us life, he gave us death, he gave us heaven, he gave us hell." He suggests that certain "trifling alterations," which he enumerates, will suffice to turn the statue into Adam, and concludes: "Is it but a question of finance? Behold the inclosed (paid bank) checks. Use them as freely as they are freely contributed."

[21] The Cincinnati Dramatic Festival ran from 30 April to 5 May 1883 at the huge Cincinnati Music Hall. The program consisted almost entirely of Shakespearean plays, performed by a group of distinguished actors and actresses culled from a number of companies—including Lawrence Barrett, John McCullough, Otis Skinner, Clara Morris, and Mary Anderson. Nathaniel C. Goodwin's performance as the first gravedigger in *Hamlet* was favorably reviewed by the New York *Times* on 5 May. Several months later when Clemens and William Dean Howells were trying to find a lead actor for their play *Colonel Sellers as a Scientist* Clemens recalled the review of Goodwin's performance and had Charles Webster approach him about the part (SLC to CLW, 2 January 1884, *MTBus*, p. 231). Howells objected to Goodwin as an actor associated with "low flung burlesques" and confessed that he would find it "extremely distasteful" to have his "name connected in any way with Goodwin's" (Howells to SLC, 15 February 1884, *MTHL*, p. 472). Howells' objections—and Goodwin's insistence that the name "Colonel Sellers," so long associated with John T. Raymond, should be changed—contributed to the collapse of negotiations.

luxury.—He soon found himself ⟨dissi⟩ falling into habits of watry dissipation & caring nothing for the other things—too cheap & abundant. Moral—make no ⟨ma[in]⟩Maine laws.

On one occasion my autograph sold for $42,480. (It was signed to a check.)

Story about triplets—girls—exactly alike—they pass along & man thinks it the same girl every time.—so he imagines he is losing his mind.[22]

We whose ⟨reputations⟩ lives are such as they are, may take solace in the thought that ⟨beyond⟩ we have a ⟨last⟩ ⟨final⟩charitable & ⟨best⟩ good friend yonder who will make all right & gracious in the end—even Death the great Whitewasher.

Paul the X-eyed, redheaded, left-handed billiardist. Could ⟨beat⟩play a better game, I judge, than his grace the saint of that name.[23]

That Col. x x x in "Cromwell" & 2 others to choose which should die. They said it would be suicide, & refused. So a little child was called & drew life for 2 & death for the third, the Colonel. By dramatic accident it could have been his *own* child. The 3 standing, faced away, the child would nevertheless recognize her father, & lovingly ⟨give⟩ put into his hand the *red* piece of paper—& then tell him so, gleefully, afterward, when he turns & sees who it is that has conferred death upon him. ("I conferred *life* upon *you*, poor ⟨unwill⟩ innocent little executioner"). Lets on to thank her & be delighted that she discriminatd in his favor.[24] [#]

---

[22] This theme recurs in an unfinished story by Clemens entitled "The Triplets" (DV 342).

[23] Clemens referred to this Virginia City gambler in an earlier notebook (N&J2, p. 448).

[24] Clemens' entry is based on Thomas Carlyle's account of Colonel Poyer's execution in *Oliver Cromwell's Letters and Speeches: With Elucidations*, 5 vols. (London: Chapman and Hall, 1870), 2:106. Clemens acquired the book in 1883. On 20 December 1883 Clemens wrote to Howells: "I read the incident in Carlyle's Cromwell a year ago & made a note in my notebook; stumbled on the note to-day, & wrote up the closing scene of a possible tragedy to see how it might work. . . . Come—let's do this tragedy, & do it well" (MTHL, p. 455). The collaboration never materialized but in December 1901

Woman manages her husband—makes him want a thing by making ⟨it⟩him believe it unattainable.

Ask where telegrams are to be sent—⟨Ri[deau] Hall?⟩ just O[ttawa][25]

Bonanza sees a hatchment & orders one.

Is deceived into attempting a morning call upon majesty.

Has a stranger played on him for the heir apparent.

Telegraph E M Bunce billiards postponed a week.[26]

He invented sin—not that I think that that was much. Anybody here—that I am acquainted with—could have done it, I reckon. Could have done it myself. *Have* invented *some* kinds.

He invented sin—he was the author of sin—& I wish he had taken out an international copyright on it. That was the *time* to start in cop—because when there got to be two people there'd be one to oppose it & then twould be too late—& (experience shows) that that other fellow he would have the most influence⟨, too⟩. And whatever profit there might be in sin that other fel would get out of it. It does seem that whoever is the author of a thing, he is the very person who has the most reason to wish he is at least in a

---

Clemens published a fictionalized version of the episode, "The Death Disk," in *Harper's* magazine. He then dramatized the story and it was produced briefly at Carnegie Hall in 1902.

[25] Clemens' entry was occasioned by a confusing series of telegrams on 19 and 20 May 1883. Lord Lorne, the governor general of Canada, telegraphed Montreal bookseller Samuel E. Dawson asking him to forward an invitation to Clemens to be Lorne's guest at his residence, Rideau Hall, in Ottawa. The occasion was the meeting of the Royal Society of Canada for the Encouragement of Science and Literature from 22 to 26 May. Clemens replied immediately to Dawson. Subsequent telegrams revealed that Clemens should have addressed his reply to Lorne. Dawson's explanatory letter of 19 May supplied the correct address—simply "The Marquis of Lorne/Ottawa/Canada." Clemens apparently then telegraphed his apologies and his acceptance to Lorne and noted on the envelope of Dawson's letter "That Marquis of Lorne blunder."

[26] Edward M. Bunce was the cashier at the Phoenix National Bank in Hartford and a member of Clemens' Friday evening billiards group.

meas not the person he really is but the other person who didn't
even do it at all—& probably wasnt there at the time,—⟨in a
measure⟩—or in a condition to retrieve his relations with—with—
but ⟨I fear I embarrass you.⟩ never mind about the rest of that
sentence ⟨—it's not⟩—let it go—it appears to have been drinking
something/body standing & in silence—standing on its head, too.
Yes I wish he had taken out a copyright on sin—just for the sake of
the parties who would infringe it.[27]

Mr Brown's "bronchial torches" in the adv.[28]

Throw your heft on the corpse.

⟨Pour kerosine down the rats [holes]— [I] reckon got to catch
'em⟩

Anything doin' in medicines?

What kind of a ⟨G— d—⟩ saw mill do *you* run?

Twichell's Deco. Day prayer—⟨G— d— that dog!⟩

He had a rat!

Lend me a knife—took door plate off ⟨coffin⟩.

Agree with him?—Why ⟨I've got him down below on the ice⟩

Filled in around him w^h fruit

Goodman & mouse

Georgia doctors decided drink just enough brandy to kill the
tadpoles. [#]

---

[27] This entry was evidently intended for Clemens' speech "On Adam," but was never
used. Only the phrase about drinking "standing & in silence" was transferred, with slight
alteration, to the finished speech. The speech is published in the 1923 edition of *Mark
Twain's Speeches* (pp. 93–97) with Albert Bigelow Paine's note: "Delivered About
1880–85. (Exact Occasion Unknown.)" Internal evidence in the speech suggests that it
was delivered in Montreal during one of Clemens' two Canadian trips in May 1883.
[28] Brown's Bronchial Troches was a patent medicine guaranteed safe for "the most
delicate female or the youngest child" and "held in the highest esteem by clergymen,
singers, and public speakers generally" (*Illustrated London News*, 26 December 1885).

Send heliotype to Major Arthur Collins.²⁹

⟨Man⟩ Liked the violin ⟨[*one word*]⟩

In High Spirits—by James Payn³⁰

Speech to the Undertakers.

Write A. Reasoner³¹
    Hoboken

Fight a duel with cats.

Write the Second Advent, with full details—lot of Irish disciples—Paddy Ryan for Judas. & other disciples.³²

Star in east. People want to know how the editor's (wise men) could see it move, while sober.

John interviewed.

55	32
32	11
110	32
165	32
1760	⟨5⟩352

A Dreadful night with a jury. [#]

---

²⁹ Clemens met Collins, comptroller and equerry to Princess Louise, during his stay at Rideau Hall. Collins' letter of 8 June 1883 acknowledges receipt of Clemens' "kind & amusing letter" and his heliotype portrait.

³⁰ Popular novelist James Payn was editor of the *Cornhill Magazine* from 1883 to 1896. *High Spirits: Being Certain Stories Written in Them* was published by Harper & Brothers in 1879.

³¹ Reasoner was an official of the Delaware, Lackawanna & Western Railroad Company. Clemens wrote to him to make arrangements for a special sleeping car to take his family from New York to Elmira for the usual summer stay at Quarry Farm. The Clemens family left Hartford on 14 June 1883 for New York and continued to Elmira on 15 June.

³² "The Second Advent," apparently written in 1881, is a satirical description of the disastrous events resulting from the Savior's reappearance in a sleepy Arkansas town. This notebook entry indicates that Clemens planned to elaborate on the existing eighty-four page manuscript, but there is no evidence that he did so. The sketch is published in *Mark Twain's Fables of Man*, ed. John S. Tuckey (Berkeley, Los Angeles, London: University of California Press, 1972), pp. 53–68.

Paddy Ryan was a heavyweight boxer from Troy, New York, known as the "Trojan Giant." He earned sudden celebrity in 1880 by winning the United States heavyweight

Louise
Ottawa May./83[33]

Henry H. Smith

35 Union Park, Boston, proposes to furnish the Congressional
investigation of Duncan by 44th Congress—extravagant salaries to
his family, &c. House Com. on Commerce, 1st session 44th Cong.[34]

Go & see the ⟨Purchis⟩ ⟨Purkis⟩ family, who still live in the
same hut where their charcoal-burning ancestors lived 1100 years
ago in the (New?) Forest & in whose cart W[m] Rufus was conveyed
to the hut when shot by Walter Tyrrell.[35] [#]

---

championship in his first professional fight. In February 1882, in his second professional
match, Ryan lost his title to a newcomer, John L. Sullivan. In the manuscript of "The
Second Advent" the role of the treacherous disciple is taken by "St. Talmage," Clemens'
caricature of the prominent clergyman and orator T. DeWitt Talmage.

[33] Princess Louise, fourth daughter of Queen Victoria and wife of the governor general
of Canada, was Clemens' hostess during his visit to Rideau Hall in the last week of May
1883. Her autograph appears here in black ink. Albert Bigelow Paine has written below
it in pencil "Signature of Princess Louise (Marquise of Lorne)." The rest of the notebook
page and its verso are blank.

[34] An interview published in the New York *Times* of 10 June 1883 entitled "Mr. Mark
Twain Excited" involved Clemens once again with his old antagonist Charles C. Duncan
(see *N&J2*, p. 35, note 26), formerly captain of the *Quaker City* and currently shipping
commissioner of the port of New York. The interview recorded Clemens' reaction to an
article which appeared in the *Times* the previous day about the investigation by District
Attorney Elihu Root of Duncan's alleged misuse of public funds. The publication of
Clemens' strongly-worded and explicit condemnation of Duncan led Duncan to bring a
$100,000 libel suit against the *Times*. Fearing that Duncan would bring a similar suit
against him, Clemens consulted his lawyers during the summer of 1883 and prepared a
defense, claiming that the *Times* reporter had completely misrepresented his remarks
and that proofs of the interview had not been submitted to him for approval before publication. The *Times's* defense consisted of proving that its statements about Duncan
were not libelous, but were in fact a matter of public record: in April 1876 Congressman
Elijah Ward of New York had presented to the House of Representatives the findings
of the Committee on Commerce exposing Duncan's appropriation of port fees for the
benefit of his own family (*Congressional Record: Containing the Proceedings and
Debates of the Forty-Fourth Congress, First Session* [Washington: Government Printing
Office, 1876], 4:2687, 3470–3475). The Duncan libel suit ended ignominiously on 8
March 1884 when the jury awarded Duncan twelve cents in damages; Duncan was subsequently dismissed from his office as a result of the investigation (New York *Times*,
9 March and 13 May 1884). Henry H. Smith, whom Clemens mentions in his notebook
entry, has not been identified.

[35] Clemens' source for this story may be Sir Francis Palgrave's *The History of*

Hunt up some other remarkable English places unvisited—that Beaver family near Henley-on-the-Thames, who lived there before the Conquest. Get abstract of both places in fac simile from Domesday Book.[36]

Bonanza calls Washington the ⟨US⟩ Gov't Asylum for (⟨impotent⟩ ⟨(homeless)⟩ the nation's paupers⟨.⟩) the nation's pauper wards. ⟨—The *head* of the country? Yes⟩

Make a game of universal *contemporaneous history*.[37] [#]

Normandy and of England, 4 vols. (London: Macmillan & Co., 1851–1864). The death of the brutal William II of England, supposedly due to an arrow shot by the nobleman Tyrrell, occurred in 1100 A.D. Palgrave adds: "[Purkis'] family still subsists in the neighborhood, nor have they risen above their original station, poor craftsmen or cottagers. They followed the calling of coal-burners until a recent period; and they tell us that the wheel of the Cart which conveyed the neglected corpse was shewn by them until the last century" (4:687). The details of Palgrave's account, which Clemens accepts as fact, are of doubtful authenticity.

[36] Clemens may be imperfectly remembering his visit in 1872 to Wargrave near Henley-on-Thames. He described the visit in a letter of 2 November 1872 to Mrs. Fairbanks: "One day we dined & breakfasted with a splendid fox-hunting squire named Broom in his quaint & queer old house that has been occupied 500 years. . . . Now years ago it used to be a curious study to me, to follow the variations of a family name down through a Peerage or a biography from the Roll of Battle-Abbey to the present day—& manifold & queer were the changes, too. But here within 2 miles of Mr. Broom, live a family named Abear who still own & farm the same piece of ground their ancestors have owned & farmed for nine hundred & fifty years! . . . There is but one other case of the kind in England—*another* small farmer" (*MTMF*, pp. 167–168).

[37] There are many entries throughout this notebook relating to Clemens' invention of a complicated history game. He described his new enthusiasm to Howells on 20 July 1883: "Day before yesterday I struck a dull place in my head, so I knocked off work & measured off the reigns of the English kings on our roadway, (a foot to the year,) from the Conqueror down, & drove a peg in the ground for each King. . . . My notion is, to get up an open-air game which shall put all these names & dates & statistics into the children's heads without the bore of study. I got vastly interested in this nonsense, & after I went to bed last night I worked out a plan for making it an indoor game also—play it with cards & a cribbage board" (*MTHL*, pp. 435–436). Clemens enlisted the aid of Orion Clemens and Charles L. Webster in researching the historical facts and perfecting the game board. The game was patented in August 1885 but Clemens apparently made no effort to market it then. In February 1891 he suddenly resurrected the history game idea. Over the next few months he obtained copyright for the instruction booklet and had Fred Hall of Charles L. Webster & Company make up some models of the game, which was now titled "Mark Twain's Memory-Builder." Hall attempted to interest toy

Mental teleg—Han's Lippersheim, of Middelburg invented & *made* the telescope, Oct 22, 1608, & exhibited it—sent it to the king. Not long afterward Jacob Adrianz, near Amsterdam claimed to have discovered the principle of the telescope 2 years earlier. And this lies in dispute between them.[38]

⟨M. T.'ˢ⟩ 4000 Historical Facts

&

Memory-Improver.

Game I.

4 columns, 100 dates in a column; 400 years, beginning with the Conquest & end 1461, end of Henry VI.

Game II.

4 columns, 100 dates in a column; 400 years, beginning with Edward IV, 1461, & ending 1884.

Same with France, Germany, the Papacy, Ancient History, &c., 400 years to a game.

RED	Length of reign & kings
[. . . . .]	10 for each hole.
BLUE	
[. . . . .]	8 ″ ″ ″
YELLOW	
[. . . . .]	⟨[6]⟩5 ″ ″ ″
BLACK	
[. . . . .]	3 ″ ″ ″

---

stores in it. By 1892 Clemens was convinced that the game had little commercial promise and he advised Hall to "put it aside until some indefinite time in the far future" (SLC to Hall, 8 March 1892, *MTLP*, p. 307).

[38] Clemens noted this information about Hans Lippershey, the inventor of the telescope, as another instance of curious telepathic coincidences, examples of which he had been collecting since 1875.

Black includes Beginning & ending of Dynasties; Revolutions, Plagues, Discoveries, introductions, inventions, & Memorable Earthquakes, Fires, Storms, & ⟨⟨C[a]⟩Memorable⟩ other Calamities. (Assassinations, Executions, ⟨Exile,⟩ Banishments. Accidents.

Dethronement is 10, (it's an end of a reign) but the death of the King, years later is but a *distinguished* death, & counts like the death of a citizen celebrity. Whereas the death of an unillustrious ⟨unroyal⟩ person counts but 1. Heirs to the throne count 3—like the *other* prince in Tower.

Game ---
Comparative History.

⟨4 columns⟩
1 column (or 2 or 4?) with 100 dates in each. Size of Umpire Chart enlarged to give events of several countries opposite each date.

A King's or President's accession counts 10; his death 10 (also, length of reign; a battle 8; a great citizen or subject, (death ⟨6⟩5 (when he flourished if can't give his date 1) (but Shakspere counts as a King;) (*above* a King) minor events 1 point. Great inventions & introductions? & revolutions. 3 points. (beginning & end of revolutions ⟨3⟩ 8 each.

1066. Hastings ⟨1⟩8; K. Harold ends, 10; K. William I begins, 10. ⟨No⟩Saxon Dynasty ends, 3; Norman ditto begins, 3.

When through, add up your score-column 10^s, 8,^{s}, 6^s, & 3^s—then add to this sum all the pins sticking in ⟨d⟩Dates & Miscellaneous, counting each of these 1 point.

Print Battles in *italics*. ⟨[S]⟩Bg. (begins to reign) ⟨E⟩Cs (ceases from reigning. ⟨D[i]⟩D (died.) B⟨o⟩ (born).

W^m· I b⟨o⟩. --- 3 He ⟨B⟩ bg. 1066 10. He C. 1087. 10.

K. Jas. III b⟨o⟩ --- 3; bg. 1685, 10; cs. ⟨1685⟩1688, 10; reigned 3 yr. ⟨3⟩1; ⟨d. --- 3;⟩ dethroned 1688, 3; d --- 3.

Hastings, Sep '66. If you name ⟨month & year, you⟩ year & fact, 8 points; if you or opponent adds the month, ⟨count 1 point for that.⟩ the person naming it counts *one* point for it. ⟨[I]⟩The *day*

of the month counts *another* point. (This is ⟨for⟩ not for the *first*
series (Outlines of History) but for the Second Series—(Elaborated,
Extended Series.)

Strong players must give weak ones odds.

Print a line down through centre, dividing points-rows into 5 on
a side. Then umpire can tell you, by the *number* of the
episode⟨-fact⟩ which hole to pin.

Umpire wont have to use pins himself in either the big game *or*
the little one.

Philip I. . . . . 1060–1108—48
Louis VI fat 1008–1137. 29
Louis Y. VII . . . . ⟨13⟩1137–1180. 43
Philip Aug. II . . . . 1180–1223—43
Louis VIII . . . . 1223–1226— 3
Louis IX . . . . 1226–1270—44
Philip III Bold, ... 1270–⟨18⟩1285—15
Philip IV Fair . . . . 1285–⟨12⟩1314—29
Louis Hutin X . . . . 1314–1315— 1½
Philip the Long V . . . . 1315–1322— 7
Chas IV Fair . . . . 1322–1328— 6
Philip VI (Valois) . . . . 1328–1350—22
John II . . . . 1350–1364—14
Chas. V . . . . .1364–⟨1370⟩1380—16
Chas. VI ins[39] . . . . .1380–⟨1378⟩1422—42
Chas. VII (Joan) . . . . 1422–1461—39
Louis XI . . . . 1461–1483—22
Chas. VIII . . . . 1483–1498—15
Louis XII . . . . 1498–1515—17
Francis I . . . . 1515–1547—32
Henry II . . . . 1547–1560—13
Chas. IX . . . . 1560–1574—14
Henry III . . . . 1574–1589—15
⟨[Louis XIII]⟩Henry IV . . . . 1589–1610—21

---

[39] For the last thirty years of his reign Charles VI was insane.

Louis XIII—⟨[1515]⟩1610–1643 —Louis XIV, 1643–1715 —Louis
XIV, 1715–1774. Louis XVI,—1774, 1793, 19 —⟨Louis XVII—1.⟩
Louis XVII. 93. Revolution 1794. Directory, '94 to '99; Consulate
99 to 1804; Empire to 1815. Louis XVIII to 1826; Chas. X to
1830. Louis Philippe to 1848.

A Sunday letter to ⟨Series of⟩ Con Journal every time his name
appears—say once a month—& be a whole month brightening them
—about being at present on a NY visit to my cousin Whitelaw—&
quote his opinions & speeches (& "he said once in the T that I'd
be a thief if I had the courage" & I laughed & said when he dug
in under Young & Greely & got their places he had the *looking*
quality, too. But he didn't like that. Edward said he had a native
Scotch dislike for unpleasant facts done up as jokes.
  Use him in story as Chief Eunuch & make him figure often.
Take out no copyright.[40]

It gives you the habit of picking up ⟨[ev]⟩a ⟨date⟩ fact or two
every day. The accumulation is handsome in a year.

No history game has really been a *game*.
Authors is nearest; but *it* isn't a game that can interest long.
This wouldn't last if it had a mere dozen or two of unchangeable
facts—but not so; you may add facts to it till you exhaust history.

Let Parker see a dragonfly the size of a man of war, ⟨[in size --]⟩
Take a journey on him. When he darts, the world disappears, ⟨so⟩
as do spokes of a wheel, so lightning-like is the movement.

Put but one or two incidents opp each year—& give their
point-value by a figure attached.
  Recommend that when you want to play the full game of the
BOOK, you play one king at a time (by choice); then you won't have
be skipping all through (the umpire won't.) [#]

---

[40] Clemens returns to his attack on New York *Tribune* editor Whitelaw Reid (see
Notebooks 19 and 20 in N&J2). The "story" referred to may be the "1002ᵈ Arabian
Night" but Clemens did not include the "Chief Eunuch" in that burlesque. Clemens
reminds himself to "take out no copyright," knowing that his projected attack on Reid
would then be widely and speedily reprinted.

Choose the monarch that shall be the trump by putting a finger at random on the board, or by the choice of the umpire. Trump facts count *double*.

Have a trump or not, as you please. But to have trumps is an incentive to *learn* all facts of all reigns.

Judas Iscariot, Guiteau, Whitelaw Reid—⟨the⟩who gets either, loses 3 points. It is called being smirched.

What this game will do.
(Increase memory, story up history.

⸻
⸻
⸻
⸻

What it won't do.
It wont cure rheumatism, colic, [&] (lot of diseases) wont bring back the hair

⸻
⸻
⸻
⸻

The ceiling is a crust of cut diamonds; the walls are single emeralds carved in arabesques; the floor a polished ruby. ⟨When he goes ⟨thither⟩ to sth[1], ⟨the⟩a Roman Emp precedes him with a torch, ⟨the⟩a Grand Lama of Thibet ⟨raises⟩ lifts up the, whilst a Pope of Rome asks a blessing—& when⟩When he goes to sth[1], a Roman Emp carries the candle, Pope Alex VI lifts up the — for him & when he gets thro he — — — — with an Irishman.

I am told, Aug. 23, 9 AM, that the Times lawyer proposed to Duncan that if he would let them off they would prove I said it all.[41] [#]

⸻

[41] Clemens' lawyer, Daniel Whitford of the firm of Alexander & Green, had already disclosed the newspaper's position in his letter of 21 July 1883 to Clemens: Duncan's

Some swells South used "store" ink—the first Tom had seen in a *dwelling* house.

Don't crowd the pinholes together.

Read only *one* reign at a time—or you will get confused.

When a king dies *and* ceases from reigning, it is *two* distinct facts & you can't play them both at once.

This game can be applied to any form of memory-practice. Meisterschaft,[42] for instance: count a point for each word of a sentence which you get right & in the right place, & your opponent get a point for each *error*-word you make.

Offer a prize (fine opera glass) to the Saturday Morning Club[43] for the highest number of points made by a member in a series of ⟨ten⟩ games; & 2^d & 3^d prizes; the same prizes to be doubled & fought for by the *same* 3 girls at a future *unnamed* date (a single game) to be *suddenly* named by me, so they will tackle it unprepared by recent cramming. This to test ⟨w⟩how much of it their memory has retained faithfully—the *proportion* that remains. Other girls' clubs.

⟨5⟩ 10 games to be played a week apart or 2 or 3 days apart as shall be preferred. [#]

---

attorney "said that the attorney for the Times called on him and told him that if he would discontinue his suit against *The Times* he would furnish him with the proper proof that you dictated the article and authorized its publication." Ironically, Clemens felt impelled to ally himself with Duncan rather than the *Times* (see note 34): he agreed to appear as a witness for Duncan at a hearing in Elmira on 22 August 1883 in order to establish "actual malice on the part of the defendant [the *Times*] in publishing said alleged libel and to increase the amount of damages to be recovered by the plaintiff" (copy of "Affidavit & order for examination of Samuel L. Clemens" dated 7 August 1883, in MTP).

[42] In the 1880s Dr. Richard S. Rosenthal published a number of exercise books based on the "Meisterschaft System" of learning languages through memorization and grammatical analysis of simple conversational sentences.

[43] An organization of young girls who met weekly, occasionally at the Clemens house, for lectures and discussions of cultural and social ideas.

Not tell each other how you are progressing, lest the forward ones discourage the others.

Opera glass, fan, work-box.

Prizes for boys.

1. Colts navy revolver; (or anything else worth the same money); [acme] skates; sled.

Offer same in a N. Y. pub school/Smith College—only 10 brightest pupils to compete.

Franklin Square Song Collection.[44]

Chas. S. Farrar, A. M, Pres't Milwaukee College could arrange History of Sculpture & Painting (Art)—see his "Topical Lessons." Townsend MacCoun, Chicago.[45]

Game of Sacred dates?

And history of the Church?

Game of Geography.

Name of country so many points. Capitals, populations, chief cities, rivers, lakes, form of government, &c.

Game of Inventions.

Printing; telescope, glass, steam, telegraph, telephone, railway, steam boat, cotton gin, &c; names & nationalities of inventors, &c.

Game of Authors & their books of each country—&

Contemporaneous universal history of authors & literature.

Games of all Histories & Countries, ancient & modern.

Among them Game of *History of Ireland.* [#]

---

[44] Harper & Brothers' eight-volume song collection, selected by J. P. McCaskey, appeared between 1881 and 1892. At the time of Clemens' entry only the first volume had appeared.

[45] Charles S. Farrar's *History of Sculpture, Painting, and Architecture: Topical Lessons, with Special References to Valuable Books* (Chicago: T. MacCoun, 1881).

Can play a⟨[l]⟩ lot of these games on the same board—only with different charts.

Chart contains 1000 facts, the book 8,000. Can sell game *without* the *book*.

Games of each of the *States?* & Canada?

Game of Celebrated Generals, lawgivers, admirals, &c.

Don't print reigns in any but *two* colors (or *one*) if too costly. Or, have *expensive* ones in all colors, the cheap ones in one.

⟨In costly ones,⟩
In all, put big events in *italics* in the chart.

In *costly* ones, make each event the *color* it counts—red for 10ˢ, black for 3ˢ, &c.

Game of great English Chancellors & judges.

Game, in *months* of French Revolution

Game of Napoleon I.

Experts play *one reign.*

In later times, *one year* or so of a reign.

B 483 ⎫
 ⎬ hotel Brunswick[46]
B 520 ⎭

Royal trick, 10; battle, 8; noble, 5; simple, 1.

$$\begin{array}{r} 4.25 \\ 1\ 00 \\ 2\ 00 \\ \hline 7.25 \end{array}$$

2

A history game is needed. After that ⟨—⟩¶ had been traveling 2 months, it turned up once more in a far-away journal, with those

---

[46] The Clemens family probably stopped at the Hotel Brunswick on Fifth Avenue in New York City on their way to Hartford after their summer stay at Quarry Farm.

same old errors "Richard II 2 yrs, Oliver Cromwell 2 yrs"—showing that scores of proof readers & printers had known no better.[47]

⟨Mail[48]
Pen
Dennison
Shoe store⟩

Let length of reign count 8? Beginning of a siege counts 8. End of it 8. No matter if it begins & ends in the same year. Name the victor or the loser counts 8. The same with a *battle*. 8. see next page.[49]

Very conspicuous happenings, count 5.

Any birth or *any* death counts 3. "So-&-so *flourished* in this reign counts 3.

Minor facts count 1.

Henry VI—1461
⟨Dis⟩Dethroned (ends the reign)—10. King again in '71—10. Dethroned in '71—10. Died in '71—3. Reigned 40—8. [#]

---

[47] Clemens described his outdoor history game in a letter of 20 July 1883 to Twichell, who indiscreetly allowed the letter to appear in the Hartford *Courant* of 24 July. Clemens was furious at his friend's meddling, noting "I shall never thoroughly like him again" (SLC note on Twichell's letter of 22 July 1883). Clemens' annoyance was aggravated by the fact that the letter was printed with two errors. Twichell had pointed out one of the errors on 24 July: "Some smarty in the [*Courant*] office changed *Richard* Cromwell into Oliver, and probably thinks he ought to be thanked for it—the ignoramus." On 8 September Twichell wrote Clemens a peacemaking letter but he continued to make light of Clemens' anger: "It was a good sin that I committed. That extract has gone and is going the rounds, as I wanted it to, and knew it would. Here it is as I cut it out of one of . . . our best religious papers only last week." Clemens' notebook entry was probably made on receipt of this clipping which evidently preserved the two errors: Oliver Cromwell was substituted for Richard Cromwell and Richard II appeared instead of Richard III.

[48] This and the three following lines appear on the first of two leaves used by Clemens for a short letter to Howells dated 20 September 1883 (*MTHL*, p. 443). The two leaves were torn from the notebook at this point and are now in the Houghton Library, Harvard University. The four notebook lines are struck through by a large X, presumably made by Clemens when he wrote the letter.

[49] The reference is to the entries from 28.11 through 29.8, which illustrate Clemens' scheme for scoring historical facts.

Chas. II. Accedes, 1660—10. Ceases to reign, 1685—10. Dies 1685—3. R'd 25 yrs—8.

W^m. III, born 1650—3. Accedes 1688—10. Ceases 1702—10. Dies 1702—3. Manner of death, result of accident—⟨3⟩5. R'd 14—8.

Chas. I suc. 1625—10. Ceases 1649—10. Dies '49—3. Manner— beheaded—5. R'd 24—8.

James III. s. 1685—10. C. 1688—10. ⟨D⟩ R'd 3 y—8. Died in exile afterward—3.

Don't use common pins, but short ones. Can handle them better.

Rev. Snoop.

Sept. 24, '83, ordered Worden & Co, 48 Wall st, to buy 100 Or Trans at 40.[50]

(Tell as facts, not a story)
6 men save six women's lives from drowning & marry them. Tell the story of their after lives.

Gravely write a story in which at intervals, hero saves his girl from ruffians, drowning, burning, & all the other stock accidents, & she persistently refuses to marry him, to his great astonishment, he never having heard of such a thing in the books. Marries her at last, & they live a cat & dog life. Sh is subject to accidents by nature or heredity or something; so she keeps ⟨suf⟩ encountering them, & other people keep saving her to her husband's irritation & exasperation, & he ⟨threatens⟩ tries to kill them instead of rewarding them. [#]

---

[50] Around January 1883 Clemens bought on margin 200 shares of stock worth about fifteen thousand dollars in the Oregon & Transcontinental Company. In the next few months Clemens watched the stock go to a high of about ninety-eight dollars a share and then begin to drop. When Clemens bought another 100 shares in the railroad company, shortly after the date of this entry, he evidently expected the stock to rally, but it continued its disastrous decline and in May 1884 Clemens finally liquidated his 300 shares for twelve dollars a share.

⟨sie⟩Sie wollte Schuhe sawgen; aber ⟨sie⟩Sie wüsste nicht wie Sie
es sawgen sollte.[51]

In this story, put the may apple, oak-ball, fox grapes, winter
grapes, summer grapes, persimmons, papaws, red & black haws,
poke berries, pecans, hickory, walnuts, butternuts, sumach-fruit,
sour-grass, hazel nuts, (no chestnuts) crabapples, wild cherries,
plums, a candy-pulling, a kissing party, skating & swimming
adventures—wreck of the Glaucus[52]—Mrs. Holliday[53] with 40
diseases & expected 4th husband & fortune-tellers. Villains *very*
scarce. Pater-rollers & slavery.

BORROWING

Borrowing—sugar, coffee, molasses, cream, flat-irons, *fire* (chunk)
COMB, &c. Drop this casually in, all along.

A Montana belle, says the Bismarck *Tribune*, being asked by a Bismarck
man if they possessed any culture out her way, replied: "Culture? You bet
your variegated socks we do! We kin sling more culture to the square foot
in Helena than they kin in any camp in America. Culture? Oh, loosen my
corsets till I smile!"[54]

Put her in a Tom Sawyer book & let Huck tell her story? Hunts
bears & things with a rifle, ⟨rid⟩ breaks horses, &c. Has some
eastern folk visit her?—or she goes east to study? Tom's far-western
cousin? Or she's a Pike-Co Californian for Swinton?[55] [#]

---

[51] This entry is difficult to translate because of Clemens' use of a nonexistent verb
form, *sawgen*. One possible translation is *She wanted to say shoes, but she didn't know*
how to say it. Clemens' *sawgen* could be a misrendering of *sagen* ("to say"), but he may
have intended any of several phonetically similar verbs.

[52] Clemens was only a small boy when the sidewheel steamboat *Glaucus* snagged and
sank at Hannibal on 12 August 1842.

[53] Mrs. Richard Holliday's husband died in California after leaving Hannibal during
the gold rush. She was promised three husbands by the fortunetellers she repeatedly
consulted ("Villagers of 1840–3," *HH&T*, pp. 31, 354). Mark Twain modeled the Widow
Douglas of *Tom Sawyer* and *Huckleberry Finn* on this woman.

[54] This anecdote is the full text of a clipping from an unidentified newspaper pasted
into the notebook here. Clemens' notes indicate that he was already considering a continuation of the adventures of Huck Finn and Tom Sawyer in a western setting. He did
not pursue the idea until the summer of 1884 when he began but did not finish "Huck
Finn and Tom Sawyer among the Indians" (included in *HH&T*, pp. 92–140).

[55] William Swinton was a journalist and historian whom Clemens had known in

Nicodemus. Millerites. Fancy ball. Tinner.

Stormfield must hear of a man who worked hard all his life to acquire heaven; & when he got there the first person he met was a man whom he had been hoping all the time was in hell—so disappointed & outraged that he inquired the way to hell & took up his satchel & left.

In costly ones Each fact MUST be printed in the color which signifies its value—this, no matter[56]

⟨No—⟨one⟩ the system must be simpler:⟩
Accessions & dethronements 10
⟨Beginning⟩
Siges; beginning of sieges; end of sieges; duration of sieges; Conquests; beginning, end, & duration of same; & *Battles*—each of these details 8
Births & deaths 3
Notable events 5

THIS IS THE CORRECT THING
No—all the markings needed will be these words over the colored bars in the corner: (Put them across *top* of board.)
⟨Accessions & retirements⟩
Throne ascended—& vacated. & Length of Reign.

10	Red

Battles & Sieges.

8	Blue

Washington, D.C., in the 1860s (*MTB*, p. 359; Swinton to SLC, 16 August 1883). He wrote to Clemens from New York City on 16 August 1883 requesting a story for his forthcoming magazine, *Swinton's Story-Teller*. Swinton wanted "a story of the old California or Nevada times—a story as good as, or better than, 'Tom Sawyer,' or 'The Jumping Frog.' " *Swinton's Story-Teller* was shortlived, only nineteen numbers being published between 10 October 1883 and 20 February 1884. Clemens sent Swinton no original matter, but two of his stories—"The Celebrated Jumping Frog of Calaveras County" and "A True Story"—were reprinted in the *Story-Teller*, presumably with Clemens' permission, on 10 October 1883 and 30 January 1884 respectively.

[56] Clemens wrote "Each . . . matter," canceled the passage, and later restored it

Any Birth or Death.

3	Yellow.

Any Great Event.

5	Black.

The blacks can be always ⟨marked with a 5⟩ put in italics in the chart & book—the others not marked at all.

⟨A Conquest is the *completion* of a Conquest, & counts 8.⟩

Double the *initial date* every time.

The ⟨boards⟩ games must be 200-years each—This gives 10 holes to each year.

   •⟨•⟩ 1066 . . . . .1. H as. H reigned months.
                       2 Ed. Con & H. descend.
   •   1066 . . . . .W^m ascended throne.
  ⟨[-]⟩ ⟨11[-]oo⟩1100. . . .W^m II r'd 13 y. 2 Descended
   •   1100⟨[-]⟩ . . . . . . .Henry I ascended.

Capt. S. finds that Hell was originally instituted in deference to an early Christian sentiment. In modern times the halls of heaven are warmed by registers connected with hell—& it is greatly applauded by Jonathan Edwards, Calvin, Baxter[57] & Co because it adds a new pang to the sinner's sufferings to know that the ⟨f⟩very fire which tortures him is the means of making the righteous comfortable.

Have king's name dimly printed on *board*—let the ignorant player have that much advantage—it will teach him ⟨that much, any⟩ the chiefest facts of history, anyway. [#]

---

with the instruction "STET," probably adding "In costly ones" at that time. He wrote the direction "OVER" to the right of "In costly ones," referring to the entries from "THIS . . . THING" (31.17) through "The blacks . . . marked at all" (32.5-6) which are written on the back of the notebook leaf.

[57] The noted seventeenth century Presbyterian divine Richard Baxter was the author of *The Saints' Everlasting Rest; or, A Treatise of the Blessed State of the Saints in Their Enjoyment of God in Heaven* (1650) in which the bliss of heaven is forcefully contrasted with the torments of hell.

Best *solitaire* game ever invented.

Board must be a pin-cushion with felting between.

Bonanza K—He killed a woman in Conn. No matter—it is a crime they do not punish there.[58]

Russell & Irwin Co.
   grape scissors.[59]

The best bunch always falls.

Sellers must pull the string out of his mouth, drunk—[60]
Also mistake a bat for a roll of greenbacks.

Publish Huck & Sawyer in one vol for $4.[61] [#]

---

[58] Throughout September 1883 the New York *Times* reported on the investigation of the murder and presumed rape of Mrs. Rose Ambler near Stratford, Connecticut. On 5 September the *Times* stated: "The atrocious murder of Mrs. Rose Ambler . . . seems likely to pass, with the Jennie Cramer and Mary Stannard cases, into the long line of Connecticut's criminal mysteries." In Notebook 20 (*N&J2*, p. 483) Clemens recommended lynching for two men being tried for the murder of Jennie Cramer in 1881. The men were acquitted.

[59] In his letter of 12 August 1883 Howells invited Clemens to invest in a pair of grape scissors which his father, William Cooper Howells, had invented (*MTHL*, p. 437). Clemens asked Charles L. Webster to search for a firm to manufacture the shears; the Russell & Erwin Manufacturing Company of New York City was one of several firms that Webster approached with no success. Webster did find a Newark toolmaker who made sixty dozen pairs of the scissors and for a time tried to sell them.

[60] There are several entries on the succeeding pages of this notebook about Clemens' current literary project, *Colonel Sellers as a Scientist*, the play on which he and Howells collaborated in November and December 1883. Clemens preserved a high opinion of the farce for years, but Howells, who shared his fondness for it, had serious doubts about its theatrical merits. Its absurd plot, which involved Sellers with all sorts of fantastic machinery on stage, defied production. Clemens later used many of the play's ideas in *The American Claimant*. There are several versions of the play in manuscript and typescript; a composite version was published in *The Complete Plays of W. D. Howells*, ed. Walter J. Meserve (New York: New York University Press, 1960), pp. 209–241. *Colonel Sellers as a Scientist* was briefly and unsuccessfully staged with the elocutionist A. P. Burbank in the title role in September 1887.

[61] Clemens revived this idea a few months later when he wrote to Charles Webster on 29 February 1884: "Let us canvass Huck Finn and Tom Sawyer both at once, selling both books for $4.50 where a man orders both, and arranging with the Pub Co that I shall have half the profit on all Sawyers so sold, and also upon all that *they* sell while our canvass lasts" (*MTLP*, p. 172). The American Publishing Company, however, insisted on such costly terms for releasing *Tom Sawyer* that the plan was abandoned.

Bring no children to the table.[62]

Children should endeavor to be smart & funny & absorb all the attention.

Never lend your teeth.

⟨⟨Do not⟩ Never eat with your knife; ⟨but⟩ (but always) acquire the habit of eating ⟨exclusively⟩ with your teeth.⟩
Do not eat with your knife.—It is not good form. Eat with your teeth.

Actress—lose your diamonds occasionally.
Keep your name going in 3-line items—smartnesses manufactured for you, old stale adventures &c.
There are persons who do this for salary.

Waiter in cheap Res'
Barber
Telephone Op
Cardriver
Doctor
S S Supt

Always say Allons! & mal apropos, &c—looks as if you knew the language.
When you tell an funny anecdote about a foreigner, tell it all in English till you get to his nub remark. Put that in the foreign tongue. That is the English style.[63]

Boil 5 min & serve cold—or hot—or—
(Some idiotic recipes.) [#]

---

[62] The following several entries are clearly notes for the burlesque etiquette book which Clemens had begun in 1881. An incomplete and fragmentary manuscript is in the Mark Twain Papers and includes two of the maxims listed here ("Never eat with your knife" [34.5] and "When you tell an funny anecdote" [34.21]).

[63] Clemens made this observation on English manners several times, evidently recalling an incident of his 1873 trip to England where at a dinner party Lord Houghton "told a number of delightful stories. He told them in French, and I lost nothing of them but the nubs" (MTA, 2:233).

In the play, cut the telegraph wire & send & receive false dispatches.[64]

Oct. 18 bought
    100 St Paul at 94¾
    100 " " 94⅛
    100 Mo. Pacif at 91½
Oct. 16, bought
    100 O T at 40.

⟨Oct 19, ordered 100 O T at 25 (order to cease with Oct.)

Told 'em not to sell me when Sage sells unless they get cost.⟩

Apl 10. Bot.
    ⟨100 St. Paul   86⅜⟩ Sold at 86⅛ Apl. 18.
    100 Mo Pacif   85⅝

May 3, '84, sold 200 Mo Pac at 80¾ & 200 St Paul at 83.—and bought 300 Western Union at 60½.[65]

RAZORS

Put the grape-scis in Charley's hands.

Tell O that dump in the b means the end of the cvass.— therefore I wish can^s to begin on the new one 1 month later—so let the dump fall Nov. 1.[66]

⟨I shan't be sat with less'n 90 p c on L of H.⟩[67] [#]

---

[64] Clemens is again referring to *Colonel Sellers as a Scientist*.

[65] Clemens added the two entries about his stock transactions on 10 April and 3 May 1884 at the bottom of the notebook page and along the right margin respectively.

[66] By the late summer and fall of 1883 large stocks of *Life on the Mississippi* were being "dumped" on the regular book trade at a lower price, and canvassing for the book suffered accordingly (*MTLP*, p. 166, n. 3). By the time Clemens made this notebook entry, in October 1883, he had resigned himself to the fact that the book was a failure, and he was willing to let Osgood "dump" the rest of the stock on the trade and begin pre-publication canvassing on his new book, *Huckleberry Finn*. Clemens, however, was so dissatisfied with Osgood's management of the subscription sale of *Life on the Mississippi* that he soon decided not to let him handle *Huckleberry Finn* at all and began making arrangements to publish the book himself through Charles L. Webster.

[67] Clemens' contract of 20 May 1881 with James R. Osgood & Company allowed him seventy per cent of the profits on the *Library of Humor*. Clemens may have been consider-

⟨Buy me 200 Am P at $1600.

Make contract with A P Co⟩[68]

Type-setter is now owned by Page—he will need capital.[69]

You have till Oct 31 to prove that you can sell books.—
But I must make my contract *now*. Therefore, turn into the
stores now, if you want to.

I want to pitch in on this book immediately, & issue it
⟨May⟩before May 1.[70]

Enter $5000 on chk book—Hubbard & Farmer "mud" on 300
sh stk.[71]

On
An deine schneeweisse Schulter.

At
An die Thüre klopfen.[72]
            to
Ich habe an ihn geschrieben. [#]

---

ing a revision of the contract to make it more favorable to himself, but his growing determination to break off business relations with Osgood precluded such a move. In February
1885 Charles L. Webster would purchase from Osgood all of Clemens' rights in his books,
including the unpublished *Library of Humor*.

[68] Clemens is probably referring to his idea of contracting with the American Publishing Company for publication of *Huckleberry Finn* (see the headnote, p. 4).

[69] Since 1877, when the Farnham Type-Setter Manufacturing Company of Hartford
first contracted with James W. Paige, the Paige typesetter had cost the Farnham company
almost ninety thousand dollars. In 1883 because of lack of capital the Farnham company
withdrew from its agreement to finance the machine ("Private Circular to the Stockholders
of the Farnham Type-Setter Manufacturing Company" dated 26 January 1891, in MTP).
It was in 1883 that Clemens became actively involved in seeking new capital for Paige's
typesetter, and in 1886 he became the machine's principal backer.

[70] Clemens is referring to *Huckleberry Finn*.

[71] The "mud" was Clemens' margin payment on 200 shares of St. Paul Roller Mill stock
and 100 shares of the Missouri Pacific Railroad purchased through the Hartford bankers
and brokers Hubbard & Farmer (Hubbard & Farmer to SLC, 18 October 1883).

[72] Clemens was apparently interested in the various usages of the German preposition
an. This entry and the following one read: *To knock at the doors. I have written to him.*
Clemens also quotes several random lines (36.12, 37.1, 37.3, 37.5–6, 37.8, 37.10) from
the group of poems entitled "Die Heimkehr" in Heinrich Heine's *Buch der Lieder*

So vergiss das ⟨[O]⟩Alte Lieben.

       on
Lieg ich jetzt an Ihren Herzen

           by or in
Kaum sahen wir uns, und an Augen & Stimme
Merkt ich dass du mir gewogen bist;

(By)
An dem Bache zirpt die Grille.

    in
Dorten an dem Bach alleine

          Der Tod, das ist die kühle Nacht,
          Das Leben ist der schwüle Tag;
          Es dunkelt schon, mich schläfert,
          Der Tag hat mich mud' gemacht.

Advertise games in Youth's Companion, Boston.

Der Gefallen gefällt wem Gefallen gefallen kann; doch gefälle dem Gefallenen nicht was mir gefiel.[73]

Sel.[74] speaks of relative 95 yr old, fell down & broke his nose— ⟨fraid 'twould disfigure⟩ fraid 'twould/come near disfigure⟨d⟩ him for life.

Sel. If you shoot at your wife in the dark for a burglar you always kill⟨s⟩ her, but you can't hit a burglar. You can always kill a relative with a gun that ain't loaded.
    (See spch)[75] [#]

(1827). The four lines beginning "Der Tod, das ist die kühle Nacht" (37.11–14) form the first verse of the poem of the same name.

[73] This rather obscure alliterative German entry appears to mean: *Pleasure pleases him who can be pleased; but what pleased me wouldn't have pleased the dead man.*

[74] Colonel Sellers.

[75] Clemens is referring to his humorous speech, "Advice to Youth," delivered about 1882, which includes a similar observation about unloaded guns: "A youth who can't hit a cathedral at thirty yards with a Gatling gun in three-quarters of an hour, can take up an old empty musket and bag his grandmother every time, at a hundred" (*MTS* [1923], p. 107).

Sel. Often the case that the man who can't tell a lie is the best judge of one.

About middle October, '83, Osgood owed me $33,250.
⟨T[---]⟩Paid me $5,000 by check.
⟨T⟩Gave me acceptances at 3 months from Oct 15, for $5,000, $10,000 & $5,000 ($20,000.)
Leaving $8,250 unprovided for.

Ladies Society for the Extirpation of Idleness, Frivolity & Other Social Evils—he shortened it & always spoke of them as the Social Evils.

Wakeman mentions a fellow who goes sneering around in heaven—nothing suits him—⟨hell⟩ hl of a place, he says. Always making suggestions of improvements.

> There is a boarding house
> Far, far away;
> Where they have ham & eggs
> Three times a day.
> O how them boardrs yell
> When they hear that dinner bell
> They *give* that lanlord—rats!
> 3 times a day.[76]

Mrs. S. L. Clemens requests the pleasure of Mrs. H. A. Perkins' company to luncheon[77] [#]

---

[76] This song is a burlesque of the first verse of Andrew Young's hymn "There Is a Happy Land," a "favorite Sunday-school song" written in 1838: "There is a happy land, / Far, far away, / Where saints in glory stand, / Bright, bright as day. / O, how they sweetly sing, / 'Worthy is our Saviour King, / Loud let His praises ring, / Praise, praise for aye' " (Amos R. Wells, *A Treasury of Hymns* [Boston: W. A. Wilde Co., 1945], pp. 220, 221). Clemens made use of this burlesque in the manuscript of *Colonel Sellers as a Scientist* and later transferred it to *The American Claimant*. In an Autobiographical Dictation of 30 November 1906 he explained the origin of the burlesque: "It was not I that wrote the song. I heard Billy Rice sing it in the negro minstrel show, and I brought it home and sang it—with great spirit—for the elevation of the household. The children admired it to the limit, and made me sing it with burdensome frequency" (*S&MT*, p. 222).

[77] Mrs. H. A. Perkins was the widow of the former president of the Hartford Bank. The occasion of Mrs. Clemens' luncheon was probably that mentioned in Clemens' letter of 4

Due Apl. 30 '84 £300.
```
"   May 30        "
"   June 30      304.7.11.
```
[78]

Songs of fair weather[79]

Uncle Remus.[80]

Paid Hubbard & Farmer J L & Co's[81] ck for $5000 Nov. 16/83.

TWICHELL at the State Prison. McManus.[82]

No earl myself, but sire of a torchlight *procession* of earls.

What is an Englishman?
A person who does things because they have been done before.
What is an American (or difference between 'em.)
A person who does things because they *haven't* been done before.

A materializzee Arctic can not only stand that climate, but the Congl investigation afterward.[83] [#]

November 1883 to Howells: "Mrs. Clemens has a menagerie on her hands from now till Tuesday Evening—the preparation & achievement of a big lunch party of old ladies to meet her mother" (*MTHL*, pp. 447–448).

[78] These amounts represent royalties, deposited in Clemens' account as delayed payments, from Clemens' English publishers Chatto & Windus.

[79] In 1883 Clemens acquired and signed a copy of this volume, Maurice Thompson's first collection of poetry, published that year by James R. Osgood & Company. Thompson's lyrics celebrated the beauty of the woods and the joys of archery. Clemens met the poet on 6 February 1885 in Lafayette, Indiana, during his lecture tour with George Washington Cable.

[80] Clemens probably intended to secure a copy of Joel Chandler Harris' second volume of stories, *Nights with Uncle Remus: Myths and Legends of the Old Plantation*, published by James R. Osgood & Company in November 1883. The book includes Harris' Georgia variant of the "Golden Arm" story which Clemens sent him on 10 August 1881.

[81] J. Langdon & Company, in which Livy Clemens inherited a substantial interest.

[82] Thomas McManus, a Hartford attorney, served as secretary on the board of directors of the Connecticut State Prison at Wethersfield. Twichell is known to have spoken there, but the occasion of the notebook entry has not been identified.

[83] In the first act of *Colonel Sellers as a Scientist*, Clemens has Colonel Sellers explain his latest scheme—that of materializing dead persons with a complicated electrical apparatus and supplying the "materializees" to world governments as policemen, rulers, and congressmen. As Sellers sees it, "if proper pains are taken in the materializing," the materialized "articles" should "remain perfectly sound and sweet a thousand years" (*Complete Plays of W. D. Howells*, p. 217).

No citizenship in America. Prof. Sloan of Princeton.[84] & the interviewer.

Twichell & the mudhole.
Beecher & $200 ck—forgave forger.

Contrast Aldrich with Sidney Smith in Lib Humor.[85]

By Capt. Eli Stormfield of New Bedford, Whaler.[86]

Man getting ready to read aloud—"Shut the window, first"—"change chairs"—40 prliminary interruptions—inspiration *all* gone.

Borrowing

Sehen veeflursist[87] [#]

---

[84] William Milligan Sloane was at this time professor of history at Princeton University.

[85] Clemens had reminded himself of a Sydney Smith witticism for the *Library of Humor* in Notebook 19 (N&J2, p. 364). Although Clemens and Howells had considered expanding the library to include "the humor of *all* countries" (SLC to Howells, 24 October 1880, *MTHL*, p. 333), the idea was eventually discarded in favor of a purely American collection. Consequently, while two sketches by Thomas Bailey Aldrich appeared in the book, the drolleries of Sydney Smith, canon of Saint Paul's and co-founder of the *Edinburgh Review*, were not represented. Clemens' notebook entry indicates that he intended to compare the wit of Aldrich and Smith, probably to the advantage of Aldrich, whom Clemens considered to have no "peer for prompt and pithy and witty and humorous sayings" (*MTA*, 1:247).

[86] Evidence in this notebook suggests that Clemens decided on the name Stormfield for his heaven-bound sea captain in 1883. Before this point Clemens referred to his manuscript informally, usually describing it as a book about "Capt. Ned Wakeman's adventures in heaven" (*MTHL*, p. 376). The name Stormfield appears for the first time in this notebook; the captain is also mentioned as "Capt. S." (p. 32), "Wakeman" (p. 38), and the conflated version, "Wakefield" (p. 56), indicating Clemens' lingering indecision. One extant version of the manuscript is entitled "The Travels of Capt. Eli Stormfield, Mariner in Heaven" (American Academy of Arts and Letters, New York City), and the hero's home port is given as San Francisco. In a much later version Clemens changed the hero's name again—to "Captain Ben Stormfield, late of Fairhaven & 'Frisco" (MTP). Clemens' captain was probably a composite creation based on the anecdotes and personalities of Captain Edgar Wakeman and Captain James Smith "of New Bedford & Honolulu" (see p. 46, note 103). Clemens had previously utilized aspects of these two nautical acquaintances for his portraits of Captain Waxman (in the 1866 *Alta California* letters), Captain Ned Blakely (*Roughing It*), and Captain "Hurricane" Jones ("Some Rambling Notes of an Idle Excursion").

[87] Clemens may be attempting a phonetic rendering of *Sehen wieviel Uhr es ist*—"See what time it is."

Bjornsen's books—Houghton.[88]

Lawrence Hutton
229 W. 34th,
$15.[89]

Bohn's Neues Bilderbuch
Esslingen—Schreiber.[90]

Clara hurts *him* & Susie hurts *sie*—then they cry.

John Alison[91]
Centre st.

Dec. 21—Furnace has been insufficient one week.

Space 2 ft 2½—6 in. tiles black & white

7 Venetian fingerbowls

Consistency.[92]

Persecution (prot.) in France.

It is a *religion*—& free here. [#]

---

[88] Houghton, Mifflin and Company published several novels and collections of stories by the Norwegian writer Björnstjerne Björnson between 1881 and 1883.

[89] Clemens wrote to Hutton on 20 December 1883: "I enclose a small Xmas present ($15) for you. Spend it judiciously for whisky & in other pious ways, & always be thankful that you have friends about you like me, who will never see you come to want" (Laurence Hutton Collection, Princeton University Library).

[90] Niklaus Bohny's *Neues Bilderbuch* (Esslingen: I. F. Schreiber, 187[-]) was an illustrated primer.

[91] Clemens secured the names of two furnace repairmen, John Alison and Charles R. Ellis, from his Hartford neighbor Newton Case.

[92] Mark Twain delivered a paper with this title concerning the ethics of party loyalty to the Monday Evening Club on 5 December 1887. It is published in the 1923 edition of *Mark Twain's Speeches* (pp. 120–130), where Albert Bigelow Paine incorrectly dates it "following the Blaine-Cleveland campaign, 1884." The relationship between the 1887 speech and the following eleven notebook entries (through "Grain . . . idiot") is unclear. These entries were evidently sparked by reports of Senator George F. Edmunds' proposal to amend his 1882 act which had denied public office to the Mormon polygamists and suspended their territorial government. Senator Edmunds' amendment was intended to make Mormon practices conform to United States law by suppressing polygamy and abolishing female suffrage in Utah. The amendment passed the Senate in January 1886.

It is backed by the Bible, & so is *not* immoral.

We say they are mistaken—Mohammedans & others say it of *us*.

They are refused a State & yet are entitled to it, for no crime is proved agst them.

If you gave them State *then* how could you find fault with their marriage laws?

Keep *Catholics* & drive out Mormons?

There ⟨never⟩ *is* no church that wouldn't break down if you took away its money power.

Utah did not go INTO U S land—their purpose was to *get* free—but the U S *enclosed* them.—Morally we have *not* the same right to boss them which we have in other Territories.

Then they ought to disendow the *Catholic* church—also the Prot.

Grain of *truth* in their relig—a promise of eternal life will catch *any* idiot.

Robinson's "Dreams." (Howells's dream when John woke up with scarlet fever.)[93]

Fairbanks[94]—at Mr. Paine's 3 W 53ᵈ. [#]

---

[93] This notebook entry and the related entries about dream and sleep phenomena which follow (43.7–44.10) seem to be the result of discussions between Howells, Clemens, and Thomas Bailey Aldrich, who was a guest at the Clemens house in mid-January 1884. Howells wrote to Clemens on 11 February 1884, evidently returning to a familiar subject: "I am having dreams, now, that are worth having" and went on to describe two recent nightmares (*MTHL*, pp. 469–470).

Hartford lawyer Henry C. Robinson read a paper on "Dreams" before the Monday Evening Club of Hartford on 21 January 1884. Howells' son John was ill with scarlet fever in January 1884. Howells later recalled his premonitory dream of his son's illness in the article "True, I Talk of Dreams" published in *Harper's* magazine in May 1895. Both Clemens and Howells explored dream symbolism and particularly recurrent and vivid dreams in later works.

[94] Possibly Mrs. Mary Mason Fairbanks. Clemens wrote to her twice in January 1884, first asking her to "come here & see us, when you arrive east" and then, when she didn't, scolding her for "this dam nonsense of shirking Hartford every 3 months & then rushing home to apologize for it" (24 and 30 January 1884, *MTMF*, pp. 255–256).

⟨A.⟩ N. A Bosworth, Page's steam heater.[95]

Townsend, ⟨r⟩crude gas.

Yung Wing[96]
  of Wᵐ H Kellogg
  80 Trumbull St

Send paper cover for Section 4 if you have one—or *any* cover.

Howells's.	Aldrich
Shock—	Need not dream all night—one dream is
⟨Worms.⟩ Worms.	all you have & it a second.
Telegraphy.	*Violence*
	Murders confessed in sleep.

⟨*Violence* in sleep.⟩

Instantaneousness of a long dream—a d is a *picture*—not words.

Never dream of a recent thing.
Telegraphy explains it *all.*
Two persons or more act individualy & talk [*one leaf torn out*]

One sees nothing in a dream which is original in shape

Not absence of violence. [#]

---

[95] Bosworth was a Hartford dealer in heating equipment and agent for the "Page steam heater" (advertisement in *Geer's* [1882], p. 264). W. H. Townsend, mentioned in the following entry, was a Hartford oil agent.

[96] Yung Wing, formerly the head of the Chinese Educational Mission in Hartford (see *N&J2*, p. 389), returned to Hartford, after a two-year stay in China, in the spring of 1883. Hartford businessman William H. Kellogg was probably a relative of the former Mary L. Kellogg, Yung Wing's wife. Clemens may have intended to confer with Yung Wing about a scheme to finance the building of a railway system in China. Clemens recalled in his autobiography that "early in 1884, or late in 1883," he "called on General Grant with Yung Wing . . . to introduce Wing and let him lay before General Grant a proposition": that of heading the syndicate of investors in the railway. Grant "would not undertake a syndicate, because times were so hard here that people would be loath to invest money so far away. . . . He said that easier times would come by and by, and that the money could then be raised, no doubt, and that he would enter into it cheerfully and with zeal" (*MTA*, 1:20–21).

⟨The Eye
       Ear
Blind don't smoke⟩
wake & snore.
Pilot.
Writing—speechmaking
faces chan—crowds melt or vanish.
Awkward situations.
Nightmare
Strong sensation.

I'll be bound *you'd* be mixed up in it, what*ever* it was![97]

'Sh! *There* they are! Lost, & sick & discouraged—pleading for
help. Huck, what did I *tell* you—what did I tell you⟨?⟩! Its the
most ⟨miraculous⟩ extraordinary triumph I've ever achieved in my
life—& yet I believed from the *start* I could do it. I've found this
whole gang! ⟨H[-]⟩(Pause)—(Impressivly). Huck, we'll be *heroes*
for this. It'll be in the papers—maybe in *books*. 'Sh! now do as I
tell you—we'll work off a *surprise* on them.

A. P.[98] Been trapsing around this hole 2 days & nights, most,
hunting for you trash.

Write Wall st play of "O. T." (With Gillette.[99] [#]

---

[97] This entry and the next (through "A. P. . . . trash.") are drafts of dialogue for
Clemens' dramatization of *Tom Sawyer*, which he completed on 29 January 1884. The
speeches, slightly modified, occur in the third and fourth acts of the play (see "Tom
Sawyer: A Play in Four Acts," *HH&T*, pp. 310, 321).

[98] Aunt Polly.

[99] The ruinous decline of the Oregon and Transcontinental Company stock in which
he had invested heavily (see p. 29, note 50) evidently struck Clemens as good material
for a play. He may have discussed possible play collaborations with his Hartford neighbor,
the young actor and dramatist William Gillette. Gillette was a favorite and frequent
visitor at the Clemens home and was indebted to Clemens for aiding him in his early
theatrical career. Part of the indebtedness was financial, Clemens having advanced
Gillette at least three thousand dollars. Gillette would write to Clemens on 29 July
1886: "I had hoped—or thought it possible, that I might do some dramatic work with
you, or assist you in some way in that line. . . . Should we arrange to do anything
together, as was once proposed, I thought this might be reckoned in against me there."
The proposed collaboration never materialized and Gillette paid off his debt to Clemens
in April 1887 (Gillette to SLC, 25 April 1887).

—put Bonanza IN this

A stranger strikes them at 3 periods—first poor, second, Enormously rich, third, beggars, but Bonanza (Villard)?) is an honorable beggar, he & his family having given up every penny to the creditors & to people who bought the stock on their recom.[100] Each time this Englishman or Frenchman or German (no, it is all *three*) have been absent on their travels a *year*.

For a play: America in 1985. The Pope here & an Inquisition. The age of darkness back again. Pope is temperal despot, *too*. A titled ⟨eccles⟩ aristocracy & primogeniture. ⟨No⟩ Europe is *republican* & full of science & invention—none allowed here.

Though he lie like a prophet.

CXLIV. *Shaks.*

Fire him out!" last line.[101]

Starving on raft. The pauper has a Boston cracker. ⟨Bonan⟩ Resolves to keep it till Bonanza is beginning to starve, then make him pay $50,000 for it. Bonanza agrees. P's cupidity excited— resolves to wait & get more; 24 hours later, ⟨Bonanza⟩ asks a million for the cracker. Bonanza agrees. P. has wild dreams of becoming enormously rich off his cracker—backs down—lies all night building castles in the air—next day raises his price higher & higher till B has offered $100,000,000, every cent he's got in the world. P. accepts. B. "*Now* give it to me." P. No, it's not a trade till you sign document relating history of the transaction & making oath to pay." While P. is finishing the document B. sees a ship.

---

[100] Railroad promoter Henry Villard had created the ill-fated Oregon and Transcontinental Company in 1881 in order to facilitate his spectacular scheme for the completion of a trunk line from the Great Lakes to the Pacific. In September 1883 Villard drove the last spike of his railroad before a crowd of notable guests. Meanwhile stock in his over-extended railroad holdings had been declining drastically. In December 1883 Villard was forced to declare bankruptcy and resign his presidency of a number of railroad companies. Although he was denounced by the press as a heartless speculator, Villard suffered considerable personal loss in attempting to repay his creditors and did not recoup his fortunes for several years.

[101] Clemens is referring to the conclusion of Shakespeare's "Two loves I have of comfort and despair" (sonnet 144): "Yet this shall I ne'er know, but live in doubt, / Till my bad angel fire my good one out."

When P. says "Sign⟨'⟩ & take the cracker"—B. smiles a smile⟨s⟩, declines, & points to the ship.

Write this story, then add it to play of Bonanza.

Make play of the £1,000,000 Banknote.[102]

In the S I story,[103] make old Commodore ⟨Smith⟩ Cyclone a frequent & red-hot letter writer, whose whirlwinds of temper are gone by the time the letter is finished. The letter reeks with blasphemy & earth-rocking profanity. But now he strikes dimly out interlines, & the letter is as mild as a sucking dove. Always put in & strike out, as in Holome's['s] temperance song.[104]

See Dr Knapp.[105]

*Daly, 490—6th ave (8 to 10)[106]

---

[102] Clemens may have planned this story as early as 1879 (see N&J2, p. 297), although it did not appear until January 1893 in the *Century*. The play version never materialized.

[103] In January 1884 Clemens plunged into a new project—writing a novel set in the Sandwich Islands, illustrating his idea that "the religious folly you are born in you will *die* in, no matter what apparently reasonabler religious folly may seem to have taken its place meanwhile & abolished & obliterated it" (SLC to Howells, 7 January 1884, *MTHL*, p. 461). The novel was to be based on the life of "Billy" Ragsdale, the half-caste interpreter to the Hawaiian parliament whom Clemens had met on his 1866 trip to the Sandwich Islands (*Following the Equator* [Hartford: American Publishing Co., 1897], p. 63; see also N&J1, p. 104). One of the characters in the novel was to be based on "Capt. [James] Smith of New Bedford & Honolulu. . . . a kind of Captain Wakeman" (SLC to Howells, 26 February 1884, *MTHL*, p. 476; see also N&J1, pp. 188 and 191, notes 18 and 19). Clemens wrote to Mrs. Fairbanks on 24 January 1884 that he had finished the novel "last week" and was currently involved in "a most painstaking revision of it" (*MTMF*, p. 255; see also the headnote to this notebook). The only relic of the Sandwich Islands story is seventeen pages of fragmentary manuscript, evidently discarded from the book. Clemens had discussed with Howells the possibility of dramatizing Ragsdale's history. Howells agreed that the novel would function "merely as a magazine to draw from for our play" (Howells to SLC, 9 January 1884, *MTHL*, p. 463). The play, if it was ever written, is not extant.

[104] In Holmes's temperance poem, "Ode for a Social Meeting, with Slight Alterations by a Teetotaler," included in *The Autocrat of the Breakfast Table*, the teetotaler has lined out words referring favorably to alcohol and substituted his own temperance language.

[105] Clemens made two short trips to New York City in the latter half of February 1884 to which these memoranda refer.

[106] Clemens wrote Augustin Daly, the playwright and producer, on 17 February 1884 to inquire about producing his dramatization of *Tom Sawyer*. Daly's reply of 19

Get a good Schiller.

Talk Gilder about Ambu[n107]

Let O retain $2500 & immediately settle everything else up & *pay.*[108]

What about the H. game?

February suggested the time and place indicated in the entry—at Daly's Theatre—for Clemens to deliver the play. Clemens' footnote to this entry, added a few lines below it (48.1), indicates that he probably asked Charles Webster to do this errand. Daly rejected the play because he thought the children's parts "would seem ridiculous in grown peoples hands" (Daly to SLC, 27 February 1884, *MTBus*, p. 236).

[107] During his illness at the Clemens home from 27 January to 15 February 1884 George Washington Cable acquired a copy of a thirty-one page pamphlet romance entitled *The Enemy Conquered; or, Love Triumphant* by S. Watson Royston (New Haven: T. H. Pease, 1845). Clemens shared Cable's delight in the book's inflated sentimental language and unconscious humor. He purportedly borrowed it to read to the girls of the Saturday Morning Club and canvassed the bookstores in order to secure a copy of his own. The two authors referred to Royston's tale as "Ambulinia," the name of the heroine. Clemens' notebook entry indicates that he had some early plans to exploit the little book but there is no record that he approached Richard Watson Gilder of the *Century* until late 1892. At that time Gilder declined to publish Clemens' long article, consisting of a critical review of Royston's book along with the text of the book itself. Clemens included the article, finally titled "A Cure for the Blues," in *The £1,000,000 Bank-Note and Other New Stories* (New York: Charles L. Webster & Co., 1893).

[108] By the terms of the 10 April 1882 contract for *Life on the Mississippi* Osgood was to retain a five per cent commission on the first fifty thousand books sold. The balance of the profits, less the cost of manufacturing the book, was to go to Clemens. Webster informed Clemens on 27 February 1884 that he had written to Osgood for his long-delayed statement of expenses; Clemens' profits could not be calculated until it was received. Osgood finally replied on 18 March: "We have rendered a detailed statement of the whole a/c to Webster, and he is coming over to Boston early next week to look into a few items which he does not understand, and we shall then arrive at an exact balance. Will you kindly write me when and how you will like the remainder of the money. If you will as before take our acceptances it would suit us a little better." An acceptance was a formal commitment to pay a debt as a time draft over a specified period. On 22 April the business was still not settled and Clemens asked Webster: "Didn't you get those acceptances out of Osgood? You will be having sharp need of that money before long [to meet expenses on *Huckleberry Finn*], & you better make him pony up. Hardly any of the sum is in dispute, & there is no propriety in his delaying to pay. He has already delayed so long that he had just about annulled any half-promise to let him give acceptances instead of cash" (*MTBus*, p. 250). Osgood's delay was indicative of the troubled financial state of his company: in April 1884 he was forced to auction off several books and plates to avert disaster, but the maneuver only served to delay the company's failure until May 1885 (Carl J. Weber, *The Rise and Fall of James Ripley Osgood* [Waterville, Me.: Colby College Press, 1959], pp. 215, 218).

*Will send W. with play.
Abonnement für die Zeitung machen[109]

Ask St. Gaudens what to do with G.[110]

Chas R Ellis[111]
  182 Centre St

48 rue La Condamine
Wm L. Hughes
Les Bébés d'Hélène[112]

⟨Saturday,⟩ Friday in the night, March 7, the telephone went out of service.

Admiral Smith (In S I story says, "When that clock of mine points to 15 min after 4, & strikes 37, it means that it is half past 10." Says it is easy enough to get acquainted with its peculiarities, & anybody is a d—d fool who thinks a blemish or two like these should ⟨injure⟩ hurt a clock's reputation.

Das lasse ich gelten (that'll do).
Viel⟨d⟩ gelten, to be esteemed
Das gilt nict   (that's not permitted)
    "   "   Ihnen ("   ⟨p[-]⟩aimed at you, meant for you)
Wie viel gilt das? (What do you value it at?)
Es gilt (it concerns) meine Ehre.
Es gilt Kampf (fight's the word)

---

[109] *Subscribe to the newspaper.*

[110] Gerhardt wrote to Clemens on 27 May 1884 evidently in response to a suggestion from Clemens: "I can't understand what chance I shall have working for St Gaudens or [John Quincy Adams] Ward. They will not allow me to compete with them, while I am an assistant, and I shall be little better than a mechanic. *I am willing and glad to start in a small way, but I must be independent, or it's the end of my career.* . . . I will show you by making a success of myself how much I appreciate and love you all, but don't make me be a second fiddle that would kill me." Gerhardt returned to New York in July 1884, leaving his wife and child in France, and immediately began to seek commissions.

[111] See p. 41, note 91.

[112] On 14 February 1884, Hughes wrote to Clemens asking his "sanction" for his forthcoming French translations of *Tom Sawyer* and *Huckleberry Finn*. He also forwarded to Clemens a copy of his French adaptation of John Habberton's *Helen's Babies*.

Es gilt mir⟨[--]⟩ gleich) it's all one to me.
Einen Lügen strafen).[113]

Write a burlesque Frankenstein—(Freestone). His uncle a
bonanza simpleton, good & kind. F. has no memory on *Tuesdays*,
but can't notice it himself because he can't remember then that
there *is* such a day as Tuesday. Engages himself to girls on that
day, forgetting previous one—appoints a dozen weddings for a
Tuesday & goes off fishing.

2 girls, one poor & honest & pious, has a hard, wretched time;
the other is a hard lot, & lives in style in the county jail, where
Women's Aiders visit her; & she earns tobacco money there with
needle & has lovely sociable times; & every time her time is up she
commits petit larceny in view of a policeman & is back again
straightway.[114]

Also during one hour each day he has no memory

Heine's works.

½ Huhn $1.
 ″ Ente— 1.
Brown Kartoffl—20 or 30c
Kauliblume   50
Kaffè au lait[115]   35

Supper—

	say.
Cucumber Salat................	60
½ b. Claret....................	1.00
Shad	60
Boild potatoes	20
Cheeze & ⟨[-]⟩Crackers	50
Appolonaris	40
Cash	5.00 [#]

---

[113] This German idiom means: *To prove to be wrong.*
[114] The idea jotted down here resembles the theme of "Edward Mills and George
Benton: A Tale," published in the *Atlantic* in August 1880.
[115] The menu includes chicken, duck, brown potatoes, and cauliflower.

Breakfast
Steak, browned pota, coffee

The Frankenstein is a fellow who has eascaped from a hotel fire
& doesn't understand who he is taken for. He steals the real F's
clothes & puts them on, & a tramp steals the Frankenstein to sell
to the Medical Collge for a subject.

The human being disrespects his kind—all through. The city
person has small respect (when shopping) in N. Y. for a person who
is from Goshen (or even Boston.)—One nation despises another—
Feji despises France. Yet they tell us these prejudices will disappear
in Heaven. Be d—d!

Rambouillon's "⟨Studies⟩ Stories of Infinity"

Let a Bonanza miser die of starvation in his treasure vault,
gnawing at leather adornments & such things, preferring them to
gems of the first water.

£1,000,000 Note.

⟨A Lost⟩
Her Second Love (Peterson, Phila)
Democracy (H. Holt.)
Rambouillon's Stories of Infinity (ask Holt *himself*.)
Life of Gray (Morley's English Men of Letters)

Tennessee Mountain Tales, by Craddock. (Houghton.)[116]

Butler   Billings   Phillips
⟨Constipation Smith⟩[117]
⟨Siphyllis⟩   ⟨Wheeler-Davis.⟩

---

[116] Four of the books on Clemens' list have been identified: Annie Ogle's (Ashford
Owen) *Her Second Love* (Philadelphia: T. B. Peterson & Brothers, 1883), Henry Adams'
Democracy: An American Novel (New York: H. Holt and Co., 1880), Edmund Gosse's
Gray, published as part of John Morley's English Men of Letters series (London:
Macmillan and Co., 1882), and Mary Noailles Murfree's (Charles Egbert Craddock)
In the Tennessee Mountains (Boston: Houghton, Mifflin and Co., 1884).

[117] Clemens' list of burlesque names, inspired supposedly by the idea of a "physician
going to write a drama" (p. 51), occupies most of seven pages of the notebook. Two of

⟨Siphillis Briggs.⟩
⟨Dysentery Jones⟩
Typhoid ⟨Ba[--]⟩Billings
⟨Malaria Johnson⟩
⟨Consumption ⟨Hoyt.⟩ Babcock⟩
⟨Asphyxia Beedle.⟩
⟨Gonorrhoea⟩
⟨Gonorrhoea Jackson⟩
⟨Diarrhea Hutchinson⟩
⟨Pneumonia Bascom.⟩
⟨Scarlatina Dodge⟩
⟨Neuralgia ⟨Garth⟩ Bliss⟩
⟨Lumbago ⟨Haynes⟩ ⟨Anderson⟩ St. Clair⟩
⟨Cancer Collins⟩
⟨Apoplexy ⟨Holcomb⟩ Anderson⟩
⟨Diphtheria Marsh⟩
⟨Vaccination Walker⟩
(Physician going to write a drama.)

160 Garden st E K Root[118]
Ich habe mich verbannt; ich komme nicht wieder bis Ihr
verdammtes Haus in Brand gesteckt wird.[119]

                    Wart
⟨Lockjaw Harris⟩
⟨Bunion Miller⟩
    Convulsion
⟨Abscess Wheeler⟩
⟨Sinapism Davis⟩
⟨Rheumatism Blake⟩
⟨Chilblain ⟨Parker⟩ Batterson⟩

---

the pages contain a clean final version of the list (53.1–31). Clemens' working notes for
"Indiantown," an undated, unfinished sketch probably written in 1899 and published
in *Mark Twain's Which Was the Dream?* (pp. 153–176), include this entry about the
character Dr. Bradshaw: "Named his children Scarlatina,—named for epidemic
outbraks—cholera morbus" (working notes in MTP).

[118] Edward K. Root was a Hartford physician.

[119] *I've exiled myself; I won't come back until your damned house is set on fire.*

⟨Cuticle ⟨Plummer⟩ Batterson⟩
⟨Quinsy Warner⟩
⟨Suffocation Billings⟩ Loomis
⟨Bowels⟩
⟨Bowels Templeton⟩
⟨Elephantiasis ⟨Aldrich⟩ Addison⟩
⟨Influenza Butler⟩
⟨Asthma Lowell⟩
⟨Liver Hopkins.⟩
⟨Cantharides Dunlap⟩
⟨Gangrene Hopkins⟩
⟨Tuberculosis Butler.⟩
Liver Hopk   Gout
Asthma Lowell   Billings   Rogers
Ophthalmia
⟨Baxter⟩
Pitts
Brigg[s]
⟨Rectum Jones⟩
⟨Major-maxillary Brown⟩
⟨General Debility⟩
⟨Ophthalmia Lewis.⟩
Indigestion Jones.
⟨Calomel
Borax⟩
⟨Bluemass Baxter⟩
⟨Diaphram⟩ ⟨Influenza ⟨Briggs⟩ Smith⟩
Abdomen St. Augustine
Scrofula
Suffocation Billings/Briggs
Hemmorrhage
  Templeton
Belladonna
Debility
⟨Paralysis Brown⟩
Epilepsy Thompson [#]

Apoplexy Addison   28
Typhoid Billings
Diphtheria Marsh
Consumption Babcock
Paralysis Brown
Malaria Johnson
Asphyxia Beedle
Pneumonia Bascom
Scarlatina Dodge
Vaccination Walker
Lumbago St. Clair
Neuralgia Bliss
Bunion Miller
Lockjaw Harris
Convulsion Wheeler
Sinapism Davis
Blister McManus.
Chilblain Batterson
Dropsy Miller
Quinsy Warner
Suffocation Loomis
Elephantiasis ⟨Addison⟩ Templeton.
Cantharides Dunlap
Gangrene Hopkins
Ophthalmia Lewis
Influenza Smith
Bluemass Baxter
Tuberculosis Butler
Indigestion Jones
—& last of all, the hero—
Scrofula St. Augustine

Codliver ⟨Hopkins⟩
Lord Asphalt
Col. Hellion
Gen. Bowels
Corporal Ashcat [#]

For a house of enchantment where humbugs & jokes are played
on a fellow; a choir sings (*appear* to sing) in his presence & he cant
hear a sound—thinks he is deaf werden.[120]

Life in interior of an iceberg. Luxuriously furnished from the
ship. (How produce heat?) Children born. Plate glass or ice
windows. Courtings, quarrels; feuds; ⟨massacr⟩massaccers. All found
dead & frozen—been dead 30 years. Flag (rag) on top. It drifts
around in a vast circle, in a current, year after year; & every 2 or 3
years they come in distant sight of the remains of the ship. They
kill bears, foxes, &c. They have a telescope. The berg consists of
mountains, levels & valleys, & is 12 miles long by 8 broad. They
live on game. They invent amusements. The children born reach
marrying age, & marry. Try to make them comprehend life on land
in the world, but wholly fail—they understand life on an iceberg
only. They tame great flocks of birds & animals to eat. Perhaps they
have no fire—eat raw. Children don't know what fire or cold are.

It must be a woman's Diary, beginning abruptly, & not
explaining how they got there.

They don't know which is Sunday?

Believing they ⟨migh⟩ should never escape, & not wishing to
curse their children with longings unsatisfiable, both families teach
the young that the elders were born on the berg & know no other
world.

By & by come questions "Whence these knives & other metal
things?" (

"Well, they are found in the egg of the Wawhawp"—so the ch[n]
often hunt for the nests of this imaginary bird.

She must speak of one young girl who is an idiot?—& who is
now found, 80 ys old?

⟨Ha⟩What religion do they teach?

---

[120] Clemens used a similar theme of a practical joke which involves an elaborate
pretense and has tragic consequences in the "Legend of Dilsberg Castle" (*A Tramp
Abroad,* chapter 19). The German *werden* in the final line of the entry means "to
become."

She visits her husband's clear-ice grave after 30 years (enabled by snowing up of a chasm) & finds him fresh & young, while she is old & gray.[121]

Of all sad words of tongue or pen, the ⟨sad⟩ verdammtest are these, Es ⟨mochte⟩ hätte sein ⟨können⟩kön'.

> Of all sad words of tongue or pen,
> The verdammtest are these, es hätte sein könn'.[122]

He said that the old forms of profanity were of no real use in learning the bi.[123] They are pale & inadequate. What we need is something stronger, something with more color—something lurid.

Second day of bi, had to go into seclusion for a while because ⟨I had⟩ there was not skin enough left on ⟨me⟩ my legs to cover my nakedness.

Expert said new & stronger forms of profanity must be created to meet the ⟨no⟩ needs of novices—the old ones are inadequate, they do not reach the case.

A fearful night (in the Sandwich Islands) The ⟨na⟩old native's smile.

Baggage goes to Xtopher st. N.Y.[124] [#]

---

[121] The theme of marooned voyagers sketched here anticipates the theme of two of Mark Twain's unfinished narratives of his later years, "The Enchanted Sea-Wilderness" and "An Adventure in Remote Seas" (*WWD*, pp. 76–86, 89–98).

[122] Clemens is paraphrasing one of the final couplets from John Greenleaf Whittier's "Maud Muller"—"For of all sad words of tongue or pen, / The saddest are these: 'It might have been!'"

[123] In May 1884 Clemens and Twichell were attempting to master bicycle riding. Clemens wrote about his unsuccessful bicycle experiences and considered submitting the article to the New York *Sun*, but soon decided against publishing the piece: "I revised, & doctored, & worked at the bicycle article, but it was no use, I didn't like it *at all*—so I tore it up. Tear up the MS. one in your possession. I will not tackle the subject again till next fall" (SLC to CLW, 6 June 1884, *MTBus*, p. 258). A typescript of the article, "Taming the Bicycle," survived and was published in *What Is Man? and Other Essays* (New York: Harper & Brothers, 1917), pp. 285–296.

[124] The Clemens family would travel from Hartford to New York City on 17 June

Plates for 3
Bread & butter for 2
Cold Roast beef for 1
Tea Oolong for 1
Strawberries 1
Currant jelly...................... 1

The fly-speck copy of the Scriptures—Pawnee—only f.s. copy in existence—worth $17,500.

A friend of Wakefied in heaven gave his note for a thousand years & kept it up till he became embarrassed & his business went into the hands of a receiver.

People in trying to justify Eternity, say we can put it in by learning all the knowledge acquired by the inhabitants of the myriads of stars. We shan't need that. We could use up two eternities in learning all that is to be learned about our own world & the thousands of nations that have risen & flourished & vanished from it. Mathematics alone would occupy me 8 million years.

⟨Mend watch-chain
Waterbury Watch
Worm-fireworks
Astoria.⟩

Small-pox (Audubon
Suicide

Sawing man in two.

Aug. 12. I think we are only the microscopic ⟨[--]⟩ trichina concealed in the blood of some vast creatures veins, & that it is that vast creature whom God concerns himself about, & not us.[125] [#]

1884 and then on to Elmira the following day for the summer stay at Quarry Farm. Their usual route from New York City was by way of the Christopher Street Ferry to Hoboken, New Jersey, where they boarded the Delaware, Lackawanna, and Western Railroad for Elmira.

[125] This entry suggests the fantasy in "Three Thousand Years Among the Microbes," not written until 1905 (published in WWD, pp. 433–553).

I lose my temper over a certain class of business (begging) letters ⟨w⟩except when they come from colored (& therefore ignorant) people. Mrs. Clemens suggests that I adopt as a motto "Consider everybody colored till he is proved white."[126]

Carter's Koal Black Ink

The calamity ⟨has cast⟩ a gloom over the whole community.

		20.		40
				7
				280
Wages[127]	300.		6000	
Expenses	300		1700	
"	600		4300	
	1200		12	
	500		8600	
	1700		4300	
			51,600	

Sell lives dearly as possible.

Paid $500 this summer—13 weeks; also paid $7 per week for washing down town.[128]

Six & 7 mos after ⟨$356.11⟩£356.11[129]

⟨Mch 29, 2055⟩ [#]

---

[126] Clemens considered Livy's maxim clever enough to report to Howells (SLC to Howells, 17 September 1884, *MTHL*, pp. 509–510).

A loose clipping from an American newspaper is interleaved near this entry, although there is no evidence to show how long it has been in this place. Under the dateline "Foo Chow, Sept. 16," the clipping reports that "the British lieutenant who was wounded when the British ship Zephyr was fired upon by the Chinese, died to-day." Details of this news item were reported in the New York *Times* of 9, 15, and 17 September 1884.

[127] These calculations of expenses were written by Mrs. Clemens.

[128] During the Clemenses' annual stay at Quarry Farm they shared expenses with the Crane family. The Clemens family left the farm on 23 September 1884 to return to Hartford by way of New York City.

[129] These are royalties due from Chatto & Windus (see p. 77, note 37).

People to see in N. Y.[130]

Dana. (*Huck Finn.* & 1,002.)[131]

Swinton, 20 Lafayette Place.[132]

Sage, or Worden & Co. 48 Wall[133]

Whitford.[134]

New York Times, or *Noah Brooks.*[135]

---

[130] Clemens' list of New York errands, through "Spring . . . Chas W" (59.14), appears near the back of the notebook, preceded by several blank leaves. The nature of the list indicates that it is out of chronological order and was made not in 1884 but just before Clemens' stay at the Hotel Brunswick in New York City in September 1883.

[131] Clemens evidently intended to see Charles A. Dana, editor of the New York *Sun*, and Richard Watson Gilder of the *Century* magazine (mentioned a few lines below) regarding possible serial publication of *Huckleberry Finn* and the "1,002^d Arabian Night," a tiresome burlesque which Clemens had completed early in the summer of 1883. The *Century* eventually published three excerpts from *Huckleberry Finn* in December 1884 and January and February 1885. The "1,002^d Arabian Night" was pigeonholed, partially because of Howells' condemnation of it (Howells to SLC, 18 September 1883, *MTHL*, pp. 441–442) and partially for lack of publishing interest in it. The burlesque is included in *Mark Twain's Satires & Burlesques*, ed. Franklin R. Rogers (Berkeley and Los Angeles: University of California Press, 1967), pp. 91–133.

[132] See p. 30, note 55. Swinton's letter of 3 September 1883 to Clemens indicates that the two had agreed to meet in New York within a few days.

[133] Clemens undoubtedly wished to confer with Dean Sage about his stock in the Oregon and Transcontinental Company (see p. 29, note 50 and p. 45, note 100), which he had bought on Sage's recommendation. Sage's letter of 1 September indicated that he was still sanguine about the stock's future: "I should advise your staying by your O. T. as I have done with mine. I believe it is as good as it ever was, intrinsically." Clemens had bought his shares on margin through the New York brokerage firm of Worden & Company.

[134] Daniel Whitford of the New York law firm of Alexander & Green was responsible for Clemens' legal affairs. Clemens probably intended to consult him in regard to the Duncan libel suit (see p. 24, note 41).

[135] Clemens probably wanted to see his friend Noah Brooks in connection with the Duncan libel suit. Brooks, a journalist on the *Times*, had been subpoenaed as a witness for the prosecution in the case. In a friendly, even conspiratorial, letter of 19 June 1883 Brooks had reassured Clemens as to his sympathies, declaring himself "a Know Nothing." Brooks's assumption was that Clemens, having cause to fear that Duncan would bring a libel suit against him as well as the *Times*, was anxious for the success of the *Times's* defense. Clemens drafted a "confidential" reply to Brooks on 23 July 1883 which he may not have mailed. The letter reveals Clemens' defection to Duncan's camp, a tactical decision which protected Clemens from further litigation (see p. 18, note 34). "The great bulk of the interview is reportorial invention," Clemens told Brooks, "& damned poor invention at that. If I am called to testify, the above will be what I shall say." Clemens

Gilder, Century. about *Huck Finn*. & 1,002.

Webster, have Munn build us a play-board. of false rubber?
Bank Note Co can print it.[136]

And he see Frank Bliss.[137]

Strike Harpers, & Ivison, Blakeman, Taylor & Co, great school
book house, for terms for the game.[138] Osgood, too.

Alex & Green[139]
Geo. Jones, 30 W 37[th][140]

Henry G. Piffard, M.D.
   408 E. 26th st
house 10 W. 35th.

Slee.[141]
Gen Grant about that fraud
Spring, 635 tel Chas W[142]

funeral obsequies
Sickening thud.

---

continued in a much revised, then canceled passage, "I write this to you as an extra cau-
tion so that you may go on with your eyes open, & I shan't have anything on my conscience. If you think the same way, tell them [i.e. the *Times*]. If not, tear this up."

[136] Munn & Company of New York City, the editors of *The Scientific American*,
provided services to inventors in securing and investigating patents. During the summer
of 1883 Charles Webster retained Munn & Company to secure a caveat on the playing
board of the history game.

[137] Clemens may have intended for Webster to speak to Frank Bliss about the publication of *Huckleberry Finn*. Clemens wrote to Webster at the end of September 1883:
"As soon as shall seem wise, come up & we will contract with Bliss for the new book.
We will keep pretty quiet about it for the present—Bliss will see the advantage of that,
himself" (*MTBus*, p. 221).

[138] In his letter of 30 August 1883 William Swinton referred to these two New York
publishing houses as "the two largest school-book houses in the world."

[139] See note 134.

[140] George Jones, one of the founders of the New York *Times*, was manager and publisher of the newspaper and determined its editorial policy. Jones, as representative of
the New York *Times* Association, was the defendant in the Duncan libel suit.

[141] J. D. F. Slee of the Langdon family coal business in Elmira.

[142] This entry is followed by two blank pages. The remaining entries in the notebook
date from 1884.

happy pair
speckled beauties
regardless of Expense
launched into Eternity
hellish purpose (gone out)
poor but resp parents (gone out)
Disciples of ⟨Izaac⟩Izaak Walton
knight of the quill
    "   "   "   sock & buskin
disc of art preservative of ⟨all⟩ arts
euphonious cognomen (gone out)
tripped the light fantas toe
devotees of Terpsichore

1 & 2ᵈ of Huck Finn very good for reading aloud.[143]

Ditto—waking Jim—84.
    "   Raftsmen fight—89½
    "   Troubled conscience & smallpox—90.
    "   Art & Bible—105, 106.
Bucking Horse.
King Solomon; Henry VIII
Jim's little girl—dumb
Hamlet's Soliloquy. [#]

---

[143] As early as 25 July 1884 lyceum manager James B. Pond had issued a circular announcing the joint appearance of Clemens and George Washington Cable "in a unique
series of literary Entertainments" (circular in MTP). The contract for the series of readings, to run from 5 November 1884 until the end of February 1885, was formally signed
on 19 September 1884. On 20 September Clemens informed Pond: "A week from to-day
I expect to make my reading-selections—that is, as soon as I reach home" (Berg). Both
Cable and Clemens chose their selections for the two-hour program carefully so that, as
Pond's circular promised, "the pathos of one will alternate with the humor of the
other, and the genius of both will be presented in a rapidly changing programme." Clemens' readings were culled from the manuscript of the forthcoming *Huckleberry Finn*,
from *A Tramp Abroad*, from his unpublished *Colonel Sellers as a Scientist*, and from a
few miscellaneous sources. This notebook list of possible selections includes readings
from *Roughing It* which were not used (see Notebook 23 for further discussion of the
1884/1885 lecture tour).

C—10
Mrs. C.—1 | —1—2

Dean Sage 142 Pearl, out of Wall.

My Steve Gillis duel.[144]
Confusing interview with A Ward?[145]
Trim & put in all of the Hank Mond & Horace Greeley
chapter—p. ⟨150⟩15[2].
178—Mexican Plug.
233—Reduce Lost in Snowstorm
329—Buck Fanshaw.
Jumping Frog.—by request
Huck—Ch. 33—"All right, I'll go to hell."[146]
Meeting of H & Aunt Sally.
(Make a whole reading from Huck).

---

[144] Clemens' humorous account of his Nevada duel, "How I Escaped Being Killed in a Duel," appeared in *Every Saturday* on 21 December 1872. Clemens later retold the story in his *Autobiography* (*MTA*, 1:354–359).

[145] Clemens' "First Interview with Artemus Ward" appeared in the New York *Sunday Mercury* of 7 July 1867 and was later collected in *Mark Twain's Sketches, New and Old* (Hartford: American Publishing Co., 1875).

[146] Huck's struggle with his conscience occurs in chapter 31 of the first edition of *Huckleberry Finn.*

XXIII

"Telling a Story As Only He Can Tell It"

(September 1884–April 1885)

ALTHOUGH THE first dated entry in Notebook 23 was written on 24 October 1884 (p. 74), it is clear that Clemens began using the notebook before that time; indeed there is probably no lapse in time between the end of Notebook 22 in late September 1884 and the initial pages of Notebook 23. Once again Clemens transferred several pages of entries—mainly names and addresses and business information—from the earlier notebook to his new one. The last dated entry in the notebook was written on 4 April 1885.

Clemens produced virtually no literary work during the period of the notebook's use. Nonetheless this was an immensely productive period for him. He confirmed his reputation as an author and lecturer and also achieved national prominence as a publisher and businessman. He grew convinced that his business success would free him from the burden of literary composition. The virulent Blaine-Cleveland presidential campaign of 1884 also revealed Clemens to his public as an outspoken man of independent political conviction—a mugwump "pure from the marrow out" as Clemens styled it (S&MT, p. 196). This reputation would grow with the coming years.

From 5 November 1884 until 28 February 1885 Clemens traveled the lecture circuit with George Washington Cable, relearning the platform skills he had not used since his London lecture engagements of 1873/1874. For the first time in a major tour Clemens departed from his practice of presenting a fairly unified lecture drawn from one work or covering one subject. For weeks before the opening night in New Haven, Clemens picked through volumes of his sketches and longer works to select a varied program of readings. Richard Watson Gilder, of the *Century*, and Cable were both asked to suggest passages from the proofs of *Huckleberry Finn*. Clemens filled pages of his notebook with lists of possible readings; the length of the pieces and their juxtaposition with Cable's selections were carefully calculated.

The program was a novelty to audiences used to didactic or expository lectures. The reviewers labeled the programs "unique" and "remarkable." The Brooklyn *Daily Eagle* called the performances "a new form of popular entertainment" in which the "elocutionary art supplements the printer's." The *Eagle* continued: "It is, in effect, a condensation of dramatic efforts in readings, where the author presents his own characters to an audience, illustrating his subject with various sidelights, such as a song or a dialect, and thus vividly picturing the scenes he projects with local color" (21 November 1884).

Of equal interest to the reviewers was the personal appearance of the two authors. Both were repeatedly and exhaustively described in the reviews, particular attention being given to Mark Twain's awkward, shambling gait, his "frowzled head" which one reviewer described as a "stubborn crop of hirsute delirium tremens," and his "conversational, slow, nasal drawl" (Boston *Evening Transcript*, 14 November 1884; Detroit *Post*, 17 December 1884; New York *Sun*, 19 November 1884). Ample notice was taken of the contrast between Cable, "the precise, alert, brisk man of style . . . one of the dapper sort, as polite as a dancing master," and Mark Twain, "the man from way back who has sat down by the stove at the corner grocery, gathered his cronies about him, and is telling a story as only he can tell it" (Buffalo *Express*, 11 December 1884).

Despite Clemens' irritation with certain aspects of Cable's personality— Clemens' letters mention Cable's parsimony, his highhandedness with servants, his strict observance of the Sabbath, his usurpation of extra time on the lecture program—the four-month lecture tour proved profitable and generally enjoyable. Clemens' profits were about sixteen thousand dollars while Cable earned five thousand (*MT&GWC*, p. 117). Clemens even considered extending his triumphant return to the lecture platform by appearing in England during the summer of 1885 or 1886. But more pressing matters—chiefly the publication of the *Personal Memoirs of U. S. Grant*—kept Clemens at home.

Clemens' split with the publishing company of James R. Osgood was definite by February 1884. On 1 May 1884 a contract was drawn between Clemens and Charles L. Webster formalizing the establishment of Charles L. Webster & Company (the May 1884 contract is no longer extant, but it is mentioned in the subsequent "Articles of Agreement" between Clemens and Webster dated 20 March 1885). The primary concern of the new company was the publication of the *Adventures of Huckleberry Finn* in February 1885. Thanks to Webster's energetic prepublication subscription canvassing, the book had a sale which even Clemens pronounced "splendid" (*MTLP*, p. 184).

While *Huckleberry Finn* enjoyed a popular success, critical reaction was surprisingly sparse and, in a few cases, decidedly negative: the book was criticized for coarseness, and even condemned as pernicious. Although the adverse criticism rankled, Clemens was quick to see its value as advertising. He wrote to Charles Webster on 18 March 1885 that the Concord, Massachusetts, Public Library's condemnation of *Huckleberry Finn* as " 'trash and suitable only for the slums' " was a "rattling tip-top puff." He added: "That will sell 25,000 copies for us sure" (*MTL*, pp. 452–453). Clemens continued in a letter to his sister Pamela on 15 April: "Those idiots in Concord are not a court of last resort, & I am not disturbed by their moral gymnastics. No other book of mine has sold so many copies within 2 months after issue as this one has done" (*MTBus*, p. 317).

The controversy about *Huckleberry Finn* was soon eclipsed by public disclosure of Webster & Company's negotiations for General Grant's memoirs. Webster had been acting as Clemens' agent in the matter since late November 1884. Both men were anxious to secure the book for their fledgling publishing house, but Grant was hesitant because of his verbal commitment to place the book with the Century Company. Grant and his son Frederick mulled over the matter throughout December 1884 and January 1885. Early in February Webster submitted a new offer to the general guaranteeing him seventy per cent of the net profits. As Clemens later recalled: "I suggested to Gen. Grant that he submit my offer to the Century & other great publishing houses, & *close with the one that offered him the best terms.* He did it, & my offer was duplicated by *several* 'regular publishers,' the Century among the number; & two firms *exceeded* my offer. But none of them could exceed my *facilities* for publishing a subscription book—nor *equal* them, either—a fact which I proved to the satisfaction of General Grant's lawyer; & that is why I got the book" (SLC to the editor of the Boston *Herald*, 6 July 1885). One of the people Grant consulted in the matter was his close friend George W. Childs, editor and publisher of the Philadelphia *Public Ledger*. "Mr. Childs said to me afterward," Clemens stated in his autobiography, "that it was plain to be seen that the general, on the score of friendship, was so distinctly inclined toward me that the advice which would please him best would be advice to turn the book over to me" (*MTA*, 1:38). Grant accepted the new offer late in February 1885, and Charles L. Webster & Company immediately began to organize the advertising and subscription canvass for what would be their most successful publication.

A more extensive agreement concerning the Webster company, to be in effect from 1 April 1885 to 1 April 1890, was drawn on 20 March 1885. Webster had written to Clemens on 25 February 1885 outlining his ideas for the new agreement: "I am now receiving twenty five hundred dollars a year; all the past business will warrant. We have now entered upon the publication of a book [the Grant *Memoirs*] that will call for an additional expendature of time and money, and its success will be largely due to my personal efforts and energy. . . . Additional care and responsibility will be placed upon my shoulders, and I must work, and think much harder." The contract of 20 March 1885 stipulated that Webster receive, in addition to his salary, one-third of the net profits up to twenty thousand dollars and one-tenth of the net profits above twenty thousand dollars. The contract, however, also included a provision which effectively immobilized much of Webster's new income: over the five-year period of the contract's life Webster would be allowed to withdraw from the company only a part of his profits each year until the final year.

Except that it originally contained eighty-six instead of ninety-two leaves, Notebook 23 is identical to Notebook 22 in design and format. It now contains 154 pages, fourteen of which are blank. Six leaves and part of one other have been cut or torn out and are missing. Three other leaves, cut from the notebook and used by Clemens for two letters to his wife, are discussed in notes 43 and 180 (pp. 78, 118). The notebook is badly worn; its front cover is detached and much of the leather is worn away from the spine. About two-thirds of the pages are inscribed in black pencil, one-quarter in purple pencil, and the remainder in grayish blue, blue, black, or brownish black ink. Use marks in black pencil, probably by Paine, appear throughout but have not been reproduced.

Clemens marked with an X passages that refer to or recount anecdotes or that sketch ideas for stories. The marks, most in black pencil but a few in black ink, occur in three forms, **X**, **⋇**, and **#**, although there is no indication that the different forms were intended to convey different meanings. (Since most

Xs precede the **✖**s, most of which in turn precede the **#**s, it may be that the three forms represent indexing efforts undertaken at different times.) Clemens usually added the Xs wherever convenient near the beginning of the passages to which he wished to call attention; in this text the Xs which clearly designate a particular entry are printed at the beginning of that entry. Three of the Xs are reported in Details of Inscription because they represent the first appearance of one form of the symbol (68.18, 79.11, and 92.11). Beyond this listing, Xs are reported in Details of Inscription only when some aspect of the symbol (as at 92.15) or of the accompanying passage (as at 80.7) requires particular explanation.

Tip Saunders
  223 W. Walnut
J M Clemens[1]
  526 W. Walnut
    Cor. Centre

1884 & 1885.

			Pays
Bk Note	cost 105—		⟨8⟩6.[2]
N. Y. Cent.	"	130½	6
Norfolk	"	105	7
Little Rock	"	105	7

---

[1] Clemens' cousins, portrait painter Xantippe Saunders and physician John Marshall Clemens, were both residents of Louisville, Kentucky. Clemens noted their names and addresses on the front flyleaf of his notebook, probably intending to visit them when he and Cable lectured in Louisville on 5 and 6 January 1885. The following notation ("1884 & 1885.") also appears on the front flyleaf.

[2] Clemens' list of current stock investments, evidently based on similar lists in previous notebooks (see pp. 7–9 in this volume and N&J2, p. 491) occupies three successive right-hand pages of the notebook.

			Pays
Am. Ex. in Eur	cost	100	6
300 West. Un.		60	7
Conn. Fire		142	10
Jewell pin Co		100	6
⟨Crown Pt		106⟩	
St Paul R Mill		110	10
Metford—		125	8
Burr Index		100	
Farnham Type Setter		100	

Am. Bk. Note certif 1701 (20 shs).	$1000
Ditto 1740 (80 shs).................................	4000
Norfolk & Western Bds 325–6–7, 1618–19	5,000
Little Rock M R & T. Bds 1530–1–2–3–4	5,000
Am Ex in Eu 500 shs, 24001 to 24,500	5000
Conn. Fire Ins (12 shs) No. 1515	1200
Jewell Pin Co 15 shs (No. 19)	1500
Farnham Type Setter 120 shs (No. 6)...................	5,000
Crown Pt. Iron Co (No. 339) 100 shs..................	10,000
Hartford Sanitary P. Co. (40 shares)	1000
St Paul Roller Mill..................................	5,000
New stock Am Ex in Europe	5000
Metford, 100 shs....................................	3,125
Burr Index Co	2,500
Beech Creek, Clearfield RR 200, par	10,000
⟨300 Westⁿ Union	18,000⟩

15 Grande rue Grande
   Montrouge, France.[3]

R. G. Brooks,
   80 Broadway

All the Am Ex in Eu was put up with Bissell & Co as security in
May '84 [#]

---

[3] This entry, noting the Gerhardts' address, and most of the following entries through
"Howells, 302 Beacon." (p. 68) also appeared in Notebook 22 (pp. 9–11).

A. O. Schwartz 42 E 14

Dean Sage 142 Pearl out of Wall
   839 St Mark's ave

East India House
   56 Summer st. Boston

Hutton 229 W 34th

Webster 214 W 125, 658 Bway

No. 603 Safety Deposit

Century $33.50 per page, 13½ p. $450.

Old China, Parke, 186 Front.

Gustav Stachert, (German books)
   Bway bet 8 & 9th.

Howells, 302 Beacon.

⟨70⟩ 1708 Chesnut st. Medallion.[4]

Brander Mathews[5]
   121 E 18th.

Carter's Koal Black Ink.

X Jewell said church would trust me to take up collection—with a bell punch.[6] [#]

---

[4] Clemens had two plans during 1884 and 1885 for portrait medallions. He approached Karl Gerhardt about making a "clay medallion," evidently to advertise the Twain-Cable lecture tour, from a Sarony photograph of Cable and himself (SLC to Gerhardt, n.d., Buffalo Historical Society). He also considered producing a portrait medallion of General Grant for sale, as entries in this notebook indicate (pp. 96, 103).

[5] Writer and critic James Brander Matthews was a frequent contributor to periodicals and a member of the Kinsmen club of New York of which Clemens was also a member.

[6] Clemens recalled this remark in a short speech in London on 13 October 1900, identifying it as "an episode which occurred fifteen years ago" in a Hartford church. The "leading citizens" of the town, excluding Clemens, were asked to pass the collection plates. Clemens "complained to the governor of his lack of financial trust" in him and the latter replied, " 'I would trust you myself—if you had a bell-punch' " (*MTS*[1910],

'84–5.

X G. asked in a Broadway place for photo of M. T.—Intelligent clerk said What's her line? "Where does she play?"[7]

X Artemus stories:

What was his other name?

Why Mother he couldn't help getting out on such a hand as that.[8]

Golden Arm[9]

1884?

1 & 2^d of Huck F. ⟨[*word*]⟩[10]

Waking Jim—84. [#]

---

pp. 189–190). Hartford resident Marshall Jewell, former governor of Connecticut and United States minister to Russia and postmaster general under Grant, attended Joseph Twichell's Asylum Hill Congregational Church until his death in 1883. The X that accompanies this entry is the first of several with which Clemens marked passages in this notebook that concern anecdotes or ideas for stories. The headnote discusses the marks in detail (see p. 65).

[7] Clemens recounted this anecdote of Karl Gerhardt's in a letter to Howells dated 7 August 1884 (see *MTHL*, p. 498).

[8] Clemens often referred to these two anecdotes by Artemus Ward in his notebooks and elsewhere. The first, a query about Adam, was published in *Cap'n Simon Wheeler, the Amateur Detective* (*Mark Twain's Satires & Burlesques*, ed. Franklin R. Rogers [Berkeley and Los Angeles: University of California Press, 1967], pp. 261–262). The second anecdote, which Clemens sometimes referred to as the "lone-hand baptism," was included in his 1871 lecture on Artemus Ward and is printed in Fred W. Lorch's *The Trouble Begins at Eight* (Ames: Iowa State University Press, 1968), p. 298.

[9] Clemens' "Ghost Story" (sometimes titled "The Golden Arm") became a staple feature of his lecture program. He included the piece in his essay "How to Tell a Story," recalling: "On the platform I used to tell a negro ghost story that had a pause in front of the snapper on the end, and that pause was the most important thing in the whole story. If I got it the right length precisely, I could spring the finishing ejaculation with effect enough to make some impressible girl deliver a startled little yelp and jump out of her seat—and that was what I was after" (*How to Tell a Story and Other Essays* [New York: Harper & Brothers, 1897], pp. 9–10). A number of the reviews of the Twain-Cable lecture tour mentioned the startling effectiveness of Mark Twain's ghost story.

[10] There are many entries in this notebook reflecting Clemens' efforts to select a program for his 1884/1885 tour. This first list (pp. 69–71) is quite similar to that which appears at the end of Notebook 22 (pp. 60–61).

Encounter with Interviewr[11]

Raftsmen fight—Missippi

Decorative Art—Spider-armed woman. H. F.

Ham's Soliloquy—H. F.

Consc & small-pox—90.

Art & Bible—105–6.

Bucking Horse.—178

King Solomon

Henry VIII

My Duel

Interv. with A. Ward?[12]

Anything from foreign travel pleases best.

⟨Make a whole reading from H. F.?
No.⟩

On a wager, *started* to ride from V C to San F in stage with several women & girls, I to play deaf & dumb. Got out early. Lost the bet. Found later they had packed the jury—men in disguise—a borrowed stage & driver.
I lied about trip to the same boys.

Trim & put in all of Hank Mk chapter—150.

Reduce Lost in Snow Storm—233.

Buck Fanshaw—329

European Guides—by request. [#]

---

[11] Mark Twain's "An Encounter with an Interviewer" was first published in *Lotos Leaves*, ed. John Brougham and John Elderkin (Boston: William F. Gill and Co., 1875) and later collected in *Punch, Brothers, Punch! and Other Sketches* (New York: Slote, Woodman & Co., 1878).

[12] This piece and the preceding selection are identified on page 61, notes 144 and 145.

Jumpg Frog (by request)

All right, I'll *go* to h— Ch 33

Meeting of H & Ant Sally

Scraps from Prang Calendar.[13]

Whistling story[14]

X Georgia doctors decided drink just enough brandy to kill the tadpols.

Decided it best to Drink considerable water, but put just enough brandy in it to kill the tadpoles. i.e. strike a ⟨ju[--]⟩judicious medium between the two extremes—

So we, between pathos & humor—kill the tadpoles.

X Paul, the red-headed, X-eyed, left-handed billiard player.

X Throw your heft on the corpse.

X The Adam Calf of the world. [#]

---

[13] Besides calendars, L. Prang & Company of Boston produced greeting cards and "Satin Art Prints" (*Publishers' Weekly*, 23 February 1884, p. 252). Early in 1884 Clemens made a contract with them to write original material for a calendar. On 29 February 1884 Clemens informed Webster: "Besides other stuff, I have written special squibs for 10 of the months & all the national holidays" (*MTBus*, p. 240). But on 4 March Prang & Company wrote Webster that Clemens' contributions were not suitable (*MTLP*, p. 173, n. 2). Two days later Clemens ordered Webster to "get the Prang contract *canceled*, right away—don't let him change his mind. You can't *imagine* what a horrible 3-months' job it would have been" (*MTBus*, p. 242). About twenty-three manuscript scraps of the Prang calendar material survive in the Mark Twain Papers. Clemens considered them for inclusion in his 1884/1885 lecture program—two of the pages have been tentatively marked for reading as a ten-minute section of the first and second day programs—but he evidently decided against using this material. Later markings indicate that Clemens returned to them when considering aphorisms for Pudd'nhead Wilson's calendar.

[14] Clemens described this story in his autobiography: "It was one which I have told some hundreds of times on the platform, and which I was always very fond of, because it worked the audience so hard. It was a stammering man's account of how he got cured of his infirmity—which was accomplished by introducing a whistle into the midst of every word which he found himself unable to finish on account of the obstruction of the stammering. And so his whole account was an absurd mixture of stammering and whistling—which was irresistible to an audience properly keyed up for laughter" (*MTA*, 2:46–47). Clemens told the story on several occasions during his 1884/1885 lecture tour, and one reviewer justly labeled it "his famous, if somewhat antique, whistling story" (Brooklyn *Daily Eagle*, 23 November 1884).

Did you ever consider the advantage of being buried in a sandy soil?

6 men save 6 women from drowning, & then marry. Tell the story of their after lives.

Something from Wakeman in Heaven?

Something from the plays of
    Tom Sawyer
        &
    Sellers as Scientist?[15]

Telephone Convesation[16]

Toast to the Babies[17]

Anecdotes—Drunk man pulls ⟨t[-]⟩thread ⟨of⟩ out of his mouth —has swallowed a small ball of it. Another tries to pay bill with a bat.

Mrs. H's husband aged 92 fell & broke nose—She said it came near disfiguring him for life.

There is a boarding house
Far, far away.[18]

Something from Ashfield speech?[19]

⟨F⟩The Tar Baby Story. [#]

---

[15] Clemens wrote to Howells around 20 October 1884 asking him for his copy of *Colonel Sellers as a Scientist* which he wanted to "get some truck out of for the platform readings" (*MTHL*, p. 511). Clemens seems to have read from the unpublished play on only a few occasions early in the lecture tour, selecting the scene from the first act in which the Colonel describes his lucrative "materializing" scheme to Lafayette Hawkins.

[16] "A Telephonic Conversation" first appeared in the *Atlantic* for June 1880 and was later collected in *The $30,000 Bequest and Other Stories* (New York: Harper & Brothers, 1906).

[17] Clemens offered this toast on 13 November 1879 at a banquet honoring U. S. Grant during the Reunion of the Army of the Tennessee in Chicago (see *MTS*[1910], pp. 64–68).

[18] See page 38, note 76.

[19] Clemens prepared a humorous speech for the Ashfield (Massachusetts) Academy dinner in August 1881 but then withdrew from the speaking engagement because of

X Hayes trying to lecture—3 interruptions—"is Mrs. B. W. Jones in the house?—husband has broken his leg. Let C come & interrupt me once or twice as introduction to it.[20]

Anything from piloting?

Membranous Croup.[21]

Paid $500 this summer ('84)—13 weeks; also paid $7 per week for washing, down town. Gave Richard, James, & David $10 each; Jimmy $2; Doyle $6.[22]

X Admiral Smith (in S. I story)[23] says "When that clock of mine points to 15 min after 4 & strikes 37, it means that it is half past 10.⟨"⟩ Except for that, she hasn't a blemish."

X I think ⟨we are⟩ the worlds that flow & swing through space are only the microscopic trichinae concealed in the blood of ⟨some vast creature's veins, & that it is that vast creature whom God concerns himself about, & not us.⟩ God.[24]

Girl of Lucerne.[25]

Hunting the sock [#]

---

the grave news of President Garfield's condition. The undelivered speech has not been further identified.

[20] Clemens told this anecdote in full in his speech at the Whitefriars Club dinner on 20 June 1899 (*MTS*[1910], pp. 380–382). The story concerns the attempts of Arctic explorer Dr. Isaac Israel Hayes to deliver a lecture despite a number of interruptions. The "C" of Clemens' entry is apparently Cable.

[21] "The Experiences of the McWilliamses with the Membranous Croup" first appeared in *Mark Twain's Sketches, New and Old* (Hartford: American Publishing Co., 1875).

[22] The reference is to the summer's housekeeping expenses at Quarry Farm which the Clemenses shared with the Crane family.The Clemens family left the farm to return to Hartford around 23 September 1884.

[23] See page 46, note 103.

[24] Clemens wrote substantially the same lines in Notebook 22 (p. 56). They suggest the fantasy developed in "Three Thousand Years Among the Microbes," written in 1905 (*WWD*, pp. 433–553).

[25] This episode, which Clemens usually referred to as "A Trying Situation," is from chapter 25 of *A Tramp Abroad* and was almost invariably included in his 1884/1885 lecture programs. The following entry refers to another episode in *A Tramp Abroad*, Clemens' blundering search in his dark hotel room (chapter 13).

X Twichell's Simsbury soldier: "I see in ⟨a⟩ about 2 minutes it warn't no place for me!"

X The village no-'count⟨: "⟩; very sick. Minister: "You ought to call ⟨upon⟩on God." "Well, I'm so kind of sick & lame I don't git out to call on anybody."

T. W. Russell, City[26]

Bret Harte's story of the naval meeting in ⟨Pets⟩Pete's restaurant—man saved another's life.[27]

Bed Guardian[28]
   manf at
      Pittsfield, Mass
        by
Geo. Campbell, Agt.
   Pat '81.

Oct 24. Saturday.

Oct. 25. To be attended to tomorrow:
Furnace doesn't heat enough.
Sell cow if she is going dry.
We not to keep 3 cows.
D. a failure; can't raise turnips & roses.

---

[26] Thomas W. Russell was a director of the Connecticut Fire Insurance Company of Hartford. He introduced Clemens at the Hartford mugwump rally on 20 October 1884 at which Carl Schurz was the featured speaker.

[27] See N&J2, p. 509, note 256.

[28] On 31 October 1884 Clemens wrote Charles L. Webster that he had been offered a half-interest in a device to keep infants from kicking off their blankets or tumbling out of bed, and he added: "I have invented a more expensive & more convenient one, & presently when I see you we will talk about it" (MTBus, pp. 279–280). Webster had to pursue the possibilities of manufacturing and marketing Clemens' improved bed clamp while burdened by negotiations for the Grant *Memoirs* and preparations for the publication of *Huckleberry Finn*, and his letter of 19 January 1885 reflects his consequent irritation: "You haven't asked my opinion, but I will say; I have no doubt that it will prove a failure. It is so entirely foreign to our business that I think it unwise to go into it, and I have already heard of one case where it has been bought and paid for and thrown aside as worthless." A few days later, Clemens replied shortly: "Damn the bed-clamp. I won't bother with it till I get home" (SLC to CLW, 23 January 1885, MTBus, p. 295). The venture was finally dropped.

Fix damp place in library shelves.
See Barnard of the Committee.[29]
Ask C to send me a full ticket.[30]
Hair cut.
Patrick, milk & alarm.
Am warum gehst
Das Bank Theilen verkaufen[31]
Hotel in New Haven.
Uncle Remus.

  Robt. Coit[32]
    New London

  Watch—
  Bank—
  Bunce
  Remus. [#]

---

[29] Henry Barnard, founder of the *American Journal of Education*, was a member of the committee established to choose a sculptor for the Nathan Hale statue in the state capitol building in Hartford. Karl Gerhardt was competing for the commission and had completed a clay model. Sometime in 1885 Clemens dictated the story of Gerhardt's imbroglio with the committee—"a 14-months' history & the funniest in the whole history of art" (SLC to William Dean Howells, 7 December 1885, *MTHL*, p. 543). In his dictation Clemens described Barnard as "an innocent ass" who "knew nothing about art . . . and if he had a mind was not able to make it up on any question." According to Clemens, Barnard withheld his approval of Gerhardt's design because Mrs. Samuel Colt, widow of the wealthy arms manufacturer, had secured his vote in behalf of Hartford sculptor Enoch S. Woods. Woods was the sexton of the Church of the Good Shepherd, a church built in Hartford by Mrs. Colt in memory of her husband. Gerhardt's letter to Clemens of 1 January 1885 claimed that "the fight is ended" because Barnard had been unable to get a majority of the committee to vote against him. But in an Autobiographical Dictation dated 1885, Clemens says that Gerhardt was not definitely notified of the award by the "dilatory committee" until March (*MTA*, 1:58). The bronze statue of Nathan Hale was finally placed in the capitol on 14 June 1887.

[30] The "full ticket" may refer to a complete list of Cable's reading selections. Within a few days Clemens received Cable's program plan for their opening night at New Haven on 5 November 1884.

[31] *Sell the bank shares*. The preceding entry may mean *Why are you going*.

[32] A member of the committee to select a sculptor for the Nathan Hale statue. In an Autobiographical Dictation of 1885 Clemens described Coit as "a railroad man, of New London, a modest, sensible, honorable, worthy gentleman, who, while wholly unacquainted with art, (and confessing it,) was willing and anxious to do his duty in the matter." Karl Gerhardt mentions Coit as one of his supporters in the competition for the commission (Karl Gerhardt to SLC, 1 January 1885).

4

Bei Lützen auf der Aue
Er hielt ⟨solch [ein]⟩⟨solche[- -]⟩solchen Strauss
Dass vielen tausend Wälschen
Der Athem ging aus;
Viel Tausende liefen dort hastigen Lauf,
Zehn Tausend entschliefen, die nimmer wachen auf!

5

Am Wasser der Katzbach er's auch hat bewährt,
Da hat er den ⟨Franzozen⟩Franzosen das Schwimmen gelehrt;
Fahrt wohl, ihr Franzosen, zur Ostsee hinab,
Und nehmt, Ohnehosen, den Wallfisch zum Grab!

6

Bei Wartburg an der Elbe, wie fuhr er hindurch!
Da schirmte die Franzosen nicht Schanze noch Burg;
Da mussten sie springen, ⟨we⟩wie Hasen über's Feld,
Und hell liess er klingen sein Hussa! der Held.

7

Bei Leipzig auf dem Plane, O, herrliche Schlacht!
Da brach er den Franzosen das ⟨Glüch⟩Glück & die Macht;
Da lagen sie sicher nach blutigem Fall,
Da ward der Herr Blücher ein Feldmarschal⟨[!]⟩.

8

Drum blaset, ihr Trompeten! Husaren, heraus!
Du reite, Herr Feldmarschall, wie Winde im Saus!
Dem Siege entgegen, zum Rhein, über'n Rhein!
Du⟨[p]⟩ ᴛᴀ⟨p⟩-ap- -fer-er ⟨D[a]gen⟩De-e-gen, in Frankreich hinein!

—

—

—

—

3

Den Schwur hat er gehalten, als Kriegsruf erklang,
Hei! wie der weisse Jüngling In'n Sattel sich schwang!
Da ist er's gewesen der Kehraus gemacht,

Mit eisernen Besen das Land rein gemacht![33]

⟨Bliss⟩
Watch
Ed Hooker pamphlet[34]
Miss Sarah Dunham.[35]
2^{d} ward times mutual
Burglar alarm.
Robt Garvie keys & locks, come or don't.[36]

Chatto's 6 & 7 mo. draft for £300 odd, given to Bissells for collection[37]

X ⟨T⟩Attribute to Frank Fuller,[38] that when he is in a car or other such place, he will allow a company of stranger to get well & deeply into a harsh criticism of some public man or some man who has been printing something—then he begins to blush & look embarrassed, & presently explains that *he* is that person!

10 Commandments
Cleveland violated 1—Blaine 9.[39] [#]

---

[33] These are the last six stanzas of a nine stanza poem by Ernst Moritz Arndt entitled "Das Lied vom Feldmarschall." This popular martial song deals with the exploits of Prussian military hero Gebhard Leberecht von Blücher during his advance into France in 1813/1814 (*A Book of Ballads on German History*, ed. Wilhelm Wagner [Cambridge: At the University Press, 1877], pp. 80–81, 146–148).

[34] Young Hartford physician Edward Beecher Hooker was the son of John and Isabella Beecher Hooker. The pamphlet referred to has not been identified.

[35] The sister of Samuel Dunham, one of Clemens' billiards partners.

[36] Garvie was a Hartford plumber whom Clemens occasionally employed.

[37] Clemens wrote to his English publishers, Chatto & Windus, on 5 November 1884: "I find your kind favor of Sept. 12 in my pocket, enclosing your 6 & 7 mo. drafts for £356. I have no recollection of ever having acknowledged the receipt of it" (Clifton Waller Barrett Library, University of Virginia, Charlottesville). The drafts were royalty payments on English editions of Clemens' works.

[38] An old friend of Clemens from the West, who was now president of a health food firm in New York.

[39] The presidential campaign of 1884 was marked by personal attacks on both candidates: Democrat Cleveland was accused of seduction and of having fathered an illegitimate child; Republican Blaine was charged with unethical and illegal conduct as a member of Congress. Clemens joined with the faction of independent Republicans, or mugwumps, in repudiating their party's choice. In the midst of the campaign, Clemens

Send game & books to New Orleans

Write a criticism of one of Shakspere's plays in the modern style
—"nothing new in situation, or plot or anything—all worn-out—
quote whence this that & the other incident was stolen. Write in
modern English, *then reduce it to quaint old English*

It's a great thing, a beautiful thing. It means moral regeneration
for the world. – – – – & there's millions in it, millions, millions![40]
I knew you had talent & a good heart,

Happy & content are Swimley's Boarders.

X You's Gen[l]. M[c]Clellan![41]

Blaine's campaign speeches.[42]

X Dream of being a knight errant in armor in the middle ages.[43]
X Have the notions & habits of thought of the present day mixed
with the necessities of that. No pockets in the armor. No way to
manage certain requirements of nature. Can't scratch. Cold in the
head—can't blow—can't get at handkerchief, can't use iron sleeve.
Iron gets red hot in the sun—leaks in the rain, gets white with frost
& freezes me solid in winter. Suffer from lice & fleas. Make
disagreeable clatter when I enter church. Can't dress or undress
myself. Always getting struck by lightning. Fall down, can't get up.
See Morte DArthur. [#]

---

wrote Howells: "To see grown men, apparently in their right mind, seriously arguing
against a bachelor's fitness for President because he has had private intercourse with a
consenting widow! Those grown men know what the bachelor's other alternative was—&
tacitly they seem to prefer that to the widow. Isn't human nature the most consummate
sham & lie that was ever invented?" (SLC to Howells, 31 August 1884, *MTHL*, p. 501).

[40] The catch phrase of Colonel Sellers' eternal speculative optimism, popularized
by John T. Raymond's performance in the *Gilded Age* play, had become almost proverbial by this date.

[41] See N&J2, p. 65.

[42] Possibly a reference to *The Words of James G. Blaine on the Issues of the Day,
Embracing Selections from His Speeches, Letters, and Public Writings*, ed. Walter S.
Vail (Boston: D. L. Guernsey, 1884).

[43] Clemens cut two leaves from the notebook following the page that ends here. He
used them for a letter to his wife dated 3 December 1884 in which he describes a call he
made on president-elect Grover Cleveland, then governor of New York, in Albany
(published in *LLMT*, pp. 221–222).

Fall of '84—while Cable & I were giving readings. Cable got a Morte d'Arthur & gave it me to read. I began to make notes in my head for a book.[44] Nov. 11 '86 I read the first chapter (all that was then written), at Governor's Island & closed the reading with an outline of the probable contents of the future book. Wrote the book (The Yankee at Arthur's Court in '87 & '88, & published it in December '89. (Shall, anyway.)

Nov. 19 '89. SL C

Turn Sellers play into a novel, & not go reading in London till ⟨'66⟩'86.[45]

✖ Jim Fisk. Would his father lie? "Well, he had moral strength up to a certain strain, like the rest of us. He wouldn't tell a lie for nine pence, but he would tell 8 for a dollar."[46] [#]

---

[44] As Cable later recollected the incident, Clemens came across Sir Thomas Malory's *Morte Darthur* while browsing through a bookstore with Cable in Rochester, New York, on 6 December 1884. Cable praised the book and Clemens soon shared Cable's enthusiasm (mentioned in Cable's speech at the memorial service for Mark Twain on 30 November 1910, *MT&GWC*, p. 135). Clemens returned to his notebook entry about the "Dream of being a knight errant," the germ of *A Connecticut Yankee*, on 19 November 1889 and added this explanation in brownish black ink.

[45] Clemens had written to Charles Webster on 15 September 1884: "Keep the Sellers play in your safe until I am done with the platform—then I will send for it & turn it into a novel" (*MTBus*, p. 277). Clemens, however, did not begin *The American Claimant* until February 1891.

For several months Clemens considered a lecture tour in England, but he was apparently uncertain of his reception by the British public. His only previous experience of formal lecturing abroad had been in 1873/1874. Clemens inquired of his English publishers, Chatto & Windus, in December 1884: "Tell me, shall I come over and try it in London in the Spring or Summer in a small hall somewhere in the West end?" (*Mark Twain the Letter Writer*, ed. Cyril Clemens [Boston: Meador Publishing Co., 1932], p. 24). He also approached Major J. B. Pond about the idea, and Pond was enthusiastic. "I had you in view both times I made a tour through England," he replied on 25 December 1884, "and never entered a book store that I did not enquire about the sale of your books and opinions as to . . . your probable success if you were to go to England to lecture. I would be ready to go in April." By 5 March 1885 Clemens had made his decision. He wrote to Orion and Mollie Clemens: "I probably shall put off the reading-trip to England & Australia till next year, as Livy does not want to take the children away from their schooling now, & I will not go without the family. Besides, I wish to be close at hand all the time while General Grant's book is going through the press & being canvassed" (*MTBus*, p. 305). See note 71 (p. 89) for further information about Clemens' projected tour.

[46] This anecdote and the one at 80.7 about the flamboyant capitalist are included

X In a train the average bride & groom are fools; but there is no such fool as the woman with her first child.

Conversations on the train:
XX Sold the oil property for $800 clean profit.
Churches.
Baby or babies.

XX ((Fisk & graveyard.

buil' a Northen Cent[l] whistle like dey got o[ne] in Elmira—den he needn't blow it only when de *rest* er de town want to sleep.

A woman with showy blue eyes (light).

XX I have not railroaded any to speak of for 15 years⟨.⟩, but have staid at home. This morning the usual new bride got aboard the train, & she began as usual her furtive love-pattings & pawings & pettings of ⟨him,⟩ her lovey-dove, proud that he was hers & willing that everybody should know it & envy her; ⟨& she would⟩ & when she wanted to ask him what time it was, or any little this-worldly trifle she would hitch her chin on his shoulder & wall her worshiping eyes up ⟨at him⟩ over his shirt collar just in the same old soft sweet railroad-honeymoon way which I remembered so well; & he, well, he stood it in the same old patient, suffering, surfeited, ⟨satiated,⟩ shamefaced martyr-like way of the railroading bridegroom of the bygone times, & wondered, no doubt, how he could ever have thought *he* knew anything about courting & keeping it up—for his courting before marriage must have seemed so pale & poor & lazy compared to hers after it. Yes, there was that same old gushy, sappy little drama going on⟨[,]⟩ before me, just in the same old, old soul-enchanting way of 15 years ago, without a change in any detail of the performance. But at last the bride tired herself out, as usual, & then as usual she cushioned the dear head under his left ear & went to sleep ⟨just⟩ as contentedly as if she had been in heaven—& it's a mighty trying position for the other fellow, & makes him feel bitterly conspicuous. But now a change

---

in W. A. Swanberg's *Jim Fisk: The Career of an Improbable Rascal* (New York: Charles Scribner's Sons, 1959), pp. 12, 117.

came—the first I had ever observed in this drama—for she began to
snore. It was an immense improvement ⟨& won back your
vanished⟩ & softened your hard heart toward her at once, because
it showed that the sleep was honest ⟨& genuine⟩, & not gotten up
for effect, as those former sleeps were. So I gratefully added that to
the long list of improvements which I have noticed in ⟨my⟩ these
six weeks of railroading. ⟨of mine.⟩ Lots of things have changed, &
always for the better. They have dry towels in the hotels, now,
instead of the pulpy damp rag of the former day, which shuddered
you up like a cold poultice; & they have electrical buttons, now,
instead of those crooked bell handles ⟨&⟩ which always tore your
hand & made you break a lot of the commandments—⟨&⟩all you
could think of on a sudden call, that way⟨,⟩; & at table they feed
you like a man & a brother, & don't bring your dinner & spread it
around your plate in a mass meeting of soap dishes; & you have the
telephone instead of the ⟨dead &⟩ petrified messenger boy. And in
many cases the cities are nobly ⟨& hand⟩ built up & architecturally
transfigured beyond recognition. And then the new light—there was
nothing like it when I was on the highway before. I was in Detroit
last night,[47] & for the first time saw a city where the night was as
beautiful as the day; saw for the first time, in place of sallow
twilight bought at three dollars a thousand feet, ⟨saw⟩ clusters of
coruscating electric suns floating in the sky without visible support,
& casting a mellow radiance upon the snow covered spires & domes
& roofs & far stretching thoroughfares which gave to the spectacle
the daintiness & delicacy of a picture, ⟨[or] of⟩ & reminded one of
airy ⟨&⟩ unreal cities caught in the glimpses of a dream. Yes, the
changes are great & marvelous, & for number are past enumeration.
And last night as I went to my room in the hotel when my
missionary work on the platform was ⟨down⟩done, I struck the
crowning blessed innovation of all, apparently—six fat green
bottles in a wire frame hanging on the wall by my door.
Gratis ⟨f⟩refreshment for the wary instructor, in place of having
to go to the bar & buy it. I took that frame down & carried it into

---

[47] Clemens and Cable read in Detroit on 16 December 1884 and in Cleveland on
the following day.

my room, & got out my lemons & sugar & calculated to have a
good solitary sociable time all to myself⟨.⟩; & says I "Here's to
prohibition—for the next ⟨missionary⟩ man that comes along the
hall." But sorrow & disappointment must come to us all; & thus
also came ⟨e⟩it even to me when I examined the label to see what
⟨kind⟩ brand of sour mash it was, & found ⟨alas⟩ that those comely
bottles were to put out another kind of fire with. ⟨S⟩But I knew
the trouble was all in the labels—my imagination would have made
everything right if it had not been for them; so I took the labels
off & carried the bottles to my fellow-missionary, Mr. Cable.

　　1. Whereas.
　　2. Wherefore.
　　3 Inasmuch
　　4 Furthermore

　　　Delay . . . . 10[48]
　　　C. . . . . ⟨1[-]⟩15.
　　　K. . . . . ⟨1[-]⟩15
　　　C. 20
　　　K. 15
　　　C. (Song *or* Nightride)—10 or 15)[49]
　　　K. . . . . 15—finis.
　　　　　　　　　　　　　⟨95⟩$\overline{105}$ & ⟨1[5]⟩10 for encs.
　　Total 115, & out at about 10.

1 page back—program.

Sellers materializer

　　"　　Swearing-pho.

This a gov'ment.[50] [#]

---

[48] It was probably during the holiday break in the lecture schedule from 19 to 28
December that Clemens filled five notebook pages with the following notes regarding
changes in the lecture program (through 85.3). In this first list "K" stands for Clemens.
The figures in the several lists represent the minutes allotted to each reading.

[49] One of Cable's pieces was "Mary's Night Ride" from his novel *Dr. Sevier*, published
just before the start of the lecture tour. He usually sang Creole songs as an encore.

[50] Pap Finn's drunken denunciation of the government occurs in chapter 6 of *Huckleberry Finn.*

Jumping Frog.

Gov. Gardner.[51]

True Story just as I heard it.

Blue-jays.

Boy-fight.

Raft-fight.

Gad'sby's Hotel

DE-parted.[52]

Fanshaw

Cable	15 minutes.
Sollermun .... ⎱	⟨[12]⟩⟨14⟩10 m.
⟨Jim's Bank⟩ Jim's Bank[53] ⎰	4 "
Cable—⟨Songs⟩	⟨[10]⟩20
(*or* songs)	
Tragic T̲a̲le ᵃ	⟨15⟩10 ⎱
Situatio̲n̲ ᵇ	15 ⎰
Night ride	13
Jumping Frog	20 tr[54]
....	10

Hang it, Huck ef I could ony c'leck de *intru*st I would let de *princi*pal GO."

1 hour for myself, 10 m for preliminary delay; 40 m for Cable.——1.50. [#]

---

[51] The anecdote about the governor occurs in "Some Rambling Notes of an Idle Excursion" collected in *The Stolen White Elephant Etc.* (1882).

[52] Clemens' discussion of German grammar from *A Tramp Abroad*, titled "Tragic Tale of the Fishwife" in the lecture program, was one of his most frequent reading selections during the tour. The preceding selection in this notebook list, the story of the "Man Who Put Up at Gadsby's," is also from *A Tramp Abroad* (chapter 26).

[53] Jim's financial experiences are in chapter 8 of *Huckleberry Finn*. Clemens customarily read the "King Sollermun" selection from chapter 14 of the book.

[54] The instruction "tr" (i.e., "transpose") and a line drawn in the left margin connect-

Sent & proposed to Pond:[55]

 Waiting for audience 12
 1. Cable 15
 2. Tw 15
 3. C 10
 4. Tw (2 pieces, a & b) 25
 5. C 13
  (Encore) 5
 6. Tw 12
             —
            107

 Wait 10
 C 15
 Trying Sit 15–17
 C 10
 1st Escape 20
 Songs 7
 2d Escape 15
 Night Ride 13
 Tragic Tale 12
             —
            112

JUMPING FROG
Call it trying sit.
Col. Sellers
Put up at Gadsby's [#]

---

ing "Tragic Tale" with a caret before "Jumping Frog" are part of Clemens' effort to rearrange this part of his program, but the exact order intended is unclear.

[55] Clemens proposed this distribution of time for the lecture program in his letter of 22 December 1884 to Major Pond. He explained at length the reasons for the revised program: "If any programs have been printed for the rest of our season, it will be necessary to destroy them; for I *must* invent some way to curtail Cable. His name draws a sixteenth part of the house, & he invariably does two-thirds of the reading. I cannot stand that any longer. He may have 35 or 38 minutes on the platform, & no more." To that end, Clemens proposed that Cable reduce or preferably cut out his second reading, which ran over twenty minutes, and that he should limit his encores to a five-minute selection of Creole songs. The entire program would therefore be shortened, Clemens reasoned, "& we send the audience home hungry instead of stuffed, surfeited, bored, weary & cursing" (Berg). Pond answered Clemens in a conciliatory tone on 25 December, promising to *"force"* Cable to "epitomize" his part but stressing Cable's value to the program: "You are

Pittsburg?[56]

If you begin exactly at 8 you can have 20 min in place of second 10.[57]

Pipe
tobacco
German book.
Shoes.
Slippers
Selections to read.
Webster envelops.
Mem. Book for Ozias.[58]
Spectacles.
Razors.
Salve.
Blanket-bag.[59]
Money
3 box cigars. [#]

---

constantly with him, & the tediousness with which he appears to you is not so much noticed by the audience, except to whet their appetite for you, & make your part of the entertainment more prominent."

[56] The Pittsburgh reading on 29 December 1884 was the first after the holiday break.

[57] Cable evidently agreed to this arrangement. Clemens wrote to Livy on 18 January 1885: "We've got a new plan, & it *works*. Cable goes on at the very stroke of the hour, & talks 15 minutes to an *assembling* house, telling them not to be concerned about *him* & *he* won't be troubled. And so, with all the encores, we have in no instance been on the stage a minute over 2 hours. The good effect is beyond estimation. (And privately, *another* thing—only half the house hear C.'s first piece—so there isn't too much of C any more—whereas heretofore there has been a thundering sight too much of him)" (*LLMT*, p. 231).

[58] Major James B. Pond's brother, Ozias W. Pond, joined the Twain-Cable lecture tour at the beginning of January 1885 as a replacement for his brother who had business to attend to in New York. Ozias was with the tour only until the end of January when he was forced to remain in Milwaukee because of illness. "For as long as he was with the tour, Ozias kept a record of events in a notebook of Twain's invention" which had been given to him by the author (Guy A. Cardwell, *Twins of Genius* [East Lansing: Michigan State College Press, 1953], p. 32). Pond's diary is now in the Berg Collection, New York City.

[59] Writing from Madison, Wisconsin, on 21 January 1885, Clemens told Livy: "It is 10 below, now—middle of the afternoon; but I am in my *bag*, in bed, & unspeakably snug & comfortable. That bag is the greatest thing in the world" (TS in MTP).

Chas. S. Cole, lawyer.[60]

✗ Have a battle between a modern army, with gatling guns—
(automatic) 600 shots a minute, ⟨with one pulling of the trigger,⟩
torpedos, balloons, 100-ton cannon, iron-clad fleet &c & Prince de
Joinville's Middle Age Crusaders.[61]

silver $1 per oz
gold $250 per pound.

Publish a bogus Vanderbilt will giving away his fortune in "tons"
of silver coin & gold coin. No other expression used—except odd
fractions of tons.—& bonds spoken of only as so many hundred
pounds of paper known as N. Y Central stock, &c.[62]

Say
✗ There is a black cat in England which has lived 300 years—
because its maintenance is charged upon the estate of a rich
bachelor without heirs, & no one is interested to prove that a new
black cat is substituted ever few years.[63] [#]

---

[60] Clemens mentioned Cole to Webster "in case you need a local lawyer to go for the
Am. Pub. Co." (SLC to CLW, 22 December 1884, *MTBus*, p. 286). Clemens was threatening to sue the company because he thought they were not adequately protecting his
copyright against an Alabama pirate.

[61] The battle occurs in chapter 43 of *A Connecticut Yankee*. Clemens was familiar
with Jean de Joinville's writings through the *Chronicles of the Crusades* (London:
H. G. Bohn, 1848), a collection of three contemporary histories of the Crusades, including
de Joinville's history of Saint Louis (Louis IX). Clemens purchased the book through
James R. Osgood & Company in October 1877.

[62] Parker L. Walter of the Pittsburgh *Chronicle Telegraph*, writing Clemens on 17
November 1887 to solicit a story for the paper, recalled the bogus will idea: "The last
time you talked to the people from the lecture platform, you suggested to me that I
should write the Vanderbilt will case, bequeathing his property by the ton, and by the
pound; I did this." Clemens evidently introduced this idea in his Pittsburgh lecture of
29 December 1884. The much publicized Vanderbilt will case began in February 1877
when Cornelius Jeremiah Vanderbilt, the Commodore's second son, and his sisters,
Mrs. Daniel B. Allen and Mrs. N. Bergasse LaBau, contested their father's bequest of
ninety-seven per cent of his wealth to his eldest son, William Henry Vanderbilt. Their
suit, and suits later in 1877 and in 1880, were unsuccessful, but William Henry Vanderbilt
voluntarily increased the portions of his sisters and brother.

[63] Clemens developed this idea in an unpublished story entitled "The Black Prince's
Cat" written about 1896.

✖ A man bequeaths a huge sum of money for the housing & protecting of cats—"& when they shall have multiplied to 1,500,000 cats." &c—then the people rose ⟨[&]⟩& wouldn't allow the cat factory to be established.

✖ To one of 2 men: ⟨"⟩O my dear *sir* did I step on your foot? The *other* man: I wish to God you had!

Rock from Mrs. G.W Nichols' house. Meerschaum crockery. Mention ⟨[--]⟩that it is NEW[64]

✖? Describe Judge Turner, Countess so-& so's rout; polyglot woman; ⟨Routledge⟩ poor Douglas Jerrold jr & his dirty shirt standing in hall with footmen. Routleg's daughters waiting in crowd to glimpse Pr of Wales. Banquet where "Viscount Falkner's here— he's *here!*"[65]

$$1$$
1st No, split in two. . . . . 10 *m.*

$$2$$
2$^{d.}$ half of it. . . . . 15 m
—————
25
3.—Songs. & encore, ... 7 min.
Night Ride . . . . . . $\overline{. . .}$ . . . . 13 to 15. m.
—————
47 *m.* [#]

---

[64] Clemens and Cable were in Cincinnati from 2 to 4 January 1885 when they visited Rookwood Pottery, an innovative ceramic plant founded in 1880 by Mrs. George Ward Nichols. Clemens was delighted with the ceramics and bought several pieces, most of which he sent to Livy. In a postscript to his letter of 7 January Clemens explained two of the items which he had forwarded: "The *red* pottery is a *new* invention—just out of the kiln. The rough piece of *rock* is what Mrs. Nichols's wonderful house is being built of" (TS in MTP).

[65] Clemens evidently considered describing some incidents of his 1873 stay in London. "Countess so-& so's rout," the "polyglot woman," and the anecdote about William Blanchard Jerrold figure in Notebook 12, S. C. Thompson's stenographic record of the Clemenses' 1873 trip (N&J1, pp. 566, 551–552). Judge Turner, identified on page 284, note 198, was in England during Clemens' 1872 visit and may have been in England in 1873 as well.

C. Inter.............. ⟨20⟩ 15 m.
⟨2. Captivity.............. 25 ″ ⟩66
3. Jumping frog ⟨20⟩ ⟨15⟩ 20
RAFTSMEN
4 Duel 20
                            ___

⟨GHOST⟩
(Synopsize *rats*.)

1st.
Sollermun
Fishwife
(Enc. Whistle).
                ___
Situation.
Ghost.

Cable costs me $550 to $600 a week—that is, $450 a week &
expenses. He is not worth the half of it.67

don't talk—don't *talk*; & then nobody 'll ever find out that ⟨ther⟩
if there *is* any intellectual difference between you & that dead twin
you been talking about, it's probly in favor of the dead one.

✖ America in 1985. (Negro supremacy—the whites under foot.)

Continue Tom & Huck. Put more of Sid the mean boy in.

Stealing a ride on the steamboat: sometimes up to Robards' mill68
—& didn't *stop*, but went to Louisiana.
4th July Excursion of Herald & Providence to Quincy.69 The
fight. [#]

---

66 Clemens occasionally varied his reading program with the account of Tom and
Huck's efforts to free Jim (chapters 35 through 40 of *Huckleberry Finn*). Clemens refers
to the piece inconsistently as "Captivity," "Escape," "Achievement," and "A Dazzling
Achievement."
67 When writing to Livy from Indianapolis on 8 February 1885, Clemens was more
specific about how much he would like to lower Cable's pay: "He isn't worth a penny
over $200. He is not a novelty anywhere. He has apparently been in every town in the
country just about twice; & that is as often as he is wanted. Especially as he offers his
same old stuff all the time" (TS in MTP).
68 Archibald Sampson Robards operated a flour mill near Hannibal in the early 1850s.
69 Quincy, Illinois, across the river from Hannibal.

John Riggin

Dress up with Whitmore & do the raftsman's brag. Wet hair & brush it down flat on forehead, in place of wig.[70]

Take ⟨Kelly⟩Riley & go to London.—pay him $50 or 60 a week⟨.⟩ & expenses

But try Dumaurier.[71]

London.

1. Du M .... 15 m.
2. K ..... K. Sol. & bank ...... ⟨1[0]⟩15 =
3. D. M .... 15 =
4. K..... Sit or Escape .... 20 —
5 Du M......................... 15
6. Tragic Tale .... 10.
   Jump Frog
   Escape
   Gardiner
   Duel
   Whistle
   McClellan

Read A True Story just as I heard it.

If it goes—then Jim's little scarlet fever daughter. & similar things.

✗? Immense sensation of Huck & Tom & the village when some aged ⟨f[arm]er⟩ liar comes there & says he has been in the Holy

---

[70] Franklin G. Whitmore was one of Clemens' billiard-playing Friday Evening Club cronies and later became his business agent in Hartford. Clemens wrote Livy on 8 January 1885: "I spent an hour, a while ago, re-writing a thing which is in the Tramp Abroad—speeches of a couple of bragging, loud-mouthed raftsmen. I cut it up into single-sentence speeches—these sentences to be spoken alternately (a lively running-fire of brag & boast) by Cable & me, for Pond's amusement, nights, in our room" (*LLMT*, p. 225). This episode is the well-known raft chapter which Clemens excised from *Huckleberry Finn*. It was not published in *A Tramp Abroad* but in chapter 3 of *Life on the Mississippi* (see p. 98, note 104).

[71] At this time Clemens was still considering a London lecture engagement (see p. 79, note 45) and possible co-lecturers for the English circuit. Before final arrangements were

Land &c!—spins long sea yarns & yarns of travl—been a sailor!
misuses sea-phrases & naval ⟨[--]⟩technicalities.

Asked the skipping & chipper young brakeman—
"Well, is she *really* pretty?—& how old is she?"
He blushed, & I knew I had rightly divined the thoughts that
had inspired his heels.

Train leaves Han 1.30 a.m.[72] gets to Ke at 4.40.
Leave K at 5.55 pm & get to Burlington at 7.30.[73]

✖ Tom Nash's confidential remark[74]

✖? There ought to be a deaf person in a play who breaks in on all
talk, never aware that she is interrupting.

---

made for the Twain-Cable readings, Major Pond had suggested Hoosier poet and lecturer
James Whitcomb Riley as an alternative to Cable (Pond to SLC, 2 July 1884). Clemens
noted on the envelope of Pond's letter: "Told him I would have nobody but Cable—or
the thing was 'off.' " By 25 December 1884 positions were reversed and Pond found
himself championing Cable: "*About England.*—I would certainly not want any one
unless a musician to make intervals, & to give you rest. . . . You will have hard work to
find any one who will hold the audience as Cable does & in a way so as to increase their
appetite for you." Clemens was evidently also considering *Punch* artist and contributor
George Du Maurier for the English tour. Du Maurier, however, did not embark on a
lecturing career until the winter of 1891 when he began a series of popular lectures on
"Social Pictorial Satire" (Leonée Ormond, *George Du Maurier* [London: Routledge &
Kegan Paul, 1969], p. 435).

[72] Clemens and Cable read in Hannibal, Missouri, on 13 January 1885. The visit was
a painfully nostalgic one for Clemens. The following day he wrote to Livy: "This visit to
Hannibal—you can never imagine the infinite great deeps of pathos that have rolled
their tides over me. I shall never see another such day. I have carried my heart in my
mouth for twenty-four hours" (*LLMT*, p. 229).

[73] On 14 January 1885 Clemens and Cable read in Keokuk, Iowa, where Clemens
visited his mother and brother. In December Clemens had arranged with Pond to cancel
the 15 January Chicago lecture date in favor of an engagement in Burlington, Iowa.
This allowed Clemens to stay over in Keokuk with his family for most of 15 January and
then, as this entry indicates, catch a train to Burlington in time for the eight o'clock
performance. Unfortunately, stormy weather delayed Clemens' train to Burlington and
Cable had to "lift a stone-dead audience out of the grave, as it were, and put life & mirth
into them & keep their spirits rising for an hour & a half all alone" (Cable to Mrs. Cable,
17 January 1885, *MT&GWC*, p. 89).

[74] Thomas S. Nash, one of Clemens' boyhood playmates, was rendered deaf and
dumb by a childhood accident. He was subsequently taught to speak but, as Clemens
later recalled, "he could not modulate his voice, since he couldn't hear himself talk.
When he supposed he was talking low and confidentially, you could hear him in Illinois"

✘? Make a kind of Huck Finn narrative on a boat—let him ship as cabin boy⟨[—]⟩& another boy as cub pilot—& so put the great river & its bygone ways into history in form of a story.

By the way, that Cleveland map of the river will come good.

✘? Invent man buying skunk in cage—[t]aking

Mad.[75]

1. Interv.
   ⟨⟨⟩⟨[E]⟩⟨Enc. Jay bird.)
⟨2.⟩4? Achievement
3. ⟨Duel.⟩ J. Frog.
⟨4.⟩ 2 ⟨S[itu] (Gov. Gardner?)⟩ Agricul Editor.[76]

════

Call *this* a gov't.?

1st n.

Chica[77]

1. Agricul Ed
2 Achievement
3 Duel   Blue-jay? 3 & Duel 4.
4. Gov. Gardner.

════

Baker's Cat[78] [#]

(*MTA*, 2:97–98). Clemens' recollection of Nash's speaking ability contrasts strangely with his account of a brief meeting with Nash in Hannibal on 13 January 1885. "At the last moment came Tom Nash," he wrote to Livy on 14 January, "cradle-mate, baby-mate, little-boy mate—deaf & dumb, now, for near 40 years, & nobody suspecting the deep & fine nature hidden behind his sealed lips—& hands me this letter, & wrings my hand, & gives me a devouring look or two, & walks shyly away" (*LLMT*, p. 229). Clemens instructed Livy to preserve Nash's letter but it has not survived.

[75] Clemens and Cable lectured in Madison, Wisconsin, on 21 January 1885.

[76] "How I Edited an Agricultural Paper Once" was collected in *Mark Twain's Sketches, New and Old* (1875).

[77] Clemens and Cable lectured in Chicago on 16 and 17 January and again on 2 and 3 February. Clemens wrote to Livy on 3 February: "You can't think what an immense burden of anxiety I have been toting around on my shoulders for the past two weeks. . . . The burden was the fact that I must exploit a new program in Chicago Feb. 2d (last night)" (TS in MTP).

[78] Clemens tried out this selection from *Roughing It* for the first time in Chicago on 2 February. He wrote to Livy: "In answer to an encore I attempted 'Dick Baker's Cat.'

1st *night*

1. How I lost Editorship[79]
2. Achievement
3. ⟨My⟩ The Blue-Jay's Mistake
4. My Duel.

The garrulous woman—or man—talk, talk, talk—never lets anybody get in more than a word—dreaded by everybody—make her or him a chief character in a (Tom Sawyer?) book.

Club Subject. Anarchists—the formidable feature of it is organization—in *that* is strength—no underlying principle needed[80]

The only time Gen Jim Lane[81] was ever profane. Explanation when he was had up before the church.
Genl. Spinner[82]

Twichell & the dog on Decoration Day.

✗ Man starting out to commit suicide is cornered by a stranger who tries to murder & rob him. Fright—desperate resistance— victory. Kills robber. "Now, d—n him, in the row I've broke my poison-vial & can't commit suicide. Consound it, why dn't I think to let him kill *me*—why what an ass I've been. I hadn't anything for him to rob me of but my poison." (It is strychnine in whisky— robber puts him hors de combat, then drinks it. Or change the whole thing & put 'em through adventures.

The Shah's visit—describe the avenues of ships—the glassy water —the early soft twilight—the manning the yards—the clothing the

---

—which I had never attempted in public before, & had no book here to refresh my memory upon—& it went a-booming" (SLC to OLC, 3 February 1885, TS in MTP).

[79] Probably "How I Edited an Agricultural Paper Once."

[80] Clemens occasionally recorded ideas in his notebook for papers to be delivered to his Hartford discussion group, the Monday Evening Club. There is no record that he ever developed this theme.

[81] Probably Confederate brigadier general James Henry Lane (1833–1907).

[82] Clemens' anecdote concerning the impressive profanity of General Francis E. Spinner, treasurer of the United States from 1861 to 1875, is recounted in Notebook 15 (N&J2, p. 150, note 74). The following anecdote about Twichell is in *Mark Twain's Autobiography* (2:210–212). The suicide story noted below became part of "Marienbad, a Health Factory," written in 1891.

ships in flags—the two-mile rank of ships saluting as we passed through—the 100 pyramids of smoke—the prodigious display of beflagged ships & pleasure boats at Dover—the Castle belching its salute & burying itself in ⟨the⟩ its own fog—the green hills encrusted with gay-dressed people till the green grass not visible.[83]

#? Confession of man who tried to derail a train—he had insured all those passengers in the Accident Co.

On train to Ottawa, man with enormous cluster-diamond scarf-pin, sleve buttons, ⟨&⟩ring, & watch charm, ⟨[(-]⟩ (2 inches across.)[84]

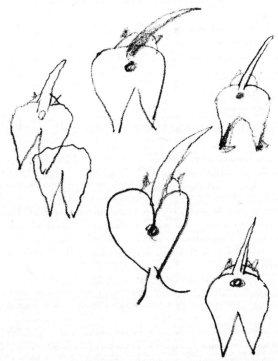

---

[83] During his 1873 trip to England Clemens agreed to act as correspondent for the New York *Herald* to cover the arrival of Nasr-Ed-Din, the shah of Persia, in London (see Notebook 12 in *N&J1*). His letters appeared in the *Herald* in July 1873 and were published as "O'Shah" in *Europe and Elsewhere* (New York: Harper & Brothers, 1923).

[84] Clemens and Cable lectured in Ottawa on 17 February. Clemens mentioned the bejeweled train passenger in his letter to Livy of 17 February 1885 (TS in MTP).

In West & Canada, the world belongs to two absolute masters, God & the cook. Cook quits at 8 pm & goes home. You can't get a hot supper as late as 11.

Feb. 20. Willsborough is where you strike Lake Champlain going north from Albany—& then you follow it for an hour to Plattsburg & beyond—say to about Rouse's Point.[85]

Put Jumping Frog &c (25ᶜ, nice cover) in *Union News Co.* at 25c.)

Room 181 1ˢᵗ floor, Everett,[86] is very choice—parlor & bedrooms (1 big & 1 little) WC & 2 *other* closets with hooks—2 *open fires.*

Extravagance:[87]
$1000 house-rent.
$10,000 rent & clerks—to do a business of $2 or 3000 a year.
Thick paper—postage.
(Turn over bank ac/.)
Osgood statement.[88]
How do you cipher over $30000 profit out of the G. book.[89]

---

[85] Clemens and Cable read in Montreal on 18 and 19 February and took the train south the next day for a reading in Saratoga, New York. As they skirted Lake Champlain, Clemens wrote to Livy describing the "divinely beautiful" winter scenery (SLC to OLC, 20 February 1885, *LLMT*, pp. 238–239).

[86] Major Pond's schedule put Clemens and Cable in the Everett House in New York City on 21, 22, and 24 February. The hotel was Pond's headquarters in New York.

[87] Clemens may have intended to discuss these instances of excessive expenditures with Charles L. Webster while he was in New York during the final days of the lecture tour in February 1885.

[88] Webster had written Clemens on 7 February 1885 that James R. Osgood & Company was preparing its overdue quarterly statement showing sales of Mark Twain's books. Webster added that he believed that Osgood had "sold but 500 books the last 6 mos."

[89] The reference is to the two-volume *Personal Memoirs of U. S. Grant*, to be published by Charles L. Webster & Company in December 1885 and March 1886. This entry begins the extensive record, in this and subsequent notebooks, of Clemens' involvement with the publication of the *Memoirs*. (Clemens' own account of the events which led to his becoming the general's publisher is found in *Mark Twain's Autobiography*, 1:26–27, 31–51). He first heard of Grant's intention of publishing his memoirs through the Century Publishing Company from a chance remark by Richard Watson Gilder, editor of the *Century* magazine. This was on an evening in 1884, probably 18 or 19 November, after

9,000 agents—do they sell a copy apiece?

J.R.[90] got agencies by letter & sold 18000 & 28,000—we travel to them & sell less.

Where are the 6000 Mississippis that are not accounted for?[91]

Exps must be brought down to $5000.

$900 for advertising—does that pay?[92]

Give me full amt of all money paid on office & wages ⟨[--]⟩ac/ since the beginning. If it is over $2,000, where is the profit? Is it business to keep an office *at all*, which doesn't pay its expenses?

Plaudern zu viel.[93]

Eure Anzug ist nicht bescheiden

Nothing done in history game—*it* might pay—the other things don't.[94] [#]

Clemens had finished his reading at New York's Chickering Hall. Clemens' lecture commitments precluded his pursuing the matter, but he enlisted Charles Webster to act as his deputy. On 28 November Webster could report some interest from General Grant and by 3 February 1885 Webster had presented an offer which guaranteed the general seventy per cent of the net profits. This offer was accepted on 27 February 1885.

[90] James R. Osgood.

[91] James R. Osgood & Company had published *Life on the Mississippi* in 1883. On 5 February 1885 Webster secured the rights to Mark Twain's books from Osgood for three thousand dollars. Clemens remained dissatisfied with Osgood's accounting for the books, complaining to Webster on 17 February: "I have *paid* Osgood for 50,000 Mississippis, bound & complete.—He has not accounted to me for more than 33,000. You speak of a remainder of 6,000. What has he done with the other 11,000?" (*MTBus*, p. 304).

[92] According to Webster, it did pay. "I put in a list of 19 papers for 1 month, an advertisement which seems to take. I carefully selected these papers and paid $900⁰⁰ for the ad. I have positive proof that it has paid for nearly every application that I get referres to some one of those papers" (CLW to SLC, 14 March 1885). The applications were for subscription agencies for *Huckleberry Finn*.

[93] *Too much chattering.* The following entry reads: *Your suit is not in good taste.* These two entries, added in the top margin and the right margin of the notebook page, are evidently additional complaints about Charles Webster and the conduct of the Webster & Company office.

[94] A hard-pressed Webster wrote that Clemens' game "was put into Munn & Cos. hands Oct. 2nd with orders to perfect the patent. They assured us that they would put it through *at once.* Now if you want some mechanical draughtsman, or whoever is the proper person to get that in shape I will do so. It is rather doubtful how popular all these things will prove, but it is not doubtful at all how your books will sell if worked properly so I have given my attention to that" (CLW to SLC, 19 January 1885). The other dubious projects referred to were the bed clamp and the perpetual calendar.

Ein Buch abschicken an[95]

    Mr. Collins, Station a[gt] at Hartford.

    Col. John Hay, Cleveland.

    HW Beecher.

    T. B. Aldrich

    Secy Lincoln

    Mr. Arthur?

    See Ital Minister

    Pitts Burt, Cincin

    Gov. Cleveland.

Make a good medallion of Gen Grant. ⟨& put on sale.⟩

Andrew Knox, 6th ave ⟨near⟩ below 42d. Shoes.

Feb. 26, '85. On the 21st I called on Gen. Grant & Col. Fred[96] his son, at 3 East 66th st (their home), to talk over the business details of the publication of the General's book. I was astonished to see how thin & weak he looked; ⟨for⟩yet as I had just read in the papers that his bad symptoms were all gone, I took for granted that the report was true, & said I had been glad to see that news. He smiled & said, "Yes,—if it had only been true." ⟨There⟩ One of the physicians was present, & he startled me by saying the General's condition was the ⟨opposition⟩opposite of encouraging.

    Then the talk drifted to business, & the ⟨President⟩ General presently said, "I mean you shall have the book—I have about made up my mind to that—but I wish to write to Mr. Roswell Smith, first, & tell him I have so decided. I think this is due him."[97]

---

[95] Evidently a list of persons to whom Clemens planned to send copies of *Huckleberry Finn.* The list includes Hartford stationmaster William Collins to whom Clemens usually sent copies of his books. John Hay thanked Clemens for the book on 14 April 1885. Robert Todd Lincoln was secretary of war under Chester A. Arthur. The Italian minister in Washington at this time was Baron Saverio Fava. Cincinnati stockbroker Pitts H. Burt, who introduced Clemens and Cable to the Rookwood Pottery at the time of the two authors' lecture engagement in Cincinnati, acknowledged receipt of a copy of *Huckleberry Finn* on 28 March 1885. Clemens' acquaintance with Grover Cleveland was slight: Cable and Clemens were in Albany, New York, on 2 December 1884 and called on Cleveland, then governor of New York and president-elect.

[96] Frederick D. Grant had resigned from the army in 1881. He was among those who assisted his father in the preparation of the *Memoirs.*

[97] Roswell Smith was owner of the *Century* magazine and director of the publishing

From the beginning the General has shown a fine delicacy toward those people—a delicacy which is native to ⟨his⟩ the character of the man who put into the Appomatox terms of surrender the words "officers may retain their side arms" to save General Lee the humiliation of giving up his sword—a delicacy which the "Century" have not well deserved. (They offered him 10 per cent royalty on his book! That was the most colossal bit of cheek the 19th century can show; & also the most cold-blooded attempt to rob a trusting & inexperienced man, since Ward's performances.[98] Gen. Grant felt under obligations to give them the book—mainly because they had suggested that he write it—a suggestion which ⟨I⟩I made to him 3 years ago.[99] And in his modesty he didn't know that when they paid him $1500 ⟨[arti]⟩for 3 articles in the "Century"[100] they were exactly as just toward him ⟨as if they had⟩ ⟨it⟩as it would be to buy a dollar bill of a blind man & pay him ten cents for it. They sent him a voluntary $1000 the other day—after the General's first article had sprung their circulation clear away up into the clouds. They could have paid him $5,000 for that article & *still* made that much money themselves.) [#]

---

activities of the Century Company. Grant had made a fairly firm commitment to the Century Company several months before Clemens' intervention. Roswell Smith had informed Richard Watson Gilder on 9 September 1884 that his recent interview with General Grant had been "in every way satisfactory" and that the general's "ideas agree with ours—to make a good book, manufacture it handsomely, sell it at a reasonable price. . . . When the book is ready he is to come to us with it" (*Letters of Richard Watson Gilder*, ed. Rosamond Gilder [Boston & New York: Houghton Mifflin Co., 1916], pp. 123–124). Rosamond Gilder adds: "The arrangements for its publication by [the Century] company were never completed. Mr. Smith suddenly found himself confronted by no less brilliant and imaginative a competitor than Mark Twain, who, by his astonishingly liberal offer and the power of his personality, succeeded in carrying off the prize" (p. 124).

[98] Ferdinand Ward, whose Wall Street dealings earned him the sobriquet of "the Young Napoleon of Finance," had been Grant's partner in the brokerage firm of Grant & Ward. The company failed in May 1884, leaving the Grant family penniless, when the fraudulent character of Ward's financial manipulations was exposed.

[99] In his autobiography Clemens recalls having proposed the idea when he and Howells visited Grant on 10 March 1882 (*MTA*, 1:26–27).

[100] Four articles by Grant were eventually published in the *Century* series, "Battles and Leaders of the Civil War": "The Battle of Shiloh" (February 1885), "The Siege of Vicksburg" (September 1885), "Chattanooga" (November 1885), and "Preparing for the Wilderness Campaign" (February 1886).

Nat Goodwin[101]—Willard's Hotel inauguration week

Make the high bindings pay a *great deal* better than cloth—$12 & $15 per set.[102]

Myself agent at large. Where genl agent delivers ⟨one book & collects money, he to have 50ᶜ—10 books $2.50; 20⟩ my books & collects, he to have 15 per cent

Use your N.Y. perforated-notice system in all cities.

⟨What went with that $1000 Indiana bond which⟩ Bissell called for?

And the $1500 of Chatto's notes?

Am Bank Note

Am Ex. in Europe. See Hawley about a sale for it. Send Charly to him.[103]

✖ Cable says restore the raft chapter to Huck Finn from Mississippi.[104] [#]

---

[101] Clemens had been considering Nat Goodwin for the title role in *Colonel Sellers as a Scientist* early in 1884 (see p. 13, note 21). Clemens wrote to Howells from Philadelphia on 27 February 1885 just before the close of his lecture tour: "Nat Goodwin was on the train yesterday. He plays in Washington all the coming week. He is very anxious to get our Sellers play & play it under changed names" (*MTHL*, p. 520). Goodwin's insistence that Sellers' name be changed had brought earlier negotiations to an impasse, but Howells now felt that the play was so problematical that Goodwin could have it on his terms (Howells to SLC, 28 February 1885, *MTHL*, p. 521). The negotiations, however, were never concluded.

[102] The two-volume sets of the *Memoirs* were issued in five bindings: cloth, $7 per set; sheep, $9; half-morocco, $11; full-morocco, $18; tree calf, $25.

[103] The American Exchange in Europe, one of Clemens' investments, promoted and protected American business and tourist interests. Clemens wrote to Webster on 31 October 1884 that he heard "whispered doubts" about the soundness of the company (*MTBus*, p. 280). Webster's inability to get any buyers for the stock in January 1885 confirmed the doubts. Joseph R. Hawley, a Hartford friend of Clemens', was at this time United States senator from Connecticut and president and chairman of the board of the American Exchange in Europe. (See p. 7, note 3.)

[104] Clemens had introduced the raft episode into chapter 3 of *Life on the Mississippi*, explaining: "By way of illustrating keelboat talk and manners, and that now-departed and hardly-remembered raft-life, I will throw in, in this place, a chapter from a book which I have been working at, by fits and starts, during the past five or six years." When Charles Webster was preparing *Huckleberry Finn* for the press he discovered that the

Mr. Lincoln[105]
312 C (Gen Hawley)
The President.
General Drum.
John Arnot.
General Sheridan
The new President.

In October, I will go to Pittsfield & read "Mental Telegraphy" to
the Young Ladies Club—a promise made to Miss Dawes. ⟨Feb.⟩
Mch 1/85.[106]

Sheridan 1632 R I Ave[107]
Wadhams 1727—19—N. W.[108]
Lincoln—14th & Mass Ave [#]

---

manuscript was considerably longer than its companion piece, *Tom Sawyer*, and was
concerned that the two books would not present a uniform appearance. Therefore he
had suggested to Clemens on 21 April 1884 that it might be "better to omit that old
Mississippi matter." Clemens replied on 22 April: "Yes, I think the raft chapter can be
left wholly out" (*MTBus*, p. 249).

[105] A list of men to whom Clemens possibly intended to send copies of the Grant
Memoirs. The list includes Joseph R. Hawley, one of the owners of the Hartford *Courant*
and senator from Connecticut, Richard Coulter Drum, adjutant general of the army at
Washington, D.C., and Elmira banker John Arnot, Jr. The last lecture engagement of
the Twain-Cable tour was in Washington, D.C., on 28 February 1885. The two authors
remained in Washington, which was bustling with preparations for the 4 March inauguration of Grover Cleveland, until 2 March.

[106] Washington newspaper correspondent Anna Laurens Dawes was a resident of
Pittsfield, Massachusetts, and president of that city's Wednesday Morning Club.

[107] General Sheridan had resided in his "roomy, picturesque, double house, on the
corner of Rhode Island Avenue and Seventeenth Street" in Washington, D.C., since
1883 (Frank A. Burr, *The Life of Gen. Philip H. Sheridan* [Providence, R.I.: J. A. &
R. A. Reid, 1888], pp. 362, 359).

[108] Cable wrote to his wife on 2 March 1885 from Washington: "Spent a long, good
day yesterday with Carrie Henderson & her husband Lieut. Wadhams. Clemens was
with us. I got him out to church at last!" (*MT&GWC*, p. 114). Naval commander
Albion V. Wadhams was married to the former Caroline Henderson, a friend of Cable's
from New Orleans. The Wadhams' niece, fourteen years old at the time of Clemens' and
Cable's visit, later recalled the occasion:

One Sunday, the family went to church, having arranged to bring the two famous
authors and a well known woman writer home for midday dinner. . . . I heard my
Uncle's key in the front door. Just a moment and he was bringing the gentlemen into
the dining room for cigars. . . . "My niece, Mr. Clemens," he said. Mark Twain's
face was one big smile. He did not shake hands but pulled me around by my braids

⟨Gen.⟩General Francis Darr, San Fran° [109]

John Mackey[110]

Geo. W. Childs[111]

A baby is left on a bachelor's hands—the complications that
ensue—his affianced arrives at last, oversees & hears his
endearments, then pitches into him. Baby turns out to be related
to one of them & has been left at the wrong address by mistake.

Make it first a mag article, then a farce.

Appoint that 2200 woman to represent me, & ⟨divide the
premium with her.⟩

India paper edition [#]

---

which he solemnly inspected. "What a funny color of hair she has," he said, and
strange to say, all my embarrassment was gone. Mr. Cable took my Aunt out to dinner
and the lady author was escorted by my Uncle. Mark Twain offered me his arm.
Just as we were seated Uncle turned to Mr. Cable and asked him to say grace which
he did. Then the great humorist solemnly remarked, "A-A-AMen." It was irresistibly
funny, as was everything he did, but what should we do? We could not offend Mr.
Cable by laughing and how could we help laughing. . . . Mark Twain was in his
element and he told stories till we were lame with laughter. (TS in MTP)

[109] Darr was probably brought to Clemens' attention by an article in the New York
Times of 3 March 1885 which disclosed Darr's plan to bring General Grant and his family to California. "The idea," said the *Times*, "was conceived by Gen. Francis Darr, formerly of New-York, but now a resident of [San Francisco]. Gen. Darr served during the
war on the staffs of Gens. D. C. Buell, Rosecrans, and John G. Foster. Since then, notwithstanding that he differs from Gen. Grant in politics, Mr. Darr has been one of the
General's warmest friends. The scheme, in which several prominent Californians heartily
co-operate, is to buy a large bearing vineyard, with a residence and other necessary buildings, and to tender the entire property to Gen. Grant as a loan. The property would be
deeded to Mrs. Grant. . . . A dispatch was received from the General last night in which
he said it would be impossible for him to make the trip at present." Darr was currently a
partner in the San Francisco wine firm of Arpad Haraszthy & Company.

[110] John W. Mackay, the Comstock Lode millionaire who had enlarged his interests
to include railroad and communications holdings, would later invest in the Paige typesetter. Clemens' entries in Notebook 24 (p. 132) indicate that he hoped to interest
Mackay in bidding for the first copy of a de luxe edition of Grant's *Memoirs* which would
include tipped-in pages of the general's manuscript.

[111] Childs, the owner of the Philadelphia *Public Ledger* from 1864 until his death in
1894, was a close friend to General Grant. Grant had consulted him about the Webster
company's proposition to publish his memoirs. Childs's *Recollections of General Grant*
appeared in 1885.

Homer Pond.[112]

Brander Matthews

Champney 337 4th ave & 25th st.[113]

In N. Y. see about have F — — W. dramatize H Finn[114]

Let Munn & Co have a game-board designed.[115]

Get General to write 100 or 200 signatures for a special edition.

The title page does not need "Personal" in it, & is a complement to Gen Sherman.[116] [#]

---

[112] Homer Pond was a brother of James B. Pond and commander of the Grand Army of the Republic units in Kansas in 1884. Clemens wrote to Webster concerning the sub-scription agents for the *Memoirs*: "Pond asks me to remind you to not forget Homer Pond, but inquire into & consider the expediency of giving him the State of Kanzas. There are 80,000 Grand Army veterans resident in Kanzas, & Homer Pond is *Grand Commander*" (n.d., between 17 February and 5 March 1885, *MTBus*, p. 305).

[113] James Wells Champney was a painter and illustrator whose opinion Clemens had solicited about Karl Gerhardt's sculptures before sending Gerhardt to study in Paris in 1881.

[114] After the close of their lecture tour in Washington, D.C., on 28 February 1885, Clemens and Cable stayed on there briefly before taking leave of each other. Clemens then proceeded to New York on 2 March to "fool around there one or two days, mainly at Webster's office" (SLC to William Dean Howells, 27 February 1885, *MTHL*, p. 520). Before returning to Hartford on 5 March, he evidently meant to see Fred Williams about dramatizing *Huckleberry Finn*. Williams, who often did stage adaptations for Augustin Daly, was one of the "dozens of dramatic hacks" who "worked as house dra-matists for all the successful theaters, and the extent of their so-called literary labors will probably never be known, for they wrote anonymously and left nothing for identification except their trashy ill-printed plays" (Marvin Felheim, *The Theater of Augustin Daly* [Cambridge: Harvard University Press, 1956], p. 148). No evidence has been discovered to indicate that Williams dramatized *Huckleberry Finn* or any other work by Clemens (see 105.8).

[115] See page 95, note 94.

[116] Sherman had published his autobiography, *Memoirs of General William T. Sherman*, in 1875. Clemens was considering making the title of Grant's book conform to Sherman's title. On 5 March 1885 Charles Webster wrote to Clemens that he had "put the title page matter before [the Grant family] in strong light," but Clemens' suggestion did not find favor. In March 1885 Grant's book was widely announced as *Personal Remi-niscences* and the book was finally issued as *Personal Memoirs of U. S. Grant*. In 1890 Charles L. Webster & Company reprinted Sherman's book and changed the title page to make it conform to that of the Grant memoirs: *Personal Memoirs of Gen. W. T. Sherman*.

Du hast mir nichts zu ⟨l⟩Leide gethan.[117]

Sie können sich vorstellen wie es mir zu Muthe wäre . . .

Ich straf⟨[e]⟩ ⟨die⟩dich Lügen!

Es kommt darauf an

Die Rache ist süss.

Fest gebunden, fest gefunden.[118]

Vor fünfzig: "⟨W[e-]⟩Wir werden alt." Nach fünfzig: "Wir sind alt geworden."

✗[119]

Charley inquire into Burr Index Co.[120]

Ask Bissell about Chatto's note.

Bed-clamp man.[121]

Schicken Sie der Herr Station-Agenten Collins einen Buch. *Also* O. W. Holmes.[122]

⟨Unser Feuer-Machine geht ganz recht.⟩[123]

ansprechend, anziehend
umfassend

---

[117] *You haven't wronged me.* The following four expressions read: *You can imagine how I'd feel. I will prove you wrong. It depends on. Revenge is sweet.*

[118] This is the proverbial expression *Safe bind, safe find.* The following entry reads: *Before fifty: "We're getting old." After fifty: "We've become old."*

[119] This X is written in black ink at the bottom of a page containing the preceding entries in German, which are written in purple pencil.

[120] A company in which Clemens owned stock (see p. 67).

[121] See page 74, note 28.

[122] Oliver Wendell Holmes acknowledged receipt of *Huckleberry Finn* in a letter of 16 March 1885, warmly expressing his appreciation of Clemens' work: "I expect great pleasure from it, as I have always found from your books, ever since I began with 'The Jumping Frog,' and I believe I have smoothed out a good many wrinkles by the inward delight and the outward relaxation of features they have never failed to produce. I hope you are well and will keep so, for you have made and will make the world happier so long as it has had your books and can hope for new ones."

[123] *Our fire machine works quite well.*

fesselnd
gebührend
geziemend
vermögend
wüthend
vielsagend?
Entzückend
Entblösst
unentbehrlich
abstossend
unwissend
überwiegend
abwechselnd
abweichend
übere[ins]t[imm]end
fl[ü]ssend
dem Name nach
herausgegeben, issued, published.
Aufgabe, edition, publication.
beförderte, promoted, advanced.
vertraut, familiar?
gelegentlich, occasionally.
anvertraut, confided, entrusted.
gewandtheit, cleverness
Antrag, proposition?
lehnte—ab, declined
bedauert[e], regretted.
in Anspruch nehmen

Versetse die Bank Rechnung.[124]

Visit Hotel Normandie, Bway & 38[th.]

Book to be copyrighted immediately.

Photographs right away, from which to make medallion of the General. [#]

---

[124] *Change the bank account.*

The illustrations & style of this book are in accordance with my father's desire & direction.

Make a type-writer copy, & keep ⟨one⟩ original in bank vault.

No, put a page of it in Each copy of edition de luxe⟨.⟩—$50 apiece.—broad 1 foot margin

Photos of self. ½ doz

Bliss put 18 girls into N. Y on Tramp. Has one man who has sold 600 in Cleveland of the new book.

Harrison[125] could canvass the ed. de luxe.
Make him a canvasser anyway & let him learn.

Write German letter to ⟨Uber⟩ Vom Fels und Meer,[126] complaining that people do not believe I know the language. In a postscript ask the editor to correct any chance mistakes I may have made. Send it through Tauchnitz.

An den Heerführer den Aufforderung stellen, dass er gütigst seine Name in meinem Notenbuch schreiben wird.[127]

Mein Gott! stellen Sie diese Thatsache vor: die $1000 welche dem Herrn General Grant durch unser Zustimme bezahlt worden waren, stand eigentlich zwischen ihm und die kahle *Nothwendigkeit!* Welch' ein ⟨groosmüthiges⟩grossmüthiges Aufruhr folgen müssen, wenn nur das Amerikanischer Volk diese abscheuliche Sache wissen können! (Dienstag, den 10ten März, 1885.)[128] [#]

---

[125] Possibly Harrison Tyrrell, Grant's Negro valet.

[126] An illustrated periodical published in Stuttgart from 1881 to 1917.

[127] *Ask the general if he would be kind enough to write his name in my notebook.*

[128] *My God! consider this fact: the $1000 which had been paid to General Grant through our agreement actually stood between him and bare necessity! What a magnanimous uproar would follow if only the American people could know of this abominable affair! (Tuesday, the 10th of March, 1885.)* Clemens amplified this remark in a 25 May 1885 dictation about the Grant *Memoirs.* Describing "a circumstance which I have never spoken of and which cannot be known for many years to come," he explained: "Appended to the contract was a transfer of the book to General Grant's wife, and the transfer from her to my firm for the consideration of $1,000 in hand paid. This was to

NY Ass Press Agt said if you will give me $500 I will put it in.[129]

Volatile liniment—50¢ bottle—flannel on breast & windpipe.

⟨⟨Send cloth to H C Bunner,[130] & ½ morocco to Brander Matthews.⟩

John Hay?
⟨O W Holmes?⟩⟩

⟨How does the postal card plan of canvassing work?⟩

Get Fred Williams to dramatize P & P or help me.[131]

Webster or I see Tiffany about changing works of watches.

Put Huck & Tom & Jim through my Mo. campaign & give a chapter to the Century.

Union officer accosts Tom & says his name is US Grant.[132] [#]

---

prevent the general's creditors from seizing the proceeds of the book." Charles Webster, thinking the $1,000 payment a mere contractual formality, had been astonished to discover that the Grant family were in need of the money to meet immediate and pressing bills (see *MTA,* 1:41).

[129] There had been some doubt expressed in a few newspapers as to the propriety of Clemens' actions toward the Century Company in the matter of the Grant *Memoirs.* In his autobiography Clemens recalled that he prepared a statement for the "Associated Press" (not related to the present-day organization), refuting the implication that he obtained the *Memoirs* "by some sort of superior underhanded smartness." When the story did not appear and Clemens inquired about it, he was told that if he "had had a friend round about the Associated Press office" his statement would have been "published all over the country for a reasonable bribe" (*MTA,* 1:55, 57).

[130] Henry Cuyler Bunner, author, poet, and editor of *Puck* from 1877 to 1896, had known Clemens at least since March 1883 when they were both inducted into the Kinsmen, a club of literary and theatrical people.

[131] See page 101, note 114. Clemens had secured a copyright on his four-act dramatization of *The Prince and the Pauper* on 1 March 1884. His interest in the play was renewed at this time by the amateur production planned as a surprise for him by Livy. Clemens wrote to Major Pond on 14 March 1885: "My boy, you ought to have been here to-night to see Susie & Clara & a dozen of the neighbors' children play half a dozen stirring scenes from the Prince & the Pauper—one of the prettiest private thatrical performances I have ever seen. Audience of 25 neighbors. Mrs. Clemens has been drilling these kids 3 or 4 weeks in their parts, & to-night the thing was sprung on me as a surprise. When it is repeated, you must run up & see it" (Berg). The production was repeated, with Clemens taking the part of Miles Hendon, on several occasions (*MTA,* 2:60–61).

[132] Tom and Huck were excluded from "The Private History of a Campaign That

How many press copies have you sent out?

Go to Chas. A. Dana's, Sunday. Ret 4.30.

⟨HAPRIS' glove store *sure*—give Charley Livy's *note*. in my pocketbook.⟩

Friday, Mch 20, '85.[133] Gerhardt & I arrived at General Grant's about half past 2 pm., & I asked that the family would look at a small clay bust of the General which Gerhardt had made from a photograph. Col. Fred & Jesse were absent, to receive their sister Mrs. Sartorius,[134] who would arrive from Europe about 4.30; but the 3 Mrs. Grants[135] ⟨looked at⟩ examined the work & expressed strong approval of it, & also great gratification that Mr. Gerhardt had undertaken it⟨, for⟩. Mrs. Jesse Grant had lately dreamed that she was inquiring where the maker of my bust could be found (she had seen a picture of it in Huck Finn, which was published 4 weeks ago),[136] for she wanted the same artist to make one of Gen. Grant. The ladies examined the bust critically & pointed out ⟨[---]⟩ defects, while Gerhardt made the necessary corrections. Presently

---

Failed," Mark Twain's account of his brief service as a Confederate volunteer in 1861 (*Century*, December 1885, pp. 193–204). According to that piece it was the approach of General Grant's regiment which prompted Mark Twain's final retreat and his decision to renounce the war. Clemens' notebook entry was made in response to a suggestion from Robert Underwood Johnson, editor in charge of the *Century's* Civil War series. In his letter of 16 March 1885 Johnson added: "I was not joking the other day in suggesting to you that you should write out your experiences in the Rebel Army. . . . Already we are roping into the Series the literary men of both sections, including Higginson and others of the Northern side, and Maurice Thompson, Cable and yourself among the eminent rebels." Clemens was not able to work on the "Private History" until the summer of 1885.

[133] Clemens' recollections of Gerhardt's work on the Grant bust, elaborating the following notebook entry, were dictated on 22 May 1885 (see *MTA*, 1:57–68).

[134] Grant's only daughter, Ellen, in 1874 had married the scion of an English country family, Algernon Sartoris.

[135] Elizabeth Chapman Grant, Jesse's wife, Ida Honoré Grant, wife of Frederick, and Julia Grant, the general's wife.

[136] Karl Gerhardt did the bust of Clemens in August 1884 at Quarry Farm in Elmira. A heliotype of the bust appears as the frontispiece to the first edition of *Huckleberry Finn*.

Mrs. ⟨U. S.⟩ General Grant suggested that Gerhardt step in & look
at the General. I had been in there talking with the General, but
had never thought of asking him to let a stranger come in. So
Gerhardt went in, with the ladies & me, & the inspection &
cross-fire ⟨of⟩ began—"There, I ⟨told you⟩ was sure ⟨his⟩ his nose
was so & so"—& "I was sure his forehead was so-&-so"—"& don't
you think his head is so & so?" ⟨I⟩ And so everybody walked
around & about the old hero, who lay half reclining, in big easy
chairs & well muffled up, & submitted to all this as serenely as if
he were used to being served so. One marked feature of General
Grant's character is his exceeding gentleness, goodness, sweetness.
Every time I have been ⟨there⟩ in his presence—lately & formerly
—my mind was drawn to that feature. I wonder it has not been
more spoken of.

Presently he said let Gerhardt bring in his clay & work there, if
G. would not mind his reclining attitude. ⟨I⟩Of course we were
glad. A table for the bust was moved up in front of him; the ladies
left the room; I got a book; Gerhardt went to work; & for an hour
there was perfect stillness, & for the first time during the day the
General got a good sound peaceful nap. General Badeau[137] came in,
& probably interrupted that nap. He spoke out as strongly as the
others, concerning the great excellence of the likeness. He had some
sheets of MS in his hand, & said "I've been reading what you wrote
this morning, General," & it is of the utmost value; it solves ⟨in [a]
few⟩ riddle that has ⟨puzzles⟩puzzled men's brains all these
years⟨."⟩, and makes the thing clear & rational." I asked what the
puzzle was, & he said "It was why Grant did not immediately lay
siege to Vicksburg after capturing Port Hudson" (at least that is my
recollection, now toward midnight, of Gen. Badeau's answer.) [#]

---

[137] Adam Badeau had been Grant's military secretary from 1864 until 1869 when he
retired as a brevet brigadier general. From 1870 until 1881 he was consul general in London, interrupting his duties to accompany Grant on the first five months of his world
tour (1887–1879). Badeau's most recent appointment had been as consul general in
Havana, a position he resigned in April 1884. Badeau had written his three-volume *Military History of Ulysses S. Grant* (New York: D. Appleton and Co., 1868–1881) partially
from records and correspondence which Grant supplied. He was currently assisting Grant
in the preparation of his *Century* articles and his *Memoirs*.

(See about inserting picture of General's birth-place.)[138]

"No *sir*—They was *receiving* that day"—(from Huck Finn.)

Sir they'd do things over a rafter 't nobody but a snake could
do—you never see anything like it—lose grip—back of your neck—
they warn't particular wher' they *fell*—They was handsome & no
harm
despised snakes—*any* kind of snakes—never made no dif to *her*
what the deno*m*
them times suspicious 'bout *everything*—been suspicious of a *cow* 'f
she'd found her comin' up out the cellar.—
not *one* little pill—*buck*shot—handful; handful at a *time*. It *was*
the most disgustin' sight!

Want Gerhardt to get measurements for a life-size bust of the
General.

Show that first printed page to General Grant.

Barrett's House.[139]

Charley at Gilsey

Gen & Charley here.

General birthplace

Charley W. see Hawley about sale of Am Ex in Europe. Money
for book?

Offer G. G.'s family $500 a month till a year hence when first
statement due—they perhaps need it.

Ask about my first page of the General's book ⟨[------]⟩

Did you see Nat Goodwin about the play?[140]

Send book to Pitts Burt, Cinncinati.[141] [#]

---

[138] An etching of Grant's birthplace at Point Pleasant, Ohio, is in volume 1 of the
Memoirs.

[139] Probably actor Lawrence Barrett, like Clemens a member of the Kinsmen club.

[140] See page 98, note 101.

[141] See page 96, note 95.

What *was* in Estes & L brief?[142]

Paid $500 this (⟨85⟩84) summer at farm—see back, many pages.[143]

Theres 4 mag articles in the Vicks one.[144]

Let *us* buy them.

Want a few pages of Genl's Ms—a dozen pages—not even paged —for 2^d volume—so you can put it in prospectus & show that the *Genl* is writing it.[145]

Hurry the Maps

Money in bank.

Offer $500 a month [#]

---

[142] On 3 January 1885 Charles L. Webster & Company had filed for an injunction against Estes & Lauriat, the Boston bookdealers, who had advertised *Huckleberry Finn* for sale before it was published and at a price below that set by the publisher. Webster wrote to Clemens on 14 February 1885 that the suit had been denied, but that he had "no particulars" (*MTBus*, p. 303). Clemens shortly informed Webster that he had "made up with Estes & Lauriat & ended that quarrel" (*MTBus*, p. 318).

[143] See page 73.

[144] During one of his visits to the general, Clemens had noticed a typewritten copy of Grant's article on the siege of Vicksburg. A rough word count convinced Clemens that the general's contract to supply the *Century* with four war articles was "most amply fulfilled already, without an additional article," since, he stated, " 'there is matter enough in this one to make two or three ordinary magazine articles' " (*MTA*, 1:50). The Vicksburg article appeared in the *Century* for September 1885. Robert Underwood Johnson, editor of the *Century's* war series, recalls visiting the general about a week before his death and assuring him "that we should gladly do anything we could for the success of the book in Mr. Clemens's hands, adjusting our plans to his. I told the General that we had willingly acceded to his son's wish that we should relinquish that part of the long Vicksburg narrative that preceded the seige—an article in itself" (Johnson, *Remembered Yesterdays* [Boston: Little, Brown, and Co., 1923], p. 223). Johnson's recollections indicate that Clemens made Fred Grant his advocate in the matter of the lengthy Vicksburg article.

[145] The dispute over Grant's authorship of the memoirs is discussed on page 205, note 71.

Young Lieut & birthplace & maps for 1st vol.
Portrait & bust & maps for 2^{d} vol.[146]

They propose to bring *all* out before we do.[147]

Put in the birthplace

Offer per month.

"*One in nine* of all insured under its Accident Policies have
received Fatal or Disabling Injuries."—Travelers Co Aver.

March 23/85. Drove at 11.30 a m to Pratt & Whitney's & told
Col. Woodruff[148] to take the offensive, now, with that terra Cotta
firm, & require of them that they pay Gerhard 65 or 70 per cent of
the *profit* on every bust of General Grant. It is the best likeness of
the General ever made, in clay, oil or any other way—in fact, *much*
the best; & it is the *last* one that ⟨w⟩ever *will* be made from the
living subject—therefore, if they hesitate about those terms, there's
plenty others who will gladly take the enterprise off their hands.

⟨The⟩On the way to Boston—noon.[149] Will telegraph Woodruff
to make no terms till I see some Boston terra cotters. [#]

---

[146] The illustrations for the *Memoirs* followed Clemens' plan with the exception of
the engraving of Gerhardt's bust of Grant, which was not included. The two other portrait engravings mentioned here depicted the twenty-one-year-old Lieutenant Grant
from an old daguerreotype "furnished the publishers through the courtesy of Mr. George
W. Childs" and a later portrait of General Grant.

[147] The *Century* was able to arrive at a compromise agreement with Charles L. Webster & Company. Webster informed Clemens on 15 April 1885: "The contract with the
Century Co is signed. All future articles [Grant's first article on the "Battle of Shiloh"
had already appeared in the February 1885 *Century*] are to be copyrighted by *us* in the
name of U. S. Grant. We are not to publish first vol before Dec. 1st next, and second vol
before Mch. 1st next giving them three months notice before publication." Grant's three
subsequent *Century* articles appeared, as agreed, with proper acknowledgment to
Charles L. Webster & Company's publication of the *Memoirs*.

[148] W. N. Woodruff was a machinist at the Pratt & Whitney iron works in Hartford.
He was in charge of the manufacture and sale of Karl Gerhardt's terra-cotta bust of General Grant. By 21 July 1885 Woodruff was able to send Clemens several testimonials from
satisfied recipients of the bust. Albert Bigelow Paine states that "the little bust of Grant
which Gerhardt worked on that day was widely reproduced in terra-cotta, and is still regarded by many as the most nearly correct likeness of Grant. The original is in possession
of the family" (*MTB*, p. 809).

[149] Clemens and his wife went to Boston to visit the Howells family on 23 March.

Actor's Fund, Phila, *afternoon* of Apl. 9, Acad Music.[150]
J. W. Ryckman, Committee
Clover Club at 5 the same afternoon, at Hotel Bellevue.[151]
C. R. Deacon, Secy. at Continental Hotel

Send book to Life[152]

⟨Hartford, March ⟨26⟩27, 1885.
Twenty-five per cent of my 70 per cent royalty on the General
Grant bust, ⟨are⟩ is to be paid over to S L Clemens, for value
heretofore received.

Karl Gerhardt.⟩[153]

Andrew White & Prof. Newbury (?)[154] [#]

Clemens was to be Howells' guest that evening at the Tavern Club, a society of writers
and artists of which Howells was president. Clemens thanked his host in a letter of 26
March from Hartford (*MTHL*, p. 524).

[150] Clemens delivered a short speech on "Obituary Poetry" at the Actors' Fund Fair
benefit in Philadelphia on 9 April 1885 (see *MTS* [1910], p. 265, where, however, the
speech is misdated). Clemens wrote to Livy from Philadelphia the same day: "It was a
superb performance, & of prodigious variety. It began shortly after noon & lasted till 4.
There were 4,000 people present, & they sat it through. I did *wish* you were there. You'd
have seen two or three of the most astonishing feats that were ever performed by human
beings" (TS in MTP).

[151] Immediately after his appearance at the Actors' Fund benefit, Clemens attended
the Clover Club dinner in Philadelphia. The Clover Club was a dinner club, founded in
1881, which met monthly at the Hotel Bellevue and was famous for the lively informality
of its members and guests.

[152] *Life*, the New York humorous weekly founded in 1883, published a caustic review
of *Huckleberry Finn*, entitled "Mark Twain's Blood-Curdling Humor," on 26 February
1885 (p. 119). "We organized a search expedition for the humorous qualities of this
book," *Life* remarked, citing several "elevating" and "delicate" episodes suitable for the
amusement of children "on long, rainy afternoons" and for "lenten parlor entertainments and church festivals." The paper continued its abuse in subsequent weeks, praising only the illustrations by E. W. Kemble, who was one of *Life's* own staff artists.
Kemble's "clever illustrations for 'Mark Twain's Adventures of Huckleberry Finn,'"
they noted, "enliven many a page of coarse and dreary fun" (12 March 1885, p. 146).
Life further commented on 9 April: "It is a pleasure to note that the Concord Library
Committee agree with *Life's* estimate of Mark Twain's 'blood-curdling humor,' and
have banished 'Huckleberry Finn' to limbo" (p. 202; see p. 113, note 161, for more information on the Concord Library's interdiction of *Huckleberry Finn*).

[153] This entry written by Clemens appears to have been signed by Gerhardt. The
entry was canceled more heavily than is usual, and the signature was canceled twice,
with additional scrawls over the initial letters.

[154] Andrew Dickson White would retire from the presidency of Cornell in 1885; John

⟨J. R. Randall,
Augusta, (Ga) Chronicle.⟩[155]

Get short-hander in New York & begin my autobiography at
once & continue it straight through the summer.[156]

Which reminds me that Susie, aged 13, (1885), has begun ⟨my⟩
to write my biography—solely of her own motion—a thing
⟨w⟩about which I feel proud & gratified. At breakfast this morning
I intimated that if I seemed to be ⟨talked⟩talking on a pretty high
key, in the way of style, it ⟨was all right⟩ must be remembered that
my biographer was present. Whereupon Susie struck upon the
unique idea of having me sit up & purposely *talk* for the
biography![157]

John L. RoBards.[158]

Mad. Square, Apl. 28 & 29—Copyright readings.[159] [#]

Strong Newberry was professor of geology at Columbia University. Clemens' reason
for noting these two names is not known.

[155] Probably in late March 1885, Clemens sent a copy of *Huckleberry Finn* to James
Ryder Randall, journalist and poet.

[156] Lecture manager and journalist James Redpath responded to an inquiry from
Clemens on 4 May 1885: "Now about the auto. When I do work by the week, I charge
$100 a week for the best I can do." Redpath, who had acquired shorthand as a youth in
Scotland, visited Clemens in Hartford in May and acted as his amanuensis for the
dictations about the Grant *Memoirs*.

[157] Clemens included much of Susy's biography in his autobiography. Her manuscript,
which ends abruptly on 4 July 1886, is in the Clifton Waller Barrett Library, University
of Virginia, Charlottesville.

[158] Clemens had known John L. Robards since childhood; at the outset of the Civil
War they served together in the hastily mustered Marion Rangers unit. When Robards
wrote him on 24 March 1885, Clemens noticed a peculiarity about Robards' signature,
letterhead, and return address ("J. L. RoBards") that amused him. On the envelope he
wrote: "This was always a poor well meaning ass—& at last has gone & stuck that big B
in the middle of his name!" Clemens ridiculed this introduced capitalization in "The
Private History of a Campaign That Failed" (*Century*, December 1885), describing a
young militiaman named Dunlap who "had some pathetic little nickel-plated aristocratic
instincts" and wrote his name as "d'Un Lap."

[159] Clemens was scheduled to read on 29 April, the second day of the two-day benefit
for the American Copyright League in New York. A number of prominent authors took
part in the benefit. Clemens read his familiar "Trying Situation" selection from *A
Tramp Abroad*.

Company at Charley Clark's[160]—his little boy of 7 runs out to a fire alarm. Back again; "Well, where was the fire, Johnny?"— "Nothing but a whore-house in Front street." Tableau. He had heard the firemen say it.

⟨"De⟩"The autopsy will show."—decide it.

Grant book must have exhaustive INDEX.

Made Hon Mem Concord Free Trade Club.[161]

⟨Hab⟩Have books been sent to Ma, Sue Crane, Pamela, Mother, &c.?

Heliotype the bust in blue or other color, & sell it?

Got matter for prospectus yet?

INDEX for book.

No ⟨[--]⟩other bust is to be made.

> ⟨*Boston,* 1ˢᵗ *Night.*[162]
> ⟨Sollermun⟩ (de Bank, Enc.)
> Fishwife.
> Trying Situation.
> Ghost Story. [#]

---

[160] Charles Hopkins Clark, assistant editor of the Hartford *Courant.*

[161] Clemens wrote to Frank A. Nichols, secretary of the Concord (Massachusetts) Free Trade Club, thanking him for the membership and noting two other honors that Massachusetts had awarded him recently: the Boston court's refusal of Clemens' injunction against Estes & Lauriat (see p. 109, note 142) and the proscription of *Huckleberry Finn* by the Concord Library Committee. Clemens sent a draft of his letter to Howells on 26 March 1885, asking him "to read it, & riddle it & scarify it with expungings & other emendations, & get it right & the way it ought to be, against the possible accident of it's getting into print, & then remail it to me straight off" (*MTHL,* pp. 524–525, 877–878). The letter appeared in the New York *World,* the Boston *Transcript,* and the *Critic* early in April and was probably reprinted elsewhere.

[162] Clemens evidently turned at random to a blank page near the back of his notebook in order to list the three following tentative lecture programs. The list interrupts the chronological order of entries and was clearly written before the surrounding entries. Clemens' and Cable's first appearance together in a major city was in Boston on 13 November 1884 for a single performance at the Boston Music Hall. They performed again in Boston at Chickering Hall on 15 November, giving a matinee and an evening reading. Clemens was apparently trying to establish a varied program for the three Boston readings.

Matinèe.
My Duel ⟨(went well.)⟩
European Guides—ditto.
Why I lost Editorship—do.
Ghost Story.
    (Enc. A Sure Cure.)[163]

2[d] *Night.*
Interviewer.
Col. Sellers.
Buck Fanshaw.
A Sure Cure.⟩

What *was* the Judge's decision in Estes case?[164]

What arrangement has been made with Century?

Got their war book?[165]

Use *new* matter in your prospectus—*not* old. What's the *idea* of using old?

Club Essay: The little man concealed in the big man. The combination of the human & the god. (nigger) Victor Hugo; Carlyle; Napolèon; Mirabeau; Jesus; Emerson & Washington ⟨&⟩(?) Grant; Mahomet;—in them (including the S) was allied the infinitely grand & the infinitely little. Carlyle, whose life was one long stomach-ache & one ⟨[-]⟩ceaseless wail over it. Gladstone—& out of courtesy to many here present, I add Blaine—Macaulay— Shakspere—Burns—Scott—Richelieu—Cromwell—[166] [#]

---

[163] Clemens identifies "A Sure Cure" in a letter to Major Pond as his "whistling stammering yarn" (SLC to Pond, [16 November 1884], Berg). The piece is described in note 14 (p. 71).

[164] See page 109, note 142.

[165] The *Century* planned eventual book publication of their "Battles and Leaders of the Civil War" series. Clemens advised Webster on 16 March 1885: "Keep on good terms with the Century people. We will presently prove to them that they can't *afford* to publish their war book themselves—we must have it" (*MTLP*, p. 184). The *Century* did, however, publish the book themselves in four volumes in 1887 and 1888.

[166] Clemens never delivered this prospective address to the Monday Evening Club. He had expressed the germ of this theme in a letter to Livy of 9 February 1885, where he described Cable as "in many ways fine & great, & splendid; & in others paltriness

51,000 Huck Finn[167]

Andrew White & Prof. Newbury, Cable.

As to short-hander Redpath, want that Free-trade reply?

Want history of the bust for pretty-soon use?

Ask about Irving dinner & Hutton do.[168]

Get out a great big quarto P & Pauper on India paper for Xmas. High price.

Also Huck, or both in one.

Get Brander Matthews after the diary of the Boston Comedian's ⟨grandfather⟩father.[169]

David Gray.[170] [#]

---

itself. In Napoleon resided a god & a little mere man" (*LLMT*, p. 235). Clemens would continue his investigations of the "paltriness" of great men, particularly Carlyle, in Notebook 25 (p. 206). The intended position of "⟨nigger⟩," which Clemens interlined below "the god" and above "Carlyle; Napoleon," is uncertain.

[167] By 24 March 1885 approximately 43,500 copies of *Huckleberry Finn* had been sold. It was not until 6 May 1885 that Webster was able to report to his brother-in-law, Samuel Moffett: "I have already sold 51000 of Huck."

[168] At the close of his American tour, a farewell dinner for Henry Irving was given at Delmonico's in New York on 6 April 1885. Clemens is not listed among the guests in the newspaper reports of the dinner. He did attend the Tile Club's New York dinner for Laurence Hutton on 31 March 1885. The menu of that dinner, autographed by Clemens, Brander Matthews, Edwin Booth, Richard Watson Gilder, Julian Hawthorne, H. C. Bunner, and other guests, is in the Mark Twain Papers.

[169] The reference is probably to a project on which Matthews and Laurence Hutton collaborated—the publication of the diary of John Bernard (*Retrospections of America, 1797–1811*, ed. Mrs. Bayle Bernard, with introduction, notes, and index by Hutton and Matthews [New York: Harper & Brothers, 1887]). The English comedian John Bernard spent most of his theatrical career in America, for a number of years managing a Boston theater. His son, Boston-born actor and dramatist William Bayle Bernard, was a prolific and popular playwright, having success with a number of farces and dramas of western American life. In *These Many Years*, Brander Matthews recalled: "I had written to Mrs. Bayle Bernard to inquire if these later reminiscences [of her father-in-law, John Bernard] were in shape for publication. She had sent me the manuscript, and we found it well worth printing" (New York: Charles Scribner's Sons, 1917, p. 215). Clemens probably heard of this project through Matthews and considered securing the book for his own publishing company.

[170] A newspaperman and poet whom Clemens had known in Buffalo in the early 1870s. Clemens sent him a copy of *Huckleberry Finn* in the spring of 1885.

Ask Mrs. Stowe if she will perform 28th or 29 Apl at Mad Square for copyright.[171]

Do you know exactly how many Miss you got from Osgood, & how many his statement must account for?[172]

⟨my father's family ⟨is⟩are of the same mind with me
      Coincide⟩[173]

Ask about *new* matter (civil *war* matter) for canvassing copy.

Full INDEX for book.

March 31. Called at Gen. Grant's & saw Mrs. Fred Grant & Mrs. Sartoris. Showed them the cover of the General's book. I took young Hall[174] with me, who writes short-hand. I had a telegraphic paragraph from this morning's Tribune, in which Gen. Jubal Early tries to take the magnanimity out of Gen. Grant's action at Appomatox in not requiring Gen. Lee to give up his sword.[175]
I hoped to find Gen. Grant well enough to tell the story of the surrender & let young Hall take it down in shorthand. I wanted to lay the suggestion before Col. Grant, but he was worn out & asleep & I would ⟨[-]⟩not allow him to be disturbed. His wife went up to see if he might be stirring, but he was still asleep; so after waiting & talking awhile, I came away. Many groups of people were

---

[171] On 6 April 1885, George Parsons Lathrop, secretary of the American Copyright League, urged Clemens to persuade his Hartford neighbor Harriet Beecher Stowe to read at the copyright benefit. Evidently Clemens was unsuccessful since Mrs. Stowe is not mentioned in newspaper accounts of the occasion.

[172] See page 95, note 91.

[173] One leaf of the notebook was torn out preceding this entry. Presumably these canceled words relate to material on the missing leaf which may have been a draft of a statement to be issued by a member of the Grant family.

[174] This entry introduces Frederick J. Hall as a stenographer for Webster & Company. In 1886 he became junior partner in the firm and in 1888 succeeded Charles L. Webster as manager, remaining until the company went bankrupt in 1894.

[175] The New York *Tribune* of 31 March 1885 reported General Early's statement that Lee's "blade was not offered to the victor" at Appomattox "for the reason that the terms of capitulation provided that officers should continue to wear their side-arms." The *Tribune* concluded that Early wished "to show that Lee owed nothing to Grant's magnanimity."

distributed here & there in sight of the house, observing the
visitors, & one reporter questioned me, but I was not able to tell
him much. Another tried to head off the coupè, but gave it up.

Webster was up till 1 this morning, notifying newspapers not to
reproduce the stolen picture of Gen Grant as a lieutenant in the
Mexican war.[176]

1601
Julian Hawthorne[177]
   Sag Harbor, L I

Get Gen's hat

Chatto's note for £178.0.6 was paid Mch 31, ⟨1⟩'85—
⟨$[8]⟩Yielding $857.[84]

Gen. Grant & Henry Watterson.[178]

Apl. 4. Gen Grant is still living, this morning. Many a person
between the two oceans lay ⟨[-]⟩ hours awake, last night, listening
for the booming of the fire-bells that should speak to the nation in

---

[176] Charles L. Webster & Company had borrowed the rare daguerreotype of young
Lieutenant Grant from Philadelphia publisher George W. Childs. It was reproduced as
an engraving for the frontispiece of volume 1 of the *Memoirs*. An unidentified clipping
in Clemens' first Grant scrapbook (Scrapbook #22 in MTP), evidently dating from
March 1885, discusses the daguerreotype and the theft of the engraving: "This engraving
has been copyrighted and carefully guarded, but by some means one of the engraved
copies in a partially completed condition came to the notice of an artist on the staff of one
of the afternoon papers, who took a surreptitious copy of it, it is surmised for publication." The article added that Clemens' attorneys, Alexander & Green, "issued a circular
warning all parties from using the picture or copies thereof" under threat of prosecution.
[177] Clemens evidently intended to send a copy of his scatological burlesque of Eliza-
bethan conversation, first printed privately in 1882, to the son of Nathaniel Hawthorne.
Julian Hawthorne was, like Clemens, a member of the Kinsmen club.
[178] Henry Watterson, editor of the Louisville *Courier-Journal*, had first met General
Grant after the latter's return from his world tour in 1879. The friendship ripened after
the general's move to New York City. "There," Watterson recalled, "I saw much of him,
and we became good friends. He was the most interesting of men. Soldierlike—mono-
syllabic—in his official and business dealings he threw aside all formality and reserve in
his social intercourse, delightfully reminiscential, indeed a capital story teller" ("*Marse
Henry": An Autobiography*, 2 vols. [New York: George H. Doran Co., 1919], 1:214).

simutaneous voice & tell it its calamity. The bell-strokes are to be
30 seconds apart, & there will be 63—the General's age. They will
be striking in every town in the United States at the same moment
—the first time in the world's history that the bells of a nation
have tolled in unison, beginning at the same moment & ending at
the same moment.[179]

> Regular 1-night.
> Richling's Visit to Kate
> King Sollermun.
> Kate & Ristofolo
> Fishwife.
> Narcisse in Mourning
> Trying Situation
> ⟨G⟩Mary's Night Ride
> Ghost Story.

In Matinee put *Duel.*[180]

Ask Pond about Snowshoe Club[181]

⟨Wa⟩What *was* in the Estes & Lauriat brief?

Properly, Capt. Rounceville comes first, & introduces the grave

---

[179] Clemens began dictating his account of the events surrounding Grant's illness and
the writing of the *Memoirs* to James Redpath about 11 May 1885 (see p. 144). The preceding paragraph is included in Redpath's transcription. It is published in *Mark Twain's
Autobiography* (1:68) where, however, it is incorrectly dated. Grant died on 23 July 1885
and the news of his death was signaled by the tolling of the fire bells in many cities across
the nation.

[180] Following the notebook page that ends with "*Duel.*" two leaves were cut out. The
first is missing, but the second was used by Clemens for a letter to his wife dated 12
November 1884 from Lowell, Massachusetts (TS in MTP).

[181] Clemens was elected a member of Montreal's Old Tuque Bleue Snowshoe Club
in November 1884. After the Montreal lecture of 18 February 1885, Major Pond, Cable,
and Clemens were inducted into the club. In a letter to his wife, Cable described their
initiation which consisted of being lifted up "in the midst of a tightly huddled mass of
young athletes, laid out at full length on their hands and then—what think you?—thrown
bodily into the air almost to the ceiling, . . . thrown up again, caught again, thrown
again—so four, five times amid resounding cheers" (MT&GWC, pp. 110–111).

pale young idiot; then comes ⟨Capt.⟩ Gov. Gardner.[182]

> Achvement.
> (*Enc.—Baker's Cat*)
> Blue-jays.
> ⟨Jumping Frog.⟩
>
> Enc   Gov. Gardner or
>   Duel
>
> Jumping Frog.

$$1^{st}\ [183]$$

King Sollermum.
Doan' a Frenchman
Tale of Fishwife + +
Ghost Story. + +
   Enc. ⟨*Hamlet.*⟩ *Gov. Gardner* use it in Boston too—⟨No⟩
A Trying Situation. +
Eng. Bret Harte's TALE. [#]

---

[182] These are characters from Mark Twain's "Some Rambling Notes of an Idle Excursion," a piece from which he occasionally read in his lecture programs.

[183] These tentative programs, marked "1st" through "5th," were intended for the first five lecture engagements from 5 through 10 November 1884 (no lectures were scheduled for Sundays) at New Haven, Connecticut; Orange, New Jersey; Springfield, Massachusetts; Providence, Rhode Island; and Melrose, Massachusetts. As Clemens pointed out to Major Pond in a letter of late October 1884: "The appearing in half a dozen small towns first is for the *purpose* of weeding out errors." The preliminary readings also provided some preparation for the first major engagement before a Boston audience on 13 November. Clemens continued in his letter to Pond: "I now send you programs for the 5 *first appearances*—thus I appear in a *new program every night* for the first five nights. Careful note must be taken of the piece *which takes* BEST *every night* during the five—& then we will make up a *permanent one-night* program out of the pieces thus *elected*" (SLC to Pond [28 October 1884], MT&GWC, p. 49–50). The small crosses which Clemens penciled in beside a number of these lecture selections may indicate particularly successful readings. Reviews of the first week's lectures, which usually included some mention of the program chosen, indicate that Clemens quickly abandoned his ambitious *"new program every night"* scheme. Although the programs for the first two nights generally follow the plan outlined in this notebook schedule, thereafter Clemens appears to have stuck to the first program—the King Sollermun reading, "Tale of a Fishwife," "A Trying Situation," and the ghost story—which was to be his most regular program.

2^d

⟨Telephone talk.⟩ +
Sellers in New Role.
   "   "   "   "

A Dazzling Achevmnt
Gov. Gardner +
⟨Whistling.⟩
   ⟨Eng.⟩Enc. ⟨*Whistling*⟩ ⟨Gov. Gardner,⟩ 41 W.E.[184] Whis

3^d

Petroleum. 57[185]	Petroleum!
Gov. Gardner. 41 +	— ⟨Essay Lying⟩
Art. Ward. 1. 306[Sk. 186]	⟨Discuticled Man⟩
Agri. Editor + +	Artemus Ward
	Agricul Editor +

4th Day.
+Digging for Facts (Inter)— +
then Tom Canty as King. +
⟨My Duel⟩ Tar Baby? + +
Ghost Story. + +

5th

Sizing Bermuda? 78[187]
Dying Soldiers, 83
Henry VIII. European Guides.
Bret Harte's Tale.
Buck Fanshaw. + +
   ⟨C⟩⟨Eng.⟩Enc. Tar Baby. + [#]

---

[184] The designations "W.E.," "Wh. E.," and Wh. El.," and the page numbers refer to *The Stolen White Elephant Etc.*, a collection published in 1882 by James R. Osgood & Company.

[185] Captain "Hurricane" Jones's interpretation of the Biblical story of the miracle of Elijah and the prophets of Baal, in which petroleum is the device which sparks the miracle, is in "Some Rambling Notes of an Idle Excursion" on pages 57 through 61 of *The Stolen White Elephant*.

[186] Clemens was using the 1883 Tauchnitz edition of *Sketches* in which his "First Interview with Artemus Ward" appears on pages 306 through 310.

[187] The anecdote about the "seven-shilling lawsuit about a cat," which, Clemens

En.

Dying Soldiers, 83 ⟨[Sketch]⟩*White Ele*
Whistling. +
Bret Harte's Tale
Wisdom—1
      "   —2
Hamlet's Solil.
Tar Baby. +
Skinned Man. + +[188]
The New Cimetery—37. Wh. E.[189]
Incorp. Co. Mean Men[190]
Bucking Horse.
Capt. Rounceville, 44 Wh. El.

Jumping Frog.

Child o' Calamity[191]
Tenn. Journalism +[192]

Ever consider sandy soil?

Brandy & tadpoles.

---

felt, served to "size" up Bermuda is in "Some Rambling Notes" in *The Stolen White Elephant* (p. 78). The story which Clemens lists next about "Dying Soldiers" was told to him by Twichell and is from the same piece.

[188] In chapter 18 of *The Innocents Abroad* Clemens describes a "coffee-colored piece of sculpture" seen in the cathedral at Milan: "The figure was that of a man without a skin; with every vein, artery, muscle, every fibre and tendon and tissue of the human frame, represented in minute detail. It looked natural, because somehow it looked as if it were in pain. A skinned man would be likely to look that way, unless his attention were occupied with some other matter." Clemens used his description of the "skinned man" in his 1868–1869 lecture "The American Vandal Abroad" (Fred W. Lorch, *The Trouble Begins at Eight* [Ames: Iowa State University Press, 1968], p. 288).

[189] Clemens recorded the conversation he overheard about the disposition of various family members in a new cemetery plot in "Some Rambling Notes."

[190] This anecdote is told by Markiss, the remarkable liar Clemens met in the Sandwich Islands, in chapter 77 of *Roughing It*.

[191] The name adopted by one of Mark Twain's pugnacious, bragging raftsmen in chapter 3 of *Life on the Mississippi*.

[192] "Journalism in Tennessee" is included in *Mark Twain's Sketches, New and Old* (Hartford: American Publishing Co., 1875).

XXIV

"The Nation Holds Its Breath"

(April–August 1885)

CLEMENS' FIRST important entry in Notebook 24, dated 4 April 1885, is an echo from the final pages of the previous notebook—"General Grant is still alive to-day, & the nation holds its breath & awaits the blow." Clemens continued to use the notebook for almost six months, the final entries being written shortly after the death and funeral of General Grant. The notebook entries attest to the complexity of Clemens' current concerns, the emphasis resting on business matters rather than literature. It is clear that Clemens too was holding his breath, acutely aware of his prominence during these months of Grant's illness. It was a supremely public moment—perhaps never before had the American people had such an intimate and sustained involvement with the passing of a national figure. Clemens was concerned that his public demeanor should be discreet and reverent; he took pains not to "furnish the shabbier half of the world a chance to say General Grant's publisher is craftily trying to advertise himself" (SLC to Karl Gerhardt, 6 July 1885, Yale).

The newspapers were inclined to doubt his disinterest. While Clemens fulminated in private over newspaper remarks, he considered it undignified to make a public disavowal. He wrote to the editor of the Boston *Herald* on 6 July 1885 asking that he be allowed to look over any articles regarding Charles L. Webster & Company's publication of the Grant *Memoirs*. "I can't reply when the newspapers make misstatements about me," he complained. "It wouldn't do—the public would quickly tire of it. . . . I seem to be fast getting the reputation in the newspapers, of being a pushing, pitiless, underhanded sharper. . . . Upon my word I have done nothing underhanded in this whole business." Clemens took rather a different tack in a letter of the same date to Robert Underwood Johnson of the *Century*. The newspaper criticisms, Clemens wrote, "will eventually convince everybody that I am the shrewdest, craftiest & most unscrupulous business-sharp in the country & now that I am become a publisher, that is the kind of reputation I need. As long as those boys merely expose my lurid morals, they are doing me valuable commercial service & winning me a golden place in the admiration of my guild" (AAA-Anderson Galleries, sale 4278, 17–18 November 1936, item 351).

On 16 June 1885 Grant and his family removed from their New York City residence to a summer cottage at Mount McGregor, New York. The two volumes of memoirs were formally completed, but Grant began a careful revision of the proofs and added considerable new material, working with his sons and a stenographer engaged by Charles L. Webster & Company. Clemens made only one visit to Mount McGregor, from 29 June until 2 July. The general's stoical composure impressed him. "Manifestly," he wrote to Livy on 1 July, "dying is nothing to a really great & brave man" (TS in MTP). During Clemens' visit Grant wrote the preface for the memoirs. Within a few days it appeared in the newspapers. The New York *Tribune* represented the general assessment of the press regarding Grant's style, praising its "frankness and simplicity": "Whoever reads that modest, unpretending, sincere Preface will be overcome with respect and admiration for the man" (8 July 1885). On 18 July Grant reviewed the final batch of proof of the second volume, made some minor revisions, and returned the whole to Charles L. Webster. Clemens and Webster were relieved: their apprehensions that Grant would not live to complete the project had been succeeded by fears that his continual revising would hopelessly delay publication. On 23 July, Grant died. Clemens remarked in his notebook that since the completion of the book, "the lack of any strong interest to employ his mind has enabled the tedious weariness to kill him. I think his book kept him alive several months. He was a very great man—& superlatively good" (p. 168). Grant's death, which for months had been hourly expected, plunged the country into mourning.

The newspaper eulogies were unanimous in their celebration of the "foremost man of the Nation" (New York *Tribune*, 24 July 1885). "General Grant's work, military and civil, will form for many ages the most striking feature in the history of his country, and the persistent determination, the manly dignity, and the quiet simplicity of this silent soldier, will give an enduring charm to the story of his life. It is, indeed, this simplicity of character, added to his heroic bearing in the long struggle with disease, and his noble fortitude in death, which now calls forth such universal admiration and sympathy" (*Frank Leslie's Illustrated Newspaper*, 1 August 1885). A single unpleasant note was struck by a brief article in the New York *Sun* of 1 August 1885 entitled "Mark Twain's Big Speculation." "The man heavily enriched by Grant's death," said the *Sun*, "is Mark Twain. He is the principal of the firm of Webster & Co., the publishers of Grant's biography. . . . The shrewd humorist had to risk his entire fortune in the enterprise, but he pluckily refused to shirk the chances of loss by dividing the possible profits, and the net result to him and his partner will be a quarter to one-third of a million dollars."

There were obvious commercial and financial advantages attached to being General Grant's publisher. The prestige of Charles L. Webster & Company increased overnight. Webster issued regular bulletins regarding the general's progress on the *Memoirs*. Statements were quickly prepared to combat rumors that Grant was not writing his own book, or to condemn the several unauthorized biographies which were published at this time to capitalize on national interest in Grant. Above all the Webster company was anxious to discredit any reports that their business was a speculation at the expense of General Grant and his family. Early in June 1885, shortly after having received the manuscript of the first volume of the book, Charles L. Webster & Company issued its circular for the *Personal Memoirs of U. S. Grant*. The circular outlined the contents of both volumes and stressed the care which had been taken in designing and illustrating the book. "This is a standard work, and all future American historians will consult its pages in compiling their histories." Emphasis was placed on the unprecedented interest in the *Memoirs* and on the publisher's openhanded and disinterested management of the book: the publisher's role was presented as that of an administrator of a public trust. "The publishers take pleasure in placing this book within the reach of the American people, who have been so long watching for its appearance and so anxiously awaiting the tidings from the sick-chamber of its distinguished author, where he has penned its pages with a characteristic determination. . . . The great bulk of the profits on this book go to General Grant himself." Specimen pages included in the circular were quickly reprinted in the newspapers.

For the moment Clemens seemed satisfied with his "agent," Charles L. Webster. To Orion he wrote: "I am right glad to see, by the way General Grant speaks *to* Charley Webster, & *of* him, that he has conceived a liking for him & confidence in him. Charley has tackled the vastest book-enterprise the world has ever seen, with a calm cool head & capable hand" (16 May 1885, printed in the New York *Herald Tribune*, 29 November 1959). He wrote to Annie Moffett Webster shortly before she and her husband sailed for Europe: "He has come through it with a superb record; & with all its array of business-inventions, ingenuities & triumphs, he has not made a single business-misstep, that I am aware of" (30 July 1885, *MTBus*, p. 331). Some of Clemens' notebook entries during this period suggest that his dealings with Webster were less than avuncular. In later years Clemens recalled only Webster's ignorance and vanity: "He was young, he was human, he naturally mistook this transient notoriety for fame, and by consequence he had to get his hat enlarged." He added: "It was unchivalrous in me to attack with mental weapons this mentally weaponless man, and I tried to refrain from it but couldn't. I ought to have been large enough to endure his vanities but I wasn't" (*MTE*, pp. 179, 180).

Clemens' involvement with the publication of Grant's *Memoirs* is evident throughout Notebook 24, but the notebook reflects Clemens' even greater preoccupation with the inventions of James W. Paige. Entry after entry records Clemens' efforts to interest capitalists in Paige's typesetter and in a lesser invention, a printing telegraph. Contractual details are noted; there are fantastic projections of the machines' applications and efficiency. In 1881 Clemens had been only one of several modest investors in the Paige typesetter. By this time Clemens and William Hamersley had undertaken to capitalize a plant to produce the machine; several hundred thousand dollars were involved. More and more, Clemens succumbed to the seductions of his new role. He traveled to New York City several times in the summer of 1885, usually on matters relative to the publishing company or the Paige inventions.

Clemens' business concerns understandably depleted his time and energy. Apart from a few benefit readings and possibly some preliminary work on "The Private History of a Campaign That Failed," he did no literary work. He did make extensive entries in his notebook for two literary projects: an essay on wit and humor (pp. 162–163, 168, 172), and a book on "Picturesque Incidents in History & Tradition" (pp. 167–168, 169, 173), but neither project was pursued any further.

Notebook 24 is identical to Notebook 22 in design and format. It now contains 180 pages. Twelve of the first thirty pages are blank because Clemens began the notebook by using the right-hand pages while leaving most of the left-hand pages blank for future entries. Two leaves and portions of three others have been torn out and are missing. Over half of the notebook is inscribed in purple pencil, with the remainder in black pencil except for a few entries in grayish blue and brownish black ink. Use marks, probably Paine's, appear throughout in black pencil and bluish black ink but have not been reproduced. This notebook is now moderately worn; one gathering is almost completely loose, and large cracks run the length of the spine.

⟨Webster 214 W 125⟩
New—109 W 126.[1]

Stedman, 45 E 30th [2]

Dean Sage, 839 St Mark's ave.

Col. W. N. Woodruff[3]
    Box 1020, Htfd.

Ch Webster
109 W 126

Calvin Tompkins,[4]
387 South st.

Howells, 302 Beacon [#]

---

[1] Charles L. Webster and his family moved into their new home—a "three story brown stone house on 126th St" (CLW to SLC, 17 January 1885)—on 17 April 1885. This and the following entry were written on the front flyleaf of the notebook.

[2] The stockbroker Edmund Clarence Stedman was known in New York literary circles as a critic and poet. He had written to Clemens on 7 January 1885 requesting permission to publish "about 15 pages" from Clemens' works—"a bit from 'The Prince & the Pauper'" and "something from your earlier & humorous works"—in a projected multi-volume anthology, *A Library of American Literature from the Earliest Settlement to the Present Time*. On 15 January, Clemens had instructed Stedman to "take from any book you want to, new or old, good or bad, Huck Finn included" (Berg). Stedman selected Mark Twain's Jumping Frog sketch and sections from chapter 27 of *The Prince and the Pauper* and chapter 18 of *Huckleberry Finn*. Clemens became more than a contributor, however, for the eleven-volume anthology was eventually published by his own firm, Charles L. Webster & Company, in 1889 and 1890. He later claimed inaccurately that Webster contracted to publish it without his approval "and thereby secured the lingering suicide of Charles L. Webster and Company" (*MTE*, pp. 191–192).

[3] Woodruff was managing the manufacture and distribution of Karl Gerhardt's terra cotta bust of General Grant (see p. 110, note 148).

[4] Clemens undoubtedly noted the name of young manufacturer Calvin Tomkins in connection with the Cornell Alumni dinner of 29 April 1885, at which Tomkins presided (see p. 137, note 35).

$$280\ 000$$
$$\underline{75}$$
$$\overline{14\ 00}$$
$$196\ 0$$
$$\overline{200.00}$$

56   36

$$\langle 452 \rangle \overline{252}\ \underline{7}$$

Apl 4, 1885.

General Grant is still alive to-day, & the nation holds its breath & awaits the blow.

Gerhardt wanted me to let him write a note & ask Col. Fred Grant's permission to make a death-mask of his father. It is something that must be done, of course, ⟨y⟩but I could not bring myself to be a party to the request, there is something so dreadful about it. So I telegraphed him to apply through Gen. Badeau, instead of making a personal application. I had before telegraphed Col Grant asking that he let Gerhardt speak with him.

A telegram from Gerhardt tonight says Col. Grant has personally given him the desired permission. I am very glad indeed; for the mask must be made when the General dies, & it is so much better that Gerhardt who is honest & whom the family know, should do it than some tricky stranger.[5]

Wenn man um ⟨half⟩halb Zwölf kommt in der Kirche an, schon

---

[5] Karl Gerhardt had informed Clemens on 1 April 1885 that sculptor James Alexander Wilson MacDonald was claiming the right to cast the Grant death mask with the intention of "vending" it. Gerhardt described MacDonald as a "cheeky unprincipled sort of man" and suggested that Fred Grant be put "on his guard" against the opportunist. He also suggested that he could take the death mask himself, making one copy only for the family. As his notebook entry indicates, Clemens did not care to involve himself in the matter, but Gerhardt easily obtained the necessary permission from Fred Grant. He made the mask immediately after Grant's death in July 1885 and placed it in the safe of Charles L. Webster & Company. In December 1885 Gerhardt and the Grants fell into a bitter dispute over rights to the mask and Clemens was asked to intervene in the matter, which threatened to develop into a law suit, by Fred Grant. Clemens proposed that Gerhardt "hand over the mask to Mrs. Grant & I will give him a receipt in full for all he owes me [which Clemens estimated at about seventeen thousand dollars] & assume also the payment of the outstanding obligations. . . . It will restore Mrs. Grant's peace of mind, &

gut; früher gibt es nichts als ⟨Flehen, Flehen, Flehen⟩ Beten, Beten, Beten, zur ganz und gar *Erschöpfung.*[6]

Write Ralph Gillett.[7]

Donkey[8]

12,000 G G for Mich sold (24,000 vols.)
8,000 sold to Iowa (16,000 vols) (40,000 vols altogether)[9]

"Suspicion of Foul Play. Geo. Herrick thought to have been poisoned. ⟨(Lunch)⟩"[10]

"A Triple Tragedy. in Chicago. A Mother-in-law & wife shot by a man who then shoots himself." ⟨(Law.)⟩

A Further particular⟨s⟩ concerning a case published yesterday—where a ⟨seduced⟩ betrayed girl's father kills the betrayer in a street car—the additional particular being the ⟨important⟩ pathetic fact

---

keep the scandal out of court & out of the papers" (SLC to CLW, 18 December 1885, *MTBus*, pp. 345–346). Clemens' plan may have soothed Gerhardt for on 21 December he instructed Webster to deliver the mask to the Grant family and the matter was not spoken of again.

[6] *If you get to church at eleven-thirty, it's good; earlier there is nothing but praying, praying, praying, to absolute* exhaustion.

[7] Gillett was president of the State Mutual Fire Insurance Company of Hartford which insured Clemens' house in 1886.

[8] Clemens purchased a donkey through Homer Pond, Major James B. Pond's brother, and had it sent from Kansas to Quarry Farm as a surprise gift for the children, particularly Jean. The donkey arrived before 18 June 1885 and was named by the children Patience Cadichon, after the philosophical donkey of the comtesse de Ségur's *Mémoires d'un âne* (1860). Clemens would celebrate the children's pet in his poem "Kiditchin" (see *MTB*, p. 822).

[9] Clemens probably got these figures from Charles L. Webster. He wrote to Livy from New York on 8 April: "You were a little afraid to have me venture on the book & take all the risks for so small a share as 30 per cent of the profits. I did not think there was any risk. These 40,000 books are ordered for only 2 States—Michigan & Iowa—wait till you hear from the other 37!" (*LLMT*, p. 242).

[10] Clemens' compilation of sensational news items from the New York *World* of 9 April 1885 occupies eight pages in Notebook 24. The list was probably drawn up in reaction to the paper's criticism of *Huckleberry Finn* in its issues of 2 and 18 March 1885. The earlier article termed the novel "cheap and pernicious stuff" and wondered "what can be said of a man of Mr. Clemens's wit, ability and position deliberately imposing upon an unoffending public a piece of careless hack-work in which a few good things are dropped amid a mass of rubbish" (New York *World*, 2 March 1885).

that the poor girl's family now admit that this was not the first time she had been betrayed.

"Shot his business Rival."

"Died with murder in his heart. (m. & suicide.)"

"A Society Man's Crime"

It will take my bks years to reach & destroy 150,000 families: but the W. ⟨does that every day—365 times a year.⟩ but the W. gets in ahead & ⟨carries its high & holy protection⟩ ⟨its⟩ saves them from my destruction—keeps them pure & sweet & holy

"Threatening to Lynch a Murderer."

"20 Chinese bady beaten"—wantonly maltreated by some white human brutes in San F.

¶ 2 daughters of prominent families run away to become ⟨strolling⟩ actresses.

"Maria Siebel's Death"—being further instructive & elevating particulars for the family circle of ⟨⟨s⟩an abortion case complicated with⟩ concerning a nameless crime—nameless in a speech, though not in a home circle newspaper.

4,000,000 ⟨in⟩ families visited in a month—50 ditto in a year

There is ⅓ of a column ⟨to tell with what generous alacrity⟩ about preparations to hang a particularly pious & Scripture-oozing wife murderer in Brooklyn.

"John J. Keller killed by an imperfectly prepared prescription"— don't see what there was imperfect about it—seems to have done its work with lamentable accuracy.

⟨Des⟩ ⟨I⟩Elevating paragraph about how one man crushed the skull of another with his boot heel.

"A Bullet in his brains"

"Half his Life spent in Jail"

¶ to tell how a man in fury flung a lamp at another man's

head—missed that man—it exploded & burned a disinterested woman to death.

"A Pretty girl's suit—she wants her recreant lover to pay $5000 for her Blighted Affections."

143,508 circu.

100,000 daily

"A Savage fight with hard gloves in New Jersey."—⅓ col.

"Eloped with his aunt"

"Hacked himself to death"—½ col.—with the gory & slaughterous details.

5 cols a in 1 issue. 10,000 words. In ⟨10 issues⟩ a week they spread ⟨the⟩ a full Huck before 1,000,000 families.—4,000,000 a month, they say. The same bulk is furnished to more than ⟨30,000,000⟩50,000,000 people by that paper in year.—while 100,000 have read H F & forgotten him.

⟨If⟩*Moral*. If you want to rear a family just right for ⟨hi⟩ sweet & pure society here & Paradise hereafter, banish Huck Finn from the home circle & introduce the N. Y. World in his place.

⟨Hart^d & Conn Western⟩
⟨L^{ve} at ⟨10.10⟩ 10.$^{15.}$⟩

Dog show at Madison Square Garden where Barnum is now begins 28th & ends May 1—Susy must see it.[11]

Get Redpath to shorthand my autobiography.[12]

As long as I am still, I am an ornament, gentlemen, & a satisfaction to the eye; but when I speak—well, a little girl was admiring a donkey, when he suddenly tuned up & began to bray. She said "I love to look at a donkey, but I don't love to hear him donk." [#]

---

[11] In her unfinished biography of her father Susy recalled going to the dog show on 29 April with Clemens and Major J. B. Pond and having a "delightful time seeing so many dogs together" (S&MT, p. 197). The show, an annual event of the Westminster Kennel Club, was attended by many prominent and wealthy New Yorkers.

[12] See page 112, note 156.

If we began to-day we could not print & bind the books that are going to be required 7 months hence. Thefore, contract at once with paper mills &c that they *must* furnish 100,000 copies per month straight along, if required.

You can't go to England—Dawson must go, if ⟨Co⟩Mrs. G will agree.[13]

What insurance against theft have you accomplished?

Will anybody insure us in $300,000.[14]

Could Dawson get up a type-setter Co in England to work in U. S.?

Better issue both vols at once?[15]

Because interest might ⟨die⟩ moderate before get out 2ᵈ.

Furnish canvassers a list of truthful & sensible things to say—not rot.[16]

Consider the edition de luxe.

⟨⅓⟩⅕ of the North have taken, say, 50,000 *sets.* That is 250,000 sets for the whole. Possibly 300,000 sets or 600,000 vols. [#]

---

[13] Clemens' objections to Charles L. Webster's trip abroad were overcome and Webster was able to leave for Europe on 1 August 1885 in order to make arrangements for English and European editions of Grant's *Memoirs.* Apparently, a secondary purpose of Webster's trip was to sound foreign interest in the Paige typesetter. Noble E. Dawson was a stenographer supplied by Charles L. Webster & Company to stay at Mount McGregor and take down Grant's dictations.

[14] Clemens was concerned that the proofs of General Grant's book be safeguarded against theft. He wrote to Webster on 11 April 1885: "No book ever stood in such peril before as this one. Long before it is out, thieves & bribers will be thick around the printing houses & binderies, ready to buy or steal even a couple of pages & sell to somebody. . . . You must think up some way whereby we can get two or $300,000 insurance against these accidents" (*MTBus,* pp. 314–315).

[15] Clemens' idea of issuing both volumes of the *Memoirs* at one time was rendered impossible within a few days by Charles Webster's agreement with the Century Company "not to publish first vol before Dec. 1st next, and second vol before Mch. 1st next" (CLW to SLC, 15 April 1885). Clemens apparently overlooked his obligation to the Century Company a few months later when he revived his proposal about simultaneous publication (see pp. 170–171).

[16] The Webster company issued a thirty-seven page pamphlet of instructions to its

To print & bind ½ of that number will take 50,000 vols a month till December. Can it be done? The binding, I mean.

100 editions de luxe at auction—knock-⟨down price $100. Or ⟨250⟩ 300 at the same k.d. price. 5 pages of MS. No canvassig.⟩

No, 100 (with 20 pp. MS) only, & sell them all at auction after thorough advertising—& have the first bid come from — — — at $500.

Send news to Mackey & others in Paris, London, Berlin, &c. Get Mackey to make a great bid for the 1ˢᵗ copy.[17]

Instead of auction, let H⟨arrison⟩ canvass 50 of them at 250 each.

⟨Have⟩
Put the type-setter in other hands & hurry it up.

Note in my portmonnaie about $2,000,000 type-writer.

Draw my own war-maps for my Missouri campaign in Century.[18]

The accident in a sitz-bath with a steel-trap to the editor of the Springfield Republican[19]

If first ed. *should* reach ½ million, can they be *made* in time. It would be 75,000 per month for ½ a year.

You didn't suggest to G. ⅓ or ½. Why?[20] [#]

---

salesmen which carefully outlined sales techniques and arguments to be used in the canvass (PH in MTP).

[17] Comstock Lode millionaire John W. Mackay led a modest, transient existence in hotels, but his expatriate wife and children lived sumptuously in Paris and entertained lavishly. Mrs. Mackay launched herself in European society in November 1877 by holding a grand reception for General Grant who was then in Paris on his world tour. Clemens was undoubtedly aware of Mackay's great admiration for Grant and counted on the capitalist's interest in an expensive limited edition of the *Memoirs*.

[18] "The Private History of a Campaign That Failed" in the *Century* of December 1885 included two roughly sketched maps by Mark Twain.

[19] Clemens was currently upset over the Springfield (Mass.) *Republican's* adverse review of *Huckleberry Finn*. Early in April 1885 he wrote a sarcastic "Prefatory Remark" for future editions of the book as a reply to the censures of the *Republican* and the Boston *Advertiser*, but Livy forbade its publication.

[20] In December 1884 Webster had offered General Grant fifty thousand dollars for

See Redpath.

Send Huck to Traveler's Record, Hart[d] [21]

Submit your circular (descriptive of the book) before you print it

Give me your dwelling address

Buy a parlor car seat for return upon *leaving the train* in NY

Buy spectacles *sure.*

CL W & Co No 2.[22]	12,673.15
" " "	12,590.91
Mt Morris B[k23]	12,000.000
Bills rec'ble	22,647.54
W. G.'s notes due ⎱	11,000.
in Sept[24] ⎰ ⟨3⟩	3,150

⟨$64,061.60⟩ $74,061.60 [#]

---

the publication rights to the *Memoirs*, but the offer was apparently not attractive enough to make Grant decide to relinquish his commitment to the Century Company. Webster countered with an offer in February 1885, which was accepted, of seventy per cent of the net profits. Clemens appeared well satisfied with the terms, but this notebook entry suggests that he had second thoughts about the liberality of the offer.

[21] A monthly magazine published by the Travelers Insurance Company of Hartford from 1865 until 1906.

[22] Charles L. Webster opened the account called "Charles L. Webster No. 2" at the United States National Bank in New York City early in January 1885 and sent Clemens a witnessed statement to the effect that funds in the account "belong in *fact* to S. L. Clemens and are simply in my hands as a trust fund for convenience" (CLW to SLC, 9 January 1885). The initial deposits in the account were the proceeds of the sale of Clemens' Western Union stock and Clemens' share of the receipts of the Twain-Cable lecture tour. The "No. 2" account allowed Webster to draw additional funds, necessitated by the company's expansion and expenses on the Grant book, for the regular Webster company account.

[23] The Mount Morris Bank, chartered in 1880 and located in Harlem in New York City, advanced Webster & Company considerable sums over the following years and was to be one of the most insistent creditors at the time of the company's bankruptcy.

[24] Clemens and Livy had invested three thousand dollars in the budding theatrical career of their Hartford neighbor William Gillette. Gillette had hoped to repay the

Send Pond $200²⁵

⟨Welche Unterstandung—auf ⟨gewöh[- - -]⟩gewöhnliche Meinung.

Haben Sie ihnen Erlaubniss förmlich gegeben *(scriftlich)* die mehrere Stücke in einem Buche zu drücken?

Nein.

Dann geben Sie es nie und nimmermehr.

Auf ⟨jen⟩ *jene* Fall, ⟨gehe ich⟩ gib ich ihnen die Erlabniss ⟨bis⟩ ohne dass sie mir *zwanzig* procent ⟨[od]⟩ König-Vorrecht, oder 75 *procent.* der profits bezahlen sollte.

⟨Wi[s]⟩Wich nicht einen blossem Zoll.⟩

Wir *sind* die unschuldigste Eseln auf der Welt—und dass *weiss* ⟨ick⟩⟨ich⟩ ich durchaus.²⁶

Wie gross ist *unser* Agentung General in und um N. Y. herum?²⁷ ✕ [#]

---

money from the receipts of the touring production of his play *The Professor* but the returns were not sufficient. Gillette's uncertain fortunes did not allow him to pay off the three thousand dollar debt in full until April 1887. There is no mention of an additional eleven thousand dollar debt in the correspondence between Clemens and Gillette; it is possible that Clemens intended the latter amount to fall under "Bills rec'ble."

²⁵ Clemens wrote to Major J. B. Pond on 15 April 1885: "I hasten to enclose the $200 which you paid Redpath for me, & which I was forgetting about" (Berg). Clemens occasionally made use of James Redpath's services as a stenographer.

²⁶ The preceding several German entries refer to Grant's four *Century* articles. The articles would be included in the *Century's* four-volume *Battles and Leaders of the Civil War* published in 1887 and 1888. In April 1885 Charles L. Webster signed an agreement with the *Century* which allowed them use of Grant's articles providing they gave proper acknowledgment to Charles L. Webster & Company (see p. 110, note 147). Clemens evidently felt that he and Webster were "asses" not to have required a substantial royalty as well. The first German entry is problematical; it appears to mean *Which agreement— of the usual opinion.* The other entries read: *Have you given them formal (written) permission to print the several pieces in one book? No. Then give it to them never and never- more. In that case, I'll give them the permission except that they would have to pay me twenty per cent royalties or 75 per cent of the profit. Do not settle for a modest royalty. We are the most innocent asses in the world—and that I know positively.*

²⁷ *How large is our general agency in and around N.Y.?* Clemens wrote to Webster on 8 April 1885: "I hope it is your idea that C L Webster & Co shall be a general agency and have New York and a fair area of territory around it, and receive the usual general agent's commission. Such a commission on fifty or 100,000 volumes would make a handsome addition to the firm's assets" (*MTLP,* p. 189).

⟨Der⟩Des Menchen der sebstgemacht ist. Umstände der Mench macht.[28]

Und um dass der unrein ⟨Zeitungen⟩Zeitungist des Westens ⟨spewed⟩ auf mich spewed hat,

Der Krieg was G G's "Umstand."
Es ⟨wa⟩ hätte MEIN ⟨were⟩wäre hatten wir einander ⟨begegnet⟩ in Missouri getroffen.

Sagen Sie Etwas begriffs Mugwumps.[29]

Lass' uns *"Schachtel der Gewehren"* und "1601" zum Alumni FEST.

Hochwürdig ⟨Bchr⟩ Beecher wird Gerhardt ins Haus nehmen lassen, und ⟨him⟩ihm Sitzungen geben so lang er solche wunschen mag.[30]

Die hauptsachliche Zug des Character Gerhardts is Undankbarkeit. Vergessen Sie diese ⟨Sagen⟩Sagung nicht. (Apl. 14, 1885.)

⟨Verkaufen Sie mir alle euer bleibenden⟩ Rechten über die Magazine Stücken—denn diese Stücken sind nur ein-zehnte bezahlt. ⟨[n]⟩Nach und nach, wenn die "⟨"⟩Jahrhundert" Streit machen soll, dann antwort ich wie oben.[31]

The severest censor has been the Boston Advertiser.[32] I am sorry

---

[28] *The man who is self-made. Circumstances make the man.* The following two entries read: *And for that the foul Western newspaperman spewed on me. The war was G G's "circumstance." It would have been* mine *if we'd come upon each other in Missouri.* In this last entry Clemens is referring to his near encounter with Grant during the Civil War (see p. 105, note 132).

[29] *Say something about mugwumps.* The following entry reads: *Let's have* "Box of Guns" [i.e., "The Invalid's Story"] *and* "1601" *for the alumni* dinner (see p. 137, note 35).

[30] *Reverend Beecher will let Gerhardt come into the house, and will give him sittings as long as he so desires.* Karl Gerhardt had secured a commission to make a portrait bust of Henry Ward Beecher and during May and June 1885 he worked on the bust regularly at Beecher's home. The following entry reads: *The principal feature of Gerhardt's character is thanklessness. Don't forget this statement.*

[31] *Sell me all your remaining rights over the magazine pieces—because these pieces are only one-tenth paid. By and by, if the "Century" should make a fight, then I answer as above.*

[32] Clemens is referring to the Boston *Advertiser's* criticism of *Huckleberry Finn* (see p. 132, note 19, and *MTHL*, p. 535, note 1).

to impute personal motives to him, but I must. He is merely taking what he imagines is legitimate revenge upon me for what was simply & solely an accident. I had the misfortune to catch him in a situation which will not bear ⟨telling.⟩ describing. He probably think I have told that thing all around. It is an error. I have never told it, except to one man, & he came so near absolutely dying with laughter that I judged it best to take no more chances with that narrative.

⟨Get full⟩

Schaffen der Name des ⟨Menshen⟩Menchen.³³

"⟨"[-]⟩Thrice have I been in the shadow of the valley of death, & thrice have I come out again." Rev. Dr Newman says Gen Grant pressed his hand & said that yesterday April 15. Ten cents to a thousand dollars he never used that form of words. This piece of misreporting comports with what that Chinese Secretary of Legation said of Newman.³⁴

Tribune version: "Thrice have I been down in the valley of death, & now I have come up." No better—gush—rot. Impossible.

See if there is any patent for indenting a waffle mould in asphalt pavement.

Write the Story of a Cub & pilot.

And of a jour printer. [#]

---

³³ *Get the man's name.*

³⁴ Methodist Episcopal minister John Philip Newman had been chaplain of the Senate from 1869 until 1874 and had been appointed inspector of United States consulates in Asia by Grant, serving from 1874 until 1876. The Grant family had attended services at Newman's Metropolitan Church in Washington, D.C., during Grant's presidency. Newman, called upon by the Grant family to attend Grant during the months of his final illness, made himself conspicuous as Grant's spiritual spokesman. His pompous and sanctimonious statements to the press naturally incurred Clemens' dislike. In an 1885 Autobiographical Dictation, Clemens repeated the speech noted in this notebook entry and remarked: "General Grant never used flowers of speech, and, dead or alive, he never could have uttered anything like that, either as a quotation or otherwise." Clemens went on to mention his chance meeting with a man "who had been connected with our embassy in China" during Newman's tenure as inspector of consulates. The man suggested that "there was some crookedness about Newman's expenditures" but he felt "not that Newman was a knave but that he was simply an ass."

Cornell dinner is at Moreli's, 8. West 28th—Ap 29 at 8 pm.³⁵

'tis by reason of *him* I have spent these 7 years in foreign wars &
*dung*eons—⟨a⟩ the very shuttlecock of privation⟨s⟩, rough
adventure⟨s⟩ & misfortune.

Lord, how soldier-like. twas *good,* twas *beau*tiful! it did warm the
cockles of my heart to *see* it.

(very simply—)

Why how near-sighted he *is*. And ⟨[n]⟩ tis but natural, no doubt
—living as he has lived &c—⟨why⟩ dear me if *I* ever

How little he *is,* ⟨poor chap⟩—& so forlorn & homeless, ⟨so
forlorn & friendless. It isn't saying much, mayhap, but such as it
is,⟩ *I'll* be his friend. I saved

How near-sighted he *is,* po thing—it was under his very nose. &
he couldn't see it³⁶

I know by instinct what you gentlemen will do.

Hendon—see next page.³⁷ [#]

---

³⁵ Major J. B. Pond wrote to Clemens on 11 April 1885 inviting him to a dinner of the
Alumni Association of Cornell University. Clemens attended the dinner, which took
place at Morelli's restaurant in New York City, and responded to the toast "The Politician." A nine-page manuscript entitled "The Politician, &c.," presumably a draft of
Clemens' speech, is in the Mark Twain Papers. It is an ironic eulogy to "our late friend,"
the "cringing & fawning" party-politician. Clemens concludes that the greatest service
performed by the politician is to stimulate a reaction against narrow partisanship by his
excesses in the service of it. The entries at pages 138.1–3 and 139.7–16 are probably
discarded ideas for the speech.

³⁶ In this and the preceding entries, Clemens is drafting dialogue for the family dra-
matization of *The Prince and the Pauper.* The dialogue was intended for a scene from
chapter 12 of the book, in which Miles Hendon learns the proper etiquette required in
dealing with the prince he has just rescued. After Mrs. Clemens' surprise production in
March 1885 (see p. 105, note 131), Clemens took a hand in the amateur theatricals,
playing the part of Miles Hendon. He "acted his part beautifully," Susy recalled, "and
he added to the scene, making it a good deal longer. He was inexpressibly funny, with
his great slouch hat and gait—oh such a gait! . . . He certainly could have been an actor
as well as an author" (*S&MT,* p. 190). The second performance of the play probably
occurred on 23 April 1885.

³⁷ Clemens' direction to "see next page" refers to the additional dialogue for the
dramatization of *The Prince and the Pauper* at 138.7–11. The preceding entry and several
of those following, however, relate to Clemens' Cornell Alumni dinner speech.

Whenever a college alumni crowd get together, they go to
"whooping up the higher ed"—as Tennyson says in his Lay of the
Last Minstrel.[38] Very well; then I propose to take the other side.

in ages—
—some here who never would be prepared to go—with credit.
quote Omar Khayam

(Confusion without—Hendon's voice heard) I *will* enter! Out of
my *way*,! ⟨I say!⟩ or I'll spit a dozen of ye as I would ⟨kidneys⟩
gizzards on a *skewer!* (Plunge in with drawn sword.) (*But how will
he reach for the* chair.
(Insert the 2ᵈ act—⟨Sue⟩Susie for Tom—I Henry VIII.)[39]

Miss Brace, teacher of Elocution at Vassar. (—Clara Spaulding.)[40]

Jim Wolf & the Cats.[41]

My general idea, in what I am about to say, is to make some of
you people mad, & liven up things up a little here.

Saturday, Apl. 25, accident—man backed almost into us—we had
to almost run into the curbstone to keep from taking his wheel off
—injured it, anyway.[42] [#]

---

[38] Clemens apparently considered delivering a burlesque speech on higher education
at the Cornell Alumni dinner, but he was eventually assigned to reply to the toast "The
Politician" (see note 35). The false reference in this entry to Sir Walter Scott's "Lay of
the Last Minstrel" is clearly intentional.

[39] Clemens evidently planned to revise the action of chapter 33 of *The Prince and the
Pauper* for the play version: in the novel the scene in which Miles Hendon asserts his
right to sit in the king's presence is considerably less lively. Clemens also indicates here
that he intended to include the scene of the meeting between Tom Canty and the ailing
Henry VIII (chapter 5 of *The Prince and the Pauper*), himself taking the role of the
monarch.

[40] Maria Porter Brace (later Kimball) graduated from Vassar in 1872, and among other
works wrote *A Text-Book of Elocution* (1892). Clara Spaulding, Livy's girlhood friend
from Elmira, had attended Vassar for a year and a half.

[41] Mark Twain's story "Jim Wolf and the Tom-Cats" first appeared in the New York
Sunday Mercury of 14 July 1867. It is included, with Clemens' history of its various print-
ings, in *Mark Twain's Autobiography* (1:135–143).

[42] This accident occurred on Friday, 24 April 1885. The following day Clemens re-
ceived a letter from J. B. Clapp, secretary of the Blodgett & Clapp Company, "Iron &
Steel Merchants" of Hartford. "I was unfortunately ran into by your carriage," wrote
Clapp, "and my own carriage somewhat injured. The carriage I have placed in the Hos-

Why dn't you fetch the cat?

Well, A cat on a chimney *looks* easy; but when you come to tackle him you find him a kind of a disappintment[43]

Grave, thoughtful, philosophic—all life was serious to him—he hardly ever smiled, he never laughed. The humorous aspect of a thing was a something which he was totally unable to see.

Sir, when you sent me the Poli for a ⟨toast⟩ text I was glad; he looked like ⟨a very fruitful &⟩ so easy a subject. I thought I could get a good deal out of him; I judged I could put my hands on him & fetch him into court without any trouble. ⟨But I had to change my mind, before I got done⟩ Ah, well, we can't always tell—in this life. Often, things that look promising—things that all circumstances, all surrounding seem ⟨to conspire⟩conspiring to ⟨make⟩ turn (any well planned effort you make) to a happy issue, a graceful & gracious success, to ——huh—⟨when I was a⟩ why muliply words—[44]

Should be but one authoritative.[45]

Refuse to endorse the other. [#]

---

pital & trust it will soon be convalescent. The Doctors bill I presume you will see in due course of time." Clemens' only comment, "Ha-ha!," written on the envelope of the letter, augured ill for the success of Clapp's petition.

[43] This entry, and probably the following one, are fragments relating to "Jim Wolf and the Tom-Cats" (see note 41).

[44] See note 35.

[45] Clemens was in New York City from 28 April until 30 April (see note 48) and during that time had at least three meetings with General Grant. This and the following six entries are probably notes for arguments which Clemens intended to present to General Grant and his family regarding the sole "authoritative" portrait of the general. Clemens' concern in the matter was sparked by an article in the New York *World* of 27 April 1885 which reported that "Col. Fred Grant engaged the services of Prof. Rupert Schmid, the Munich sculptor," and that the artist had four sittings with the general and had almost completed a portrait bust. Schmid's commission came inopportunely at the moment when Karl Gerhardt's terra cotta bust of General Grant, which had been made on 20 March 1885, was to be offered for sale (see pp. 106–107). Clemens considered Gerhardt's bust "the best likeness of the General ever made . . . & it is the *last* one that ever *will* be made from the living subject" (p. 110). The four German entries which follow read: *Let G make a life-mask* ("Lassen . . . machen"); *It should not be done by a foreigner* ("Sollte . . . sei"); *He says in his first sentence, that he was a genuine American* ("Er . . . sei"); *I would think G had promised you a per cent* ("Ich . . . verheisste"). Clemens apparently hoped to persuade the Grants that their endorsement of Gerhardt's bust

Lassen Sie G ein Lebenmass machen.

Sollte nicht beim Fremder machen sei.

Er sagt in seine Erste Satz, dass er echter Amerikaner sei.[46]

G's is Art—das andere is poppycock & sham

Ich dächte G hatte ⟨ihrem⟩ Ihnen eine pro cent verheisste.

L Po'k 9.48 per Central
L Fiskill⟨,⟩ ⟨10⟩Landing 10.30 reach Htfd. 2.25.

L. N. York at 10.30 am[47]

Oil of peppermint 2 oz in each roof-pipe, & 2 kettles of boiling water, then plug the pipe with rags & go down & smell. Saturate the inner surface of the pipe with the oil.

May 1/85, at Vassar Vorlas A Trying Situation & Ghost Story.[48]

Quel gaz!

Can follow that.

Moncoon. [#]

---

constituted an exclusive authorization and that Schmid, being a foreigner and a stranger to the family, should be barred from selling his bust. Clemens' statement that Schmid's work was "poppycock & sham" probably refers to the sculptor's remark in the New York *World*: "'The face has a somewhat worn look, but I shall remove that, and I feel confident that I will, after one more sitting, be able to present a faithful likeness of Gen. Grant as he appeared before he was prostrated by the cancer.'" Gerhardt's bust was completed with only one sitting and captured, without idealization, the features of the suffering general.

[46] Clemens is referring to the opening sentence of Grant's *Memoirs*: "My family is American, and has been for generations, in all its branches, direct and collateral." Clemens was evidently impressed by this direct statement and made use of a similar remark to open *A Connecticut Yankee*.

[47] This schedule is for the rail trip from New York City to Poughkeepsie for the Vassar College reading engagement and return to Hartford (see note 48).

[48] Samuel Lunt Caldwell, the president of Vassar College, wrote Clemens on 3 April 1885: "I am gratified to know that you have consented to meet our young ladies on Founder's Day, & read to them." The Vassar reading trip was the conclusion of a four-day excursion. Clemens, Livy, and thirteen-year-old Susy went to New York on 28 April 1885 for a combination of shopping, entertainment, and business. Clemens discussed business with Charles Webster and General Grant, read at the authors' benefit for the Copyright League on 29 April, and attended the Cornell Alumni dinner. Susy's share of the amuse-

Long dog.

Broke rake handle

$5! ⟨d[--]⟩Put the s— of — b— out

Write a Damon & Pithias short story, & then enlarge it. 2 twins are enough.

We say Ach Gott, you say Goddam.

Why d'nt you bet a *million*—you'd a won it!

Apl. 28—Chatto's draft for £178.0.5. paid—$861.35. This I take it, is the *second*, & that the first was paid a month ago—about the end of March.[49]

26th & Madison ave (University Club)—send note there to Hamersley, Wednsday.[50]

Heiliger Gott! ich glaub' es wohl.[51]

If all one dog, mighty long dog.

May 1, '85. ⟨58,⟩ 60,000 sets of Gen. Grant's book (or 120,000 single vols) which ⟨we are to⟩ I am to publish next December, are already ordered by a region comprising one-fourth of the territory lying between Canada & Mason & Dixon's line, & the Mississippi river & the Atlantic Ocean. At this rate, the rest of that territory

---

ments included a visit to General Grant, a dog show, a play, and the trip to Poughkeepsie on 1 May for the Vassar reading. Susy recalled the occasion in her biography of her father: "Papa read in the chapell. It was the first time I had ever heard him read in my life—that is in public. . . . He read 'A Trying Situation' and 'The Golden Arm' [also called the "Ghost Story"]. . . . I enjoyed the evening inexpressibly much" (*S&MT*, p. 200). "Vorlas" in Clemens' notebook entry may be his notation for *Vorlesung*, the German for "lecture."

[49] In September 1884 Clemens' English publishers Chatto & Windus had sent him these two time drafts for royalties payable in March and April 1885 (see p. 77, note 37).

[50] Hartford attorney William Hamersley was president of the Farnham Type-Setter Manufacturing Company and one of the earliest investors in the Paige typesetter. He and Clemens were attempting to buy Paige's rights in the machine and capitalize a new typesetter company, an endeavor which was never successful. Clemens wrote Charles L. Webster on 4 April 1885: "Hamersley is going West for 3 weeks, but will send you a copy of the Pa[i]ge contract when completed" (*MTBus*, p. 308). Clemens' notebook entry indicates that Hamersley had returned from his trip and was in New York City.

[51] *Holy God! I believe it indeed.*

will take 180,000 sets more—240,000 sets in all, or 480,000 single
volumes. The vast West, & the body of Southern States, ought to
take, together, 120,000 sets, perhaps⟨.⟩—say 600,000 single volumes.
If these chickens shall really hatch out according to my count, Gen.
Grant's royalties will amount to $420,000, & will make the largest
single check ever paid an author in the world's history. Up to the
present time, the largest one ever paid was to Macaulay on his
History of England ⟨£[5]0,000⟩£20,000. If I pay the General in
silver coin (at ⟨$12 per 0⟩ $12 per pound) it will weigh 17 tons.[52]

April 15, 1889. Have just read the preceding. How curiously
accurate a prophecy it was. ⟨Those⟩ We sold about
⟨$6[1]0,000⟩610,000 single volumes. We paid Mrs. Grant somewhere
between $420,000 & $450,000, I do not remember the exact figures.
When I talked with Gen. Grant in November, 1884, thirteen
months before his first volume was published, I ciphered on the
sales achieved by my own books, & told him that by my reckoning
his book must sell 600,000 single volumes.

Canvassers must be given streets or *portions* of streets in New
York—all outying districts to be canvassed *first*—then the cream of
the city to be given ⟨to be given⟩ to those canvassers who have
done the best.

Mention in ⟨cir⟩prospectus that 5 proofs have been submitted to
authorities.
Also put World lie & General Grant's *facsimile*
contradiction.[53] [#]

---

[52] In later years Clemens recalled that the propensity for awe-inspiring statistics was
one of Charles L. Webster's vanities: "He loved to descant upon the wonders of the book.
He liked to go into the statistics. He liked to tell that it took thirteen miles of gold leaf
to print the gilt titles on the book backs; he liked to tell how many thousand tons the
three hundred thousand sets weighed" (*MTE*, p. 186). Apparently Clemens was not
immune to such statistical gymnastics. For information about Macaulay's famous royalty
check see note 55.

[53] In a column headed "National Capital Gossip," the New York *World* asserted that
General Adam Badeau, Grant's secretary during the Civil War, was writing the *Memoirs*
for him (29 April 1885). At first Clemens wanted to sue the *World* but his lawyers advised
him that litigation "would be long, expensive, and annoying, not only to us, but to Genl.
Grant" (CLW to SLC, 2 May 1885). General Grant's letter of denial, dated 2 May 1885,
was printed in the New York *World* of 6 May and was included in the publisher's pros-

Get my watch

Canadian Copyright *now*.

Get the necessity of notifying an American—accessory—pirate removed.

What do they teach you in the high school, my son?
Pisciculture, ⟨as[s]⟩ ⟨astrology⟩astronomy, love of count -ry

Her Majesty the King (German) *"She"* &c—page 68 Drei Musketiere.

Her Eminence the Cardinal ("She" &c)

Get the rest of Dumas at the German Buchhandlung.

Euer or Ihrer ergebenster—Your most ⟨truly⟩ devoted?—nicht wahr.

By & by advertise Memoirs on bulletin boards ⟨appro⟩ just outside N.Y on all railroads.

Auf ⟨der⟩das Gesangbuch—Seite 233 [54]

Die Versammlung mangelte an Anzähle.

Die Geschickte Mary Bacons—

Macaulay's great Check was for £20,000—& is still preserved by Longmans as a curiosity. *346 vol. II.* Was it for the whole 5 vols? The edition mentioned is only 25,000 copies or 30,000. [55] [#]

---

pectus for the *Memoirs* along with an extract from the New York *Sun* of 7 May which praised Grant's "peculiarly compact, distinct, picturesque and telling English style" and stated that the published "contradiction seems to us unnecessary." Clemens soon wrote Charles L. Webster that he noticed that the *World's* allegations were not reprinted elsewhere and they apparently "fell dead & did no harm." Clemens concurred in the decision against bringing suit: "I recognize the fact that for General Grant to sue the World would be an enormously valuable advertisement for that daily issue of unmedicated closet-paper" (SLC to CLW, n.d., *MTBus*, p. 323).

[54] *In the songbook—page 233.* The following entry reads: *The gathering was lacking in numbers.*

[55] Clemens garnered these statistics from *The Life and Letters of Lord Macaulay* by G. Otto Trevelyan, 2 vols. (New York: Harper & Brothers, 1876), 2:345–346. Macaulay received his check for £20,000 in March 1856 from his publishers, Longmans, Green, and Company. The first two volumes of Macaulay's *History of England* were issued in 1849;

Club subject—"The insincerity of Man"—all men are liars, partial hiders of facts, half tellers of truths, shirks, moral sneaks.— When a merely *honest* man appears, he is a comet—⟨he⟩his ⟨sta⟩ fame is eternal—needs no genius, no talent—mere honesty—Luther, Christ, & maybe God has made 2 others—or one—besides me.

May 11 or 12, began dictating.[56]

L. D. Haymond, Liberty, Bedford Co., Va. Have said if he will come for 2 days in first week of June, I will try to go to him for 2 days in the fall.

Ch send expert from Elmira or N. Y.[57]

Macaulay's grand Edition weighed 45 tons. Our first issue (Dec. 1) ought to weigh 300 tons.)

Teleg. Ch & Norv. Green or Watterson.[58]
P. to bind himself to give me the 15-150[ths] *anyhow* if I require them before March 1, next.
Ch. to return $\frac{1}{2}$ to me at 7,500/at cost if I make the demand before Mch 1, '86.
Ch can require me to take the *whole* 15,000 back at cost if he chooses, *after* Mch 1, '85.

---

the third and fourth volumes appeared in December 1855 in an edition of twenty-five thousand copies, "weighing no less than fifty-six tons," and it was for these later volumes that Macaulay received his famous royalty check; the fifth volume of the *History* was published posthumously ("Sketch of the Life and Writings of Thomas Babington Macaulay" in *The History of England*, 5 vols. [Philadelphia: J. B. Lippincott & Co., 1869], 5:16, 21).

[56] See page 118, note 179.

[57] On 4 April 1885 Clemens had written to Charles L. Webster that the Paige typesetter was "in perfect working order" at last and that capitalization of a company to manufacture the machine could now begin. Part of the process involved the testing of the machine's performance by a number of mechanical "experts."

[58] Norvin Green had been president of the Western Union Telegraph Company since 1878. Henry Watterson was editor of the Louisville, Kentucky, *Courier-Journal*. "Ch" may be George W. Childs, owner of the Philadelphia *Public Ledger*. Clemens hoped to interest these men in underwriting the manufacture of the typesetter. The following notes reflect Clemens' flurry of interest in another invention by Paige—an electric telegraphic apparatus. Clemens traveled to Albany, New York, probably on 20 May, to discuss the new invention with businessman Dean Sage. On Clemens' behalf, Sage asked for an opinion from Alonzo B. Cornell, former governor of New York and an executive of Western Union. On 21 May Cornell responded: "I can only say that the domain of Teleg-

On the *further* condition that Ch shall take 10,000 at his *sole* risk, I being responsible for no part of it—and

1 year later I am to return the 15000 if required (& take back 15-25^{ths} of the thing); ⟨but⟩ or, if both parties are satisfied, then I am to have ½ the ⅓ interest (25,000) to have & keep for ⟨12,000⟩12,500.

If T.-S. ⟨fails⟩ wins, ⟨[I]⟩ P. to give back to me the 15,000 or leave it in the Tel, *at my 12-months* OPTION.

(⟨If⟩But if T.-S. fails, of *course* the 15,000 remain⟨s⟩ in the Tel.) ⟨& part[--]⟩

And the 10,000 *also*, in any & all cases.

These ownerships include foreign countries also.

Read these in Morgen;

What were the former terms offered the N.Y. men?

Give me a year, provided Nov. 1 fails.

Sell me the 25000 outright.

Give me a piece of writing to that effect.

And another stating that this fulfills my trade with Hamersley & Paige—signed by both?

If Dean don't want half, let him sell a part of his.

Telegraph Dean—& Peyton.[59]

Let Peyton tell Laffan.[60]

Ham give me ⟨l⟩authority to offer Pton 10 per cent to be shared between us. We want him to work for *us*. [#]

---

raphy has been so thoroughly exploited that nothing valuable remains to be secured however meritorious any specific device may be in its operations. The competition has exhausted all chances of profit and I would not give $100. for the best invention extant." This opinion dampened Clemens' ardor for the investment.

[59] William A. Paton was publisher of the New York *World* from 1877 to 1881 and was currently business manager of the *Century* magazine. He had been interested in the Paige typesetter since 1881 and had used his influence then and in 1883 to seek out capital for the machine. In December 1884 Paton had started a new campaign to secure investors.

[60] Journalist and art connoisseur William Mackay Laffan was the publisher of the New York *Sun* and a friend of Clemens'.

You people go up & let P explain to why it would be stupid & dangerous to remove to N. York.

The ⟨s⟩thing is safe *here*, because the details are recorded & *promised*—but would kill it in foreign lands—any description printed, or public *use* of machine. It is usd now as a test.

I have given Gerhardt several thousand dollars' worth of my time, & a good deal of trouble besides. *I* ought not to ⟨f⟩⟨c⟩ charge for that, neither ought he to fail to remember it. Look at the bother & lost time over that Committee business, & also that Steinbild von mir.[61]

⟨400⟩100, & draw on W for $400[62]
   $200 to J. (Total $1365)
   100 ″ ″   & $5000
   65 um Wasser kur⟨[-]⟩
⟨400⟩200 ″ Vereinigten Halle.
   100 in odds & ends. when going to Phila & New York.

Note of $1000 to Goodwin Bros.[63]

$2 or 300 to sail to Paris with.

Formerly the new Co were to create the plant & have only the privilege of making & selling 1000 machines, & on these they had to pay a royalty of $600 each to the old Co. The old Co wanted to require that *they* inherit the plant when the 1000 machines had been finished & sold. [#]

---

[61] Karl Gerhardt returned to the United States in the summer of 1884 after a three-year course of study in Paris at Clemens' expense. Gerhardt's main concern was to secure large commissions so as to enable him to support his wife and child and repay Clemens. But commissions proved difficult to find and he continued to depend on Clemens financially. The "Committee business" which Clemens refers to in this entry was the competition for the Nathan Hale statue (see p. 75, notes 29 and 32). The "Steinbild von mir" (*statue of mine*) was a statuette of Echo which Gerhardt completed in Paris and shipped to Clemens; Gerhardt reclaimed the Echo at least twice in order to exhibit it.

[62] The notes through "$2 . . . Paris with." (146.18) refer to money advanced to Gerhardt and his wife Hattie Josephine (known as "Josie") by Clemens and Charles L. Webster & Company. The amounts include $65 *for the water cure* and $200 *for the union hall.*

[63] The Elmwood, Connecticut, firm which produced and distributed Gerhardt's terra cotta bust of General Grant.

We have now procured documents allowing us to absolutely *sell* the ⟨patent⟩ whole thing, out & out (for the U.S.) No limit upon the number to be manufactured.

If the former machine had been perfect in all its several functions, it would still have been far less valuable than is the present one, because of the new invention which will not allow a weak or imperfect type to enter the machine. That ⟨h⟩defect has been the rock upon which all former type-setters have gone to the devil.

This machine will set the whole alphabet—*the other one wouldn't.*

There are 11,000 papers & periodicals in America.

Justifying will become an "expert" trade, & this person will be the only expert left or required in type setting & distributing.

This type-setter does not get drunk.

He does not join the Printers' Union.

He does not distribute a dirty case, he does not set a dirty proof.

A woman can operate him.

He can snatch up late matter, 8 "takes" at a mouthful at 3 in the morning when the paper is in a hurry to get to press.

The "type-tester" is *new.*

The Catholic pr's speech to Sunday School about the Prot & Cath ships sailing out of port together, & the storm came, the Prot foundered, but the Cath came safe into port with all her sails standing—"*Why?*—Because she was founded upon a rock⟨.⟩, me childer."

Ein Tochter Russlands

Erster Liebe

Fruhlingsfluten[64]

Auf die Höhe⟨n⟩ (Auerbach)[65] [#]

---

[64] This and the preceding two titles are short works by Turgenev—*A Daughter of Russia, First Love,* and *Spring Floods.*

[65] Berthold Auerbach's melodramatic novel of illicit love, guilt, and expiation was first published around 1865.

Boots & Saddles
E. B. Custer[66]

Wm. M. Hunt's 3 horses & naked colored man leading them—
very fine, very spirited—this group made by H himself one day in
⟨(   )^s⟩Garibaldi^s/⟨stone cutter⟩ studio, ⟨b⟩Boston—Vanderbilt
has a bronze of it & there are other plaster ones. Here close by is a
photo of them made 25 yr ago! The frescoes in the capitol were
made 8 yrs ago. After G's death a great many sketches of these
horses in different attitudes were found. So, after a quarter century
he put them in ⟨the⟩ as part of a fresco in the Albany capitol—&
prepared for it as for the great work & monument of his life.[67]

Bekken's Erzählungen aus der Alten Welt.[68]
Dr. Porter.

The Russians at the Gates of Herat (Franklin Square).[69]

There is a good old anecdote which used to be very popular
among the disciples &c.

Send books to the ⟨Shakes⟩Shakers.[70] [#]

---

[66] Elizabeth B. Custer's "*Boots and Saddles*"; or, *Life in Dakota with General Custer*
was published by Harper & Brothers in 1885.

[67] William Morris Hunt made a number of studies for his large painting *Anahita*,
named after the Persian nature goddess. The painting depicted Anahita seated on a cloud
driving three fiery horses, one of which was held by a "swarthy male attendant." The canvas was destroyed in the Boston fire of November 1872 but Hunt's plaster model of the
horses survived. In 1878 Hunt was commissioned to fresco two walls in the Assembly
Chamber of the New York State Capitol in Albany. He derived the subject for one of the
huge frescoes, *The Flight of Night*, from the lost *Anahita*. The frescoes were completed,
after two months of grueling work, in December 1878 and were instantly acclaimed as a
triumph of mural art. Unfortunately the leaking roof of the badly constructed Capitol
building caused large sections of Hunt's work to flake off; in 1888 the marred frescoes were
walled up during the renovation of the structure.

[68] Karl Friedrich Becker was the author of this early nineteenth-century children's
book, a collection of tales from ancient mythology.

[69] A book by the English writer Charles Thomas Marvin published in America by
Harper & Brothers and Charles Scribner's Sons in 1885. It notes an alarming pattern of
Russian expansion toward British India, a topical subject in the spring of 1885 when both
imperial powers threatened war over the "Penjdeh incident," an Afghan border clash.

[70] Clemens evidently visited the large Shaker community at Watervliet, New York,
near Albany when he made a brief stay with Dean Sage (see p. 144, note 58). Sage wrote

Translations of ⟨Genl⟩General's book

By the Morse system, names are as a rule spelt wrong by the receiving operator. Why is it?

If God is what people say, there can be none in the universe so unhappy as he; for he sees, unceasingly, myriads of his creatures suffering unspeakable miseries,—& besides this foresees all they are going to suffer during the remainder of their lives. One might well say, "as unhappy as God."

The telephone must be driven out, for it is useless—at any rate at night when the electric lights are burning.

Find Richards, formerly of Colt's.[71]

After Pton, try Col. Chas. Fairchild.[72]

After Gov. Cornell, see Gen. Eckert.[73]

Letter from Watterson to Norvin Green some time or other.

Slee—Charley.[74]

Chief telegrapher here.

The Scotch boy & Westminster Abbey.[75]

Tom Beecher's Hairdresser story.[76]

Buckner lent Genl Grant $50—& after war said he had done

---

to Clemens on 23 May 1885: "We enjoyed your short visit very much & dont want you to forget your promise to the Shakers, the fulfilment of which will of course involve the long promised visit here of Mrs Clemens & yourself."

[71] Possibly Francis H. Richards, a mechanical engineer at the Pratt & Whitney iron works in Hartford.

[72] The Boston broker Charles Fairchild was a close friend of William Dean Howells'.

[73] See page 144, note 58. Thomas T. Eckert, an expert in telegraphic matters, was at this time vice president and general manager of Western Union.

[74] J. D. F. Slee was an official of the coal firm of J. Langdon & Company, of which Charles Langdon, Livy's brother, was the head.

[75] This anecdote is told in full in an unpublished manuscript entitled "Information About Westminster Abbey" in the Mark Twain Papers (see also p. 155, note 96).

[76] Thomas K. Beecher was the pastor of the Congregational church in Elmira of which the Langdons were prominent members.

more for him than any other man—had lent him $50 & given him 15,000 men &c.[77]

Hartford, den 25ten Mai
Frau — —
Gewiss ist Ihre Schwester noch am Leben. Vor zwei Jahren wurde⟨n⟩ ⟨Sie⟩ sie verheiratet, ⟨wahren⟩ während sie noch in unser Dienst ⟨geblieben⟩ war, dann ging⟨en⟩ sie sogleich in die Familie ⟨ihres Mannes⟩ ⟨des Vaters⟩ ihres Schwiegervaters⟨.⟩, wo sie jetzt wohnt. Ihr Mann ist ein ⟨ziehmlich⟩ziemlich wohlhabender ⟨Landsmann⟩Landmann, und es scheint mir dass Rosa/die Ehepaar ganz ⟨glüchlich⟩glücklich und zufrieden ist. ⟨(sind.)⟩ Sie wohnen ungefähr eine halbe⟨n⟩ Meile von unser Sommeren Aufenthalt entfernt, ⟨die⟩⟨der⟩ der im Staat New York ist.

⟨Die⟩Der Name und Adresse Rosas ist "Mrs. Horace Terwilliger, Elmira, N.Y."

⟨Ich zweifle mich ob Sie meine unwissendhalfter Deutch verstehen können; ⟨aber⟩ denn ich habe kein Fähigkeit in diese Sprache.[78]

Resp⟩ [#]

---

[77] Clemens recalled this story in an Autobiographical Dictation of 1 June 1906. Confederate general Simon B. Buckner had been a West Point classmate of General Grant. Some time later Grant "found himself in New York, penniless. On the street he met Buckner and borrowed fifty dollars of him. In February 1862 Buckner was in command of the Confederate garrison of Fort Donelson. General Grant captured the fortress by assault and took fifteen thousand prisoners. After that, the two soldiers did not meet again until that day at Mount McGregor twenty-three years later" (MTE, p. 184). In his 1906 dictation Clemens erroneously stated that he was present the day of Buckner's visit and heard Buckner's comment about General Grant: "He has one deadly defect. He is an incurable borrower and when he wants to borrow he knows of only one limit—he wants what you've got. When I was poor he borrowed fifty dollars of me; when I was rich he borrowed fifteen thousand men" (MTE, p. 185). The date of General Buckner's visit was 10 July 1885 (Thomas M. Pitkin, The Captain Departs: Ulysses S. Grant's Last Campaign [Carbondale and Edwardsville: Southern Illinois University Press, 1973], p. 83). Clemens was with his family at Quarry Farm on that date. Furthermore, the notebook entry itself antedates the Grant-Buckner reunion by nearly two months.

[78] Clemens evidently drafted this letter in response to a query regarding Rosina Hay, Susy's German nursemaid who was hired in 1874 and accompanied the Clemens family to Europe in 1878. The German reads: *Certainly your sister is still alive. Two years ago she was married, while she was still in our service, then she went to the family of her father-in-law, where she now lives. Her husband is a rather well-to-do farmer, and it seems to me*

Jas H Rutter[79]
    778 Madison ave

See if Dana wants to look into the matter.

See Cornell?

Depew?[80]

Martin?

Paton.[81] **x x x x x x x x.**

The Philada machine.

Geo. W. Childs?[82]

Paton?

Balt & Ohio Tel. Co.[83] [#]

---

that Rosa/*the couple is completely happy and satisfied. They live about a half mile from our summer residence, which is in the state of New York.*

Rosa's name and address are "Mrs. Horace Terwilliger, Elmira, N.Y."

Clemens canceled the following remark at the end of the letter: *I doubt whether you can understand my ignorant German; because I have no ability in this language.*

[79] Rutter had succeeded William H. Vanderbilt as president of the New York Central and Hudson River Railroad Company in 1883. The demands of this office soon impaired Rutter's health. By late May 1885 he lay gravely ill at his country home in Irvington, New York. He died on 12 June 1885. Clemens was probably unaware of Rutter's illness. This and the following several entries date from Clemens' trip to New York City at the end of May 1885. One of his major concerns on the trip was to interest investors in James W. Paige's printing telegraph and in the typesetter, which was now supposedly ready for demonstration.

[80] Chauncey M. Depew for several years had been attorney for the Vanderbilt railroad empire. In June 1885 he succeeded James H. Rutter as president of the New York Central Railroad, a position he held until 1899.

[81] See page 145, note 59. Since December 1884 William A. Paton "had called on nearly every man he could think of who would be likely to take an interest" in Paige's typesetter, but the investors, having been twice persuaded to view an obviously imperfect machine, were no longer attracted (Daniel Whitford to SLC, 11 June 1885). On 20 June 1885 Paton withdrew entirely from the financial affairs of the typesetter.

[82] George W. Childs, owner and publisher of the Philadelphia *Public Ledger*.

[83] The Baltimore and Ohio Telegraph Company, created in 1877, was a subsidiary of the Baltimore and Ohio Railroad. Clemens undoubtedly thought that the railroad directors, who had implemented Samuel F. B. Morse's first transmission on his electric telegraph in 1844, would be interested in Paige's printing telegraph invention.

See shirt makers

See Norvin Green

W^m A Paton, 15 W. 19.

Gold & stock tel Co.

Ross Winans.[84]

Charley
109 W 126th

I did not know that this was the future General Grant, or I
would have turned & attacked him. I supposed it was just some
ordinary Colonel, of no particular consequence, & so I let him go.
It was probably a great mistake.

General said he read my article first & all the family afterward.[85]

(It is curious & dreadful to sit up this way & talk cheerful
nonsense to Gen. Grant & he under sentence of death with that
cancer. He says he has made the book too large by 200 pages—not
a bad fault—a short time ago we were afraid it would *lack* 400 of
being enough. He has dictated 10,000 words at a single sitting, &
he a sick man! It kills me these days to do half of it!—May 26/85.

Translations of the Memoires.

Stepping off train in front of ein Ehepaar:[86] "Bless your soul *I*
didn't know your wife wanted to."

Mrs. H. J. Brooks—[87]
35 W 11th [#]

---

[84] Ross Revillon Winans, a Baltimore capitalist whom Clemens hoped to interest in
Paige's inventions (see p. 198, note 51). Clemens had been acquainted with Winans'
father, Thomas De Kay Winans, and grandfather, Ross Winans, both of whom were inventors and railroad entrepreneurs connected with the Baltimore and Ohio Railroad.

[85] Clemens is referring to his article "The Private History of a Campaign That Failed"
(see p. 105, note 132). The words "General . . . afterward." were squeezed in vertically
along the inner margin of the page next to "I did not . . . mistake." and were evidently
added later. General Grant seems to have seen an early draft of the article. It was not
published until the December 1885 issue of the *Century*.

[86] *A couple.*

[87] Mrs. Brooks was an old friend of Livy's.

May 27—Called on Postmaster Henry J Pierson[88]—a very young looking man—42, but looks 10 yrs younger

May 26 '85.—This date, 1858, parted from L, who said "We shall meet again 30 years from now."[89]

To-day talked with General Grant about his & my first Missouri campaign in 1861 (in June or July.) He surprised an empty camp near Florida, Mo., on Salt river, which I had been occupying a day or two before. How near he came to playing the devil with his future publisher![90]

May 27. Called on Postmaster Pierson (New York City)—a very young man—is 42—but I have already made this note.)

Then called on D[r.] Norvin Green, President of the Western Union Telegraph Co & had a long talk about James W. Paige's printing telegraph.

One of the Virginian ⟨Wise's⟩Wises was there—a very pleasant gentleman. We were on good terms at once, because one of my tribe of Clemenses shot one of his tribe of Wises in a duel once— or was shot himself by a Wise, I don't remember which, & didn't like to ⟨let on⟩ appear ignorant, so I didn't betray that I didn't

---

[88] Henry G. Pearson was postmaster for New York City from 1881 until 1889.

[89] Laura Wright (later Dake) was a young girl with whom Clemens enjoyed a brief idyll in New Orleans in 1858. Almost fifty years later he still recalled her affectionately. On 26 May 1906 Isabel V. Lyon noted in her journal:

This afternoon when Mr Clemens picked up the Times, & noticed the date he said, "This is one of my anniversaries. 48 years ago I said good bye to my little sweet heart." Then he told me how he had said that he wouldn't see her for years—2 or 3 years—& she had given him a little gold ring, & then he went away. Laura Wright was her name, & she was very young. In all these 48 years he has never seen her. There werent many romances in his life, "just those two early ones: Laura Wright & Laura Hawkins." (Isabel V. Lyon journal, January–June 1906, Humanities Research Center, University of Texas, Austin)

Shortly after he made these remarks, Clemens came to the aid of Laura Dake in a time of financial distress (see *N&J1*, pp. 89–90, note 41).

[90] Clemens' experience as a Confederate irregular in Missouri occurred some time between 12 June and 10 July 1861; on 18 July 1861 Clemens left Saint Louis for the West. Since General Grant did not arrive in Florida, Missouri, until early August, Clemens' tale of a near encounter is exaggerated (John Gerber, "Mark Twain's 'Private Campaign,'" *Civil War History*, March 1955, pp. 39–40, 59–60).

know, because this might have been the very ⟨[--]⟩identical Wise himself.[91]

May 27. Major Pond tells me there is an article in the Boston Herald telling all about Geo. W. Cable's sickness at our house 18 months ago, but saying nothing about his not reading for international copyright—& fortunately nothing about Ponds gift of books in Cable's name to Dr Davis[92] who attended Cable 2 or 3 weeks free of charge. The whole thing was an unwarrantable publication. Our papers are where the London ones were 100 years ago.[93]

Daughter of (rebel) General Morgan Smith called on me. Bright & pretty—aged 17½.[94]

Depew's yarn about Lord Roseberry in Duke of Buccleu's box—Hamlet—the call on Irving in dressing room to inquire what becomes of Hamlet—got a Shakspeare & reformed. Lord R told

---

[91] Probably John Sergeant Wise, a Virginia lawyer and politician, who later settled in New York City and became legal adviser to the leading electrical companies.

[92] G. Pierrepont Davis was the medical examiner for the Travelers Insurance Company.

[93] There was a gossipy attack on George Washington Cable in the Boston *Herald* on 7 May 1885. The article accused Cable of petty stinginess both while he was ill at Clemens' home early in 1884 and during their joint reading tour. There was also a criticism of Cable's conduct in not taking part in the copyright benefit readings of 28 and 29 April 1885. The reporter suggested that Cable "considered . . . that the lack of a copyright law would not harm the sale of his books, and he didn't propose to aid his guild without cash down for his services." Cable demanded—and obtained—a retraction of the damaging article by the editor of the *Herald* (Arlin Turner, "Mark Twain, Cable, and 'A Professional Newspaper Liar,'" *New England Quarterly*, March 1955, pp. 26–31). Cable telegraphed, then wrote, to Clemens on 15 and 16 May requesting that he too refute the newspaper allegations, but Clemens, who was very likely the source for the rumors about Cable, chose to treat the matter lightly. He advised Cable not to give himself "any discomfort about the slander of a professional newspaper liar." He added: "I do assure you that this thing did not distress me, or even disturb the flow of my talk. . . . To take notice of it in print is a thing which would never have occurred to me. Why, my dear friend, flirt it out of your mind—straight off" (Guy A. Cardwell, *Twins of Genius* [East Lansing: Michigan State College Press, 1953], pp. 108–109). Although Clemens' notebook entry suggests that he first heard of the matter from Major Pond in New York on 27 May, he had in fact been aware of the *Herald* article for almost two weeks.

[94] Morgan Lewis Smith, brigadier general of Union, not Confederate, forces during the Civil War, died in 1874. Miss Smith wrote to Clemens on 1 June 1885 mentioning their pleasant meeting.

this to Depew himself—probable—no, possible—future prime minister of England.[95]

⟨M⟩Scotch boy & Westminster Abbey.[96]

Gen. Grant told me it was at Salt River his heart was in his mouth but from that day forth he never had a tremor again in war. He had been in war before, but this was the first time he was *responsible*.

Write to Prince Bismarck in German, through Am. Minister.

By & by, ask for *perpetual* copyright on General's book, restricted to his heirs. An heir of Cromwell died poor the other day. C. ought to have written a book & had perpetual copyright on it.

At that port near Sebastopol we saw Russian ladies strip themselves stark naked for a sea bath & walk down into the water so.[97]

May 28—At Western Union building ⟨sa[-]⟩was introduced to

---

[95] Clemens may have heard Chauncey M. Depew tell such an anecdote in his lecture on "Poetry and Politics in the British Isles" at the Hartford Opera House on 15 May 1885. Clemens and several other prominent Hartford citizens were seated on the lecture platform. Depew's lecture included diverse impressions of Ireland, Scotland, and England, interspersed with many personal anecdotes. Archibald Philip Primrose, fifth earl of Rosebery, in 1894 would succeed Gladstone as prime minister. "Irving" is of course the renowned actor Henry Irving.

[96] See page 149, note 75. In "Information about Westminster Abbey" Clemens feigns ignorance of Westminster Abbey to the astonishment of his inquisitor—one of his fellow passengers during an Atlantic crossing, "a Scotch lad of sixteen." Chauncey Depew, in his speech at the Lotos Club's 10 November 1900 dinner to Mark Twain, said that a dinner guest, "an English gentleman," once mentioned to him a shipboard encounter with a traveling American by the name of Clemens who professed no knowledge of Westminster Abbey. Until Depew identified Clemens as Mark Twain, the Englishman had considered the encounter evidence of the singular obtuseness of American travelers (John Elderkin, Chester S. Lord, and Horatio N. Fraser, eds., *Speeches at the Lotos Club* [New York: privately printed, 1901], pp. 389–390).

[97] Mark Twain described the unselfconscious bathers of Odessa in a letter to the *Alta California* published on 3 November 1867. He omitted the episode in *The Innocents Abroad*.

Jay Gould, & lunched with his son. Damned insignificant looking people.[98]

Tell the *truth* about ⟨Cable⟩ & Bret Harte's visits here.—
⟨& stop⟩[99]

E. Whistling.   Begin with ghost, IF *house all quiet.*
Gov. Gardner.
Duel.
Blue Jays.[100]

G. G.'s first idea was to put in portraits of prominent Generals, but he got so many letters from Colonels & such asking to be added, that he resolved to put none in, & thus avoid the creation of jealousies.

Have a Chapter on English & American lecture audiences.
American humorists I have known.
Why the West & South have produced the chief (low-comedy) humorists. [#]

---

[98] Gould had acquired control of the Western Union Telegraph Company in 1881 and maintained offices in the Western Union building in New York City. His son, George Jay Gould, reached his majority in 1885 and joined his father in his business enterprises. In an Autobiographical Dictation of 28 January 1907 Clemens would characterize Jay Gould as the "first and most infamous corrupter of American commercial morals" (*MTE*, pp. 73–74).

[99] Clemens discussed Harte's several visits to the Hartford house, in particular his extended stay in late 1876 when the two were collaborating on *Ah Sin*, in his Autobiographical Dictation of 4 February 1907 (*MTE*, pp. 274–280).

[100] On 1 June 1885 Clemens accepted an invitation by the Art Society of Hartford to give a benefit reading of his works (SLC letter of acceptance printed in the Hartford *Courant*, 2 June 1885). The two readings were on 5 and 6 June 1885. The *Courant* reported on 6 June: "The entertainment last evening at Unity hall was most heartily enjoyed by an audience which included many of the best-known and most intelligent and cultivated people in the city. They were untiring in their demands for more, and called out Mark Twain after each reading. . . . Mark Twain is one of the best story tellers in the world." Clemens' final selections for the benefit differed from the tentative list in this notebook entry. He used some of the most popular readings from his 1884/1885 lecture tour: the King Sollermun selection from *Huckleberry Finn,* the "Awful German Language," "A Trying Situation," the whistling and stammering story ("A Sure Cure"), and the Governor Gardner anecdote from "Some Rambling Notes." He concluded with the "Golden Arm" ghost story.

⟨F⟩*Tom. Fitch.* Try the Journal of Ham in the Ark again—&
make him only 10 yrs old in *fact* though 100 by the family Bible.[101]
And try also that other old tale begun in Edinburgh.

Gerhardt—big statue.[102]

Osgood's $1800. Let W. make the offer to *me*. It should come
from him.[103] [#]

---

[101] Thomas Fitch was a lawyer and politician whom Clemens had known in Nevada.
He and his wife wrote Clemens on 27 May 1885 praising *The Prince and the Pauper* as
a work that would "live" beyond all of Mark Twain's other works, having the triple merit
of being a "suggestive" allegory, a history, and a romance. Fitch concluded: "You have
money enough. Instead of 'potboilers' why dont you write another such a book as 'Prince
& Pauper.'" Clemens evidently valued Fitch's opinion; he noted on the envelope of the
letter: "The 'Silver-tong[ued] orator of the Pacific.' High praise for Princ[e and the]
Pauper." Clemens' notebook entry suggests that he was considering returning to some
abandoned literary projects of the allegorical-historical-romantic style. His "Journal of
Ham in the Ark" does not survive, but it was probably part of the series of Adam Family
papers (a number of related Adam Family fragments are published in *Letters from the
Earth*, ed. Bernard DeVoto [New York: Harper & Row, 1962], pp. 62–114]. The "old
tale begun in Edinburgh," mentioned in Clemens' next entry, was part of the same series.
Clemens recalled in April 1909: "As to that 'Noah's Ark' book, I began it in Edinburgh
in 1873 [Paine's footnote states: "This is not quite correct. The 'Noah's Ark' book was
begun in Buffalo in 1870."]; I don't know where the manuscript is now. It was a Diary,
which professed to be the work of Shem, but wasn't. I began it again several months ago,
but only for recreation; I hadn't any intention of carrying it to a finish—or even to the
end of the first chapter, in fact" (*MTL*, p. 488).

[102] Clemens wrote to Karl Gerhardt on 4 June 1885 with a suggestion: "You *must* have
the first Grant statue—& you must have it *finished & ready to be presented* to the City
of New York 4 or 5 months from now, if possible. Go now to Webster & tell him to find
business with General Grant *two or three days in succession*—& you go *with* him every
time, & get a chance to see the General sitting, walking, standing, &c. . . . I will contribute a tenth of the cost of said statue if I can get people to give the rest, & I haven't
the shadow of a doubt that I can" (New-York Historical Society, New York City). There
is no evidence that Gerhardt obtained a commission for such a statue.

[103] James R. Osgood's publishing company had announced its failure on 2 May 1885
and on 2 June a settlement of the firm's debts, at a third of their value, was agreed upon
(Carl J. Weber, *The Rise and Fall of James Ripley Osgood* [Waterville, Me.: Colby
College Press, 1959], pp. 218–219, 223). Clemens had severed his relations with the
company earlier in the year and had repeatedly asked Webster to secure Osgood's overdue final statement. Clemens wrote to his mother from New York City on 8 June: "I
didn't know Osgood owed me anything, but I find out today he owes me $1,800. Very
sorry Osgood failed—mighty nice man" (TS in MTP). It is apparent from this entry and
a nearby entry ("Take the Osgood thing, collect the 30 pc & give yr note for the rest.")
that Clemens considered that the balance of the eighteen hundred dollars—after the

You persistently neglected to get that statement for more than a year. Acting for yourself w^d you have done that?

It would be a simple thing to hand that game to Munn—I've got to bring Orion east to do it.[104]

Prang's War pictures.[105]

Take the Osgood thing, collect the 30 pc & give me yr note for the rest.

Pope mentions &c &c.

See Slote about the gummed ribbons or blanks, & talk with Norvin Green about them.[106]

See Col. Hamilton.

See Balt & Ohio people.[107]

See Whitford about Mr. Paton—& have a distinct understanding with Paton.[108]

Perhaps talk with the Harpers. [#]

---

payment of the third allowed to creditors—should be paid to him by Charles L. Webster & Company.

Clemens left Hartford for a three-day business trip to New York City on 8 June and evidently conferred with Charles Webster about the matters mentioned in the following several entries.

[104] Charles L. Webster informed Clemens on 19 January 1885 that the history game had been in the hands of Munn & Company, who were to "perfect the patent," since October 1884. Clemens was dissatisfied with the lack of progress and was considering using Orion, who had been helping to research the game, as his agent in the matter.

[105] Clemens may have hoped to secure publication rights to L. Prang & Company's "War Pictures," a series of eighteen prints of the Civil War. The series was advertised for subscription sale only, the final print to be "accompanied by an elegant portfolio of special design, and a copy of an excellent souvenir picture of Gen. U. S. Grant, illustrative of his military career from West Point to Appomattox" (*Publishers' Weekly*, 25 September 1886, p. 439).

[106] Clemens is referring to Daniel Slote & Company of New York City, manufacturers of his pre-gummed scrapbook. The Slote company wrote to Clemens on 29 May 1885: "Herein please find samples of gummed paper as we understood your description given us yesterday." Clemens apparently was interested in adapting the gummed paper for use as Western Union telegraph blanks.

[107] See page 151, note 83.

[108] See page 151, note 81.

Put the thing in Osgood's hands for London?[109]

Or in Gilligs—no, Gen. Hawley's.[110]

⟨Gun⟩ Ginn, Heath & Co
    New York
(Expurgated Shakspeare.[111]

3-vol Shak $1.20 per vol.

Write D. Appleton & Co from Webster's

Perfect: Abou ben Adhem & the Rubiyât.

And Sir Ector de Maris's eulogy of Launcelot du Lak

And Gettysburg speech[112]

Sir Walter Scott paid debts amounting to £120,000 out of his numerous copyrights, but not out of one or two volumes.

Uncle Tom's Cabin sold 200,000 in this country. "Nurse & Spy" ditto. Headley's History of the War ditto.[113] [#]

---

[109] James R. Osgood announced publicly on 10 June 1885 that he would soon join the firm of Harper & Brothers. Osgood became Harper's London representative in the spring of 1886.

[110] Joseph R. Hawley was president of the American Exchange in Europe and Henry F. Gillig was vice president and general manager.

[111] The Reverend Henry N. Hudson's *Plays of Shakespeare Selected and Prepared for Use in Schools, Clubs, Classes, and Families*, 3 vols. (Boston: Ginn Brothers, 1870–1873).

[112] Charles Hopkins Clark, assistant editor of the Hartford *Courant*, wrote to Clemens on 8 June 1885: "Your enclosure received. It is a fine thing—fine all thro' but, it seems to me, especially so in spots. I'm going to use about half and return th whole when th half appears. The reason I cant use all is that so much *stuff must* be printed." Clark was evidently referring to Clemens' eulogy ot General Grant, apparently prepared and delivered to the *Courant* in June against the possibility of Grant's death. The *Courant* printed the abridged eulogy on 24 July 1885. Clemens quoted at length Sir Ector de Maris' eulogy from Malory's *Morte Darthur*, describing the passage as one "whose noble and simple eloquence had not its equal in English literature until the Gettysburg Speech took its lofty place beside it."

[113] S. Emma E. Edmonds, *Nurse and Spy in the Union Army: Comprising the Adventures and Experiences of a Woman in Hospitals, Camps, and Battle-Fields* (Hartford: W. S. Williams & Co., 1865); Joel Tyler Headley, *The Great Rebellion: A History of the Civil War in the United States*, 2 vols. (Hartford: American Publishing Co., 1865–1866).

Caesar's Commentaries (on the Gallic War & the Civil War) are the only books that rank with this. Like this, it is noted for its "simplicity, naturalness & purity" of style.

Get Carlyle's "Essays."

Merivale's History of the Romans—first 2 vols (Caesar).

Froude's Caesar[114]

13 Haynes st—Paige. Telephone him through Sykes & Newton[115] *Thursday noon,* whether to come to the house that afternoon or next day.

"Mexicans not so discriminating—sometimes picked off his Juniors[116]

Paper contract for 2 years let to Warren & Co, Boston, at ⟨6½⟩6⅓ cents per pound—they charged Osgood 8½ for the same paper for Life on the Mississippi at a time when the market was lower than it is now. We ⟨sha⟩ may possibly want 600 tons of it—we *already* require 300 (June 9/85.)
Called on Gen. Grant to-day (9th June.)

Journalist in insane asylum.

D. H. Bates, Prest & Gen Man Balt & O Tel Co, N. Y.

Make 1000 de luxe at $100 apiece.

ASK JOHN HAY. to write the first notices, to appear, say Dec 3 & Mch 3. [#]

---

[114] James Anthony Froude's *Caesar: A Sketch* (1879). The preceding two works mentioned are Thomas Carlyle's *Critical and Miscellaneous Essays,* published in 1838, and Charles Merivale's seven-volume *History of the Romans Under the Empire,* issued between 1850 and 1862.

[115] James W. Paige was living at 13 Haynes Street, Hartford. Clemens intended to reach him by telephone through druggist Philo W. Newton at the Allyn House Drug Store (formerly Sykes & Newton), a block away from Paige's home.

[116] "My regiment lost four commissioned officers, all senior to me, by steamboat explosions during the Mexican war. The Mexicans were not so discriminating. They sometimes picked off my juniors" (Ulysses S. Grant, *Personal Memoirs of U. S. Grant,* 2 vols. [New York: Charles L. Webster & Co., 1885], 1:163).

3 average compositors will set 20,000 ems in a day of 10 hours; & distribute the same in 2¼ hours. The day, then, is 12¼ hours long. The machine, (with its 2 men, operator & justifier), will most easily & set & distribute 37,000 ems in 12¼ hours; that is to say, more than 5 men's work. On reprint, it will easily do *six* men's work.

On the Sun ($1600 a week composition bills,) it would save $1000—or $50,000 a year. Say $40,000. on *all* copy.

Mach will set & distribute ⟨[40],000⟩50,000 of *reprint* in 12¼ hours, easily.

Watch at Tiffany's

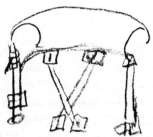

Advise agents to give out no press copy till 3 or 4 days after distribution.

Upper ferry—Xtopher street.[117]

Cards-Kards.
Tree calf

Papa, couldn't you go out & ask those people to be more quieter?

Though a man live as long as an astronomer, ⟨y⟩he must yet die at last.

Bret Harte's miner: *"Son* of a ——!⟨"⟩ Shake!"[118] [#]

---

[117] The Clemenses usually went from New York City to Hoboken, New Jersey, by way of the Christopher Street ferry, on their way to Quarry Farm each summer. They arrived in Elmira for the 1885 summer stay on 19 June.

[118] The complete anecdote is included in Clemens' Autobiographical Dictation of 4 February 1907 (*MTE*, pp. 270–272).

Bet. Aitkin & Arnold—*not* Vantine's. Little Jap. store—a small
water heater $4.50 & pd for it.[119]

Exp. pkgs—2
Shirts.

⟨Teleg for cigars⟩

Alexander 6th ave[120]

"H—l you say!"
"Deaf as damn!"

Courtlandt Palmer[121]
  Stonington.

Wit & Humor—if any difference, it is in *duration*—lightning &
electric light. Same material, apparently; but one is vivid, brief, &
can do damage—tother fools along & enjoys elaboration.

Punch's adv. "Don't." That is the *obvious* remark—the element
of surprise is almost lacking. To this day I remember the first time
I ever saw it. It didn't strike me as being anything better than a
horse might say; it ⟨didn't seem⟩ is just horse-wit, & nothing more.
The joke was very very old before Punch was born[122]

---

[119] Clemens wrote to Charles L. Webster on 24 June 1885: "Your aunt Livy bought
a little *water heater* in Broadway, the other day, at a small Japanese store between Aitkin's
& Arnold & Constable's (*not* Vantine's). . . . Please send & hunt up that place right
away & have them start that water-heater along immediately" (*MTBus*, p. 327). Thomas
Aitken, diamond setter, Arnold, Constable & Company, the huge drygoods emporium,
and A. A. Vantine & Company, merchants of rare Japanese and Chinese goods, were all
on or near Broadway and Nineteenth Street in New York City.

[120] Probably Henry Martyn Alexander, senior partner of Alexander & Green, Clemens'
lawyers.

[121] A wealthy New York lawyer and resident of Stonington, Connecticut, Palmer
wrote to Clemens on 21 June 1885, asking him to address the Nineteenth Century Club
"next winter on the subject of American Humor or some cognate theme." Palmer was
founder and president of the club, which the New York *Times* described as "a debating
society devoted to the discussion of social, literary, artistic, theological and scientific
problems in the spirit of the broadest liberality" (24 July 1888). Although Clemens jotted
down the following entries on "Wit and Humor" for the speech, he later declined to
appear (see p. 185, note 20).

[122] *Punch's* famous "Advice to Persons About to Marry,—Don't!" first appeared in
Punch's Almanack for 1845. These fairly extensive notes on wit and humor anticipate

No humor in Pickewick papers except the kind the clown makes in the circus—I mean the humorist is a million times funnier to himself than ever he can be to any reader. Every line in the book says: "Look at me—ain't I ⟨too⟩ funny!"

Dif. bet. Eng & Am humor, E is conscious, Am is ⟨carefully concealed.⟩ ostensibly unconscious. English methods of explaining jokes with italics, parentheses, &c.

Sidney Smith, Aldrich, Lamb, (Bitter enmity against the hated name of Sidney Smith).[123]

Advantage to Jeff Davis if he'd never been born.

Advice to people about to marry—*do*. There is no wit & no sense in either form of it, yet one. form is faintly funny—makes you smile, & then you are ashamed of yourself for doing it.

⟨G— d—⟩ the *old* ⟨old⟩ jokes, the jokes that never die—that tortured Cain & brought murder into the world—⟨[-]⟩&c. The mother in law—big footed girls—he lit the fire with petroleum, funeral at 3.

Common room along with all the other tramps. I was so ⟨dis[a]⟩disgusted. Why in such circumstances I'd always been used to having a cell to myself.

Drop in the Scotch boy & Westminster conversationally here & there.

Clysmic for farm

Reginald Scott's Discovery of Witchcraft: 1584.[124] [#]

Clemens' remarks in "How to Tell a Story," published in October 1895 in the *Youth's Companion*.

[123] Sydney Smith's deprecatory opinion of the country's cultural achievements had angered many Americans in the 1820s. Though he praised American educational and governmental institutions, he was remembered for his arrogant query in the *Edinburgh Review*—"Who reads an American book?"

[124] The first edition of Reginald Scot's *Discoverie of Witchcraft* appeared in 1584. The book was the first practical study of legerdemain and included instructions and illustrations describing this supposedly occult art. As such it constituted a direct refutation of witchcraft. The edition of 1584 was quite rare; there were two seventeenth century editions. The fourth English edition, edited by Brinsley Nicholson and issued in a limited number by Elliot Stock, did not appear until 1886.

Katy give me Baby Days[125] with cover torn off;

2. Pattern of Jean's Mother Hubbard coat.

3. Did she find any ⟨bugs in⟩ George's ⟨bed.⟩

Found a few, & cleaned everything, sold the bed⟨stead⟩ & had the bedstead varnished &c.

De Luxe. Call it a *very limited* edition & make it 2000 at $50.

Put in a dozen full page pictures not hadable or getable elsewhere.

Picture of the statue?

Presentation copies to potentates &c.

July 6, '85. Privately subscribed $500 to G. statue.[126]

Character. Woman with a pet prejudice—forever dragging it in, by the head, the heels, the testicles—anywhere she can get the ghost of a hold—like Miss L with her half-instructed prejudice against the German language. (Anyway she gets—perhaps what she's after—a chance to air what she does know about it. And this is of value, since the things she knows are scarce.

(June ⟨8⟩28th, Gen Grant telegraphed me & I went to him next day—a long trip, from Elmira to Mount Gregor.[127] Left the hill-top at Quarry Farm at 6 a.m., & arrived at Gen Grant's cottage 14 hours afterward, 8.20 p.m. The business was a letter from the Century—⟨not w⟩exactions about the Century articles. I devised one method, ⟨F⟩Col. Fred Grant another. We fixed it up. [#]

---

[125] *Baby Days* was a collection of "songs, stories, and pictures, for very little folks," including music, selected from the children's monthly magazine, *St. Nicholas* (New York: Scribner & Co., 1879).

[126] See page 157, note 102. Clemens wrote to Gerhardt on 6 July: "I wish to subscribe $500, but that is for interest in you, & love & pride in the object—so my name does not need to go on the subscription list and furnish the shabbier half of the world a chance to say General Grant's publisher is craftily trying to advertise himself, or give a personal friend a lift toward fame in art" (Yale).

[127] General Grant and his family had moved to the cottage at Mount McGregor in upstate New York on 16 June 1885 in order to spare Grant the rigors of a New York City summer.

I was ready to return next morning, but waited 24 hours for Jesse Grant to return from New York, who wanted me to furnish money for him to go to Turkey with. It appears that a year or more ago Gov. Stanford of California was dining with the Sultan when the latter offered him a franchise for a RR from Constantinople to the Persian Gulf—strongly pressed it upon him. Stanford came home full of the project; then his son died, & he at once lost all interest in life. So he gave the chance to Jesse Grant & offered to join General Grant in furnishing Jesse letters to the Sultan.

I had to leave before Jesse could get back, but I shall furnish the money for the experiment. (July 10) General Grant has written the Sultan.[128]

⟨Give Charley's [-]⟩

4⟨½⟩ men 2600 per hour

$$\begin{array}{r} 10 \\ \hline 26000 \end{array}$$

½ man   3250

$$\begin{array}{r} \hline 29250 \end{array}$$

It distribs 30,000 in 10 hours—1 man's work[.]
Does 5½ men's work. reprint.

Give Cassel's letter to Charley—& don't forget.[129]

Telegraph Redpath

550 per h. MS,
4 men 2200 ″   ″ 22,000 in 10 h.
Mach the same
Take ½ a man to distribute it in 10 h.
Mach does 4 & maybe 4½ men's work on manuscript. [#]

----

[128] On 13 July 1885, Webster counseled Clemens against this project which had "been thoroughly sifted by several gentlemen here months ago and dropped." Clemens did not immediately heed this advice: he financed Jesse Grant's October exploratory trip, which only got as far as London (see p. 202, note 59).

[129] Cassell & Company, the English publishers, may have been interested in securing the English rights to the Grant *Memoirs*. The rights were eventually won by Sampson Low, Marston and Company.

In the hands of a young *expert* it can do *far* better.

Must be a delicately proportioned combination of audacity & pathos. I don't say a word—not a word. ⟨"I⟩"I lay my in her hand & burst into a flood of tears."

Write a blast against the temperance (& other) "pledge" folly.[130]

Write a pamphlet about the goverment of children[131]

(Nearing.) He could live a year on an onion & a ---- & at the ⟨end of⟩ end of the year he'd have the --- left.

⟨Your⟩ Deine Mutter hatte Schwillinge—ein Knabe und ein ----   Der Knabe starb—ach, wie du bist vergrössert![132]

Miss Mary H. Norris.[133]

Money-down payments are—Munn & Co.[134]

Gt. Britain	$100
France.	100
Belgium	100
Germany.	100
Austria	100
Canada $40 . . . . or	80 [#]

---

[130] Clemens would not act on this idea until 1886 when he produced a fifty-nine page manuscript entitled "Concerning a Reformed Pledge: A New-Year Sermon" (see p. 254, note 89, and p. 264, note 127).

[131] An article in a June 1885 issue of the *Christian Union* concerning the difficulties of a certain couple in managing their unruly offspring prompted a reply from Clemens. Clemens' letter, which appeared in the *Christian Union* on 16 July 1885 under the title "'What Ought He to Have Done?': Mark Twain's Opinion," was a tribute to Livy's loving but firm governance over their children (reprinted in the *Twainian*, May 1944, pp. 2–3). It was written and published without Livy's knowledge or consent and elicited a number of letters of approval as well as some protests. In particular one letter (Thomas Twain to SLC, 21 July 1885), which Clemens believed to be from the father of the child in the original article, written in the most insulting language, caused Livy to regret Clemens' invasion of her privacy.

[132] *Your mother had twins—a boy and a ---- The boy died—oh, how you've grown!*

[133] Since 1873 Mary Harriott Norris had written several popular children's books. In 1880 she founded a private school in New York City of which she was principal until 1896.

[134] The following figures may refer to the cost of registering patents in each country. Munn & Company was handling the history game patent, but Clemens may have also had them investigate patent rights for Paige's typesetter or the printing telegraph.

Some day make a little book, call it ⟨"⟩Picturesque Incidents in History & Tradition (of all countries.)[135] For instance:

Describe what England was like during the 6 years wherein no church bell was heard ⟨in⟩—John & his whole realm being under papal curse & interdict. Cyclo. Britan.

The Irish rage yet over what they call the tyrannical siezure of their country 700 years ago by Henry II—forgetting that Ireland was *given* to that King in 1156 by their beloved god the Pope—& that Henry went over in 1171 & claimed & took his own with but little opposition from the pope's Irish slaves. Am. Cyclo. H II⟨[-]⟩

Picture England during the 30 days (1216) that no human being appeared in public view without wearing a wreath of flowers—a garlanded nation! Prince Louis of France held London, & so Henry III could not be crowned in Westminster Abbey,—so his crowning at Winchester was but a symbol, & temporary. There was no unction, no laying on of hands—& his crown was of flowers. And a command was issued begarlanding the nation for 30 days. ⟨—⟩(Memorials of Westminster Abbey.[136]

At the coronation of Geo. III (1760) the biggest jewel in his crown dropped out—an omen which made some people shudder. It was known *later* that this foretold the loss of America. (M of W. A.)

Was it William, or was it Caesar, who, when he fell, on ⟨the⟩ landing in England, pretended to have thrown himself down to take siez[ure] of the land? (W I think).

Origin of Order of Knights of the Bath. (M of W. A.)

Ditto Garter.

---

[135] Clemens wrote to his nephew Samuel E. Moffett on 21 July 1885 with a suggestion for Sam's budding career as a historian: "I have a subject which I am not competent to handle, but you are: to wit, *Picturesque Incidents in History & Tradition;* a 500 or 600-page octavo, to be written by you & published (with illustrations) by Chas. L. Webster & Co., by subscription. . . . You can draw from the history & traditions of *all* countries & epochs; & such a book, ingeniously contrived, captivatingly written, will sell handsomely, largely, & will *keep on* selling, permanently." Clemens included as examples some of the historical incidents in the following list. There is no indication that Moffett ever pursued the project. In his notebook entries Clemens refers to the book as "P. His" and "P. H."

[136] *Historical Memorials of Westminster Abbey* by Arthur Penrhyn Stanley, 5th ed., with the author's final revisions (London: John Murray, 1882).

The Boy-bishops of Salisbury.

The Children's Pilgrimage to Palestine.

To please Richard III, a priest of Westminster invented (or allowed) the quibble that *sanctuary* was a refuge for only those who were guilty of crime—& so, poor little Henry V[137] having committed no crime had no right to that protection!—wherefore the child was taken out of the sanctuary & delivered to his uncle to be smothered in the Tower.

Two Henry III^s of England. One (son of Henry II) was crowned in his father's lifetime with that title, & governed some of the French provinces, but died before his father. It was he who said, when H. II waited behind his chair at his (the prince's) coronation banquet, "It is but meet & becoming that the son of an Earl should wait upon the son of a King." This is always called a malicious & mannerless speech. I think it was more likely the prince's little joke & made a laugh which spread to the furthest borders of England & Normandy & gave the prince the reputation of being *the* humorist of his generation.

(Go back a few pages— —Essay on Humor.)

I have no sense of humor. In illustration of this fact I will say this—by way of confession—that if there is a humorous passage in the ⟨pickwick⟩Pickwick Papers, I have never been able to find it.

On board train, Binghamton, July 23, 1885,—10 a. m. The news is that Gen. Grant died about 2 hours ago—at 5 minutes past 8.

The last time I saw him was July 1st & 2^d, at Mt. McGregor. I then believed he would live several months. He was still adding little perfecting details to his book—a preface, among other things. He was entirely through, a few days later. Since then, the lack of any strong interest to employ his mind has enabled the tedious weariness to kill him. I think his book kept him alive several months. He was a very great man—& superlatively good.[138] [#]

---

[137] Actually Edward V.

[138] Clemens wrote to Livy from New York City on 24 July: "The second volume was finished last week, to the last detail; & was formally delivered to Charley Webster at Mt. McGregor last Saturday [18 July]. General Grant having not another interest in this world to live for, died" (TS in MTP).

GET A DONKEY.[139]

Johnny Skae, once worth $10,000,000, has just died in San F
penniless. Arrested once & locked up in default of $5 to pay his
fine—a year ago.[140]

P. His*ᵗ*. The delivery of the French oath by cannon throughout
little France.

The flags of a continent at half mast, & the continent clothed in
mourning draperies, & the bells of the continent tolling 5 minutes
after Gen. Grant's death. Last April the fire bells would have been
struck simultaneously by electricity.[141]

P. His. Turning the clock back to defer the 4ᵗʰ of March till the
bill retiring Gen Grant as General could be passed.[142]

Have Charley lay rope for setter in London.[143]

Get donkey. [#]

---

[139] See page 128, note 8. Clemens evidently planned to purchase another donkey.
Clara recalled: "Starting with dogs large enough to be harnessed and pull a little express-
cart, we progressed to a couple of donkeys (called 'Kadichan' and 'Polichon')" (*S&MT*,
p. 211).

[140] The report of Skae's death and a sketch of his career, including all the facts which
Clemens noted in this entry, appeared in the New York *Times* of 18 July 1885. Skae had
made a fortune from the Comstock Lode, but a few years later during a speculative
panic he "became in one week virtually a pauper." The *Times* reported that he died in
San Francisco "in poverty and obscurity," but the obituary in the San Francisco *Call* of
17 July 1885 stated that Skae had later recouped a part of his millions and made valuable
investments in San Francisco real estate.

[141] By the end of March 1885 Grant's throat cancer was dangerously advanced. For
several days bouts of choking, coughing, and hemorrhaging had weakened him. During
the first week of April death seemed imminent, and the country hourly expected news of
the event. But Grant rallied and by the middle of April his condition, though still serious,
showed signs of remission.

[142] The Senate bill to place Grant on the army's retired list with full pay as a general
was moved up on the agenda, passed in the House, and signed by President Arthur on
3 March 1885, the day before the close of the second session of the Congress.

[143] On 1 August 1885 Charles Webster sailed for Europe in order to arrange for the
foreign rights to the Grant *Memoirs*. Clemens also wanted Webster to do some preliminary promotional work for the Paige typesetter in England. Clemens explained to
Webster on 28 July 1885 that he hoped to secure advance orders for the typesetter from
a number of American newspapers. "With these promises in my hands," he added, "I
will go to the capitalists & ask them to come in & organize a company. If it works, I will
repeat the plan in England" (*MTBus*, p. 331).

Inquire for Gen Wallace[144]

    (Pauld[ine] on the Horle[au]

Inquire of Alexander & Green about the road.

Go to Hartford & get document for 2 years, with ½ one gets. For May 1—not compulsion but privilege.

Teleg Pg[145] to come Sunday.

Teleg Bunce come to-night.[146]

C L W. put ⟨2 or⟩ $3000 in Mt Morris bank for me.

⟨The⟩ A better name than the Empire City for New York would be the Ill-mannered City.

All men in New York insult you—there seem to be no exceptions. There ⟨are⟩ exceptions—of course—*have* been—but they are probably dead. I am speaking of *all* persons there who are clothed in a little brief authority.

Home (Hartfd) July 25/85 (Saturday) noon. James W. Paige has just told me that I can dispose of his telegraphing machine & have half of the proceeds for my trouble. Each of us is to give a certain share of said result to Hamersley.

Will get up a T. S. Co who will *rent* machines at $8 a day apiece.

I think we must issue *both* vols Dec 1—to beat Wannamaker & the book stores[147]—if the General agents like the idea. [#]

---

[144] Lew Wallace, the Civil War general and author of *Ben Hur*, was minister to Turkey from 1881 until his resignation in the spring of 1885. Wallace arrived in New York on 3 July. Jesse Grant wrote to Clemens on 18 July: "I saw Lew Wallace and he thinks it sensible for me to go [to Turkey, in the interests of the Turkish railroad scheme]—he says the Sultan is anxious for the road to be built." Clemens and Grant probably hoped to secure Wallace's direct intercession with Sultan Abdul Hamid II regarding the projected railroad (see p. 165, note 128).

[145] James W. Paige.

[146] Edward M. Bunce was cashier of the Phoenix National Bank in Hartford and a regular member of Clemens' Friday evening billiards group.

[147] Wanamaker had opened his hugely successful prototype of the modern department store in Philadelphia in 1877. Clemens' fears regarding unauthorized sales of the Grant

In that way we could dump 50,000 sets onto those people.

Otherwise many a man would back down from taking the second vol because he had seen the first in a book store at $2.

The General Agent, knowing both were to appear at once, would load up the bookstores—a thing he can't well venture to do, otherwise. This would beat all the pirates, too.

Charley must come to Elmira.[148]

⟨Ask the Marquis of Lorne[149] to subscribe to the setter stock.⟩

Did Charley attend to the patent of the game?

⟨Go to Depew with the setter scheme.⟩

Importance of the Prang Chromos.

Aug. 6/85. Tallked an hour with Gen. Sherman. He spoke in terms of prodigious praise of Gen. Grant's military genius. "Never anything like it before." I think those were his words. But he said this talk of Grant's never listening to indelicate stories was bosh. Said ⟨G⟩he had seen Grant listen & laugh by the hour at Governor (Jim) Nye's yarns. They were seldom delicate, as I well remember, myself.[150] [#]

---

book were justified: in the summer of 1886 he would attempt—unsuccessfully—to secure an injunction preventing Wanamaker from selling the book below the list price (see p. 250, note 77).

[148] Eager to discuss the idea of issuing both volumes together, Clemens sent a telegram on 27 July asking Webster to come to Elmira. Webster replied: "Perfectly impossible for me to come to Elmira. If important you must come here. If I come to Elmira I can't sail Saturday & we can't publish in Dec, which will damage us one hundred thousand dollars" (*MTBus*, p. 328). Before sailing for Europe in order to make arrangements for foreign editions of the Grant *Memoirs*, Webster supplied several arguments against Clemens' idea, including the claim that the binders could not get both volumes ready by December 1885 and that Webster & Company was legally bound by its contract with the Century Company (see p. 131, note 15).

[149] Husband to Queen Victoria's daughter, Princess Louise, and governor general of Canada from 1878 until 1883. In May 1883, Clemens had spent a few days in Ottawa at Lorne's invitation.

[150] James W. Nye was territorial governor of Nevada from 1861 until 1864 when he became the United States senator for the state. Clemens' recollections of Nye in his

Send Huck Finn to Harrison,[151] % Col. Grant, Mt McGregor.

Somebody has said, "Wit is the sudden marriage of ideas which before their union were not perceived to have any relation."[152]

⟨Nasby⟩ Merely refer to & quote from Nasby, Josh, Derby, Burdette, Bill Nye, (& that forgotten Tennessee humorist)

Sidney Smith
Major Dalgetty (good on stage, no doubt,)
Capt Cuttle is good anywhere, & so also of all Dickens's humorous characters except those in Pickw Papers, & the body-snatcher in Tale of 2 Cities.[153]

Aug. 15.

To Johnson. I did what I could in the photo matter, but I found that there was more behind it than I had supposed; so I dropped it. Any judicious person would have done about the same, I judge. I did not call on you again because a business which I was expecting to arrange with Hartford people Tuesday I arranged Sunday, & so came away Monday morning.[154] [#]

Autobiographical Dictation of 2 April 1906 characterize him as "a very remarkable talker, both in private and on the stump" (MTA, 2:305). In a letter to Livy from New York City written on 6 August Clemens mentioned that he had met General Sherman, among others, at the Fifth Avenue Hotel and "talked army life & anecdotes & Grant & the war, for an hour, over whisky & cigars, & had a very good time" (TS in MTP).

[151] Probably Harrison Tyrrell, General Grant's black valet.

[152] Clemens makes some additional notes for his projected essay on wit and humor (see pp. 162–163, 168). He may be recalling Sydney Smith's discussion of the nature of wit which first appeared in his 1803 Edinburgh Review article, "Edgeworth on Bulls." Smith remarks that "wit discovers real relations that are not apparent" and that the "pleasure arising from wit proceeds from our surprise at suddenly discovering two things to be similar in which we suspected no similarity" (The Works of the Rev. Sydney Smith [London: Longmans, Green, Reader, and Dyer, 1869], p. 76). Clemens may have come across Smith's definitions of wit when researching works for his Library of Humor in 1880 and 1881—they are included in William Evans Burton's Cyclopedia of Wit and Humor, one of the anthologies Clemens consulted at that time.

[153] Captain Dugald Dalgetty is the pedantic soldier of fortune in Sir Walter Scott's Legend of Montrose; good-hearted Captain Edward Cuttle appears in Dickens' Dombey and Son; the "body-snatcher" is also Dickens' creation, Jerry Cruncher.

[154] For their deluxe edition of the Memoirs, the Webster company intended to use what Clemens believed to be the last photograph taken of Grant. Webster wrote Clemens on 1 August that another copy had been made, surreptitiously according to him, by the

The English. The arrogant nation. The ⟨French⟩ Parisians, the adulterous nation. The Americans, the material nation. The Germans, the patient nation. The Russians, the ⟨stupid⟩ unclassifiable nation. The several Roman Catholic countries, the ignorant nations. The French, the ⟨thrifty⟩ volatile nation. The Scotch, the get all you can & keep all you get thrifty nation. The Italians, the hot-blooded, kind-hearted nation. The Irish, the nation of chaste women &

P. H. The last thing after Gen Grant's body was laid to rest in the receiving vault, a bugler stepped out all alone in front of the tomb, & blew "taps" ("put out the lights"). This in the presence of a great host of war veterans who had heard it every night in the camps & battlefields of Grant's campaigns of a score of years before.

I was not there. I saw the great procession (Aug. 8) but was not at the tomb.

P. H. King Knut saying to the Ocean "Thus far shalt thou come & no farther."
P. H. The boy Bishops of Salisbury.
The Children's Crusade.

The new Co shall put up $1,100,000 cash, & with this extra $100,000 buy a $\frac{1}{10}$ from Paige, ⟨Hamersley & me. $60,000 to P. & $20,000 each to H & me.⟩ The new Co wd then own just one half.

P H Discov of microscope 1608. Robinson Crusoe leaves the bag of doubloons in the wreck; a fine literary point, but untrue. No ⟨man⟩ ⟨poor⟩ man would have done that.

P. H. Plague & Fire of London. Copy from Pepys. Also see 315 Taine's English Literature[155] [#]

---

photographer. He had given it to the Century Company and they proposed to publish it in their October issue. Clemens had his lawyer, Daniel Whitford, investigate the legal complications of the affair. Whitford concluded that "we can prevent Howe [the photographer] from printing, but in return he can prevent us" (Whitford to SLC, 27 August 1885). In the end the *Century* decided not to use the picture.

[155] Clemens owned a two-volume Chatto & Windus edition of H. Van Laun's translation of Taine's *History of English Literature*. The reference on page 315 has not been identified.

With 2,000,000 machines rented, P would *own* $\frac{3}{10}$,—they would be worth $20,000,000, & his ownership in them would be $6,000,000, whereas on the old plan he would have received $600,000 in royalties & $100,000 down, & there an end.

He gets the same old royalty of $300, but gets it *permanently* per annum.

They must have the attachment to count the ems.

Aug. 8. Witnessed the imposing funeral pageant of Gen. Grant from our office windows in 14th st.,[156] Union Square, five hours, then plowed through the sidewalk crowd up Fifth avenue to 40th st.

Send Memoirs to

F. E. Griffith $\Big\rbrace$ D L & W
Billings & $\Big\}$ Hoboken
A Reasoner $\Big\}$

Mr. Collins, sta Master, Htfd [157]

---

[156] The offices of Charles L. Webster & Company were on East Fourteenth Street in New York City.

[157] Clemens gave instructions to the Webster company to send presentation copies of the Grant *Memoirs* to the three officials of the Delaware, Lackawanna & Western Railroad who each summer handled the arrangements for the Clemenses' special railway car to Elmira, and to William Collins, the Hartford stationmaster.

XXV

"My Fiftieth Year"

(August 1885–March 1886)

CLEMENS BEGAN using Notebook 25 around 20 August 1885 and continued to make notes in it until 25 March 1886. Much of his attention during this period was given over to the major business of Charles L. Webster & Company: the publication of the *Personal Memoirs of U. S. Grant*. Clemens played an active role in all stages of the preparation of the book, including the reading of proof. Except for his persistent aggravation over the attempts of rival publishers to divert the public to competing works and his understandable anxiety about meeting the publication schedule, Clemens enjoyed his preoccupation with the *Memoirs*, particularly since the subscription canvass quickly indicated that sales of the book would justify his most sanguine expectations. On 2 December 1885, the day after the first volume of the *Memoirs* was issued to tumultuous acclaim, Clemens told Howells: "We've bound & shipped 200,000 books; & by the 10th shall finish & ship the remaining 125,000 of the first edition. . . . This is a good book to publish" (*MTHL*, p. 540). And on 27 February 1886, the anniversary of the signing of the Grant contract, Charles L. Webster & Company paid Mrs. Julia Grant $200,000 in a single check, less than half of what the Grant heirs were ultimately to earn. The orchestration of this resounding business and personal triumph is a recurrent motif of Notebook 25.

The optimism and self-confidence produced by the success of the Grant *Memoirs* impelled Clemens further into his ever-deepening commitment to development of the Paige typesetter. On 10 November 1885 he gave orders for the dispatch of a check for $3,500 to William Hamersley, another typesetter investor, instructing Webster to "make a particular entry of it to remember the circumstance by, for it finishes the type-setter business in a very satisfactory fashion" (*MTBus*, p. 338). Nevertheless, Paige's invention continued to require finishing, at the rate of some $2,000 to $5,000 a month, for years to come. Clemens had no doubts of its final success, however, and on 6 February 1886 he signed an agreement by which he assumed the entire financial responsibility for its development. Throughout Notebook 25 he compiled lists of the machine's virtues, elaborated terms for its rental or sale, devised schemes to promote its economy and efficiency to the world's newspaper publishers, and drafted assurances of continued employment for the human compositors it would inevitably have replaced.

Clemens' literary impulses at this time were consistently interrupted by his business affairs. The recent publication of *Huckleberry Finn* satisfied his need to appear before the public as an author, and it was only after repeated insistence from Robert Underwood Johnson of the *Century* magazine that he agreed to turn his reminiscence of Civil War experiences, stimulated by the close association with Grant, into "The Private History of a Campaign That Failed" (*Century*, December 1885). Toward the end of 1885, Howells reported that preparation of *Mark Twain's Library of Humor* was nearing completion, but, almost as if he wished to have a work in reserve for an anticipated fallow period, Clemens decided to "pigeon-hole it & wait a few years & see what new notion Providence will take concerning it" (SLC to Howells, 18 October 1885, *MTHL*, p. 539).

On 18 January 1886, after a visit to Hartford, Howells urged Clemens to write instead of merely contenting himself with talk about writing: "That notion of yours about the Hartford man waking up in King Arthur's time is capital. There is a great chance in it. I wish I had a magazine to prod you with, and keep you up to all those good literary intentions" (*MTHL*, p. 550). In fact Clemens had begun what was to become *A Connecticut Yankee* the previous month, for on 16 December 1885 he had notified Webster: "I am plotting out a new book, & am full of it; so unless there is use for me down there, I shall not come yet awhile" (*MTBus*, p. 343). But other matters intervened and it wasn't until around 13 February 1886 that he was able to follow Howells' prompting. On that date he wrote to Webster: "For the first time in a long while, I am so situated that I can't well leave home. I have begun a book, whose scene is laid far back in the twilight of tradition: I have saturated myself with the atmosphere of the day & the subject, & got myself into the swing of the work. If I peg away for some weeks without a break, I am safe; if I stop now for a day, I am unsafe, & may never get started right again." By 22 February he was able to entertain his family with "the beginning of his new book, in manuscript . . . founded on a New Englanders visit to England in the time of King Arthur and his Round Table" (Susy Clemens' biography of her father, quoted in *S&MT*, p. 219). Notebook 25 contains several early notes for *A Connecticut Yankee*, but their submersion in details of business affairs reflects Clemens' wavering attention.

Despite the business concerns that frequently kept him away from home and prevented sustained creative effort, Clemens made time for the pleasurable duty of family occasions. On 27 November 1885 he interrupted a business trip to New York to return to Hartford for Livy's fortieth birthday celebration. Three days later his own fiftieth birthday was given a special splendor by tributes in the *Critic* from Oliver Wendell Holmes, Charles Dudley Warner, and others. In thanking Holmes, Clemens noted that his poem had "drawn the sting of my fiftieth year; taken away the pain of it, the grief of it, the somehow *shame* of it" (*MTB*, p. 829), but such distress was probably more conventional than real. For at fifty, Mark Twain was comforted by an affectionate family and by an awareness of his own accomplishments as an established author, eminent publisher, and innovative capitalist. As author he was pleased, despite some rankling criticism, with his performance in *Huckleberry Finn* and, as time allowed, was moving in a new direction toward *A Connecticut Yankee*. As publisher he basked in acclaim for his dramatic deathbed rescue of Grant from insolvency, achieved with profit for himself and the promise of future lucrative ventures for his publishing company. And as backer of the Paige typesetter he felt himself on the verge of a success that would dwarf all of the others. Clemens might well have wished to pause at such a pinnacle of maturity and achievement, for as Charles Dudley Warner observed in his *Critic* birthday greeting: "You may think it an easy thing to be fifty years old, but you will find it's not so easy to stay there" (*MTB*, p. 287).

Notebook 25 is identical to Notebooks 22 and 24 in design and format. It now contains 180 pages. The last thirty-seven pages and two others are blank, while two leaves have been torn out and are missing. Like most of the notebooks of this period, Notebook 25 has deteriorated from age and use. The front cover is almost detached and the leather on the spine is cracked and worn.

Except for some entries in grayish blue ink or black pencil and the last five pages in black pencil, it is inscribed in the purple pencil which Clemens began using in Notebook 23. A few of the purple entries are heavily boxed in black pencil. Use marks in black pencil, probably Paine's, appear throughout but have not been reproduced.

Draper 19 E 47.[1]
Send Memoirs to
F. E. Griffith,⎫
Billings & ⎬ D. L. & W.
A. Reasoner ⎭ Hoboken.
Collins, RR Station, Hartford

All the Am Ex in Europe was soaked with Bissell as security in '84.

115 E 23^{d}
Mrs T M Wheeler[2]

Henry A. Taylor
3 or 5 Wall st.[3] [#]

---

[1] William Henry Draper was a prominent physician and professor of clinical medicine at the College of Physicians and Surgeons of New York. This reference list of memoranda and addresses, many repeated from previous notebooks, appears on the back of the front flyleaf and the first page of the notebook. With the exception of the third and fourth entries, the list seems to have been inscribed on a single occasion.

[2] Mrs. Candace Wheeler, a close family friend associated with Louis C. Tiffany & Company, had advised the Clemenses on the renovation of their Hartford home in 1881. In the last week of August 1885, Clemens and his wife visited Thomas and Candace Wheeler at Mount Onteora in the Catskills near Tannersville, New York. The Wheelers returned the visit in early October.

[3] Henry A. Coit Taylor, New York financier, whose office was at 3 Wall Street. Taylor

R. G. Brooks, 80 B'way.

⟨Webster, % Brown Shipley & Co.⟩[4]

Also 109 W 126th.

Stedman, 45 E. 30th.

Dean Sage,[5] 939 St. Mark's ave. & 142 Pearl st out of Wall.

Col. W. N. Woodruff, P.O. Box 1020.[6]

⟨Gerhardt, Mt. Vernon, N. Y.⟩

Howells, 302 Beacon.

East India House 56 Summer[7]

No. 603 S. D. Co.[8]

Century, $33.50 per page.[9]

Old China, Parke, 186 Front. [#]

---

and Clemens may have conferred in early September about Jesse Grant's projected Turkish railroad (see p. 202, note 59). Only Taylor's address appears to be in Clemens' hand.

[4] Charles L. Webster had left for England on 1 August 1885 to arrange European publication of the Grant *Memoirs*. Brown, Shipley & Company was a merchant banking firm with offices in London, Liverpool, and several United States cities.

[5] Clemens and Livy spent the night of 24 August 1885 at the Albany home of Dean Sage, the lumber executive who sometimes acted as Clemens' broker. The following day Sage and his wife accompanied the Clemenses to Mount Onteora to visit Candace Wheeler.

[6] William N. Woodruff, a Hartford machinist and contractor, was managing the successful sale of reproductions of Karl Gerhardt's portrait bust of General Grant. In July 1885, at Gerhardt's instigation, Woodruff also undertook to initiate a subscription fund for a life-size statue of Grant to be placed in the Capitol in Washington. Woodruff's plan was to solicit nominal contributions totaling $26,400 from each of the 5,280 past commanders of the Grand Army of the Republic. Despite early enthusiasm, this subscription, opposed by Grant's widow, was not realized and Gerhardt apparently ceased to pursue the commission in 1887.

[7] A Boston dry-goods establishment from which, according to an 1885 bill, Livy had recently purchased "2½ yds Pink Arab cotton."

[8] Clemens' box number at the Connecticut Trust and Safe Deposit Company in Hartford.

[9] Mark Twain's next contribution to the *Century* magazine would be his "Private History of a Campaign That Failed" in December 1885.

Gustav Stachert, German books, B'way bet 8 & 9$^{th.}$

[A]

Paige reminds me (Aug. 20) that the $3000 I sent him the other day was $1000 too much. Does he mean that I have paid ⟨$1[5]ooo⟩$16000? My impression was that I had with that paid but $13000   *Correct.*

See Mr. Geo. P. Rowell⟨'s⟩ & Co's directory reports 13,494 newspapers in the U. S or one for every 3,716 inhabs.[10] 25 yrs ago, in 1860, only 5,253 papers—one to every 6,000 of population. The business trebles in 30 yrs at this rate; which means that in the next ten years, the number of papers will increase to 20,000. or ⟨27,000⟩25,000.

Where let by ems, machine must get ⟨12^c⟩10^c per 1000 for setting.

Per year or less $3 per day ⟨—or⟩ straight ahead—or ⟨$1085⟩$1095 per year.

For the first 200 machines, no rent will be charged for the first ⟨60⟩ 30 or 60 days if we can't furnish skilled labor.

? What am I to get for introducing the telegraphic machine? Apparently I was to have half, for I was going to give J. R. G. 10 or 20 p^c of my interest to introduce it for me.[11]

If B & O income is $50,000 a day (the other has reached 5 times that) we could reduce the expense ⅓. Rent the machines on a ⟨daily⟩ yearly royalty equivalent to the cost of the mach? Or, a tenth of the cost & *they* make the mach—provided they ⟨either⟩ pay on 5000 whether they use them or not.

None but 30,000-ems-a-day papers need or can afford the machine. —& then ⟨only⟩ all in one-size type. [#]

---

[10] Clemens borrowed his statistics from the preface to *George P. Rowell & Company's American Newspaper Directory*, 17th annual volume (New York: George P. Rowell & Co., 1885), page iv.

[11] No record now exists of Jesse R. Grant's involvement with the printing telegraph machine invented by James W. Paige.

All that use 30,000 in one type can set it in 8 or 10 hours, & pay operator $1.75 & justifer ⟨$1.2⟩ $1.25 & mach. $3 a day. Total, $6. The same, done by ⟨[-]⟩ 6 men, would cost at least $9.

100 compositors require 100 lights.
15 machines will do their work with 30 lights.

If the first require but 50 lights, the latter will require but 15.

Offices that now use 3 Morse's can do with 1 Paige. That is the basis to estimate upon.

No use in the small intermediate offices where only one Morse is used

⟨Gov. Fuller—could he put that tel on the market?⟩ [12]

Cipher it down to me, if possible, how a station which employs but one mach can better afford to have it than the Morse?

Send Mrs. T. M. Wheeler, Tannersville, Greene Co N.Y a letter of Cable's. [13]

I felt as embarrassed as Lazarus when he had to get up before folks in such an outfit.

Have a youth practice on
tion ⎫
in ⎪
im ⎬ & other combinations till he can set them without thinking.
and ⎪
the ⎭ [#]

---

[12] Clemens never seriously approached Frank Fuller about Paige's telegraphic device. On 28 September, perhaps in reference to this invention, he advised Fuller to "run up here & stop over night & let me tell you how I think you can make a considerable stack of money," but despite Fuller's immediate interest he failed to furnish further details. Finally, on 11 November he informed Fuller: "I dropped that scheme I wrote you about. . . . I was afraid it would hamper & delay a scheme of mine of 4 years' standing [the Paige typesetter] which absorbs all my love, & interest, & spare time" (Berg).

[13] While visiting Candace Wheeler in late August, Clemens must have entertained with anecdotes about George Washington Cable's often irritating behavior during the lecture tour of 1884/1885. He probably intended to send one of Cable's letters as evidence of the idiosyncrasies he had described.

Let this begin his apprenticeship, & not go on the alphabet till
he has got this *pat.* Then the Alphabet backward & forward.

a good authority in the publishing business.

Mr. R S, who has built up the C to its present dizzy height of
prosperity, ⟨said to me⟩ ⟨sho⟩ ought surely to know good terms
from poor ones; & he said to me shortly after the contract was
signed, "I am glad on GG's account that there was somebody with
pluck enough to ⟨pay⟩ give such a ⟨price[.]⟩ figure[;] I
⟨would⟩should ⟨not have liked to venture it."⟩ have been
⟨[wary]⟩chary of venturing it myself."[14]

I saw he liked the offer; he said he supposed it was enough.

One would have supposed, from the tears of grief & shame shed
⟨in some⟩by some ⟨tender-hearted⟩ some newspaper correspondents
at that time that in persuading ⟨him⟩ the ⟨robbed &⟩ ⟨abused⟩
⟨hero of the war⟩ plundered & impoverished old war-chief
⟨standard-bearer⟩flag-bearer of the vanished ⟨[- -sts]⟩⟨[chil]⟩⟨hosts⟩
children of victory to burn a contract which ⟨promised⟩promised
him a pittance & a publisher a fortune, I had[15]

that in persuading the plundered & impoverished old soldier—⟨the
only hero in the world's history who had never been whipped⟩ to

⟨I was guilty of⟩ I had done a mean & disgraceful act. [#]

---

[14] Mark Twain may have been revising an extensive Autobiographical Dictation of
May 1885 which included information about the Grant *Memoirs* noted here and in the
following entries (see *MTA*, 1:26–57). The dictation contains a more elaborate version
of Roswell Smith's testimonial, but despite Mark Twain's claim that "I've got Smith's
exact language (from my notebook)" (*MTA*, 1:54), this is the only record of the comment
in the extant notebooks. Furthermore, Clemens evidently misremembered Roswell
Smith's remarks here. In a statement of 6 July 1885 prepared for the editor of the Boston
Herald, Clemens had admitted: "My offer was duplicated by *several* 'regular publishers,'
the Century among the number; & two firms *exceeded* my offer. But none of them could
exceed my *facilities* for publishing a subscription book—nor equal them either . . . &
that is why I got the book."

[15] The complex evolution of this passage, almost certainly involving intervention by
Albert Bigelow Paine, is described at length in Details of Inscription entries for 182.12
through 183.1–2.

If I had the tears, now, that were shed by the holy crocodile that edits the Boston Ad.

I perceived that this 10 pc contract would give the publisher two or three dols to G. G.'s one. I had known him a long time, & could speak with a measure of freedom; but if I had known him for but a day, I would still have ventured to show him ⟨wherein⟩ that the only hero in ⟨40 centuries who ha⟩ the world's history who had never been whipped in war was on the verge of being whipped ⟨in⟩and badly whipped in a humbler sphere of activity. I committed that crime without a qualm of conscience, & have never had one since.

I suggested that examination myself. It was not in G G's nature to be willing to pry into people's private business affairs—least of all for his own protection.

N. B. Thousands of people have lately been induced to subscribe for bogus biogs of G G under the false pretence that they were the genuine Memoirs or "companions" to the Genuine Memoirs. I offer them the hint that they are not obliged to make good those subscriptions, unless they choose to do it.[16]

If I may be allowed one more ⟨com[---]⟩ word, by & by, I shall desire to mention those fraudulent publishers by name, & characterize them.

Some of the fraudulent pubs have been ⟨very⟩ movingly pathetic, in their circulars, over the hard fate of our gen^l agents in being bonded to sell more books than they could by any possibility sell, & ⟨must⟩ would therefore become bankrupt & go to the poorhouse for our benefit. Let these tears cease to flow; let these breaking

---

[16] Throughout the writing and promotion of the Grant *Memoirs*, Clemens was exasperated by persistent rumors that Grant was not their true author, by allegations that there was not enough matter for the promised two volumes, and by the efforts of other publishers, including the American Publishing Company, to capture the market with rival biographies. This entry and the three that follow were drafted in late August in reply to a circular signed "Appomattox"—actually the Historical Publishing Company of Philadelphia—which offered eleven reasons why the *Memoirs* were not attractive to canvassers and general agents and would not be welcomed by the public.

hearts cease to suffer & be healed: those poor bondsmen were bonded to sell 204,000 sets of the book; they have already sold 250,000. Each of them can buy a poorhouse if he wants to.

G G told me before he went to McGregor, that ⟨he had⟩the two volumes were *more* than complete, ⟨now,⟩ at that date, because he had written more than we could get into the second one. I said we would find a way to get it all in; ⟨if ordinary book-backs wouldn't stand the strain, I would try boiler iron—issue an edition of iron-clads.⟩ & we did. That matter is all in; & both vols are larger than our original advertisements promised they should be.

One thing we have constantly had to fight was reports that the Gen had not written matter enough to complete the 2^d vol.

10 p c.

⟨This was a perfectly fair & honorable offer, for it was based upon a possible sale of 25,000 sets. But I was not figuring on 25,000, I was figuring on a possible 300,000. Each of us could be mistaken, but I believed I was right.⟩

Great fear that ⟨the pub of⟩ G G's ⟨book⟩family will not get large enough share—so they illogically ⟨discourage⟩encourage the people to fly to *their* book, which pays G G nothing *at all*

Jean killing the unjust ant.[17]

Jean requests me to tell a story to be based upon a kind of business copartnership between a "bawgunstrickter & a burglar."[18] [#]

---

[17] In 1906, Clemens attributed this act to Clara in a canceled passage of the unpublished "Family Sketch":

In my turn I admonished the children not to hurt animals; also to protect weak animals from stronger ones. . . . When Clara was small—small enough to wear a shoe the size of a cowslip—she suddenly brought this shoe down with determined energy, one day, dragged it rearward with an emphatic rake, then stooped down to examine results. We inquired, & she explained—
"The naughty big ant was trying to kill the little one!"
Neither of them survived the generous interference.

[18] In his Autobiographical Dictation of 8 February 1906, Clemens recalled his service as a "romancer to the children" expected to produce "absolutely original and fresh" stories, "hot from the bat":

Sometimes the children furnished me simply a character or two, or a dozen, and required me to start out at once on that slim basis and deliver those characters up to

Oct 7, 11 a. m., Wednes. Morning Club, Pittsfield, ⟨Caroline⟩ Pingree, Secy.[19]

Courtlandt Palmer—I have tried—have not succeeded to my liking, & have given it up. Therefore shall have to be excused; & will make no ⟨pr⟩more promises nor half promises.[20]

Patents

Patenting In Canada can *wait*, for one year.

In England, $100 patents the thing for 4 years. Don't have to work the patent there.

In France, you have 2 *years* in which to begin work.

In Belgium don't have to work the patent till within *one year* after it has been worked abroad.

In Germany, you have 3 *years* in which to begin to work.

In Austria, *one year* in which to begin work.

So there is no hurry *any*where. You merely take out all these patents at once (except Canada,) & go to working them by & by, in from 1 to 3 years.

Sept. 8, '85 sent to Bissell & Co for collection, Chatto's notes:
⟨[d]⟩Due Feb. 27 '86—£300 paid Mch 25 ($145[8]
"   Mch "   300   "   Apl 10, $145[6].54
"   Apl "   368.10.5. [#]

---

a vigorous and entertaining life of crime. If they heard of a new trade, or an unfamiliar animal, or anything like that, I was pretty sure to have to deal with those things in the next romance. Once Clara required me to build a sudden tale out of a plumber and a "bawgunstrictor," and I had to do it. (*North American Review*, 19 October 1906, p. 710)

[19] On page 196 of this notebook Mark Twain planned his travel arrangements for a Pittsfield, Massachusetts, appearance at the Wednesday Morning Club, a young women's literary society. Mark Twain had agreed in March 1885 to give this October reading (see p. 99).

[20] Courtlandt Palmer was president of the Nineteenth Century Club. Clemens had made some notes for a speech to the club (see p. 162, note 121), but on 23 September 1885, soon after this entry was made, he declined to appear. He continued to resist Palmer's importunings through the fall and winter of 1885, noting "Distinctly *no* sir!" on the envelope of one request and issuing a definitive "Nein!" in a letter to Palmer on 20 January 1886.

Now that our houses are become so elaborate, there ought to be a professional tinker under wages of a whole street—visit daily & repair all.[21]

Could not a full line of creatures be made of paper pulp cast in moulds, for the use of city schools & families whose members can't go insect-&-snake-hunting to get their own specimens for study?

The costly sets could be accurately colored by hand, the cheap ones left plain.

Bodies, legs, antennæ, &c could in some cases be made separate & the pupil could put them together.

Might some be made of celluloid?

On the humorous essay for Nineteenth Century Club I have "nearly 9 months" from June 27. Can choose my own date, I believe.[22]

If it will set, in good average hands, 3000 an hour, we agree to take so many (for 1 – to 5 yrs) at $3.
If ⟨[$]⟩ 3,500,—$4.
If 4,000   —5
Price of $3 m is $10,000
     "   "   4 " "   15,000
     "   "   5 " "   20,000

2 cnts a 1000 for power.

Composition by operator will in each case be 10 cents per 1000. Justifier 8 cents per 1000. Leading costs 0. About 10^c per 1000 for machine. [#]

---

[21] In "Wanted—A Universal Tinker," an open letter to the *Century* magazine (December 1885, p. 318) signed "X.Y.Z.," Mark Twain proposed the creation of this home-maintenance post at a cost of three dollars a month to "each of forty or fifty house-holders along a street or in a neighborhood." For a "trifle of wages" and a "trifle of material" subscribers would gain "rest and peace" after "years of fretting and harass-ment." In early January 1886, the *Century* forwarded to Clemens a circular from a Universal Tinker Company of Kansas City, which had begun operation in response to his letter.

[22] Repenting momentarily of his recent decision not to address the Nineteenth Century Club (see note 20), Clemens recalled Courtlandt Palmer's promise of 27 June: "You see you have nearly nine months (if necessary) ahead of you as any time next winter will avail."

If we can engage the first 300 or 500 for New York, Brooklyn, Boston, Philada, Balto & Wash (refusing to take any ⟨other⟩ other orders till these are filled) we can have a year or two in which to decide about prices, because we can let these at 10 c per 1000, & ⟨co⟩send a man every month to collect.

Ask Mr. Childs if he wants to go on paying ⟨40 or⟩ 46 while his neighbors pay only 30.[23]

Spin a wonderful yarn (detective?) of a man with a scent like a hunting-dog.[24]

Order of Procedure to followed Thursday, Sept. 17:

1. Get lay-out of $\frac{2}{5}$ for Gt. Britain; consideration, I pay all foreign pat costs & ⟨[-]⟩give H $\frac{1}{10}$ out of mine. Maybe get the same lay-out for other foreign countries, I to pay all expenses of raising the cap.

1.a. Pay other $2000.

2. Take out all the patents immediately.

3. Remove the m. to Trow's in N. Y. Get him to put on a nimble young fellow. Throw the m open to the public.[25]

4. Get 500 contracted for.Atlantic cities at 10 c per 1000 ⟨fo⟩ ems for the m.

5. Sell $\frac{4}{10}$ of the property for the necessary cap. Sell half of this to N. Y. newspapers & printers like Harper, & the other half to N. Y. *non*-printers (& Elmira.)

6. Do you want to sell $\frac{2}{10}$? ⟨[-]⟩Can I have what I can get⟨,⟩ over $100,000?

7. Get the number of "union" members in the several Atlantic cities, & the prices paid per M.

---

[23] George W. Childs, a close friend to Grant, was the proprietor of the Philadelphia *Public Ledger* and a potential customer for the Paige typesetter. The figures here, like those in previous entries, refer to the cost per thousand ems of printed matter.

[24] This entry appears alone on a page, interrupting the following sequence of typesetter notes at 188.29 after "*distributing*," in the manuscript notebook. Mark Twain also recorded ideas for such a story in Notebook 26 (p. 235) and in Notebook 41, kept in 1897. Around 1899 he wrote the fragmentary "A Human Bloodhound" (*HH&T*, pp. 67–68) and in 1902 he published *A Double-Barrelled Detective Story* (New York and London: Harper & Brothers), both of which deal with this unusual gift of scent.

[25] John Fowler Trow, printer, bookseller, and publisher, best known for the famous directories of New York which he published for many years. Mark Twain evidently hoped to demonstrate the Paige typesetting machine at Trow's New York printshop.

⟨7⟩8. Get cost of plant;
      size & cost of buildings;
      superintendent⟨s⟩;
      foremen;
      number of men needed.
      Wages of all these.

9. Then get cap enough to build 200 m before any income begins to come in.

10. Propose Web for Pres; Bunce for Treas, & Woodruff for Supt.[26]

11. And that Pratt & Whitney make foreign plant at a lower cost.

12. Get number of men employed in each big N. Y. daily office, & each paper's weekly composition bills.

13. *Mem.* After Mr. Trow, the first papers that order will be the first served, & the first who can drop composition at once to 30 cents & be a year or so ahead of the rest.

14. Repairs must be paid for, & malicious damage; ⟨& loss of time where paying us per M.⟩ ⟨& $600 a year if not used(?)⟩ (take away mach if not fairly used). $1,500 each must be paid for destroyed M (malicious.

15. We insure all M's agst fire.

(Mem. The Concord RR pays 10 p c & sells at 212 & can't ever declare a higher div, by its charter. T. S. will pay 100 to 150 ⟨e⟩in 5 years—possibly sooner.)

Bissell acknowledged receipt of Chatto's 3 notes Sept. 9, '85.

16. How much will the steel for a mach cost?
(a. *All mach can be estimated at 10 h. per day, for the printer who sets 7½ h on the Sun, puts in 2½ h more, distributing.*
                                  b.

17. (2[d] year) Takers must sign a contract to pay $1000 for one year (quarterly); pay all repairs, & pay $1500 down if the m be injured beyond repair during said year.

c. The m will not diminish the number of printers, but increase composition & make it much lighter work for both body & mind.

---

[26] Charles L. Webster, Edward M. Bunce, William N. Woodruff (see p. 179, note 6).

d. A 12-page Sunday Tribune contains only 180,000 ems of *reading* matter. So there must be more than as many more in daily new advertisements & discarded matter.

18. Ask Mr. Trow to exhibit the m (*rent it?*) & take $100,000 stock, in place of 24 mach.

E. No injury *can* befall the m except it be done *purposely.* Awkwardness can't break or ⟨cripple it⟩ injure it.

Sieh da! Wir werden nur EIN ⟨ZEHT⟩ZEHNTEN der Besitzung Herr P. verkaufen. Es ⟨ist⟩ wäre ganz und gar nöthigt dass wir in Eigen Händen ⟨de⟩die Mehrzahl der Actien-Theilen aufbewahren sollen. Ausser wir sie zu eiginen Freunden ⟨[be]-⟩ verkaufen: z. B., Charley, John Arnot, Bunce, Whitmore, Robinson, Gen. Magee, Mrs. Grant, Webster, Alex & Green, McCook.[27]

Arrived about June 22, '85 at the farm: 6 in our party. Left for home Sept. 15. Ich habe ein jeder ⟨Deiner⟩Diener und Dienerin (vier) Zehn Thaler⟨.⟩, ⟨bez⟩ gegeben. I ⟨have⟩habe um Fleisch und Brot und Bett ⟨Sieben⟩ Fünf Hundert und 50 Thaler bezahlt.[28] ($550.)

Lass uns Whitmore an die Telegraphiren Gesellschaften schicken.[29]

Auch kann er reise mit mir[30] & make contracts with the newspaper men. [#]

---

[27] *Look here! We will sell Mr. P[aige] only a tenth of the ownership. It would be completely necessary that we keep the majority of the shares in our own hands. Except we sell to a few friends.* Among the friends not recently identified were: Charles J. Langdon; John Arnot, Jr., an Elmira banker; Franklin G. Whitmore, Clemens' business agent in Hartford, who in 1886 would supervise construction of the Paige typesetter at the Pratt & Whitney works; Henry C. Robinson, a lawyer and former mayor of Hartford; George J. Magee, former paymaster general of New York State, who was in the coal and railroad businesses in the Elmira area; Alexander & Green, the New York City law firm which represented Charles L. Webster & Company; the Reverend John James McCook, rector of Saint John's Church in East Hartford and professor of Latin in Trinity College.

[28] *I gave each servant and maid (four) ten dollars. I paid ⟨seven⟩ five hundred and 50 dollars for meat and bread and bed.* These were Clemens' Quarry Farm expenses for the summer of 1885.

[29] *Let us send Whitmore to the telegraph companies.*

[30] *Also he can go with me.*

19. ⟨Is⟩Are those old Engineering Co buildings for sale?

a. Or that abandoned brick factory down somewhere on the Consolidated road?

b. Which W. shall we have for President? The capacity of *one* we already know. Can try & prove that of the other on the telegraph.[31]

20. Put W^h on a salary of --- per week & let him go to getting up type statistics.

21. Sit down & cipher with Wh.

22. Turn over to Howells mein funf tausend Thaler Theil in der alten Farnham Gesellschaft. Dies ist $\frac{1}{40}$ Theil des alten Gesellschaft, und wird in ⟨fun[g]⟩funf Jahren $50,000 werth werden.[32]

23. Whi= has long been a director of the Conn fire Co[33] & built their new building, superintending the work personally. He ought to make a good Pres, & would take care of our interests.

24. Get $100,000 taken in ⟨H⟩Elmira to vote with us.

25. Wollt er nicht mir ein Drittel oder ein ⟨Half⟩Halb der Englischen ⟨or⟩oder Fremden Actien-Theilen geben? Dann werden wir nur vier-zehnten dort verkaufen, und so Herrschaft behalten, wie in Amerika.[34]

26. Ask Bunce & Robinson as to W^h's capability?

----

[31] The men referred to here are Charles L. Webster and Franklin G. Whitmore, probably in that order.

[32] Turn over to Howells *my five thousand dollar share in the old Farnham Company* [the Hartford typesetter company which originally sponsored Paige's machine; Clemens first invested in it in 1881]. *This is $\frac{1}{40}$ share of the old company, & will be worth $50,000 in five years.* In 1881 Clemens had agreed to pay Howells $5,000 for collaboration on *Mark Twain's Library of Humor.* In mid-October 1885, when Howells was forced to withdraw from the desultory project because of a contract to write exclusively for Harper & Brothers, he proposed that Clemens pay him $2,000, in addition to $500 previously advanced, for work already done. Clemens immediately agreed, but asked to postpone payment until 1 January 1886 since until he began to receive proceeds from the Grant *Memoirs* "every dollar is as valuable to me as it could be to a famishing tramp" (*MTHL,* p. 539). Although Clemens claimed that he had long had the $5,000 secretly invested for Howells (SLC to Howells, 7 December 1885, *MTHL,* p. 543), this entry suggests that he considered a stock transfer only as a means of paying Howells in full without paying him in cash. Clemens did not attempt to implement this scheme, instead paying Howells $2,000 on 2 December 1885.

[33] The Connecticut Fire Insurance Company of Hartford.

[34] *Wouldn't he give me a third or a half of the English or foreign shares? Then we will sell only four-tenths there, and so keep control, as in America.*

27. Don't mention the *m* to W^h until the telegraph is wholly disposed of ⟨[o]⟩& out of the way.

28. ⟨Let⟩Lassen wir Charley V. Präsidenten machen, auf dass der P. kann mit mir nach England reisen und die Englische Gesellschafft stiften.[35]

29. Wir können eben so wohl ein ganzen zehnten verkaufen wenn wir es unter eignen Freunden theilen.[36]

30. Ich werde W^h $\frac{1}{10}$ von meine Theil der Telegraphe geben und ein Sold von − − − Thaler monatlich datzu.[37]

31. Keep the justifier back 15 years & then introduce it & thus give the mach another 17-year lease of life?

32. The price must be ⟨$15,000⟩$12,000 each, *now*.

Mr. Hall.[38] Keep reiterating the fact that the book issues Dec. 1.

$7\frac{1}{2}$ h setting, & $2\frac{1}{2}$ h distributing, is 10 work. The printer sets & distributes 5,500 & gets $2.53 for it. If he can set 40,000 on the m in 10 h, he should get $6\frac{1}{4}$^c per M, or $2.50 for 10 h work, & the justifier $5\frac{1}{2}$ per M or $2.20 for 10 h work. (No, better be $7\frac{1}{4}$ & $6\frac{1}{2}$?)

This is $4.70 for 40,000 . . . . .4.70
Machine 4.50
Power 50
                                                                              $9.70

As against $18.40 by hand at case.

We *may possibly* be able to charge $4 a day, but not $4.50.

If we can charge $4, we can let each m go for nothing the first 3 months & charge $1000 for the rest of the year.

To Printers.

You will make as much as you did before.

---

[35] *Let us make Charley V. [Vice] President, so that the President can go to England with me and establish the English company.* Probably Charles L. Webster who was already a candidate for president of the proposed company.

[36] *We can just as well sell a whole tenth, if we divide it among our own friends.*

[37] *I will give Whitmore* $\frac{1}{10}$ *of my share of the telegraph and in addition a monthly salary of* − − − *dollars.*

[38] Frederick J. Hall acted as head of Charles L. Webster & Company while Webster was in England contracting for European publication of the Grant *Memoirs*.

You can sit at your work.

Perfectly cleanly. Your work can be done in a drawing room.

There will more & bigger papers, & more men required.

Printers are peculiarly well instructed men. They all know the history of the great labor saving & speed-enhancing inventions, & they know that no hostility in the world can stop such a machine from coming into use, or even notably delay it.

⟨A man⟩

A person should always have a hobby. Observe how a sweetheart fills every waking moment to the brim & makes life a jubilation. Observe the miser & the successful stock speculator ⟨&⟩ & projector of vast money-making industries of various. ⟨T⟩Observe the student in a specialty—in bees, ants, bugs, fossils—*any* specialty that is absorbing. But the hobby must not be, the *result*—no, only the pleasure of working *for* the result, & the final triumph of *accomplishing it.*

At 40,000 in 10 hours:

Setter	per M	....	$6\frac{1}{4}$
Justifier	" "	....	$5\frac{1}{2}$
Machine	" "	....	$11\frac{1}{4}$
Power	" "	....	$1\frac{1}{4}$
⟨P⟩Total per M		....	$24\frac{1}{4}$

July 24—Depos in Mt. Morris bank $3,000.

Total........................ 15,000.

71 Broadway

Conductor 119.

⟨2_⟩24 min to 12 m.

Let me aboard, then pushed the children back. & tried to hold me back from following them.

33^{d} st station

G P Lathrop[39]

78 E 55th [#]

---

[39] George Parsons Lathrop had organized the April 1885 Authors' Reading for the American Copyright League in which Mark Twain had participated. Clemens was now

Go to Stedman for a sub. to type setter.

See Jno Russell Young[40]

912 Garrison ave St.L.[41]

Last resort, Col. Will Willimantic Barrows[42]

Mr Clemens to Pay all expences for patenting the Typesetter in foreign countries and for maintaining the same. He is also to pay all expences ⟨all⟩ directly, and indirectly connected with the introduction and sales of ⟨m⟩ such machines in said foreign countries during the life of said patents, and is to receive ⟨[th]⟩ in full payment therefor one half of the net profits accruing from the use or sales of said machines

James W. Paige.

Hartford, Sept. 19 '85[43]

Nelson
P. i. Mungo Park
   Ireland. [#]

---

probably trying to make Lathrop, literary editor of the New York *Sun,* a proponent of the Paige typesetter.

[40] A prominent journalist and diplomat, Young was currently on the editorial staff of the New York *Herald.* The Paige typesetter was undoubtedly a topic of discussion at a dinner the Clemenses gave for Young at Hartford soon after this entry was made. The two men surely also discussed the Grant *Memoirs* since Young had been a personal friend of Grant's and was the author of *Around the World with General Grant* (1879).

[41] The address of General William T. Sherman. In September 1885 Clemens and Sherman were corresponding about possible publication of Sherman's European travel notes of 1871–1872. In early October, Sherman agreed with Clemens that they did not merit publication.

[42] Colonel William E. Barrows was the former president of the Willimantic Linen Company of Willimantic, Connecticut. Clemens did not approach him for a typesetter investment at this time, for it wasn't until 1887 that Barrows learned of the machine. On 21 September of that year he wrote Clemens that "a mutual friend . . . told me that you were building a type setting machine on which you had expended three or four hundred thousand dollars" and "that these expenses had used up your spare cash." Barrows was moved to help Clemens out of this financial "embarrassment" by passing along an opportunity for involvement with a perpetual motion machine.

[43] The Clemens family had just returned to Hartford from Quarry Farm after a stop-over of several days in New York City. With the exception of the dateline, added by Clemens, this draft of a typesetter agreement is in Paige's hand. Clemens did not tear the tab from the leaf on which it appears—although he consistently removed the tabs from surrounding leaves—probably to facilitate subsequent reference to it.

Without justifier the tariff shall be 10ᶜ per M.

With justifier, 25 c per M., & throw *in* the leading machine, & ⟨sell⟩ rent that with this machine alone.

The machine offered will only be the former, & we will ⟨b[an]⟩ offer ⟨only⟩ subscriptions for only 5 or 6 in the Sun, & others in proportion.

Sun—⟨6⟩ . . . . 6.
Herald 12
Tribune 10
Times 10
World 12
Eve Post 10
3 others 10
⟨1⟩ Brooklyn Eagle 10

4 Boston 20
4 Philada 20
3 Baltimore 15

Cincin—2 or 3 25
Chicago 30
N.O. 2 20

⟨These will pay $17.50 per ⟨M⟩ machine per day at 25ᶜ per M.—$3,500 per day for [200] machines.⟩ ⟨2,000 machines will yield $12,000,000 a year.⟩ 2,000 would pay $5,000,000 a year.

Renters must pay $1500 each for destroyed machines—& we will agree to replace them as fast as possible after every destruction.

The M that can earn ⟨$6,000⟩ $2,500 a year cannot be sold at less than ⟨$60,000⟩$25,000.

At 4000 per hour, the setters wage would be 6½ c per M.

Machine . . . . ⟨2[6]⟩24
Power . . . . ⟨2½⟩
                                                                                    ———
                                                                                    30

This *with* automatic justifier. (Nothing allowed for power & oil.

That would be $8.40 per 10 h for the M. That ⟨is⟩ ⟨just⟩ is $2,500 a year *rent* for the m—about.

2000 M would yield $5,000,000 a year⟨.⟩—if they were all in NY—but they *won't* be.

John Hay[44]
Stedman
Howells
Warner.

Bram Stoker's yarn about the Irish christening.[45]

Lafayette Yseult.

Paige go with me to newspaper⁀men & attend to the details of making contracts for work at so much per M. per mach.

Power costs 5 dollars a month for 10 mach. Oil costs ⟨$1.50⟩ $15 a month for 10 mach.

E ⟨V⟩O Eve Orion

Rev. Madison Square Mallory & the Philada man want stock in the type-setter.[46]

Telephone Reform League.

Sept. 20 or 21, paid $1000 on the $7,000 contract, (in advance,)

---

[44] In Notebook 24 (p. 160), Clemens had reminded himself to ask Hay "to write the first notices" of the *Personal Memoirs of U. S. Grant.* He may have considered making similar requests of Edmund C. Stedman, William Dean Howells, and Charles Dudley Warner.

[45] The basis of Mark Twain's "Christening Yarn" (DV 7), a "*long* anecdote with a smart surprise at the end" which Paine titled and dated "90s." The story is about a minister whose bombastic predictions of masculine glory are deflated when he learns that the infant to be christened is a girl. A version of this anecdote is printed in the 1910 edition of *Mark Twain's Speeches* (pp. 149–150).

[46] The Reverend George S. Mallory, an Episcopal clergyman and formerly one of the owners of New York's Madison Square Theatre, the "home of the 'Sunday-school drama'" (George C. D. Odell, *Annals of the New York Stage*, 15 vols. [New York: Columbia University Press, 1927–1949], 12:222). In 1882, George S. Mallory and his brother Marshall had been briefly interested in the play that became *Colonel Sellers as a Scientist* (see *MTHL*, pp. 411–412).

for these payments do not begin till Oct. 1, 1885. They close March 1, 1886, or will then be assumed by the new Co.

Next payment (if in advance) is due along about Nov. 20.

(6th, no doubt)
Guest of W[m] R Plunkett, Pittsfield, for the reading is the 7th at 11 am.[47]

Leave Hartford at 5.55. by the Hartford & New Haven
Leave Springfld at 9
reach Pittsfld at 11.09 by Boston & Albany.

⟨L. Spr. at 4 p. m & get to Pitts at 6.15.
(L. Hartford at 2.24. get to Spring at 3.02. p.m.⟩ *Won't do.*

The *proof* that 5000 an hour can be done on the M is that 1000 is the average by hand.

Any machine on which an average of 35,000 in 10 hours for 50 consecutive working days has been done—they shall not pay us any rental for that first 50 days.
Or shall we charge nothing for the 1st month & apply the test on the 2[d]?

Rental. We to have 66 per cent of the amount *saved* ⟨per⟩ on each 1000 over the cost of the 1000 a year ago. If the 1000 costs you 10 cents now, we take 66 per cent of 36 cents & leave you 34 per cent of ⟨it⟩ the 36 cents.

No type-setter to be removed from the town it is hired for

Oct. 3, '85. I think I've struck a good idea. It is to ⟨make⟩ reduce a series of big maps to mere photographic fly-specks & sell them together with a microscope of ¼ to 1 inch focal distance. By this means I could conveniently examine my ⟨cynchromatic⟩synchromatic map which is 36 ft long.[48] [#]

---

[47] William R. Plunkett was a leading citizen and public official of Pittsfield, Massachusetts. Clemens was to appear at the Wednesday Morning Club there on 7 October 1885.

[48] Clemens may have hit upon this idea while drawing the maps that appeared in the December 1885 *Century* magazine as part of "The Private History of a Campaign That

5.60

4.60

⟨T⟩Operators *guess* at many words.

Two men can hold situations on the same machine. One may work from 10 am to 5.45; the other from 5.45 to 2.30 a. m. This cannot be done at the case. Two men could never agree about the distributing.

At ⟨42⟩46 cents, the man ⟨[woul]⟩ who can set 10,000 (1500 an hour) in 7½ h, makes $4.60 & works 2½ h more at distributing, for which he gets nothing. (10 *h work*).

At 12c the man who could set 6,000 an hour would make $5.60 —& work *only* 7½ *hours*, instead of 10.

Collect telegrams with errors in them.

Must require that papers shall pay to operator not more than *one-fourth* ⟨& one-twelfth⟩ & a fraction what they ⟨are⟩ have been paying the compositor the best part of the year before the introduction of the machines.

So the Sun (now 46) would pay 11½ & 1 cent—that is, 12½. We get 18^c

The Hartford Times & Post (now 30) would pay 7½. We get 12½ The Courant (now 35) ⟨8¾.⟩8½. We get about 15^c

Papers that now pay 40 must not pay over ⟨10.⟩ 12.[49]

Clara, St Stephens
11th st.

⟨C⟩Eckhardt's
Main st.[50] [#]

Failed." The "synchromatic map" was evidently the large map of the Mississippi River which at one point Clemens had planned to use in *Life on the Mississippi* (see *N&J2*, pp. 455–456).

[49] Written at the top of an otherwise blank page. Presumably Clemens left space for further notes but never returned to add them.

[50] J. H. Eckhardt & Company, a Hartford "Fine Art Store," dealt in artists' materials, offered framing and restoration services, and advertised a gallery "constantly filled with rare and choice Oil Paintings, Etchings, Engravings, Colored Photographs" (*Geer's*[1886], p. 225).

See Ross Winans.[51]

1   2
Call—dinner 6.

3
Drive at 4.
======
4 Hawley & Warner.[52]
    (or Twichell)
======
5 Go to club & order it.

Union Lines tel.

Go to Fox & get the mahogany towel rack & dining room door done this week.[53]

Go to Mrs. Perkins.

Take Twichell on the way.

What is a printer paid for waiting? In Wash^n, 40 c (20 per cent of 1000)

The above shows that the average man *averages* 1000 per hour. So we must see that he makes *present* wages per hour.

This makes ⟨12⟩ 11½ (not 12⟨½⟩) cents per M fair in N.Y.

That is, at 4000 per hour, he makes ⟨48^c⟩46^c. The *fast* man, at 5,000, makes ⟨60⟩ 57½ [#]

---

[51] Ross Revillon Winans was the grandson of Ross Winans, the prominent railroad mechanic and inventor who had died in 1877. Clemens visited him in Baltimore on 1 December 1885 to discuss the Paige typesetter. On 8 December Winans wrote Clemens that he had decided against investing in the machine because "the conservative path which I have always laid out for myself in monetary matters excludes all investments of such a nature."

[52] United States senator Joseph R. Hawley and Charles Dudley Warner were partners in the Hartford *Courant*. Clemens was apparently arranging a dinner meeting at the Hartford Club, a private men's club of which Hawley was president, to discuss the *Courant's* possible interest in the Paige typesetter.

[53] Fox, Brusselars & Company, a Hartford home furnishings and interior decoration firm which had previously done work for the Clemenses in March 1885.

$7\frac{1}{2}$ & is fair for him where 30^c is now the price. He makes 30.

P. S. He makes ⟨36⟩35.

⟨9⟩ $8\frac{3}{4}$ is right, where wages are now 35.

Sun	12	
Trib	18	
Times	15	
World	20	
Herald	25	
Post	10	100
Harper	25	
⟨Trow	15⟩	
Eagle	18	
Little[54]	25	
Several others	32	
	200	

Agree to *sell* no more in New York (to be *used* there.)
And rent only to be used in the town rented for.

The man who *owns* makes his own terms with his operator; but the lessee doesn't.

Orion—heaven-scraping exaltations, followed by ⟨hell⟩ ⟨depressions⟩ depressions which sunk his spirit⟨s⟩ to the lowest hell.[55]

All other M depend on gravitation—fall from a height by its own weight to its place.

Or, where positive ⟨action⟩ mechanical action is used to move the type into position, only one type can be moved at a time, & *it* has to be turned from flatways to edgeways.

No other machine distributes directly into the case without human manipulation. & ⟨none⟩ no other distributes into the case in proper position for setting.

---

[54] J. J. Little & Company, printers for Charles L. Webster & Company.

[55] The extant letters from Orion Clemens for this period do not indicate any particular instance of this characteristic alternation of mood.

No other m provides for broken or breakable type or foreign matter.

No other m tests the strength of the type.

No other is used which does not make pi w^h has to be distrib by hand.

No other m regulates the amount of matter to be distrib into the case.

No other m automatically distrib & justifies.

(There *is* a m wh automatically justifies, but it does not auto^y distrib.)

⟨All the m we know of are limited in the number of different characters they can handle.⟩

This is the only m ⟨who⟩ using type with so small a nick as to not weaken the type.

A list of all the patents (with description) foreign & domestic, issued since the first one in March 1822, can be seen at this office.

We have an automatic nicking-machine which we will furnish to type founders. They say they will nick the type free of charge.

Economy of room, gas, rent, &c

Mach occupies about the space of a single stand—a trifle longer but not so wide.

10 ft 3 in long.

29 in wide.—⟨4[0]⟩41 call it to oil it.

Space to stand in, 9 ft widthways & 15 lengthways, which allows plenty floor space.

3 abreast in 30 ft room 45 feet long accommodates 9 mach.

A room 36 wide & & 45 ft long amply accommodates 12 machines.

12 gas burners.

And will set the same amount of type that 60 compositors at 60 stands would ⟨(for each has 2 sets of cases on his stand.⟩

A stand wants about 9 ft length by 6 or 7 width of floor space.

Double stand, back to back, wants 9½ ft floor space. Room ⟨150⟩

75 ft long, with double stands down both sides & imposing stones in the middle, should be about ⟨30⟩40 or 45 ft wide.

	41	15 ft
	⟨[-]⟩	8 between
		23
Width of room		12
Space for 8 standing back to back		35
15 feet endwise—second row 15		

2
———
30   So the room is 30 × 35 ft & contains 16 machines.

A compositor & single set ⟨oc⟩of cases occupy 12¼ square. The machine occupies 24—just double.

Pic His. Once on the Rapidan when North & South were ⟨ca[p]⟩camped on opposite sides of the Rapidan. In the early evening the Yanks began to sing Yankee Doodle; the Rebs broke in with "Dixie;" soon the sweet tones of a ⟨[h]⟩cornet ⟨p[la]⟩ clove the discords with Home Sweet Home" & ⟨then⟩ immediately the two armies burst out & sang it together.[56]

Eustace Conway
⟨⟨[16]⟩18⟩ 18 Exchange PLACE[57]

Col Grant.[58] [#]

---

[56] A further episode for inclusion in the collection of "Picturesque Incidents in History & Tradition" which Mark Twain began planning in the preceding notebook (p. 167).

[57] The eldest son of Moncure Conway was at this time practicing law in New York City. Moncure Conway and his daughter Mildred visited the Clemenses on 14 October, at which time Clemens probably noted this address.

[58] On 29 September Frederick J. Hall had informed Clemens that Colonel Frederick Grant "contemplated writing the life of his father, taking it up where the Autobiography left off, and carrying it down to the time of his death. He said that he had talked with other publishers in regard to this book and that they were very anxious to get it, but that he felt that he would prefer to talk with you before making any arrangement." Clemens chose to leave the direct negotiations to Charles L. Webster, however. When Grant's demands exceeded a generous offer, Webster advised Clemens to "let him go, its no fun publishing a book for nothing when we can get plenty for something" (CLW to SLC, 29 October 1885). Frederick Grant's proposed biography was never published.

⟨Se⟩ See Jesse Grant[59]

Mrs. Wheeler

Dr. Roosa in Beziehung auf meinem Daumen und mein Ohr[60]—sharp 9. AM

The Gerhardt note.[61]

Edition de luxe.[62]

Gen. Sherman[63]

Orion send me that boy that sets 1200 an hour.[64]

1st—Enders, ⟨[c]⟩ about O'Neil.[65] [#]

---

[59] For several months Jesse R. Grant had been providing Clemens with information about a projected enterprise: the construction of a railroad from Constantinople to the Persian Gulf. Ignoring a warning from Webster and the negative opinion of his lawyers, Clemens made $5,000 available to Grant in September 1885 through the formation of a dummy firm, the Wolfe Contracting Company. In early October, Grant used these funds to finance an investigatory journey. He only got as far as London before he was forced to return "simply because of the elections in England and the revolutions in Turkey which must terminate ere I could do anything." He claimed, however, that he had "made very satisfactory arrangements in London as to our business," and asked for a meeting with Clemens "in the near future" for "I have so much to tell you" (Grant to SLC, 13 October 1885). Although by 21 October Clemens had received Grant's report cordially, there is no record of his further interest in the venture.

[60] This phrase reads: *Dr. Roosa about my thumb and my ear.* Daniel Bennett St. John Roosa, president of the New York Post Graduate Medical School, was an important medical educator and innovator and an eye and ear specialist.

[61] On 5 October 1885, Clemens instructed Frederick J. Hall to have a note for $1000 due to Karl Gerhardt endorsed to Charles L. Webster & Company and then placed "to my private credit." This note was from Goodwin Brothers, the Elmwood, Connecticut, firm which manufactured Gerhardt's bust of Grant. In Notebook 24 (p. 146) Clemens noted a thousand dollar indebtedness to the same firm.

[62] An edition of the *Personal Memoirs of U. S. Grant* which was to have specimen manuscript pages bound into each volume. It was never published.

[63] Mark Twain was communicating with William T. Sherman about a projected volume of travel writings (see p. 193, note 41).

[64] During this period Orion Clemens was making himself useful to his brother by gathering statistics of the work speed of newspaper compositors. On 28 September 1885 he had reported that compositors in the Keokuk area "average about 1000 [ems] an hour for 7½ hours. One, a boy, in the [Keokuk] Democrat office, sets 1200 an hour and keeps it up."

[65] Thomas O. Enders was president of the United States Bank in Hartford. Clemens

2^{d}. Safety Depos & see what those say as to European ownership in setter.

3. Then, if necess & tell P the report from Cornell.[66]

Boot—letter in pocket

[key] Robinson

Shave

Flynn—⟨cases⟩Case's 2^{d} ⟨gardiner⟩gardener[67]

Dated Tuesday Oct 27th 3 nos come due Jan. ⟨F⟩Jam. 29$^{\mathrm{th.}}$
Paper dated ⟨25⟩24 Oct. come due, 27th ⟨March⟩ February.
Telegraph S. G. Dunham 66 State st[68] if we can take care of these dates.
Also, do we want any to come due in 5 months.
                                        (March)
Get the notes ⟨signed &⟩ made out to the order of S. L. Clemens & endorsed by S. L. Clemens.
Send them to S. G. Dunham 66 State street by registered letter, & he will return the proceeds by registerd letter to Webster.
Make 4 pieces of $5000, & call the rest $10,000.

⟨⟨[3]⟩[1]⟩ of the 5000 to come due, one in Jan, ⟨⟨one⟩ 2 in

---

apparently sought Enders' opinion of John O'Neil who was about to become the Clemens family gardener (see p. 206).

[66] Clemens refers to a negative estimate of the potential for Paige's telegraphic invention by Alonzo B. Cornell. He had known of Cornell's opinion since May 1885, but evidently had not informed Paige (see p. 144, note 58).

[67] Clemens was considering candidates for the gardener's position at the Hartford house, in this instance an employee of Newton Case, president of the Case, Lockwood & Brainard Company, Hartford printers and bookmakers, and a Farmington Avenue neighbor.

[68] Samuel G. Dunham, a director and the treasurer of the Dunham Hosiery Company of Hartford, was a friend of the Clemens family. The notes referred to here and below in Clemens' instructions to Webster were for loans totaling $100,000 to cover publishing expenses of the Grant *Memoirs*. On 22 October 1885, Clemens cautioned Webster: "I am making myself personally liable; therefore I desire that the books, both finished & unfinished, be kept insured *fully*—I mean, get all the insurance you can on them" (*MTBus*, p. 334).

Feb & *can* make one in March if you choose⟩ & the rest as you
please—but better make them Feb to save interest.

All the $10,000 notes can come due in Feb ⟨or [-]⟩ or Jan.—put
some in March if you choose. Don't put too much of it in Jan (too
early for the firm of Wbestr)

If this paper ought to be *dated* in New York, destroy these notes
& substitute others.

This paper is to be dated 3 months, 4 months, & if necessary 5
mos (some of it). Paper dated 4 mos must be dated back to Oct
24; (⟨o⟩to avoid Sundays.)

$20,000 or $30,000 can go 5 months if you choose.—

The paper must be made payable at one New York ⟨band⟩bank.

S. ⟨[-].⟩ G. Dunham will remit the proceeds of these notes to
W Wednesday.[69]

Oct. 26, '85. Up to date, 320,000 sets of General Grant's book
have been subscribed for—that is to say, 640,000 single volumes.

Oct. ⟨26⟩21. '85 Borrowed $100,000; $15,000 payable 29th
⟨the⟩ January, $85,000 payable 27th Feb. interest 6 per cent. Sent
the notes to S. G. Dunham by the office boy, per 4.30 train

Got 12 more presses to work; this makes 20, that are going night
& day; if we could get 37, we could print a complete volume every
second; but it is impossible to get them.

We have got 7 binderies at work—all large ones. One of them
turns out 1500 volumes per day in sheep, by hand. This one
occupies 3 large floors, & works upon nothing but this book. The
building was rented, the machinery bought new, & the hands
brought from Philadelphia,—all for this book. We are being well
scolded by other publishers, for they have to send their printing
and binding to other cities.[70] [#]

---

[69] That is, 28 October 1885. On 29 October, Webster informed Clemens: "We have
recd the proceeds from the notes all right."

[70] Clemens did not exaggerate the arrangements required to meet the booming sales
of the Grant *Memoirs*. On 24 October Webster had reported: "If you could see the *piles*

The letter written to General ⟨Ba⟩Grant by Gen. Badeau last spring, & the General's pulverizing reply, are still in existence; I have read them; & it is within the possibilities that they will creep into print some day, unless Badeau learns some wisdom. It will be a sorry day for him when General Grant's letter sees the light.[71]

Oct. 26. Saw Salvini in Othello. His was a grand performance, but his support was wretchedly poor. They might as well *all* have talked Italian—or Sanscrit, for that matter—nobody could understand what they said.[72] [#]

---

of stock at the printers and binders and see the hundreds of men boys and girls at work upon it . . . what you would see would astonish you. . . . I have telegraphed for paper in large quantities and am using the set of plates that I had made for Canada while another set is being made for them. . . . I shall *drain* this city of printers & binders. All the other publishers are howling about me they are obliged to send their Christmas books out of town to get them bound."

[71] The subject of this acrimonious exchange of letters was the extent of Adam Badeau's contribution to the *Personal Memoirs of U. S. Grant* and the remuneration he expected. In a letter of 2 May 1885, Badeau had appealed to Grant, his old friend and patron, to renegotiate the private agreement by which he was to receive "$10,000 out of the profits if they should amount to $30,000" as payment for his labors. He pleaded "the immense sale assured, the unexpected work put upon me, the unanticipated damage done to my life's labor [his well-regarded but unprofitable *Military History of U. S. Grant*]," and the destruction of "what I have spent my life building up—my reputation as your historian." Claiming responsibility for transforming Grant's "disjointed fragments" into a "connected narrative" and asserting that "if you cannot yourself finish the work, nobody can do it fitly but me," Badeau asked for "$1,000 a month, to be paid in advance, until the work is done, and afterward ten per cent of the entire profits." On 5 May, Grant replied, recalling his own vital contributions to Badeau's *Military History* and denying that the *Memoirs* were disjointed. He noted that Badeau was "petulant, your anger is easily aroused, and you are overbearing, even to me," and questioned Badeau's disposition to work if paid in advance. Grant then rejected Badeau's demands, concluding that it was "impossible for us to be associated in a work which is to bear my name. It would be a degradation for me to accept honors and profit from the work of another man, while declaring to the public that it was the product of my own brain and hand." Although Grant promised that "this correspondence between us may be unknown to the world if you choose," his family made it public through the New York *Herald* on 17 March 1888 after Badeau took legal action to collect the $10,000 originally promised him. On 30 October 1888 the dispute was settled out of court and Badeau received payment after withdrawing "offensive allegations of joint authorship" and agreeing "to limit his claim to that of suggestion, revision, and verification" (New York *Tribune*, 31 October 1888). Webster was also familiar with these letters in 1885, for on 29 October he wrote to Clemens: "If the Badeau letters come out at the right time it will boom our book. We can take a back seat & see the fun go on and seem to have nothing to do with it."

[72] Clemens expressed the general opinion of this production of *Othello* staged at the

5 Exp Hamlets.[73]

Animals for Jean

Call on Col. Grant.

Col. Crabbe.[74]

Oct. 28. Wrote Webster to see what a barrack for the soldiers who guard Gen. Grants tomb would cost; & proposed that I would contribute $500 toward that instead of the Monument.

Monday Oct. 26. '85 John O'Neil came to work—$50 per month & find himself.[75]

Make an article composed of Carlyle's whines & complaints. "⟨[O],⟩It is my nerves, my nerves!" Had the belly-ache all his life. George Elliott's ditto[76] [#]

Metropolitan Opera House in New York on 26 October 1885. The acclaimed tragedian Tommaso Salvini delivered his lines in Italian to an English-speaking cast which the New York *Herald* of 27 October called "a rather weak support for a star in any language, apparently engaged to resist rather than support him."

[73] The Clemenses were planning one of their theatrical entertainments and evidently considered a version of *Hamlet* expurgated for children. In mid-December 1885, Clemens indicated an alternative selection in a letter instructing Charles L. Webster to "Please send your boy in to Samuel French's next door to you on the corner of University Place, & buy 8 acting Macbeths—pamphlets—& mail to me" (*MTBus*, p. 344). Nevertheless, when the family did put on a play it was not Shakespeare, but rather a performance of *The Prince and the Pauper*, presented on 13 January 1886 before an audience that included William Dean Howells and many of their Hartford friends.

[74] The officer in charge of the guard at Grant's tomb in Riverside Park in New York City. On 20 October 1885, the New York *Times* reported:

> The soldiers on guard at Gen. Grant's tomb were promised some time ago a wooden barracks to shelter them from the cold, damp winds that blow strongly at night on the heights. Plans and specifications were made and were accepted by the Park Commissioners and by the War Department, and each asked the other to go ahead and build. The officials of the War Department imagined that the Park Commissioners would defray the expenses and the latter seemed to be under the impression that the War Department would foot up the bill. Meanwhile the soldiers catch cold at night and sneeze and cough during the day.

[75] Clemens' new gardener, who was to serve the family for many years.

[76] Clemens owned James A. Froude's *Thomas Carlyle: A History of the First Forty Years of His Life, 1795–1835*, 4 vols. (New York: Charles Scribner's Sons, 1882), as well as his *Thomas Carlyle: A History of His Life in London, 1834–1881*, 2 vols. (London,

62 men on Tribune composition, Sep 5/84

⟨In N. Y.

Send special messenger to Mr. Beecher & get my Auto MS.⟩[77]

Write A. Reasoner.[78]

Louvet's "Chevalier de Faublas."[79]

See Shirt man.

Hall take down in sht-hand?
How many had been bound July 1?

1884), both of which include numerous descriptions of Carlyle's mental and physical states. Livy had recently been reading John W. Cross's *George Eliot's Life as Related in Her Letters and Journals*, 3 vols. (New York: Harper & Brothers, 1885) and was annoyed by "constant mentions of ill health" (OLC Diary, 7 June 1885). There is no further record of the article Clemens proposed to write.

[77] On 8 September 1885, Henry Ward Beecher had written Clemens asking to see "the Grant autobiography, so far as published" as an aid in preparing a eulogy of Grant which he was to deliver in Boston on 22 October. Beecher also asked Clemens to include any "special ideas suggested by Grant, in your dealings, or observation" and expressed particular interest in stories of Grant's "intemperate habits." Clemens replied at length on 11 September, explaining that he was unable to send the *Memoirs* because the printers and binders had been ordered to deny all access to the manuscript. He did, however, confirm Grant's early drinking problem, provided details of the writing of the *Memoirs*, and enclosed "some scraps from my Autobiography—scraps about Gen. Grant—they may be of some trifle of use, & they may not." These scraps were part of the Grant matter Clemens had dictated in the spring and summer of 1885 (see *MTA*, 1:11–70). By late October he had become uneasy at Beecher's delay in returning the autobiographical materials. Clemens lightly canceled this notebook entry, evidently after prompting Beecher by messenger or letter, for on 9 November 1885 Beecher wrote admonishing him to "Sit down & be silent! You speak after the manner of the foolish—I *do* know where the MSS are—they are safe—and will soon be on their way home. Were it not for these wanton aspersions on my habits—I should say how much they helped me—& how much I am obliged for your generous pains to aid me—but you have forfeited these sentiments —until I hear that you wash with ashes & sit in sackcloth."

[78] The Delaware, Lackawanna & Western Railroad official who usually arranged for the Clemens family's special car to Elmira each summer. The Clemenses made a shopping and business trip to New York City in late October and may have wished unusual accommodations since Livy "had the cholera morbus lately" (SLC to Annie Webster, 28 October 1885, *MTBus*, p. 336).

[79] *Les amours du chevalier de Faublas* (1787–1790), a celebrated erotic novel by the French revolutionary and politician, Jean Baptiste Louvet de Couvrai.

Of what styles?

2. July 7? ⟨88⟩8? &c

You said you had got the biggest bindery in N.Y & told me he could do 10 or 12000 a week. I warned you *then*, before you went to Europe, that this w^d take 7 mos to bind the *bonded* books.

How many are bound now? Give me exact figure—not loose guesses.

You will find there are not 150,000.

If you had *known* every week, what the week's binding had been, instead of merely guessing, you would have been hunting binderies long *before* the 15^h October.

Saturday you reported orders for 298,000—exactly the same report made to me 30 days ago.

The truth is, you don't know but by loose guesses, the condition of your business.

Mr. Hall must give me a statement of books *bound, every day*. If there isn't time, so much the worse for the next man's business, for I will have mine attended to.

You could never find time to give me a weekly report, & here is the hellish result—asleep over a volcano⟨e⟩.

You will not get to printing vol 2 before Jan 1. At your present rate it will take you 8 months to bind it.

I ordered 6 sets of plates—and think I remember your taking the responsibility on yourself of disobeying it.

If the papers give us a black eye we don't want to be 50,000 behind orders—they'll be countermanded. I know more about that than you do.

I will dictate a daily (weekly) report & see how long it takes. (for Hall.)

How many presses?

37 Bullocks?

Then they can do the 300,000 in a single day of 24 hours.
1 Bullock can do it in 40 days.
2 Adams in 40.
Your printers have been using 1 press, & that not all the time.

These 300,000 should all have been ready Sept 1, using a single
bullock press

Lot of presses?—You only needed 1.

I undertook the most gigantic publishing enterprise, & here you
are calmly & undistressedly *proposing* to make a gigantic failure of
it. I *don't*—& *won't.*

The ⟨24ᵗʰ⟩20ᵗʰ July a book was bound. People will have a full
right to laugh when you tell them that with a big printer
pretending to be at work, ⟨[i]⟩sheets for less than 200,000 were
ready 3½ months later, ⟨Oct⟩Nov. 14
There was no occasion to be *short.* We should be ⟨ad⟩ahead. At
the time of the funeral I gave orders to keep 25,000 ahead of orders
all the time—& here we are 150,000 be*hind* orders. It is ridiculous,
& totally unnecessary & inexcusable—from my point of view.
Extenuate it—no doubt you can.
Tell me exactly ⟨wha⟩ how many orders now⟨;⟩, still unfinished;
2. How many of these under contract?
3. Take the remainder, add 30,000 to it, & make contracts
requiring their production Nov. 29.
It will cost heavily? Of course it will. Let it cost. It *shall* be
done, at any cost.
You & Whitford have been asleep.

Has a written understanding been arrived at as regards the
emoluments of ⟨[N]⟩the N.Y. General Agency?

Hat man eine Scriftbar Einverständness in Beziehung auf die
Gelteinnehmen der New Yorker Gemein-Geschäfft bekommen?[80]

You expect a shortage of only 50,000. At what date? Dec. 15? [#]

---

[80] Clemens here translated his preceding question to Webster into German.

We will issue Dec. 15. It will not be safe or well to issue Dec. 1.[81]

We want 200,000 made in 30 days. Apportion them & get to work—make stringent contracts.

Make 6 more sets of plates if necessary.

Make 30-day contracts for engravings, too—of course *they* are behindhand.

We must have 50,000 per week made—25,000 in N. Y., & 25,000 in Boston & Phila.

Ditto engravings.

How many sets of brass binders' plates have we got?
Make some more—night & day.

One printer & binder should take the contracts on 2ᵈ vol, & be responsible under penalties to furnish 50,000 complete copies a week.

Better go to Boston, first, perhaps, on account of proximity of paper.

Thousands of these books have been ordered as Xmas presents & may be thrown back on our hands.

A fine triumph for die Hundertjahr Leute,[82] if we make a botch.

Plates not yet gone to Canada, & only 2 weeks to spare—it is simply hellish apprentice-work. You are unsuited to a job of this size.

Try Brooklyn & Jersey City & Paterson & all big near towns.

This necessity is brought on us by damned carelessness & stupidity.

Ask the President if he will not give me a note to the govt. printer. [#]

---

[81] Despite Clemens' misgivings the first volume of the Grant *Memoirs* was issued on 1 December 1885.

[82] Clemens' attempt at *die Jahrhundert Leute: the Century people.*

Get 100 etching plates made & several sets of book plates.

All on the Wilderness from the Rapidan to the James to come back in galleys

Insertions to be made in *corrected* galleys, & then printed a*gain* in galleys.

Nov. 18. '85. There was an understanding with Gen. Grant, in Col. Fred's presence, that *we* should run the N. Y. Genl. Agency instead of appointing a Genl Agent, & that we should take 80 per cent of a Genl Agent's commission, & give the Genl the other 20%. But this have never yet been *signed*, though written out & sent to Mrs. Grant by Col. Fred some time ago. Yesterday—no, I believe it was day before yesterday—Webster asked Col. Fred about it in my presence in our office, & Col. Fred said he believed he had mislaid that paper somewhere, & added, "But you needn't be uneasy about it; mother understands it & I understand it, & know that that agreement was made; & that it isn't signed is only an accident. Mother was perfectly ready to sign it; & you are safe, because it will be carried out, whether it is ever signed or not."

That was entirely satisfactory to me, & also to Webster, & we said so.

Nov. 19. Called on ⟨the⟩ President Cleveland at the White House, by appointment, with Johnson of the Century Magazine & Geo Walton Green, Chief of the Authors' League. By little & little I wandered into a speech—having got speedily warmed up by the first remark or two made on international copyright—which remark or two I made myself without intending to say anything further. Then there was a 4-cornered talk of an hour. The President showed great interest in our subject & will do it as good a turn as he can in his Message. I ventured to urge him to make I.C. the child of his administration, & nurse it & raise it.[83] [#]

---

[83] On 3 November 1885, George Walton Green, a New York lawyer and secretary of the American Copyright League, had written asking Clemens to "give your associates on the Exec. Comit^e much encouragement" by attending the league's annual meeting on 7 November. Clemens noted "Got a cold" on the envelope of Green's letter and did

Send full morrocco to Sherman & Sheridan, with their names printed in gilt on them. General W. T. Sherman ⟨Lieut⟩ Lieut. Gen. P.H. Sheridan.

R. L. Blakeman
Rennselaer Polytechnic Institue—Troy.[84]

Go to Mrs. Wheeler & hurry those curtains to Mrs. Brooks.[85]

Get up a burlesque symposium on some silly question

That story for boys—The Strongest Man in the World.[86]

⟨Offer to renters of 200, for 5^c p M is it don't justify, & 10^c if it does.⟩

No, 15 if it does, & 10 if it doesn't.

Whoever ⟨s⟩takes $5000 stock can rent a M at 7^c per M. Others pay ⟨15^c.⟩ more than double that.

A country paper can pay ⌐ompos 5^c & then he earns in 7 hours within 15 cents of what he used to at 35^c. The "C" could hire at 15^c, pay 5 to operator, & save 15.

City paper must probably pay 8^c to compos.

Get Susy a Shaksp^{re} [#]

---

not attend. On 17 November, however, while in New York on business, he wrote Livy that his return home would be delayed by this trip to Washington to "talk international copyright to the President. One must not refuse an office of that kind, when asked—a man who prides himself on his citizenship *can't* refuse it. . . . In the circumstances, you will not object, & so I don't need to holler for pardon." In late January 1886, Clemens returned to Washington to appear before a Senate committee on copyright.

[84] In a letter of 22 September 1885, Blakeman had pedantically criticized Clemens' playfully literal retranslation of "The Jumping Frog" from French to English (*Mark Twain's Sketches, New and Old* [Hartford: American Publishing Co., 1875]). Although Clemens characterized Blakeman as a "Singular ass" on the envelope of the letter, he evidently took pleasure in encouraging him, corresponding briefly with him about the French language and receiving foolishly inflated replies on 29 September and 14 November 1885.

[85] Candace Wheeler specialized in the design of tapestries and fabrics for Louis C. Tiffany & Company. Clemens performed this errand for Mrs. H. G. Brooks on 23 November 1885 while in New York City on business.

[86] Clemens had previously noted his intention of writing such a story in 1880 (see *N&J2*, p. 379).

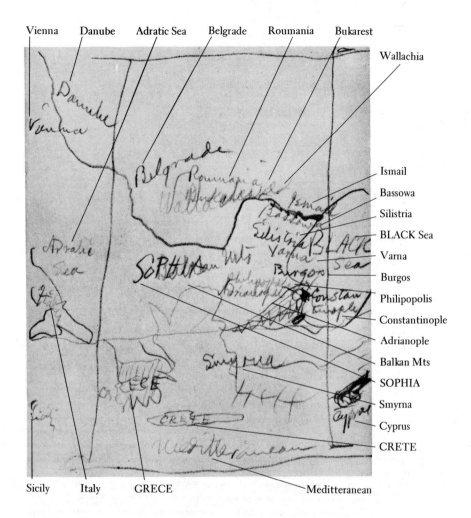

Vienna Danube Adratic Sea Belgrade Roumania Bukarest

Wallachia

Ismail

Bassowa

Silistria

BLACK Sea

Varna

Burgos

Philipopolis

Constantinople

Adrianople

Balkan Mts

SOPHIA

Smyrna

Cyprus

CRETE

Sicily Italy GRECE Meditteranean

[*Clemens' source for this map has not been determined. He evidently drew or copied it as an aid in following complex political developments in the Balkan area in 1885–1886 which for a time threatened to touch off a general conflict. In September 1885 a bloodless revolution in Eastern Rumelia, an autonomous province of the Turkish Empire, had reunited it with Bulgaria, from which it had been separated by the Congress of Berlin of 1878. In the middle of November 1885, shortly before Clemens made this entry, Serbia, which also claimed Eastern Rumelia, declared war on Bulgaria. Serbia was defeated, and the eventual settlement, achieved in 1886, involved Turkey's tacit surrender of Eastern Rumelia to Bulgaria.*]

Copy the OWH letter for mother.[87]

Buy several copies of OWH poem.

Give that MS back to Laffan.[88]

Have the press books all been sent out?

About that index.

Each Mach will pay a rent of over $1500⟨.⟩, at 15

Until 2000 are in use, there will be no price but 15 for city or country—& maybe *never* any other price.

Write President George Williamson Smith[89]

To Lyceum Courses.

A minister with 16 sexual indiscretions proved against him, ⟨is willing⟩ is wishes to lecture. Stereopticon views. Terms $600 per night. Address ⟨Rev.⟩ W. B. W. S office[90]

Go to Century & read that proof again[91] [#]

---

[87] On 1 December 1885, Oliver Wendell Holmes wrote Clemens that he was "so glad you and your family are pleased" with the "little verses"—"To Mark Twain (*On His Fiftieth Birthday*)"—which had appeared in the *Critic* of 28 November, along with other tributes. Although "I had twenty three letters spread out for answer," Holmes reported, "I stopped my correspondence . . . until the lines were done. So glad they pleased you!" Clemens was presented with the original of this poem which, he told Holmes, raised "me up to remote and shining heights" in the eyes of "the wife and children" and "has drawn the sting of my fiftieth year" (*MTB*, pp. 828–829).

[88] An unidentified manuscript evidently submitted to Charles L. Webster & Company through Clemens' friend William M. Laffan, publisher of the New York *Sun*. This work may have been a preliminary version of an elaborate art catalog Laffan was to offer to Charles L. Webster & Company (see p. 273, note 157).

[89] A clergyman and, since 1883, president of Trinity College in Hartford, Smith was a member of the Monday Evening Club.

[90] Possibly a sly allusion to the scandal that reached a climax in the first half of 1875 when Henry Ward Beecher was sued by Theodore Tilton for alienating the affections of his wife. Rumors of Beecher's adultery with Elizabeth Tilton had circulated for years and were not entirely laid to rest by his acquittal. Clemens may have been moved to make this note by an annoying recent letter from Beecher (see p. 207, note 77).

[91] The *Century* magazine for December 1885 included two contributions by Mark Twain, "The Private History of a Campaign That Failed," and the open letter, "Wanted —A Universal Tinker," attributed to "X.Y.Z."

Scribner & Welford—Gulliver,—*not* cloth.

Write Gen Longstreet? Gainesville, Ga.[92]

An Italian in Spain—Putnam's Sons.[93]

Rennet Hotel, Balto.[94]

Jos. Casey
788 3rd Ave
N. Y. City

I left my stuff to my friend Howells & he betrayed my confidence.

W ⟨H⟩D. H.

At first I was aghast at taking up so much space; but after reflection I perceived the justice of Mr. H's judgment, ⟨& became reconciled⟩ —as far as it went; & ⟨then⟩ so was reconciled; & not only reconciled but presently began to feel annoyed that he had

---

[92] Former Confederate general James Longstreet was a West Point cadet at the same time as Ulysses S. Grant and served with him during the Mexican War. After the Civil War, Longstreet became a Republican and a political supporter of Grant, who appointed him surveyor of customs of the port of New Orleans. Longstreet had published an article in the *Century* magazine's "Battles and Leaders of the Civil War" series in July 1885 and would contribute others in 1886 and 1887. Clemens may have offered him the opportunity to expand his articles into a book for Charles L. Webster & Company. Between 1886 and 1888 the firm published works by or about Generals George B. McClellan, Philip H. Sheridan, Samuel W. Crawford, and Winfield Scott Hancock.

[93] Probably *Spain and the Spaniards* by Edmondo de Amicis (trans. Wilhelmina W. Cady [New York: G. P. Putnam's Sons, 1885]). The Langdon family gave this "book which I more wanted than any other book that could be named" to Clemens for Christmas 1885 (SLC to Jervis, Julia, and Ida Langdon, 28 December 1885).

[94] Clemens was planning a trip to Baltimore with William M. Laffan, publisher of the New York *Sun*, to see the recently developed Mergenthaler Linotype. The trip was originally scheduled for the first week of January 1886, but after a postponement by Laffan the two men were evidently unable to agree on an alternative date. Laffan finally inspected the machine alone and on 25 January informed Clemens that "I saw the Baltimore machine set type . . . I incline to the belief that every daily in [New York] will be set up by that machine inside of twelve months. The *Tribune* will have 12 of them ready by Feby 15th and I have applied and have secured 2[d] place on the list. This is confidential; but you'd better haul in your lente and festina like hell." On 26 April 1886, after the *Tribune* Linotypes had proved slow in arriving, Clemens noted on the envelope of Laffan's letter: "O lame & ineffectual prophet. About 2½ months are sped, & none of those machines are visible yet,—& I, unaffrighted, am still at work building my (Paige) type-setter."

not been intelligent enough to put in some more of me. However, let it go—it is no matter. M. T.[95]

Give Webster Col. Woodruff's account.

Wouldn't fight the knight with a lance, "but I will just try him a whirl with a hay-fork—& I bet I'll show him that I warn't brought up on a ⟨Conneci[t]⟩Conneticut farm for nothing"

(Bring out as a holiday book.
Title, "The Lost Land."

First part written on ancient yellow parchment, (palimpsest) the last chapter on fresh new paper, laid, hand-made, with watermark, British arms & "1885." In palimpsest one catches remnants of monkish legends. ⟨[¶] [T]h⟩Get them from W^m of Huntingdon.[96]

He mourns his lost land—has come to England & revisited it, but it is all changed & become old, so old!—& it was so fresh & new, so virgin before. Winchester does not resemble Camelot, & the Round Table (has at least seen a life-size picture of the one there in James I's time (See State Trials)[97] is not a true one. Has lost all interest in life—is found dead next morning—suicide

He is also grieving to see his sweetheart, so suddenly lost to him. Maledisant? But not Isolde. Elaine? No, she is dead. He saw her arrive.

Valentino. Ch. Scribner Sons.[98] [#]

---

[95] The notes in this entry record the formula Howells and Clemens agreed upon in early December 1885 as humorous explanation of Clemens' extensive representation in *Mark Twain's Library of Humor* (see *MTHL*, pp. 541–544). Although neither epigraph was used when the much-delayed volume was finally published (New York: Charles L. Webster & Co., 1888), their facetious spirit was preserved in the introduction and in Mark Twain's "Compiler's Apology." This entry is in grayish blue ink and is written over the preceding penciled address, which was apparently entered at random in an unknown hand.

[96] Clemens owned a copy of Thomas Forester's translation of *The Chronicle of Henry of Huntingdon* (London: Henry G. Bohn, 1853).

[97] *Cobbett's Complete Collection of State Trials*, compiled by Thomas Bayly Howell and Thomas Jones Howell, 33 vols. (London: R. Bagshaw, etc., 1809–1826).

[98] *Valentino: An Historical Romance of the Sixteenth Century in Italy*, by William Waldorf Astor, was published by Charles Scribner's Sons in 1885. This was the first of several literary works by the millionaire son of John Jacob Astor.

Start printing office—diagram of a "case." Arthur.

Country placed under an interdict.

Why not let him arrive just as the dumb boatman arrives with Elaine's body?

Miss Frame
    232 W 22^d

Dec. 11. '85. Howells says: "I'm reading Grant's book with a delight I've failed to find in novels." And again:
"I think he is one of the most natural—that is, *best*—writers I ever read. The book merits its enormous success, simply as literature."

Mrs. A. W. Fairbanks
    506 Willson ave
        Send 2^d vol.

Twichell

House—care
    Jno A. Pitman
    Club Cha[mb]ers
        Hong Kong

Send Mrs Laffan's book—½ mor.[99]

The German Verb-Drill. D. Appleton & Co[100]

Fanny C. Hesse[101]
    ⟨Smith College⟩ Hatfield House
        Northampton
            Mass.
2^d vol. cloth. [#]

---

[99] On 21 December, Clemens repeated his order for a complimentary copy of the Grant *Memoirs* for Mrs. William M. Laffan. "If the first vol has been sent . . . it has miscarried," he wrote Webster. "A cloth copy will answer, if you are short of ½ morocco" (*MTBus*, p. 347).

[100] This book by Adolphe Drey was published in 1885.

[101] Fanny C. Hesse was Charles Dudley Warner's sister-in-law. In the 1870s she had served as Clemens' secretary.

Prime ⟨E⟩38 E 23[102]

Give the order again for Gen. Magee's book—I misdirected it.

Aber die Frau Generalin sterben mochte—dann konn' man Mühe mit die Erben habe.[103]

"The First Napoleon" by John Ropes.[104]

Add negotiable paper.

⟨Sen⟩Explain that clause about proportions of expense. Give illustration.

Send word to Alexander.[105]

Why did canvass stop, Oct. 15? The Elmira one has not stopped —why others? [#]

---

[102] The New York address of the "gushing pietist," William C. Prime, who "was always under the influence of religion. Seldom actually drunk with holiness but always on the verge of it, always dizzy, boozy, twaddlesome" (*MTE*, p. 349). Clemens had attacked Prime's idealized *Tent Life in the Holy Land* (New York: Harper & Brothers, 1865) in chapter 48 of *The Innocents Abroad*. In late 1885 and early 1886, Prime was representing General George B. McClellan's widow in negotiations for rights to *McClellan's Own Story*, published in 1887 by Charles L. Webster & Company.

The subject of the drawing that precedes this entry, and the possible relationship of the drawing to any notebook entry, are unknown. A faint curved line within the drawing may be an arrow to indicate clockwise motion.

[103] *But the general's wife might die—then there could be trouble with the heirs.*

[104] John Codman Ropes's *The First Napoleon: A Sketch, Political and Military* (Boston and New York: Houghton, Mifflin and Co., 1885).

[105] Henry M. Alexander of the firm of Alexander & Green, lawyers for Webster & Company. On 15 January 1886, Alexander wrote Clemens: "It seems to me wise that you should come to some conclusion in regard to the partnership matter upon which we conferred. . . . I think you had better telegraph me yes or no." This was a reference to Jesse R. Grant's wish to become a partner in Charles L. Webster & Company "as a consideration" before the firm would be allowed to publish Ulysses S. Grant's letters to his wife (SLC to CLW, 20 December 1885, *MTLP*, pp. 195–196). Clemens was unenthusiastic about Jesse Grant and, influenced by Webster's reluctance to accept him, let the matter drop in the spring of 1886 (see notes 110, 111, and 114).

Why don't canvassers advertise their addresses?

⟨If⟩ When canvass actually HAS stopped, let's give all agents liberty to put into the trade.

Make the new G contract.[106]

Consult about Paige's machine.

Have the law bill charged to you.

Stillson Hutchings is here. Can we find him? You send to the Tribune & see.[107]

Both machines are needed, I judge.

Meeting of Hamersley, Paige & Clemens in my billiard-room, Jan 20 '86, pm. Paige says "Every expense connected with making the model machine *cannot* reach $30,000—can't possibly go *over* it." This includes every possible cost of wages, drawings, building the machine, taking out *all* the patents, ⟨e⟩&c.

Get Club box from Hamersley.[108]

Get old contracts from Safety Deposit.

Revolutionary
Aurora Borealis
Massachusetts
⟨Shinneat[e]es⟩S[k]inneat[e]es. [#]

---

[106] In December 1885 Clemens had begun urging Webster to "Sign & seal a contract [for Grant's letters to his wife] before you sleep. . . . Get it, & sign it, & seal it, & shove it in the safe" (SLC to CLW, 18 December 1885, *MTBus*, p. 346). On 1 February 1886 he informed Webster that "Livy thinks Mrs. G's letters ought to be put off a year. We have talked it over, & I am of her mind. The public curiosity could be sharply whetted up, by that time; but now the Memoirs supply the public appetite for Grant-material. . . . I think you had better make the contract for the letters, & at the same time ask [Mrs. Grant] her preference in the matter of date of issue" (*MTBus*, pp. 351–352).

[107] Stilson Hutchins was the founder and editor of the Washington *Post* and one of the principal founders of the Mergenthaler Linotype Company. As the following entry suggests, Clemens may have been seeking reassurance about the Paige typesetter's potential market.

[108] William Hamersley was a vice-president of the Hartford Club, where Clemens had earlier held a typesetter business dinner.

Mollie Fancheron
Gates ave.

Dr West, principal of a school, on Montague st (Young Ladies
school) Brooklyn.[109]

Say "Cemetery" instead of "Appendix"—Mr. Prime's accidental
characterization. Therefore, say, ⟨"For⟩ "further in this connection,
⟨the⟩ will be found in the Cemetery at the end of this volume."

Ich werde G. ein $\frac{1}{50}$th um \$25,000 ⟨barre⟩baare Geld verkaufen
und ihn schützen vom Schaden; oder $\frac{1}{25}$th um \$50,000 $\frac{1}{2}$ in baare
Geld und keinem Theil davon schützen.—(den anderen $\frac{1}{2}$ kann
Man ⟨von aus Dividends⟩ upon delivery of the stock oder von aus
Dividends bezahlen.) Erlange wir nicht, so verliere seine \$25,000.[110]

We say Ach Gott, you say Gott dam.

Pottstausand! "Der Herr Jesus Christus, if I should hear my son
say that, I would die of horror!"

Get that partnership paper from W.
=Mem. Sell his stock.[111]
=A credit on P's salary.[112]

---

[109] Charles Edwin West, an innovator in the field of higher education for women,
was president of the Brooklyn Heights Seminary.

[110] *I will sell G. a $\frac{1}{50}$th for \$25,000 cash and protect him from the loss; or $\frac{1}{25}$th for*
\$50,000, $\frac{1}{2}$ in cash, and not protect any share.—(the other $\frac{1}{2}$ can be paid upon delivery of
the stock or *from the dividends.) If we get nothing, he would lose his \$25,000.* This scheme
was one of Clemens' responses to Jesse Grant's desire to become associated with Charles
L. Webster & Company.

[111] On 19 March 1886, Clemens informed Webster: "It will be necessary that I see
you first, & take your opinion on the propositions" before a scheduled conference with
Jesse Grant about a possible partnership in Webster & Company (*MTBus*, p. 357).
Webster's reply the next day scotched any notion Clemens may have had of reducing
his nephew's share in the firm in favor of Grant. "I would go very slow about taking in
new partners," Webster cautioned. "I don't want to part with any of my interest but
if you wish to sell any of yours I have no objection to the Grant boys, but they should
have *nothing* to say about the conduct of the business." Webster's remarks suggest that
Fred Grant was also a potential partner. Both Fred and Jesse had been considered in
the summer of 1885, but discussions had not then reached a serious level.

[112] In the following notes: "P" is James W. Paige; "Colonel" is probably William

⹀Propose a London syndicate to Colonel
⹀Buy up the old F. stock
⹀Should CW be told about the rebate checks?

Marsh-mallow.
    By Dora Wheeler.[113]

N. Woodruff; "F." is the Farnham Type-Setter Manufacturing Company of Hartford,
originally sponsors of Paige's invention; and "CW" is Charles L. Webster.

[113] Clemens' caption for the ink sketch of marsh mallow flowers by Candace Wheeler's
artist daughter, Dora, was written with the notebook inverted. The sketch was probably
done in early October 1885 when the Wheeler family visited Hartford. The pencil sketch
of a flower on the facing page may have been done by Clemens. The illustration has been
reduced by somewhat less than one-half.

Man ⟨bildet⟩ stellt ⟨vor⟩eine Gesellschafft vor, die eine Capital ⟨au⟩welche aus 100,000 Theilen besteht um $50 per Theil ($5,000,000). Nun, um $50,000 baares Geld were ich ihnen 1000 Theile ⟨kauf⟩ verkaufen, mit Vorrecht diese zu verwechseln, nach 18 Monaten, gegen ¹⁄₁₀ Theil in C L Webs & Co. (Oder, nach machine drei Monaten in N.Y. angeschaut haben solle.)[114]

King Sollermun
German language
Trying Situation
Ghost story
Whistling Yarn[115]

4 tablespoonsful of saleratus to 2 qts water—soak 15 min. Cut away dead nail, apply 2 drops & let it dry. ⟨E⟩One application a day till well.[116]

Con-flag-rat-shun[117]
Tell   -e-   fun
W^m   letter
           most
           used.
Un (French 1)-inn-Tell-lie-jib-bill-i-tie.
Inn-sub-ordination
Chant-i-cleer.

---

[114] The entry reads: *Imagine a company which consists of 100,000 shares at $50 per share ($5,000,000). Now, for $50,000 cash I will sell them 1000 shares, with the prerogative to exchange them, after 18 months, for a ¹⁄₁₀ share in C L Webs & Co. (Or, after the machine has been demonstrated three months in N.Y.).* This draft of a note to Webster made purchase of Paige typesetter stock a prerequisite to any acquisition of interest in Charles L. Webster & Company by Jesse Grant. The plan was intended to discourage Grant, for on 8 February 1886 Clemens had told Webster he meant to offer Grant "a one-tenth interest" in the company for a price he "*ought* not" to pay (*MTBus*, p. 353).

[115] A tentative program for the appearance Clemens had decided to make at West Point on 3 April 1886.

[116] A treatment perhaps suggested by Dr. Daniel Bennett St. John Roosa (see p. 202, note 60).

[117] The following notes probably record some of the charades performed by Clemens, Karl Gerhardt, Jesse Grant, and Frank Warner at Susy Clemens' birthday party on 19 March 1886. Susy described the occasion in a portion of her biography of Clemens which he published in the *North American Review* of 7 June 1907 as part of his autobiography.

Inn-can-descent
Ill-lustration
Condem-nation
Pole-k. (polka.)
's!-indicate.
Croquet
   (soit)
Ma['⟨-⟩]ss-a-saw-it.
(mass)
'M-ass (mass.)
(deaf & dumb signs.)
foe-rum (forum)
Inn-jin (Indian)
Con-few-shun (a mixed discordant dance—or *songs*).

McCann 2,350 in 3 hours; Barnes, 2,000-odd in 3. Phila,
Mch 25[118]

"I'm a *feather-duster* man." Prof. Sloan.[119]

---

[118] In late March 1886 a typesetting tournament was being held in Philadelphia. Among the competitors were Joseph McCann and William C. Barnes, compositors on the New York *Herald* and the New York *World* respectively.

[119] William Milligan Sloane, professor of history at Princeton University, was an acquaintance of Clemens'. References to anecdotes told by Sloane appear intermittently in later notebooks.

XXVI

"I Do Not Expect to Publish"

(March 1886–June 1887)

WITH PUBLICATION of the *Personal Memoirs of U. S. Grant* triumphantly accomplished, Charles L. Webster & Company had become a publishing house of note. Clemens enjoyed his new fame as an eminent publisher, and although he diverted many of the attendant responsibilities to Webster, Notebook 26 bristles with allusions to his own part in the firm's many current or contemplated enterprises. As a result of its prosperity, the company expanded on 28 April 1886 when Frederick J. Hall, one of its employees, became a junior partner. Clemens' connection with Webster & Company was not always gratifying, however. In March 1887 belated discovery of the gradual and systematic embezzlement of some $25,000 by a trusted bookkeeper aggravated Clemens and led him to give vent to his simmering displeasure with Webster. He outlined his grievances in this notebook, then protested some of Webster's business practices and angrily requested adjustments in their business relationship. Clemens complicated a difficult situation with complaints that he was not kept fully informed, conveniently ignoring his stipulation, written into a succession of partnership agreements, that Webster not bother him with details. A series of irascible entries in Notebook 26 anticipates the disillusionment and bitterness that would remain with Clemens long after the dissolution of Charles L. Webster & Company. This aura of impending crisis is documented by note-

224

book evidence of Clemens' and Webster's propensity to squander reputation and capital in ill-advised ventures, such as the publication of the *Life of Leo XIII*, which seemed to promise large profits but did not produce them.

In addition to the affairs of the publishing company, there was Clemens' enduring infatuation with the Paige typesetter, which was reportedly costing him $5,000 a month in this period (see SLC to Orion Clemens, 7 September 1887, *MTLP*, p. 229). As was the case with Notebook 25, a large portion of this notebook, used from the middle of March 1886 until the beginning of January 1887, is given over to Clemens' plans to perfect, test, market, and promote the typesetter. His interest in the rival Mergenthaler Linotype, first evident in Notebook 25, intensified here as he monitored the copy it produced for the New York *Daily Tribune* in 1886, confident of the ultimate failure he thought he could predict from tallies of typographical imperfections and presumed mechanical difficulties. Even summer days at the Elmira, New York, farm the family called "Rest-&-Be-Thankful"—usually devoted to literary work—were not free from the anxiety of this watch over the competition. Clemens recorded his observations and deductions in this notebook before reporting them in letters to Franklin G. Whitmore, his Hartford business agent, to James W. Paige, and to sympathetic friends. Clemens' preoccupation was so great that it left no scope for the kind of evocative, retrospective notes of potential literary importance to be expected from a brief return to the Mississippi and a Clemens family reunion in Keokuk, Iowa, in July 1886.

The consequence of Clemens' immersion in business was an almost total cessation of literary activity. Notebook entries in 1884 (p. 78) and 1885 (pp. 216–217) had shown Clemens beginning to work on *A Connecticut Yankee*, but his rate of progress was unimpressive. By 16 November 1886 he still had little to show, for he then told Mrs. Fairbanks defensively:

> Only two or three chapters of the book have been written, thus far. I expect to write three chapters a year for thirty years; then the book will be done. I am writing it for posterity only; my posterity: my great grandchildren. It is to be my holiday amusement for six days every summer the rest of my life. Of course I do not expect to publish it; nor indeed any other book—though I fully expect to write one other book besides this one; two others, in fact, if one's autobiography may be called a book—in fact mine will be nearer a library. (*MTMF*, p. 258)

The "other book" was "Captain Stormfield's Visit to Heaven," which Clemens had begun years before, but there is no indication that he felt moved to return to it in 1886 or 1887. Several notes for his autobiography which occur in Notebook 26 were not followed up for a considerable time. Clemens' willingness to divert his creative energies into commercial channels is implicit even in his

most sustained literary endeavors of this period. The only extended literary
entries in Notebook 26 are concerned with Clemens' and Howells' effort, in
May of 1886, to refurbish their play, *Colonel Sellers as a Scientist.* It took all of
Howells' artistic integrity, his belief that "the thing will fail, and it would be a
disgrace to have it succeed" (*MTHL*, p. 557), to overcome Clemens' determination to see the play produced. With Howells' assistance, the much-delayed
Mark Twain's Library of Humor was completed, but Clemens' contribution
was merely editorial and did not involve the writing of original material. When
finally published in 1888, the anthology did not appeal greatly to the international audience Clemens had established for his own books. His more funda-
mentally creative efforts at this time were not extensive. In April 1886 he wrote
"Luck," a sketch about a military officer whose pronounced stupidity results in
repeated success and great fame. This trivial piece was not published until 1891
when it was given to *Harper's* magazine as part of "the general house-cleaning
which took place after the first collapse of the [Paige] machine" (*MTB*, p.
1106). He also produced three papers which he read at meetings of the Hartford Monday Evening Club, one of them a version of a piece called "Concerning a Reformed Pledge: A New-Year Sermon." A failure of literary judgment is
apparent in Clemens' repeated notebook references to this meandering and
dreary work which he did not tire of showing around and which he tried unsuccessfully to publish. In April 1887 he did publish "English As She Is Taught"
in the *Century* magazine, but this article demanded little of Clemens since he
merely provided a framework and running commentary for the children's misstatements and malapropisms sent to him by Caroline B. LeRow, a Brooklyn
schoolteacher. In explicit acknowledgment of her initiative he sent her the
Century's payment of $250. Ideas for other literary works appear infrequently
in this notebook, but Clemens deferred most and forgot others. Notebook 26
presents a record of the concerns of an often-harried investor, publisher, public
figure, and family man who was also, intermittently, an author.

Notebook 26 is identical to Notebooks 22, 24, and 25 in design and format.
It now contains 176 pages, twenty-three of them blank. Four leaves have been
torn out, three of which are missing. One of the torn-out leaves, used by Clemens for a letter to his wife in October 1886, survives in the Mark Twain Papers.
The entries are mostly in black pencil, but there are also inscriptions in purple
pencil and in black, brownish black, grayish blue, and blue ink. Use marks in
black pencil, probably by Paine, appear throughout but have not been reproduced. Notebook 26 has suffered from age and use: the front cover, together

with the front flyleaf and the first two leaves, is detached from the notebook, some leaves and several gatherings have come loose from the binding, and the leather on the spine is cracked and worn.

Eugen Meyer[1]
 ⟨⟨[31]4⟩154, East 56th⟩

R. G. Brooks, 80 Bway, 35, ⟨[E --]⟩W 11th
Webster 109 W 126th
Stedman, 45 E 30th
Dean Sage, 939 St Mark's ave
 & 142 Pearl out of Wall.
Century, $33.⁵⁰ per page
Howells, 302 ⟨Beekman⟩ Beacon
Laffan, 335 Lexington ave
House, 350 W. 32^d st, bet 8th & 9th aves.
Mme H ⟨U⟩M. Abry, 125 W. 16th⟨(?)⟩
Robt. W. Allen, 1215—19th st.
Mr. Burghardt, 389 Bowery[2]
Mrs. Gen. Custer, 148 E. 18th [3]
R. S. Paynter, 107 Fitzhugh st. Rochester [#]

---

[1] Piano teacher for Susy and Clara Clemens. This entry appears alone on the verso of the manuscript notebook's front flyleaf. The balance of this list of names and addresses, some transferred from the preceding notebook, appears on the first page and was compiled during the period of this notebook's use.

[2] A New York furniture dealer from whom the Clemenses purchased a "very desirable" sofa in April 1886 (OLC to CLW, undated letter, *MTBus*, p. 358).

[3] In 1886 Clemens and Webster were considering publication of work by Elizabeth Custer. On 30 December Clemens suggested that if Mrs. Custer's *"Boots and Saddles"; or, Life in Dakota with General Custer* (New York: Harper & Brothers, 1885) and her

Die Arbeit is gär (done)

⟨Sept. 8, '85, sent to Bissell Chatto's notes—due
Feb. 27, '86, £300 (paid Mch 25, $1457.)
Mch 27, £300 (paid Apl 10, $1451.54.)
Apl. 27, £368.10.5.—paid May 10, $1,786.22⟩

Gänse-hirt.
   "   -wein (water).
Danksagungsgesundheit. (grace-cup)
Sprüch-wort (judgment or sentence)
WAHN (false or erroneous opinion, illusion) -BILD (portrait,
likeness, picture) Wahn-bild, *phantom.*

Jim & the strainin' rag.[4]

Calvin H. Higbie, Greenville, Plumas Co. Cal.[5] [#]

---

husband's *My Life on the Plains* (New York: Sheldon and Co., 1874) were "put into one
volume" and nothing was said "about their being second-hand, we could risk 25 cents per
copy on it—& I would like to do it for *her* sake, for she needs money" (*MTBus*, p. 371).
This impractical plan was abandoned, however, and in 1887 Charles L. Webster & Company published a new work by Mrs. Custer, *Tenting on the Plains; or, General Custer in
Kansas and Texas.*

   [4] In her biography of her father, Susy Clemens included this anecdote as "a little
scene way out west":

   "Aunt Sal!—aunt Sal! Jims gone got the new strainin rag roun his sore schin. A.S. You
   Jim, take that ar strainin rag off you sore schin, an renc it out, I allers did dispise nastiness." (Clifton Waller Barrett Library, University of Virginia, Charlottesville, PH
   in MTP)

Clemens later noted that the incident was actually "a reminiscence of my boyhood-life
among the slaves" ("About Susy's Biography," PH in MTP).

   [5] This entry was squeezed in at the top of the manuscript page around 4 December
1886 when Higbie, Clemens' Nevada mining partner, the "honest man . . . genial
comrade and . . . steadfast friend" to whom *Roughing It* was dedicated, wrote to ask
"without any circumlocution" for a loan of $20,000 to rescue an eleven-year investment
from some "vilianous" mining partners. Noting reports that Clemens had become a
millionaire, Higbie explained that he had "kept pegging away at mines, but have never
found anything before now, that was worth much. and am afraid that I Shal loose that
If I cannot get assistance." He offered Clemens a half interest in the mine he expected
to sell for "50 or $60,000 easy" before settling down "in some quiet retreat." On 16
December, Clemens replied: "Lord, it's good to hear from you again! It brings back the
pleasantness of the old times, with the pains and the privations left behind. I would most
certainly help you if I could, and I believe you know that to be the truth. I know it to be

Mrs Zadel Barnes Gustafson[6]
30 Cromwell Grove
  West Kensington Park
    London W.
Or "Pall Mall Gazette"
  "Personal."

Send latest news about Pope's book.

Also, photograph of SLC.

Aug.	7.	T.W.[7]	16.	C.	35.
	10	" "	16.	"	38.
	12	" "	16.	"	42
	11	" "	38	"	38
	13	" "	14	"	48
	14	" "	25	⟨46⟩48	[#]

---

the truth. But I alone am responsible for the capital of my firm in New York. . . . For the next twelve months this will make it necessary for me to sail just as close to the wind, financially, as I possibly can. . . . We have one book in preparation [*Life of Leo XIII*] which will require every cent I have in the world and perhaps more. . . . Oh, dear, why did you ever let anybody have control of the property? You were always too trustful." Clemens closed his reply with a suggestion that Higbie contact Robert M. Howland, another Nevada mining friend, who "has been in New York very lately—and prospering. He seems to be always having the luck to sell a mine to somebody or other. Don't you think he could be of use to you in this difficulty?" (SLC letter quoted from Michael J. Phillips, "Mark Twain's Partner," *Saturday Evening Post*, 11 September 1920, p. 74).

  [6] The poet and journalist, Zadel Barnes Gustafson, was a world traveler, lecturer, and suffrage advocate who frequently contributed to *Harper's* magazine and in 1886 was a special correspondent of the *Pall Mall Gazette*. In the summer of 1886 she solicited an interview with Clemens for that newspaper. After he offered to help bring her to Elmira she suggested that he instead "make a brief flitting to Hartford. . . . as that is your real home it must be to you, as its shell is to the tortoise. . . . and you could show me over the house & rummage among your treasures & souvenirs & tell me all about them & all that you willingly could about yourself. . . . and we can go out & get a quiet cup of tea when the visit is done" (Zadel B. Gustafson to SLC, 25 July 1886). Although when business took Clemens to Philadelphia in the first week of August (see p. 250, note 77) he asked Mrs. Gustafson to meet him there instead, he evidently made a special trip to Hartford to see her. No interview appeared in the *Pall Mall Gazette*, but two years later, on the basis of their brief acquaintance Zadel Barnes Gustafson asked Clemens to lend her $5,000. He ignored her repeated appeals, commenting on the envelope of her final letter: "God damn this tedious woman."

  [7] Probably Theodore W. Crane. This list may be a record of Crane's and Clemens' scores at one of the parlor games popular during summers at Quarry Farm.

M. Allen, 287 W. 19$^{th.}$

Gänse-hirt. gooseherder.

Will sell a $\frac{1}{200}$ (250 shs) interest (American pat.) for $25,000,
⟨pay⟩ keep or retire from the purchase Jan. 1, 1887.

Basis of a capital of $5,000,000.—50,000 shares of $100 each.

Telegram to Houghton for Howells's address about Apl. 7 or 8
not to be paid for—that or the explanation sent Apl 10.[8]

The P.S. does the work of 5 men; a slow operator dos the work
of 5 slow men; a fast one the work of 5 fast men: therefore the new
wages should be $\frac{1}{5}$ of the old; 9 cents per 1000 on morning papers,
⟨& [⟨8⟩⟨7⟩8] ⟨on⟩in book offices⟩ & ⟨5 or⟩ 6 c in book offices,
because at ⟨5,000⟩ 4,500 an hour he would make $2.70 a day (he
gets full 10 *hours'* work) as against $2.40 & $2.50 now.

Whoso pays us 10 cents & his man 9, saves ⟨24^c⟩27^c on a M
paper; ⟨& the same in⟩ a book office paying us 10 & its man 6,
saves 24^c out of the present 40.

When the (later) M p's pay us 15 & the man 9, they will save
22^c. The (later) book office paying us 15 & the man 6, will save 19
cents per 1000 out of 40.

A Courant man (good one) now sets ⟨[9]⟩nearly 9,000, (at 35) &
makes from $3 to $3.15. Makes about 40^c an hour for 7.$\frac{1}{2}$ h. He
ought to get 8^c on the P.S., & set ⟨[-]⟩ 5,000. They should pay us
⟨⟨1[2]^c⟩10^c & save 15.⟩ ⟨11^c & save⟩ 10^c & save 17$^{c.}$ (half.)

The *established & permanent* terms after the first 600 machines
shall be 15 cents for New York, (& Washington & N. Orleans &
Frisco) 12 for other large cities & 10 for the country. And a lease
shall lapse if a machine be removed from the town for which it was
rented. [#]

---

[8] Since the middle of March 1886, Clemens and Howells had been attempting to
schedule a meeting of their families in Hartford. In early April, the Howells family was
at the Murray Hill Hotel in New York, on their way home from Washington. An exchange of telegrams and letters between the two men at that time failed to establish a
satisfactory date. It evidently wasn't until the weekend of 1–2 May that Howells finally
visited Hartford, accompanied only by his daughter Mildred ("Pilla").

Sell 800 to London papers or to an English syndicate at $6,000 apiece, $\frac{1}{2}$ cash—but not sell the foreign patents at all.

"Making even" will cease—no take less than $\frac{1}{4}$ column long will ever need to be given out.

Peck—"take your horses & go to hell with them!"—soft & gentle up to this point.

Charley stir up Am Pub Co.[9]

⟨By⟩Buy 1000 *sh.* F. T. S. co?[10]

Write Tom Fitch[11]

trading (or borrowing teeth)

Hopkinson Smith[12]
    150, E. 34[th.] [#]

---

[9] Clemens must have been agitated about belated royalty payments from his former publishers. In late April 1886 he was able to inform Webster: "Am. Pub check received" (*MTBus*, p. 360, letter of 20 April apparently misdated 22 April).

[10] The Farnham Type-Setter Manufacturing Company of Hartford, the firm that originally sponsored the Paige machine.

[11] On 20 February 1886, Thomas Fitch, an old Nevada associate, had sent Clemens the manuscript of a play written by his wife, the novelist Anna M. Fitch. The Fitches wished Clemens to "send it to some theatrical manager or personage, with such endorsement of it as will secure its being read" for "with an introduction from you it will at least gain a favorable inspection." Clemens passed the play—about Washington life and politics—on to his friend Laurence Hutton, former drama critic of the New York *Mail.* On 11 March, Hutton reported: "Its not a bad play of its kind But its a poor kind. What they call in our day 'a farce-comedy in 5 acts.' . . . But something *might* be made out of it in the proper hands. There is a Daisy-Miller-Lotta-Minnie-Palmer-girl who might be elaborated to suit some of the hoyden-banjo-playing-jig-dancing-monstrosities who call themselves actresses in this last half of the 19th Century. . . . A great many worse plays have drawn crowds for months." Hutton advised that the play be sent to one of the companies "who romp thro' five acts of that sort of thing all over the country every night." Clemens subsequently offered it without success to William Gillette.

[12] On 13 April 1886, Smith wrote inviting Clemens to attend a gathering of "a few hungry spirits," including William Dean Howells, in honor of Edwin A. Abbey. "The gorge begins at 7 P.M April 22[d] Thursday at my house," he informed Clemens, "Please say yes." A subsequent entry in this notebook (p. 234) suggests that Clemens and Howells divided their evening between Smith's affair and an Authors Club dinner, at which Clemens spoke briefly on "Our Children and Great Discoveries" (*MTS*[1910], pp. 69–70).

Mr Twichell, they've made him county clerk!

The young fellow who won & married the Bermuda girl.[13]

tr.

Der Herr Jesus Christus! *if I should hear*[14]

Martin McGinnis making his great speech at Gettysburg.[15]

"Go & see Dicky's Darling—1^s"—Irving & Toole & the asphyxiated stranger.[16]

My visit to Augustin Daly, & encounter with the porter & 125-lb dog. —My Bench Show at New Haven.[17]

The two darkies shoveling snow for Jewell & ⟨Gil⟩ Newton Case.[18] [#]

---

[13] Clemens included the tale of the courtship of "a soft-headed young donkey who had been reared under Mr. Twichell's spiritual ministrations" in an Autobiographical Dictation of 15 March 1906 (*MTA*, 2:206–210).

[14] Clemens added "tr." in the top margin of the page above this paragraph and drew a line between "tr." and *"hear."* He may have intended to transpose the English and German phrases or to translate part of the entry. Clemens noted the remark more fully in Notebook 25 (220.14–15).

[15] On 4 May 1885, President Grover Cleveland, accompanied by several members of his administration and a number of Civil War veterans, visited the battlefield and National Cemetery at Gettysburg, Pennsylvania. One of the speakers that day was Martin Maginnis, a survivor of the Gettysburg battle and a Montana congressman. No explanation has been discovered for Clemens' note about Maginnis' speech which, although eloquent, does not seem to have been exceptional.

[16] "Uncle Dick's Darling" was a play written by Henry J. Byron for the English comic actor J. L. Toole. The anecdote alluded to here was reportedly told by Henry Irving and concerned Toole's continual efforts to publicize the play. Pretending to be a doctor, Toole administered to a drunken man unconscious in a gutter. After performing "with impressive accuracy the whole professional routine," Toole departed, leaving an admiring crowd to discover labels bearing the following advertisement on the afflicted man's face: "*Uncle Dick's Darling*, Gaiety Theatre, every evening" (Joseph Hatton, *Reminiscences of J. L. Toole* [London: Hurst and Blackett, 1889], pp. 193, 318–321). Clemens had met Toole in London in September 1872.

[17] Clemens told the story of this encounter of "two or three years ago" at a dinner at Daly's Theatre in New York on 13 April 1887. He claimed that when a dog-fancying Irish porter denied him access to Daly he won the man's confidence with a calculated allusion to a New Haven bench show which featured a one hundred forty-five pound Saint Bernard (see *MTS*[1910], pp. 79–82). Mark Twain included a version of the anecdote in chapter 45 of *Following the Equator*.

[18] Marshall Jewell, a wealthy manufacturer and public official who died in 1883, had

⟨2⟩Procession of men hired to follow a ⟨[-]⟩the corpse of an unpopular man at $2 apiece, & look down sorrowing; if they looked up, to be docked half. There was an evil smell. Finally they agreed that one should look & they would stand the loss between them. They found they had switched off & were following a night cart.

Texas girls lassos wild horse[-] & rides home; Boston girl captures codfish & rides him home astride. Burdette—"This accounts for the peculiar smell of the codfish."

"Wie fühle ich? Ich fühle unbeschreiblich wohl."

Weisst du warum du ⟨gleichest ein⟩ die ≈ eine Frau gleichest? Weil ⟨du siehst so⟩ du so viel besser ⟨aus als⟩ fühlst als du aussiehst."[19]

⟨What⟩Which is the biggest county in the world? The county of Kent, in England—because it includes the whole of what is now the United States. In 1782 Sir James Marriott, a judge of the Admiralty Court, ⟨co⟩quoted the fact, in parliament, in justification of the war, that the first colonization, in Virginia & all subsequent ones, were under one form of royal charter & authority, "to have & to hold, *as part & parcel* of our Manor of East Greenwich in the county of Kent"—& the judge held ⟨the[r]⟩that therefore the American colonies were *not* taxed without representation: they were represented by the knights of the shire for the county of Kent.[20]

Hi! mars Jesus, how's yo' pa?

Get 2 stylographics (without gold.) [#]

---

been a Hartford acquaintance of the Clemenses'. Newton Case, their Farmington Avenue neighbor, was president of the Case, Lockwood & Brainard Company, Hartford printers, publishers, and bookbinders. Clemens expanded this note in "The Snow-Shovelers," an unpublished dialect sketch about two indolent laborers distressed at "Anerkis en Socialis'" proposals that "everybody git along 'dout work."

[19] *"How do I feel? I feel indescribably good."*
Do you know why you're like a woman's ≈ ? Because you feel so much better than you look."

[20] Marriott's "pedantic folly" caused "great merriment" on 15 March 1782 during bitter parliamentary debate occasioned by a series of British military reverses, including the climactic defeat at Yorktown in the American Revolutionary War (Philip Henry Stanhope, *History of England from the Peace of Utrecht to the Peace of Versailles: 1713–1783*, 5th ed., rev., 7 vols. [London: John Murray, 1858], 7:135–139).

Tiffany—watch.[21]

Fool—Why dn't you bet 1,000,000—you'd a won it.

I guess I can follow that.

Aldrich's cripple with the strip of walnut beading.[22]

Mikado Music.[23]

Photo of 3 little maids f'm school.

He broke a rake handle the other day.

33 Wells, bet the bridge & Mulberry.[24] Over Jones's (pattern maker)—up 2 flights stairs.

H. C. Leland (No admittance).[25]

Author's Club 10 W. 24[th.]
    Apl. 22—Howells.
     8 to 12 PM.

Tell Smith how the Boston Ad man got his —— caught in the steel trap.

⟨Whst⟩Whist. Frenchman heard them say "We are two" "We are two too." "Nice language—sounds like a flute."
    Italian said in Italian, "Nice soft language—*Cellar*-do-or."

Ned House 2132 6th ave. May 8 or 10[26] [#]

---

[21] Evidently the watch belonging to Livy that Clemens had sent for repairs several months before, explaining: "The watch which Mrs. Clemens bought of you some days ago keeps too much time, sometimes, & the rest of the time it doesn't keep *any*. Will you please take out its present works & put in some of a more orthodox character" (SLC to "Dear Sirs," 26 December 1885).

[22] Clemens recorded this anecdote in detail in Notebook 18 (see *N&J2*, p. 335).

[23] The Clemenses were in New York City during the weekend of April 16–18, 1886, to see the popular D'Oyly Carte production of *The Mikado* at the Fifth Avenue Theatre.

[24] The business address of several Hartford artisans, including a brass founder, a furniture repairman, and the firm of R. M. Jones & H. B. Little, "wood turners, pattern and model makers" (*Geer's*[1886], p. 118).

[25] Henry C. Leland was a Hartford printer.

[26] Clemens' friend Edward H. House was confined by illness to his New York City residence. During the spring of 1886 Clemens called on House several times while in

⟨See Gilder about Miss Larned.⟩[27]

Do you know why Balaam's ass spoke Hebrew? Because he was a he-brayist.

Blongs to ⟨the⟩that Monday Evening Club & Nat Shipman,[28] Chas Warner, Mk Twain, Corneil Dunham,[29] & a lot more d—d cranks ['t] don't know nothing about business—& they just stuffed him *full.*"

Next Saturday Howell's & ⟨Palla⟩Pilla will come & stop over Sunday.[30]

⟨Wenn⟩Venn ze Frenchman hunt ze tigèr, ze sport is grande— ven ze tiger hunt ze Frenchman—mon *Dieu!*

Write a sober account of the man with a blood-hound's ⟨s⟩marvelous scent.[31]

⟨See Pond about his "Benefit."⟩ [#]

New York on business. He also encouraged several of their mutual acquaintances to pay similar cheering visits. On 29 June, John Hay passed on such a suggestion from Clemens to Whitelaw Reid. Reid replied on 2 July that he had already seen House and provided a description of his condition: "His knee-joints were kept bent so long by gout that they have solidified. It has been years since he has stood on his feet and he can never hope to move about, even on crutches. It comes the nearest to a living death of any case I have ever seen, and is most pitiful. Yet his mind seems perfectly clear and his ways and talk have even more than their old gentleness. Looking at him in his present state, it is impossible to care for or think of the old escapades when he was crazed with drink and the mischief he wrought" (John Hay Collection, Brown University, Providence, R.I.).

[27] Harriet Beecher Stowe had recently referred a Miss Larned, an aspiring writer of children's stories, to Mark Twain for assistance in getting "an opening into some magazine or paper for the young" (Harriet Beecher Stowe to SLC, 6 April 1886). Clemens intended to transmit the request to Richard Watson Gilder, editor of the *Century* magazine.

[28] Nathaniel Shipman, judge of the United States Court for the district of Connecticut.

[29] Austin Cornelius Dunham was a Hartford wool and hosiery manufacturer.

[30] Clemens and Howells met in New York City on Saturday, 17 April 1886, to arrange this visit to Hartford. Although this entry suggests that the dates Clemens originally had in mind were 24–25 April, the visit took place on 1–2 May. Mildred ("Pilla") was Howells' fourteen-year-old daughter.

[31] Mark Twain's eventual literary development of this idea is discussed on page 187, note 24.

Call on Hutton & ask about Fitch's play.[32]

⟨Call on Howells & insist that Mrs. H. come too.⟩

⟨Order hack for to-morrow morning.⟩

⟨Call on Webster & ask about Pamela.⟩[33]

E. S. Cleveland, Hammond Trumbull, Prof. Riddle & D[r.] Gatling ⟨[met]⟩ surrounded an unprotected stranger in a lonely place, & ⟨surr⟩ ere help arrived it was by several hours too late. The remains have been sent to the family.[34]

⟨There was⟩ I once saw a man ⟨who got⟩get up before a weary & sweltering audience to ⟨make speech No. 22—just⟩ *add* a speech which was not down in the long, long list of speeches in the regular program—uttered his opening sentence, & fell dead in his tracks. I never saw an assemblage⟨—⟩so startled(?)—so deeply moved—so sincerely grateful. I would win *your* gratitude. I cannot die, but I will resign.[35] [#]

---

[32] Despite Laurence Hutton's tepid initial response to Anna M. Fitch's play (see note 11), in mid-April Clemens may have been encouraging him to place it with an appropriate theatrical company.

[33] Clemens wished to verify the itinerary of Pamela Moffett who was to begin an extended stay with her daughter, Annie Webster, and son-in-law, Charles L. Webster, on 24 April 1886. She would visit the Clemens family in Hartford from 13 to 20 May before returning to the Websters' New York City home to remain until the middle of June.

[34] Four prominent residents of Hartford: Edward S. Cleveland, Connecticut state senator, who in late 1886 was unsuccessful as Democratic candidate for governor; J. Hammond Trumbull, scholar, president of the Connecticut Historical Society, source of the multilingual chapter headings in *The Gilded Age*; the Reverend Matthew B. Riddle, Hosmer Professor of New Testament Exegesis at the Hartford Theological Seminary; Richard Jordan Gatling, a non-practicing physician, inventor of the Gatling gun. In a notebook kept in 1892 and 1893, Mark Twain remarked on Trumbull's garrulity, a trait evidently shared by the other distinguished men.

[35] Clemens used a variation of this approach to good effect while attending Fourth of July festivities in Keokuk, Iowa, in 1886. "The man who makes the last speech," he told the holiday crowd, "has the best of the other speakers as he has the last word to say, which falls like a balm on the audience . . . and though I can't say the last word, I will do the next best thing I can and that is to sit down" (Fred W. Lorch, "Lecture Trips and Visits of Mark Twain in Iowa," *Iowa Journal of History and Politics*, October 1929, p. 538).

Thursday week Annie comes.[36]

The contract was signed in Rome about April 22, 1886, & by my firm in New York ⟨about⟩ May 4.[37]

Went to West Point May 5.

Kahler, opp. Stewart's, 9th or 10th st B'way—shoes. Gen. Merritt.[38]

Advertise it everywhere & prominently as "*A Farce in 3 acts.*"[39]

Oh, did I step on your foot?" "No—(said the *other* fellow "I wish to God you had!"

⟨Try that chair—⟩
"I have invented a chair which is light, portable, graceful in shape, & so strong than elephant can sit in it" (chair breaks down under De Boon) or Hawkins.)—"This isn't the one."

Telegram from north end of the city—dated day before yesterday

---

[36] Annie Moffett Webster and her daughter Jean accompanied Pamela Moffett to Hartford on Thursday, 13 May 1886, for a week's visit.

[37] The contract for Bernard O'Reilly's *Life of Leo XIII* (New York: Charles L. Webster & Co., 1887), which Clemens mistakenly believed would be more profitable than the Grant *Memoirs*. Clemens learned of the signing on 5 May 1886 when he and Twichell stopped in New York City on the way to West Point where he was to repeat a platform success of early April. "The issue of this book will be the greatest event in the way of book publishing that ever occurred," Twichell wrote in his diary, reflecting Clemens' misplaced optimism, "and it seems certain, M.T. will make a vast amount of money by it." But he added later: "(P.S.—Proved quite otherwise in the event.)"

[38] General Wesley Merritt, superintendent of West Point and Mark Twain's host on 6 and 7 May 1886, had probably recommended the Kahler shoe store in New York City near the famous department store founded by Alexander T. Stewart.

[39] With the exception of the following anecdote and the entry at 237.13–238.2, entries through "trouble with the machinery" (238.16) are notes for Clemens' and Howells' play, *Colonel Sellers as a Scientist.* During the first half of May, the two men were attempting to rework the play for a production featuring A. P. Burbank, whom Howells characterized as "a clever and charming elocutionist" (William Dean Howells, *My Mark Twain* [New York: Harper & Brothers, 1910], p. 26). Revisions jointly conceived in Boston on 10 May were insufficient to overcome Howells' misgivings about the play's quality. On 11 May he definitively requested that Clemens withdraw it from Burbank and from Daniel Frohman of the Lyceum Theatre. The following year Clemens backed a new production of *Colonel Sellers* which was presented unsuccessfully by Burbank and a traveling company.

—Curious, but it's a fact: you can get a dispatch from China quicker'n you can from the other end of your own town.

Uncle Danl

Sarcasticises [&] the telegraph boy: How'd you leave your folks at home?—All pretty well, hey? You going ⟨right⟩ *back* with another message? Ah well,—You been gone a good while you know —you'll find a good many changes—it's a world of change⟨—I wish to God it was a world of *small* change⟩

Boy says something in an inaudible voice. ⟨S.⟩ Uncle Danl. stoops & boy whispers. ⟨S.⟩D. (Has an ⟨[a]⟩exhaustive fit of ⟨5⟩2 minutes of laughter—not loud, but shaky & destructive—toward the end broken by)—I said—said—'twas a world of change, & he said (another long earth-shaking attack)—said—said—he wished to gosh it was a world of *small* change! (another fit.) Exit in the fit.

People are always happening into that room. That telegraph comes often & always get into trouble with the machinery.

⟨Turn Phillips over to Charley.⟩

Ask Charley to convey my thanks to Mrs. Grant & to Mr. Alexander the binder.

Ask Charley to tackle Geo. Fawcett Rowe.[40]

Go & see James Russell Lowell, Minister Phelps, Penfield, & Consul General Waller.[41]

Never mind Mrs. Stowe & Sutherl.

My books are water; those of the great geniuses is wine. Everybody drinks water.[42] [#]

---

[40] George Fawcett Rowe was an actor and an undistinguished dramatist. Clemens may have wished to consult him concerning *Colonel Sellers as a Scientist.*

[41] James Russell Lowell had been minister resident to England from 1880 to 1885 when he was succeeded by Edward J. Phelps. Frederick C. Penfield was the American vice-consul and Thomas M. Waller the American consul-general in London. This entry may be an instruction to Webster who was to leave for England on 23 June 1886 on the first stage of his journey to Rome for a papal audience concerning the *Life of Leo XIII.*

[42] Mark Twain amplified this metaphoric assessment of the appeal of his writing in a

Inquire of Gilder how he liked the Ode.

Go to House[43]—& Charley's.

Then to Mrs. Grant's.

Then to Mr. Dana's.—25—60th? Cor. Madison ave.[44]

Ask F. G.[45] about horses.

Go & see Laffan.

See Battle of the Monitors[46]

Studies for that article:[47] Balzac, Shakspeare, Saint Simon⟨.⟩;
One believes St. S. & Benvenuto, & partly believes the
Margravine of Bayreuth. There are things in the Confessions of
Rousseau which one must believe.

What is biography? Unadorned romance. What is romance?
Adorned biography. Adorn it less & it will be better than it is.

A *narrative* novel is the thing, perhaps: where you follow the
fortunes of two or three people & have no plot more than real
life has.

The private who imagined he stood by & advised Gen. Grant all
through Chattanooga. [#]

---

letter to William Dean Howells on 15 February 1887, some nine months after he noted
it here (see *MTHL*, pp. 586–587).

[43] Clemens paid this second May 1886 visit to Edward H. House in the last week of
the month while in New York City on business.

[44] Clemens probably wished to see Charles A. Dana, editor of the New York *Sun*,
in connection with the *Life of Leo XIII*. Dana had played an intermediary role in securing
that book for Charles L. Webster & Company.

[45] Probably Fred Grant.

[46] "A panorama of the fight between the Merrimac and Monitor" had been "set up,
in late January at Madison Avenue and 59th Street" and remained on display through
the summer of 1886 (George C. D. Odell, *Annals of the New York Stage*, 15 vols. [New
York: Columbia University Press, 1927–1949], 13:135, 137).

[47] Mark Twain was evidently contemplating an article about the relationship of
biography to imaginative literature. His interest in the subject may have emerged from
his most recent attempt at autobiography, the 1885 "Grant Dictations" (see *MTA*,
1:13–70).

Well sir, I felt as surprised as a clergyman in hell.

If the matter resolves itself finally into a raising of capital, neither Winans nor Mackay is the man, but Andrew Carnegie. He is *experienced* in manufactures in both Europe & America.[48]

Topics
The adventures of those runaway apprentices with the boy Jesus.

Review "Luxilla" that hogwash novel from the South.[49]

Leave New York 1 pm; change at New Haven at 3.12.

Sell that Rolling Mill stock.

Give W.[50] a note of all securities & let him keep watch of them.

Bring down Tolstoi[51]

Get "The Midge" by HC Bunner.[52]

Brer Whitmo "get canvassers to carry the petition. [#]

---

[48] Clemens had failed to interest Ross R. Winans in the Paige typesetter in December 1885 (see p. 198, note 51). Despite the negative impulse of this entry, he did approach his old Nevada friend John W. Mackay, the spectacularly successful Comstock miner who had become a prominent banker, railroad director, and telegraph entrepreneur. It wasn't until 1890, however, that Mackay made $5,000 available to Clemens, a sum that represented little more than a month's maintenance of the Paige machine and fell far short of the investment Clemens envisioned. There is no reason to believe that Andrew Carnegie ever became a sponsor for the typesetter.

[49] Clemens refrained from drawing attention to George Ernest Miller's *Luxilla: A Romance* (Mobile, Ala., 1885), fifty-four pages of melodramatic prose and doggerel about the unconsummated infatuation of Marion Ipsellee, count of Inexplane, for the mysterious Luxilla, queen of a subterranean kingdom inhabited by thieves, bombastic spirits, and a dwarf sorcerer.

[50] Franklin G. Whitmore, Clemens' Hartford business agent, who handled many of Clemens' investments.

[51] Howells had devoted most of his "Editor's Study" in the April 1886 *Harper's* magazine to praise of Tolstoi's commitment to truth and realism, especially in *Anna Karenina* and *My Religion*. Clemens undoubtedly felt challenged by Howells' passing remark that the apt criticisms of nineteenth-century life in *My Religion* "give one pause, but probably an average American humorist could dispose of his arguments in a half-column funny article" (*Harper's*, April 1886, pp. 808–809).

[52] Henry Cuyler Bunner's sentimental novel, published by Charles Scribner's Sons in 1886.

The said *itching piles*. 1 part litherage
to 2   "   ⟨[--]⟩lard.

Carbolic acid.

Cigars.—200 more to Elm.[53]

Postman send letters to Elmira till 20th, then to K till further notice.

⟨Give House the Wirt pen to exchange—H W Smith & Co. 173 Bway.⟩[54]

Show Clark the pen.[55]

⟨$583.³⁴⟩$583.³³—⟨pay to Paige July 10.—as usual.⟩[56]

⟨Write for field glass to Whitmore.⟩[57]

Carbolic acid.

Get condensed ⟨both⟩beef. [#]

---

[53] Clemens noted this and the following four reminders around 15 June as the family was starting for New York City on the way to Elmira. The following week they traveled to Keokuk, Iowa ("K" in the next entry), for a short visit with Jane Lampton Clemens and the Orion Clemenses.

[54] Agents for the "Paul E. Wirt Fountain Pen," advertised as "Absolutely Durable, Practical and Reliable." Mark Twain thought it "a great pen . . . the only fountain pen in the world that can be left open by the week without its' drying up" (SLC to George Standring, 25 August 1886). In late 1886, at Paul E. Wirt's request, Clemens wrote a testimonial for the pen. For many years advertisements included Clemens' remarks: "With a single Wirt Pen I have earned the family's living for many years. With two, I could have grown rich."

[55] Probably Charles Hopkins Clark, assistant editor of the Hartford *Courant* and an associate of Howells and Clemens in *Mark Twain's Library of Humor*.

[56] By the typesetter contract of 6 February 1886, Clemens had agreed to pay James W. Paige an annual salary of $7,000 in equal monthly installments. Payment began on 10 April 1886 and was to continue until Paige realized "a net yearly profit" from the machine equivalent to that salary.

[57] Clemens wrote Franklin G. Whitmore from New York City on 15 June: "I came off and forgot my field-glass—and I particularly need it on the lake trip [see notes 60 and 62]. Won't you express it to me at ELMIRA, N.Y. I suppose it is in the billiard room, though I don't remember seeing it ANYwhere lately" (MTM). The following notes, through " 187 West NY." (243.19), were made in New York City.

⟨2ᵈ (gift) vol.⟩

Send Julia 2 to 4.[58]

⟨Get ⟨$500⟩$100 at Webster's.⟩

Derndst fool; you know, he'd go & try to warm himself by a hotel register.

Take children to Monitor fight.

Stafford's Commercial ink

No. 3284—$110 Ged House
  3285. ⟨47.⁸⁵⟩45.⁸⁵
   6 Sypher & Co. $10.
   7. Vantine & Co. 49.¹⁰
   8 Sellf (Crane) 500.
   9 K. S. Cook 28.38.
   90. H. ⟨W.⟩M. Smith & Co $5.
   91 T. P. Carpenter $242.
   KKBK 300
   Burley & Co 85.[59]

2 pens ⟨?⟩to KKK.[60]

---

[58] Julia Langdon, Clemens' niece, was the fifteen-year-old daughter of Charles J. Langdon. This gift, evidently of books, remains unidentified.

[59] A list of checks written by Clemens in New York City. Among other expenses were the family's hotel bill at the Gedney House and a purchase of Wirt pens at H. M. Smith and Company. Clemens provided himself with five hundred dollars in cash to give to Theodore W. Crane as an advance on his share of summer costs at Quarry Farm. He may also have planned to deposit three hundred dollars in a Keokuk bank ("KKBK") for use during his visit there.

[60] On 21 June, the Clemens family set out from Quarry Farm for Keokuk, Iowa, to visit Jane Lampton Clemens and Orion and Mollie Clemens, accomplishing the journey in part by Great Lakes steamer and Mississippi River steamboat. They remained in Keokuk from 2 until 7 July 1886, attending the elaborate local Independence Day celebration and a reception in their honor at Orion's home. Clemens' notebook is disappointingly devoid of information about this family reunion. The "days & nights of hell-sweltering weather" (SLC to Franklin G. Whitmore, 12 July 1886) were probably too filled by the demands of family and friends to be easily captured in notebook entries, just as they proved distracting to Susy Clemens' precocious biography of her father, which breaks off at this time with the tantalizingly unfinished observation: "We have arrived in Keokuk after a very pleasant . . ." (S&MT, p. 231).

⟨⟨Telegram to⟩
Go to Mayor
   ″   ″ ⟨Dentist⟩
    ″ ⟨Locksmith⟩
     ⟨Barber⟩⟩
150 cigars to KKK
Pair easy shoes.
Ship-chairs? Write.
Also box provis[ns]

In Rochester go to Powers house to dinner.[61]

1. oz. aconite
2 trunk straps.
Shave.

Olives
Alcohol—1 quart.
Fruit—cherries, strawber ⟨or[a]⟩
Champagne

H. S. Billings, 187 West
           187 West NY.

Send Innocents Abroad to Capt. E. Mooney, Lake Superior Transit Co. Buffalo, & write name in it.[62]

9.30 am & 12.[30] noon—trains from Clinton to Chicago.
   If you don't get a train at Rock Isl, go on to Clinton, (Revere House.)[63] [#]

---

[61] Probably the home of Daniel William Powers, the eminent Rochester banker and broker who was a leading eastern financier and one of the greatest art collectors in the United States. Dinner with Powers was a last occasion to discuss Paige typesetter business before the Clemenses continued on to Buffalo to begin the steamboat segment of their trip to Iowa.

[62] Edward Mooney was captain of the *India,* the freight and passenger vessel which took the Clemens family from Buffalo across Lakes Erie, Huron, and Superior to Duluth, Minnesota, where they stopped briefly before going on by railroad to Saint Paul to make Mississippi River boat connections for Keokuk.

[63] Clemens probably made this entry, his only Keokuk note, shortly before departing for Elmira. The family returned to Elmira by train with a stopover in Chicago.

Mrs. Edith R. Somerville
  Drishane
    Skibbereen
      Co. Cork
        Ireland.
Compiler of Birth-Day Book now waiting in Hartford. Write her again when I see it.[64]

Thursday, Nov. ⟨8⟩11, *8. PM*[65]
⟨["]⟩*Governor's Island, N.Y. Harbor.*
Military Service Institution."
Gen. ⟨F⟩T. F. Rodenbaugh, Secretary.
Gen. James B. Fry, invitation committee.

July 21, '86. Read at the Reformatory:[66]
  King Sollermun.

---

[64] In June 1886, Edith Somerville had sent Clemens a copy of her *Mark Twain Birthday Book* (London: Remington and Co., 1885), a selection of quotations from his works in a calendar format. Her accompanying note, forwarded from Hartford, was awaiting Clemens in Elmira when he returned from Keokuk. On 15 July he wrote Edith Somerville, explaining that he had not seen the book because "I am allowing my printed mail matter to accumulate in Hartford . . . but I want to thank you now, both for sending it to me & the compliment which you have paid me in making it. I have a high curiosity to see it, for you have accomplished what I once failed in [see p. 71, note 13]. I contracted to compile such a book, but was obliged to get myself released: my books grew suddenly & disastrously barren & empty: I couldn't find the requisite material in them. It was a sharp wound to my self-love. I shall look to you to heal it" (Houghton Library, Harvard University, Cambridge, Mass.). Clemens may not have felt so gratified when he saw the *Mark Twain Birthday Book*. The *Saturday Review* of 21 February 1885 had already confirmed his own earlier apprehensions, complaining that the Somerville work "is rather to be recommended as a proof of the strength of a fashion than for its own merits. Mr. Twain does not show to advantage when quoted in lines" (p. 257).

[65] On 14 July 1886, Clemens accepted an invitation from General James B. Fry to appear before the Military Service Institution of the United States, an organization of "some 11 or 12 hundred officers & ex-officers, working *gratis* for the military welfare of the country, and the entertainment of old soldiers" (James B. Fry to R. L. Ogden, 18 June 1886). Clemens made this entry after receipt of a letter of 19 July from General Theophilus F. Rodenbaugh providing details of time and place. On 11 November 1886 a large and enthusiastic audience heard Clemens read the first chapter and selected excerpts from "a still uncompleted book": "the autobiography of Sir Robert Smith of Camelot, one of King Arthur's knights, formerly a manufacturer of Hartford" (Hartford *Courant*, 13 November 1886).

[66] The New York State Reformatory for men at Elmira, an innovative penal institution founded in 1876.

German lesson
Trying Situation.
Whistling Story.
Time 1 hour & 15 min.

Proposed bill, next time:
Mexican Plug.
Buck Fanshaw.
Jumping Frog.
Tom Bowling's yarn.[67]
Ghost Story.
(Twichell's Bermuda girl?)[68]
(The Irish Christening? Mary Ann.)[69]

25 M to line.—40 line to 1000
Tribune column of the medium type is ⟨4,500⟩ ⟨6,000⟩ 4,500
ems. ⟨5⟩ ⟨3¾⟩ 5 inches of this solid matter is 1000.

22 M to line—45 lines to 1000
The big editorial type is ⟨5½⟩ ⟨4⅝⟩4¾ 4¾ inches (solid) to the
1000; ⟨4,000⟩4,700 solid in a column. possibly 4,800

28 M to line—34 to 1000
The smallest reading-type is ⟨6,300⟩ 8,000 to the column;
⟨[3½]⟩2¾ inches to the 1000. 2¾ (short 2¾ inch to 1000

1ˢᵗ page—(medium) . . . . 27,000.
2: ½ large, ½ smallest, . . . 12000 & 19,000
                            ⟨[21],000⟩31,000;
3ᵈ—(mainly smallest) . . . . 38,000.
4ᵗʰ (2 Col. Medium)   9,000
Total reading in 4 pages, . . . 108,000.
Double it: 216,000 ems.
Add 2 pages new ads: 75,000.
Total about 300,000.

---

[67] The anecdote about "Governor Gardiner" which Clemens noted in Notebook
13 (N&J2, p. 18).
[68] This anecdote is identified in note 13.
[69] Bram Stoker's story (see p. 195, note 45).

Bogus, 50,000.

Grand total 350,000 ems a day[70]

350,000 ems a day is possible in the Tribune; add Sunday &
extraordinary bogus, & it may be near 3,000,000 a week.

2 *type* (of all sorts) make an *em*. There are 43 & 44 type in a
Tribune editorial line all the time—& there are 22 ems in a line,
by Van's[71] measurement.

5,000 solid of the big editorial type ⟨is⟩becomes 6,000 when
leaded. When you lead 1,000 solid, it becomes 1200.

Alice, $28.16—3329.

Mrs. Z. B. ⟨Barnes⟩ Gustafson,
% Duane Barnes,
    Middletown, Conn.
between 1ˢᵗ & 6ᵗʰ Aug.

#3331—Mrs. Freese, $30.[72]

⟨Send Memoirs to Station Master Collins, Hartford—both vols.⟩

Special providence! That phrase nauseates me—with its implied
importance of mankind & triviality of God. In my opinion these

---

[70] Clemens derived this figure from his original set of calculations beginning with
"Tribune column of the medium type is 4,500 ems" (245.14). The computation would
be reasonable if all the type were to be leaded, but in fact the New York *Tribune* at this
time used a combination of leaded and unleaded type in almost every article. Clemens
revised his initial figures, apparently to reflect the greater amount of type the *Tribune*
would set if all its columns were unleaded, but he did not re-calculate the grand total.
Instead he seems to have begun restoring the original numbers by writing "STET" across
the entry about medium type. He did not mark the entries about big and small type.

[71] Charles G. Van Schuyver, a retired printer who was employed to determine the
efficiency of the Paige typesetter. Charles E. Davis, the Pratt & Whitney engineer who
supervised manufacture of the machine, later recalled: "The final arrangement of the
keyboard for setting type by syllables and words . . . was the result of an analytical
study of the language, covering all subjects, made by Charles G. Van Schuyver . . . and
to his patient work all praise is due" (Lucien A. Legros and John C. Grant, *Typographical
Printing-Surfaces* [London: Longmans, Green and Co., 1916], p. 378).

[72] Madame Cécile Freese was a Hartford French teacher and an acquaintance of the
Clemens family. Clemens' check may have been in payment for French lessons for Susy.

myriads of globes are merely the blood-corpuscles ebbing & flowing through the arteries of God, & we but animalculae that infest them, ⟨&⟩⟨dis[s]⟩disease them, pollute them: & God does not know we are there, & would not care if he did.[73]

Tuesday, Aug. 10 '86. All is set with brand-new matrices, every projection & hair-line clean-cut & handsome. Bran-new dress. For the first time, the alignment is good—almost good enough for book-work (except 4 or 5 first lines). Now let's see how long the letters will remain perfect & the alignment good.[74]

58[75]

3,400

1,500

1,500

Montreal, ... 140,000 8
Toronto . . . . 6 . . . . 86.
Halifax 34
Ottawa 4 27
                        18

Mexico 4 225
Havana 4 230
Lima 101
Santiago (Ch) 150
Buenos Ayres 300
Rio Janiero 4 275
                        12   [#]

---

[73] Mark Twain developed a variation on this theme in "Three Thousand Years Among the Microbes," written in 1905 (see *WWD*, pp. 430–553, especially pp. 454, 473).

[74] Clemens was keeping a watchful eye on the performance of the New York *Tribune's* Mergenthaler Linotype. Related observations occur on pages 251, 259, and 288.

[75] The following list of cities records their populations, in thousands, and the number of typesetting machines Clemens estimated would be required in each. The four numbers preceding the list, which Clemens added in the margin above "Montreal," are approximate totals of the number of machines in four sections of the list: "58" for "Montreal" through "Copenhagen," which is the first column in Clemens' list; "3,400" for "London" through "Liège," Clemens' second column; "1,500" for "Paris"; and "1,500" for the remaining cities.

Christiania 6 122

Stockholm 6 177

Bergen 40

St. Petersburg, ...   10 900
Moscow 612
Warsaw 400

Copenhagen 6 240
                                       28

London, ... 3,000 5,000,000
Glasgow . . . . ⟨20⟩25 . . . . 511.
Liverpool 20 552
Manchester, ... 25 400
Birmingham 20 400
Dublin 30 340
Leeds 20 300
Sheffield 10 300
Edinburg 50 230
Bristol 4 206
Belfast 8 174
Bradford 6 180
Dundee 3 142
Newcastle 5 145
Hull 161

    ⟨C[o]p[en]⟩ Netherlands:
Amster 50 330
Rotter 25 157
Hague 25 123

    Belgium:
Brussels 50 400
Antwerp 50 163
Ghent 133
Liège . . . . ⟨[2]22⟩[1]22 [#]

Paris . . . . 1500 . . . . 2,269.
Lyons . . . . 25 . . . . 376.
Marseilles 25 360
Havre 10 105

Madrid 25 400
Lisbon 10 250

Berlin, ... 500 1,122
Hamburg 100 410
Breslau 25 272
Dresden 25 220
Munich 20 230
Eberfeld 189
Cologne 145
Leipsic 50 150
Stuttgard 10 117
Frankfort 30 164
Strasburg 25 104
Bremen 10 112

Vienna 300 1,103

Geneva 20 68
Basle 20 61
Berne 20 44
Zurich 76

Naples, ... 500 30
Milan 321 30
Rome 300 30
Palermo 245
Turin 253 30
Florence 169 10
Genoa 179
Venice 133 10
Bologna 123 5

[#]

Bombay,. 773 20
Calcutta 684 25
Madras 406 10
Benares. 200
Delhi. 173

Melbourne 300 30
Sydney 224 10
Adelaide 38

Europe 6,500

60 American towns & cities, (maybe a few *capitols* where a small
market.

Say 500 needed outside of the 8 big cities. 1700 needed
⟨outside⟩ by the big cities. ⟨2000⟩2200 for all the US.

Prop. of Aug. 17/86. On the day that W.[76] sets & justifies on the
mach itself, within 30 days after it reaches N. Y., 42,000 in 6
consecutive hours (copy as it comes from that morning's papers),
I give him $300; & on any appointed day thereafter (though it be
the next) that he does 48,000 in 6 consecutive hours, I give him
$300 more.

Him? Grasping? Insatiable? That man wouldn't be satisfied if he
had the contract to furnish hell with fuel![77] [#]

---

[76] Franklin G. Whitmore's son William was being trained to operate the Paige typesetter for a planned New York City exhibition. Clemens repeated this prize offer in a
letter to the elder Whitmore also dated 17 August. "My dream," he explained, "is that
Van shall show the public what the average man can do on the machine, & that Will
shall show what the fast man can do on it." By training an inexperienced youth to use
the typesetter, Clemens probably hoped to prove the claim he made to Edward H. House
in a letter of 11 August 1886: "Our machine is a mechanical miracle; when a body sees it
work, he says 'it's poetry;' & yet it is so simple & sure, that a crossing-sweeper can put
down his broom & set type on it."

[77] Probably a reference to "that unco-pious butter-mouthed Sunday school-slobbering
sneak-thief John Wannemaker, now of Philadelphia, presently of hell" (SLC to William
Dean Howells, 15 July 1886, *MTHL*, p. 572). On 21 July 1886, Charles L. Webster &
Company had sought a preliminary injunction restraining the Philadelphia department
store owner from selling sets of the Grant *Memoirs* below subscription price. Wanamaker's self-satisfied advertisements for the book, which condemned subscription publishing while commending his own service to the public, infuriated Clemens as much as

Aug. 9,[78] struck the idea of renting on a basis of dividing with
the lessee the saving on each 1000 ems set—every 1000 recorded by
the machine to count as 1250—(because the machine sets solid
& the lessee must do his own leading.)

Aug 21. Proposed that we overcome the 2-line-letter difficulty by
having the 2-line letters cast in exact fractions of an em; set quads
in their place & stick the letters in in the galley, afterward.

T. O. E.[79] to be head chief & borrow of Chemical,—& have a
$\frac{1}{500}$ interest. WML to sell 800 here at a com^n of $50 each—⟨& as
many⟩ he to make the contracts & collect the $1000 bonus (if we
have any difficulty in doing it ourselves. Give him the same com^n
on 1200 in Europe.

Aug. 21. '86. Within the past few days the Tribune has ceased
from using its first set of matrices; it was quite time, for they were
worn out. The first I heard of that machine setting Tribune matter
was last december—or maybe a month earlier—it was still in
Baltimore then. Got it from Laffan. But ⟨their⟩there was never
an evidence in the Tribune itself until one month ago (July 23.)[80]
Now whether they wore out that set in 8 months or 1 month, the
fact remains: it's a costly luxury to its employer.

The Trib introduced 2 new sets lately—the first ⟨in⟩ about the
first ⟨week⟩ of this month—the other a week or two later. [#]

---

the interference with Webster & Company's elaborate sales apparatus. On 3 August
Clemens was in attendance in the United States Circuit Court of Philadelphia when legal
arguments were heard. On 9 August the injunction was denied, a decision that was influenced by Webster & Company's known history of selling to trade outlets.

[78] Clemens apparently intended to write "Aug. 19."

[79] Clemens was counting on Thomas O. Enders, president of the United States Bank
in Hartford, to help raise capital for the Paige typesetter. He was also expecting assistance
from New York Sun publisher William M. Laffan, who had evidently reconsidered an
earlier commitment to the Mergenthaler Linotype (see p. 215, note 94). Laffan must
have been as disillusioned as Clemens was pleased by the New York Tribune's difficulties
with the Mergenthaler machine, described in the following entry and recurrently in this
notebook. By May of 1888 Clemens would convince himself that Laffan could earn
"$210,000 in ten or twelve months" (see MTLP, p. 246) selling the Paige machine. Never-
theless, there is no indication that Laffan agreed to become Clemens' salesman.

[80] The first Mergenthaler Linotype was installed at the New York Tribune on 3 July
1886.

Aug. 31, 1886. Revealed to Livy[81] my project of buying the remains of Christopher Columbus & placing them in the base of the Statue of Liberty Enlightening the World, in New York harbor. No—rotunda of the Capitol at Washington.

"I don't see *why* they would have those tunnels. I wish they would *take* those tunnels *away*."[82]

"She's a very *un*spirited (uncivil) cat. (S. M.)"

"Golden Rod. He's got the prettiest face—& &—the nicest manners of all the cats."

"Week after month"

"Why the very *idea* to ass' you to make a fire." (Aunt Sue told me to.) Well I shouldn't think you *would*. (What *would* I do?" (Why, *read* & take your time).

⟨"I wish they would *take* those tunnels away."⟩

"If you pat old S M on the body she'll gramble."

"Zoraster Morning Glory Stanchfield"

100 isn't much from 40—it is for *dollars,* but it isn't to *count.*

Shep—"He is a very *nice* dog—in his *manners.*"

P. B. Bromfield[83]
Newspaper Advertising
21 Park Row. N.Y. [#]

---

[81] Clemens initially wrote "L"; "ivy" was added later, perhaps by Clemens but possibly by Paine, who included this passage in *Mark Twain's Notebook* (New York and London: Harper & Brothers, 1935), p. 190. In notebooks of this period, Clemens occasionally used "L" to refer to William M. Laffan.

[82] Entries through "Shep . . . *manners.*" (252.18) were intended as additions to the "Record of the Small Foolishnesses of Susie & 'Bay' Clemens," which Clemens had intermittently compiled between August 1876 and September 1884. These notes, several of which concern the family cats—Sour Mash, Golden Rod, and Zoraster Morning Glory Stanchfield—were not added to the "Record."

[83] In order to determine the market for the Paige typesetter, Clemens had instructed Frederick J. Hall to employ "some advertising agency" in a confidential inquiry to pro-

Sept 3—Through Mr. Hall, have offered Bromfield $325 for the whole work, including the dailies of N.Y. city

The Family Cat.

No advertisements admited.

monment to 2000 killed in 12 yrs by the Board of Assassins.

GERHARDT.[84]

Diana of the Xroads—by Geo. Meredith.[85]

Prince Otto, by author of Kidnapped.[86]

Pay the bill at Fitch's

John Bodewin's Testimony by Mary Hallock Foote.—(if they've got it.)—Don't send for it.[87] [#]

---

duce a list of "every *daily* newspaper in the U.S. and Canada that contains fully *2 pages of new matter daily*" and "*about* how many 1000 ems of new matter each of said papers prints daily" (SLC to Hall, 19 August 1886, *MTLP*, p. 203). When Bromfield produced responses to about one-third of the requests for information, Clemens professed himself satisfied, although not without commenting that facts would have been more pleasing than "romance" (SLC to Hall, 30 September 1886, *MTLP*, p. 208).

[84] On 7 September 1886, after months of deliberation, the Israel Putnam Monument Commission awarded a contract for an equestrian statue of the colonial soldier to Karl Gerhardt. Always alert to possible new projects, Gerhardt wrote Clemens on 10 September asking advice about using his Putnam success to influence a pending assignment.

[85] Clemens was probably acquiring *Diana of the Crossways* (1885) for Livy. Albert Bigelow Paine reported that "Mrs. Clemens and her associates were caught in the Meredith movement and read *Diana of the Crossways* and the *Egoist* with reverential appreciation. The Meredith epidemic did not touch Mark Twain" (*MTB*, p. 847).

[86] The works by Robert Louis Stevenson were published in 1885 and 1886 respectively.

[87] A romantic novel set in the Arkansas silver-mining region in the 1870s (Boston: Ticknor and Co., 1886).

Law to forbid all but whistles inside of buildings & on locomotives.

Chatto's 2 notes:
£200. Dated Aug. 24. Falls due ⟨6 months later⟩ Feb. 27, '87.
£271:16:9. Dated Aug. 24. Falls due March 27, '87.

Send Molly for Mr. S. $100 Jan 1 '87, & the same every 4 months thereafter.[88]

1000 to 1 that I do one of 2 things: I will either cure him or prove to him that he hasn't got as much reasoning-faculty as a cat. There is only one vice which I except; that is the p. m's,[89] his possession of it is proof that he lacks the raw material for a cure.

profanity given up—on account of fatigue
one all comprehensive cataclysmal curse
sesquipedalian

Wise business men drop harassments in bed—the others get softening of the brain [#]

---

[88] Clemens began to absorb some of the medical expenses of Mollie Clemens' father, William Stotts, before January 1887. On 16 November 1886, Orion Clemens reported that every Sunday he was accustomed to visit Mr. Stotts, who was confined to Saint Joseph's Hospital in Keokuk, "and pay the sisters five dollars, which, but for your generosity would have been a cramping business this month." On 25 November Mollie Clemens added her thanks for "such a surprise in a check . . . more than we really needed. . . . Pa just cried like a child and asked how you came to do that. I told him, I could not see any other way for your doing it, only because you were so good to us, and to him. He said 'I don't know why he should be so good to me.'" Stotts, a pioneer, public official, and popular resident of Keokuk, died in Saint Joseph's Hospital on 13 June 1888 at the age of eighty-eight.

[89] Mark Twain's abbreviation of "pledge-maker's." This passage was evidently drafted for "Concerning a Reformed Pledge: A New-Year Sermon," an unpublished piece written and revised in the fall and winter of 1886. In that article, Mark Twain hoped "to make as strong and earnest a protest as I can against pledges to cease from bad habits, & pledges to never begin bad habits," arguing that such pledges were necessarily ineffective because of one's "dumb yearning to shake himself free of his shackles & be a man again." The fragmentary notes in the following entry were for a discussion of curing profanity in the same piece.

N. Y. Errands.[90]
Examine Johnson Heat Regulating Apparatus.[91]

⟨18⟩ 17 years practice
I know that ⟨applying s[o]⟩⟨⟨a[p]⟩assaulting so small a trouble
with so large a⟩ so large a remedy to so so apparently small a
trouble ⟨is⟩was rather like hunting ⟨rabbits⟩ cats with artillery, but
I will explain that my colds in the head were not of the regulation
size; they were a kind of cyclone, & they blew ten days; they left
nothing behind but wreckage & devastation. Moderate remedies
had no effect upon them.[92]

Sept. 14, '86
Rev. J. Chester:
Your⟨s⟩ confession received. The Arab proverb says: When a
man deceives me once, it is his fault; when he deceives me twice, it
is mine. When you play your confidence game on me again
(Bunco-steerer" for "Christ." It's safer.[93] [#]

---

[90] The Clemens family planned to spend 17 through 27 September in New York City
while returning from Elmira to Hartford.

[91] During the summer of 1886, Clemens had considered methods of modifying the
inadequate heating system of his Hartford home. He was particularly concerned about
his furnace, which he reported to Whitmore in late July, "was born bad & *can't* be improved." The "Johnson Heat-Regulating Apparatus," advertised as "equal in importance
to the telephone," was a thermostat which Clemens examined in the fall of 1886.

[92] A very rough draft of a passage ultimately deleted from a discussion of the uses and
means of fasting in Mark Twain's unpublished "Concerning a Reformed Pledge: A New-
Year Sermon."

[93] Since 1882 Clemens had contributed to the support of several Negro students at
Lincoln University in Chester County, Pennsylvania, and in 1886 was also helping one
of its graduates complete studies at Yale Law School. He came to regard the Reverend J.
Chester, the unctuous financial agent of the school, as a "humbug," a "clerical fraud,"
and a "bilk," however. When Chester reported on 7 September 1886 that a student
Clemens was sponsoring had decided to stay on at Lincoln University for post-graduate
theological study, Clemens refused further assistance, explaining: "Of course I made no
stipulation that would hamper my student in the slightest degree in the choosing a profession—I would rather starve a man than curtail his liberty in any way. No, I merely
hoped he would make choice of some useful occupation; he has disappointed me, & I
feel no further interest in him" (SLC to Chester, 10 September 1886). On 14 September,
Clemens sent a version of the letter he drafted here, for the following month Chester

Pier 8 North river.

From Rector st to ⟨Oce⟩ Sandy Hook by boat. Then train to Spring Lake, which is (6 miles) next station beyond Ocean Grove. 2 hours. 11 oclock boat is *good*. Avoid the 1 pm boat.[94]

J. Wells Taylor
    Bergh Society.[95]

Prof. Stowe says under "Illustration D" of his "Illustrations to Chapter 3" of his "History of the Books of the Bible" that a fac simile of no part of the *New* Testament (Vatican Bible) has ever been permitted to be taken, though fac similes from the *Old* have been allowed, & he furnishes a specimen. Good thing if we could get a scrap for the Pope's ⟨life⟩Life.[96]

But Stowe adds that (⟨about 1870⟩1867 1867) Prof. Tischendorff was about to issue the Vatican B. parts of *both* Testaments to be in fac simile. Was it done?

Get checks for baggage through to Hartford. ⟨Pay 40 cents per piece transportation ($2) in Elmira.⟩

The police-captain's book.[97] [#]

---

replied: "What you mean by my '*confession*, I do not understand. The 'Arab proverb' is all right, but its application I don't see" (Chester to SLC, 15 October 1886).

[94] A one-day excursion to Springlake Beach, New Jersey, which the Clemenses planned to undertake while they were stopping in New York City. This entry was made before the family left Elmira on 17 September 1886.

[95] No information has been discovered about Clemens' business at the New York office of the American Society for the Prevention of Cruelty to Animals. Henry Bergh, the society's founder, was still its president at this time. J. Wells Taylor has not been identified.

[96] Bernard O'Reilly's *Life of Leo XIII* did not include an Old Testament reproduction. The facsimile of both testaments to be prepared by biblical scholar Constantin Von Tischendorf, mentioned in the following entry, was not published.

[97] A book "likely to attract attention" by George Washington Walling, retired New York police superintendent. On 3 September 1886, Fred J. Hall wrote Clemens that Walling's work "gives the inside of a great many celebrated cases" and "the inside history of the Police and Detective Bureaus of the City for a great many years . . . without gloves." It was offered to Charles L. Webster & Company by a member of the firm which had intended to publish it, but "some of the statements made were so strong that they were afraid that it would raise a storm, and as Superintendent Walling did not wish to

Letter from Gen. Drum.[98]

⟨Mrs. Jas. Beecher
  Bayport, Conn
  Prince & P.[99]

$57.85. *TWC*[100]

orto for Sue

Brer W send 50 cigars to Murray Hill & 450 home.⟩[101]

Apple Trees.
Harvest Apple Trees.
Fall pippins ⎫
King apples ⎬ Get the best varieties of these.
Greenings. ⎭

Farm: Estimated the family (6 persons) in bulk at $40 per week,
& the pony at $3. (Add $50 to the whole to cover possible
overlookings.

William $18; Richard & Ernest $12 each. [#]

---

modify it any, they did not dare to publish the book in its present state." Clemens proposed tentative terms for Walling's book and suggested that Webster & Company's
lawyers "read it and mark the worst of the libelous passages for expunging" (*MTLP*, p.
206), but he wanted the final decision to await Webster's return from Rome. Webster
evidently disapproved, for *Recollections of a New York Chief of Police* was published
in 1887 by the Caxton Book Concern, the publisher originally interested in it.

[98] At Clemens' request, Richard C. Drum, adjutant general of the United States
Army, had made inquiry to determine if a letter from Clemens had reached General
Philip Sheridan. On 10 September 1886, Drum wrote Clemens at Elmira, apologizing for
neglecting "to communicate the [affirmative] result of my inquiry to you" because of
"sickness in my family which has taken much of my time." Clemens may have been attempting to arrange a meeting concerning Sheridan's *Personal Memoirs*, which Webster
& Company was trying to secure in the fall of 1886 (see note 105).

[99] Clemens' condolence gift to the widow of James C. Beecher, Congregational clergyman, missionary, Civil War infantry officer, who had committed suicide on 25 August
1886 while under treatment, at the Elmira water-cure, for chronic mental disturbance.

[100] Here and below (257.13–16), Clemens noted his financial obligations to Theodore
W. Crane for summer expenses at Quarry Farm. A related set of calculations appears on
page 296.

[101] Clemens sent this directive to Whitmore on 16 September 1886, noting that the
Murray Hill Hotel in New York City was to be "our address for the next 10 days."

Mrs. W^m. Gillette
    Care Mrs. Hatch
        18 W 51st st.

Fremont is writing a book.[102]

Dr. J. N. Farrar[103]
Apartment 1
    Rensselaer
B'way & ⟨3^d⟩32^d st

Buy a gun.

How many copies sold

3360. Mrs. S. E. Urie 93^90

Bocard (Mrs. C) will be glad this af or eve.
    325—4th ave.
Come at once.

Furniture covers at 42 E 14.

See House.

E. I. Horsman[104]
cor Maiden Lane & William.
Buffalo tricycle.

S[105] & I meet the others *in* Webster's office at 11.^30 [#]

---

[102] Frémont's *Memoirs of My Life* (Chicago and New York: Belford, Clarke & Co., 1887).

[103] John Nutting Farrar was a New York physician and dentist who was about to begin a program of corrective treatment of Clara Clemens' teeth. He first examined Clara in mid-September 1886 while the Clemens family was in New York City. On 29 September he informed Clemens that the protracted work Clara required "is among the most difficult in the profession and must be done right or, no good." He estimated that the cost would be "somewhere from 350 to 400 [dollars], more probably 400, but not exceeding it."

[104] A dealer in bicycles and tricycles located at 80 and 82 William Street in New York City.

[105] Possibly General Philip Sheridan. This meeting may have been scheduled to discuss publication of his *Personal Memoirs* by Charles L. Webster & Company. Sheridan signed a contract with the firm in early November 1886. His work appeared in 1888.

Sunday Sept 26 the Tribune contains a page of leaded *minion* done on a machine. So they've at least 2 sizes of matrices, whether they've 2 machines or not.

Old Jim Howland's Speech.

Closed his ⟨S. S. school⟩ first "Experience-meeting⟨["]⟩⟨"⟩" speech after conversion with: "And as for ⟨one,⟩ me, *I* hope to live to see the day when ⟨the⟩this whole ⟨wide⟩ world will be one brotherhood in Christ; & when the terms Christian & s—— # ——s will cease to be ⟨no longer⟩ synonymous."

Clarence King's remark, as quoted by Kate Jenkins—speaking of some wealthy families of contented animals occupying rows of rocking chairs on the verandah of a summer resort, "their countenances softly lighted with the peace of gold which passeth understanding."[106]

Jean—'Scoose me."

Hist Hartford[107]

Tues, Oct 5, 1.30 PM
Dʳ Farrar J. N. 1271 B'way

3381—(Ad Ex) Maltby & Co
    Atlas, Phila—$25

Pretty girl & ugly girl were asked which they'd rather be, homely or homeless. Stumped them both. Couldn't arrive at a decision

⟨R⟩C L W reply to Curtis.

Are German plays at Thalia?[108] [#]

---

[106] Katharine Jenkins' work was collected in *Stories* (Baltimore: John Murphy & Co., 1892). Clemens' source for her quotation of this remark by Clarence King, the eminent geologist, mining engineer, and author, remains obscure.

[107] Probably a reference to the *Memorial History of Hartford County, Connecticut,* 2 vols. (Boston: Edward L. Osgood, 1886), edited by Clemens' acquaintance, James Hammond Trumbull.

[108] Beginning on 1 October 1886 and continuing into January 1887, the Thalia Theatre in New York City presented a series of German operettas described as "waves of frivolity" (George C. D. Odell, *Annals of the New York Stage*, 15 vols. [New York: Columbia University Press, 1927–1949], 13:276).

Anne Brown, 715—5th av.

The canvass for a book—*any* book—utterly ceases 15 days after issue & is *never* resumed.

John's man began Oct. 8.

Charley—
Kalakaua's book.[109]

Charley, what did you find out about the deeds to our property?

Geo. Standring[110]
   8 & 9 Finsbury st
   London, E.C.

Psychical Society
14 Dean's Yard
   London.
   Prof. Barret.[111] [#]

---

[109] On 11 November 1885, Clemens first informed Webster that Rollin M. Daggett, an old *Territorial Enterprise* associate and a former United States minister to Hawaii, had "constructed" a book about "the (historical) Traditions and legends of the natives" with the assistance of Hawaiian king David Kalakaua, whom Clemens had met in 1866 (see N&J1, p. 230). "It is fresh ground—untouched, unworn, and full of romantic interest. . . . With a sufficient concession from [Kalakaua], I would rather have this book than any that is offering now. It can be fascinatingly illustrated," Clemens noted, perhaps recalling his own "illustrated Sandwich Islands book" which had failed to interest a publisher in 1866 and 1867. Webster agreed that the "book would have a market value, and would undoubtedly have a large sale," but only if "the King's name appeared as author" (*MTLP*, pp. 192–193). It was finally published by Webster & Company in 1888 as *The Legends and Myths of Hawaii: The Fables and Folk-Lore of a Strange People*—"By his Hawaiian Majesty Kalakaua; edited and with an introduction by Hon. R. M. Daggett," but did not achieve the anticipated success.

[110] A London printer and political writer who edited a magazine first called the *Republican* and later renamed the *Radical*, Standring was an admiring correspondent of Mark Twain's. In the summer of 1886, Clemens had asked Standring for a copy of his *People's History of the English Aristocracy*, which evidently became an important source for *A Connecticut Yankee* (see the discussion of Standring in Howard Baetzhold's *Mark Twain and John Bull* [Bloomington: Indiana University Press, 1970]). Clemens had also asked Standring to provide him with information about the rates paid English newspaper compositors, obviously as an aid in assessing the Paige typesetter's international appeal.

[111] Sir William Fletcher Barrett, the British physicist and professor at the Royal

Honorary Member of Scottish Society of Lit & Art—Glasgow. Oct '86. Alfred J. Weyman, Secretary. (Journalist.)[112]

Look in at Arnold Constable & correct bill. (in this notebook.)

Eliz Cady Stanton & daughter gone to Europe to write "Woman's Version of the Bible."[113]

R. M. Daggett,
 Virginia, Nev.
Write him.[114]

The beads were blessed by the Pope, Saturday July 10, '86, at 5. p.m. at a PRIVATE audience.[115] [#]

College of Science in Dublin, was a founder of the Society for Psychical Research. On 4 October 1884, Clemens had accepted Barrett's invitation to become a member of the society, expressing "strong interest" in "Thought-transference, as you call it, or mental telegraphy as I have been in the habit of calling it . . . for the past nine or ten years" (*Journal of Society for Psychical Research*, October 1884, p. 166). Records of the society indicate that Clemens remained a member until 1902.

[112] On 27 September 1886, Weyman had notified Clemens of his unanimous election as a "Corresponding member of the Society" whose purpose was "the cultivation of Literature, Music, Elocution, and Art generally." Clemens undoubtedly found the honor easy to accept since the rules of the society, enclosed by Weyman, specified that "Corresponding Members shall be exempt from all subscriptions," and "shall not have any voice in the Society's affairs."

[113] Elizabeth Cady Stanton, a pioneer in the women's rights movement, was the principal editor of *The Woman's Bible*, 2 vols. (New York: European Publishing Co., 1895, 1898), a controversial analysis of the Bible's disparaging depiction of women. Her daughter, Harriot Stanton Blatch, a suffrage leader, was not among those who assisted as members of the work's "Revising Committee."

[114] On 21 October 1886, Clemens wrote congratulating Daggett on the "good persuading" he had done, evidently a reference to a successful effort to convince King David Kalakaua to appear as author of the book of Hawaiian legends Webster & Company wished to publish (see note 109).

[115] As a memento of his papal audience, Webster had presented the Clemens family with a rosary blessed by Pope Leo XIII. On 18 October 1886, Clemens wrote to Annie Webster:

> The Pope's rosary has created such another stir in this household as was before utterly unimaginable. I would not take a thousand dollars for it—& I guess your aunt Livy's price would run higher still. We have three excellent girls in the house, & I believe they value more the telling their beads on that rosary than they would the handling government bonds that fell in their laps as a free gift. (*MTBus*, p. 367)

The three girls mentioned were Clemens family servants.

Oct. 16, '86, subscribed for $3,000 of Laffan's telegraph stock.[116]

Saturday Morning Club—our house—November 6th.

Ask Webster if he sent 2 Uncle Toms.[117]

One train leaves N. Y side at 1, the other 3.40.

Be at Desbrasses at 3.30[118]

Miss Minnie D. Louis
   66 W. 56th

Get a tree calf Uncle Tom from Charley.

Curious survivals:
Giving out hymns;
   "   " appointments;
Church bells.
⟨No probation⟩ ⟨Hell.⟩

Ask Mr. Dana about the man who offered to Associated-press an ad for $500.[119] [#]

---

[116] On 7 December 1886, at Laffan's request, Clemens remitted three thousand dollars to the treasurer of the International Telegraph and Cable Company. The investment was unfortunate, for on 3 October 1887 Laffan wrote: ". . . as to the great cable invention . . . let me explain to you in person, when I see you next, what a Goddamned humiliating and degrading fizzle it proved to be . . . and how the first of experts are the cream of asses, and how I am now fully trying to get the money back."

[117] On 22 October 1886, Webster informed Clemens that he had sent two copies of *Uncle Tom's Cabin* to Hartford for inscription by Harriet Beecher Stowe. One of the books was for Mrs. Jesse R. Grant, the other was for Webster himself. "I think this is the first instance where I have bothered you on the autograph question," Webster apologized, "and it will be the last."

[118] Desbrosses Street in New York City was the site of a terminal for ferries to Jersey City. The purpose of this trip has not been determined.

[119] Clemens was seeking further evidence of a practice he had condemned in 1885 in an unpublished section of his Autobiographical Dictations about the Grant *Memoirs*. He claimed there that when he tried to place a statement rectifying inaccurate reports of his acquisition of Grant's book, an employee of the "Associated Press" (not related to the present agency):

read it over, hesitated, said it was certainly a matter of great public interest but that he couldn't see any way to make the statement without its being also a pretty good advertisement for General Grant's book, and for my publishing firm; but he said if we would

⟨What is the price of Blaine's book?⟩[120]

Go & see Laffan.

⟨Telegraph Ebbitt House.⟩

Give me $30.

⟨Send & buy me a ticket.⟩

My Sermon[121]

Set Will W at work at 7 cents.[122]

Get order for admission to Governor's island.[123]

Have that man get judgment & then refuse to compromise. We will give him a more valuable interest ($\frac{1}{25}$ than they *can.*

Get John M.[124] to furnish 3 or 4 M at 5 p/c a year & 3 or 4 per cent of the whole profits.

Or—which is preferable—get 500 taken here & give 10 per cent of American profits.

500 in Great B & 10 pc there. 200 in France & Germany & 10 per cent of all profits that shall accrue in those countries. [#]

---

pay $500 he would send it over the wires to every newspaper in the country. . . . This pleasant offer was declined.

Albert Bigelow Paine included another account of the same incident in *Mark Twain's Autobiography* (1:56–57).

[120] After his defeat by Grover Cleveland in the presidential election of 1884, James G. Blaine had written the second volume of his *Twenty Years of Congress: From Lincoln to Garfield* (Norwich, Conn.: Henry Bill Publishing Co., 1886). On at least one occasion Webster & Company used this subscription book as a yardstick in pricing a work of its own.

[121] The unpublished "Concerning a Reformed Pledge: A New-Year Sermon" (see p. 254, note 89; p. 264, note 127; and p. 275, note 164).

[122] William Whitmore, whom Clemens was having trained to operate the Paige typesetter (see p. 250, note 76). Clemens here proposed to increase young Whitmore's pay for each 1000 ems of type set in the course of the informal apprenticeship. He had begun at a rate of two cents for each 1000 ems.

[123] Clemens was to be on Governor's Island on the evening of 11 November to read at a meeting of the Military Service Institution (see p. 244, note 65).

[124] John W. Mackay, whom Clemens hoped to interest in the Paige typesetter (see p. 240, note 48).

Go down ⟨Thursday⟩ Friday morning:[125]

Call on Gen. Fry;

"   "   Mrs. Grant;

"   "   Laffan;

Provide drawing room tickets for next day;

Receive mother ⟨[f]⟩next morning at Murray Hill ⟨or RR station⟩ at ⟨[10.4]5.⟩12.15. Friday.

Get spectacles.

See Gen. Fry.

⟨Charley, give me address of Genl. Agent for Conn—for D[r.] Snow.⟩[126]

See Ac & Co about this bill.

Give the sermon to Mr. Bacheller.[127] [#]

---

[125] In fact, Clemens went to New York on Thursday, 11 November, to keep his speaking engagement on Governor's Island. He stayed over in the city, probably at the Murray Hill Hotel, and on Friday, 12 November, saw General James B. Fry, Mrs. Julia Grant, and William M. Laffan, and met Mrs. Jervis Langdon. The following day he returned with her to Hartford, where she was to spend part of the winter of 1886/1887.

[126] Gustavus N. Snow was a Hartford dentist. Clemens tore out a page from the notebook following this entry on 26 October 1886 for a hurried letter to Livy from New York City. He reported that he had just returned from Washington, where he had evidently conferred with Philip Sheridan about Webster & Company's publication of his memoirs. "I am just in from the 6-hour night-trip," Clemens wrote, "& mighty tired & sleepy, because I slept badly last night. Goodbye—I love you, darling."

[127] On 8 September 1886, Irving Bacheller had asked Clemens to "write a short article suitable for publication Christmas Day for our syndicate of newspapers. . . . Anything you might feel disposed to write on any conceivable subject even if it were very short we would be glad to get." A week later Clemens noted on Bacheller's request: "Wrote that I had a sermon. Would wait a month & if it then *could still bear my own inspection* would forward it." "Concerning a Reformed Pledge: A New-Year Sermon" survived this scrutiny, accomplished partly through a reading on 11 October to the Monday Evening Club. After extensive revision, Clemens dated it "Hartford, Christmas, 1886" and had it printed by the Paige typesetter before attempting to publish it. Frequent references to the "Sermon" in this notebook indicate Clemens' satisfaction with it and his wish to see it in print. Never heless, its excessive length as well as its general banality, evident in Clemens' humorless insistence that one could "tire out" an unhealthy desire by thinking of something else "& then it will not come back any more," apparently caused its rejection by Bacheller and others.

Challenge Mr. Dana to billiards.
Show him the sermon.

Spectacles.

Gen. Fry.

⟨Telegraph both Charley.⟩

Call for mother Friday morning.

Write Waring[128] before Wednesday.

Horace King,[129]
Thompsonville.

Get 3 (?) drawing-room tickets Friday for Saturday.

Miss M. R. Samuel,
    218 E 46th,

Gen. James B. Fry
30 East 63[d][130]

In Wales the parson came to collect tithes.[131] The ⟨wom⟩

---

[128] George E. Waring, Jr., was a prominent "Consulting Engineer, for Sanitary and Agricultural Drainage" and the author of numerous scientific works and several volumes of travel pieces and literary sketches. A friend of the Clemens family's, Waring arranged some work on their Hartford home in the spring of 1886.

[129] A man who had applied for rights in Clemens' Kaolatype process. On 25 August 1886 Clemens instructed Frederick J. Hall to "sell the unsold United States rights in the Kaolatype patent to him on the terms proposed by him. . . . As to whether he is 'good' or not, it isn't of any consequence to me" (*MTLP*, pp. 204–205). And on 3 September he repeated the order to Webster, again expressing indifference about King's reliability. This entry suggests that the matter was still pending around mid-November 1886.

[130] "We will be most happy to have you stay with us," General Fry had written Clemens on 5 November 1886, "when you come to this city to read a paper before the Military Service Insti. on the 11th instant. We are a family of three, a dog, a woman, and a man. If children are necessary to your comfort you had better bring them, as I don't know that I could even borrow one for the occasion." Clemens probably refused this invitation, preferring to stay at the Murray Hill Hotel, where he intended to meet Livy's mother (see note 125).

[131] Clemens' reaction to the November 1886 Welsh protests against Church of England tithes influenced his generally unfriendly portrayal of the clergy in *A Connecticut Yankee*. He used the ancedote about the farmer's wife in chapter 20 of that work.

farmer's wife said "Parson, I have 11 children—will you take one of them? You take the tenth pig; will you have the tenth child?" And is "tithes" a tenth of *all* a man's crop, live & otherwise? However, call it a tenth of the animal crop of livestock only, & think what a frightful tax it is—on a poor man. It *does* leave a gap as if one of his family had been taken.

Read the anecdote in Oct or Nov. '86

Suppose God had levied this tax upon the incomes of the rich? How long would it have remained in force? A week? ⟨I⟩Try to imagine ⟨godly⟩ rich godly Englishmen paying from $10,000 to $800,000 a year to the church, & making no murmur, raising no hell about it. What a pity God didn't levy the tax upon the rich alone. *I* would. However, he knew the rich couldn't be forced to pay it & the poor could. With all his brutalities & stupidities & grotesqueries, that old Hebrew God always had a good business head. He always stopped talking shop (that is, piousness,⟨⟩⟩ sentiment, sweetness & light), & came right down to business whenever there was matter concerning shekels on hand. His commercial satisfaction in the clink of the shekel runs all through his Book—that book whose "every word" he inspired, & whose ideas were all his own; among them the idea of levying a one-tenth income tax upon paupers. We hear a great deal about the interior evidences of the "divine origin" of that Book. Yes; & yet the tithe-tax could have ⟨been⟩ originated in hell if interior evidences go for anything.

Taking for granted that Lowell knew, is no sufficient defence. He should have distinctly *told* him that what he said would be printed. If he did not do that, his case is serious—his act was a crime most easily describable (at the proper time) & punishable in but one way. The question for the Committee is mere that one: Did he plainly *tell* Lowell that what he said would be printed? or did he merely *intimate* it in some darkling way, hoping it would not be understood   If he merely *intimated* it, ⟨& in so⟩ I conceive that that was not sufficient. However, in any case, let him give his exact language & *prove* it.[132]

---

[132] On 24 October 1886, the New York *World* published "Lowell in a Chatty Mood,"

Also, did he send a proof? If he didn't, his act is a crime, &
nothing can excuse it.

Instead of brickbatting H. he ought to libel the World.[133]

J. W. Schuckers
  % Ewing & Southard
    155 Bway, or
Belleville, N.J.[134]

Brer W., add to the list the Securities in Elmira. [#]

---

an interview with James Russell Lowell conducted by Julian Hawthorne, the paper's
literary editor. In the course of the interview Lowell, the recently retired United States
minister to England, commented injudiciously upon English royalty and nobility, public
officials and farmers, artists and writers. His published remarks caused Lowell acute embarrassment and, claiming not to have been informed that he was speaking for quotation,
he protested: "The reporter has made me say the reverse of what I really must have said
and of what is the truth" (New York *World*, 27 October 1886). Hawthorne insisted, however, that Lowell had been neither misled nor misrepresented. The *World* prolonged the
resultant controversy through most of the month of November by reproaching Lowell
directly and by reprinting remarks from other newspapers which were also offended by
his seeming desire to placate the English. On Thursday, 11 November, the day Clemens
went to New York City for his Military Service Institution reading, the *World* published
a lengthy letter in which Hawthorne gave particulars that Lowell had not been able to
refute. The paper commented editorially: "We have in our possession letters and telegrams from Mr. Lowell, which are not to be published because they are personal, which
show exclusively that Mr. Lowell must have understood the purely journalistic basis upon
which he was approached by Mr. Hawthorne." The committee mentioned in this entry
was evidently named by the Authors Club, to which Hawthorne, Lowell, and Clemens
belonged, to investigate the matter. Clemens planned to attend a club meeting on the
evening of 11 November at which expulsion of Hawthorne was to be considered. No such
action was taken, however, for Hawthorne was still a member of the club in 1887.

   [133] Clemens was probably recalling the Charles C. Duncan-New York *Times* lawsuit
of 1883, which the Hawthorne-Lowell disagreement closely resembled. In preparing for
possible legal action after his harsh remarks about Duncan appeared in the *Times*, Clemens had resorted to a claim that the newspaper had not sent him proofs of the comments
it attributed to him (see p. 18, note 34).

   [134] In late November 1886, Clemens, Franklin G. Whitmore, and James W. Paige met
in Hartford with J. W. Schuckers of the Printer Composing Machine Company. They
were particularly interested in a spacing device which Schuckers had developed. Although
there was amicable consideration of the acquisition of rights to Schuckers' machine, possibly through consolidation with his firm, discussions were broken off on 30 November because of "the constructive incompleteness of your machine, and the many difficulties that
have presented themselves toward any negotiation" (Whitmore to Thomas Ewing, 30
November 1886). Thomas Ewing and M. I. Southard comprised the New York law firm
which represented Schuckers. Ewing was also majority stockholder in Schuckers'
company.

Mr. Hurd, 231 Main[135]

[es]. Blackbird.

Stationers Dinner—Bram Stoker's Christening?[136]

Stationers & Publishers Dinner, Hotel Brunswick, Thursday Feb.
10, at 7 p.m.
Henry B. Barnes.
Alexander Agar.

"What do you think of CHICAGO!"[137]

A story wherein the pantaletted little children talked the stilted
big-word sentimental hifalutin of Walter Scott's heroes & the other
& older ⟨novel[i]s⟩novels (Pamela &c).

$10 to ⟨Susy⟩Susan Corey,[138] Paris. [#]

---

[135] Charles F. Hurd & Company, Hartford dealers in "crockery, china, etc."
(*Geer's*[1886], p. 115). The "Blackbird" may have been an addition to the Hartford
house collection of bric-a-brac.

[136] On 20 November 1886, Clemens informed Henry B. Barnes, president of the Stationers' Board of Trade, that he "would like very well indeed to be present" at the board's
annual dinner "with the *speech* requirement left out. Being a publisher myself, I should
like to meet & get acquainted with fellow-craftsmen; & would also like to get up & talk,
in case the spirit moved me to approve or assail things dropped in the course of other people's speeches; but I could not respond to a toast. A toast makes preparation necessary, &
I am too old & lazy to make even the triflingest preparation for a speech. I have reached
that stage where one would rather make a bad off-hand speech than a good painstakingly-
constructed one." Barnes accepted this condition and on 6 December Clemens promised
to attend. This entry and several later entries in this notebook indicate that despite his
disclaimer, Clemens did not intend to arrive unprepared for the Stationers' Board of
Trade dinner. On 10 February he entertained with a rambling, although only partially
extemporaneous, speech in which "Bram Stoker's Christening" (see p. 195, note 45) did
not figure.

[137] In an Autobiographical Dictation of 10 October 1906, Clemens recalled that at the
1879 Chicago banquet of the Army of the Tennessee the man sitting next to him "was
very hard of hearing, and he had a habit common to deaf people of shouting his remarks
instead of delivering them in an ordinary voice. He would handle his knife and fork in
reflective silence for five or six minutes at a time and then suddenly fetch out a shout that
would make you jump out of the United States." This habit produced a startling effect
when, at the climax of someone else's story about a gruesome murder, the deaf man suddenly interrupted, screaming: "How Do You Like CHICA-A-AGO?!!!" (*North American
Review*, September 1907, p. 9).

[138] A friend of the Clemens family who occasionally gave piano lessons to Susy
Clemens.

Send tickets to Beecher & Warners.

Go see G.'s statue.[139]

Send $20 to Walt Whitman, poet.[140]

Send $ or or 3 to the gate-tenders.

Also to the car-drivers

Speak to Br. W[h] about listing my Elmira securities.

Send copy of M[c]Clellan's book[141] to
   Mrs. Gen Custer
      148 East 18th St.
       New York

Send to me & to Mr. Collins.

"Who de devil send de hoss dah?"—(Lewis.[142]

⟨Telegraph Webster Livy says send that article[143] by Wednesday or it won't reach here in time.⟩

Get ⟨Warner[144] &⟩ Livy & go see the statue [#]

---

[139] Here and below (269.15) Clemens referred to Gerhardt's statue of Nathan Hale, which in December 1886 was apparently ready to be cast in bronze. It would be placed in the Connecticut State Capitol building on 14 June 1887.

[140] Clemens was probably reacting to stories of Whitman's financial distress current in mid-December 1886. On 17 December the New York *Times* reported Whitman's complaint that the New York newspapers "gave exaggerated ideas of his depleted financial condition," noting also, however, his willingness to accept "testimonials" and "return his heartiest thanks therefor." It is not known if Clemens aided Whitman at this time, but on 28 May 1887 he contributed fifty dollars, and offered more if needed, to a fund to build a summer cottage for the poet. Clemens had previously assisted Whitman in August 1885 by joining in a subscription to buy him a horse and buggy.

[141] *McClellan's Own Story* was ready for publication by Charles L. Webster & Company in December 1886. This paragraph ("Send . . . New York") is not written in Clemens' hand.

[142] John Lewis, the Negro tenant farmer at Quarry Farm. Clemens here paraphrased the remark with which Lewis ended a dispute about divine responsibility for the runaway carriage incident of 1877 in which he figured so heroically (*MTHL*, pp. 194–198).

[143] Possibly a bureau that Livy had commissioned Charles L. Webster to purchase for her in New York City around the middle of December 1886.

[144] Charles Dudley Warner was a member of the commission that had awarded the Nathan Hale statue assignment to Karl Gerhardt.

Twichell's irascible D[r.] who came home from China & waded into the mud pile in the front yard. *Had just stopped swearing.*

(If comments on my *sermon* should give me a text. Instance the story of the D[r] (see preceding page) in proof of—*what?*) Well, he stood that strain—so he knew he was all right for the rest of his life —the superior to it couldn't be invented. (He only cursed his half-drunk driver in dumb show, if at all.)[145]

Badeau's Book (?)[146]
⟨Get a sponge.⟩
Charley need Richard?[147]
Make up annual ac/.
See Laffan.[148]

Trust no order-book business to —— witness all my Grants, & this unbound M[c]Clellan to Courant.[149]

Charley give me a lot of Grant statistics:[150] Presses 41; binderies

---

[145] Clemens may have contemplated using reaction to "Concerning a Reformed Pledge: A New-Year Sermon" as the basis for his speech to the Stationers' Board of Trade. The entry about "Twichell's irascible D[r.]," who was a reformed swearer, occurs on the preceding page in the manuscript notebook and presumably would have provided a vivid example of the efficacy of Mark Twain's modified pledge.

[146] Clemens and Webster had begun considering publication of Adam Badeau's *Grant in Peace* in the fall of 1885. Although a contract was finally signed on 25 January 1887, Badeau withdrew when Webster, fearing possible revelation of the bitter Badeau-Grant feud of 1885 (see p. 205, note 71), insisted that he agree to "alter the matter in such a way that it will be unobjectionable" to Mrs. Julia Grant (New York *Sun,* 7 March 1889). *Grant in Peace* was published in 1887 by S. S. Scranton & Company of Hartford.

[147] On 26 December 1886, Clemens wrote to Webster: "If you should want an assistant porter in the new office, I know of a bright, strong & phenomenally active young mulatto who is out of work. Writes a good hand." In the same letter he wished the office staff a "Merry Christmas to all, & to all a good morning!" and added "Now trot out our first annual statement, & let's see!" (*MTBus*, p. 371).

[148] Clemens expected confirmation of his suspicion that the New York *Tribune* was having difficulty with its Mergenthaler Linotype. On 6 December Laffan had written that he was "to see [Whitelaw] Reid tomorrow and may find out something. If you are right it is the most busted machine in existence."

[149] The offending Webster & Company staff member has not been identified. This entry was made around 26 December 1886 when Clemens complained to Webster: "Whoever sends out the McClellan press copies needs to be careful—an unbound, but no bound, copy has come to the Courant" (*MTBus*, p. 371).

[150] Clemens evidently wanted to have such statistics on hand for his scheduled ap-

⟨8⟩6; tons 1,000: one firm made all the paper & presented no bill till we owed them $80,000—if then. So many thousand old soldiers & widows divided $1,000,000 among them & would have dividd more but for Wanamake[r.] [151]

Two. big checks. 1000, ⟨[o]⟩pages of MS—worth so much per page. In silver coin Mrs. G. would have receivd – – – tons.

Can't publish my own books.

700 tons of books in 2 years—sold them at $5000 a ton.—580,000 single vols.

Poem about Wannamaker

Casting vote. "So, 350,000,000 heathen are to be damned because they have never happened to hear of that close-fisted Conneticut Yankee's stinking little religion."

Write a "French" novel—37 cases of adultery, & they all live happy to the end.

The Englishman 100 years ago."
The Englishman of To-Day

Henry Clews's book.? [152] [#]

---

pearance at the Stationers' Board of Trade dinner in February 1887 since he planned to attend in his capacity of publisher (see p. 268, note 136, and p. 275, note 166).

[151] John Wanamaker had recently bested Clemens in a court test over department store sales of the Grant *Memoirs* (see p. 250, note 77). In a short piece he called "A Suggestion," written during this period, Clemens noted inaccurately that "a United States Court has convicted [Wanamaker] of being a pirate" and that "this odorous pilgrim . . . is the only individual in a population of sixty millions who is known to have picked the pockets of the heirs of the dead General Grant. . . . Before they had got a penny of [profit from the Grant *Memoirs*], this occasional moral instructor of youth . . . had his scrofulous hands on it. John Wannamaker helped himself first; the family had to wait" (printed with some alterations in *MTE*, pp. 348–349). In fact, Mrs. Grant's returns were not affected by Wanamaker's sales of five hundred sets of the *Memoirs*. Clemens and Webster feared, however, that the availability of discounted books would cause a general repudiation of purchase agreements by subscription customers. This would have occasioned a substantial loss to everyone involved, including any "old soldiers & widows" among Webster & Company canvassers.

[152] Henry Clews was a prominent New York banker. His *Twenty-Eight Years in Wall Street* was offered to Charles L. Webster & Company in November 1886 whereupon Clemens advised Webster to "make perfectly conscienceless terms with him—terms which will absorb all the profits—and take his book. He choused me out of a good deal of money, 13 years ago as cooly as ever any other crime was committed in this world" (*MTLP*, p. 208). Clemens had not forgiven the suspension of currency payments to

How is Grant selling?
Back.

No of ⟨of⟩*copies* of that & McClellan sold?

What's gone with my "Sermon?"

Ole Bull & the Queen of Naples.[153]
I & the colored RR porter who took me for Gen McClellan.[154]

Aldrich ordered one dozen bottles of the effervescent stuff he had seen Fitz James O'Brien order. There was a mistake made—(*he* ordered the wrong stuff)—it frightfully physicked him & his eleven young bohemian comrades who were his guests.

Get Bryant's Homer (⟨[r]⟩no—only Odyssey)[155]

(My "Sermon.")

Beecher's Auto.[156] [#]

----

depositors by Clews's bank during the great financial panic of September 1873. News of the suspension had reached Clemens and Livy in London, catching them disturbingly short of funds. Clews's book was published in 1887 by the Irving Publishing Company.

[153] Clemens had met the popular Norwegian violinist Ole Bull at a luncheon at the Boston home of James T. Fields in April 1880. Amidst the "uproarious story-telling gayety" of that afternoon (William Dean Howells to his father, 17 April 1880, *MTHL*, p. 301), there was probably allusion to Ole Bull's encounter with the Dowager Queen of Naples. The queen had offended Bull by talking loudly as he was about to play at a private recital, causing him to rebuke her. When he was afterward summoned by her: "The Queen opened the conversation by remarking that she supposed they had a great many bears in Norway, to which Ole Bull replied that he had himself had the good fortune to be nursed by one, and that he should always hold in grateful remembrance its tender devotion to him" (Sara C. Bull, *Ole Bull: A Memoir* [Boston and New York: Houghton, Mifflin & Co., 1882], pp. 63–64).

[154] This incident occurred in 1870 (see *N&J2*, p. 65).

[155] William Cullen Bryant's translation of the *Odyssey* (originally published in 1871) was to be a gift for Susy Clemens. On 19 March 1884, Livy had given her Bryant's translation of the *Iliad* (originally published in 1870) as a birthday present.

[156] On 3 January 1887 Webster informed Clemens that Henry Ward Beecher was considering an autobiography: "Beecher seemed to think that it might be a pretty good thing to do, and he also seemed to think that other things being equal, he would rather have us publish it than any one else. . . . I do not love Beecher any more than you do, but I love his money just as well, and I am certain that that book would sell." Webster & Company acquired the rights to the book, but after Beecher's death on 8 March 1887, the firm settled for the unprofitable *Biography of Henry Ward Beecher* (1888), by his son, William Beecher, and his son-in-law, Samuel Scoville.

Laffan's book.[157]

Henry Clews' book.

Col. Grant editing papers?

How many M{c}Clellans sold?

How is Grant selling?

Annual statement.

(Look back 4 pages.)[158]

⟨Stir up Am Pub & Slote.⟩[159]

⟨Why didn't you answer W. Miller Owen?⟩ ⟨Too many of these complaints.⟩
(Letter in this book.)[160]

The Unitarian Herald says Herbert Spencer has [deter] to autobi-

BRING WITH ME.

Get ⟨y⟩ 1 dozen of yellow, & 1 dozen of red twisted candles at the block above or below Mitchell Vance & Co.

Also 1 dozen cut glass bobéche (things for tallow to drip into.) [#]

---

[157] A catalog of the vast art collection of William Thompson Walters, a Baltimore merchant and railroad and steamship developer, which William M. Laffan was encouraging Clemens to publish with lavish color illustrations. Clemens hoped to have Walters advance funds to cover all publication costs and foresaw "a probably three quarters of a million dollars profit. . . . There's a dead-certain half-million, I judge" (SLC to CLW, 13 January 1887, MTLP, p. 213). Only around one thousand copies of the catalog were to be published, each to sell for $1,000. Clemens later excoriated Webster for avoiding this "greenback-mine" (see MTE, pp. 189–190).

[158] Evidently a reference to the "Grant statistics" on pages 270–271.

[159] Clemens was recurrently dissatisfied with royalty payments on his books still controlled by the American Publishing Company and with his earnings from sales of Mark Twain's Self-Pasting Scrapbook, marketed by Daniel Slote & Company.

[160] William Miller Owen had written Clemens in December 1886 seeking re-publication of his In Camp and Battle with the Washington Artillery of New Orleans, a Civil War narrative originally issued by Ticknor & Company in 1885. On 14 December Clemens issued instructions to decline, but Webster evidently did not do so promptly. No letter of complaint from Owen is now in the manuscript notebook.

Also, ½ done candle-shade standards

Miss Goldthwaite—"She's so d—d punctual!"

"We say Ach Gott, you say Goddam.

First 100 at	50	5,000.[161]
2^d	60	6,000
3	70	7,000
4	80	8,000
5	90	9,000
6	100	10,000
7	110	11,000
8	125	12,500
9	138	13,800
10	152	15,200
		$97,500

By any other system the cream would be skimmed & the business discarded.

⟨⅓ or ½ the⟩

No solicitation should be made till the name could be taken & the book delivered at the same moment.

Price, 1,000. At half that price, reduce the above terms by half.

Ask D^r O'Reilly about book with gold back.[162]

We pay for it & get great folk to present it.

Write some dialect sketches in the character of

Lowell a "monotonous speller"—"I allays 've noticed in his letters to me he ⟨allays⟩ spells his words the same way every time." [#]

---

[161] In this table and in the following two paragraphs Clemens devised tentative terms and conditions for publication of the William T. Walters art catalog (see note 157). The table consists of his calculations of escalating commission payments to the "single individual"—evidently William M. Laffan (see pp. 339–340), an established art expert—who was to do "all the canvassing" for the book (SLC to Frederick J. Hall, *MTLP*, p. 245).

[162] In June 1886, Clemens had suggested a gold-bound copy of Grant's *Memoirs* as a suitable gift for Webster to bring to Pope Leo XIII, but that had proved impractical.

The Twins. A. Story. (But there is really only one twin; she changes her dress & becomes the other twin.)[163]

L. What went with my sermon?[164]

See the new presses

Falk-photos.[165]

Gold binding Pope

Charley, you go to that dinner & use those statistics.[166]

Get addresses of Mrs. D^r· Draper & the other daughters.

Granular Effervescent Citrate of Caffeine.
17 Speck's Fields

250 is broadest—5½ inches.

Speak to Laffan about Lucius C. ⟨Rice⟩Ryce, with New Haven Morning News & correspondent of Sun. Knows Chester S. Lord,[167] I think.

Grant & McClellans.
The Pope's.

He now seems to have been considering a gift of an equally lavish version of Bernard O'Reilly's biography of the pope (see 275.6).

[163] In Notebook 22 (14.6–8), Clemens had also noted an idea for a sketch about multiple identities, in that case involving triplets.

[164] Clemens evidently offered "Concerning a Reformed Pledge: A New-Year Sermon" to William M. Laffan for the New York *Sun* after it was declined by the Irving Bacheller syndicate (see p. 264, note 127).

[165] A photograph of Mark Twain taken by Benjamin J. Falk, the prominent New York photographic artist and innovator, possibly around the time of this entry, survives in the Mark Twain Papers.

[166] On 26 January 1887, in response to Clemens' request (see 270.15), Webster sent a number of curious statistics about the Grant *Memoirs*. He noted, for example, that the paper used "would make a ribbon . . . one inch wide which would stretch seven and one third (7⅓) times around the world." Clemens ultimately refrained from any mention of the Grant *Memoirs* at the Stationers' Board of Trade dinner on 10 February, simply noting: "I am here in the character of author and publisher, but I think I will let that rest. . . . Oh, I can tell you a great deal about publishing, but I don't think I will. I am rather too fresh yet. . . . I am at the honest stage now, but after a while, when I graduate and grow rich, I will tell you all about it" (New York *World*, 11 February 1887).

[167] Managing editor of the New York *Sun*.

The General's.[168] (   )
Life of Christ.[169]
H. W. Beecher's Autobiography.
General Badeau's Grant in Peace.
Mrs. General Custer's book.
General Crawford's book.[170]
General xxx's *Letters*.[171]
Grant Memoirs *de luxe*.
Library of Humor.[172]

Re-write the parable of the talents (those now praised went short in the Wall street of that day, got fleeced, & the only one that got any praise was the one that kept his money in a napkin.)

Do the quarrelsome "Five times one are *five!*"

Ar-chi-bald-⟨as⟩As-kin.

⟨Write Howells—⟩[173] [#]

---

[168] Philip Sheridan's *Personal Memoirs*, published by Webster & Company in 1888.

[169] In late January 1887, Webster advanced Henry Ward Beecher $5,000 for his proposed *Life of Christ*. The book had not been finished when Beecher died on 8 March 1887 and after lengthy negotiation the Beecher family withdrew the manuscript and returned the money. Beecher's autobiography is discussed on page 272, note 156.

[170] Samuel W. Crawford, *The Genesis of the Civil War: The Story of Sumter, 1860–1861* (New York: Charles L. Webster & Co., 1887).

[171] Possibly Mrs. Grant's planned volume of correspondence from her husband (see p. 219, note 106). By August 1887, some six months after Clemens made this list of Webster & Company projects, the firm no longer thought a collection of those letters would be profitable since "there is not much, if anything, in them. . . . As great as Grant was, the people . . . have had enough of it" (Frederick J. Hall to SLC, 10 August 1887). The "Grant Memoirs *de luxe*," which were to have manuscript pages bound into each set, were also abandoned.

[172] Throughout 1887, Clemens grew increasingly insistent that *Mark Twain's Library of Humor* no longer be delayed in favor of works by others. He even entertained Howells' proposal that they give the book to Harper & Brothers, a suggestion which Webster rejected because: "It would never do to publish that out of our house; as you are a partner it would look as though we had had a row or as though you doubted the ability of your own house" (CLW to SLC, 17 February 1887). The *Library of Humor* was finally published in 1888.

[173] A letter of 15 February 1887 informed Howells that his suggestion about publishing the *Library of Humor* with Harper & Brothers had been passed on to Webster.

& the poet Forest.

Another coffin-box story. Judge Gray's "box" doesn't arrive with him. Telegraphs undertaker, (being routed out at 4 a.m) "Where in hell is my mother in law?

Why don't Missionaries go to the Esquimaux.

Sell a $\frac{1}{500}$ to Cl. L. S$^{t.}$ at $10,000.[174]

Stewart's place
8 Warren st—barn-door.

Scheemann
23 John—Russian Wedding feast.

Dora Wheeler.[175]

237—5th ave
Prof. Loisette.[176]

3. East 66th st.

715 Fifth ave. [#]

---

[174] Livy's friend Clara L. Spaulding had recently married John B. Stanchfield, "a gentleman five years younger than herself. . . . She is 36, while he is only 31," who had "wanted her for ten years, but she did not love him" (Pamela Moffett to Samuel E. Moffett, 15 May 1886). Stanchfield, a prominent Elmira attorney and mayor of Elmira from 1886 to 1888, was Clemens' business associate and personal lawyer in the early 1900s. This entry probably plans their first business connection, an investment by Clara Stanchfield in the Paige typesetter. In September 1889 she actually did invest $5,000, entitling her to receive a royalty of five dollars on each machine rented or sold. Clemens increased her potential royalty to six dollars in compensation for a loss she suffered in one of his previous unsuccessful ventures, the Kaolatype Engraving Company.

[175] The Clemenses invited Dora Wheeler to visit them in February 1887. Clemens sat for a portrait by her, evidently in late 1886. The Literary News for March 1889 used a reproduction of that portrait as its frontispiece.

[176] Under the pseudonym Alphonse Loisette, Marcus Dwight Larrowe, whom Clemens had known in Nevada, conducted "The Loisettian School of Physiological Memory" at this address in New York City. Clemens became an enthusiastic pupil around February 1887, receiving instruction in person and by mail. He provided an endorsement of the method for Loisette's advertisements and allowed his name to be used in promotional materials in 1887 until the number of inquiries directed to Hartford became intolerable.

⟨My sermon.⟩

Telegraph John M. Holcombe—Yale Dinner[177]

"Did I step on your foot?" "I wish to God you had!"

Damn a man that's always tying his shoe!

Alex. Agar (Stationers) 112 W^m st.(?) Don't send carriage.

Send enclosed letter to Professor.[178]

See Gilder & tell him am going to use that article.[179]

⟨Telegraph for room.⟩[180]

⟨Telegraph Fogarty.⟩[181]

⟨Telegraph Mrs. Gay.⟩[182]

"G— d— it all, I've left it at *home!*"

⟨Make the basis [1]o[o,oo]o shs of 100 each.⟩

Go to Senator Jones first.[183] [#]

---

[177] An 1869 graduate of Yale University, John M. Holcombe was a Hartford resident
and secretary of the Phoenix Mutual Life Insurance Company. He was a member of the
committee planning the Yale Alumni Association dinner held at Seminary Hall in Hartford on the evening of 8 February 1887. Clemens must have declined an invitation from
Holcombe to attend the dinner since he expected to be in New York City that day.

[178] Evidently a letter about memory development which Clemens forwarded to
Loisette.

[179] A reference to Mark Twain's "English As She Is Taught" which would be published
in the April 1887 *Century* magazine, edited by Richard Watson Gilder. Clemens included
an excerpt from it—the schoolboy's composition "On Girls"—in his 10 February 1887
speech to the Stationers' Board of Trade.

[180] Clemens stayed at the Victoria Hotel while in New York from 8 to 11 February
1887 to attend to business and appear at the Stationers' Board of Trade dinner.

[181] The exclusive New York dressmaker who made clothing for Olivia Clemens.

[182] Maria C. Gay of Farmington, Connecticut, was a member of the group of women
"away above the intellectual average" (SLC to Mrs. Fairbanks, 22 March 1887, *MTMF*,
p. 261) who met at the Clemens home in 1887 for Mark Twain's weekly readings of
Robert Browning.

[183] During the next few years, Clemens persisted in trying to secure a substantial type-

Call on Rev John W. Chapman, 38 Beekman st—City Missions.[184]

Der—die   das   die
des—der   des   der
dem—der   dem   den
A. den—die   das   die

KINSMEN dine March 17. (Osgood.)[185]

Sei auf Deiner Hut—keep on the look-out.—

Pass-auf! (look out?—take care?)

Lasst gut sein! (Never mind—or never mind that.)

Rose Bonheur's Horse-Fair & Stewart's other pictures at 6 East 23ᵈ st till Mch 23.[186] [#]

---

setter investment from Senator John P. Jones. Finally, in 1890, after inspecting the machine in one of its operative intervals, Jones made a token investment of $5,000. At about the same time a contract was drawn up in which Jones and Clemens agreed to organize a Paige typesetter corporation.

[184] On 7 February 1887, the Reverend John W. Chapman, an assistant chaplain of the City Missionary Society of New York, sent word of the death of Clemens' distant cousin, Jesse M. Leathers (see *N&J2*, p. 51) in Charity Hospital on Blackwell's Island. Leathers had died of tuberculosis complicated by alcoholism. "He called here a few weeks ago," Clemens told Chapman on 12 February, "and sent up word that he wanted $50, and was going out to a hospital in Kansas. But I was never able to believe his statements, and I did not believe this one; otherwise I would have paid his way. I sent down $15, believing it would carry him as far as he really wanted to go" (published in John W. Chapman, "The Germ of a Book: A Footnote on Mark Twain," *Atlantic Monthly*, December 1932, pp. 720–721). On 14 February Chapman sent Clemens an account of Leathers' last months and noted: "I should be glad to see you . . . when you are in the city, and to take you to the ward where he died if you care to go."

[185] The Kinsmen was an informal club of actors, artists, and writers which met periodically for lunch or dinner. Clemens had become a member in 1883 at which time James R. Osgood was also admitted, after much mock protest that he was only a publisher.

[186] The extensive art collection assembled by department store magnate Alexander T. Stewart, whose widow had died on 25 October 1886, went on display at the galleries of the American Art Association in New York City on 21 February 1887. It was disposed of at an auction sale held from 23 to 25 March 1887. Rosa Bonheur's *The Horse Fair*, the "most famous [painting] in the entire Stewart collection" (*New York Times*, 27

Old London street
Ned House.
Laffan—sermon.
Casino.
Larowe—Meinz—Loisette
Mrs. Grant
Dentist.
Gilder—Century—My play.[187]

Peck nice eat^g apples.
½ dozen bananas
1 doz oranges.

Pic="9010":[188]

The place on the Hartford's (?) deck which is always saluted.

Surgeon Warden of the Northumberland quotes O'Meara as saying Napoleon's pulse never rose above 62 when he was in health (& he was always that.[189]

It was to Warden (as per his little book of Letters, published 1817, four years before N's death, that N. said, "I found a crown in the kennel, I cleansed the filth from it & ⟨put⟩ placed it on my head.

9010. At the table at Longwood was always an empty chair in the place of honor. It represented Marie Louise. [#]

March 1887), was purchased for $53,000 by Cornelius Vanderbilt who presented it to the Metropolitan Museum of Art.

[187] Clemens' *Meisterschaft*, which he originally wrote to entertain his family, did not appear in the *Century* magazine until January 1888.

[188] The material in this entry was probably intended for the volume of "Picturesque Incidents in History & Tradition" which Clemens suggested as a project for Samuel E. Moffett (see p. 167, note 135).

[189] William Warden was the surgeon on board the *Northumberland*, the ship which carried Napoleon to Saint Helena. Warden reported this comment by Barry E. O'Meara, Napoleon's physician, in *Letters Written on Board His Majesty's Ship the Northumberland, and Saint Helena* (Philadelphia: M. Thomas, 1817). The following remark by Napoleon and the information about the chair at his Saint Helena residence which stood empty in honor of his second wife also appear in Warden's book.

T J V up Wash[190]
7 k a b k—Adams.
⟨Wash.⟩
Dficit—Jefferson

The   Old   London Street.
⟨[1]⟩ ⟨[o]51⟩⟨O51⟩51 ⟨502102⟩5 21 2 014 e 1.

First Saturdays.

March . . . . . ⟨6⟩5 Will Dan daub a niche?

April . . . . 2 Now boy, touch a numb mouse⟨?⟩

May . . . . 7 Aback tore a naughty knave?

June . . . . 4 Hero taught Davy Noel.

July . . . . 2 Same as April.

In a hot

August . . . . 6 A shy dame knows a knock.
    night

Sept . . . . 3 My days take newer might.
    because cool weather.

In Oct . . . . 1 Do have Dull Nanny Nebo

Nov. . . . . 5 Same as March.

Dec. . . . . 3 ⟨Se[p]⟩Same as September.
    because very cold. [#]

---

[190] This cryptic notation and those that follow (through 282.8) are evidently exercises from the "Loisettian School of Physiological Memory" (see note 176). In a testimonial

⟨2 [num]bers⟩
They lie low, nay c r i n g e amid loam.

1	5	5	2	7	4	⟨6⟩2	3
J.	F	M	A	May	J	J	

They lie low, nay, c r i n g e a m i d   l o a m.

| 1 | 5 | 5 | 2 | 7, 4, | 2, 7, | 3, | 1 | 5, | 3 |
| J | feb. | Mch | Ap. | M.J. | J. Aug. | Sep. | Oct. | Nov. | Dec. |

an

"The man who says that he cannot form an ⟨unbiassed⟩unbiased opinion any given set of facts, simply shows the shallow quality of his mind."—N.Y. Trib.—On Jury System.[191] (Be he deep *or* shallow, he ca*nnot* form an unbiased opinion upon "any set of facts" involving a ⟨political⟩ party or a religious (?) This makes his ability to form a valuable opinion on *any* question doubtful.

Dinner at Daly's theatre Apl. 13.[192] [#]

---

prepared in early 1887, Mark Twain noted that "Loisette, among other cruelties, requires you to memorize a great long string of words that haven't any apparent connection or meaning—there are perhaps 500 of these words, arranged in maniacal lines of 6 to 8 or 9 words in each line." The samples recorded here suggest that the system, kept secret by Loisette, involved the substitution of digits for groups of phonetically related letters.

[191] This remark appeared in "How Juries Are Obtained in This Town," an editorial of 10 March 1887 in the New York *Daily Tribune*, which lamented the misapplication of the "liberal and sensible" law defining the qualifications for jurors.

[192] A midnight supper on stage at Augustin Daly's Fifth Avenue Theatre to celebrate the one hundredth night of Daly's production of *The Taming of the Shrew*. General

Periodicals of all kinds, including dailies, of course, in France, 2,500. Of these, 1,500 are published in Paris.

There are only 120 dailies in France that are worthy the name even from the French view—& 60 others, unworthy the name from even the Central African view.

In fact there ⟨is⟩ are only 5 or 6 *real* dailies, & one machine could set them all up in 8 or 10 hours.

		should have been
U.S. in 1790,	4,000,000	
" 1820,	9,600,000—	8,00000
" 1850,	23,000,000	16,000,000
" 1880,—50,000,000	32,0000	

In ⟨1880⟩1881, England had ⟨28,000,000⟩38,000,000;
" 1841 " " 27,000,000.
" 1880, Germany " 45,000,000.

Thursday 31$^{st.}$ 4 p.m. Susie[193]

Print Tribune machine Editorial & place it alongside the original —for contrast in type-face.

The money taken, up to say the middle of Dec was doubtless from Huck Finn.[194] [#]

William T. Sherman served as toastmaster and Mark Twain was prominent among the speakers. His remarks on this occasion are discussed on page 232, note 17.

[193] Clemens may have intended that his eldest daughter accompany him to Boston on 31 March 1887 to observe his participation in an afternoon of Authors' Readings on behalf of the Longfellow Memorial Fund. Susy Clemens was ill at the time, however, and did not attend.

[194] In this entry, the following one, and in the entry at 285.1–4, Clemens alluded to the embezzlement of some $25,000 by Frank M. Scott, cashier and bookkeeper for Charles L. Webster & Company. Scott was arrested on 11 March 1887 after it was discovered that he had been diverting considerable sums each month since joining the firm in July 1885. On 25 March, Webster informed Clemens that he hoped to recoup "in the neighborhood of $6,000" from disposal of Scott's personal property, including a house under construction in Roseville, New Jersey. "I feel," Webster wrote, "that he should at least be sent to States Prison for as much as five years. . . . I think it would be a miscarriage of justice if he was sentenced to a shorter term; . . . five years would sufficiently

The man was suspected when Thorndyke Rice's prospectus of his Lincoln book appeared—a counterfeit of ours—he got access through Bromfield.[195] I connect the 2 events. He was again suspected while Webster was in Europe—say August or September. At any time during the next 6 months, so simple a device as a decoy letter or a detective would have captured him in 24 hours. But the advice of the Wise Whitford[196] must be asked, & nothing said to me. Whitford said, as usual, of course—"don't disturb Ch with these annoyances—you will spoil his good time."

Put in the summer on the past 2 years of my Autobi. Also write & *publish* the vol. relating to my life up to marriage.

Write up Mrs. Gillis's boarding house & its boarders in *full*. But never publish it.[197]
& add Judge & Mrs. Turner.[198]
Also some Carson & Va boarders. [#]

---

punish him, as it would dis-franchise him and hold him up as an example to others." On 23 April, Webster was able to report: "Scott was sentenced . . . to six years at hard labor in Sing Sing States Prison yesterday." Late in 1890, Clemens and Webster petitioned Governor David B. Hill of New York to pardon Scott and restore him to his wife and three young children.

[195] Charles Allen Thorndyke Rice, the ambitious young editor and publisher of the *North American Review*, had hired Bromfield, a Webster & Company bookkeeper and "a poor, weak tool" (CLW to SLC, 7 November 1885), in order to acquire information about the company's subscription publishing methods. Webster called Rice "a persistent sneak" and accused him of repeated interference in company affairs, particularly in connection with the Grant *Memoirs*. In 1885, Rice compiled his *Reminiscences of Abraham Lincoln by Distinguished Men of His Time* (New York: North American Review, 1886) which included anecdotes provided by Fred Grant from the manuscript of the *Memoirs*, had a cover resembling that of the *Memoirs*, and was sold by subscription. Although Webster reported that "Mr. Scott has been invited out to dinner several times by Bromfield" at Rice's instigation, there is no surviving evidence that Scott conspired with Bromfield against Webster & Company.

[196] Daniel Whitford, a lawyer employed by the New York firm of Alexander & Green which represented Charles L. Webster & Company.

[197] Clemens briefly alluded to the period when he boarded at Angus Gillis' San Francisco home in an unpublished passage of his Autobiographical Dictation of 19 January 1906 (see N&J1, p. 68). He apparently never wrote the contemplated full account.

[198] George Turner was chief justice of the Territorial Supreme Court while Clemens was in Nevada. In an Autobiographical Dictation of 2 October 1906, Clemens recalled that it was his burlesque of Turner's "exceedingly flowery style" of oratory that led to

$\frac{9}{10}$ of the steal *before* Feb. 27, '86, was mine, no doubt; but I had no money there after that; all that was there was the Company's; it was borrowed from me (a forced loan,) & ⟨[so]⟩⟨they⟩ it is the company that loses it. I also want interest on it.

Write—
            "The Banqueteer's Handbook."
Don't have an ass for a chairman.
Have a brass band to chestnut-bell long-winded speakers.
Have a claque to start the applause which is the sign to the band to break in.
⟨Autho[r]⟩Speakers ⟨m⟩for regular toasts must have their speeches by heart—volunteer speeches are worthless & an insult.
Ch^n *must* furnish volunteers a text. It *must* be in the form of a *question.*—not an ungraspable generality.
Form for inviting Howell's to get up & talk; Warner, Holmes, Aldrich, &c.
Form-speech to be used by a grocer, a plumber an author, &c in responding. (Forms for *soldier & all* sorts of people.)
Author's readings must consist of only 6 authors of 10 minutes each & end in 1$\frac{1}{2}$ hours.[199]

Story to be built on the game of "gossip." A trifle starts; is told confidentially to A; who tells it to B; B. to C &c, till it finally ruins the family originally mentioned in it. All sorts of people are in the list of tellers—educated & uneducated, high & low; they all tell

---

his employment by the Virginia City *Territorial Enterprise* (see MTE, pp. 390–391). When he made this entry, Clemens may have been thinking of the unfortunate circumstances in which Mrs. Turner once found herself while accepting a late-night bribe of $10,000 on behalf of her husband. She reportedly "spread out her voluminous nightgown, and the sack of gold was emptied into it. The weight proved too heavy for the garment. It was torn completely from her body, leaving Mrs. Turner as naked as a worm, with hundreds of twenty-dollar gold pieces at her feet!" (Effie Mona Mack, *Mark Twain in Nevada* [New York: Charles Scribner's Sons, 1947], p. 192).

[199] Clemens may have had in mind the Longfellow Memorial Fund readings in which he participated on 31 March 1887. He later recalled that the affair began at two o'clock and "at 6 o'clock half the audience had been carried out on stretchers, and . . . the rest were dead—with a lot of readers still to hear from" (see MTHL, pp. 589–590).

the story as accurately as they can, but all distort it. Tell *all* their stories—& this will make a *story*.

A. & G.[200] are your private counsel; I pay the bulk of their fee to get ⟨them⟩ to advise—

1. That I be never shown a statement;[201]

2. That all attempts to get my money be resisted upon one pretext or another.[202]

3. That we make a new partnership & still ⟨make⟩ not clear up accounts & start fresh.

4. That they advise you to keep a thief's hand in my pocket ⟨while y⟩ till you return from Europe.

I *must* work thro' an agent or lawyer. It is what you have always done & still do.[203] [#]

---

[200] Alexander & Green, lawyers for Charles L. Webster & Company.

[201] On 25 March 1887, Webster explained that modifications in the Webster & Company business agreement, including the acceptance of Frederick J. Hall into the firm, had extended the period covered by the annual statement to 28 April. He further explained, somewhat too easily, that responsibility for monthly statements had belonged to the discredited bookkeeper, Frank M. Scott: "He made out such statement[s], showed them to me, and as I supposed, sent them to you, as I gave him the orders to do so, and as I understood he did. If this is not the case, it is not my fault." Webster closed with the promise of a "clean statement" from an "expert accountant" which "will clearly show every dollar which has come into the firm and which has been expended, and for what it has been expended. It will also show the firm's indebtedness to you, as *author*."

[202] Around 27 March 1887, Clemens demanded "A tri-monthly complete statement, with check, *imperative*" (*MTLP*, p. 215) in response to Webster's offer to provide periodic accountings of "all profits due Mr. Clemens as partner in the business & sums due Mr. Clemens as Author on account of royalties due on his books together with a check for the same." In a contract signed on 1 April 1887, however, Clemens, Webster, and Hall agreed that accountings and payments would be biannual. Despite his complaints of being by-passed, this new contract retained from previous ones the stipulation that "in consideration of his furnishing the capital" for Charles L. Webster & Company, Clemens "shall not be called upon to perform any service or to take any supervision of said business." Webster was to "have the entire management of the active business of said Firm," including the making of "all contracts for work or material."

[203] In late March 1887, Clemens demanded "A desk in the office for my agent, & free access to the books, balance-sheets, & every detail of the business." He promised to furnish capital to the firm as needed, after the amount had been "proven in a plain, clear, business-like way, to me or to my agent." On 8 April, in a long "STRICTLY PERSONAL"

Apl. 12, '87. Day before yesterday I encountered Mrs. Harriet Beecher Stowe on the sidewalk, & she took both of my hands in hers, & said with a strong fervency that surprised the moisture into my eyes, "I am reading your Prince & Pauper for the fourth time, & I *know* it's the best book ⟨of⟩for young folk that was ever written."

⟨About⟩ In the second week of April '87 we got judgment against some swindling general agents of ours in Philadelphia for about $45,000.[204]

Go & call on Rev. Mr. McCook as soon as we return.[205]

The artic Explorer Hayes.[206]
Cheney's bill of fare[207]
Whittier's drown climax.

---

letter, Webster protested: "I cannot deal with my partner in business through the intervention of an agent. . . . no business can succeed where partners deal with each other at arms length. . . . I must say frankly that I do not think you are doing your duty by me in neglecting to come to the office and talk matters over with me and be intelligently informed." Webster demanded a private interview to show Clemens how profitably their "magnificent business" was being managed. "Now you are talking a language which I understand," Clemens responded by telegram on 10 April, "I will come down in a day or two." And on 17 April, after their meeting, Clemens wrote: "Everything is on the pleasantest possible basis, now, & is going to stay so. I blame myself for not looking in on you oftener in the past—that would have prevented all trouble. I mean to stand to my duty better, now" (*MTBus*, p. 379).

[204] On 12 April 1887, Webster & Company received awards totaling this amount in separate suits against Hubbard Brothers and J. M. Stoddart & Company, who had failed to make payment on the grounds that John Wanamaker's sale of the Grant *Memoirs* (see p. 250, note 77) caused losses which Webster & Company were obliged to prevent. In June 1887 Webster accepted "$6,500 in cash, and $4,700 in notes" in settlement of the $13,200 claim against Stoddart (CLW to SLC, 14 June 1887). It wasn't until 9 February 1888 that he could report an out-of-court settlement with Hubbard for "all that could be possibly obtained," $25,000 "in cash and property" of a $32,000 indebtedness.

[205] The Reverend John James McCook of Hartford. In 1885 Clemens included McCook in a list of "friends" to whom he was willing to sell Paige typesetter stock (see 189.13). The trip alluded to was probably the visit to West Point in April 1887.

[206] Clemens provided some of the details of this anecdote about Isaac Israel Hayes on page 73.

[207] Probably Frank Cheney, a Hartford silk manufacturer who was a member of the Monday Evening Club.

Twichell's naval sw[ea]re
"So'm *I*, but I'm not a *fool.*
Bermuda young man.

T. W. Higginson

Article suggested by a talk with Mrs. Capt. Price.[208] Head it
"Don't talk Shop."

Toward end of Apl. '87, Tribune introduced new brevier &
minion matrices—didn't notice about agate. The account stands:
New matrices 23ᵈ July '86; about 1ˢᵗ Sept. '86; & end of Apl '87.
Always going to require $4,500 worth a year?

May 10, '87. Charley reports Livy's balance at J L & Co's a trifle
under $55,000.
⟨About⟩ $3,487.14 subject to draft at any time.

Connecticut in ⟨the "Comm⟩ "American Commonwealth"
Series—Alexander Johnston, Houghton Mifflin & Co.[209]

Tribune G W S letter, May 15, '87. Text for a mugwump speech:
Goldwin Smith in London Times: "The American . . . . .
politician is in most cases a political slave." Change that to ALL
cases, & change "politician" to "voter," & the statement is exactly
true.[210]

Show the San Francisco school-teacher's letter to Gilder. [#]

---

[208] Captain Philip M. Price was stationed at the United States Military Academy at
West Point. On 17 April 1887, General Wesley Merritt, superintendent of the academy,
invited Clemens, Livy, and Joseph Twichell to come to West Point at the end of the
month. The Clemenses probably took that opportunity to return a visit to Price and his
wife, who had called upon them in Hartford earlier that year.

[209] Alexander Johnston, *Connecticut: A Study of a Commonwealth-Democracy*
(Boston and New York: Houghton, Mifflin and Co., 1887).

[210] On 15 May 1887, the New York *Daily Tribune* had published European correspondent George Washburn Smalley's report of Goldwin Smith's remarks to the London
Times. Smith, an eminent historian and political writer, had commented on "things
Canadian and American," observing in particular that "the American and Canadian
politician is in most cases a political slave. The Irish vote is largely responsible for this.
The Irishman is the worst of citizens in the United States, and Canada is becoming
politically an Irish Republic."

If he doesn't want it, offer it to Laffan.

Show Laffan ⟨[P]⟩the type-setter prospectus. & Standring's letter.

Show ditto to Geo. Jones?[211]

Get statement & new contract from Webster.[212]

Call on Jo. Jefferson.[213]

J. F. Cornish, a Master of Christ's Hospital.[214] [#]

---

[211] Evidently in hopes of eliciting support for the Paige typesetter from William M. Laffan, publisher of the New York *Sun*, and George Jones, manager and publisher of the New York *Times*, Clemens intended to show them a letter of 7 May 1887 in which George Standring had asserted: "There *is* a big market in Europe for any man who succeeds in making a simple, reliable, & not too costly [typesetting] machine."

[212] This entry and others that follow intermittently indicate that Clemens was not content with the Webster & Company contract dated 1 April 1887 which, among other provisions, had raised Webster's annual salary from $3,000 to $3,800. His dissatisfaction was in part produced by repeated delays in the preparation of the required statement, "a long laborious task on account of the loss of a cash book which Scott destroyed and also on account of a missing ledger entry so that we are obliged to pick the items out one by one in a sales book" (CLW to SLC, 26 April 1887). On 24 May, after visiting Hartford, possibly with the statement in hand, Webster forwarded another contract, noting: "I now see nothing in the way of a long and prosperous business." And the following day Clemens wrote: "Everything is satisfactory, now, & everything shall be done on our part to keep it so" (*MTBus*, p. 383).

[213] On 8 May 1887 Joseph Jefferson offered his autobiography to Clemens for publication by Charles L. Webster & Company. On 28 May, Clemens reported to Webster: "Joe Jefferson's MS is delightful reading, & I see that it has this additional great advantage: it is quite largely a book of *foreign travel*, & the illustrations can be made to show up that feature prominently, & the advertisements can further whoop it up" (*MTBus*, p. 383). Clemens instructed Webster to conclude an agreement with Jefferson, but by the time an offer was finally made in October 1887 the actor had made other arrangements. *The Autobiography of Joseph Jefferson* was published by the Century Company in 1890 and reissued several times.

[214] On 13 April 1887, J. F. Cornish had written to Clemens remarking on the "similarity, amounting in one or two cases to identity, between some of the answers quoted by you [in "English As She Is Taught" (*Century* magazine, April 1887)] and some quoted by me in an article that appeared in 'Cornhill' of June last on 'Boys' Blunders.'" Cornish wondered if Caroline LeRow, the schoolteacher who compiled the comical children's mistakes Mark Twain used in his article, had seen the *Cornhill* piece, "jotted down a few specimens & forgot their source." "I need hardly say that I make no sort of complaint," he commented graciously. Clemens forwarded Cornish's letter to Caroline LeRow, requesting "a letter to me which I can send to him, answering his question." The content of the joint reply to Cornish is not now known.

The stranger's reason why as "*Christ* has been here once" (Holy Land) the 2^d Advent would take place elsewhere.[215]

"The very stones of Jerusalem would cry out."[216]

May 17/82[217] Greeley (Depew told this last night at dinner at Chas. A. Dana's house) turned on the man who was collecting money to "save millions of your fellow creatures from going to hell": "I won't give you a d—d cent; there don't half enough of them go there *now*."

You get ⅕ of the profit—do you pay ⅕ of the expenses?

Everything was on a ¹⁄₁₀ basis up to Jan '86.[218]

May 23^d, '87. Mrs. Stowe came on the Ombre & said "I am reading the Prince & Pauper for the sixth time." (See a previous remark.)[219] She asked about such matters & I referred to Perkin Warbeck & Lambert Simnel.

She was already losing her mind.   SLC [#]

---

[215] Clemens used this joke in a letter from Jerusalem which appeared in the *Alta California* on 5 April 1868, omitting it later from the corresponding section of *The Innocents Abroad*. Its appearance here reflects his persistent impulse to burlesque the notion of a second coming. Although he did so in "The Second Advent," a sketch written in 1881 (*Mark Twain's Fables of Man*, ed. John S. Tuckey [Berkeley, Los Angeles, London: University of California Press, 1972], pp. 50–68), further ideas for that piece or a related one appear intermittently in his notebooks.

[216] A paraphrase of Luke 19:40, which is the basis of an anecdote about a "perfectly serene" guide of "simple faith" in chapter 54 of *The Innocents Abroad*. Clemens recalled the punchline of his anecdote more exactly at 294.7.

[217] Clemens inadvertently wrote "May 17/82" instead of "May 17/87."

[218] A contract signed on 21 January 1886 had modified an earlier agreement by which, over a five-year period, Webster was to receive one-third of Webster & Company profits up to $20,000 and thereafter one-tenth. The January 1886 accord stipulated that the "provisions as to twenty thousand dollars and ten per cent" would apply "solely to the Personal Memoirs of U. S. Grant." On all other publications Webster was to receive an unrestricted one-third of profits, which he could withdraw annually. In addition, his yearly salary was increased from twenty-five hundred to three thousand dollars. Clemens evidently calculated that the effect of these provisions was to give Webster one-fifth of the firm's profits. There is no mention of that figure in the January 1886 contract or in the surviving subsequent ones.

[219] Clemens had recorded a similar comment by Harriet Beecher Stowe on 12 April 1887 (287.1–6). In an Autobiographical Dictation of 23 March 1906, he would recall this period when Mrs. Stowe's "mind had decayed and she was a pathetic figure" (see

How could you draw all out & I not. You say mine could not be ascertained—then how did you ascertain your own?

Does not the present contract require you to make statement now & *pay* me? Then before we ⟨begin⟩ go further, pay me; & afterward we will agree upon a present sum to advance to you to work with.

This new contract is what *you* proposed to W:[220]

    1. A stated capital;

    2. 50% royalty on my books.

    3. ⟨All⟩ Grant to come into ⅔.

What ⟨we⟩ you are adding is a clause never seen in a contract before. It would seem that you *expect* to bust.

How *many* Missippis at 60ᶜ?

Who owned them?

Then how do they come to be sold as *firm* property?[221]

(No doubt under ⅔ arrangement as not being *published* by the firm. But that won't do, for the firm never bought them, & own no part of them. The firm *did* buy them, but have ignored the trade, after the fashion of the ⟨G⟩Col. [#]

MTA, 2:242–243). It was possibly around that time that he added the final line of the present note, written diagonally in ink across the original pencil entry.

[220] Webster had evidently instructed Daniel Whitford, one of Webster & Company's lawyers, to draft a revised partnership agreement. The terms noted here were probably incorporated in the contract signed in late May 1887, with which both Webster and Clemens professed satisfaction (see note 212). The third item on Clemens' list suggests that this new contract dropped the limitation on Webster's share of profits from the Grant *Memoirs* imposed by the 21 January 1886 pact. Webster and Clemens would then divide Grant earnings on a straight one-third to two-thirds basis. The clause which Clemens protested in the next entry remains obscure.

[221] On 23 April 1887, Webster had jubilantly informed Clemens: "I have sold the whole batch of the Mississippi's over 9000. for more than cost, a splendid sale and mighty glad to get rid of them as I needed the room." Clemens apparently believed that these remaindered copies of *Life on the Mississippi*, acquired in 1885 from J. R. Osgood & Company, were his personal property and not part of the stock of Charles L. Webster & Company. Here he conjectured that his right to two-thirds of the company's profits had been used to justify disposal of *Life on the Mississippi* as company property. Clemens' profound confusion seems apparent in the contradictory statements which conclude this agitated entry.

Books "not published" by the firm are *bought* by it—but *this* case would be a *gift*.

⟨When⟩ Who could endure a French Christ?[222]

O ⟨*sigh*-ye-⟩ yas-me no-*sigh*—good night[223]
Sighyenarrah . . . .   "   "
Combangwah . . . .   "   "
Ohio—good morning.

Sam¹. L. Clemens[224]
Clara L. Stanchfield
Sa
Samuel L. Clemens
Samuel L. Clemens
Samuel L. Clemens
Lilly G. Warner.
S L Clemens

Publish daily report of condition of telephone.[225] [#]

---

[222] In early June 1887, Grace King, who was visiting the Charles Dudley Warners, described a conversation with Mark Twain: "His talk drifted all around and talking about affairs in general & black and white affairs in particular, I asked him if he did not think Providence was a darkey—He laughed and said he had made a note of a reflection of his the other day—He pulled out his note book and read me 'Could we endure a French savior?' He said he wondered over the question himself—We had had a Jew who had been satisfactory, but fancy a Frenchman saying 'Come unto me all ye who are heavy laden'—& then he thought of an Irishman—wouldn't do at all. And so all through all nations" (Robert Bush, "Grace King and Mark Twain," *American Literature*, March 1972, p. 33).

[223] Edward H. House (see p. 234, note 26) and his adopted Japanese daughter Koto were guests at the Clemens' Hartford residence for six weeks in 1887, arriving from New York in mid-May. A language lesson by Koto probably prompted Clemens' phonetic rendering of these Japanese phrases: *o yasumi nasai*, good night; *sayonara*, goodbye; *komban wa*, good evening; *o hayo*, good morning.

[224] The following signatures were probably the product of a social evening at the Clemenses' home. The first two signatures and the last one are in Clemens' hand. The false-start "Sa" and two of the "Samuel L. Clemens" that follow are in Clara L. Stanchfield's hand. Responsibility for the third "Samuel L. Clemens" has not been determined. Lilly G. Warner, one of Livy's close friends, signed her own name.

[225] It was in this period that Mark Twain conceived the form for the weekly "Report . . . of the condition of the telephone" which Albert Bigelow Paine printed in *Mark Twain: A Biography* (facing p. 838).

Write a Rollo with a Jonas in it who is sodden with piety & self-righteousness.[226]

F. E. Church
Hudson, N.Y.[227]

Teleg—
Catskill Station on Hudson River RR.

Webster look for Alexandrè's organs.

Take 'em to South Beach & *drown* 'em.[228]

Christenig Yarn.

Bermuda lover—Twichell.

Don't put your shovel in where you hain't got——

Pulling Annie M⸗Dannold out of the mud.

Getting into Daly's the back way.

Hand the "Nobility" book to a publisher.[229]

The N.O. preacher's sermon.

The naval swearer who reformed. [#]

---

[226] Clemens frequently considered writing a story that would include Rollo and Jonas, two of the characters featured in Jacob Abbott's sentimental children's books, which were enjoyed by the Clemens offspring. The satirical impulse evident here is not always present in Clemens' notes for a story in the Abbott mode.

[227] In the second week of June 1887, the Clemenses, the Charles Dudley Warners, Joseph Twichell, and Grace King visited Frederick E. Church at "Olana," his imposing mansion near Hudson, New York. On 11 June, a day after returning to Hartford, Clemens began an unfinished letter to Church: "It was an ideal holiday, in a Garden of Eden without the Garden of Eden's unprotection from weather."

[228] Evidently the punchline of an anecdote told by John Greenleaf Whittier which Clemens recalled as "Whittier's drown climax" (287.13). References to this story also appear in later notebooks.

[229] Clemens' high regard for George Standring's *People's History of the English Aristocracy*, whose attack on the nobility furnished him material for *A Connecticut Yankee*, resulted in a plan to republish it himself as part of a lavish multi-volume set of political writings (see p. 295). Clemens later conceived alternative plans for the dissemination of Standring's book, among them the possible inclusion of a copy with each *Connecticut Yankee* sent to a newspaper for review.

Joseph Warner,
    Major Com^{dg} PP.[230]

The Whittier Yarn.

"Breaking the news" to Mrs. Higgins.

Why the Second Advent won't occur at Jerusalem.

Jack Van Nostrand yarns.

"This is one of the stones that *would* have cried out."

H. Greeley— "⟨Ain't⟩ Don't half enough go to hell *now*."

Dinner at Chas. A. Dana's to Osgood, with Chauncey Depew, May 17 '87.

Moncoon.
Origin of the Irish.

Postman's instructions Wednesday afternoon.

800 compositors on the daily press of Chicago. Two papers employ 150 each on Saturday nights.

Knew a democrat stole the ½ beef; been a Repub he'd stolen *all* of it.

Scotch boy in Westminster Abbey.

Pollinaris "tas' like yo' foot's asleep."

Stewart's recipe for capturing an Irish lady's consent.

  Miss Davenport—tea Sat. aftnoon & 4. to 6 to meet her sister Mrs. Fackler, from N.Y. [#]

---

[230] In May of 1886, Clemens had been elected a life member of the Putnam Phalanx, a social and ceremonial military organization named for Israel Putnam. Joseph Warner, a contractor at Colt's Patent Fire Arms Manufacturing Company in Hartford, was "Major Commanding" of the Putnam Phalanx in 1887. In early June of that year he may have invited Clemens to accompany the group to New Haven, Connecticut, where on 17 June it was prominent at the dedication of the soldiers' monument.

See D^r· Roosa.[231]

Also Dentist

Novel about the Esquimaux ⟨[-]⟩nabob who owned 5 flints. Told by Jahn in that old Icelander's English.[232]

⟨Discharge the lawyers. We can't afford legal advice at these figures.⟩

What are you doing with Library of Humor?[233]

Webster call on Joe Jefferson.

Let us publish the Memoirs of Saint-Simon, elaborately & beautifully illustrated—4 big vols at $8 to $12 the set, according to binding.

Add the ⟨little⟩ English printer's little book as another volume, & call the whole "Royalty & Nobility Exposed." Later add Taine's Ancient Regime & Carlyle's French Revolution?

Add the White Slave[234]—Mining life in Wales—Margravine of Bayreuth.[235]

Don't know as much as a lady's watch. [#]

---

[231] Clemens had been treated by Daniel Bennett St. John Roosa, a noted New York eye and ear specialist, in the fall of 1885 (see p. 202, note 60).

[232] Evidently a note for the story that became Mark Twain's "Esquimau Maiden's Romance" (*Cosmopolitan*, November 1893) in which the wealthiest man of the tribe owns twenty-two iron fishhooks.

[233] Clemens had received the manuscript of *Mark Twain's Library of Humor* from Howells on 9 May 1887, at which time he wrote: "I think of putting the book in the printers' hands about a month hence" (*MTHL*, pp. 592–593). The necessity of arranging for illustrations and for permission to use copyrighted material caused considerable delay, however, as did additional editorial work on the manuscript by Charles H. Clark, Clemens' Hartford *Courant* collaborator. *Mark Twain's Library of Humor* was finally issued in 1888.

[234] *The White Slave; or, Negro Life in the Slave States of America*, by Richard Hildreth, originally published in 1836 as *The Slave; or, Memoirs of Archy Moore*.

[235] Mark Twain thought highly of the memoirs of Frederica Sophia Wilhelmina, the margravine of Bayreuth, which William Dean Howells had edited in 1877 (see *MTHL*, p. 211). Charles L. Webster & Company did not publish any of the books noted here.

Somers Bros, mfr's of fine metal boxes, Brooklyn. Tin—for historical game. Or gun cotton.[236]

The Wisconsin youth who explained the steamboat in detail, & afterward ⟨f⟩discovered me steering, & "By God!" & not another word.[237]

"The mills of the gods grind slow, but they get there just the same."

$$13 \quad ^{238}$$
$$\frac{40}{520}$$
$$\text{pony} \quad \frac{40}{560}$$
$$\text{add } 40\text{—}600$$

1 Porter—2

2 1

  1 ⟨w[--]⟩Kellner—2 & Rahm.

  1 . . . . . . ″ 1

Antithesis. (for charade)

---

[236] Guncotton, or nitrocellulose, is primarily an explosive material produced by the treatment of cotton fiber with a mixture of nitric and sulphuric acids. When dissolved in camphor, nitrocellulose forms celluloid, the material Clemens probably had in mind for the manufacture of his history game.

[237] This incident occurred during Mark Twain's 1882 return to the Mississippi River. An entry in one of the notebooks kept on that trip describes Clemens' victim as a "passenger from Nebraska" (*N&J2*, p. 526).

[238] These calculations of summer expenses at Quarry Farm were made in pencil on one of the final pages of the notebook, which Clemens also used to test his pen. A slightly different set of figures appears on page 257 of the notebook.

XXVII

"Curse All Business. I Can't Understand Even the ABC of It."

(August 1887–July 1888)

THE DECLINE in the fortunes of Charles L. Webster & Company, signaled in the preceding notebook, is substantiated and documented in Notebook 27, which Clemens used from late August 1887 until around the middle of July 1888. Clemens devoted much of this notebook to expression of his disgruntlement over the firm's large expenditures and small profits, objecting repeatedly to the misscheduling of its publications and to the grandiose offices and staff Webster thought appropriate to its place in the world. In fact, the glory days of the Grant *Personal Memoirs*, when Webster had to worry about the danger of keeping too much money in unreliable banks, were long past. Sales of books reported in the hundreds and bank balances precariously maintained in the low thousands made Clemens demand monthly, and even weekly, statements of the business's financial condition and prospects in an attempt to provide the direction he thought lacking. Notebook 27 is punctuated with the evidences of this effort: notations of publishing house credits and debits and angry instructions to Webster to cut costs. A consequence of the dismal state of affairs was the further deterioration of the relationship between Clemens and Webster. In this notebook, Clemens not only reproached his nephew for current difficulties but resurrected old complaints with new vehemence. Finally, in February 1888, Clemens could record his relief at Webster's agreement to withdraw from the business temporarily to recruit his impaired health, a retirement made permanent at the end of the year.

Perhaps the most irksome failure of Charles L. Webster & Company was its inability to provide Clemens with ready funds for investment in the Paige typesetter. The business which he counted on as a resource had become a complementary drain on his finances, already severely taxed by the cost of Paige's interminable tinkering with the machine. Unable to withdraw the infrequent profits which provided working capital for the publishing house, Clemens consoled himself with dreams of the riches to be harvested from the typesetter without any clear notion of when they would be forthcoming. With a wary eye on the progress of the rival Mergenthaler Linotype, already in operation, and keen to the newspaper industry's desire for a device to cut composition costs, he pressed Paige in vain for commitment to a firm completion date.

Clemens' dual business entanglements followed wherever he went. Removal to Quarry Farm for the summer of 1887 helped somewhat, however. Despite a progression of often distressing reports from Webster & Company and letters from Franklin G. Whitmore, sometimes twice a day, reporting typesetter developments, Clemens advanced the manuscript of *A Connecticut Yankee* far enough to project completion by 15 November. Unfortunately, a return to the distractions of Hartford and New York in late September soon made him abandon that goal. Not surprisingly, Clemens' other literary work was minimal. In December 1887, "A Petition to the Queen of England," partially drafted in this notebook (p. 329), appeared in the "Editor's Drawer" of *Harper's New Monthly Magazine,* but this humorous complaint against the English income tax was not memorable. Nor was *Meisterschaft,* the brief play originally written as a family entertainment, which the *Century* magazine published in January 1888. Evidence of Clemens' continuing concern for *Mark Twain's Library of Humor* abounds in Notebook 27, but his interest in it was that of publisher, not author.

Clemens was at this time more a man of letters prominent in literary affairs than a practicing writer. He participated in readings, two in Washington in March 1888, to promote the cause of international copyright. He expended much effort and filled several notebook pages in the course of writing four articles, only one of which saw print, debating the need for international copyright with Brander Matthews. And when asked to defend America against Matthew Arnold's harsh criticisms in "Civilisation in the United States," Clemens produced a profusion of disconnected manuscript. Although some of this eventually found its way into *A Connecticut Yankee,* Clemens could not manage a publishable magazine piece in response to Arnold. Notes for other unwritten articles also appear. The most ambitious of these, perhaps planned only for personal amusement, proposed a "cipher" along the lines of the Bacon-Shakespeare controversy to prove that John Milton was the actual author of John Bunyan's works.

On 25 June 1888, just as he was preparing for a summer of writing at Quarry Farm, Clemens' spirits were raised when Joseph Twichell notified him that "the Corporation of the Yale University, now in session, have just decreed you the honorary degree of Master of Arts (M.A.)." Clemens reported himself "vain" at being "the only literary animal of my particular subspecies who has ever been given a degree by any College in any age of the world, as far as I know" (SLC to Charles H. Clark, 2 July 1888, *MTL*, p. 495). He accepted the award gratefully in his own name and on behalf of all the American humorists whom Matthew Arnold had recently branded "a national misfortune." "A friendly word was needed in our defense," Clemens wrote to the university on 26 June, "and you have said it, and it is sufficient. It could not become us—we being in some ways, and at intervals, modest, like other folk—to remind the world that ours is a useful trade, a worthy calling: that with all its lightness and frivolity it has one serious purpose, one aim, one specialty, and it is constant to it—the deriding of shams, the exposure of pretentious falsities, the laughing of stupid superstitions out of existence; and that whoso is by instinct engaged in this sort of warfare is the natural enemy of royalties, nobilities, privileges and all kindred swindles, and the natural friend of human rights and human liberties. We might with propriety say these things, and so hint that in some degree our calling is entitled to respect, but since you have rehabilitated us it is not necessary" (Hartford *Courant,* 29 June 1888). In this mood of renewed purpose, Clemens resumed work on *A Connecticut Yankee.*

Notebook 27 is identical to Notebooks 22, 24, 25, and 26 in design and format. It now contains 176 pages, two of which are blank. Four leaves have been torn out and are missing. The entries are predominantly in black pencil, but there are a number in brownish black ink, mostly in the first half of the notebook, and others in blue and grayish blue ink in the last quarter. Clemens

marked fifteen entries in this notebook with symbols. Although their precise
meaning is not clear, the symbols fall into two groups. A small group accompanies entries that deal with proposals for publishing an art catalog and for the
underwriting of the Paige typesetter (see notes 119 and 120), while a longer
series accompanies lists of punch lines and anecdotes (see note 179). All are
reproduced in this text in positions that approximate their manuscript placement. Use marks, probably by Paine, also appear in the notebook but have not
been reproduced.

A. P. Bur—227 - E. 14.[1]

Kinkley Locomo. Co.
    439 Albany st. Boston.

Next May, write Prof. Francis Wayland that I am ready to pay
the young colored man Chas. W. Johnson's way through the Yale
Law School.[2] [#]

---

[1] Alfred P. Burbank, the actor and elocutionist, wrote Clemens from his "little flat
at this address" on 18 September 1887, having just returned from trial performances of
Colonel Sellers as a Scientist in Rochester and Syracuse. Although obliged to report
that the play was received "kindly, even cordially in some instances" by "uniformly light"
audiences and that "the newspapers have not been so kind," Burbank remained optimistic about its prospects. He invited Clemens to observe a performance at the Lyceum
Theatre on 23 September, promising elaborate arrangements to keep his attendance
secret, but Clemens sent Franklin G. Whitmore, his Hartford business agent, instead.
The disparaging response from New York critics to that production helped convince
Clemens to abandon further attempts to produce the play at this time.

[2] On 29 September 1887, Francis Wayland, dean of the Yale Law School, forwarded
to Clemens a letter of application, evidently from Charles W. Johnson. Wayland asked
Clemens, who had already provided two years' support to another Negro student, "to
put the writer down for your kind assistance." Clemens and Wayland agreed, however,
that Johnson should "spend the coming year in earning & saving money, so that he might
come to us, if he chose, at the end of that time, with money enough in hand to prevent

100,000 shs at 100, is 10,000,000
"Lambs" 34 W. 26[th][3]

Stilson Hutchins,
1603 Mass[ts] ave.[4]

Robert Louis Stevenson   Apl. 19 to 26th
St. Stephen's Hotel East 11[th.][5]

Rev. Henry Hopkins,
Kansas City (College at Springfield, Mo.)[6]

562 - 8th st. Oakland (Moffett)[7] [#]

---

him from being wholly dependent on charity" (Wayland to SLC, 1 October 1887). This plan evidently was not realized, for Charles W. Johnson does not appear on the roster of Yale Law School graduates.

[3] The Lambs' Club was a popular New York meeting place for theatrical people. Clemens' business there is not known, but the calculations which precede this address suggest that he had an engagement to discuss a scheme to raise capital for the Paige typesetter.

[4] Hutchins, the editor of the Washington *Post,* was one of the founders of the Mergenthaler Linotype Company. In early 1886 Clemens had indicated a desire to confer with Hutchins about their potentially competitive composing machines (see p. 219).

[5] Stevenson later recalled his April 1888 meeting with Clemens as "that very pleasant afternoon we spent together in Washington Square among the nursemaids like a couple of characters out of a story by Henry James" (Stevenson to SLC, [16 April 1893], *Twainian,* September–October 1950, p. 1). In an Autobiographical Dictation of April 1904, Clemens remembered that Stevenson's "business in the square was to absorb the sunshine. He was most scantily furnished with flesh, his clothes seemed to fall into hollows as if there might be nothing inside but the frame for a sculptor's statue. His long face and lank hair and dark complexion and musing and melancholy expression seemed to fit these details justly and harmoniously, and the altogether of it seemed especially planned to gather the rags of your observation and focalize them upon Stevenson's special distinction and commanding feature, his splendid eyes. They burned with a smoldering rich fire under the penthouse of his brows, and they made him beautiful" (*MTA,* 1:247).

[6] The Reverend Henry Hopkins, pastor of the First Congregational Church at Kansas City, was a trustee of Drury College, a coeducational institution in Springfield, Missouri, founded by Congregationalists in 1873.

[7] The address of Pamela A. Moffett while in California in 1888 and 1889 to be near her son Samuel, a member of the editorial staff of the San Francisco *Examiner.* The earliest surviving evidence of her stay there dates from April 1888. Clemens' entry may have been made around that time.

Aus seinem After kommt ein grellendes poo-o-o-o! und dabei
fängt er an die "From Greenland's Icy Mountains" zu singen——
mit dem *zweite* Nota beginnend, als ob die *Erste* schon gesungen
sei![8]

Dickens to Hen. Robinson: "G'way, little boy, g'way!"[9]

What have ye in yer bahsket, says I. Fish, s'she. They stink, says
I. You lie! s'she. To hell! says I. Whoo-oo-oop!

Fireman wants the widow to put off her son's funeral a day
because the boys want to turn out on that day, & must lose the
chance to turn out for *him* (a member) otherwise. ⟨Asks leave
[to]⟩The widow explains that the weather being warm, is afraid
Jimmy won't keep. The fire-laddie asks to examine the body—the
weeping widows stands by:

(Bends over body & snuffs.) Smf! smf! ⟨Hell!⟩ Sweet as a nut!—
keep a week!

"Organize! — — you, & pay James T. Hedley &c"

See Charley Clark about finishing Library & reading proof.[10] [#]

---

[8] *From his rear comes a hard poo-o-o-o! and with that he begins to sing "From Greenland's Icy Mountains"—beginning with the <u>second</u> note, as if the <u>first</u> had already been
sung!*

[9] The punch line of Clemens' anecdote about Henry C. Robinson, his Hartford friend
and billiards partner. Clemens claimed that upon being urged to describe an 1842
encounter with Charles Dickens, Robinson responded as follows:

> "The meeting was brief; & yet, fleeting as it was, I can never forget it. It was a beauti-
> ful day; one of those days which soothe the spirit, which make the heart happy, which
> endear existence to man, & man to his kind. I was passing by the City Hotel, in my
> ancient town of Hartford, when suddenly I stopped, as one that is paralyzed; for there,
> in the great bay window, alone—& meetly solitary in a greatness which could be no
> otherwise than companionless—sat one whom all the universe knew—Dickens!
> Eagerly I pressed my face against the pane, & in one moment was lost, absorbed,
> enchanted. Presently I saw his lips begin to open: was he going to speak to me?—to
> *me?* I verily held my breath. And—gentlemen—he *did* speak to me!"
> (Immense applause—thunders of applause—in the midst of which it was noticed
> that Robinson was blandly walking off the platform. Voices—"Hold on, hold on!—
> what the nation did he *say?*")
> "Well, he only said, 'Go 'way, little boy, go 'way!'" (SLC to F. G. Kitton, 8 Novem-
> ber 1886, Berg)

[10] Clemens probably made the sequence of business entries which continue, with
some interruption, to "Lib. of Humor postponed till next year." (305.3) in preparation

Can Library be canvassed from Sept. 15 to Dec. 10—if so, take it at ⟨45. But if *either* date fails, then 50.⟩

Can you begin canvass for Yankee Jan. 15 & issue Ap. 1 if I furnish the copy Nov. 15?[11]

Leo—start fresh & issue in ⟨25¢?⟩ numbers.[12]

How would it do to issue Lt. Gen[13] & Library Humor in parts—especially former.

Royalty & Nobility Exposed.[14]

See Joe Jefferson—10 p.c.[15] [#]

---

for Frederick J. Hall's visit to Elmira on 30 August 1887 to discuss Webster & Company projects. Memoranda prepared at that time called for issuance of the *Mark Twain's Library of Humor* prospectus on 1 January 1888 with book publication on 1 March. If this proved impossible, the prospectus was to appear on 15 January and the book itself on 15 March. Profits from the *Library of Humor* were divided on an equal basis between Clemens and Charles L. Webster & Company, the second of the two arrangements noted in the next entry.

[11] Clemens was hoping that his summer of work on *A Connecticut Yankee* would enable him to finish it in the fall of 1887. But Webster & Company's many commitments would have made it impossible to publish *A Connecticut Yankee* in the spring of 1888 even if Clemens had been able to avoid business and social distractions successfully enough to complete it on schedule. As early as 5 September 1887, he conceded to Webster and Hall that the only remaining "choice date for a canvass to begin is Jan 1, '89" (*MTLP*, p. 228).

[12] A plan to stimulate sales of the *Life of Leo XIII*. Clemens was concerned about the disposal of this book, from which the great profits anticipated were not being realized, and had Hall send him regular reports of its sale. He evidently was not entirely comforted by Hall's assurances that the book was doing well considering that it "was published during the hot and dull season" of the year (Hall to SLC, 10 August 1887).

[13] At their meeting on 30 August 1887, Clemens and Hall agreed to issue the prospectus for Lieutenant General Philip Sheridan's *Personal Memoirs* on 1 September 1888 with publication scheduled for 1 December of that year. The prospectus was actually ready by mid-June 1888 so as to permit an extended canvass. Neither Sheridan's book nor *Mark Twain's Library of Humor* was published serially.

[14] Clemens' tentative title for a multi-volume edition of some favorite political writings which he had conceived as a possible project for Charles L. Webster & Company (see p. 295).

[15] On 15 August 1887, Clemens had instructed Hall and Webster to offer "only 8 per cent" for the autobiography of comedian Joseph Jefferson (*MTLP*, p. 223). Although he was now willing to increase his offer to "the highest royalty I ever got (while I was green)" (*MTLP*, p. 223), Webster & Company lost Jefferson's book through delay in communicating their interest in it.

⟨Purchase American magazine?⟩

Visit Ned House.[16]

Talk with John.
And with Patrick—⟨.⟩(break.)⟨.⟩—on the big carriage.[17]

Call on Laffan.

How soon ⟨Calico's⟩Kalico's book?[18]

McGlynn, Beecher, the King, & now Stanley. Let's insure
Lt. Gen.[19]

Am Pub Co 5% dividend

"Put on your shoes & give the cheese a chance." [#]

---

[16] Edward House, who had spent six weeks in Hartford with the Clemenses in the
spring of 1887, was now staying at the home of their neighbors, the George Warners. On
8 September, House wrote to Livy in Elmira: "I should promise myself the pleasure of
going over to welcome you on your arrival, next week, if I were not apprehensive that I
might disturb you. . . . Perhaps I will ride over, and wait at the front door,—see you
into the house, and then retire;—and make a real visit as soon as I hear that you are ready
to receive friends."

[17] Upon his return from Elmira in mid-September, Clemens intended to consult his
gardener, John O'Neil, and his coachman, Patrick McAleer, concerning tasks assigned
through Franklin G. Whitmore. On 9 September, Whitmore reported: "I have attended
to the brake on the carriage and have planned it all out for the workmen. I think it will
do the business all right. John O'neil has had the Gun & I suppose he has killed a good
many sparrows & perhaps eaten a pie or two of them."

[18] Probably *The Legends and Myths of Hawaii: The Fables and Folk-Lore of a Strange
People*, nominally written by David Kalakaua, the Hawaiian sovereign, but actually
prepared by Rollin M. Daggett (see p. 260, note 109, and p. 261, note 114). Webster &
Company originally planned to publish this book in the fall of 1887, but immediately
began a series of postponements in favor of works that seemed more lucrative. Daggett's
increasing impatience would finally force Hall to shift from a policy of stalling to one of
active deceit. In the fall of 1888 he proposed "to have a die made and bind up a few
volumes. . . . We can easily dispose of these, send three or four of them to [Daggett],
and that will keep him quiet" (Hall to SLC, 17 September 1888). Once this was done
Webster & Company could "secure the copyright, and push the work after we get over
the Sheridan rush" (Hall to SLC, 21 September 1888). Daggett's book was finally published late in 1888. It was "an absolute and flat failure" although Webster & Company
"tried in every way to make it sell, both by subscription and through the trade" (Hall to
SLC, 22 November 1890).

[19] A wishful impulse to protect Webster & Company's interest in Sheridan's *Personal
Memoirs* from the sorts of perils which had upset or threatened planned works by the
other men noted here. Edward McGlynn, Roman Catholic clergyman and social

"You may think a dude is vain of his leg. Well, he is; but not so much so as ⟨an⟩ military officer is of his—the one he lost in battle.

Lib. of Humor postponed till next year.

He has set up for a gentleman—⟨travels⟩ carries his own soap. (when he travels.)

God himself exhibits no originality. Look at people; all alike, & he keeps repeating them.

Courant always remarks contemptuously that Ingersoll's arguments are "old." So is the argument that God must have loved the world or he would not have given his only begotten son, &c. The grumbler in California who was tested with a pile of "slugs"; finally examined their dates & said disparagingly, "Shucks, they're old!"

Rev. Alex Campbell, founder of the Campbellites, gently reproved our apprentice, Wales MᶜCormick, ⟨once,⟩ on separate occasions, for saying Great God! when ⟨"⟩Great Scott would have done as well, & for ⟨us[in]⟩ committing the Unforgiven Sin when *any* other form of expression would have been a million times better. Weeks afterward, that inveterate light-head had his turn, & corrected the Reverend. In correcting the pamphlet-proof of one of Campbell's great sermons, Wales changed "Great God!" to "Great Scott," & changed Father, Son & Holy Ghost to Father, Son & Caesar's Ghost. In overrunning, he reduced it to Father, Son & Co., to keep *from* overrunning. And Jesus H. Christ.[20] [#]

---

reformer, had evidently ceased to be attractive to Webster & Company when he was excommunicated in July 1887 for supporting Henry George's candidacy for mayor of New York. Henry Ward Beecher had died on 8 March 1887 before finishing either his autobiography or the biography of Christ he had promised the firm. Hawaiian king David Kalakaua, whose book would be reluctantly issued in 1888, was challenged, in the summer of 1887, by a revolutionary movement which left him on the throne but effected a severe constitutional limitation of his authority. And through August 1887 rumors were circulating about the death of Henry M. Stanley while in Africa at the head of an expedition to rescue Emin Pasha from extermination by Sudanese rebels. Although Stanley had turned down a Webster & Company proposal in December 1886, Clemens persisted in thinking of him as a potential book-contributor. Stanley survived his African excursion to reject Webster & Company's further overtures in 1890.

[20] Clemens frequently recalled the irreverent pranks of Wales McCormick, his fellow

"Isaac, shall I wash for high neck, or low neck?" (Purim ball.)

The British Navy (1878) had 297 ships in commission, & 332 Admirals in full pay on the active list (3 grades, Admiral, Vice & Rear.) An admiral for every ship, & 35 to spare.[21]

The army conisted of 151 regiments. To command it it has on the active list, under full pay: 96 full Generals; 154 Lt. Generals; 435 Major Generals; 925 Colonels; 2250 lt. Colonels; & 1475 majors.

That is, a General for every 2 regiments, & 20½ to spare; ⟨2⟩⟨[3]⟩one lt. Gen for each reg & 3 over;

    3 Maj. Gens."   "   "   lacking 18;
    6 colonels   "   "   & 19 over;
   15 lt. Cols   "   "   & 44   "
    9 majors   "   "   & 116 ⟨over⟩over

In the year 1885–6 the army & navy cost £18,000,000.

⟨Admirals⟩Generals Generals 96
Generals 154
Lt. Gen[s] .435
Cols. 925
Lt. Cols .2250
Majors 1475

5,335 field officers to command 151 regiments, & ⟨335⟩332 admirals for 297 ships.

Father Adam & the apple—he didn't know it was loaded.

Gahsh (or Gosh) ⟨[-]s⟩is ⟨20⟩ 100,000 miles high & swings in a ⟨hammock and⟩ swing. ⟨The proportions are 10 times 15 or 1600 now. So that his shoe-sole instead of being 15 or 1600 feet long, as formerly, is now ⟨1[0]⟩15 or 16,000 feet.⟩

The Gospel of Gahsh.

His foot-ball is suspended in front of his face, & ⟨when he⟩ every time he winks his eye it is ⟨dark⟩ night on it. His speech is thunder

---

apprentice on the Hannibal *Missouri Courier*. Extant letters from McCormick indicate that Clemens regularly provided him with financial assistance in the middle and late 1880s.

[21] Clemens' authority for these statistics of the British army and navy was chapter 33 of George Standring's *People's History of the English Aristocracy*, an important source for *A Connecticut Yankee*.

& they run into their holes. His shoe-sole is 13 or 14,000 miles. So is his face.

The Yank will be ⟨$[-].25⟩$3.25 cloth & be accompanied *gratis* by a thin-paper 12-illustration (full page) copy of the complete Legends.[22]

Han . . . . 8,000 . . . ⟨5,000⟩7,000 . . . . . 8000 ⟨20,000⟩18,000
Custe . . . . . . .14,000 . . . . 5,000 . . . . . 7000 25,000
Kox . . . . .10,000 . . . . 7,000 Cox 6000 20,000
Bchr . . . . 6,000 . . . . ? 15,000
Kalakaua . . . . 2,000 . . . . ⟨2[0],000⟩
Lib. Humr . . . . ⟨[40],000⟩20,000 . . . . .or ⟨20,000⟩25,000
Life of Chr. . . .13,000 . . . . 5,000 . . . .13,000 30,000
Old stock . . . . 10,000? 20,000

           $81,000 $56,000[23]

Rip Van Jefferson[24]

Royalty Exposed.[25]

Bills receivable?
Phila. & Iowa debts?[26] [#]

---

[22] A plan to enhance the effect of *A Connecticut Yankee* by including with each copy a volume of Malory's *Morte Darthur.* Clemens later also considered George Standring's *People's History of the English Aristocracy* as a possible companion work to his own book.

[23] These cryptic calculations pertain to the following Webster & Company works: *Reminiscences of Winfield Scott Hancock,* by Almira Hancock (1887); Elizabeth Custer's *Tenting on the Plains; or, General Custer in Kansas and Texas* (1887); Samuel S. Cox's *Diversions of a Diplomat in Turkey* (1887); *A Biography of Reverend Henry Ward Beecher,* by William C. Beecher and the Reverend Samuel Scoville (1888); *Legends and Myths of Hawaii: The Fables and Folk-Lore of a Strange People,* by King David Kalakaua and Rollin M. Daggett (1888); *Mark Twain's Library of Humor* (1888). Henry Ward Beecher's *Life of Christ* was aborted by Beecher's death on 8 March 1887 and Webster & Company negotiated the return of a $5,000 advance in 1888.

[24] Joseph Jefferson, the comic actor who had offered his autobiography to Webster & Company, was most famous for his stage portrayal of Rip Van Winkle.

[25] See page 303, note 14.

[26] A reference to money owed to Webster & Company by Hubbard Brothers of Philadelphia and R. T. Root of Iowa, book agents for the Grant *Memoirs.* Litigation against Hubbard Brothers would lead to a settlement in February 1888 (see p. 287, note 204). The claim against Root was not settled until January of the following year (see p. 390, note 306).

Leo in *parts*.

N.Y. Genl Agency.

⟨Give me guesses on all these⟩

Rule—Canvassing bks *ready* 2 weeks before *issue*.

Ask Charley Clark to go & get Am. Pub's permission to use matter.[27]

Tell them they are liable for not completing my copyrights & I will sue.

Farm—estimate: 6 persons at
    $40 per week each, 13 weeks......$520.
Pony, $3 per week 40
Add $40 to cover extras............ 40
                           $600

(Last year, W^m $18 & ⟨& Ernest⟩Richard & Ernest[28] ⟨$1[8]⟩$12 each ⟨&⟩.)

This yr. W^m $20, & the others $12 each.

Simplified, it is $1 a day for each person & 3 a week for pony.

Nasby's yarn: "Man don't even get his seed back."

Moncoon

Pleasant, to have a body follow you with "The way *I* heard it was."

Cable's & my adventure with (first, *him*self,) my abuse of somebody for telling me the most ancient of all ⟨humories⟩humorous stories—then ⟨Na⟩ Tom Nast telling it that night at dinner—then Cable's hearing it at the reception in Buffalo —then next March when the President was to arrive, I said something chaffingly about a "stranger always tells me that old tale

---

[27] Charles H. Clark, one of the editors of the Hartford *Courant,* did much of the actual assembling of the manuscript of *Mark Twain's Library of Humor.* Clark also had a part in the sometimes difficult task of securing publishers' permissions to use copyrighted material, in this case selections from Clemens' own early work.

[28] Individuals employed at Quarry Farm.

if he 〈has〉 is with me 15 minutes—don't be gone long." The
President entered the one door as Cable stepped onto the stage
from the other. 〈Ten or 15〉Twenty minutes later, as I stepped
onto the stage as Cable stepped off it, I was able to remark in his
ear, "He told it to me."[29]

Traded teeth.)

Bermuda girl.

They've made him County Clerk!

Putnam's wolf-hunt descendant.

Martin McGinnis making his great speech at Gettysburg.

Scotch Christening.

Bacon-Shakspere

Suggestions for a Charade
CAMP. Soldiers cooking, sentries on duty. The Guard-mount.
Roll-call. The colors. Drums. Bugle calls. Songs: John Brown &
Marching through Georgia.
MEETING. Noisy (nominating *or* ratification) republican
convention—a Mugwump finally makes a speech. Comes in &
inquires what kind of meeting it is, & a joker deceives him. He tells
that story about the stolen beef. Cries of What do you mean?
What does this man mean? Look here, sir, are *you* a republican?
Republican?—no, I am a Mugwump! (Riot—they fire him out.)

CAMP-MEETING.
Get that young fellow to dress up & sing & play that lovely
thing of his; & *remain;* then I break in with 〈you'll〉You'll be an
angel by & by. A circle of a dozen to do the shouting & amen-ing.

---

[29] The occurrences of this irrepressible unidentified anecdote date from Mark Twain's
1884/1885 lecture tour with George Washington Cable. According to the chronology
noted here, the story was told at Thomas Nast's Morristown, New Jersey, home on 27
November 1884, again at an after-lecture dinner in Buffalo on 11 December, and finally
by the recently elected president Grover Cleveland in Washington in the first week of
March 1885.

No use for to weep & *cry* in de morn,
   You'll be an angel by & by,
Dig up de *ta*ters, hoe *up* de corn,
   You'll be
Strap on de armor, armor of de Lord
   You'll be
Clap on de helmet, grip on de sword,
   You'll be—
Ole Satan's a-*comin*', *don't you run*—
Heave/Slap on de *ar*mor, *git* yo' gospel gun—
Keep *on* a-*blaz*in', *hear* de rifle crack!
Aim for his *bo*som, hit him *in* de back!
     For ENCORE:
Put on de *robe* an' frizzle *up* yo' har—
Git OUT yo' *coup*on *for* de gospel k'yar—
Snatch *on* de *ar*mor, armor *of* de Lord
Lay *for* de *Pull*man, pile *on* board—

Pratt & Whitney's bill for August, '87, is $1567.23.[30]

"Well, the *Savior's* been here *once*." (2[d] Advent.)

Arkansas Girl. "Look here, I ain't no more particular'n most folks, but all the same I can't stand only jist *so much*, & I got to have a *limit* set up. Now, all in jist this ⟨fust⟩⟨f[ir]st⟩fust week we've had ⟨Schütz⟩, & ⟨Fahrt⟩ ⟨& Konnt.⟩ I don't wish to crowd marters ⟨[-]⟩& 'pear to be ⟨putting on frills⟩ *over*-finicky, ⟨but with my bringin' up⟩ but I want to give you notice here & *now*, that I'm goin' to draw the *line* at a-h.

Sept. 1, '87. Two ⟨books⟩ in a year & a half. Loss upon the one, $32,000; profit on the other, $15,000. Expenses, $30,000. Net loss, $17,000.[31] See scheme of this time. [#]

---

[30] For work done on the Paige typesetter. Clemens also paid $1,691.82 for miscellaneous related expenses in August, including expenditures for development of a dynamo and for preparation of a patent application. In addition he paid Paige his monthly salary of $583.33.

[31] Webster & Company actually issued three books in the period between March

Up to this time there had been absolutely *no* system. Everything was done by guess; nothing was *calculated.* We are forced to suddenly change from 2 in a year & a half to an attempt to *do 7 in 9 months!*[32]

Let us stop all questionable & silver-gilt account-keeping. Would it be honest to show that August report to a would-be purchaser—with its 4 months' sales of 21,000, when 8,000 went ⟨[unsold]⟩ *below cost?* Then why make up such an account for *anybody?* You should have said, We *sold* 12,000, we *gave away* 8,000.[33]

Memoirs sur les Prisons.
Deux Amis.[34]

The first trouble—& from it grew the permanent disagreement—originated in your telling me a lie & knowing you were going to get caught in it at cost to me of $1800 interest-money. You told me,

---

1886, when volume 2 of the Grant *Memoirs* appeared, and September 1887. These were Samuel W. Crawford's *The Genesis of the Civil War, McClellan's Own Story,* and the *Life of Leo XIII.* Only the second of them was profitable. Even it could hardly have met expectations, however, despite Hall's 10 August 1887 assertion that it had "paid well." Although Clemens here lamented his firm's dismal output, on at least one occasion he himself decided to delay acceptance of "a good book . . . we ought to have" since "our hands will be more than full with the Pope's and General McClellan's books" (SLC to Hall, 12 July 1886, *MTLP,* p. 198). It was only when these works failed to produce the anticipated profit that he questioned the wisdom of such a policy.

[32] The books scheduled for publication between 20 September 1887 and 30 May 1888 are listed on page 307. Clemens and Hall had agreed upon that schedule on 30 August 1887.

[33] In an attempt at reassurance, Hall had informed Clemens on 10 August 1887: "We have sold since April 1st. to August 1st. 21577 books and prospectuses. It must be borne in mind that these months are hot, unprofitable and considered the dullest of the year." Hall's figure included about 1,100 prospectuses which brought no profit since they were sold to agents at cost. Hall had evidently been forced to concede the further damaging adjustment of statistics noted here while conferring with Clemens in Elmira at the end of August.

[34] *Mémoires sur les prisons,* two volumes in the *Collection des mémoires relatifs à la révolution française,* edited by Saint-Albin Berville and Jean François Barrière, 67 vols. (Paris: Baudouin, 1820–1827); *Histoire de la révolution de France . . . par deux amis de la liberté,* 19 vols. (Paris: Garnery, etc., 1792–1803), actually the work of several authors.

the middle of October that you had orders for 298,000 sets (forgetting that you had told me the same thing a week or so before,) & that they were increasing at the steady rate of 3,000 a day. I said we must borrow $100,000 at once. "You said wait—no hurry"—which was *true*, because you had been lying; otherwise it would *not* have been true. We had 55 days before us: 3,000 sets a day—*how* could we get along without $100,000? ⟨Tha⟩The thing would have been impossible. But you knew you were lying, & that we already had money enough. But you were caught where you couldn't get out of your lie, & wouldn't confess; so you had to let me go & borrow $100,000 which we hadn't the slightest use for. The 298,000 *remained* at that figure thenceforth, without change.[35]

You never could tell how many presses & binderies you were employing ⟨at⟩without lying about it.

You suspected S before he'd had been there 3 months & *told me* so.[36]

We talked over & decided upon a project of mine (you knowing all the time the smartness which you meant to forestal it with) to pay Mrs. G. a lump sum of $500,000; & by & by you sneaked in & paid her $200,000, & wrote your note to Field or somebody signing *your* name alone. It was *you* who paid it her—& you owned a $\frac{1}{10}$th interest![37] [#]

---

[35] In October 1885, Clemens had been forced to borrow $100,000 from Samuel Dunham, a Hartford acquaintance, to meet production costs for the Grant *Memoirs* (see p. 203), the first volume of which was published on 1 December of that year. The necessity annoyed Clemens, but Daniel Whitford, lawyer for Webster & Company, reminded him on 24 October 1885: "Charley is legally correct when he says that *you* are bound to furnish all the capital." Surviving business records do not suggest any intentional misrepresentation of sales by Webster. Nor do surviving sales figures for the period include the total Clemens recalled here. On 6 October 1885, Frederick J. Hall reported that 250,258 sets of the *Memoirs* had been sold as of the first of the month. By 24 October, Webster could claim 296,497 "ORDERS for FIRST delivery" and total sales of over 300,000, a figure Daniel Whitford amplified to 319,000 that same day.

[36] For a discussion of the offenses of Frank M. Scott, a Webster & Company bookkeeper imprisoned for embezzlement, see page 283, note 194.

[37] Although a half million dollar profit for Mrs. Grant was considered possible—she eventually received "some four hundred thousand dollars" (CLW to Frederick Grant,

And you played the same trick next time—paying her $150,000 without consultation, though you attributed it to the firm, this time.

Never could get a statement. No *time* to get one up. When S defaulted, you said you always supposed I had one regularly. Which was a lie.

The money-borrowing previously referred to two ⟨bac[k]⟩pages back,[38] made bad blood for this reason. I went home & borrowed it, & gave notice of the fact, & got some impudence in return. I sent a rude telegram. It brought me a brutal letter—the letter of a hog —which you are, & were so born.[39]

As your letter when you first wanted the contract reorganized, will prove. I have saved it.[40] [#]

---

19 January 1888)—Webster had a reason for neglecting Clemens' scheme to allow her earnings to reach that amount before payment. On 26 February 1886 he explained to Clemens: "I dislike to carry so large a bank account, so I have decided to give Mrs Grant a check on account for $200,000⁰⁰. . . . I do not for a moment think there is any danger with either of our banks here still such a thing is possible and . . . the safest way is to pay now. This will be over double the largest amtt. ever paid an author in one check so we should be satisfied with the record." Webster later acknowledged that in giving this celebrated first check to Mrs. Grant on 27 February 1886, he "strained a point, and overpaid her by five or six thousand dollars, to make it an even two hundred thousand dollar payment" (CLW to Frederick Grant, 19 January 1888). He compounded the adverse effect his autonomous decision had on Clemens by announcing the record royalty in a personal letter to Grant's friend Cyrus W. Field, who published it in his New York *Mail and Express* on 27 February 1887.

[38] Clemens alludes to the incident described on pages 311–312.

[39] Although extant business correspondence confirms that there was hard feeling between Clemens and Webster about the October 1885 loan of $100,000 to cover production expenses for the Grant *Memoirs*, neither Clemens' rude telegram nor Webster's brutal letter has been discovered. A double line connects this paragraph and "interest!" (312.22) on the facing page of the notebook.

[40] On 25 February 1885, two days before the signing of the Grant contract, Webster wrote to Clemens noting that success of the *Memoirs* "will be largely due to my personal efforts and energy in the making of the book and conduct of the business. Additional care and responsibility will be placed upon my shoulders, and I must work, and think much harder." Consequently, Webster requested a share of company profits in addition to his annual salary of $2,500 (the details of his proposal are discussed in the headnote to Notebook 23).

JL & Co's Notes, made to Mrs. C: $17,750; 8,000; 25,000; 2,410.
($53,160.)

George Herbert:
Do well & right, & let the world sink.
(Country Parson.[41]

There is one humorist whom this book makes no attempt to
keep up with; & that is Mr. Burdette.[42]

Sir F. W. P. Napier, 1785–1860. Napoleon's troops fought in
bright fields, where every helmet caught some beams of glory, but
the British soldier conquered under the cool shade of aristocracy; no
honors awaited his daring, no despatch gave his name to the
applauses of his countrymen; his life of danger & hardship was
uncheered by hope, his death unnoticed. (Peninsular War.)[43]

In summer of '85 (early), you told me Scott professed to be
speculating in Wall⟨s⟩ st & also that anonymous letters had warned
you he was a thief. You said you meant to shadow him with a
detective *or* trap him with decoy letters containing remittances.

You now pretend that ⟨that⟩the first you heard against Scott was
in Oct., ⟨'87⟩'86, when you returned from Europe. If that were
true, it would have been *then* that you proposed detectives and
decoys, whereas the *only* thing you proposed was an expert
examination of the books, & *that* you had already ordered.

Being capable of only one idea at a time, you waited more than
4 months over ⟨the⟩this volcano, to get the expert. Through the

---

[41] George Herbert employed this apothegm at the close of chapter 29—"The Parson
with his Church Wardens"—of A Priest to the Temple; or, The Country Parson, His
Character and Rule of Holy Life, first published in 1652.

[42] The prolific Robert J. Burdette at this time contributed a regular column to the
Brooklyn Daily Eagle. Clemens' draft of a disclaimer addresses the difficulty of adequately representing Burdette in Mark Twain's Library of Humor. In fact, only Clemens'
own work appeared more extensively in that anthology. Clemens indicated his intention
of being generous with Burdette on page 321.

[43] Clemens copied this passage from the conclusion to chapter 3, Book 11 of General
William Francis Patrick Napier's History of the War in the Peninsula and in the South of
France, from the Year 1807 to the Year 1814, originally published between 1828 and 1840.

wisdom of A & G.,[44] (by whose brains, almost exclusively[,] the business has always been run), Mr. H. had already waited a couple of months (after *new* warnings) for your return, so as not to "disturb" the serenity of your mind while charming Pope & Cardinals with the peculiar graces of your Fredonian English. Mr. H was so accustomed to the office-policy of ignoring me, that he never once mentioned the new anonymous letter to me.

In March & April '87, you had 3 times the office-force necessary for your (absence of) business, yet in spite of my appeals I was obliged to get *my* information about the defalcation from your sentimental newspaper interviews, in which you posed as a suffering but magnanimous hero, & decided to be lenient in Court with a thief who hadn't robbed you but *had* robbed me.[45]

You have a rare faculty for being generous at other people's expense. When you imagined that Scott had stolen $4,000 from you, albeit you could produce no evidence of it,) you handsomely called on me to make up the loss by an advance of wages—which I did; being an ass.[46]

---

[44] "A & G." is the New York law firm of Alexander & Green, which represented Charles L. Webster & Company. "Mr. H." (315.2) is Frederick J. Hall who had become a junior partner in Webster & Company in 1886. Hall had been put in charge of company affairs in the summer and fall of 1886 while Webster was in Rome conferring about the *Life of Leo XIII*. Clemens had been pleased then by Webster's successful diplomacy with the pope and cardinals, but that was before the biography's lack of appeal became evident.

[45] On several occasions Webster had publicly expressed sympathy for Frank M. Scott's wife and three children. But it was probably a statement attributed to him by the New York *Daily Tribune* of 19 March 1887 that Clemens alluded to here. "Mr. Webster," the paper reported, "did not think [Scott] ought to be allowed to escape. Still, he felt more for Scott's wife and children than he did for the loss of the money. If Scott would come to this city without a requisition and would plead guilty and give no further trouble Mr. Webster said he was willing to use every means in his power to have his punishment made as light as possible." Webster's behavior, however, was not consistent with this tolerant attitude. Although he did not attach Mrs. Scott's personal property in settlement of the claims against her husband, Webster was adamant in demanding Scott's conviction and imprisonment and expressed satisfaction at the six-year sentence imposed by the courts. Only after Scott had served several years did Webster and Clemens join in an appeal for remission of the balance of his penalty (see p. 283, note 194).

[46] One of Webster's claims against his defaulting bookkeeper was that Scott had charged him with an $8,000 withdrawal from company profits when in fact he had withdrawn only around $4,000. He asserted that Scott had then destroyed the cashbook in

You have been sowing the wind ever since you became a beggar on horseback, & all in good time you shall reap the whirlwind.

You got the G. book! *You* told him it would ⟨see⟩sell 300,000 sets! Then how do you explain the estmate in your celebrated letter —when you "would not have made such a contract with me if" you had ⟨d⟩imagined my profits would exceed $60,000.[47] You, a mere apprentice,—with the trade half learned, proposed to strike for a full third of the profits, did you?

The Pony. We leave Sept. 13, Tuesday, after 78 days' stay at the farm, & the pony Vix leaves that night, the U.S. Express Co taking him straight through to Hartford—all charges paid here in advance: $30. Usual rate, $35.

The D. L. & W. RR furnish me 13 *through*-checks to Hartford.

U. L. Dr Sir: Biography is not worth a dam. [It] cannot speak the truth. It ought to read, Concealment of the Life of —

Anna Keary novels   Jennette's Home, Castle Bailey, & others. McMillan.[48]

Next Door, by Clara Louise Burnham.

---

which the actual transaction was noted. In a letter of 29 December 1887—indicating that the issue still rankled almost four months after this entry was made—Webster recalled that Clemens had offered him the opportunity to take the additional $4,000 Scott had charged to him. This misguided proposal, which balanced Webster's account but doubled the company's loss, had become the basis of a final settlement. Webster rejected the single payment plan because "I could not get at the exact amtt. I thought it would be easier for the firm to pay me $800 a year extra, this method would take five years to pay me what you offered to let me take in one and what I could have legally taken could I prove the amtt. but the books having been destroyed I could not."

[47] This letter is not known to survive. The estimate and language here attributed to Webster do not appear in the 25 February 1885 letter in which he requested a one-third share of publishing house profits. At the time Clemens made this entry, his share of the Grant *Memoirs*' profits had long since exceeded $60,000. By the spring of 1887 he had already earned $93,481.34 as compared to Webster's $25,942.37 and Mrs. Grant's $394,459.53.

[48] Several novels by the English author Annie Keary, including *Janet's Home* (1863) and *Castle Daly: The Story of an Irish Home Thirty Years Ago* (1876), were published in London by Macmillan & Company. Clemens may have wished to acquire copies of them, as well as Clara Louise Burnham's *Next Door* (Boston: Ticknor and Co., 1886), for his daughters.

Mendellsohn's Letters 2 vols.[49]
Country Doctor—Balzac[50]

JL & Co have been paying out money on the new colliery right along for 3½ years now (Aug. '87) & will continue to do it 3 or 4 more.

2 notes. Now in pocket-book.

Chatto's note ⟨£2[3]5.[50]⟩£200., due Feb. 27, '88; & his note for £230.5.10, due March 27, '88. Both placed in Bissell's hands for collection about middle of Sept.

Farm. 6 person & washing $1 per day each $49 per week
Pony $3 per week.
Mr. Rice for carrying washing, trunks, &c, $10.
W^m. $20; the others $12 each.
Doyle $5.

Adjustable speech to be used on all occasions.[51]

to add my weak/broken voice to the jubilations/lamentations of this spirit-stirring/crushing occasion.

I am called up suddenly & am not prepared—was not expecting to be called ⟨to ad⟩ upon, but will do what I can upon so short a call. Agriculture, sir, is after all but the palladium of our political/ spiritual liberties. By it, economically/spiritually speaking, we live &

---

[49] Felix Mendelssohn-Bartholdy, *Letters from Italy and Switzerland,* trans. Lady Wallace (originally published in 1862); *Letters of Felix Mendelssohn Bartholdy from 1833 to 1847,* ed. Paul Mendelssohn-Bartholdy and Karl Mendelssohn-Bartholdy (originally published in 1863).

[50] A translation of Balzac's work by Katharine Prescott Wormeley was published in 1887 (Boston: Roberts Brothers).

[51] A draft of the "Patent Universal Climate-Proof Automatically-Adjustable Oration" which Mark Twain demonstrated before the Congregational Club of Boston on 20 December 1887. This speech, he noted, was designed to "fit every possible public occasion in this life to a dot, and win success and applause every time." All the speaker had to do was "change three or four words . . . and make his delivery anguished and tearful, or chipper and facetious, or luridly eloquent, according to the occasion, and then turn himself loose" (quoted in Frank M. Flack, "Patent Adjustable Speech," *Twainian,* November–December 1951, pp. 1–2).

move & have our being/—our ending. Without it our political
existence were short/long indeed, & subject to manifold ills/
vicissitudes/curses too multitudinous for enumeration here. All that
we have been, all that we are, all that we hope to be, has had, has,
& must continue to have, its spring, its growth & its fruition in
that purest/saddest, sublimest & most elevating/depressing of the
activities/potentialites of man, thrice glorious/sorrowful Agriculture/
Death. While we have life, while we have soul, & in that soul the
sweet & hallowed sentiment of gratitude, let us with generous
accord attune our voices to songs of praise, perennial outpourings of
thanksgiving for that most precious gift/profitable monitor/[b]oon
whereby our bodies/morals/intelligences thrive, whereby our
ambitions are nourished/modified, whereby our otherwise
sterile/sinful lives are made rich, & strong, grand, & aspiring, &
⟨filled⟩ are adorned with a mighty & far-reaching & all-bracing
grace & beauty & purity & loveliness. I—I—but the time is late &
I will not detain you, sir.

Post-prandial oratory.

Only *one* good impromptu speech—that was when Chaplain was
closing a long, labored prayer & a dog bit him. "___ __ _ __!"
He was a reformed journalist.

See Gilder & ask who is President of the New England society
this year.[52]

Say the kind word for it, Horatio.—Hamlet, Act 2. sc. ⟨5⟩v.

Barber.
Telegraph Gillette[53]

---

[52] The New England Society of New York City was a literary and charitable organization founded in 1805. Its president in 1887 was Cornelius N. Bliss, a wealthy merchant
prominent in Republican politics. On more than one occasion, Clemens had addressed
the annual dinner of the society, held on 22 December. He may have considered an appearance in 1887 in order to test his "Adjustable speech" (see note 51).

[53] This list of errands was probably made around 13 September 1887 as the Clemens
family prepared to leave Quarry Farm for their customary visit to New York City before
returning to Hartford. In that month William Gillette was appearing at New York's Star

Call at [C]L W & Co
See Gilder Century
Back & see Whitmore.
RR tickets
Jean—Central Park
RR tickets

Has had another letter from F. G.[54]

Make a NOTE. I will have nothing to do with that Iowa bond business.[55]

Show me list of *what* this money has been paid out for, since Aug. 1, when balance was $35,000? & is now but $21,000.[56]

Is money coming *in* all the time on these sales, & does *it* add itself to the "balance" & then go out, make the *apparent* expense of $10,000 a month in reality 11 or 12?[57] [#]

Theatre in his Civil War drama *Held by the Enemy*. On 15 September he wrote to Clemens: "Only rec. your telegram on arrival at theatre last night—8 p.m.—too late to send up. I stationed a man at door who *said* he knew you—but he did not—for he came back and reported that you had not arrived. Sorry not to have had the pleasure of sending seats for the family."

[54] In the summer of 1887 Frederick D. Grant had become insistent in questioning Webster & Company's handling of profits from the *Personal Memoirs of U. S. Grant*. He claimed to have discovered a discrepancy in their accounting of the amount due Mrs. Julia Grant and objected to certain expenses which she had been asked to share, particularly expenditures for legal counsel. The resultant disagreement continued through much of the winter of 1887/1888, with Grant pressing his claims and threatening legal action and Webster rejecting all demands and defying Grant to proceed with a law suit. The matter seems to have been resolved without court proceedings.

[55] Clemens here referred to Webster & Company's difficulties with R. T. Root, an Iowa general book agent for the Grant *Memoirs* who had defaulted on book payments for which he had given his bond. A settlement with Root was not achieved until January 1889.

[56] Clemens misrecalled the Webster & Company bank balance reported by Frederick J. Hall on 1 August. He recorded it correctly at 323.14–15. Entries through "Show former writing" (321.4) are notes for a visit to the offices of Charles L. Webster & Company which Clemens planned to make while in New York in mid-September 1887.

[57] Even Clemens' highest estimate falls short of Charles L. Webster & Company's expenditures. A "Cash Statement" of 1 October 1887 would show disbursements of $105,328.10 since the previous April. Profits during the same period were $18,934.40.

Have either of you drawn anything but salary since settlement of Apl. 1?[58]

If so, it must count to me Oct 1.[59]

You *issue* H. Sep 20? Is it bound & *paid* for?[60]

The others? Are they in the *air*—or bound & paid for?[61]

What has that Lib of Lit cost, thus far? How much *more* will it cost?[62]

Now add paper & binding.

It is not going to pay.

Must have the artists at work right away.

Get *their* contract-dates & No of pictures, & then see that you furnish the MS on time.

Stir Clark right up.[63] [#]

---

[58] 1 April 1887, the date of the most recent Webster & Company accounting. At that time a new "Memorandum of Agreement" was signed specifying the responsibilities and privileges of the three partners.

[59] In this period when the Paige typesetter was making heavy demands on Clemens, he was frequently resentful of the requirement that he provide capital for Charles L. Webster & Company. This obligation effectively prevented him from withdrawing his share of the firm's profits. He was consequently jealous of Webster's and Hall's freedom to withdraw their smaller earnings at the appointed times, the next of which would be 1 October 1887.

[60] Almira Hancock's *Reminiscences of Winfield Scott Hancock* was ready on schedule, for on 21 September 1887 Hall reported that it "came out yesterday, so that so far there has not been a moment's delay." According to the "Cash Statement" of 1 October 1887, Charles L. Webster & Company expended $3,012.79 to produce and advertise Mrs. Hancock's work.

[61] By 1 October 1887, $7,238.24 had been expended on the six other works which, with the Hancock *Reminiscences*, comprised Webster & Company's list of projected publications (see p. 307). The "Cash Statement" of that date shows bindery expenses only for the *Biography of Reverend Henry Ward Beecher*.

[62] Between 1 April and 1 October 1887, Webster & Company invested $9,692.74 in the *Library of American Literature*, the eleven-volume anthology edited by Edmund C. Stedman and Ellen Mackay Hutchinson. This was the work whose costliness Mark Twain later claimed "secured the lingering suicide of Charles L. Webster and Company" (*MTE*, p. 192).

[63] Charles Hopkins Clark, Clemens' associate on *Mark Twain's Library of Humor.*

Have *all* publishes given permission in wrting?

Get those at once or tell Clark to leave them out.

Take all this down in writing.

Show former writing

5 lbs Oolong, 40 or 50¢
5 " English breakfast 40 or 50¢

> While though this chain so harsh clanks
> It bindeth me to thee, dear Marjoribanks
> These lips of mine, then, dumbly,
> Do make appeal to Cholmondeley
> That he the same will break ⟨so⟩ right soon
> And shall expect of good Colquhoun

We must have Bill Nye in—& Burdette's very latest & best. *Lots* of *Burdette.*

"Avoid swinish sounds at table, with ⟨spoons,⟩ soup, peaches, &c.; snuffling, embarrassed laughter, & requiring butter where butter is not"

Get a book fm B'dette

IN THE TRADE.[64]

Harte's greatest sale was his first book, "Luck of Roaring Camp" —26,000. Royalties $3,000.

Bad Boy—is Aldrich's biggest sale; in 10 years, 13,000 copies. Royalties $1,500.

Howells's biggest sale of a single book was 12,000. Royalties $2,400. Took several years to accomplish this.

Bayard Taylor's Royalties in Goethe's Faust were $1,000.

We shall *always* sell twice as many copies of *any* book as the trade can sell. We shall always sell at ⟨dou⟩about double the price the trade would venture to charge.

Therefore, 5% from us is twice as good as 10% in the trade. [#]

---

[64] The following notes were the basis of "a systematic and orderly scheme" of royalties which, Clemens informed Webster & Company on 18 September 1887, "I have worked at

No, we must run our *own* general agency.
Re-arrange the Sheridan bindings.[65]

Chicago   Genl Agency.
New York   "   "
(Chicago $2,500!)
   Am. Pub Co $600.

Reduce C's to what ⟨is⟩it was before—$3000.[66]

I got $46,000, you $30,000.

You always take care of No. 1.

Century advertisement.[67]

Reduce your force.[68]

Show me the day-book of expenses from $13th Sept, when cash
balance was $21,000.

I want a minutely detailed statement, Oct. 1, including old stock
as asset.

Sell that Scott house. [#]

---

a good deal, the last two days, and have finally got it to suit me. It cannot easily be improved, if at all" (see *MTLP*, pp. 232–234).

[65] Webster & Company planned to issue the *Personal Memoirs of P. H. Sheridan* on
1 December 1888.

[66] The partnership agreement of 1 April 1887 had increased Charles L. Webster's
annual salary from $3,000 to $3,800 in an ill-advised effort to rectify one of the effects of
Frank M. Scott's embezzlement (see p. 315, note 46). Clemens was not successful in im-
plementing the reduction noted here, but in December 1887 he tried another approach
to the same end. When Webster then insisted upon hiring a subscription sales manager,
Clemens suggested in vain that Webster personally pay $800 of the new man's salary, a
proposal which did nothing to improve the eroding relationship between the two partners
(*MTLP*, pp. 241–242).

[67] On 21 September 1887, Frederick J. Hall reported to Clemens: "On consulting with
Mr. Webster, we thought that during the dull months of the year, say from April to the
1st. of October or November, it would not pay us to engage a page in the 'Century'. It is
a very expensive advertising medium, costing $250.00 a page, and if we use it during the
busy months of the year, it will do just as much good as using it constantly."

[68] Clemens felt that Webster had an exaggerated notion of the office and staff appropriate to Charles L. Webster & Company. In a letter of 24 December 1886, Webster had
boasted to his brother-in-law Samuel E. Moffett that the firm had "the finest subscription

3,814   Sept 22 H M & Co $100[69]

You have had an offer of $11,000?[70]

Aug 10.[71]

"Pope's book was issued during the hot & dull season".

"We don't owe a single cent except the undrawn profits due you."

"Stuff on hand cost $15,000."

"$5,000 paid Beecher, & $8,000 Stedman"

"Hancock is *all* paid for."

"All cuts & steels for Sheridan are *paid* for."

"Kalakau's pictures are all *paid* for."

"All of Steadman's pictures are *paid* for."

"Also Beecher's are all *paid* for."

Aug. 1st. Cash:

$$31,506.94$$
$$(B.R.) \ 9,351 \ 26$$

Last m.s. ⟨13,1[2]8.42⟩⟨13,178.42⟩13,108.42

---

publishing office in the world" and that "I have about 14 clerks in the office and it is a pretty busy place."

[69] On 22 September 1887, Charles H. Clark sent Clemens a copy of a letter from Houghton, Mifflin & Company requesting a "pecuniary consideration" of $100 for permission to include works by James Russell Lowell, Oliver Wendell Holmes, and Bret Harte in *Mark Twain's Library of Humor*.

[70] Charles L. Webster was planning to complete and sell a house in Roseville, New Jersey, "the finest suburb of Newark," begun by Frank M. Scott with funds appropriated from Webster & Company. The property's value, "less the mortgages and liens which we were able to find," was $5,285. Webster intended to "put it into the market at $12,500, selling it at $12,000, if we can get it" (CLW to SLC, 25 March 1887). It evidently was not until around 15 November that an acceptable offer was received, however, for on that date Webster sent Clemens a deed to be signed, requesting its return "as soon as possible."

[71] Entries through "Also Beecher's are all *paid* for." (323.13), alluding to planned Webster & Company publications, are either quoted or paraphrased from a long letter of 10 August 1887 in which Frederick J. Hall had attempted to allay Clemens' apprehensions about the publishing company's prospects. With unconscious prophecy, Hall assured Clemens then that "we are now laying the real foundation of our business. . . . Of course

Where is this?[72]

Donelly's book.[73]

Mark Twain's Lib of Humor.

See note on green card.

Cox mainly paid for.[74]

Sept. 13, in bank $21,000, & everything paid for.

Then what has gone with the other $23,000 in 6 weeks?

Show me the day-book from Aug. 1.

Do you own ⅓ of the stock? And have I given you $30,000 twice over in 2 years?

You had 35,000 in bank about June 1st when the new contract was made in Hartfd,[75] & only $13,000 a month later.

Let us see the day-book from ⟨J⟩May 1.

Whence *came* the addition which raised $13000 in July 1 to $31,000 ⟨one [or]⟩ 30 days later, making $44,000? [#]

---

our reputation is established thoroughly and is world-wide, still this is really our formative period, which once past we will stand on a sure foundation, which nothing but very bad management can undermine."

[72] Clemens' cryptic abbreviations in this entry expand to: "Bills Receivable" ("B.R.") and "Last month's statement" ("Last m.s.").

[73] Clemens had decided on 9 July 1887 that Webster & Company did not want Ignatius Donnelly's *The Great Cryptogram: Francis Bacon's Cipher in the So-Called Shakespeare Plays* (Chicago, New York and London: R. S. Peale & Co., 1888). Webster had also, later, "thought it best to decline it, especially as the author wanted all the profits" (Frederick J. Hall to SLC, 10 August 1887). By the fall of 1887, however, Clemens had forgotten his original lack of enthusiasm for Donnelly's work and in a letter to Orion Clemens on 7 September condemned Webster's "hardihood" in making a decision that merely confirmed his own (*MTLP*, p. 230).

[74] Samuel S. Cox's *Diversions of a Diplomat in Turkey* was scheduled for publication by Charles L. Webster & Company in November 1887. On 21 September Frederick J. Hall reported: "We calculated that it would cost from $2500.00 to $3000.00 to make the plates of this book. We find that so far we have spent $1600.40 on it; fully three-quarters of the work is completed, so that we over-estimated the cost of this book."

[75] No Charles L. Webster & Company contract of 1 June 1887 is extant. Although the latest surviving contract was signed on 1 April 1887, it was evidently modified in late May of that year (see p. 289, note 212). Clemens' entry may refer to that revised document.

How is it that $4,000 have been advanced to D^r O'Reilly?[76]
And *when?*

Sell that house—for $11,000.

⟨Protestant—cast off for that.⟩[77]
⟨Music,⟩
Father a scrivener *(writer).*
Set up in Bread st., 1600.
(Wills, marriage-settlements &c.)
⟨Lent m⟩ Invested money for people.
Married Sarah Jeffrey, 1600.

The widowed mother, Ellen, came ⟨in ⟨17⟩1610⟩, to live with them, but could not stand it—lasted only 10 years.

John lived in Bread st his first 16 years—which were the last 16 of James I—& absorbed *music.* John was diligently instructed by his father & educated.

His tutor (⟨to hi[s]⟩domestic) was a university graduate—John under him several years & also all this time he was a pupil at Pepys' St Paul's school, near by.

At 16 John was scholarly & accomplished. & handsome. Compare Milton at 12 with Bunyan's frontispiece.

Began to poetize before 16. Went to Cambridge at 16; & a month later, Apl 9, '25, James I died.

Abundance of Latin & Greek there, & scholastic disputation & drill in logic & philosophy, but with little physical science & mathematics.

A fellow of Chirist's college was Mr. Joseph *Meade*[78] *a commentator on the Apocalypse!*

---

[76] Bernard O'Reilly, author of the *Life of Leo XIII.*

[77] This long entry, which runs through "He was a clandestine duck—every time." (328.17–18), contains Mark Twain's notes for a projected "cipher" identifying John Milton as the actual author of John Bunyan's *Pilgrim's Progress.* Clemens was undoubtedly influenced here by his recent consideration of Ignatius Donnelly's book supporting the theory that Bacon wrote Shakespeare's plays (see note 73). His notes about Milton's life were made from the biographical essay by David Masson in the ninth edition of the *Encyclopaedia Britannica.*

[78] Joseph Mead, or Mede, a wide-ranging scholar and a prolific biblical commentator, whose important *Clavis Apocalyptica ex innatis et insitis visionum characteribus eruta et demonstrata* first appeared in 1627.

7½ years in College, to July 1632—24 yr old.

Was satirically called "The Lady of Chri's College" he was so pretty & graceful & prudish, & the haughty fastidiousness of his tastes & morals.

By 1628, high reputation for scholarship & literary genius.

(His *signature in the* University ⟨register⟩Register 1632 compare with Bunyan's.)

He then knew Latin, Greek, French, Italian, Hebrew, & was *an expert swordsman.*

The lines "On Shakspeare" written 1630.

(Note some more, page 325.)

Lived at Horton with his old father from July 32 to Apl 38.

Disgusted with Laud,[79] wouldn't be a preacher; then gave up idea of law.

At 23 sent a sonnet to a beloved & admired friend, who then remonstrated with him on his "belatedness," & his persistence in "⟨a life of mere⟩ a life of mere DREAM & study." It cut deep. So, near 50 years later it prevented his giving his name to his immortal *Dream.*[80]

Windsor & London in walking distance from Horton.

Now he goes into physical science & mathematics.

It is an interesting fact that his very first public appearance in the world of English authorship was in so honorable (?) a place *as the second folio edition of Shakspeare in 1632.* ⟨The f⟩His enthusiastic Eulogy on Sh. written in '30,

(See 326)

The *furtive Bacon* got him & Ben Jonson to play into his hand. He knew Bacon's secret, admired it, & afterward borrowed the idea without credit. (No—in cipher *gives* credit.)

His frequent writing & helping to rehearse stage-plays called Masques, enabled him later to make his Dream bristle with incident & situation like a drama. 1634.

at Ludlow Castle.

Compare Comus with the Dream.

---

[79] William Laud, archbishop of Canterbury from 1633 to 1640.
[80] That is, Bunyan's *Pilgrim's Progress*, first published in 1678.

As early as '37 he had got poisoned with the secretive, & so published Comus without his name.

⟨(On the⟩ other hand, who wrote P L?

Why Bunyan done it.

Even his noble Lycidas was published '38, with his *initials* only—thus "I. M"—he knowing that *that* was ⟨[- -]⟩perfect concealment.

He went to Italy '38—B. never did.

This gives the sea-phrases—whereas B. never saw anything but a canal boat.

Just as he was leaving came the tremendous news of the Covenant, banding all ranks in Scotland against the ecclesiastical innovations of Charles & Laud. Without question this colossal cloud-burst roused & roared in him & inspired the Dream not printed till 36 years later.

By *that* time he was a developed & booming Puritan & *could* not print it—since it is a *covert* argument in support of the Established Church, & against Puritanism & non-comformity of all kinds.

This has never been suspected before, but the Cipher makes it plain. The Dream must be read between the lines—then it becomes a grisly & almost Hudibrastic Satyre.

He went to Paris—B never did. Paris is the "⟨Delect[i]ble⟩Delectable City."

B was never *in* a city.

In the neighborhood of Florence he "found & visited" old Galileo, old & blind & still a nominal prisoner of the Inquisition. And there he loaded up with the fine astronomical errors which we find in the Dream.

Next he goes to Rome—where B never was. Hence his "Eternal City." There he met up with all the great & learned & polished, & reproduces these very characters (first column, page 327) under the fictitious names of – – – &c.

Staid a month in Venice—where B never was. Hence the "City ——."

Next, Geneva a red-hot Protestant City (see his "City of —") to show them the part of his Dream written.

Got back home Aug '39—16 months

His great Continental Tour enabled him to imagine the travel in the Dream—& no stay-at-home could ever have done it. Notice the accuracy of his descriptions

And how he could draw!—for that day. Compare the two men's work in that line.

⟨Both King &⟩ Chas. Deodati ⟨were⟩was just now dead,[81] & you find the pathetic result in Chap. — of the Dream.

The latter he publicly celebrated in his sublime Epitaphium Damonis—but if you want to see the *real* thing look in Ch —.

"He used to always jerk a public poem to divert attention from what he meant to do some day in the Dream".

Bottom of 327.

Now read those verses,[82] turning the Trojans, &c into *Christian*[s] cruising around, & they immediately *mean* something. But they have never meant anything before, because people not knowing he was riddling, took him at his word, & looked for a vast poem on the whole range of Arthurian & British legend. ⟨He⟩ He was a clandestine duck—every time.

Biogs of Milton—Toland, Todd, Symmons, D^r. Johnson, Mitford, Keightley (London, '59, & Mason's London '59 '71 (lit hist of the time.[83] *Southey's Bunyan.*

Cousin Sally Dillard[84]
Harp of 1000 Strings
Flush Times in Alabama. [#]

---

[81] Edward King, whom Milton knew at Christ's College, Cambridge, died in 1637. Milton dedicated "Lycidas," published in 1638, to King. Charles Diodati, a friend of Milton's from their days together at St. Paul's School, died in 1638. Milton addressed him in several poems, including the famous "Epitaphium Damonis," published in 1645.

[82] David Masson's translation of verses from "Epitaphium Damonis" containing Milton's plan for the British epic Clemens describes (*Encyclopaedia Britannica*, 9th ed., 16:327–328).

[83] This notation of Milton's biographers—including David Masson, author of the massive *Life of John Milton, Narrated in Connexion with the Political, Ecclesiastical, and Literary History of His Time*, 6 vols. (Cambridge and London: Macmillan and Co., 1859–1880)—derives in part from the *Encyclopaedia Britannica's* reference list and suggests the degree of preparation Clemens contemplated for his "cipher," if only for his own amusement.

[84] Hamilton C. Jones's comic piece about a witness at a trial. Clemens had considered

I have met the P of W once, but it was not in any familiar way but in a quite casual & informal way, & was ⟨most likely⟩ of course a surprise to us both. It was in Oxford street, just where you come out of Oxfd into Regent Circus. ⟨He was at the head of a procession, &⟩ just as he turned up one side of the circle ⟨I went⟩ at the head of a procession, I went down the other side on the top of an omnibus. ⟨If he remembers the man that sat at the driver's⟩ He will remember me, on account of a gray coat with flap pockets that I wore, as I was the only person on the omnibus that had on that kind of a coat; & I remember him of course as easy as I would a ⟨comet⟩ ⟨prominent⟩the Matterhorn. I have seen the P. L. here on our side of the water, & noticed how natural & pleasant she was, & ⟨like the⟩ interested in everything going, & taking more trouble for other people than she did for herself. And once I called on your Majesty, but you were out.

He looked pretty proud that day, but that is not to be wondered at, he has a good situation.[85]

Better have an expert accountant go through the books & furnish a detailed statement which will show everything so a cat can understand it.

Placard, "For sale for $11,000 cash—apply to CLW & Co."[86]

Whereas, his ⟨[d]⟩Divine Hiness, the Deputy First Assistant ⟨God Almighty⟩ ⟨God⟩ Sup. B. (otherwise known to men as the Boston & Albany Railroad Company) has in His inscrutable

---

it for *Mark Twain's Library of Humor* in 1880 when he was first planning that work. He was now again thinking of including it, along with selections from Samuel P. Avery's humor anthology, *The Harp of a Thousand Strings* (New York: Dick & Fitzgerald, 1858) and excerpts from Joseph G. Baldwin's *The Flush Times of Alabama and Mississippi* (first published in 1853). Ultimately, none of these works were represented in *Mark Twain's Library of Humor.*

[85] A partial draft of the playful petition dated 6 November 1887 in which Clemens addressed Queen Victoria in protest of the income tax mistakenly levied upon his English royalties (see *MTB*, pp. 852–854). The last sentence here was added as an afterthought. Clemens worked a revision of it into his description of the Prince of Wales before the petition appeared in the December 1887 *Harper's*. In the published version Clemens did not mention Princess Louise, whom he had met in May 1883 (see p. 18, note 33).

[86] Intended for the Roseville, New Jersey, house which had belonged to Frank M. Scott, Webster & Company's dishonest bookkeeper (see p. 323, note 70).

wisdom visited the ⟨act⟩ shabby act of 16 Hartford males, of low
⟨degree⟩degree & character, upon the town itself, & commanded
that henceforth & forever no ⟨invidual⟩ citizen of ⟨all⟩ the 45,000
can ⟨[¶] [1].⟩ Have a drawing room seat reserved for him at the
Boston office either with or without prepayment of the dollar;

2. Nor ⟨with⟩ upon any terms whatever but just these, to-wit:
the cash purchase ⟨&⟩in Boston of a through ticket ⟨and⟩ to New
York *and* a draw seat;

⟨Therefore,⟩ And whereas, This is but the simplest &
straightforwardest way ⟨in the world⟩ divinable, of calling Gen
Hawley & Gen Franklin, & CD. Warner & the Bishop of
Hartford, the President of Trinity—& Mrs. H B Stowe & the other
45,000 citizens of Hartford, swindlers⟨-⟩&⟨-⟩not-to-be-trusted-by-a-
railway-Co, or treated as it treats its other slaves ⟨subjects⟩ along
the route.

And Whereas this attitude is a shade over-righteous for a
railroad whose ticket-seller in Boston has been caught paying false
change to a hurried passenger, & seemed to show by his air of
comfortable indifference that getting caught in that sort of theft
had ages ago lost its novelty in his office—

Now Therefore, O, Deputy First Asst. ⟨God Almighty⟩ S. B.,
the ⟨obj⟩ prayer of this petition is, that Thou wilt now stay Thy
hand, & not add to our punishment ⟨as one reports⟩ & our
humiliation the further device that has been reported⟨—⟩ as being
under consideration—to-wit, a cattle-car, to be named the
"Economical City" & labeled "Hartford Special—2 cents extra per
bench—⟨advance-pa[y]⟩ no pay if not occupied."

It was quite manly—⟨B. & A.⟩ manly—& quite ⟨godly⟩ plucky
—⟨B & A⟩ ⟨godly⟩ ⟨style &⟩ quite—to visit the sin of 16 incipient
bunco-steerers upon the 45,000 clean & honest men & women of
Hartford, but it would have been still manlier & still braver &
still less incredibly & unspeakably & grotesquely & ridiculously
donkeyish/asinine/kittenish, to publish the names of the 16 & let
the rest of the town alone.

It has been said by one of old that it is always bad to lodge
despotic power in the hands of the ⟨⟨ignorant⟩ small-souled &
the⟩ stuck-up childish. [#]

And what is the Holy War but an attempt to do P Lost over again[87]

fine & heroic & sublime

Call & insist on the statement being full & *delivered* to me Oct 1, if it takes 50 men & I have to stand over them myself.[88]

Call on Sypher. It is not a "chandelier"—we never chose it—they must pack it & take it away at their own expense.

Give me the pay-roll in detail. Names, & length of service. Do not these people tell tales out of school?

Schreiben Sie Frau Peeve an.[89]
Auch Sypher.

Monday, bank balance $18,900; the following Thursday (Sept. 29) it was $18,000-odd.

K: $1800; H. $1200; $2,500; rent $500; rent increased to $1000; rent in 14th st. $1500; ⟨[f]⟩New contract, salary $3,000. New quarters, $3000; ⟨new⟩asks me to make up to him Scott's theft of $4000 by raising salary to $3,800.[90] [#]

---

[87] A stray note for the Milton-Bunyan "cipher" which Clemens outlined on pages 325–328.

[88] By 3 October 1887, Clemens had still not received the required financial statement from Charles L. Webster & Company. On that date the firm reported: "We hoped to send you the full account to-day, but our book-keeper says it will not be ready until tomorrow."

[89] On 28 September 1887, Clemens went to New York with Joseph Twichell "to see the race between the English yacht 'Thistle' and the American 'Volunteer,'" scheduled for the following day (Twichell Diary, 28–29 September 1887, Yale, TS in MTP). They stayed at the Yonkers home of a Mr. and Mrs. Peeve, friends of Twichell's, returning to Hartford on 29 September after unsuitable wind conditions caused postponement of the race. On 30 September the *Volunteer* retained possession of the America's Cup for the United States with a decisive victory over the *Thistle*, actually a Scottish challenger. Clemens reminded himself here to write thanking Mrs. Peeve for her hospitality.

[90] Clemens here noted a number of Webster & Company operating costs. The first item, "K: $1800," was not actually a business expense, however, referring to the monthly check for $155 which the firm sent to Keokuk, Iowa, on his behalf. Of this amount $100 was for the support of Orion and Mollie Clemens, $50 was for Jane Lampton Clemens, and $5 went to one of Clemens' cousins. In calculating the annual sum sent to Keokuk, Clemens evidently overlooked this last amount. "H." in this entry is evidently Frederick

Oct. Nov. Dec: 3 books: 30,000 copies, $30,000. Of Han & Cust, $2000 each come back to us for plant ($4,000); divide the $16,000, leaves us $8,000; (total $12,000). Pay KX[91] $3,000 & retain $7,000; (grand total, $19,000. Subtract $6,000 expenses & $3000 extras, leaves $10,000 profit. Now subtract previous 9 mos expenses, & the ⟨loss is⟩ profit is eaten up & as much loss takes its place.

D[r.] Rice cut my palate.[92]

? —Heading.

Have we a *Whelker.* among us? (Translation of "?" to be closing sentence.)

Let us charitably believe that Mr. Newman[93] is not a burglar, not a highwayman, not a pickpocket⟨;⟩—⟨for these operate upon the living/do battle with the⟩ at risk—but only a Whelker—⟨a careful W, a cautious W, a judicious W & "lays" for the friendless dead⟩

I will presently try to answer that ? —but ⟨now⟩ just now I must talk a page or two upon other matters. ⟨In the heart⟩ Wanderers

---

J. Hall. The contract of 1 April 1887 had set his annual salary at $2,000. It may previously have been only $1,200 and subsequently may have been increased to $2,500. Charles L. Webster's yearly salary, set at $3,000 by the 1 April agreement, had been increased to $3,800 to offset an alleged loss to Frank M. Scott (see p. 315, note 46, and p. 322, note 66).

[91] Probably Samuel S. Cox, author of *Diversions of a Diplomat in Turkey*, published by Webster & Company in 1887.

[92] Clarence C. Rice of New York City was physician to the Clemens family. He was also Clemens' personal friend, responsible for introducing him to Henry H. Rogers, and eventually became an investor in the Paige typesetter. On 14 October 1887, Clemens informed his business partners that "I had my palate cut out several days ago, and it promises to never get well again" (*MTLP*, p. 235), but the exact nature of this unspeakable surgery by Dr. Rice, perhaps in treatment of an abscess, remains uncertain.

[93] Although referred to here and later as Newman, Clemens intended to direct his satire against James King Newton, professor of modern languages at Oberlin College. In "A Private Letter and a Public Postscript" (*New Princeton Review*, January 1888), Mark Twain presented evidence that Newton was a plagiarist. He demonstrated that in "Obligations of the United States to Initiate a Revision of Treaties Between the Western Powers and Japan" (Oberlin, Ohio, 1887), Newton had borrowed entire passages from Edward H. House's "The Martyrdom of an Empire" (*Atlantic Monthly*, May 1881). Clemens did not, however, proceed with the satire proposed here. He may have been deterred by the impropriety of identifying his chronically ill friend House with the pillaged dead of the fictitious Whelkers. Clemens evidently derived the name for his savage tribe from the whelk, a marine snail which feeds on dead or dying sea creatures.

report that in ⟨the⟩ a remote & almost unvisited spot in the forest solitudes of Central Africa, there is a small tribe of savages called Waelkers or Whelkers; who have this peculiarity: they respect the property of the living, but rob the dead. As soon as the breath is out of a man's body, it is no disgrace for even the nearest friend to steal the corpse's personal effects, provided he isn't caught at it. If caught, he is held up to derision for his awkwardness. ⟨in that region, therefore,⟩

Sun. What did you pay for your 6 new presses? $240,000. It did not cost $18,000 to build them. Will they *save* ⟨their cost⟩ 24,0000 in 2 years, & then *add* $220,000 to your annual savings after that? Well, the T. S. will do it, every time.

Mail these letters[94]

One who robs the dead in the service of God. Pictures of it & of Newton showing points of resemblance.

See Gilder abt play.[95]

What the prices of the 4 books & mine?

See Laffan & invite.[96]

"Ein Tropfen Gift."[97] [#]

---

[94] This line appears at the top of an otherwise blank page.

[95] On 28 September 1887, Clemens submitted *Meisterschaft*, the three-act play he wrote for the amusement of his family, to Richard Watson Gilder of the *Century*. Gilder accepted the play for the *Century* of January 1888, but only after insisting that Clemens accept correction of the "ungroomed" German, "not a part of the fun in this case—but rather a distraction," and deletion of "a few expressions which would run off very well on the stage . . . but when served up in cold Century type would surely grieve" (Gilder to SLC, 29 October 1887).

[96] Clemens wished to see William M. Laffan in response to a letter from him of 3 October 1887. Laffan had reported that a spokesman for the Mergenthaler Linotype Company recently "told me the machine was now a go: that it had surmounted all obstacles and swept aside all difficulties and had entered on its career as a patent reaper. There are 12 of them now in the *Tribune* shop and the company is now ready to take orders and put in machines on a basis of 10¢ for 1000m. . . . I hope to hear from you. . . . Composition has gone up to 50¢ for 1000 ms on all the papers and we are all ready to talk machines. How are you and how is your machine?"

[97] This play by Oscar Blumenthal was presented at New York's Thalia Theatre, which made a specialty of German drama, from 3 October to 15 October 1887.

$229.47—Whitmore send this to A. P. Burbank.[98]

Dress up some good actors, as Apollyon, Greatheart, &c & the other Bunyan characters; take them to a wild gorge & photograph them—Valley of the Shadow of Death; to other effective places & photo them along with the scenery; to Paris, in their curious costumes, place them near the Arc de l'Etoile, & photo them with the crowd—⟨city of⟩ Vanity Fair; to Constantinople, Cairo, Venice, Jerusalem, & other places, (twenty interesting cities,) & always make them conspicuous in the curious foreign crowds by their costume. Take them to Zululand. It would take two or three years to do the photographing, & cost $10,000; but this stereopticon panorama of Bunyan's Pilgrim's Progress could be exhibited in all countries at the same time & would clear a fortune in a year. By & by I will do this.

> How doth the little busy bee
> Improve each shining hour⟨[?]⟩b'gosh,
> Gathering honey all the day
> From many a lovely flower b'gosh.[99]

⟨Sep⟩ October 4, 1887.

If, in 1891 I find myself not rich enough to carry out my scheme of buying Christopher Columbus's bones & burying them under the Statue of Liberty Enlightening the World, I will give the idea to somebody who *is* rich enough.

The envious will say there is some pretty poor German in this play. Well, never mind about that, there are all sorts of prejudiced people.[100] [#]

---

[98] Clemens was evidently reimbursing Burbank's expenditures for the 23 September 1887 Lyceum Theatre production of *Colonel Sellers as a Scientist* (see p. 300, note 1), which was to cost "about $250.⁰⁰ if we have no door receipts" (Burbank to SLC, 18 September 1887). The play must have been as unattractive to the paying public as it was to the critics.

[99] Clemens' modification of a stanza from the twentieth of Isaac Watts's *Divine Songs for Children*, "Against Idleness and Mischief."

[100] This draft of a comment for Mark Twain's explanatory note to *Meisterschaft* became superfluous when Richard Watson Gilder refused to publish the bad German that was originally part of the play.

Make a strong defence of Newman. Brer.

⟨Get match-box.
Fix the gun.
Pay Burbank⟩

Davy Twichell must imitate the mechanical bear & squirrel—&
other mechanical toys.

Tin lock-box for papers.
Bib. Sacra. Jan.[101]
Is Newman at Springfld?

See Gerhardt[102]—& the crockery man.
⟨Ammunition⟩
CHALEY CLARK

Get a N.Y. Directory through B. & Gross.[103] or Chly.

⟨Have Dʳ· Rice cut my palate, or pull it out by the roots.⟩

Send bk balance & week's expenses every Monday & I shall get
it Tuesday morning.

Change *form* of offer to "Will pay you⟨["]⟩ 15 to ⟨["]⟩17½ cents
per copy for 1ˢᵗ 10,000."[104] [#]

---

[101] The pamphlet by Oberlin professor James King Newton which Mark Twain
exposed as a plagiarism of Edward H. House (see note 93) originally appeared as "Japanese Treaty Revision: Its Necessity and our Responsibility Therefor" in the January
1887 number of *Bibliotheca Sacra*, a journal primarily devoted to biblical scholarship.
Clemens evidently thought that Newton was attached to the faculty of Drury College,
a Congregational institution in Springfield, Missouri. In his *New Princeton Review*
article he mistakenly identified Newton as a clergyman.

[102] On 22 September 1887, Karl Gerhardt had written Clemens: "The author of
'Marching through Georgia' surely deserves a statue and if you should favor me with an
order, it not only should be my very best work but you should have it at your own price
above actual expenses." Gerhardt may have wished Clemens to commission a statue of
Henry Clay Work, author of "Marching through Georgia" and other popular songs, for
presentation to the city of Hartford. Work had received part of his education in Hartford and served as an apprentice in Elihu Geer's printshop there. He died in Hartford
in 1884 and was buried in the city's Spring Grove Cemetery.

[103] Brown & Gross, Hartford booksellers and publishers.

[104] The "systematic and orderly scheme" of royalties which Clemens proposed to
Charles L. Webster & Company on 18 September 1887 (see 321.19–30) originally allowed

List.[105]

C.D. Warner . . . . 2,000.

Chs. H. Clark 2,000

JH. Twichell . . . . 1,000 G

WD ⟨[-]⟩Howells 1,000

Sourmash Stan. . . . . 1,000 G

T. W. Crane 5,000

C. J. L. 2,000 (preferred) 5,000
        from *me*

Slee (courtesy-offer). 2,000

Young Geo. Jones. 25,000

Ned Bunce. 2,000

Whitmo'. . . . . 2,000 ½G —24 hours' notice—.[106]

Br. Robinson 10,000

⟨Geo. W.⟩ Will Gillette. 5,000

Harpers. 15,000

Hawley 3,000

Hubbard. 2,000

S. E. Moffett . . . . 1,000 ⎫

P. A. M. . . . . 1,000 ⎬ G

O. ⟨C.⟩Cl . . . . 1,000 ⎭

⟨C L W. . . . . 10,000⟩

---

an author of a $3.50 book "On the first 10,000 copies, 5%——$1750" (*MTLP*, pp. 232–233).

    [105] A listing of potential investors in the Paige typesetter with Clemens' projection of the amount each would invest. Among those not previously identified in connection with the typesetter or with Clemens' other affairs and those not readily identifiable from Clemens' notation here are: Clara Spaulding Stanchfield, designated "Sourmash Stan" for a Clemens family cat given to her (the $1,000 investment noted here is discussed on page 277, note 174); Charles J. Langdon ("C. J. L."); J. D. F. Slee, a partner in the Langdon family coal firm; Henry C. Robinson ("B[re]r. Robinson"), Hartford lawyer and a personal friend of Clemens'; Senator Joseph R. Hawley, one of the proprietors of the Hartford *Courant; Courant* managing editor Stephen A. Hubbard; Samuel E. Moffett, Clemens' nephew; Pamela A. Moffett ("P. A. M."); Orion Clemens ("O. Cl"); Charles L. Webster ("C L W."). "Young Geo. Jones" may be a reference to Gilbert E. Jones, son of New York *Times* publisher George Jones. Clemens had been trying to interest the senior Jones in the typesetter since 1881. Arnot is evidently M. H. Arnot of Elmira, New York, who in 1889 invested in the typesetter. "G" is Clemens' abbreviation of "gift."

    [106] This phrase is written lengthwise in the margin to the right of "Whitmo' . . . [Mr.] Hall . . . 1,000" (336.13–337.1).

[Mr.] Hall 1,000
Our draughtsmen .... 1,000 each—G.
S G Dunham................. 3,000.
⟨Hawley—⟩
George,..................... 1,000.
Bunce
S. Dunham—
Senator Jones, ... 25,000
Arnot,...................... 100,000
D. Sage, ... 25,000
   Gov't Printing office the largest in the world. They get all the new machinery

Have you seen Laffan about art book?[107]

Tell Burbank to take Fulton up.[108]

In my pocket is estimated difference ⟨P⟩between Paige & McMillan machines—to show to George.[109]

Skip Ch. LXXVII, page 344.

Get Livy a tin box.
& Wine-list from Lane[110] [#]

---

[107] On 17 October 1887 Clemens transmitted this query to Charles L. Webster & Company. The book in question was the contemplated catalog of the art collection of Baltimore railroad executive William T. Walters (see p. 273, note 157). In his letter of 3 October 1887, William M. Laffan had asked Clemens: "When can Webster talk figures on that Baltimore book?"

[108] On 11 October 1887 Alfred P. Burbank passed along an offer from Chandos Fulton, minor novelist, playwright, and historian, to rewrite *Colonel Sellers as a Scientist* for a fee of $300, the right to produce and direct it, and a one-quarter share of profits from that production, not to exceed $5,000. Despite the positive response indicated here, Clemens declined Fulton's proposal.

[109] On 3 October 1887 William M. Laffan had sent Clemens a long article from the Albany *Journal* of 26 September devoted to the history of the McMillan typesetting and distributing machines in use in the *Journal's* composing room. The machines were the creations of John Loudon McMillan, a twenty-eight-year-old inventor who had been engaged in developing typesetters for eight years. Clemens may have intended to explain the advantages of the Paige typesetter over the McMillan machines to George Jones, publisher of the New York *Times*.

[110] Joseph G. Lane was a Hartford "Importer and Wholesale Dealer in Groceries and Liquors" (*Geer's*[1886], p. 324).

Do you promptly send first copies to Congressional Library for Copyright?

Tuesday, ⟨[-].⟩a.m., Oct. 18, 1887, Paige showed me (& Whitmore, North, Earl, & two or three others,) an experiment with his new dynamo & motor, to prove that one of the laws laid down in the electrical books is not a law at all. He thinks it a great discovery that he has thus made; & proposes to apply it in a machine which shall show surprising results.[111]

Still no weekly expenses & bank balance ever comes.

Get Devinney's History of Printing.[112]

Is it as a *charity* you desired me to retire from 70 per cent, I paying the money & running the risk?

Seen Jefferson yet? ⟨I will see him.⟩[113]

I will put that receipt up & borrow money on it.

Put not a penny of expense on 2^d vol L of Xst until you have the MS.[114] [#]

---

[111] In the summer of 1887, while perfecting a dynamo for his typesetter, James W. Paige claimed to have discovered a revolutionary electro-magnetic motor which, when developed, "would give *us* all the money we should need in starting the Type Setter" (Franklin G. Whitmore to SLC, 18 July 1887). Clemens became interested in sponsoring Paige's motor, but at the urging of Franklin G. Whitmore sought to limit any financial involvement. An agreement dated 2 July 1887 specified that Clemens would provide support up to three thousand dollars in return for a half-share of profits on the motor. Clemens, following Whitmore's advice, refrained from signing this contract although not from temporarily underwriting Paige's experiments. On 16 August, however, he became party to an agreement by which Paige was to proceed with this invention at his own expense, allowing Clemens to claim a half-share in it by executing the 2 July contract and reimbursing him if the motor proved successful. Among the people who attended the 18 October demonstration noted here were Charles R. North, inventor of the typesetter's automatic justifier, and Charles I. Earll, one of the draftsmen employed in the development of that machine.

[112] *The Invention of Printing*, by Theodore L. De Vinne, first published in 1876.

[113] Clemens did not yet know that Webster & Company's long delay in making the offer he had suggested in August 1887 (see p. 303, note 15) had cost them the opportunity to publish Joseph Jefferson's autobiography. On 20 October 1887 Jefferson wrote to inform Webster that he had contracted elsewhere.

[114] The manuscript of Henry Ward Beecher's *Life of Christ* had been left incomplete when Beecher died on 8 March 1887. The Beecher family eventually withdrew the manuscript and returned the $5,000 advance paid them.

⟨[St]⟩Have you the MS of Mrs. Custer's book?

Send for Steve Gillis.[115]

Is that house sold?

Get $100.

Also list of questions made by Whit[more]

Error in No. 3. $62,362.53. It should read $62,926.53.[116]

Does October show that you need all those clerks?

Dʳ Burton's Yale Sermons[117]

Write Fred Grant.[118]

See L & offer him $100,000 for 600, & $200,000 for 1000, & myself the same. Use both countries.[119]

                              [#]

---

[115] Clemens may have thought to put his old friend from the Virginia City *Territorial Enterprise* to work testing the Paige typesetter. There is no surviving correspondence between the two men to indicate that such a plan was even discussed.

[116] The latter amount was reported as Clemens' undrawn share of Webster & Company profits on 1 April 1887. By late October, when Clemens received the firm's tardy financial statement, this amount evidently had not changed, a circumstance which prompted the following irascible query about expenses.

[117] In late October 1887 Webster & Company was preparing to issue *Yale Lectures on Preaching, and Other Writings* (1888) by the Reverend Nathaniel J. Burton of Hartford, who had died on the thirteenth of that month. Webster and Clemens disagreed on the desirability of publishing this book, but Clemens' conviction of its merits carried the day. Years later, Burton's son Richard, a minor poet and critic who edited the book, recalled that he had offered a version of it to the Century Company "when Mark Twain hearing about it, sent for me at once and . . . spoke as follows: 'You take that manuscript right away . . . and bring it to me; then root around in your father's barrel of sermons, pick out a dozen of those splendid preachments of his, and we'll add them to the Yale Lectures, and make a big portly volume of it. . . . we'll charge a price for it that will be a *damned outrage*, and we'll make it a religious classic!' . . . The Webster Company published it and the royalty to my mother was ten times better than if it had been brought out in the usual ten percent trade way" (Richard Burton, "Mark Twain in the Hartford Days," *Mark Twain Quarterly*, Summer 1937, p. 5).

[118] Clemens undoubtedly had decided to reply personally to Frederick D. Grant's contention that Webster & Company was amiss in its accounting of profits from his father's book (see p. 319, note 54). No letter from Clemens to Grant at this time is known.

[119] On 3 October 1887 William M. Laffan had written that he intended "to go away

⟨Return the⟩ Decline the Enclosed Chicago book.

On 300, pay $1000 down & knock $1000 off the other end.

On 2ᵈ, the same, or both can come in & advance $2000 & knock it off the other end.

On final 400, the same, or all can come in & advance $3000 & knock it off the other end.

⟨[D]⟩Take the contracts to Europe & double the orders. by showing them.

Do you want a fund of $100,000 um dass man Vorsätzer ⟨dabe[u]⟩dabei bestochen wird?[120]

Or divide one or two thousand Theilen among them—or *both*.

P. must give L a 400ᵗʰ, & I the same—& I can cancel P's indebtedness for it. My giving it was a pretext to get him interested for the general benefit.[121]

Decline Chicago. [#]

Pariswards and take a week or two with the French etchers," evidently prompting Clemens to devote this entry and, with one exception (340.1), the notes through "by showing them" (340.8) to marketing plans for the William T. Walters art collection catalog. He had previously developed a different commission system for the work (see Notebook 26, p. 274) and would discuss the idea further in a letter to Frederick J. Hall on 7 May 1888 (*MTLP*, pp. 245–246). The symbols with which Clemens marked several of the entries that deal with Laffan accompany those entries here.

[120] Clemens' puzzling German might mean: *in order to lure backers*. These schemes were perhaps related to a plan for Laffan to act as international agent for the typesetter (see p. 251, note 79).

[121] In an agreement dated 12 March 1888 Laffan was assigned 1/200 interest in the Paige typesetter, with Clemens receiving in exchange a similar share "in the profits which shall accrue from the patents of a certain invention for quadruplexing telegrams, whenever the interest of said Laffan in the same shall have been defined and acquired."

Paul Boyton. No terms till we see the MS—& not then, perhaps, for it would occupy a valuable date.[122]

Jo Jefferson.

Pope 80%!

⟨Dibble.—"Our great work."⟩[123]

⟨Show me all of Charley Clark's letters.⟩

Longstreet—Oct. 19.[124]

⟨(Capt. Boyton?)⟩

Man sollte der Herr Karl Dickens einladen. (und seine Tochter.)[125]

Get clerk list for June '85 & Oct. '85.[126]

Next year capture 500 Kaolatype infringers. [#]

---

[122] In April 1887 Clemens had rejected *The Story of Paul Boyton* . . . *A Book for Boys, Old and Young* (Milwaukee: Riverside Printing Co., 1892), in which Boyton described his adventures paddling the waterways of the world in a rubber suit. Clemens had not been won over by Boyton's promise to generate publicity by swimming "one hundred miles at sea on the day the book is published" (CLW to SLC, 26 March 1887). Webster liked the work and apparently renewed his efforts to persuade Clemens, arousing his ire instead (see 347.20–24). The "valuable date" is one Clemens had already allotted, at least in his own mind, to publication of the William T. Walters art book.

[123] Probably W. E. Dibble, a Cincinnati subscription publisher from whom Charles L. Webster & Company purchased rights to Edmund C. Stedman's *Library of American Literature*. In December 1887, Dibble would begin an undistinguished connection with Webster & Company, first as manager of the firm's New York subscription agency and afterward as merely a canvasser.

[124] Clemens probably had an appointment on this date with James Longstreet, formerly a Confederate general, to discuss a possible book for Charles L. Webster & Company (see p. 215, note 92).

[125] *Mr. Charles Dickens should be invited. (and his daughter.)* Charles Dickens, the son of the novelist, was in the United States giving readings from his father's works. The Clemenses invited Dickens, his wife Bessie, and his daughter Sydney to visit them in Hartford on 10 November 1887. On 5 November, Dickens responded from Boston, where he had recently read, accepting the invitation with "sincere pleasure" on behalf of "that portion of my extensive family which accompanies me."

[126] Clemens wished to compare past Webster & Company salary expenditures with present ones, which he considered excessive.

Whitmore take entire charge of Dick Burton's book.[127]
Correspond with Webster & Co. & all.

Our insurance—is it in W[128] or Webster's hands?

Get November North American

At the Author's Reading in New York, tell the Hank Monk story
5 times—& (Encore) whistling story[129]

Tell Burbank to introduce the hideous laughing, idiotic
screeching & pious & profane ejaculations of a Polly-crackering
parrot *as absent-minded musings & unconsciousnesses.* Every time
he begins to walk the stage absently, the audience will get ready to
laugh, for they know that at longer or shorter intervals the brown
silence will be broken by a hideous or funny parrot remark or
explosion—& one particular oft-repeated parrotism can be made as
common in the press & public as "There's millions in it!"[130]

X Gerhardt's check.

Got money for only 3 weeks?

Got Laffan's paper ready?

X Got that canvasser yet?[131] [#]

---

[127] Probably to take better advantage of the expected local appeal of Nathaniel J.
Burton's *Yale Lectures on Preaching* (see note 117), its manufacture and subscription
canvass were managed in Hartford.

[128] Daniel Whitford, one of Webster & Company's New York lawyers.

[129] An authors' reading for the American Copyright League was held in New York
City's Chickering Hall on 28 and 29 November 1887. On 31 October, Clemens agreed to
participate, stipulating that "my date shall be the 29th, *not* the 28th" and that "my reading shall occur either No. 2 or No. 3 on the program, & shall *not* occur *later* than No. 3"
(SLC to Robert Underwood Johnson, 31 October 1887). For the reason noted at 347.18–
19 Clemens actually appeared on 28 November, giving the first reading after James
Russell Lowell's introductory speech. He entitled his contribution "The Fatal Anecdote"
because of the deadly effect that suppression of the Hank Monk story has on a would-be
teller in chapter 20 of *Roughing It*.

[130] A suggestion for the planned revision of *Colonel Sellers as a Scientist* (see p. 337,
note 108).

[131] On 27 October 1887, Clemens proposed a unique method of handling the subscription for Nathaniel J. Burton's *Yale Lectures on Preaching.* "We will have no general

How long take to make Dr Burton's portrait?

O Laffan name a staving lawyer for me.

Write the House-Newton article.[132]

Shall Whitmore contract for the Burton plates here? Then give us the exact dimensions of page & number of lines on page. Give specimen

You have spent what, since Oct. 1? And what have you got to show for it?

You will have to cut down the office expenses, beginning with the head.

You have spent how much a month since Apl. 1?

How has the Chicago office managed to cost $2400?

Does the Chi man an old resident of Chic, or an importation to make enemies?[133]

For Princeton Review—to be written in April '88. If you attempt to ⟨build⟩ create & build a wholly imaginary incident, adventure or situation, you will go astray, & the artificiality of the thing will be detectable. But if you found on a *fact* in your personal experience, it is an acorn, a root, & every created adornment that grows up out of it & spreads its foliage & blossoms to the sun will seem realities, not inventions. You will not be likely to go astray; your compass of fact is there to keep you on the right course. Mention instances where you think the author was imagining. Others where he built upon a solid & actually *lived* basis of *fact*.[134] [#]

---

agency," he informed his business partners, "but use a canvasser only. I am on the track of the one we want: a young insurance-policy canvasser, who hunts the State on his bicycle, is a member of Burton's church" (*MTLP*, p. 238). In the same letter Clemens noted: "This is a case where a steel portrait is a quite valuable addition to a book." At 344.6 he recorded the desired information about how long preparation of the portrait would take.

[132] This article is discussed at length on page 332, note 93, and on page 335, note 101.

[133] C. S. Olcott was manager of the Chicago branch office of Charles L. Webster & Company. The reason for Clemens' challenge to Webster has not been determined.

[134] This accurate statement of the foundation for Clemens' best writing dates from

⟨Sold that house?⟩

See Gilder about Comedy, & Johnson about reading "The Fatal Anecdote."[135]

Give me the items of what each book has cost—*all* the books.

Have 3 book arrived from Webster?

Nov. 1. Will take 3 or 4 weeks to make D^r B's steel—$300.[136]

Balance ⟨Oct. 31⟩ Nov 1, 13,221.71

Fix alarm clock *again*.

Write Mr. Dickens Uncle Remus,[137] &

Bro. Robinson come & play billiars & read Brusnahan's letter. Propose that I write him another.[138] [#]

---

around the beginning of November 1887. Clemens planned to expand it either for the May 1888 or July 1888 number of the *New Princeton Review*. On 10 April 1888, A. C. Armstrong, publisher of that journal, would inquire of Clemens about "the progress of the article which you kindly promised for our pages. We trust that it is well in hand, or at least quite planned, and that before long we shall have the pleasure of receiving your manuscript." Clemens wrote "Great Scott!" on the envelope of Armstrong's letter and on 11 April formally withdrew from fulfilling the forgotten commitment.

[135] Clemens planned to consult Richard Watson Gilder about *Meisterschaft*, which would appear in the *Century* in January 1888. He wished to see Robert Underwood Johnson about the American Copyright League benefit scheduled for 28–29 November 1887. (See p. 333, note 95, and p. 342, note 129.)

[136] The frontispiece for *Yale Lectures on Preaching* by Nathaniel J. Burton.

[137] Clemens reminded himself here to invite Charles Dickens to Hartford (see p. 341, note 125) and to write Joel Chandler Harris about permission to include selections from his work in *Mark Twain's Library of Humor*. On 14 October Clemens had instructed Webster & Company to write Harris, promising to take him "by the hair myself" if he didn't consent (*MTLP*, pp. 235–236). Evidently Harris hadn't replied satisfactorily to a company appeal of 15 October.

[138] John Brusnahan was a foreman in the New York *Herald* composition department whose connections on the New York *Tribune* enabled him to provide Clemens with information about the *Tribune's* Mergenthaler Linotypes. Clemens had written to Brusnahan on 15 October 1887, telling him that the Paige machine was nearing completion. On 31 October Brusnahan replied, assuring Clemens that even when perfected the Mergenthaler machines "would not be what is required, for they take up too much room and have too many attachments." It was this comforting letter that Clemens showed to his Hartford friend Henry C. Robinson, occasionally mentioned in notebook entries as a potential typesetter investor.

"Although I say it myself, who shouldn't, this was the first & only capital crime which I have ever committed."[139]

Burdict,
Stoddinger
O'Hara
Whitney
Kirk left & instead of giving us a man in his place, you took his bench-room for other work.
Franzen, Parker & Marlow have been crowded into our assembling room in order to give their bench-room to other work
The work has been "delayed."
Davis told Bates[140] in the start that if ever he needed tracings, give notice, & if he was keeping any back for his convenience he would meet the difficulty at once.

No more red lines in title-pages.

Have my pen fixed.

Get some tobacco.

Bal. Nov. 5, 10,224.41.

Brander Matthews
121 E 18th[141] [#]

---

[139] A draft of a close for Mark Twain's "Fatal Anecdote" reading for the American Copyright League on 28 November 1887. The reference is to his destruction of a "poor wanderer" by compelling him to withhold the Hank Monk story in chapter 20 of *Roughing It*.

[140] Charles Ethan Davis was a draftsman who had "charge and control of the drawings and mechanical engineering work connected with [the Paige typesetter], and superintended its manufacture from the first stage of development, down to the completion and operation of all the models and machines which were built" (Lucien A. Legros and John C. Grant, *Typographical Printing-Surfaces* [London: Longmans, Green and Co., 1916], p. 378). George A. Bates was a Pratt & Whitney foreman. The other men mentioned in this entry were machinists engaged on the typesetter.

[141] When he noted Brander Matthews' address in early November 1887, Clemens and Matthews were disagreeing on matters relating to international copyright. Matthews had asked Clemens for "facts and statistics concerning English piracies" of his books, but after reading Matthews' "American Authors and British Pirates" (*New Princeton*

Write article on the phonograph?

A.C. Armstrong, N. P.[142]

On what date shall my canv. bk be finished. Is it begun?
Begin it.[143]

All crimes should be ⟨punishment⟩punished with humiliations—
life-long public exposure ⟨to⟩ in ridiculous & grotesque situations—
& never in any other way. Death/Gallows makes a hero of the
villain, & he is envied by some spectators & by & by imitated.

Chap IX—"1988."[144] (the preceding chapters have not been
written yet & ain't going to be—"The thing that struck me, was
their methods of punishing criminals."

—in place of flowers, hymns, proxy-marriages, conversions,
scaffold-eloquence, shrine (grave) pilgrimage, (date made a public
holiday)—*this* was the reason they ⟨changing⟩changed hanging to
insult, humiliation &c — — Sense of ridicule is bitterer than death
& more feared—met commit suicide daily to escape it. (Lingg.)[145]

Review, September 1887), an article condemning English publishers, Clemens expanded
his intended personal response into "A Private Letter and a Public Postscript." This
article, as well as Matthews' rejoinder, "An Open Letter to Close a Correspondence,"
appeared in the *New Princeton Review* in January 1888 under the heading "American
Authors and British Pirates."

[142] A. C. Armstrong was the publisher of the *New Princeton Review* (see note 134).

[143] The prospectus for *Mark Twain's Library of Humor*, scheduled for publication in
early 1888.

[144] Notes through "Mention this on machine?)" (347.16–17) suggest plans for an
imaginative work about the future that would complement Clemens' treatment of the
past in *A Connecticut Yankee*.

[145] On 11 November 1887, after one of the most celebrated of American political
trials, four of seven condemned anarchists were executed by hanging for their alleged
complicity in the 1886 Chicago Haymarket bombing, where seven policemen were killed.
Two defendants had their death sentences commuted to life imprisonment and the
seventh, Louis Lingg, committed suicide in prison the day before the scheduled execution, apparently by detonating a "fulminating cap" in his mouth with a lighted candle.
A quarter of a million people lined the route of the funeral procession, and a monument
was commissioned for the grave site. Prominent among the mourners was Vassar-educated
Nina Van Zandt, the daughter of "well-to-do residents of Philadelphia" (New York
World, 12 November 1887), who had married defendant August Spies by proxy after
a courtroom romance.

Hanging is not based on knowledge of human nature   When death penalty was instituted ⟨it was⟩ revenge was the object, & passionate quick revenge. But now when our object is deterrent, *not* punitive, the death pen is an anachronism & is irrational & ridiculous. It ⟨pun⟩ is the opposite of a deterrent, ⟨ab[-]⟩ often.

(The shave a woman's head, make her wear rubber tubing back of both lips,—& stop there. She would rather be in hell.)

Chap. XX. The phonograph. Neither printed newsp. nor books left—except as curiosities. Salacious daily news furnished in a whisper to any that want it. But the character of each sort of news is marked by signs indicating "pure", "hellish["] &c. Portraits & pictures transferred by light, accompany everything.

The Ph goes to church, ⟨takes⟩ conducts family worship, &c.
⟨Appoint me to see Edison?⟩[146]
Teaches foreign languages. Pops the question.
(Ph holds copy for compositor, who⟨se⟩ loses time now. Mention this on machine?)

Mem. I *must* be put ⟨[a]h⟩back to Nov. 28 in the readings[147] —dinner to the Hawleys.

What about *Laffan's* book? Inquired since? Only once? Been a Boyton book for babies how many times would you go?
Or to Jo Jefferson?
Or Donnelly.
Loss, $100,000 on 3.

The cessation of hospitalities to traveling English? Because English manners could not be endured.

You had *no* subject; but if you⟨r theme⟩ wanted a prodigious theme, why didn't you take "English Breeding as Exhibited in the

---

[146] Clemens would again remind himself to see Edison about the phonograph in entries made in February (374.1), May (386.1–2), and June 1888 (390.5). He attempted to see Edison in late May, but the two men did not actually confer until early June.

[147] The authors' readings for the American Copyright League (see p. 342, note 129, and p. 345, note 139). United States senator Joseph R. Hawley was among the possible Paige typesetter investors Clemens listed on pages 336–337 of this notebook.

United States?"—& call for statistics. You could have made all England blush; as it is, you have simply given your own country cause to blush.[148]

Ask Am Pub Co *personally* for permission to use matter from my books. Carry Mr. Hall's letter for signature.[149]

Call on Laffan. Make an appt.

Balance, Nov. 11, noon, 11,297.21

Old Pavey's[150] negro preacher chopping wood back of the tavern: "Make yo' callin' & election sure "brethren & sistern."

"We lean on de railin's o' heben & look down & ⟨s[aw]⟩sees 'm a fryin' in hell."

Stop Patrick's batteries & get dry ones from Boston.

Knock that woodcut of me out of that Library.[151] [#]

---

[148] This entry and the previous one were made while Clemens was considering a response to Brander Matthews' September 1887 *New Princeton Review* article on "American Authors and British Pirates" (see note 141). In his published remarks Clemens did not digress from consideration of literary piracy to a discussion of English breeding, but he did preserve the intent of this entry by insisting that Matthews' article unwittingly emphasized the real justice of British copyright law as opposed to the imperfection of the American system. "Don't you know," he admonished Matthews, "that as long as you've got a goitre that you have to trundle around on a wheelbarrow you can't divert attention from it by throwing bricks at a man that's got a wart on the back of his ear?" ("A Private Letter and a Public Postscript," *New Princeton Review*, January 1888, p. 52).

[149] Evidently a letter drafted by Frederick J. Hall, to be signed by the American Publishing Company, giving Charles L. Webster & Company permission to use selections from Clemens' early works in *Mark Twain's Library of Humor*.

[150] The proprietor of a Hannibal hotel, "a vicious devil of a Corsican, a common terror in the town" (*MTA*, 1:118), Pavey is mentioned several times in Mark Twain's notebooks and in some of his unfinished writings (see *HH&T*, pp. 33, 362).

[151] On 15 November 1887, Clemens demanded that Charles L. Webster & Company "leave out that woodcut of me from the L of L [Edmund C. Stedman's *Library of American Literature*]. The more I think of the gratuitous affront of wood where steel is lavished upon the unread & the forgotten, the more my bile rises. Don't leave it out, simply—put it in the fire" (*MTBus*, pp. 388–389). In fact most of the illustrations in the *Library of American Literature* were done from woodcuts. On 24 December 1887 Clemens accepted a new woodcut of himself.

Inn-Tell-lie-gents.
Whole Intelligence. (Office).

Get Am. Pub Co's consent Jan 1st.

See Gilder & say use that Burton Agnosticism or give it up.[152]

Long primer now $.1.30 per page for comp & electrotyping—1400 ems. Is mere steretyping cheaper? 40 reading-lines on page.

Charade—
    Dumb (orchestra, with a Thomasonian leader.[153]
    Belles—Susie, Clara, Daisy, Julie
    Dumb-Bells—use those up garret—Gillette & I—exhibition.

Mrs. Hannah Coffin
  % Mrs. Custer
    55 W 10th st.

⟨R. M. Howland 1327 Walnut.⟩[154]
⟨Dr Bacon⟩[155]
⟨⟨L⟩Sloane's telegram⟩[156]

---

[152] The Century Company had had an opportunity to publish a volume of writings by Nathaniel J. Burton before Clemens captured it for Charles L. Webster & Company (see p. 339, note 117). Richard Watson Gilder had retained rights to a Burton essay entitled "Agnosticism," which Clemens probably heard at an 1881 meeting of the Hartford Monday Evening Club, for publication in the *Century* magazine. It was not published in the *Century*, but did appear in Burton's *Yale Lectures on Preaching*.

[153] Theodore Thomas was a controversial and dedicated conductor and music educator whose orchestra was beginning a season of thirty-six concerts in New York City in November 1887. Clemens may have been referring here to Thomas' habit of becoming taciturn when under attack, for his shrewdness and intelligence were widely recognized. The occasion for these elaborate charades, involving Susy and Clara Clemens, Daisy Warner, and, evidently, Julia Twichell and William Gillette, has not been identified.

[154] Robert M. Howland had been a Nevada acquaintance of Mark Twain's. No correspondence between the two men survives to explain this notation, possibly of a Hartford address.

[155] Probably William T. Bacon, a Hartford physician.

[156] William Milligan Sloane, professor of history at Princeton, was the editor of the *New Princeton Review*. His telegram was presumably in connection with Clemens' appearance in the January 1888 number of that journal (see p. 345, note 141) or with Clemens' promise to contribute to a subsequent number (see p. 343, note 134).

⟨Letter to Miss Dickens⟩[157]
Miss Trumbull[158]
See my doctor[159]
⟨Robt Garvie—Mahogany⟩[160]
⟨Buell—Clock.⟩[161]
⟨Gen. Hawley's address.
Hotel Buckingham, N.Y.⟩

On machine, use nickle or soft iron type, & then case-harden it.

Nov. 18—9,689.89

Nov. 18/87. Jesse Grant came in & spoke of an offer he had
received to publish⟨er⟩ his mother's book—(Gen Grant's letters &c)
elsewhere,[162] & asked if we would object. He said would not do it if
we objected. We did object, & said we thought it would us & the
General's book. Whereupon he said he would write at once &
decline the offer. He sat down & wrote a letter & carried it away
with him. Wrote it on plain paper; asked for that saying he did not
care that it should be known the letter was written in our office.
He asked if it would be any harm to put some of the matter in a
magazine. We said it would do harm; I believed the General's
Century articles cost the family $100,000.

The paper in a 600-p book costs 15ᶜ; the printing 5ᶜ; binding,
(cloth) 22ᶜ; 35 in sheep; 75 to 80 in half. mor; $[1.]20 in full m.

---

[157] On 14 November, after the Dickens family's visit to Hartford, Miss Sydney M.
Dickens wrote to Clemens requesting an inscribed photograph. On 18 December she
wrote to thank him for sending it.

[158] Annie Eliot Trumbull, daughter of the Hartford historian and philologist J.
Hammond Trumbull, was a friend of the Clemens family's.

[159] Probably Clarence C. Rice, who had recently performed surgery on Clemens'
palate (see p. 332, note 92).

[160] Robert Garvie, a Hartford plumber and gas-fitter, did a variety of work on the
Clemens house.

[161] Dwight H. Buell was the Hartford jeweler who first brought the Paige typesetter
to Clemens' attention.

[162] Charles L. Webster & Company had once been eager to publish Ulysses S. Grant's
letters to his wife, but in August 1887 had decided that public interest in Grant had
worn too thin to justify such a collection (see p. 219, note 106, and p. 276, note 171).

The Burton book, 3.75 or 4 in cloth, ⟨$5⟩$4.50 sheep, & $5 in ½ mor.

Apparently, requisites for Victoria X, are that he shan't be a private, & *shall* be by birth a "gentleman." Say this in King Arthur —& furnish the statistics in an appendix.[163]

Canvass Dʳ Burton NOW.[164]

Make a single scene—monologue or dialogue—Queen Elizabeth, & play the part myself. "Hells-bells! &c."

Boston man (Tyler) makes gas at 7 cents per 1000 to run factories with.

Book about Chas II & Kerouaille, translated by Mrs. M. G. Crawford, pub by Scribner & Welford.[165]

A superb Geschäfft ruined in zwei Jahren, und sechzig tausend Thaler Schuld gemacht.[166]

PAR-(pa) SIGH-MONY.

IN-DIG-NAY-SHUN.
Coro(t)-may-shun.

Get me (⟨[5]⟩650 pages)
Composition (1500 per page)

---

[163] Clemens did not include this information in *A Connecticut Yankee*, presumably because he discovered it to be incorrect. The Victoria Cross was instituted in 1856 as a reward for individual acts of bravery performed by lower-grade officers, non-commissioned officers, soldiers, marines, and seamen. There was no class prerequisite.

[164] A few days after he made this note Clemens had a change of heart (see 354.2–3) and it wasn't until 24 December that he informed Webster that the canvass for Burton's *Yale Lectures on Preaching* had begun "with good promise" (*MTLP*, p. 240). This entry concludes a page in the manuscript notebook. Clemens tore out the leaf which followed, probably on 19 November 1887, for a note to Bram Stoker who was in New York managing Henry Irving's engagement at the Star Theatre.

[165] Louise Renée de Kéroualle was the mistress of Charles II of England. The book referred to is *Louise de Kéroualle, Duchess of Portsmouth, in the Court of Charles II*, compiled by Henri Forneron; preface by Mrs. G. M. Crawford (New York: Scribner & Welford, 1887).

[166] A superb *business* ruined in *two years and a sixty thousand dollar debt created.*

Printing per 1000 volumes
   (for 4,000.)
Binding, cloth per vol.
   (with steel portrait).

Combination sentence for Van[167] to compete with a hand-man
with:
Through consecration of the nation to inflation the degradation
of the nation is occasioned.—(27. per mach; 92 movements by
hand.)
There are many men of many minds; & where this is the case, a
minimum of deliberation promises a minimum of confusion.

IN-DIE-JEST-SHUN.

Him a marksman! Can't hit a pile with a pile-driver!

Joe's Mr. Shaw: I guess the man cheated me (referring to his
lame horse). What did you g—— "O, he *give* him to me!"

What does the American Electric Lighting Co pay the Ass
Press?[168]

N. Y. *They* pay/paid the compositor 60^c for the 1500, & sell it
to us at 80. They charge 40 more to electrotype it. They charge 88
for the comp. *now.* The printing is 30^c for 250 sheets turned &
printed on both sides.
This would make 4,000 printed pages, which would make
6—650-page books, & each book would cost 5^c. [#]

---

[167] Charles G. Van Schuyver, a compositor who assisted in the development and
testing of the Paige typesetter.
[168] For several years Clemens had suspected employees of this organization of accepting bribes to circulate advertisements as news items (see p. 262, note 119). His entry here
may have been prompted by a report carried in the Hartford *Courant* of 22 November
1887 noting, in a fashion that might well have seemed promotional, the great prosperity
of the American Electric Manufacturing Company. The American Electric Light Company was an unrelated and unproductive firm whose dissolution had been announced
in the summer of 1887. Clemens' confusion of the two firms, a common error, can be
attributed to the *Courant* article's omission of the former company's full name.

Nov. 22, ⟨9,6[1]1.12⟩9,591.12.

$4,000 due; & also the house 4 or $5,000 more.

Ben to have the *whole* afternoon the 28th. Shall take her there (Dr. Farrar's) about or before 2.[169]

Go & see "Pete" at Harrigan's.[170]

Nov. 26⟨.⟩—9060.97.

Mary Barton,
Mrs. Hawley
   ″   Warner
   ″   Warner
Geo.   ″
Ward Foote
Gen. Hawley
Joe Twichell.
Twichell boys (imitations).
Koto (bring Jap. dress & *talk* Jap.[171]

Get that 400th interest from P.

S— H. says Bram Stoker's story of the Christening is the best he ever heard & the sharpest surprise at the end.

Clara go to Tiffany's & get a dozen of those dinner-cards— without fail. 12 of *some* kind, anyway.[172] [#]

---

[169] Clara Clemens was receiving extensive treatment from John Nutting Farrar, a New York dentist (see p. 258, note 103).

[170] *Pete* was Edward Harrigan's melodramatic "play of Southern life" which became enormously popular, running at Harrigan's Park Theatre in New York from 22 November 1887 until 21 April 1888. Harrigan himself "made a great hit as the faithful negro servant," the title role (George C. D. Odell, *Annals of the New York Stage*, 15 vols. [New York: Columbia University Press, 1927–1949], 13:458).

[171] This list, evidently of guests expected at the 29 November 1887 dinner for Senator and Mrs. Joseph R. Hawley, includes Mr. and Mrs. George Warner, Susan Warner (Mrs. Charles Dudley Warner), and Koto, Edward H. House's adopted Japanese daughter.

[172] Clemens was delegating to his thirteen-year-old daughter, Clara, the selection of place cards for the 29 November Hawley dinner party. The Tiffany establishment on the corner of 4th Avenue and 25th Street was only a short walk from the office of Dr. John Nutting Farrar with whom Clara had a dental appointment on 28 November.

Buy 3—4.30 seats on arrival.

Do not begin on the Burton book till the MS is *all* ready, & the words carefully counted.

$$
\begin{array}{r}
650 \\
\underline{365} \\
3250 \\
3900 \\
\underline{1950} \\
237,250
\end{array}
$$

Twichell's soldiers doing the hollering when man was having tooth pulled.

Dying soldiers that played smart for coffins.

Twichell's 2 sets of soldiers.

Martin McGinniss (See   **X**[173]

Well, the Savior's been here once.

Negro sermon, "Make yo' callin' & election sure."

Cable's Man. In my Father's house are many mansions; IF it were not so, I would have told you.[174]

The *only* calf—the seed calf of starving nations, the ⟨The⟩ Adam calf of the ⟨world⟩universe.

Busy bee, b'gosh.

Shaw's horse (Joe.

Blind Tom.[175] [#]

---

[173] It is unclear what X Clemens' instruction refers to, though it is likely a reference to one or more of the symbols with which he marked several other lists of punch lines and anecdotes in this notebook (see note 179).

[174] Clemens here recalled a sermon he had heard in the New Orleans church attended by George Washington Cable (see N&J2, p. 507).

[175] The subject of a Clemens anecdote which had appeared in the San Francisco *Alta California* on 1 August 1869 (reprinted in the *Twainian*, July–August 1949, pp. 4–5). Thomas Greene Bethune was a blind musical prodigy who had perfect pitch, an ear of extraordinary accuracy, and, reportedly, a piano repertoire of seven thousand pieces.

Wakeman—Prophets of Baal & Isaa[c]
    ″   Hanging the English mate
    ″   Courtship.
    ″   Daniel in Lion's den.
    ″   Stealing Clipper ship.
    ″   Shipping as a boy with the saint.[176]
Whistling story.
Christening the Baby.
⟨[-]⟩John Hanicks' laugh.[177]
    ″   ″   Giving his "experience"
"I had a miscarriage."

⟨See Gilder, Monday Dec. 5, & say he must give up the Burton article, for we shall issue by Jan. 1.⟩

A Manual for Beginners in Dinner-Table entertainment. Leave Sydney Smith out,—in America.[178]
(Banquet-Management) [#]

Clemens told the *Alta* that while traveling "from Galena to another Illinois town to fill a lecture engagement," his enjoyment of the smoking car was disrupted by a Negro passenger who entertained himself with a frenzied and compulsive reproduction of "the groaning and clattering and hissing of a railway train." Finally, after enduring the exhibition "until I was becoming as crazy as he was and getting ready to start an opposition express on my own hook, I inquired who this barbarian was, and where he was bound for, and why he was not chained or throttled? They said it was Blind Tom, the celebrated pianist—a harmless idiot to whom all sounds were music, and the imitation of them an unceasing delight." At about the time Clemens made this entry, Bethune was giving a series of concerts in New York, first at the Athenaeum from 24 through 26 November 1887 and then at Knickerbocker Hall on the last three days of the month.

[176] Clemens' relationship with and literary indebtedness to Edgar Wakeman are discussed at length in Notebook 7 (*N&J1*, pp. 241–243). With the exception of the second anecdote, a version of the tale that occupies chapter 50 of *Roughing It*, the stories listed here are told or alluded to in chapters one, two, four, eight, and eleven of *The Log of an Ancient Mariner, Being the Life and Adventures of Captain Edgar Wakeman*, ed. Minnie Wakeman-Curtis (San Francisco: A. L. Bancroft & Co., 1878). Clemens included Wakeman's tale of the "Prophets of Baal & Isaac" in the installment of "Some Rambling Notes of an Idle Excursion" which appeared in the *Atlantic Monthly* in November 1877.

[177] John Hannicks was the original of the Negro drayman whose cry "S-t-e-a-m-boat a-comin'!" rouses the sleepy river village in chapter 4 of *Life on the Mississippi*. The two anecdotes about Hannicks noted here have not been recovered.

[178] Clemens had previously proposed compiling a burlesque "Banqueteer's Handbook" (see p. 285). The present modification of that idea presumably called for an

"Cried—*so* hard. But I gave him my little finger & he quieted right down——though all he got was just his own juice.

Opera.[179] Sing "Your Royal Highness the plumber has come to collect 3 sequins for mending the hole in the busted gas pipe. (Make the company jump out of their clothes.

HOW DO YOU LIKE CHICAGO!

Boy with Molasses (boo-hooing) "Mam! pap! --- |Moncoon

Don't care a —— if I *never* git to Texas.

Scotchy & Westminster Abbey.

Whittier—"Take 'm & drown 'm."

Mrs. S. "Ever read Uncle Tom⟨["]⟩? *Tried* to.

"j'you think I come out here for my health?

How the editor of the Springfield Republican got his Nüsse caught in the steel trap. [#]

---

anthology of comic pieces suitable for after-dinner reading. In planning to exclude Sydney Smith, the English clergyman, journalist, wit, and author of much quotable table-talk, from the American edition of such a work, Clemens was probably thinking of the annoyance Smith had caused with his famous remarks: "In the four quarters of the globe, who reads an American book? or goes to an American play? or looks at an American picture or statue? What does the world yet owe to American physicians or surgeons? What new substance have their chemists discovered? or what old ones have they analyzed? What new constellations have been discovered by the telescopes of Americans? What have they done in the mathematics? Who drinks out of American glasses? or eats from American plates? or wears American coats or gowns? or sleeps in American blankets? Finally, under which of the old tyrannical governments of Europe is every sixth man a slave, whom his fellow-creatures may buy and sell and torture?" (review of Adam Seybert's *Statistical Annals of the United States of America* in the *Edinburgh Review,* January 1820, pp. 79–80).

[179] The symbol that accompanies this entry is the first of twelve in this notebook that mark lists of punch lines and anecdotes. They take various forms—asterisks, Xs, crosses, and hatch marks—and most of them are boxed. Their placement suggests that Clemens drew most of the symbols at the time he wrote the lists, rather than adding them later.

W & Co send a set of my engravings to Chatto & Windus.[180]

Get patent leathers shoes at Alexanders, 6 ave. & 23ᵈ—or 52 West 10, MᶜComber.

⟨⟨[-o-] with⟩Write the Chamberlaines of Concord.[181]

Pratt & Whitney's gauge-book. Get one or two.

Dec. 1/87. ⟨16,198.78⟩16,196.78.

La Terre. Zola. N. Y.   W. R. Jenkins.[182]

For next Authors' Readings: "Bram Stoker's Yarn."
ADJUSTABLE Speech.
ALSO obituary of Thos. P. Afterall. See black wallet in my pocket.

⟨Ho[--]t[--]⟩Chilblains.

Call on Mr. Geo. Keller.[183] & MᶜDonald.

Get "Fliegende Blätter."[184]

Car-whistle. (horse)

Look out for copyright on Library.

Whitmore get me that apple-wood.

"Don't even get your seed back." [#]

---

[180] The illustrations for *Mark Twain's Library of Humor*, which was to be published in London by Chatto & Windus.

[181] The Clemenses had met Mr. & Mrs. Augustus P. Chamberlaine in 1878 while on the European tour which produced *A Tramp Abroad*.

[182] Clemens hoped to acquire a copy of Zola's recent novel from the William R. Jenkins Company, New York publishers and importers of French, Italian, and veterinary works advertised as "excellent, pure, tasteful, and cheap" (*Publishers' Weekly*, 30 July 1887, p. 157).

[183] George Keller was a Hartford architect.

[184] A German humor magazine published in Munich.

The "Burning Shame."

Jean praying for a pair of goats, & to have the stomach ache discontinued.

X^n & shts cease to be synonymous.

I had a mskrj.

"Go & see Dicky's Darling—1$ & upward.[185]

Is Mr. JONES in the audience?

Does you shovel SNOW by de hour?[186]

Jim Lane's speech—explanation of it to his Methodist Church.

Michael McGinniss.

Lawrence Barrett's Irish funeral.

Broke a rake handle other day.

"Proset."

Joe Tw—prayer when dog interrupted.

Louise de ⟨P⟩Keroualle.
Scribner & Welford.

—Prophesy—[187]

1910. In the South, whites of both sexes have to ride in the smoking car (& pay full fare,) the populous & dominant colored man will not ride with them.

The colored brother has succeeded in having severe laws against miscegenation passed.

There is no such thing as a free ballot. The whites have to vote as they are told, or be visited by masked men & shot, or whipped,

---

[185] Clemens here recalled an anecdote about the British actor J. L. Toole which is discussed on page 232, note 16.

[186] This question was part of the anecdote that became "The Snow-Shovelers," Mark Twain's unpublished sketch about two leisurely and sociable laborers who agree on the wisdom of being paid by the hour, not by the job (see p. 232, note 18).

[187] This heading may have been added by Albert Bigelow Paine.

& house burned & wife & d ⟨stripped na[k]⟩ turned out in their night clothes.

More religion than ever with both colors.

Dec. 9—15,076.79. Draft & notes due, $554.

What do you allow "off" on my book & General's? 50 & rebate?

Dec. 17—14,000.

If that's all one dog, it's a

Moncoon. The old Queen Ann gun.

Whittier's story, "Drown them!"

Automatic Oration, Boston

⟨Man can't save his seed.⟩

Man don't even get his seed back.

Capt. Wakeman's rats (jiggering in procession along chain-cable & finally hauling up sick rat in a rag) ⟨deserted⟩deserting noble clipper ship & joining an old "basket"—gap & see the waves—if overhead, rat fall in your mouth. Basket survived her voyage & he didn't *say* but what the other did.[188]

Sent $100 to K. Xmas. Repeat this Apl. 1, as the outlay is $29 per month.[189]

Canvassed a ⟨bo⟩bk that had no existence—Bchr.[190]

---

[188] Mark Twain recorded Captain Edgar Wakeman's tales of ships' rats at length in a notebook he used in 1866 while aboard Wakeman's steamer, the *America* (see *N&J*1, pp. 252–256). He then incorporated them into a letter to the San Francisco *Alta California* (reprinted in *Mark Twain's Travels with Mr. Brown*, ed. Franklin Walker and G. Ezra Dane [New York: Alfred A. Knopf, 1940], pp. 28–33).

[189] Clemens' gift to Jane, Orion, and Mollie Clemens, residing together in Keokuk, Iowa.

[190] Webster & Company had prematurely canvassed the *Biography of Reverend Henry Ward Beecher*, by William C. Beecher and Samuel Scoville. The book appeared too late in 1888 to allow delivery of early orders, occasioning a considerable loss to the firm.

Hancock.[191]

Pub. next to nothing during 2 years & then pile everything in together & make one bk kill another.

Lib Humor ought to have issued & sold 100,000, fall of '86, stead of being balled-up with Custer & Cox in the winter of 87–8.

Paying rent in 4 places.

Haven't made a cent in 2½ years, yet salaries twice increased, & now bigger than J. L. & Co.[192]

Slee's sal & yours is the same. C. L's smaller. Kelley, Prest of a RR & a coal Co., gets less.[193]

What did you print the Custer book for?[194]

Did you bind it?

3 times times the money lying idle in Library that ought to be.[195] [#]

---

[191] This sarcastic entry alludes to the slightness of Almira Hancock's *Reminiscences of Winfield Scott Hancock.* Large type, more than a score of full-page illustrations, and appendixes bulking almost as large as the text itself were necessary to bring the book up to acceptable size.

[192] J. Langdon & Company, the Langdon family coal business.

[193] J. D. F. Slee and Charles J. Langdon were partners in J. Langdon & Company. Langdon was also chairman of the board of the Clearfield Bituminous Coal Corporation of Elmira. William D. Kelly was president of the latter firm. The railroad he served in a similar capacity has not been identified. The doubtful assertions about salaries in this entry were probably noted in response to a 29 December 1887 letter in which Charles L. Webster protested that his salary, then $3,800 annually, "has always been small. I think I can say without fear of contradiction that *no* man in the city of New York having any where near the cares & responsibilities that I do works for a salary of less than $5,000 a year."

[194] On 24 December 1887, Frederick J. Hall reported that Elizabeth Custer's *Tenting on the Plains* "is all printed and paid for, which made quite a heavy item in this week's expenses." Clemens was annoyed by this expenditure since Mrs. Custer's book was to be held back temporarily to avoid interference with a good response to Samuel S. Cox's *Diversions of a Diplomat in Turkey.* On 29 December, Clemens wrote to Webster & Company: "It occurs to me that it will not be best to bind the Custer book for some months yet, as it cannot now be canvassed, and we can use the money to better advantage in other ways" (Miriam Lutcher Stark Library, University of Texas, Austin, Tex.).

[195] In 1887, with Clemens' unenthusiastic approval, Webster & Company had invested $8,000 in the acquisition of plates for the first five volumes of the *Library of American*

Money also in L Christ.[196]

Everywhere that it ought not to be.

Since moved to 14,[197] always kept a useless double force of people & desks to keep up appearances.

You said you had to keep these people (2 years) to be ready for business ("the rush") when it should come.
Upon my insistence you at last discharged   3   in fall of '87.

Got robbed for a year right under your nose.

Alexander & Green get part of *your* salary. The idea of a one-horse pub house keeping a lawyer!

How much copyright to pay Jan 1?

If ⟨[A]⟩Chas. Francis Adams would let Ike Bromley (literary manager of the U. P. RR) or W^m· D. Bishop, Bridgeport, still better. write up the inside of the ⟨Union⟩ Central Pacific business for Century—[198] [#]

Literature, which was then being abandoned by Cincinnati publisher W. E. Dibble. On 24 December 1887, Hall reported that "the 'Library of Am. Lit.' will in the course of a month or six weeks begin to make some return, as we intend to put the first two volumes to press very shortly." By 12 May 1888, Hall could inform Clemens: "The 'Library of American Literature,' ten volumes, is going well. . . . I think this book is going to pan out big eventually, as the results attained so far have come without any particular pushing." Nevertheless, sales of this work never offset the continual demands it made on company resources.

[196] Webster & Company had advanced $5,000 to Henry Ward Beecher for his projected *Life of Christ.* After long negotiations with the deceased clergyman's family, the firm recovered its advance and relinquished rights to the unfinished book in December 1888.

[197] Webster & Company offices at 3 East 14th Street in New York.

[198] Charles Francis Adams was at this time president of the Union Pacific Railroad. Isaac H. Bromley, the well-known journalist, was his assistant. William Darius Bishop, former president of the New York & New Haven Railroad was still on that line's board of directors and was also president of the Naugatuck Railroad in Connecticut. On 31 December 1887, the New York *Times* carried a lengthy account of the findings of a three-man presidential commission appointed under a Congressional act of 3 March 1887 to investigate "the books, accounts, and methods of railroads which have received aid from the United States." Among the economically distressed railroads most severely

Ask Laffan about Associated Press.[199]

Write an Elaborate Essay on Lying, with instances patly illustrating each breed of lie.[200]

Dec. 31, balance about 14,000. Royalties & other bills will reduce this some 3,000.

Bal., Jan 3/88—13,293.28.

Go to some publisher & get the facts.[201]

12860 48 Jan 7.

Look & send those Burton advance-sheets to Chatto. [#]

---

condemned for comprehensive dishonesty, speculative financial mismanagement, and unfair business practices were both the Union Pacific and the Central Pacific. The *Century* magazine did not publish the article suggested here.

[199] Clemens was seeking further evidence of the suspected unethical practices of this agency (see p. 352, note 168).

[200] Clemens never produced this expanded version of "On the Decay of the Art of Lying" (*The Stolen White Elephant*, 1882). In that essay, originally delivered to the Hartford Monday Evening Club on 5 April 1880, Clemens remarked playfully that it had been his intention "to mention names and give illustrative specimens, but indications observable about me admonished me to beware of particulars and confine myself to generalities."

[201] The facts gathered from various publishers appear in the long sequence of entries about "previous publication" ("PP," "P.P.," "pr p."), running almost without interruption to "The above applies to *my* books, too." (368.5). These notes were made while Clemens was evolving three unpublished refutations of the views on international copyright which Brander Matthews set forth in two articles on "American Authors and British Pirates" (*New Princeton Review*, September 1887 and January 1888). These unpublished pieces—which amplify "A Private Letter and a Public Postscript" (*New Princeton Review*, January 1888), Clemens' response to Matthews' first article—are: "Mr. Matthews's Second Article," a lengthy, contentious, sometimes derogatory "reply by annotation"; "Concerning the British 'Pirate'" (Doheny), a more finished and documented presentation of Clemens' views; and "P.P.S. A Recapitulation," a brief summary of the opposing positions and Matthews' errors. Clemens' compulsion to have the last word, if only in private, is illuminated by Matthews' recollection that "I was studiously courteous, refraining from any retort in kind to Mark's humorous personalities. Nevertheless Mark took offense and for a year or two he seemed to avoid me. Like most humorists, he was inclined to take himself seriously" (Brander Matthews, *These Many Years: Recollections of a New Yorker* [New York: Charles Scribner's Sons, 1917], p. 231). Matthews made similar observations even more trenchantly and at greater length in "Memories of Mark Twain" (*The Tocsin of Revolt and Other Essays* [New York: Charles Scribner's Sons, 1922], pp. 255–260).

H O & Co²⁰²—always do P P & never go to Canada. Dʳ· Holmes was the last to go Can to get *Eng* cop—1867. "Guardian Angel."

In ⟨1880⟩1878 *began* a great Eng business & did it on PP alone.

Part of their *contract* (invented by themselves) ⟨req⟩ *includes* P. P. & a royalty to author. ⟨They 40% of their ne[w boo]ks in England.⟩

Century protects them   Cable, Eggleston, Stockton, & Mrs. Burnett   Howells.

Burroughs.

Last 8 or ten years everybody who has published serially in C has been pr p. copyrighted. there.²⁰³

Once in a while we send over 6 of an unknown author (with Eng *imprint*) & place 5 in library & advertise & ⟨sell⟩ offer the other one for sale.

Not aware of any case where a PP has been stolen in whole or in part or mutilated or name changed, or introduction added.

To show how they respect PP, we sent the plates to Cassell for edition de luxe Longfellow, & he had to teear those costly plates to eliminate later poems PP'd by Long & sold to Routledge.²⁰⁴

Lee & Shep—Higginson.²⁰⁵ [#]

---

²⁰² Houghton, Osgood & Company, forerunner of Houghton, Mifflin & Company. Clemens explained in "Concerning the British 'Pirate'" that he "went to Boston to collect instances" of successful use of previous publication. Much of the information from publishers noted here and below was elaborated in that unpublished article.

²⁰³ In "Concerning the British 'Pirate'" Clemens noted that he had collected these facts about the *Century* magazine himself: "they were easy to get at, for it is only a hundred steps from the editor of the Century to the Century's publisher."

²⁰⁴ "As an indication of the respect in which the law in its present state is held in England, this piece of history may be cited. Mr. Longfellow sold to Routledge, of London, a few poems, & these were secured by P.P. Upon the great bulk of his poems there was no English copyright. Houghton, Mifflin & Co sold to Cassell, of London, a set of plates of the *de luxe* edition of Longfellow, but before Routledge would let Cassell publish, he required him to break into those costly plates & remove those copyrighted poems. Mr. Cassell complied" ("Concerning the British 'Pirate'").

²⁰⁵ In "An Open Letter to Close a Correspondence" ("American Authors and British

& Harpers.

Get Publisher's Weekly Jan. annual

We think we pub ⟨10 or ⟨a⟩12⟩ 15 or 16 *new* authors a year.
Then it would cost little or nothing to P. P. protect *all of them.*

Therefore author⟨s⟩ may be to blame on first book, but even
then his pub is still more to blame.

First books of unknown & *partially* known *people*: 15 or 16
books.

It may be a good thing sometimes for an author to have *one*
book pirated & a scramble made—I think it true. Look at my first
book.[206]

Douglas. Takes everything, & pays on all—even when public
property, if a profit results.

An Englishman ⟨is⟩ has written a history & *has* no publisher but
his American H O H & Co[207]—& *they* provide him an Eng
publisher.

Roberts Bros—⟨Miss [- - - - -]⟩ for 15 years; have used P P & not
a miscarriage. [#]

Pirates," *New Princeton Review,* January 1888), Brander Matthews cited Thomas Went-
worth Higginson's *Common Sense About Women* (Boston: Lee and Shepard, 1882) as
an example of a book that had gone through several pirated and abridged English editions
until all market for a legitimate English version was destroyed. In the unpublished "Mr.
Matthews's Second Article," Clemens composed a "Parable of the Scholar & the Rats"
comparing Higginson's failure to arrange for English copyright through previous English
publication to the embarrassment of a sage "Equipp'd with all of those sorts of Knowledge that be Great & Fine & High" who wrote "a great Book" and left it "out Doors to
Dry, where abode divers Rats." After the rats had "made a Continuous Whole through
his Book & Devour'd a many Chapters & Defil'd the rest," the scholar was overcome with
grief and reviewed "in Harrowing language the Particulars & Details of his Misfourtune,"
unable to explain his failure to "protect the Book with this Rat Trap . . . here near at
Hand unused."

[206] Clemens here alludes to the commercially successful piracies of *The Celebrated
Jumping Frog of Calaveras County, and Other Sketches* by George Routledge and Sons
in 1867 and by John Camden Hotten in 1870. These successes occasioned a competitive
"scramble" by Routledge and Hotten to secure Clemens' authorization for English
publication of his future works.

[207] H. O. Houghton & Company was a Cambridge, Massachusetts, printing firm.

They frequently P. P.

Routledge can prevent H O H from publishing Lonfellow in England without eliminating *his* copyrighting.

⟨A great London pub—says We consider it perfect, but don't⟩ Use Lon if you want to.

It might cost $3000—a single book.

No doubt about P. P by a dozen copies & no cost to author.[208]

Aldrich chasing little dog round circle in dark & shouting for help. Both scared to death.

Aldrich buys 6 bottles of citrate of magnesia & treats his card party by the goblet.

Aldrich's bald-headed grandfather, prize (& only) pear, & the good-marksman monkey.

Fields's man, boy, & can of peaches.

Twichell & the ostler.

Aldrich's man who painted the fat toads red, & the frantic naturalist trying to catch them.

I would like to go to the State House

Adventure with U. S. Marshal in Chicago who had a bill for $21

Aldrich & the crutch. [#]

Henry O. Houghton, a partner in that establishment, was also a partner in Houghton, Mifflin & Company. It is the publishing company that Clemens intended here and below (365.2–3) as the publishers of Longfellow.

[208] In "P.P.S. A Recapitulation," directed at Brander Matthews, Clemens wrote: "An author is entitled to a dozen copies or so of his book free of cost. Let his publisher send these to a London house, with instructions to place five of them in the great libraries, as required by the law, & advertise the rest & place them on sale twenty-four hours before the book is issued here. A 'previous publication' copyright, on these terms, is within the reach of any author whose book has had merit enough to secure an American publisher."

Twichell's naval officer who stopped swearing for 3 years.

In the mines, if you neglected for a certain time to work your claim, it was held to be abandoned, & anybody could take it. It did not hurt the character of the taker. He was not a thief. The "pirate" who takes an American's abandoned book is not a thief. You have no reasonable complaint against him.[209]

If you had leveled your complaint agst the Am. author & publisher you'd have *had* a complaint.[210]

Ticknor & Co. We P P all books that seem to be worth the trouble. We do this for *future* value—the Bk may become valuable some day, so we protect it for 5/6 & postage &c on ⟨½ dozen⟩ 6 copies in paper.

One publishers says "They expose it in the window; *that* advertises it; ⟨n[ow] boy comes in & bu⟩ take it to ⟨Simpson⟩Simpkins & Marshall & subscribe it—(See copy)

Story of "Margaret Kent".[211] Griffin & Farren published it not knowing it was copyrighted; whereupon Trübner & Co. called their attention to the fact & ⟨they⟩ Ticknor allowed them to sell the edition (it was already printed) by buying the right. He *instantly accepted* the *situation* & said "⟨Ass[-]⟩What have I got to pay." They are very nice people & not pirates.

This is the only case thus far & *it* was a mistake. [#]

---

[209] Clemens also compared abandoned to pirated property in "Mr. Matthews's Second Article" and in "Concerning the British 'Pirate'" (Doheny), but used a more common nautical metaphor, identifying "an abandoned vessel & cargo" with "an abandoned American book."

[210] "When you speak of the 'misdeeds' of certain British publishers, the word has no meaning. The blame belongs with the American author; it is he that deserves the lash. *The American author is the father, the creator, of the so-called British 'pirate.'* He begot him, he is his own child; he feeds him, nurses him, coddles him, shelters him, protects him; & if he did his plain simple duty & withdrew this support, the 'pirate' would in that instant cease to exist in *fact* as he has already & long ago ceased to exist in *law*" ("Mr. Matthews's Second Article"). Mark Twain used a similar argument in "Concerning the British 'Pirate.'"

[211] *The Story of Margaret Kent*, a popular novel by Ellen Warner Kirk, who used the pseudonym Henry Hayes, was originally published by Ticknor and Company in 1886. It was later also published by Houghton, Mifflin & Company and went through at least forty-five editions.

Ticknor. "P. P. is a burden to nobody. ⟨It⟩ No author is so poor or so obscure that he cannot PP if he have an Am publisher."

T & Co

"And P. P is enough. We make no Canada trips."[212]

The ⟨⅚⟩5/6 ⟨is⟩ fee is charged to author by ⟨T &⟩Ticknor & Co.

T & Co. "When we sell an edition to London, *they* pay that 5/6 fee.

"When we have sold say 1000 copies to L & are pressed for time, we mail 6 or 6 copies & PP—& then take our time to ship the rest."

⟨"You⟩ The substance of the English is: the book must be delivered at the British Musem within a month after ⟨af⟩publication—the copies to the other libraries are to be delivered *if demanded.*

So Brit M would seem to be sufficient (in law) but custom acts otherwise

⟨Our (say 1860) law was 50 cents damages for every ⟨page⟩ sheet (8ᵛᵒ or 16) 320 pages 16ᵐᵒ would be $10 a copy & the pirate must pay that for every copy *in his possession* whether sold or not.⟩

Now it is exemplary damages—& weak.

You are pirated. You sue. The pirate proves that although he sold a good many, he made no profit. Then there is no ⟨p⟩damage proved, & nothing to collect it from. You could not prove damage by showing how many you *might* have sold if you hadn't been pirated. Our law is absolutely worthless. And yet even ⟨the⟩ a *shadow* (when it's law) is a protection—people are afraid to infringe it. [#]

---

[212] In "P.P.S. A Recapitulation," Mark Twain reproved Brander Matthews on this point: "You think I admit that the American author must go to the expense of a journey . . . to Canada in order to get English copyright; but what I said [in "A Private Letter and a Public Postscript" (*New Princeton Review,* January 1888)] will not permit that interpretation. If you want both English *and* Canadian copyright you must make that journey, & that is what my language makes clear; I explained . . . that 'previous publication' in England would secure English copyright—no journey necessary."

The English law—in substance: (as to *importing* a copyrighted book.) Every copy is forfeited; the offender is fined £10 for every such offence, & double the value of every copy. (And they destroy the book—don't try to collect duty on them.) The above applies to *my* books, too.

Book of Birds?

SHAVE.

Get 2 or 3 Sept. New Princetons.[213]

See Gilder about editorial work for R. E. Burton.[214]

Get tickets for night & morning Opera.

229 ⟨—⟩W. 34ᵗʰ Hutton

SHAVE. Get $100. Op. Book.

Read for Historical Class last Monday in February.

Jan. 16, about $10,000.

Jan 21— 9,798.
    25—10,352

Chas Warren Stoddard & his horse-scene on the stage:

Young Roe's Sunday trip with the girls & the sick mare to Sunday Church.

⟨A⟩Isaacs Menken & her horse on Va City Stage.[215] [#]

---

[213] The *New Princeton Review* for September 1887, in which Brander Matthews' initial article on "American Authors and British Pirates" had appeared.

[214] The son of the late Hartford clergyman, Nathaniel J. Burton. Richard E. Burton had recently edited a volume of his father's writings for Charles L. Webster & Company (see p. 339, note 117). Clemens planned to request the assistance of Richard Watson Gilder, editor of the *Century*, in finding further work for Burton.

[215] Clemens here recalled the scantily-clad equestrian appearances of Adah Isaacs Menken in Henry M. Milner's melodrama, *Mazeppa*. He attended her performances in both Virginia City and San Francisco in the early 1860s.

Jo's soldiers having teeth pulled.

Pff! Sweet as a nut—Keep a week!

The preacher's "Stone soup" of doctrine.[216]

My darkies & the snow-shovel.[217]

Bill—Bill—Bill—give—me—that h-a-n-d-spike—A—men! Anthem.

Whittier yarn.

Bogus Jay Gould & the brakeman

 Last Mon Feb.

Do dish-yer k'yah go to de town limit?

Bram Stoker's yarn last.

The German Lesson—Fishwife.[218]

Aunty Cord's story.[219]

Hunting sock.[220]
Lucerne⟨.⟩ girl.
Buck Fanshaw. [#]

---

[216] "Stone Soup" is a Belgian folk tale. It has numerous permutations, but usually involves a hungry traveler and a niggardly household which refuses to furnish him with a meal. Under the pretext of producing soup from a stone, the traveler tricks the occupants of the house into providing a pot of water and a succession of ingredients until a hearty soup results. The preacher referred to by Clemens has not been identified.

[217] Clemens' unpublished piece, "The Snow-Shovelers" (see p. 358, note 186).

[218] Mark Twain's "Tale of the Fishwife and Its Sad Fate," part of his attack on "The Awful German Language" (Appendix D, *A Tramp Abroad*).

[219] Aunty Cord, a freed slave, was the cook at the Elmira home of Theodore and Susan Crane, where the Clemenses spent their summers. Mark Twain's "A True Story, Repeated Word for Word As I Heard It," an account of Aunty Cord's reunion with one of seven children sold away from her, appeared in the *Atlantic Monthly* of November 1874. It was his first contribution to that journal.

[220] Mark Twain's account of the nocturnal pursuit of a sock in a Heilbronn hotel room appears in chapter 13 of *A Tramp Abroad*. His embarrassing Lucerne encounter with a young woman traveler is described in chapter 25 of the same work. Buck Fanshaw's death and funeral are the subjects of chapter 47 of *Roughing It*.

6th ave L to Cortlandt St ferry. 3.40 train. No SEAT

Jan. 25. This morning's Trib. contains 36½ col. of reading &
commercial matter, of which ⅓ i.e. 12½ col. were set by *hand*. They
have 27 machines, & say that they ⟨u[s]s⟩*use* 23 of them. Reid
says they use but 12 of them. Well, at *that* rate, each machine sets
but 2 col (10 or 11,000 ems) in 8 hours.

Knock out the leads, & the machine-matter in this issue (6 pages,
a large proportion of it leaded),—Jan. 25), amounts to but little
over 100,000 ems. ⟨U⟩That is to say, the 12 machines averaged
something over 1000 ems per hour each. *With* the leads the matter
amounts to only 125,000 ems, which is about 1250 ems per hour for
the 12 machines—(8 hours.)

Jan. 21. Mr. Crane bought four drawing room for 11 a. m. They
sold him 4 for 9 a.m. ⟨He⟩Mr. Halstead redeemed ($1 apiece) C's
2, but Clara already had hers. She took the 11 am & found her
tickets no good. These tickets were sold for a train which was
already gone.

Pope's Life for Alice

Paige invent stove—coal stove

80% of coal mined is stove, 30% is chestnut—& so chestnut is
scarce & the former dull.

Miss, would you be so kind as to ft here & go outside & shit[e]

Blind Tom.

Twichell & the hostler.

"Parker's the minister for *me*.²²¹

"I live over in the pest house. [#]

---

²²¹ The subject of this unrecovered anecdote was probably Edwin Pond Parker, the
prominent Congregational clergyman. Parker had been pastor of the Second Church of
Christ in Hartford since 1860.

Chicago prices & Courier-Journal, 41 for ⟨[n]⟩day, 46, night.
Cincinnati, 39½ ⟨[ni]⟩day, 42½ night.

"Wh— house in Front st"²²²

Trib. Jan. 30/80, Monday.

Hand—　96,200.⎫
Machine, 116,000.⎭

Mach. Non.　39,700.⎫
　　　　　　37,000⎬ 2 ems of nonpareil
　　　　　　76,700⎭

　　Min.　14,400⎫　to
　　　　　16,800⎬ 1 of minion.
　　　　　31,200⎭

　　　　　76,700
　　　　107,900

　Brev.　8,000⎫
　　　　115,900

The Eclectic—anually.²²³

The chicken-trial in Bermuda.²²⁴

& Maybe more from the same source.

My Duel.²²⁵ [#]

---

²²² The punch line of an anecdote about Charles H. Clark's young son. Mark Twain recorded the complete story on page 113.

²²³ The *Eclectic Magazine of Foreign Literature*, published from 1844 to 1907.

²²⁴ Clemens noted this event, involving cats as well as chickens, in detail in the notebook he kept during his 1877 trip to Bermuda (see N&J2, p. 28). He included a version of the anecdote in an installment of "Some Rambling Notes of an Idle Excursion" (*Atlantic Monthly*, December 1877).

²²⁵ Mark Twain described this supposed near-fatal encounter with James L. Laird of the Virginia City *Daily Union* in an Autobiographical Dictation of 19 January 1906 (*MTA*, 1:355–359; also *Mark Twain of the "Enterprise,"* ed. Henry Nash Smith [Berkeley and Los Angeles: University of California Press, 1957], pp. 24–28, 191–203).

Blue-jay.[226]

Jan. 28—9,538.76

Get a rubber sprinkler.
Write Chatto.[227]
Get a knife
Inquire about B^r alarm

Feb. 7, Van[228] set 6,356 solid Brevier (7,355 leaded, Herald) in exactly 1 hour on his board.

Der Herr Jesus!
Bret Harte's proof-reader.[229]
"S— of b—!"
"If ever go to hell I want to go in ox wagon".
"Adam? What was his first name?
Jean says there is a difference in things—even snakes. "Now the rattlesnake is a very good KIND of a bad *thing.*"

Feb. 8, Van set ⟨[ag,]⟩ 997 in 1 hour by hand—solid—& distributed it in 25½ minutes.

Courant wages now, are 40 cents. Case Lockwood,[230] 34 cents— mainly because book work is pretty nearly *always* leaded.

What returns from the Pope in foreign lands?

Chatto contract [#]

---

[226] This favorite platform yarn is in chapter 3 of *A Tramp Abroad.*

[227] Webster & Company was making arrangements for English publication of *Mark Twain's Library of Humor* by Chatto & Windus, Clemens' regular English publishers. On 27 January 1888, Andrew Chatto had written Clemens reminding him of "the steps necessary to be taken to secure copyright in Great Britain, Canada, & the US."

[228] Charles G. Van Schuyver, the experienced compositor who was one of Paige's assistants.

[229] Evidently a reference to the anecdote about Bret Harte's unfortunate experience as a proofreader which Clemens included in an Autobiographical Dictation of 4 February 1907 (see *MTE*, pp. 268–269).

[230] The Case, Lockwood & Brainard Company, Hartford printers and binders.

Several books to decide on?

Decide *date* for my book.[231]

See Pond.

Talk with U. Johnson on A.M. Palmer's proposition.[232]
And Pond's.

And the League's own.

If you pub my pamphlet, you want to first send word to all
Custom Houses on border.[233] [#]

---

[231] *Mark Twain's Library of Humor* had originally been scheduled for publication on
15 March 1888. The lengthy process of securing permission from excerpted authors and
their publishers, still continuing in mid-February 1888, was causing delay. There were also
complications in coordinating prior British and Canadian publication of the book so as to
establish Clemens' foreign copyrights (see p. 376, note 248).

[232] Robert Underwood Johnson, associate editor of the *Century* magazine, was secretary of the American Copyright League. Albert Marshman Palmer was a prominent New
York theatrical manager who organized the Washington authors' readings for international copyright of March 1888 (see p. 376, note 249). The propositions by Palmer and
James B. Pond mentioned here were probably related to those readings, part of the
league's 1887–1888 campaign to secure Congressional passage of an international copyright bill. Although the desired legislation was passed by the Senate in the spring of 1888,
the House of Representatives failed to act on it. An international copyright act was not
passed until 1891.

[233] In 1889 the American Copyright League published Brander Matthews' two *New
Princeton Review* articles on "American Authors and British Pirates" in pamphlet form.
They may have considered including Clemens' "A Private Letter and a Public Postscript"
and possibly one of his three unpublished pieces on the subject (see p. 362, note 201).
One of these, "Concerning the British 'Pirate,'" closes with Clemens' comment that
"inasmuch as England has for twenty years given American authors perfect copyright at
cost of one penny & no trouble, it may not be improper or unpatriotic to hope that Congress will see & believe that our government ought now to respond in kind. And it seems
to me that the best & rightest way to do this would be to . . . pass the just & liberal bill
urged by our Authors' League" (Doheny). Clemens' reference to custom houses emerged
from a December 1887 dispute with a United States customs official over procedures to
stop foreign piracies of *Roughing It* from entering the country. Clemens resented the fact
that although his rights to *Roughing It* and his right to deny entry to a pirated edition
were recognized he was expected to pay the import duty on the books before confiscating
them. He now wished to warn the American Copyright League that if they did not file "in
the several police offices along the border, proof of ownership of the originals" of any
pamphlet subsequently pirated, the United States government would simply collect its
duty from the pirate and allow his goods to "circulate in this country" (see SLC to H. C.
Christiancy, *MTL*, pp. 479–482).

See Edison?[234]

Chas. Giblin, 424 W. 55th.[235]

Feb. 10— ¼ of Trib to-day is handwork.

Tell W. Mrs. C. will sign checks[236]

Have Van do 4 hours every other day.

Look for Watterson.[237]

W. bring down satchel.

In Topeka the Typothet [238] employ 300 persons—⟨[as]⟩doubtless 200 ⟨or [more as]⟩ compositors.

Feb. 16, 1888. On the 13th we at last got Webster to retire from business, from all authority, & from the city, till April 1, 1889, & try to get back his health. How ⟨log⟩ long he has been a lunatic I do not know; but several facts suggest that it began in the summer or very early in the fall of '85,—while the 1st vol of the Grant Memoirs was in preparation & the vast canvass[239] [#]

---

[234] Since November 1887, Clemens had been planning to consult Edison about use of the phonograph as a literary subject (see pp. 346 and 347). The present entry, made in February 1888, is evidently a further reminder of the same errand.

[235] On the evening of 15 February 1888, Charles Giblin, a young "wireworker" and "native of Ireland" living at this address, wounded grocer Valentine Goelz in the shoulder and jaw and fatally shot Goelz's wife Madeline in a struggle over a counterfeit five-dollar bill with which he had attempted to buy some pastry (New York *Times*, 16 February 1888). Police found what they claimed were counterfeiting tools at Giblin's residence and accused him of belonging to "a gang that has been disposing of raised bills" (New York *Times*, 18 February 1888), that is, currency whose denomination had been increased. On 21 June 1888, Giblin was convicted of first-degree murder. Four days later he was sentenced to death by hanging. Clemens would allude to subsequent developments in this sensational case in a notebook entry of September 1889 (see p. 520, note 124).

[236] While he was in New York, Clemens intended that Livy sign the checks with which Franklin G. Whitmore was to pay typesetter and other business costs.

[237] Henry Watterson, for many years editor of the Louisville, Kentucky, *Courier-Journal*. Clemens had already noted that paper's compositor-expense (371.1) and probably intended to describe the Paige typesetter's virtues.

[238] A local chapter of the United Typothetae of America, the national association of master printers.

[239] Since the summer of 1887, Charles L. Webster had frequently been absent from business because of a chronic condition diagnosed as acute neuralgia. In a letter of 29 December 1887, Webster himself attributed the physical deterioration to his efforts on

Write Theodore Roosevelt.[240]

Kinsmen meeting
229 W 34th, Tuesday
21st Feb at 4 pm.[241]

Give me the *other* Chatto contract.[242]

Get Kinglake's Crimean War—v small vols—Harper[243]

"I want my Blaine!—I *will* have my Blaine!" [#]

---

behalf of the Grant *Memoirs:* "I am not whining but I have actually ruined my health by the hard work which I did two years ago." And he noted: "if it is thought that I do not earn my salary I am willing to make some arrangement to retire from the firm." Nevertheless, he closed with a plea for continuation of the partnership, explaining that "while I have nothing but kind feelings for you my duty to wife & family tells me I must not relinquish any part of my share." Given the antagonism toward Webster evident in this notebook and in Notebook 26, the suggestion of retirement must have been irresistible to Clemens. Although Webster's disengagement was, as noted here, planned as a temporary measure, he was never again allowed to become an active member of the firm. In late December 1888, after involved negotiations, Webster was persuaded to sell his share of the business to Frederick J. Hall.

[240] Clemens may have thought to entice another author from the Century Company as he had previously done with Grant and Nathaniel J. Burton (see p. 339, note 117). Roosevelt, unsuccessful candidate for mayor of New York in 1886, had already published his first books and by early 1888 his "Ranch Life in the Far West" was being serialized in the *Century.* Any overtures by Clemens were in vain, however, for Roosevelt's next book, *Ranch Life and the Hunting Trail,* was published by the Century Company in 1888.

[241] This meeting of the Kinsmen was to be at the home of Laurence Hutton, who had introduced Clemens into the group in 1883.

[242] Webster & Company had been discussing arrangements for English publication of *Mark Twain's Library of Humor* with Chatto & Windus since the fall of 1887. The English publishers had originally proposed that Webster & Company supply "electros of the illustrations at the same rate as we paid you for those of 'Huckleberry Finn' and we paying Mr Clemens the same royalty" (Chatto & Windus to CLW & Co., 3 October 1887). Webster specified, however, that "we should probably want a somewhat different arrangement from that on 'Huckelberry Finn'; at least, we would want you to account to us, and not to Mr. Clemens, as our partnership arrangement is now such that we will be obliged to have the account made in the manner indicated" (CLW to Chatto & Windus, 19 October 1887). Nevertheless, a contract drafted by Chatto & Windus for the *Library of Humor* and received on 7 February 1888 "duplicated . . . the agreement made for 'Huck Finn' and 'The Prince and the Pauper'" (Andrew Chatto to SLC, 27 January 1888). Another contract was not received by Webster & Company and forwarded to Clemens until 6 March 1888.

[243] Between 1863 and 1888, Harper & Brothers published three six-volume editions of Alexander W. Kinglake's *Invasion of the Crimea: Its Origin, and an Account of Its Progress Down to the Death of Lord Raglan.*

History of the Inquisition—2 vols ready. (Harper.) Henry
C. Lea.[244]

Also, his "Sacerdotal Celibacy."

Depew's "Ready Speaker"—*now* is the time.[245]

Howells, 46 W. 9[th.]

Dinner—Dana—March 11, Sunday, 7.30 p.m.[246]

Go & see Geo. Iles.[247]

Chatto publish April 19th.
Pub in Canada the 20th
　" here about the 〈[3]〉23[d].[248]

Read in Washington Mch. 19.[249] [#]

---

[244] Henry C. Lea, *A History of the Inquisition of the Middle Ages*, 3 vols. (New York: Harper & Brothers, 1887). *An Historical Sketch of Sacerdotal Celibacy in the Christian Church*, by the same author, was originally published in 1867.

[245] Clemens was interested in a selection of speeches by Chauncey M. Depew, lawyer, president of the New York Central Railroad, and a celebrated wit and after-dinner speaker. Webster & Company was not able to secure rights to Depew's book. Issued by the Cassell Publishing Company in 1889, *Orations and After-Dinner Speeches of Chauncey M. Depew* was successful enough to twice require new editions.

[246] A dinner given by Charles A. Dana, owner and editor of the New York *Sun*, for the English actor Henry Irving. Irving and his company were in New York at this time for an extended engagement at the Star Theatre.

[247] George Iles—later an editor, anthologist, and scientific writer—had been manager of the Windsor Hotel in Montreal where Clemens stayed in 1881 while arranging for Canadian copyright of *The Prince and the Pauper*. Iles moved to New York City in 1887 and Clemens may have planned to see him there. It is possible, however, that at the time this entry was made Clemens was unaware of Iles's relocation and thought to renew their acquaintance in Montreal in April 1888 while copyrighting *Mark Twain's Library of Humor*.

[248] Here and below (377.7–9), Clemens planned the publication schedule for *Mark Twain's Library of Humor*. The English edition was published by Chatto & Windus on 20 April 1888, but the Canadian edition, published by Dawson Brothers of Montreal, was held up by an error in the shipment of printer's plates. On 21 April, Hall expressed relief at word that "no harm has been done" and assured Clemens, who was in Montreal to secure copyright, that Webster & Company had "four copies of the book ready to make publication with" in the United States "at any time."

[249] On 17 March and again on 19 March 1888, Clemens participated in authors' readings in Washington on behalf of the American Copyright League which was trying to convince Congress to pass an international copyright bill. On the day of the second reading,

Chas H Bass
  104 Albany ave
Dr. Edward H. Hooker.[250]

Speak to Gilder about Dawson's labors for copyright.[251]

Siamese Twins

Mrs. Cabell $10[252]

Chatto issue Apl. 20.
Dawson   " 21.
We, Apl. ——— 23.

⟨Letters about 3 books ([W to pnt.)]⟩

⟨Return it to Rev. Leopold Simonson, Hartford High
School.⟩[253]

Monday midnight March 26, (88) Delmonico's—supper to
Irving & Miss Terry—by Daly.[254] [#]

President and Mrs. Cleveland greeted the authors at a White House reception attended
by cabinet members and other government officials.

[250] On 2 April 1888, Clemens would receive a letter from Edward B. Hooker, a Nook
Farm neighbor, thanking him for attempting to find work for "my friend the engraver.
. . . You will be pleased to learn, I am sure, that Mr. Bass has, after considerable anxious
waiting, secured a position in Boston, so that for the present at least he is not in want."

[251] On 5 March 1888, Samuel Dawson, Clemens' Canadian publisher, wrote to Clemens of his long commitment to international copyright and his long service to American
authors. Dawson recalled that he had made his views on international copyright available
to Roswell Smith of the *Century* through copies of an original lecture, *Copyright in
Books: An Inquiry into Its Origin, and an Account of the Present State of the Law in
Canada* (Montreal: Dawson Brothers, 1882). Smith "was polite enough to write me that
he thought highly of it. . . . I asked him to notice the lecture which he did not do. Probably an obscure Canadian was not worth a notice. Nevertheless I feel that I have contributed a great deal more to the elucidation of this question than many who have been
airing their knowledge (or ignorance) of it. It seems to me that I have got very little credit
or thanks for it in the literary papers." Dawson enclosed two copies of his lecture which
convinced Clemens to plead the publisher's case with Richard Watson Gilder, who had
made the *Century* a primary force in the movement for international copyright.

[252] Probably Isa Carrington Cabell, a friend of the Charles Dudley Warners. This
transaction has not been identified.

[253] A teacher at the Hartford Public High School. It was probably his class that Clemens had entertained in late February 1888 (see 368.13).

[254] On 7 March 1888, Augustin Daly wrote to Clemens: "I'm going to give Mr. Irving
& Miss Terry a parting supper after the play on Monday night March 26th at Delmonicos

7th chap. Rob Roy—
269 Apl Hopes.[255]

⌗   The Bashaw of Bengal, 260 days out from Calcutta,
—homeward bound!—the ⟨m⟩Mary Ann, 3 days out from
Boston—only goin to Liverpool.[256]

Ask about Washington hotels—of Gilder?

See Geo. Iles.

BEECHER—take out Canadian copyright.

Chianti—*Maspero.*
University Place below W 9th.

The Land of the Morning Calm, Ticknor.[257]

Mme. Bovary—Translated by Mrs. Marx Aveling—English
Edition[258]

Pas de lieu Rhône que nous.[259] [⌗]

—and I shall be very glad if you will come. Indeed I'll be lost if you dont." Clemens noted
"*Yes*" on the envelope of Daly's letter.

[255] Clemens evidently meant to contrast Dan Mavering's enraptured praises of Alice
Pasmer on this page of Howells' *April Hopes* (New York: Harper & Brothers, 1888) with
Francis Osbaldistone's cautious response to Diana Vernon in chapter 7 of Scott's novel.
Both of these authors were to be included in a stylistic study Clemens contemplated on
page 379.

[256] An allusion to an anecdote from chapter 35 of Richard H. Dana's *Two Years Before
the Mast* which Mark Twain came to invest with great poignancy. Dana told how "a mean
little captain in a mean little brig," who vainly and needlessly "insisted on speaking a
great, homeward-bound Indiaman," received his comeuppance when required to identify
his own insignificant ship in turn. On 10 July 1907, shortly after the award of his cherished
Oxford degree, Mark Twain was given a farewell dinner by the lord mayor of Liverpool.
He closed his speech on that occasion with a moving amplification of Dana's anecdote,
comparing himself, in his disparate moods, to both the humble vessel "cargoed with vege-
tables and tinware" and the "stately Indiaman, ploughing the great seas under a cloud of
canvas" (see *MTS*[1923], pp. 372–374).

[257] *Chosön, the Land of the Morning Calm: A Sketch of Korea,* by Percival Lowell,
originally published in Boston by Ticknor and Company in 1886 and re-issued in 1888.

[258] This translation of Flaubert's novel by Eleanor Marx-Aveling, daughter of Karl
Marx, was published in London by Vizetelly & Company in 1886.

[259] This French nonsense phrase reproduces the sound of "Paddle your own canoe."

Murray Hill Hotel, New York., March 14, '88. I came down
here from Hartford, Saturday the ⟨11ᵗʰ⟩10ᵗʰ,—to dinner to
Henry Irving at Charles A. Dana's Sunday evening, & the
memorable ⟨b[u]zzard⟩blizzard has snow-bound me here ever since.
Not a train here from Hartford since early Monday morning.
Mrs. Clemens was to come down to-day, & we were going to
Washington to-morrow. Of course she will not come till everything
is smoothe again. I can't get a telegram nor a telephone to her nor
she a message to me. A Boston friend is better off: he cabled
Boston through London, & got an answer back promptly over the
same long road.[260]

R. M. Johnson, Uncle Remus, Cable, Howells, Clarence King,
(Harte, artificial) Stowe (Sam Lawson) Grant, (simple)
    Hardy, (Haggard, hideous) Stephenson (Kidnapped), Uncle Tom
(earlier, & dialect bad)
    Howells (truth).
    Pilgrim's Prog. Scott. Defoe (tone)
    Derby (Doesticks)[261] [#]

---

[260] When Clemens made this entry, New York City had hardly begun to dig out from
the massive snowstorm that began in the early hours of 12 March 1888 and continued
through the day. The city was paralyzed by a reported snowfall of nearly three feet and
by winds said to have reached speeds of sixty miles an hour. Most telegraph lines were
down or otherwise inoperable, streetcars were not running, elevated trains were blocked,
and many businesses and the New York Stock Exchange had been forced to close. Clemens filled most of a scrapbook with articles about the storm clipped from New York newspapers. On 16 March he wrote to Livy: "I have only just this moment given you up. All
these years since the blizzard ceased I have expected you 'next day,' & next day, & next
day—until now. I give it up. I no longer expect you. It is perfectly manifest that that road
will not be open for one or two—or possibly 30 days yet. So I will go along to Washington
this afternoon in the special car with the rest of the menagerie [authors participating in
readings for the American Copyright League (see p. 376, note 249)]. . . . Blast that
blasted dinner party at Dana's! But for that, I—ah! well, I'm tired; tired calling myself
names. Why, I could have been at home all this time. Whereas, here I have been, Cruso-
ing on a desert hotel—out of wife, out of children, out of linen, and out of cigars, out of
every blamed thing in the world that I've any use for. Great Scott!" (*LLMT*, pp. 249–
250). Hotel bills and correspondence suggest that Livy joined Clemens in Washington
around 18 March.

[261] Clemens evidently had in mind some extended comparison of the prose styles of
the writers listed or alluded to here. He is not known to have written such a piece.

⟨1 & 2—36. tickets (13)⟩

MARCH, 1888.[262]

Mrs. Ralph ⟨X⟩ ⟨T⟩X Johnson[263]

1735 I st. Saturday 5 pm

⟨Col. Alexander Bliss, 820 Conn Ave Wednesday 9½ pm.⟩[264]

Bancroft—evening

⟨Fortnightly 8 this pm.
Mrs. Lucius Tuckerman[265]
1600 I st⟩

8.30 Mrs. Kaufman (next Saturday evening.)—literary club—
Gen. Greeley essayist.[266]

8 Lafayette Sq—⟨([?])⟩ ⎱
Thursday night   ⎰ (?)

Com. on Enrolled Bills—Senator Bowen—on Senate floor.[267]
Senate. Adair Wilson. Wednesday, 2 p.m.[268] [#]

---

[262] The following engagements were to be kept while Clemens was in Washington,
D.C., for the 17 and 19 March 1888 American Copyright League authors' readings. Surviving hotel bills indicate that he remained in Washington until 26 March.

[263] The wife of Ralph Cross Johnson, the lawyer and prominent art patron who lived
in Washington.

[264] Alexander Bliss was the son of Mrs. George Bancroft by her previous marriage. As
the next entry indicates, Clemens also visited the aged historian while in Washington.

[265] Elizabeth Wolcott (Gibbs) Tuckerman, the granddaughter of Oliver Wolcott, a
signer of the Declaration of Independence. Her husband, Lucius, was an iron manufacturer.

[266] "Mrs. Kaufman" was probably the wife of Samuel Hay Kauffmann, one of the pro-
prietors of the Washington *Evening Star* and a member of the Washington Literary
Society. Brigadier General Adolphus Washington Greely, Civil War veteran, arctic ex-
plorer, and scientist, was author of the *Report on the Proceedings of the United States
Expedition to Lady Franklin Bay, Grinnell Land* (1888), as well as *Three Years of Arctic
Service* (1886), accounts of the arctic weather study he commanded in the early 1880s.
In 1888, Greely helped found the National Geographic Society and became a prolific
contributor to its journal.

[267] Thomas Meade Bowen, Republican senator from Colorado. Clemens evidently
had an appointment to speak with him about the international copyright bill under
consideration by the Congress.

[268] Adair Wilson had been a reporter for the Virginia City, Nevada, *Daily Union* while
Mark Twain was on the staff of the *Territorial Enterprise*. He was Colorado state senator
from 1886 until 1890.

Miss Clymer, Thursday, 4 p.m.

Thursday, dinner, Sec'y Whitney.[269]

Friday afternoon, Soldiers' Home.

Leave cards at Tuckerman's in afternoon Thursday.

Friday, dinner, 7.30—Mr. Hitt.[270]

Ck—4069. T. E. Roessle 110.[20] [271]

 Decoration Day

"Nothin' left to do in this life but keep it green. And I'm goin' to keep it green, by God, if I have to *paint* it." (Text of "He was jest wrapt up in Jim.")

Also Dec. Day—G⟨.⟩— ⟨G⟩D— that dog!

"I wish to God you *had!*"

Photo of M. T. "Where does she *play?*"[272]

"Name of the ship?"

Rabbi ben Ezra.[273]
Andrea del Sarto.
Up at a Villa.
The Mother & Poet. (Mrs. Bwⁿ

---

[269] "The Secretary of the Navy, William C. Whitney, is the moneyed man and entertainer of the Cabinet. . . . In society he is not only a liberal entertainer, but a man of very ready wit and fine conversational powers" (Randolph Keim, *Society in Washington: Its Noted Men, Accomplished Women, Established Customs, and Notable Events* [Washington, D.C.: Harrisburg Publishing Co., 1887], p. 45).

[270] Probably Robert R. Hitt, Republican congressman from Illinois, whom Clemens had met in Paris in 1879 when Hitt was serving as first secretary of the American legation there (see *N&J2*, p. 299).

[271] T. E. Roessle was manager of the Arlington, the hotel at which Clemens stayed in Washington. On 23 March 1888, Clemens paid a bill of $110.20 for a week's room and miscellaneous services. On 26 March he paid a second bill of $78.85 that included charges for 2¾ days' room and services, and for railroad tickets.

[272] The complete version of this anecdote occurs in Clemens' letter of 7 August 1884 to William Dean Howells (see *MTHL*, p. 498).

[273] Clemens evidently made this selection of poems for a scheduled meeting of his Browning circle. The entry at 383.1 indicates that he did not read them as planned.

In a Balcony.
 " " Gondola.

⟨A 1-1000ᵗʰ interest is worth \$1,000,000—sell it for 1/10ᵗʰ or
\$100,000.⟩

Smells like J. G's breath when ⟨his morals are working.⟩ ⟨he is
working his morals.⟩ his morals are working.

"He shot his wife & then himself."

Apl. 9/88. Now after 6 wks apprenticeship, Fred Whitmore has
set 40-odd-000 in 7 hours.[274]
Sept. 8, '88, he set 11,200 in 1 hour.

Fowle's trial, page 112.

Lippincott—

Carbolic acid.

Pads.—*take vial.*

Me Leddy—& the last one.

Dukesboro' Tales.[275]

Unfair trials of aristocrats

⟨Advowson's⟩Advowsons. B[low] Cathedrals.

Telegraph Charley Lang[276] [#]

---

[274] One of the sons of Franklin G. Whitmore. Clemens had previously employed
another son, William Whitmore, as a Paige typesetter operator (see p. 250, note 76).
The following sentence was, of course, added later.

[275] Richard Malcolm Johnston's volume of Georgia dialect sketches, originally published in 1871. Clemens included a tale from the 1883 edition of Johnston's work, "The
Expensive Treat of Colonel Moses Grice," in *Mark Twain's Library of Humor.* The immediate stimulus to Clemens' notation here was probably William Dean Howells' discussion of Johnston in the April 1888 *Harper's* magazine. In his "Editor's Study" Howells
noted that Johnston was "one of the truest humorists of a country superabundant in
humorists, and he has unfailingly the racy local flavor of the Southern humorist. *The
Dukesborough Tales* long ago gave proof of this" (p. 806).

[276] Clemens may have telegraphed to inform Charles J. Langdon of the state of Mrs.
Clemens' health. Around mid-April she was still suffering the effects of what Clemens
called "a savage combined attack of dipththeria & quinzy" (SLC to Candace Wheeler,

No Browning next week.

? Snow-photographs.[277]

Xn religion & whisky. Both good, in wise hands; the reverse in bad. Let good men do without, in the best interest of the unwise, & vote prohibition.

Gazetteer—"Maidenhead."
Dose of Medicine—Dr James Dic$^{[nar]y}$[278]

"The Egoist"—Meredith[279]

⟨Pencils—No 1.⟩

Mrs. C's umbrella at station.

Matthew Arnold's civilization is *superficial polish.*[280]

Torrens's book on India.
Lord Elgin's Diary & Letters.
Article in Nineteenth Century—within 7⟨—⟩yrs—first article of a certain number—on England's rule in India.[281] [#]

---

19 April 1888, Clifton Waller Barrett Library, University of Virginia, Charlottesville). The Browning class cancellation noted in the following entry was probably occasioned by that illness.

[277] Presumably photographs of the blizzard that crippled New York City in March 1888 (see p. 379).

[278] Robert James's *A Medicinal Dictionary; Including Physic, Surgery, Anatomy, Chymistry, and Botany, Together with a History of Drugs,* 3 vols. (London: T. Osborne, 1743–1745). On page 415, Clemens recorded a plan to use James's curious treatments in *A Connecticut Yankee.*

[279] Clemens probably intended to acquire this book for Livy (see p. 253, note 85).

[280] In early April 1888, Lorettus S. Metcalf, editor of the *Forum,* approached Clemens for an article in rebuttal of Matthew Arnold's criticisms of America in "Civilisation in the United States" (published in London in the *Nineteenth Century* for April 1888 and reprinted in the New York *Evening Post* on 9 April 1888). Clemens wished to comply, but on 13 April wrote to Metcalf that Livy's attack of "dipththeria" had "stopped the Arnold-article on the spot. . . . Therefore let us consider that all the chances are against having the article for your next number." Clemens did not complete an article for the *Forum,* although he did produce a quantity of somewhat diffuse manuscript on the subject. Indeed, he had so much to say that by June he would consider turning his reply to Arnold into a book (see p. 391, note 311).

[281] William Torrens McCullagh Torrens, *Empire in Asia, How We Came by It: A Book of Confessions* (London: Trübner & Co., 1872); *Letters and Journals of James,*

Japan siezed a coolie ship with 1100 & liberated them.

Sirry Harry Parkes (at bottom) forced a cholera ship in & cost 100,000 lives in 6 mos.[282]

A World "Want" page contains 42,000 without the rules, ⟨add 3,[3]oo.⟩ & ⟨45,000⟩45,500 or 46,000 *with* them.

The 13 Want pages could be set by 13 good men in 7½ hours.

Tribune page, smallest type, 36,000.

No, there *is* no reverence with us.[283] I remember once in a dream I went to Heaven, & noticed there that it was an ordinary thing for Americans to hail Michael the archangel as he went by with a hearty & friendly "Hello, Mike!"

to refer to M the A simply as "Mike."

When the machine is setting 5,000 an hour, it is doing the work of 6¼ men, because it ⟨al⟩is also distributing; 4 machines thus do the work of 25 men; 8, the work of 50 men; 16, the work of 100 men. This will hold good on book work all the time.

An English hermit of the Middle Ages—"Whip & Spur," Waring, 191.[284] [#]

Eighth Earl of Elgin, Governor of Jamaica, Governor-General of Canada, Envoy to China, Viceroy of India, ed. Theodore Walrond (London: John Murray, 1872). "The Spoliation of India," a series of three articles by J. Seymour Keay which provided detailed criticism of England's activities in that country, appeared in the July 1883, April 1884, and May 1884 numbers of the *Nineteenth Century.* Clemens apparently planned to extract damaging examples of British civilization from these articles and books to use in his reply to Matthew Arnold's "Civilisation in the United States."

[282] Sir Harry Parkes was a prominent British foreign officer in China and Japan during the middle years of the nineteenth century. In 1878 Parkes was charged with responsibility for a Japanese cholera epidemic that occurred during disagreements over enforcement of quarantine regulations. The accusation was later dismissed as absurd.

[283] Clemens responded here to Matthew Arnold's belief that "if there be a discipline in which the Americans are wanting, it is the discipline of awe and respect," a condition he blamed in part upon the "addiction to 'the funny man,' who is a national misfortune there" ("Civilisation in the United States," *Nineteenth Century,* April 1888, p. 489). In late June 1888, Clemens would accept the award of an honorary Master of Arts degree from Yale University as a refutation of Arnold's aspersions and an affirmation of the humorist's "worthy calling" and "serious purpose" (see the headnote to this notebook).

[284] An account of the holy life of the seventh century English prelate, Saint Chad, part of a piece titled "In the Gloaming," appears on this page of *Whip and Spur* (Boston:

617 towns in U.S. of 4,000 & upwards.

970 dailies in US.

Sat., May 5, '88, the World had 185 compositors at work. It would take 37 machines to supply their place.

⟨New time-table.⟩

Fix watch.

Send watches & coat.

Ask D^r. Smith[285] about Greek & Latin for Susie.

Burglar alarm—11—Vassar alarm.

1 dozen malt to Montowese. take bottle.[286]

⟨Jean—picture writing-paper⟩

Description of the boarding house in "Pere Goriot."

There is a boardin" house
　　Far, far away[287]

⟨1 or 2, $15,000 apiece⟨. All⟩; 3 & upwards, $12,000?⟩[288]

4143, Wm Bryan & sons
　　May 14.—$80.20. [#]

James R. Osgood and Co., 1875), a collection of sketches by Clemens' friend, George E. Waring, Jr.

[285] The Reverend George Williamson Smith, president of Trinity College in Hartford. Clemens may have been seeking advice about a suitable program for sixteen-year-old Susy to follow as preparation for eventual college enrollment. Later in 1888 he also queried Joseph Hall, principal of Hartford Public High School, for on 24 August Hall advised him that "while we do not allow beginners to take two languages at once, for the reason that in most cases it would be too hard for them, I do not see that there would be any objection to allowing your daughter to take Latin, French, and Algebra next term and for the remainder of the school year, as she has already been over the Latin once and it will therefore be much easier for her than it would if she was beginning it."

[286] In the second week of May 1888, Clemens and Livy were at Montowese House at the shore in Branford, Connecticut. It was hoped that rest and changed surroundings would hasten Livy's recuperation from a recent illness (see note 276).

[287] Clemens probably recalled these verses as he made the preceding note about the shabby *pension* in which Goriot lived. For a discussion of the source of Clemens' song see page 38, note 76.

[288] Evidently proposed terms for sale of Paige typesetting machines.

Thos. A. Edison,
Llewellyn Park, N.J.[289]

World Manufacturing Co 122 Nassau st. Send me a $6 roller
organ.

The man that lost his false teeth ⟨[in]⟩over the brook-bridge
when on his way to propose to the widow.

The man that picked up Miss Reverdy Johnson's 3,000 tracts, &
"I believe you dropped these, Miss!" returned them to her.

4144. Twenty. J. Quin[290]

Army of the Cumberland,
Geo. W. Smith, Sept. 20.
Room 45, 99 Randolph st. Ch.[291]
Their last meeting was in 1868.

Stop at 19 Dey st.[292] [#]

---

[289] On 21 May 1888, Clemens wired Edison from the Murray Hill Hotel in New York,
attempting to make an appointment to see him about his phonograph. On 24 May,
Edison replied from his Orange, New Jersey, laboratory: "Will be glad to see you this
afternoon or any time to-morrow convenient to yourself. Am here all the time." Clemens
had already returned to Hartford, however, and did not see Edison until the following
month. His plans for the phonograph in the writing of *A Connecticut Yankee* are discussed in note 292.

[290] J. Scrugham Quin, Hartford ticket agent for the New York, New Haven & Hartford Railroad.

[291] The Chicago address of the Society of the Army of the Cumberland. On 21 May
1888, George W. Smith and the four other members of the Committee on Toasts invited
Clemens to take part in the society's first meeting in twenty years by speaking at its dinner
on 20 September 1888. Clemens planned to attend and on page 391 noted a possible
speech topic.

[292] The address of the New York office of the Edison Phonograph Company. Clemens
ordered one of their machines, but on 6 June 1888 Ezra T. Gilliland, general agent for
the company, explained: "Changes in the form of the phonograph have delayed the issue
of the machines. . . . You will receive an instrument from among the first ones that are
put out. . . . Our efforts to deliver it promptly will not be diminished by the knowledge
of the fact that one of 'Mark Twain's' books is dependent upon it." Clemens entertained
the notion of dictating *A Connecticut Yankee* to the phonograph. On 27 July 1888
Andrew Chatto, Clemens' English publisher, wrote to encourage him in such an experiment: "I hope you will soon tell the story of Smith of Camelot to Edisons phonograph
& let us have it." But on 30 July Clemens finally abandoned this scheme, canceling an
order for two phonographs which another firm, the North American Phonograph Com-

See Laffan.[293]

As to "Preface"

⟨[H]s⟩As to $20,000 lawsuit.

⟨A⟩One chapter of Sheridan to "Scribner?"[294]

⟨W⟩ Is canvassing matter in type? When will it be ready?[295]

Heard from Johnson?[296] [#]

---

pany, had been unable to fill. In 1891 he actually tried to dictate *The American Claimant* using a phonograph, but found the results unsatisfactory (see *MTHL*, pp. 637–641).

[293] Clemens evidently wished to have William M. Laffan's advice about some Webster & Company matters. It is not known what counsel he sought regarding the preface to the *Personal Memoirs of P. H. Sheridan*, which was scheduled for publication in the winter of 1888. The lawsuit may be an action for $30,000 against R. T. Root, a defaulting Iowa general book agent for the Grant *Memoirs*. In early June, Webster & Company attempted to negotiate a settlement of its claim (see p. 390, note 306).

[294] In the first half of 1888, Webster & Company was inconvenienced by Charles Scribner's determination to exact compensation for an unfulfilled contract in which Philip H. Sheridan had agreed to produce a book for his firm in collaboration with James B. Pond. In late June, wishing to avoid any threat to Sheridan's *Personal Memoirs*, Webster & Company promised to pay Charles Scribner's Sons $5,000 out of that work's eventual profits, half to come from Sheridan's share, and to allow selections from the book to appear in *Scribner's Magazine*. In return, Scribner would release Sheridan from all previous obligation. It wasn't until 3 August 1888, however, that all parties could settle on suitable excerpts, ones that would prove attractive to readers of the magazine without reducing the book's appeal. Sheridan's "From Gravelotte to Sedan," incorporating part of chapter 15 and all of chapters 16 through 18 of volume two of the *Memoirs*, appeared in the November 1888 number of *Scribner's Magazine*.

[295] On 14 June 1888, Frederick J. Hall was able to assure Clemens that "the [Sheridan] prospectus will be ready this afternoon."

[296] Probably Robert Underwood Johnson of the *Century* magazine. On 14 August 1888, evidently renewing previous overtures, Johnson would apply for permission to use selections from the Sheridan *Personal Memoirs* in the book version of the *Century's* "Battles and Leaders of the Civil War" series. In return Johnson promised that the magazine would consider a manuscript "autobiography of a slave" offered to Clemens by Mary Duncan, an impoverished and ailing Tennessee woman. Clemens' response to this proposal is not known, but on 24 August he offered Richard Watson Gilder the desired Sheridan material in return for hiring Mary C. MacDonald, an aspiring artist he wished to assist, "for a few months to do general utility work for you in her line of art" (American Academy of Arts and Letters, New York City). On 5 September Johnson responded for the *Century*: "We accept your proposition and I will write details to-morrow." That same day, however, Frederick J. Hall protested that the *Century* book would provide undesirable competition for the Sheridan work. He recalled that Colonel M. V. Sheridan, Philip H. Sheridan's brother, who was handling many of the details on the *Personal Memoirs*,

You'll have to do the Department, & turn the rest over to Wright.[297]

Title of Sheridan's book.[298]

All prices same as Gen. Grant's.[299] [#]

---

had expressed a similar reservation, which constituted a sufficient reason for withdrawal from the *Century* agreement. On 6 September, Clemens wrote to Johnson: "Oh, hang it, I've got to withdraw that guaranty of mine, now that Col. Sheridan objects, as Mr. Hall writes me" (New York Public Library). Mary C. MacDonald's sketches did not appear in the *Century* magazine, nor did any part of Philip H. Sheridan's *Personal Memoirs* appear in the *Century* book.

[297] On 19 May 1888, Hall had written at length to Clemens about "certain glaring defects in the organization of our Subscription Department." Chief among these was the performance of W. E. Dibble, recently hired at Webster's insistence to manage subscription sales. Although Hall found him "a thoroughly conscientious man" of unimpeachable "honesty, integrity and willingness," Dibble "lacks education and culture, and is positively slovenly. He seldom wears a cravat, washes his hands semi-annually, and never cleans his nails nor cuts them; he is continually smoking, not a good cigar, to which there would be no objection, but the cheapest sort of a weed. He talks ungrammatically, and his letters are unique specimens of illegible chirography, poor composition and bad spelling." Dibble had "a knack of getting hold of men," but was not able "to retain good canvassers after securing them." Hall proposed that Dibble be replaced with "a first-class man, one who would take entire charge of the selling of our books, whip up our General Agents when they lagged and get rid of them when they were not satisfactory, drive our canvassers, and make every part of the country pan out just so much." He noted that he had formerly done all this, but with Webster gone he had to devote himself to the department that "dictates the general policy of the office, deals with the authors, manufactures the books and attends to the finances" and could "give but little time to [the subscription] branch of the business." Beginning in June 1888, Arthur H. Wright, the company "Cashier" who prepared Clemens' brief monthly statements, began to send him extensive reports of the firm's financial condition and activities, signaling at least some implementation of the shift in responsibilities Clemens called for here. Nevertheless, Dibble remained manager of the subscription department through 1888.

[298] As this entry and the following two show, Clemens was conscious of the advantages of associating the *Personal Memoirs of P. H. Sheridan* with Grant's very successful work of similar title. Hall, equally aware of the benefits of such an association, also recognized its dangers. On 19 May he had observed that "the way we handle [Sheridan's book] will either increase the good reputation made on the 'Grant Memoirs' or destroy it." He warned Clemens that while "people are so tired of 'war-literature' that something extraordinary is required to command large sales . . . General Sheridan will probably take Grant's 'Memoirs' as the standard by which to judge of the success of his own."

[299] On 5 June 1888, in response to Clemens' order to this effect, Hall proposed that the Sheridan work sell for "$3.00 a volume, $6.00 a set" since it "will make a scant 500 pages to each volume, and the volumes will probably be a trifle thinner than the 'Grant.' . . . You will remember that we had a great many complaints about the price of the Grant book, and . . . all whom I have talked with advise lessening the price of the

Save MS for de luxe—don't let it be given away.[300]

4145—June 2—$6. Norwood House.

"Aus zwei Übeln das Kleinste⟨[-s]⟩ wählen."[301] Übereilen Sie
sich nicht, don't hurry.

Durch Überfall einnehmen, take by surprise.

Einer Sache überdrüssig seyn, got enough of it, tired of it.

I cannot see how a man of ⟨l⟩any large degree of humorous
perception can ever be religious—except he purposely shut the eyes
of his mind & keep them shut by force.

Ings Complete Works.[302]

Shall I go to Washington & get that Preface to Gen. Sheridan's
book?[303]

Have you got that canvassing book ready?[304]

You ceased to send me proofs.

Why am not I put down for an *immediate* copy of every book
issued?

How is Custer selling?[305] [#]

Sheridan. . . . The difference to us is very slight as the 50cts. extra on each volume
goes principally to the General Agent and the canvasser." The price for the Sheridan
Memoirs was set at the figure Hall preferred.

[300] Webster & Company had planned, but did not publish, a deluxe edition of the
Grant *Memoirs* with manuscript pages bound in.

[301] *Choose the lesser of two evils.* Clemens provides translations of the other idioms
which follow.

[302] Mark Twain may have considered a collection of Robert G. Ingersoll's lectures on
agnosticism for publication by Charles L. Webster & Company.

[303] On 15 June 1888, Frederick J. Hall wrote Clemens about progress on the Sheridan
Memoirs, noting "the importance of getting a short manuscript preface from the General," who was seriously ill at this time. Although the preface that appears in Sheridan's
work is dated 2 August 1888, a first draft was actually written in Washington on 13 May
and revised on 3 August, only two days before Sheridan's death.

[304] Webster & Company sent Clemens a copy of the Sheridan prospectus on 15 June
1888.

[305] Webster & Company had only recently begun selling Elizabeth Custer's *Tenting
on the Plains,* which was printed at the end of 1887, having held it back so as not to interfere with the sales campaigns for Samuel S. Cox's *Diversions of a Diplomat in Turkey*

Iowa lawsuit.[306]

Have a dozen of my mem. books made, Whitmo.[307]

Cipher on the cost & *see* if you can make the General's book
at $3.

See Edison.

See the type-machine in 4th or 9th st.

Get Jean a "Liberty."

Get Clara a jewel.

Make appointments with D^r. Rice for L & S afternoon 22^d.

Habberton's book.[308] [#]

(1887) and *Mark Twain's Library of Humor* (1888). On 4 June, Hall was pleased to report
that the firm had "gotten rid of" a satisfying number of books, including "a little over
100 Custer, all within the last two weeks." Mrs. Custer was not satisfied with the company's unproductive efforts on behalf of her book, however, and in December 1888
offered to buy the rights to it in order to place it with another publisher. Her offer was
refused.

[306] The $30,000 lawsuit against R. T. Root, an Iowa general book agent who had failed
to make payment for the Grant *Memoirs*. On 11 June 1888, Hall reported to Clemens
that Webster & Company lawyers advised that "if we can get fifteen, or even twelve
thousand dollars, it is best to accept it." No such settlement was achieved, however, and
court proceedings were continued. In January 1889, Webster & Company won a judgment of $31,433.33 against Root, but agreed to settle for $9,000 when it became clear that
his property could not yield much more. After paying the Grants their share of the settlement, Webster & Company retained only $2,000.

[307] On 11 July 1888, Whitmore informed Clemens: "I ordered 12 Memorandum books
of the Plimpton Cy. for you at a cost $11.^{25} This is about as cheap as they can be gotten
up & made first class as per your own as sample." On 16 July, Clemens acknowledged
Whitmore's report, commenting: "It was eminently just like me to order 12 memorandum books when 4 would answer." The Plimpton Manufacturing Company of Hartford
actually billed Clemens $11.00 for these tab-page notebooks of his design, eight of which
are known to survive (Notebooks 29 through 36). Clemens' manner of using this style of
notebook is described in the headnote to Notebook 22.

[308] John Habberton, a member of the editorial staff of the New York *Herald*, was the
author of the immensely popular *Helen's Babies* (1876), based on the mischievous activities of his own two sons, as well as fifteen books of lesser fame. On 16 May 1888 he wrote
to Clemens "to ask whether your publishing house could stand a new war book—one with
scarcely a sign of a battle in it, but full of the life and incidents over which the old boys of
both armies chat most. I am about finishing such a story, of over 100,000 words. . . . As I
went through three different branches of the service—half the time as a private soldier—

Cheney's, Wed. June 13. Train leaves here 5.10. & returns at 10.10.

⟨Suspendrs.⟩

Murray Hill telegraph the Delavan for me.[309]

For Chicago speech.—"It was a campaign lie."[310]

Title of book. "English Criticism on America. Letters to an English Friend."[311]

13 & 14 Dr. Rice is in Canada—will see L & S—⟨n⟩afternoon of 22 bet 5 & 6. 115 E. 18th C. C.

There is a very prominent English town whose name is barred to ears polite[312]

4146—Delavan House, June 8—$2.25.

Collection Schick
L. Schick, publisher, Chicago.
get it of C. Schoenhof, 144 Tremont st Boston.[313] [#]

I think I know it all, so far as the life of camp and field go." Clemens had a fervent dislike for *Helen's Babies,* as late as 17 January 1887 calling it "the very worst & most witless book the great & good God Almighty ever permitted to go to press" (SLC to Belle C. Greene), and refused Habberton's war book, which was never published.

[309] The Delavan House was a hotel in Albany, New York. The entry at 391.12 suggests that Clemens sent a check to that hotel to hold a reservation. It is not known if he actually went to Albany.

[310] The title of a speech for delivery to the Society of the Army of the Cumberland on 20 September 1888 (see p. 386, note 291). Clemens almost immediately changed his subject, however, and made the notes that appear below (392.4–13) for a speech on "The American Press." A few days before he was to attend the society's dinner, however, he was forced to withdraw after Theodore Crane suffered a paralytic stroke.

[311] A tentative title for the book Mark Twain considered writing in reply to Matthew Arnold's recent criticisms of the United States (see p. 383, note 280).

[312] Probably Maidenhead. On page 383, Clemens noted the appearance of this town's name in a gazetteer.

[313] Carl Schoenhof was a book importer and publisher from whom, on 25 July 1888, Clemens would order a number of volumes of the *Collection Schick: Novellen, Humoresken und Skizzen,* 23 vols. (Chicago: Louis Schick, 1884–1888), a paperbound German anthology, and *Deutsche Grammatik für Amerikaner,* by Carla Wenckebach and Josepha Schrakamp, 4th ed. (Boston: Carl Schoenhof, 1887). On 28 July, Schoenhof notified Clemens that the order "has reached me and will be attended to in a few days." Almost two months later, Clemens noted on Schoenhof's postcard: "Hasn't come yet (Sept. 23)."

⟨W⟩"German Grammar for Americans" by Carla Wenckebach—
same place.

Scribner, 2 pm 21st. Murray Hill.[314]

Rede.[315] By the absence of an irreverent press Europe for 1000
years has ⟨been⟩ existed merely for the advantage of half a dozen
7th rate ⟨folk⟩ families called monarchs, & some hundreds of
riff-raff sarcastically called noble. Our papers have one peculiarity—
it is American—it exists nowhere else—their irreverence. May they
never lose it & never modify it. It is irreverent toward what[?]
Pretty much everything. But ⟨for⟩where it laughs one good thing
to death, it laughs a thousand cruel & infamous shams &
superstitions into the grave; & the account is squared. Irreverence
is the champion of liberty, & its only sure defence.

Zum Vorlesen.[316] The Ant.

The criminal classes ⟨of Europe⟩—I refer to the nobilities &
royalties of Europe—

  4147. June 29. Mme H. M. Abry[317]—$462.50.

  4307—July 9. Schoenhof, $2.80.
  4308   "   "   Cowles,[318] Secy. 25.00. [#]

---

[314] Clemens intended to confer with Charles Scribner about the matters discussed on
page 387, note 294.

[315] This entry contains the germ of "The American Press," a speech (Rede in German)
Clemens planned to deliver to the Society of the Army of the Cumberland (see p. 386,
note 291, and p. 391, note 310). Here Clemens replied to Matthew Arnold's lengthy
criticism of American journalism in "Civilisation in the United States," particularly the
comment: "I should say that if one were searching for the best means to efface and kill in
a whole nation the discipline of respect, the feeling for what is elevated, one could not
do better than take the American newspapers" (Nineteenth Century, April 1888, p. 490).
Clemens later incorporated "The American Press" into chapter 10 of The American
Claimant, where it appears as a speech delivered at a debate of the "Mechanics' Club."

[316] For the reading. Clemens probably intended to read from his extended discourse
on ant behavior and intellect in chapter 22 of A Tramp Abroad. The occasion has not
been determined.

[317] Possibly a dressmaker employed by Mrs. Clemens.

[318] James L. Cowles was secretary of a tariff "Reform Club" recently organized in New
Haven, Connecticut. On 1 July 1888 he wrote inviting Clemens, as one of "the mugwumps of 1884," to join the association in support of Cleveland's tariff program. "We
shall need a great deal of money," he noted, "and shall be compelled to perform an im-

1888.

The London Standard says there are now 13,600 periodicals in Europe, & 12,000 in America.

But give yourself no uneasiness; there was never a monarch yet, insane enough to try it.

Stag—Whis[k]
A C Dunham
Sam Dunham
Brer Robinson
Brer Whitmore

My Duel.
Interview.
Bram Stoker

$$151$$
$$15$$
$$\overline{755}$$
$$\langle 115 \rangle 151$$
$$\overline{\langle 2905 \rangle 2265}$$
$$44$$
$$\overline{2249}$$

$$151$$
$$9$$
$$\overline{1359}$$
$$116$$
$$\overline{1475}$$

$$265$$
$$250$$
$$\overline{13250}$$
$$530$$
$$\overline{66,250}$$

Earned in 3 years.

---

mense amount of labor to insure success but we shall succeed." Clemens evidently responded affirmatively to Cowles's plea that "you take hold with us."

XXVIII

"Just Burying Myself . . . in a Book"

(July 1888–May 1889)

NOTEBOOK 28 differs significantly from the notebooks which immediately precede it. Unlike the previous notebooks, largely devoted to Clemens' business affairs, the present one is predominantly literary and reflects his preoccupation with the matter of *A Connecticut Yankee*. Offended by Matthew Arnold's criticisms of America in "Civilisation in the United States" and called upon to prepare a rebuttal (see p. 383, note 280), Clemens made many entries about English social failings which worked their way into his novel. "I am just burying myself as well as I can in a book," he wrote to Orion Clemens from Elmira on 2 July 1888. And after he completed his summer's work there he told his English publisher: "I had a sort of half-way notion that I might possibly finish the Yankee at King Arthur's Court this summer, but I began too late, & so I don't suppose I shall finish it till next summer. We go home to Hartford a week hence; & if at that time I find I am two-thirds done, I mean to try to persuade myself to do that other third before spring" (SLC to Andrew Chatto, 17 September 1888, British Museum). Clemens resumed work almost immediately upon arrival in Hartford, arranging in the first days of October for a workroom in Joseph Twichell's house in order to avoid the distractions of his own home. At about the same time, in refusing an invitation to a dinner in honor of James Whitcomb Riley, he noted: "I am finishing a book begun three years ago. I see land ahead; if I stick to the oar without intermission I shall be at anchor in thirty days; if I stop to moisten my hands I am gone" (SLC to "W. D. Foulke and Others," 3 October 1888, published in Marcus Dickey, *The Maturity of James Whitcomb Riley* [Indianapolis: Bobbs-Merrill Co., 1922], p. 231). Although this estimate was overly sanguine, Clemens easily made good his earlier prediction of completion by spring. On 16 April 1889, Webster & Company was able to report that two typescripts of "your new book" had been prepared.

Clemens wanted to bring another project of several years' duration to a successful conclusion at the same time as *A Connecticut Yankee*. In letters of this period he sometimes wishfully linked completion of his book with perfection of the Paige typesetter, hoping or expecting the machine would be done in August, September, October, then December 1888, and afterward in January, March, and July 1889. This notebook closes before he was disillusioned of that final date as well, for the machine would be completely disassembled in August 1889 before the cycle of promised readiness began again. While he was using Notebook 28 Clemens disposed of other investments, selling stocks at a disadvantage, in a desperate attempt to provide capital for the voracious machine. On at least one occasion he made provision to divert some of Livy's money into the typesetter as well (see p. 459, note 170). He persisted, without success, in efforts to extract large investments from wealthy men—some of them acquaintances, others merely glad to meet Mark Twain—and did not hesitate to approach close family friends and relatives, occasionally with modest results. He also turned to Webster & Company, but to no avail, for the publishing house was in no condition to assist him. In fact, it required his repeated assistance in the form of his signature on notes to the Mount Morris Bank in New York City. Frederick J. Hall continued to make optimistic predictions, however, when not excusing poor performance with a refrain which pleaded a perpetual dull season of the year. At times business was so bad that insurance payments for sheets or books destroyed in bindery or warehouse accidents were greeted as windfalls. Great returns were anticipated from the *Personal Memoirs of P. H. Sheridan*, but even before the book came out in December 1888 a survey of book agents necessitated a more realistic appraisal of its prospects.

With the permanent retirement of Charles L. Webster, settled after long negotiation at the end of December 1888, Clemens' interest in the firm's affairs seemed to wane. Frederick J. Hall bought Webster's share of the business for $12,000, at least partly advanced to him by the company, and Clemens predicted: "You and I will never have any trouble" (SLC to Hall, 11 January 1889, *MTLP*, p. 252). But on more than one occasion Hall found it necessary to prompt his partner repeatedly to elicit replies to pleas for assistance or direction. And when he was responsive Clemens was likely to offer dubious advice, such as a suggestion that men with placards advertising Webster & Company publications be sent out into the streets as a means of increasing sales. In one of the few references to Charles L. Webster & Company in this notebook, made even before Webster agreed to retire, Clemens planned a reduction of his interest in the firm and even proposed a total withdrawal. Then in an adjacent entry he considered assuming full control of the publishing house, a typical ambivalence of business purpose.

Despite his determined effort to finish *A Connecticut Yankee*, his continual concern with the Paige typesetter, and the intermittent attention required by Charles L. Webster & Company, which collectively made large demands on him, Clemens found time for family pleasures and duties. In the fall of 1888 Grace King made a welcome stay of seven weeks in Hartford, spending more than a month with the Clemenses and the balance at the nearby home of the Charles Dudley Warners. But the Clemens family had other, less cheering, visitors as well. Theodore Crane, who had suffered a disabling illness in September 1888, was at the Clemens home with his wife Susan that fall and, when not in New York City to consult physicians, remained in Hartford through much of the winter of 1888/1889 to receive treatment there. On 30 December 1888 Clemens wrote to Mrs. Mary M. Fairbanks:

> Theodore Crane has been here a month or two in a precarious state, because of a stroke of paralysis. Sometimes he picks up a little, & then for a day or two it is a cheerful house; after that, he drops back again, & the gloom & the apprehension return. It is pulling Susie Crane down a good deal, & Livy also, of course. These two women will get sick if this continues. (*MTMF*, pp. 262–263, with corrections from the original at the Henry E. Huntington Library, San Marino, Calif.)

Livy in fact suffered a lingering case of pinkeye early in 1889 and Clemens himself was sometimes not well, making notebook reminders to schedule appointments with doctors.

Clemens was partly able to escape the gloom of his household in literary work. In addition to *A Connecticut Yankee* he busied, and aggravated, himself with the details of a contract of 3 January 1889 with Abby Sage Richardson for a dramatization of *The Prince and the Pauper*. He may at this time also have worked on a play set during the Franco-German War of 1870–1871 for which he made notes in the summer of 1888. And he welcomed frequent opportunities to appear in public, speaking at banquets and giving unremunerated readings for a variety of causes. On the latter occasions, Clemens sometimes read selections from the manuscript of *A Connecticut Yankee,* undoubtedly hoping to whet his public's appetite while testing its reaction to his first book in almost five years.

Notebook 28 is identical to Notebooks 22 and 24 through 27 in design and format. It now contains 176 pages, fifteen of which are blank. Four leaves have been torn out and are missing. The entries are in black pencil, except for a number in brownish black ink, one in blue ink, and one in a pale greenish black ink. A small proof sheet of a passage typeset on the Paige compositor, with Clemens' comments written on it (see illustration, p. 442), was interleaved in the notebook at the page where he wrote and signed his enthusiastic "**EUREKA!**" after seeing movable type "*spaced & justified* BY MACHINERY" for the "first time in the history of the world." Use marks in pencil and in ink, scattered throughout the notebook, are probably by Paine and have not been reproduced.

Eugen Meyer, 403 Lexington ave

562, 8th st. Oakland,. Mrs. Moffett

Prices.

First   500, $12,000 each.

"   600,   11,000   "

"   700,   10,000   "

"   800,   9,000   "

"   900,   8,500   "

"   1000,   8,000   "

After that we reserve priv. of returning to original price. [#]

For 300,000 ems, to be done in 7½ hours, 3 sizes of type, you want 6 or 7 operatives, with 3 machines for *each* operative; so that machines only, & never *men* will stand idle.

First price for 21 machines, $252,000; final price, $168,000.

Worked *all the time*, 7½ hours a day, in New York, a machine will ⟨earn⟩ save its cost in 20 months (first price); it will save its *final* cost in a year & 6 weeks.

If you work it *half* the time, it will save its final cost in 2¼ years.

Allow a man the *leads* at 50ᶜ M & he will set you a page of the Tribune on our machine *for nothing*.

At $8,000, on a N.Y. daily—8 hours a day, it saves its cost in 16 months; at $12, in 22 m.

Army of the Cumberland. Last meeting was in 1868. Geo. W. Smith, Sep. 20. Room 45, 99 Randolph st.[1]

Here is a counterpart of what you call your "civilization", (Quote slave-making ant.)[2]

Yours is the civilization of slave-making ants. (Copy note from little book of English-German.) It says there is no supreme merit but in accident; that there is more merit in accident than in the mightiest achievements of intellect & conscientious endeavor. (Darwin) (King, duke, &c.) What is the value of a civilization ⟨which⟩ ⟨makes the sublimest merit stand with its hat in its hand⟩ howsoever artificially high & fine which carries with it a degradation like this & the shabby/mean spirit to approve it & be contented with it.—(Routledges waiting ½ hour to see Pr. of W.—Grant.)[3]

---

[1] Clemens planned to address the Society of the Army of the Cumberland in September 1888, but withdrew shortly before his scheduled appearance (see p. 391, note 310).

[2] Notes through "a very good Eng." (402.24) were made for Clemens' unfinished reply to Matthew Arnold's "Civilisation in the United States" (see p. 383, note 280). The opinions and ideas recorded here, and similar ones which occur later in this notebook, also found expression in *A Connecticut Yankee*.

[3] Clemens recalled this incident more fully in a notebook entry of early 1882 (see N&J2, p. 461).

What a curious admixture of cur & lion is the English character.
The unicorn in the coat of arms is an error. (Picture of it—
corrected.)

(How superbly brave is the Eng in the presence of the awfulest
forms of danger & death; & how ⟨mean & shamelessly⟩ abject in
the presence of any & all forms of hereditary rank.)

Are we asked to believe that the vote of a whole nation would
voluntary saddle upon itself any form of hereditary monarchy &
hereditary nobility? Then we must also believe that it would in the
same way approve the restricting the officering of ⟨ar⟩its armies &
navies to persons of "noble" degree—which is on its face impossible,
absurd.

Rank in the army is still restricted to the nobility—by a thing
which is stronger than law—the power of ancient habit &
superstition. Let a commoner become an officer—he will be
snubbed by all his brethren, ostracised, driven out. (1889)

The ⟨[c]r⟩Victoria cross—who gets it? Intrepid commoners? Do
not deceive yourself. Examine the V. C. records.[4]

The kingly office is entitled to no respect; it was originally
procured by the highwayman's methods; it remains a perpetuated
crime, can never be anything but the symbol of a crime. It is not
more entited to respect than is the flag of a pirate. A monarch,
⟨whether good or bad⟩ when good, is entitled to the consideration
which we accord to a pirate who keeps Sunday school between
crimes; when bad, ⟨or a nullity⟩ he is entleed to none at all.

Does Mr. Childs use the old hand-press yet? No? How could he
reconcile it to his conscience to adopt steam & turn so many men
out of a job?[5] [#]

---

[4] Examination of these records indicates that although the Victoria Cross was sometimes conferred upon high-ranking officers, presumably members of the nobility, the vast
majority of awards between 1857 and 1889 were to lower-grade officers, noncommissioned
officers, soldiers, marines, and seamen as specified upon institution of the decoration in
1856. Commoners were evidently well represented among this group. Clemens had previously noted a plan for an appendix to *A Connecticut Yankee* based on a mistaken
assumption of a class prerequisite for the Victoria Cross (see p. 351).

[5] This brief note concerning the Paige typesetter interrupts the long series of entries

—but if you cross a king with a prostitute the resulting mongrel ⟨is⟩ perfectly satisfies the Eng idea of "nobility." The ducal houses of G. B. of to-day are mainly derived from this gaudy combination.[6]

To this day Eng revere the memory of Nell ⟨Quin⟩Gwin & speak of her with a smack of unconscious envy. ⟨of her⟩ They seem to consider her a ⟨⟨pet⟩ darling of fortune.⟩ one of the peculiarly fortunate of this world. They keep her portrait at Hampton Court, among some more treasures of the same sort; they study her picturesque history with affectionate pride; they value any rag or relic which her touch has made holy; they are as excited & pleased over the discovery of any new fact concerning her ⟨as they would be over⟩ as a devotee ⟨is⟩ ⟨wo⟩wd. be over a clout which his favorite saint had ⟨pissed on⟩ used.

—has not in him the making of a gentleman.

As between the Second Advent & a glimpse of the ⟨Pr of W.⟩ Queen, the average—female—commoner would have no hesitations. She would ⟨sieze⟩ elect for the bird in the hand—she would bless ⟨enchant⟩ her ⟨[-]⟩ worshiping eyes with a ⟨glimpse⟩ view of her proprietor, & chance seeing her Savior later.

I will explain that Marlborough House is not a hotel.[7] If it were that, & the Pr kept it, he would be in better business than he is, for he would be earning an honorable living, a new departure for princes.

Ours is the only civilization yet produced in this world which could look God in the face at the judgment day ⟨&⟩; for it is the

---

on the subject of monarchy. (Clemens, or possibly Paine, drew a line from "all." at 399.25 to "—but if" at 400.1, bypassing this paragraph.) Clemens was occasionally sensitive about the potential displacement of human compositors by the Paige machine and alleged that the device would result in more, not less, income for them (see for example pp. 191 and 197). Here he testily reproached George W. Childs, owner of the Philadelphia *Public Ledger*, for inconsistency. Childs was known as "the beloved champion of the typographical union" (New York *Times*, 13 May 1888).

[6] A recurrent theme of George Standring's *People's History of the English Aristocracy* (1887), an important influence on *A Connecticut Yankee*.

[7] Marlborough House in London, the residence of Edward, Prince of Wales, was the gathering place for fashionable society.

only one not founded in cold hard selfishness, the only one where ⟨the system ⟨degrades⟩ does not degrade the many to exalt the few,⟩ the system has ⟨not⟩ for its end the degradation of the ⟨few⟩ many to exalt the few, the misery of the many for the happiness of the few, the cold & hunger & over-working of the useful that the useless may live in luxury & idleness.

⟨You⟩ There are shams & shams, there are frauds & frauds, but the transparentest of all is the sceptred one. We see ⟨monarch[i]s⟩monarchs meet & go through solemn ceremonies farces with straight countenances; but it is not possible to imagine them meeting in private & not laughing in each other's faces.

The ⟨c[--]⟩system of our Indians is higher & juster ⟨than yours⟩; for ⟨[----]⟩ only merit makes a man a chief, & his son cannot take the place if there is another man better fitted for it.

Observe how monarchies & nobilities are sprung upon a heedless & ignorant people. Chiefs rise by the one divine right—capacity, merit. One of these shows merit for ⟨command⟩ war & government above all the rest. He conspires with a faction of the Chiefs, & is made king—⟨other factions, &⟩ ⟨dissent⟩ ⟨[of]⟩ the body of the people ⟨not⟩ ignored, allowed no vote, their desires in the matter held to be of no consequence by these upstarts. The conspirators make the succession permanent in this king's family—he erects *them* into a perpetual nobility— —& the crime is complete. It is the same sort of crime that ⟨invasion⟩ surprise & siezure of a ⟨weak⟩ weak community's property by a robber gang & the ⟨sale of the⟩ conversion of the community itself into slaves is. All monarchies have been so built; there was never a throne which did not represent a crime, there is no throne to-day which does not represent a crime. A monarchy is perpetuated piracy. In its escutcheon should always be quartered the skull & cross-bones.

W^m the Conqueror—examine his "right"—trace his line down—through Mrs. FitzHerbert—& see that this piracy is not even "legitimate" piracy.[8] [#]

---

[8] George Standring had already accomplished this genealogical study in *The People's*

Magna Charta⟨!—haha⟩

The "war-lord"—Kaiser W^m II^s first utterance—proclamation to
army & navy upon ⟨as[cen]⟩ assuming authority.[9]

What a funny thing is Mon, & how ⟨queer⟩ curious its
assumptions. It commits a crime, & ⟨assumed⟩assumes that lapse of
time removes the criminality; it does a dishonest thing & assumes
that lapse of time removes the taint, as if it were a mere smell, &
perishable; it does a shameful thing, & assumes that lapse of time
transfigures it & makes it a thing to be proud of. It assumes that a
wrong, maintained ⟨intact⟩ for a dozen or a thousand years,
becomes a right. It assumes that the wronged parties will presently
give up, & take the same view—that at least their descendants will.
Now, By an effort, we can imagine a family of bears taking pride in
the historic fact that an ancestor of theirs took violent possession of
a bee tree some centuries ago, & that the family have had a right
to it ever since. We can get that far without any trouble, but there
the allegory fails; for the bees would attack the bears every day for
a thousand years. You can make a man understand how time turns
a wrong into a right, but you can't make a bee understand it—in
his present undeveloped stage. ⟨If you will load a nation down
sufficiently with the "thrill of awe," ⟨that⟩ you can warp its
judgment about anything you please, but it is different with a
bee⟨s⟩.⟩ What the bee lacks is the "thrill of awe".[10] He will get
that, by & by, & then he will be a very good Eng. [#]

History of the English Aristocracy (published in 1887), noting that, despite all claims to
the contrary, "not a single peerage dates back to the Conquest" (quoted from second, and
only available, edition [London: Robert Forder, 1891], p. 4). Maria Anne Fitzherbert,
twice a widow, married George, Prince of Wales (later George IV), in 1785. This union,
considered illegal because of Mrs. Fitzherbert's Catholicism and the prince's minority,
did not impede their reception by society and by members of the royal family. Despite
the prince's second marriage in 1795, he and Mrs. Fitzherbert lived together until 1803.

[9] On 16 June 1888, after acceding to the German throne, William II sent individual
communications to the army and navy reaffirming their indissoluble ancestral commitments to their sovereign. He reminded the army in particular of the "firm and inviolable
attachment to the war lord" which was his hereditary due (New York *Times,* 17 June
1888). William's statements were in keeping with his well-known belief in divine right
monarchy and his dislike of government by popular representation.

[10] "But if there be a discipline in which the Americans are wanting, it is the discipline

9 times married—& none of 'em satisfactory.— —It's a risk, but I've got to do it. All my life I've sighed for an heir.[11]

Father looked younger, even as a corpse; & he died at 98—& not grown, yet.

No grown yet?

No—& he was 11 feet high.

What!

I measured him[,] myself.

Do you mean to say when he stood on the floor ⟨his⟩the crown of his head was 11 above it?

(Disgusted)—*Naw!*—he stood on the bureau.

Picture of the war-map in the show-bills. French, red—Prussians blue.[12]

Lines of Prussian retreat, yellow.

French ⟨killed⟩ losses, red; the other blue.

Map 6 feet square.

Publish Original sketch in the playbill—"Die Belagerung."[13]

Marie—"He's a bad man" [#]

---

of awe and respect. An austere and intense religion imposed on their Puritan founders the discipline of respect, and so provided for them the thrill of awe; but this religion is dying out" (Matthew Arnold, "Civilisation in the United States," *Nineteenth Century*, April 1888, p. 489).

[11] Clemens probably intended to add the material in this entry and the following one to his "Encounter with an Interviewer," originally published in *Lotos Leaves: Original Stories, Essays, and Poems*, edited by John Brougham and John Elderkin (Boston: William F. Gill and Co., 1875).

[12] With several exceptions, Clemens' notes through "& supplements to Appleton." (405.18) were intended for a play about the Franco-German War (1870–1871) to be based on Alphonse Daudet's story, "Le siège de Berlin." Daudet's melodramatic piece described how Colonel Jouve, an ailing octagenarian veteran of Napoleon I's forces, is temporarily kept from suffering a fatal seizure by his doctor's and granddaughter's elaborate pretense that France is besieging Berlin and winning the war. Their efforts fail when the old soldier arises from his sickbed, expecting to witness the triumphant return of the French army, and sees German forces enter a siege-crippled Paris. The introduction of Pierre/Gaston and the suggestion of a love story are Clemens' contributions. His notebook entry at 461.13–14 suggests that he actually completed this dramatization. No manuscript is known to survive.

[13] *The Siege.*

⟨Split that scene & show his success & defeat before Kaiser &c?⟩

Bring home the Original sketch.[14]

Also, Washburne's book (Scribner)

"Why the thing is ⟨absolutely⟩ *cob*-webbed with Prus'n *retreats!*"[15]

The Congress of Death.[16]

Mayor, Old Mortality

X bones[17] Congress escutcheon [#]

----

[14] Daudet's story was probably most readily available in *Le siège de Berlin, et d'autres contes*, published in 1888 by the William R. Jenkins Company, a New York firm which Clemens patronized (see p. 357, note 182). Elihu B. Washburne's *Recollections of a Minister to France, 1869–1877*, 2 vols. (New York: Charles Scribner's Sons, 1887), provided details of the siege of Paris, which lasted from 19 September 1870 until the armistice of 28 January 1871.

[15] A remark for Clemens' dramatization of "The Siege of Berlin." The reference is to the map of Germany on which, in Daudet's story, Colonel Jouve's granddaughter plots the imaginary maneuvers which defeat France's enemy and keep the old veteran alive.

[16] Entries through "in favor of Bridgeport." (405.4) were probably made around the middle of July 1888 as Clemens was formulating a statement of grievances against the city of Hartford intended for newspaper publication. The immediate stimulus to his anger was an irritating alteration in street lighting proposed at that time and effected some months later (see pages 427–428). After addressing himself to that issue, Clemens went on to note other instances of mismanagement. One that particularly rankled was neglect in the disposal of sewage, which, he asserted, had lethal consequences, leading him to comment: "If I had my way, no city government should ever own stock in the cemeteries." He then observed that the inefficiency of the police force had made Hartford "a burglars' paradise" where housebreaking "is the most thrifty of all our industries. . . . You can't tell the burglary-list from the bills of mortality." These remarks suggest the process of Clemens' association of Hartford's mayor with Old Mortality, the subject of Scott's novel of that title, who fanatically devotes most of his life to the repair and erection of headstones. Clemens' allusion here to Bridgeport, Connecticut, is illuminated by the charge in his statement that local policies served to "banish" industry from Hartford to that city. Clemens' bill of complaints was not published.

[17] Before writing "X bones," Clemens drew what appears to be a circled X, perhaps to represent the "escutcheon" (possibly a skull and crossbones), and then canceled it.

Undertakers wanted

Burglarville.

The control was in my hands; I followed city govt precedents & threw it in favor of Bridgeport.

Scene, a richly furnished library. Last scene change to parlor.

They discharged all the other servants. This is recorded at beginning of –––– act.

Sword-fight between Col & Pierre—who only defends himself.

—or for practice.
or reminiscence—illustrating how it happened.

"Take your cane—I'll show you."

"But you don't let me get *to* your breast"
"It is habit monseiur—I can't help it"

Gaston, instead of Pierre.

"(love-sick look)—listening—"I know that voice"—various huggings & caressings of his broom."

Look in Cyclo. Britan— for Franco-Prus'n war.

& supplements to Appleton.

Speech advocating 21 yrs residence for citizenship—⟨no taxes/heavy taxes meantime.⟩ Military service? Exactly as a miner is. Look at the movement for parochial schools. "Let me educate your children & I will ⟨prophecy your⟩ determine your ultimate form of gov't"—instead of the "songs"—make a paraphrase.

Arrogance.   Chicago speech.[18]
Club Paper "The English Trade-Mark"—Trait? Characteristic?
A Buffon in mentalism would take a million mental ⟨s[a]⟩skeletons

---

[18] Notes for a speech Clemens planned to deliver to the Society of the Army of the Cumberland (see p. 391, note 310). Clemens evidently also considered this a possible subject for elaboration before the Hartford Monday Evening Club, but did not carry out this plan.

& know the Englishman by that ⟨to⟩ bone. In the American, according to Arnold & his procession of predecessors, it is Brag; in Spaniard, Pride. Frenchman, ⟨Vanity (effeminate)⟩ nastiness; &c *Alibi*, German—Patience?

Lady & Gentleman—that anecdote is the American idea.

Chicago speech

Try to imagine an English Christ.[19]

Many things put a nearly unbearable strain upon the imagination. (Above)

That worm-eaten & dilapidated social structure in England which Mr. Arnold regarded as a "civilization"

Trait—mixture of cur & lion—unicorn an error.

English is hybrid—⟨lion⟩ bulldog at front, cur at [i]t tail. Ox, Lion (Spanish) American Peacock. French Polecat. Russian— ⟨sheep?⟩Wombat

insolent   Russian—wombat.

Bull-dog at front, with a cur's tail tucked in between the hind legs.

This attitude before no nation or royalty or caste or even well-earned & heaven-high distinction in the ⟨[outer]⟩ outer world, but only before his own ridiculous royalty & nobility.

George Knight has quit starring & gone with E E Rice in Evangeline.[20]

They would ⟨[notice] a⟩ Jee[m]s the movements of a cross between a Zulu Kaffir & a Chimpanzee, ⟨of⟩if it had a title, & was the earl of something or duke of something & wore a snip of ribbon at its buttonhole to show that it had been decorated into

---

[19] A variation upon an old theme (see p. 292).

[20] *Evangeline, or, the Belle of Acadia* was the burlesque of Longfellow's poem written by Edward E. Rice, a composer, promoter, and theatrical manager, in collaboration with dramatist J. Cheever Goodwin. The play had been a staple of the American light theater for more than a dozen years and, in March 1888, had passed its five-thousandth perform-ance. George S. Knight was a comic actor famous for his German dialect roles. The de-cline in Knight's fortunes suggested here is substantiated by the fact that early in 1889

some noble order or other whose first & last & only qualification was that the member ⟨should⟩could prove that his tribe had been loafers for four generations. ⟨of no-accountness in his tribe.⟩

But Mr. Blaine the most notorious ⟨man⟩⟨busy-body &⟩ blatherskite in America can go there ⟨⟨[--]⟩& ⟨⟨get⟩ [-----]/arouse no⟩ more ⟨[----tion] ⟨[----]⟩& get no⟩ ⟨excitement &⟩ ⟨pow[---]⟩ attention, rouse no/get no more ⟨[homage]⟩ enthusiasm than would a⟩ & get no more attention/homage than would a brass farthing in the Bank of England.²¹

⟨Bert⟩ Cosmopolitan Club²² "Yes-me-lord,"—"No-me-lord."

& the awful spectacle of Douglas Jerrold's son at the grand evening blow-out ⟨in⟩of the noble bitch with the Italian name. I was ⟨[---]⟩ into that business through that ass Judge Turner. Polyglot woman there.²³

Andover & ⟨G⟩people in charge ⟨those unsp⟩ of Girard College, who rob the corpses of ⟨the⟩ ⟨great⟩ their noble dead in the ⟨name of⟩ interest of religion,²⁴ & are applauded for it by those

---

"a matinée benefit to poor, disabled George S. Knight" was staged, producing gross receipts of $1,834 (George C. D. Odell, *Annals of the New York Stage*, 15 vols. [New York: Columbia University Press, 1927–1949], 14:288).

²¹ James G. Blaine traveled in Europe in 1887 and 1888 before returning to the United States to accept the position of secretary of state in the administration of Benjamin Harrison. Considering his own dislike of Blaine (see *MTHL*, pp. 501, 508–509), Clemens might have been expected to congratulate, not criticize, the English for neglecting him.

²² A London club, frequented by prominent politicians and literary men, the Cosmopolitan was founded in 1852 and "for about half a century . . . remained the London paradise of the intelligent foreigner" (T. H. S. Escott, *Club Makers and Club Members* [New York: Sturgis & Walton Co., 1914], p. 169).

²³ Clemens' meeting with this woman occurred during his visit to England in 1873. The event was recorded in the stenographic notebook of that trip kept by S. C. Thompson, as were Clemens' comments upon the "awful spectacle" of William Blanchard Jerrold, son of the English humorist Douglas Jerrold (see *N&J1*, pp. 551–552). Clemens also recalled these incidents in Notebook 23, page 87.

²⁴ Stephen Girard's will had left $6,000,000 to the city of Philadelphia in 1831 for the establishment of a school for white orphan boys. Girard insisted that no representative of any religious sect ever be employed by the school or even be admitted as a visitor. His intention was to spare its pupils the pernicious effects of the conflict of doctrines. In *Girard's Will and Girard College Theology* (Philadelphia, 1888), Richard B. Westbrook, himself a Doctor of Divinity, introduced evidence that "the present system of religious

two unspeakable shams, buttermouthed hypocrites, ⟨[J]h[e]⟩ John
Wanamaker & ⟨the⟩ his Sunday School Times.

Let us ⟨in fancy⟩ take the present male sovereigns of the earth—
⟨the male ones⟩—& strip them naked⟨; also⟩⟨.⟩; Mix them with
500 naked mechanics, ⟨50 dancing masters, 50 quack doctors &
then march the whole⟩ & then march the whole around a circus
ring—charging a suitable admission, of course—& desire the
audience to pick out the sovereigns. (Nobles, ditto)

The new government on a desolate island. This is the way
monarchies are created; & their "rights" transmitted.

⟨You⟩They couldn't. You would have to paint them blue. You
can't tell a king from a cooper, except you differentiate them
exteriorly.
Royalty & nobility in *our* day!—⟨Do⟩ These Dodos &
pterodactyls!

Every time in a book I happen to speak of a king differently
from the way one speaks of God, or of a noble differently from the
way one speaks of the Son of God, it is stricken out of ⟨the⟩ the
European reprints.—Seems to give the ⟨poor⟩   ⟨j[ec]t[e]d⟩
proofreader the ⟨cold shudders.⟩ dry gripes.[25]
    ⟨Those castrated peoples!⟩ [#]

---

instruction in Girard College is in palpable violation of the conditions of the Will of the
Founder" (p. iii), noting resemblances to the dogma of the Protestant Episcopal Church.
Westbrook also commented on another instance of violation of an institution's religious
mandate. This was the case of five professors at Andover Theological Seminary who, in
late December 1886 and early January 1887, were compelled to face charges of having
departed in their teachings and writings from the stated creed of the school. In late July
1888, at Clemens' request, Westbrook sent him a copy of *Girard's Will and Girard College Theology.* Clemens made extensive marginal notes in this book (see the *Twainian,*
May–June, July–August 1968). The *Sunday School Times* was a weekly newspaper "devoted to the pedagogical problems of the Sunday school and the weekly exposition of the
lesson" (Herbert Adams Gibbons, *John Wanamaker,* 2 vols. [New York and London:
Harper & Brothers, 1926], 1:191–192). John Wanamaker had been owner and publisher
of the *Sunday School Times* from 1871 to 1877.
    [25] Clemens anticipated that *A Connecticut Yankee* might be subjected to this sort
of tampering. On 16 July 1889 he would complain to Andrew Chatto that England was

When we look abroad over far-reaching, historic Europe, & contemplate those castrated peoples—

London July 1, '88. "The Liberals welcome the passage of the Local Government bill through committee as almost a revolution which transfers the control of county affairs from the privileged few to the people. G. W. S.[26]

There—the handwriting on the wall! There's a day coming!

Neil Burgess has accepted a new play.[27]

You take royalty & nobility, you people bred up in its shadow; you don't see the fun of it. It is brim full of fun, if you will only move off a piece & get a perspective on it. It's as funny as seeing quacks & prostitutes ⟨playing the p⟩ ⟨solemnly⟩ gravely doing the rôles in a miracle-play.

$$
\begin{array}{r}
3.75 \\
5 \\
\hline
18.75 \\
7 \\
\hline
131.25 \\
\end{array}
$$

20
$140 [#]

"thin-skinned. It causeth me to smile, when I recal the modifications of my language which have been made in my English Editions to fit it for the sensitive English palate." (See also the headnote to Notebook 29.)

[26] Clemens adapted this remark, which he dated incorrectly, from a 21 July 1888 dispatch to the New York *Tribune* from London correspondent George Washburn Smalley. Smalley's report appeared in the *Tribune* on 22 July 1888.

[27] Neil Burgess was a popular actor who specialized in playing middle-aged women. "A big man, without the slightest trace of good looks, he could, without difficulty, seem the woman he was playing, whether making a pie in the kitchen, giving a piece of her mind to an interfering interloper or starting a young couple on the way to matrimony. Nothing of the effect, somewhat unpleasing, that one associates with the young 'female impersonator' of vaudeville inhered in Burgess's wholesome, jolly characterisations" (George C. D. Odell, *Annals of the New York Stage*, 15 vols. [New York: Columbia University Press, 1927–1949], 14:56). Burgess' new play, *The County Fair*, "a hilarious, clean comedy" by Charles Barnard, opened at Proctor's Twenty-third Street Theatre on 5 March 1889. In it he had the role of a mortgage-burdened spinster available for matrimony.

But you are 83.

Tis nothing. Methuselah (Do you know how old he was when he co[u]rted his first wife?

⟨*First?*—why he never had but one⟨.⟩, ⟨⟨if⟩You don't know what y⟩

Him? It grieves me to hear you expose your education like that.⟩

⟨Well, then⟩ *How* old?

⟨He [w]⟩A stripling of— of— well he was a couple of hundrd yrs old.

By Catholic law you cannot take office in heaven till you can show four generations of inertia, decay & rottenness; curiously enough, holding military office in France was restrited to just these same terms.

Monarchy & nobility (hereditary) is a laughable departure from the law of survival of the fittest—a law obeyed in all other cases.

But I have seldom heard of a king who ever did anything worth remembering, except perhaps at the General Judgment

"And such a sight as he was,—" said she; "there he sat, almost stark naked—not a thing on ⟨him⟩ but a pair of spectacles." Paused, & added, musingly, "and one of *them* was broke, & you could see him right through it."

On ferry boat 0; in ferry house 150 feet above sea. 5th floor, 90; no noticeable difference between Webster & the brunswick— 175–200.

Water-Gap *station* 200 above sea.

Pocono⟨[es]⟩ summit nearly ⟨1400⟩1600 ⟨odd⟩ ⟨(ab[- -t])⟩ above sea.

Highest point a little beyond—1700

Scranton ⟨1700⟩   1700

A little west of Scranton, 1800 ft above sea level

Binghamton 700 ft high[28] [#]

---

[28] Clemens had probably observed these altitudes while traveling by train to Elmira, New York, in the last week of June 1888. The Clemenses took the Delaware, Lackawanna

quiet. Would you look for a joke
neus^{r}[29] that laughs. Does this descrip^{n}
that played-out anachronism & impudent swindle.—
—⟨s⟩certainly the English human herd are as dumb & patient as
their own cattle.
—& impudent insult to common sense,
squalid invention of machine

What is the chiefest privilege remaining to nobility? That you
shal not laugh at it. No other class is exempt. If you wd know how
vast a priv it is, observe that to accord it to any ⟨usurpation⟩ thing
or being or idea is to give it eternal life.

No god & no religion can survive ridicule. ⟨No god,⟩ ⟨no
religion,⟩ no political church, no nobility, no royalty or other fraud,
can ⟨confront⟩ face ridicule in a fair field, & live.

Show me a lord, & I will show you a man who you couldn't tell
from a journeyman shoemaker if he were stripped; & who, in all
that is worth being, is the shoemaker's inferior; & in the shoemaker
I will show you a ⟨dumb⟩ dull animal, a poor-spirited insect: for
there is enough of him to rise & throw/chuck his lords & royalties
into the sea where they belong, & he doesn't do it. [#]

---

and Western Railroad, whose route cut across the northeastern corner of Pennsylvania,
passing the Delaware Water Gap, then Mount Pocono and Scranton before reaching
Binghamton, New York, and going on to Elmira. The record of relative altitudes begins
with the previous entry, which refers to the ferry that took the family from Manhattan
to the railroad terminal in Hoboken, New Jersey, and compares the heights of Webster
& Company's offices and the family's rooms at the Hotel Brunswick, an elegant New York
establishment.

[29] A miswritten abbreviation of "newspaper." Clemens was considering a reply to
Matthew Arnold's recent remarks about "the absence of truth and soberness" and "the
poverty in serious interest" in American newspapers ("Civilisation in the United States,"
Nineteenth Century, April 1888, p. 490). Some of the fragmentary notes in this entry were
expanded in "The American Press," a speech prepared in rejoinder to Arnold's article (see
p. 392, note 315). In it Clemens noted that the most valuable quality of American journalism was its "frank & cheerful irreverence. . . . For its mission—overlooked by Mr.
Arnold—is to stand guard over a nation's liberties, not its humbugs & shams. And so it
must be armed with ridicule, not reverence. . . . I believe it is our irreverent press which
has laughed away, one by one, what remained of our inherited minor shams & delusions
& serfages after the Revolution, & made us the only really free people that has yet existed
in the earth."

412   Notebook 28

Take that Atlantic & make showing of how much a day's wages would buy. *Death-rate*.[30]

⟨[4]⟩6 sous a year "king's twentieth" payable by *every* individual in the land⟨.⟩; say ⅓ of a day's wages. Would produce to-day $40,000,000, here.

See a leech to cure the Abbot's squeeze
                    Name the Abbot.
Finds the leech at the Abbey before leaving.

Speech introducing Hawley in Elmira—see Courant.[31]

Carl Shurz in Htfd—Times.[32]

"Consistency."[33]

Write a 7th one on Woman.

Babies.[34]

Weather.[35]

Negro Woman (⟨Ne[-]⟩N. E. dinner) [#]

---

[30] A reference to Edward Jarvis' "The Increase of Human Life," a study of the beneficial effects of improved sanitation, wages, education, clothing, food, and housing on human mortality. Jarvis' work, a source for *A Connecticut Yankee*, appeared in the October, November, and December 1869 numbers of the *Atlantic Monthly*.

[31] On 18 October 1879, Clemens had introduced United States Senator Joseph R. Hawley to a Republican meeting in Elmira, New York. Two days later the Hartford *Courant* printed Clemens' speech praising Hawley's patriotism, honesty, and integrity, including the following comment, partly attributable to Livy (see *MTHL*, p. 277): "The presence of such a man in politics is like a vase of attar of roses in a glue factory—it can't extinguish the stench, but it modifies it." The reason for Clemens' notation of this old speech, and those recalled in the following seven entries, is not known.

[32] Clemens served as chairman of a 20 October 1884 mugwump meeting in Hartford at which Carl Schurz appeared. A description of the occasion and an account of Clemens' remarks can be found in Albert Bigelow Paine's *Mark Twain: A Biography* (pp. 780–781).

[33] Clemens' final paper for the Hartford Monday Evening Club, read at a meeting on 5 December 1887 (see *MTS*[1923], pp. 120–130, for a version of this piece, incorrectly assigned to 1884).

[34] This response to a toast was given on 13 November 1879 at an Army of the Tennessee banquet in honor of Ulysses S. Grant (see *MTS*[1923], pp. 58–62).

[35] Clemens delivered a speech on New England weather at the seventy-first annual dinner of the New York City chapter of the New England Society on 22 December 1876 (see *MTS*[1923], pp. 53–57). At the society's seventy-seventh annual dinner, he spoke on

Adjustable Speech.[36]

If the Honi Soit incident happened now, what would a gentleman do? Put the motto into modern phrase & say, ⟨"⟨This⟩ A woman's garter is indilicately suggestive, but I am too delicate a person to remark upon the fact"⟩ "To the indelicate only, does a woman's garter suggest the indelicate⟨,"⟩. It doesn't suggest it to me, & so I yell right out & say so." This was the first exhibition of delicacy that had ever been seen in England, & so to keep it in mind, it was raised to a place in the British escutcheon, to stay there until some Englishman should do a delicate thing again. It is observable that It has not been taken down yet.

English manners are characterized for all time in the motto of the Escutcheon; ⟨English pluck in the lion.⟩

Said I, ⟨"Lance"—⟩"Lance|"lot—

Had an octroi at every gate of every town & that tax went to the baron who owned there. See "1792"

As for me, I believed God was a Presbyterian, & sh^d always believe it—but I would not force mine on others—so I started a church of each breed

Free trade, says I.

They were actually taxing salt & medicines timber & clothes—of course for the benefit of some baron. A brutality in any country. They stuck to it. I says All right, I'll tax your breath—& I did till they couldn't afford to draw it. Then we struck up a compromise.

An excommunicated person—carry him through what he had to stand. We assist him—& here begin my troubles & long fight with the church, & my eventual defeat. [#]

"Woman—God Bless Her." In the course of this speech, referred to in the following entry, he described "the savage woman of Central Africa," noting her habit of wearing "just her complexion. That is all; it is her entire outfit. It is the lightest costume in the world, but is made of the darkest material. It has often been mistaken for mourning. It is the trimmest, and neatest, and gracefulest costume that is now in fashion; it wears well, is fast colors, doesn't show dirt" (Hartford *Courant*, 25 December 1882).

[36] This speech is discussed on page 317, note 51.

The Interdict continues 6 yrs; no bell heard in the land, no burials with religious services—business & everything at a standstill —grass grows in the streets—people flit about, avoiding each other & speech—no marriages. A mute solemn bell; ruined lives; many went mad.

Run across the slaves again—auction & speeches.

There are in Conn, at this moment & in all countries, children & disagreeable relatives chained in cellars, all sores, welts, worms & vermin—cases come to light every little while—2 recent cases in our state. This is to suggest that the thing in man which makes him cruel to a slave is in him permanently & will not be rooted out for a million years. To admit that slavery exists in any country is to admit that you may describe any form of brutal treatment which you can imagine & go there & find it had been imagined & applied before you.

Find absolute power unrestrained by a trained public opinion & you will know without going to inquire, that le Droit du Seigneur exists there. Observe, it existed in Scotland, there are traces of it in England, you find it lodged in the big medicine man of various savage tribes.

In some savage tribes it was an *honor* to the girl & her family. In modern times it is an *honor* to a subject to be reigned over (that is, ⟨made a slave⟩ have his liberty debauched—) by a family called royal—a family with no decenter right than the medicine man. The stupid loyalty of to-day is the same sentiment, unaltered, that made le Droit possible, & the degradation is the same in quality & quantity—the form of it is changed, that is all.

Loyalty is a word which has worked vast harm; for it has been made to trick men into being "loyal" to a thousand iniquities whereas the true loyalty should have been to themselves—in which case there would have ensued a rebellion & the throwing off of that deceptive yoke.

Loyalty to a party *name* is pure royalty—& silly.

Competitive examination for a 3^d lieutenancy—Who was your

father? Grandfather? Brewer Greatgrandfather? Great-grreat-great gr?
Mother? Prostitute. Grandmother &c.

Able to show a tie as to nobility & number of generations.

Question then on quality of the blood. Mixture of whore & king
decided it.

"But sire, *neither* of these idiots knows anything of *military*
matters. Here is a commoner who *does*."

"No good—must be noble."

Same terms for saintship.

I offer a pupil from my West Point.

No-no, he isn't noble.

All-right—I will abide my time & not force you. I'm not yet
equipped anyhow

I make a *peace*ful revolution & introduce advanced civilization.
The Church overthrows it with a 6 year interdict.

A revolution cannot be established under 30 years—the men of
old ideas must die off.

Skip from this trip at once to civilization, ten years later.

The leech gives him recipes from James's medical Dictionary.[37]
Result bedrids him 2 months.

The first thing I want to teach is *disloyalty* till they get used to
disusing that word *loyalty* as representing a virtue. This will beget
independence—which is loyalty to one's best self & principles, &
this is often disloyalty to the general idols & fetishes.

Brunor the Abbot.

Marinel—the leech hermit   very celebrated—sought by the
whole world.

Artigal, The Bastard. ⟨one Expert⟩ whom I hadn't washed.

Gander, an expert [#]

---

[37] Robert James's *A Medicinal Dictionary; Including Physic, Surgery, Anatomy,
Chymistry, and Botany,* 3 vols. (London: T. Osborne, 1743–1745). "A Majestic Literary
Fossil," Clemens' article on "this deadly book," appeared in the February 1890 *Harper's*
magazine.

I used compulsion in Establishing my several breeds of Prot. Churches, because no missionarying has ever been accomplished except by force which was not contemptible by comparison of the paltry results with the gigantic outlay of cash & labor.

I gave the leech his choice—become a Presbyterian or hang. He said true holiness consisted in doing disgusting things, living in a disgusting way, making oneself as unpleasant as possible. To be a Presby ⟨&⟩*and* a hermit would lay out anything ever yet attempted in the way of the repulsive, so he elected to ⟨forego the⟩ forego the lighter fate & be a Pres. hermit.

Stylites must be a Free-Will Baptist or I would degrade him from his pillar & put the Presbyterian up there⟨.⟩; but I remitted the baptism.

I made a Campbellite out of the skunk man, for this would require him to bathe & keep clean.

Others I started in business as Methodists, Quakers, Episcopalians, ⟨Congregat⟩Congrega &c. And I *taxed* ⟨all⟩ their churches, too, & all the buildings & land they might own. A thing which ought to be done everywhere.

This was giving me immense trouble with the Estab church. Up to now I hadn't collected much.

Cathedral struck by lightning—they had just removed my thunder-rod, a mob led by priests.

Advowsons & lithographed sermons—found they were for sale.

Impressment of sailors & soldiers. Vol. 3, last pages.[38]

The building of the Mansion House. A Dissenter could not be Sheriff of London, because he would have to ⟨subscribe⟩ take the Sacrament according to the Anglican rite. The City passed a bye-law, fining any man £400 who refused to run, when asked, & £600 for refusing to serve, after being elected. A blind man & a

---

[38] The final chapter in volume 3 of William E. H. Lecky's *History of England in the Eighteenth Century,* 8 vols. (New York: D. Appleton and Co., 1878–1890), contains a lengthy discussion of the impressment practiced to fill the ranks of the British army and navy (pp. 580–586). The same chapter was the source for the information in the following entry (pp. 538–539) and for the note about exemption from impressment at 417.9–10 (p. 580).

bedridden one were thus robbed of £1000 each. In this way £15,000
were collected—enough to build the whole Mansion in that day—
100 yrs ago.

I try to stop impressment. But the pay is trifling & volunteers
can't be had. So I am answered that the press is necessary & there is
no way to get rid of it. So I have some nobles pressed "by mistake."
It is promptly decided that a system which offers opportunity for
such mistakes must be instantly abolished—& is.

By the law, in impressment for *the army, the man with a vote
for a M P was excepted by a special Clause.* I[ts].

His Extreme R H the Hellion of H drove in the park
flapdoodle for Royalty.

Good stand for a hermit

4th issue of paper.

584 vol 3—18th cent.

Connect H V³⁹ Cam & --- by tel- now. & phone.

There were Schools attached to the monkeries, & nunneries &
⟨other [busin]⟩—taught Latin ⟨to speak,⟩ but not to read Eng. &
chatechism.

Sir Galihud &c &c arrived in town last night & are stopping with
our genial host of the ⟨Goose & Borax⟩ Blue Boar.

(Electric bells, light &c put into Blue Boar—puff of it in the
paper

(Name some new places Telegraphville, &c.

Advertise for continued story for the paper—which is a weekly
with a patent inside.

That civ is permanent which comes up by the appointed &
regular steps; so I started with balls & a Franklin, & would come
up through the Ramage & the Columbia to the mile-a-minute.⁴⁰ [#]

---

³⁹ The Valley of Holiness. The telephone connection to Camelot is accomplished in
chapter 24 of *A Connecticut Yankee*.

⁴⁰ This note for *A Connecticut Yankee* provides a capsule history of printing. Ink
balls, made of leather stuffed with wool or horsehair, were early devices for applying ink
to type. The Franklin press Clemens alludes to was probably the sort of simple wooden
screw press used but not invented by Benjamin Franklin. Although around 1726 Franklin

Hello Exchange!—Gentleman wishes to speak with the Lady of Shalott.

Grumersome, this old bounty-jumper[41]

Some of the royal poor kin walked in the park.

The bicycle.

Journal items:
Grayling parties going out.[42]
       "   Relief expeditions.
$10,000 reward for Boss.
Search expeditions.

Journal The Sunburst
            Electri Light.

Ck! & take a ride![43]

Clara Tues 11th—
Reform^y Wed 12th—
Leave Thurs 13th[44] [#]

---

devised a copperplate press to print paper money, that machine was hardly one of "the appointed & regular steps" in general printing press evolution. A Franklin press, named because its inventor received his inspiration from Benjamin Franklin in a dream, appeared in 1856, too late for the early chronological place assigned here. Wood and wood-and-iron screw presses manufactured by Adam Ramage began appearing at the turn of the nineteenth century. The Columbian, invented by George Clymer around 1813, was the first iron hand press made in America. By "mile-a-minute" Clemens may have meant one of the large rotary presses developed by Robert Hoe & Company, possibly the "Quadruple" press which reportedly produced 48,000 eight-page or 24,000 ten- to sixteen-page newspapers in an hour. The first of these was adopted by the New York World in 1887.

[41] Sir Grummore Grummursum, or Grummorsum, "a good knight of Scotland," appears briefly, although not as a "bounty-jumper," in book 7, chapters 26 and 28 of Malory's Morte Darthur. Clemens would incorporate part of the latter chapter, including the Scottish knight's defeat in a tournament, into chapter 9 of A Connecticut Yankee.

[42] That is, the "holy grailing" expeditions noted at the end of chapter 9 of A Connecticut Yankee.

[43] Clemens was evidently recalling "S'klk! G'lang!," the "loving though humble and squalid poem" he sent to Clara Spaulding on 1 September 1886, along with some "brave & true horse-car tickets," as a wedding gift (manuscript owned by Stanchfield Wright, Earleville, Md.). The poem has been published in Arthur L. Scott's On the Poetry of Mark Twain (Urbana and London: University of Illinois Press, 1966), pp. 101–102.

[44] This note records a preliminary plan for the Clemenses to leave Quarry Farm on 13

In a constitutional—figure-head—monarchy, a royal family of Chimpanzees would answer every purpose, be ⟨idolized⟩ worshiped as abjectly by the nation, & be cheaper. I propose that, & send for a chimpanzee couple. Arthur has no children. Carry out the project. It is not ⟨generally⟩ known & is now revealed for the first time that this was the origin of the present royalty. It arrives at W^m through the tanner's daughter

Midland. British Volcano—1st irruption.[45]

"The lion walks alone; the jackals herd together."

Instead of giving the people ⟨work &⟩ decent wages, ⟨they⟩ church & gentry & nobility made them work for them for nothing, pauperized them, then fed them with alms & persuaded themselves that the alms-giver was the holiest work of God & sure to go to Heaven, whereas one good-wage giver was worth a million of them to a state.

The treacherous treatment of Napoleon.[46]

Market dull in rich girls from the republic—several offering, no takers. Shady dukes going at a fair rate for cash.

This leech had hermited in Arabia & could read & write. He wrote his prescriptions & Sandy filled & administered them with a dipper. [#]

September 1888, evidently after an Elmira Reformatory reading by Mark Twain on the previous day. Departure was postponed around 6 September, however, when Theodore Crane suffered the paralytic attack that eventually resulted in his death. The Clemens family was not able to leave Elmira until 24 September 1888.

[45] Possibly a note for *A Connecticut Yankee*. The Midlands area of England was the scene of numerous eruptions, which occurred, however, long before the sixth century setting of Clemens' book. There are several allusions to volcanoes in *A Connecticut Yankee in King Arthur's Court*, including the newspaper that Hank Morgan introduces in chapter 26 called the "Camelot *Weekly Hosannah and Literary Volcano*."

[46] Here Clemens probably recalled William Warden's *Letters Written on Board His Majesty's Ship the Northumberland, and Saint Helena*, which he had read in early 1887 (see p. 280, note 189). In that work Warden reported Napoleon's complaints of "the severity with which he was treated, in being consigned to pass his days on the Rock of St. Helena, buffetted by the winds, and amidst the waste of waters; and that he could not comprehend the policy or the apprehensions of England in refusing him an asylum, now that his political career was terminated" (p. 12).

Competition of bards. Break, break, break; the Fair Maid of
Astolat; some exploit of Launcelot, (to curry favor with Queen⟨(⟩)
from Idyls. Sensation. Hint that I was "prepared." I demand an
instant competition. The bard breaks down, showing that his
barbarous previous effort had been memorized. I whirl in some
more Tennyson, with a touch of Shak & Browning & take the cake.
King says, "Strike the lyre"—I lay him out.

"Why, Jean what have you got on such thin clothes for?"
"Mamma, ⟨[-]⟩I saw the sun signed (signified) a hot day."
        Sept 1/88.

The device of "loyalty" to king or party should be a sheep. He is
the counterpart & exactest twin & representative of the king's slave
& the party's slave. Follows his leader—to hell or heaven, it's all
one to him, he hasn't got independence enough to think it any of
his business.

Einräumen, to put into a house—to permit, to give up.
Anwenden, to apply
Verwaltung, management.
unterhandeln, negotiate
Meditate, sinnen, nachdenken
        -tion, Nackdenken
Multitude, Menge, Haufen
Anstellen, Geschäfft, occupation
sich besinnen, to recal, remember[47]

Sept. 12. /88: Read Browning last night in a private house to 130
people, the ladies in the majority.
Have made speeches several times at banquets where half were
ladies.
Have read & lectured a good many times at matinès, where of
course ladies were largely in the majority.

---

[47] This expression more properly means "to recollect oneself" or "to recollect one's
thoughts." In the previous line, Clemens intended to write *Anstellung*, meaning "place,
post, situation," instead of the verb *anstellen*, meaning, among other things, "to place"
or "to appoint." The other words and definitions in this list, except for some minor faults
in transcription, are correct.

In all such cases, failure may be counted upon. In fact, hardly anything can prevent it but a carefully organized *claque*. Not a half-hearted claque, but a brave one—a claque which will not allow itself to be discouraged.

For several reasons. To begin with, ladies are cowards about expressing their feelings before folk; men *become* cowards in the presence of ladies. Here then, is what you are to expect: Your first piece goes well—the men forget themselves & applaud. Consequently you go at your second piece with good heart & do it well. This time the applause has an undecided flavor about it: the men have not reasoned that it was the *ladies* who failed to support them when they applauded before, they have merely noticed that the support was lacking. After that, they are afraid, & a dead silence follows the third reading. You are as exactly equipped now for the fourth piece as if a bucket of cold water had been poured over you. If you are wise, you will ⟨not⟩now tear your audience all to pieces with a roaring anecdote; then say you are smitten with a killing headache, & dismiss them; for no man can read or talk against ⟨[irr]esponsiveness⟩unresponsiveness. If you try to go on, you will *earn* ⟨irresponsiveness⟩unresponsiveness, for you will do your work so poorly as to make ⟨irresponsiveness⟩unresponsiveness your only just reward.

And so one should make the following his rule, & never depart from it: If ladies are to be present, *and* a brave, instructed, & well organized claque of a dozen men, all right; if ladies are to be present, & no organized claque, decline with thanks.

The Elmira ⟨r⟩Reformatory contains 850 convicts, who are there for all manner of crimes. People go there & lecture, read, or make speeches, & come away surprised & delighted. They can't understand it. They have astonished themselves by the excellence of their own performance. They cannot remember to have ever done so well before. Afterward, they always say that for a splendid audience give them a housefull of convicts, it's the best audience in the world. They puzzle & puzzle over it & are not able to get away from the apparently established fact that an audience of convicts is the most intelligent & appreciative in the world. Which is· all a mistake. The whole secret lies in the absence of ladies. Any 850

men would be just as inspiring, where no dampening female
person was in sight, with her heart full of emotion & her
determined repression ⟨keep⟩ choking it down & keeping the signs
of it from showing on the outside. There is more inspiration in an
audience of male corpses than in a packed multitude of the livest
& brightest women that ever walked.

Who made the greatness of England—& indeed of the ⟨whole⟩
civilized world? Name their great names. Was it Wellington &
Nelson? No; these shrink into a pitiful insignificence when placed
alongside the mighty names of Watt, Arkwright, ⟨Eli Whitney⟩ &
Stephenson. ⟨Daguerre⟩ To whom does England raise statues &
monuments? To her creators? No; to her Georges & ⟨her⟩ Prince
Alberts.

The book-house equipped will pay $5\frac{1}{2}$ to 6^c per M—the
unequipped 43; the equipped journal will pay $7\frac{1}{2}$ to 8^c, & the
unequipped 50. A formidable competition? Yes!   .

233 vol 6. Elizabeth's law regulating occupations. Universal
suffrage would have annulled it instantly.[48]

Law of James I empowering magistrates to fix wages.[49]

A law of our day ⟨p⟩made the public treasury *pay* part of the
wages. [#]

---

[48] "During the whole of the eighteenth century the famous law of Elizabeth determining the conditions of industry was in force. It provided that no one could lawfully exercise
any art, mystery, or manual occupation without having served in it at least seven years as
an apprentice; that no one should be bound as an apprentice who was not under twenty-
one years, and whose parents did not possess a certain fortune; that every master who had
three apprentices must keep one journeyman, and for every other apprentice above three,
one other journeyman; that no one should be engaged as a servant or journeyman for less
than a year; that the hours of work should be twelve in summer, and from dawn to night
in winter, and finally that wages should be assessed for the year by the justices of the peace
or town magistrates, who were also directed to settle all disputes between masters and
apprentices" (Lecky, *Eighteenth Century*, 6:233). Clemens' confidence in the summary
effect of universal suffrage may have been misplaced, for Lecky noted that "it was especially the workmen who appear to have clung" to this act, and to the one noted in the
following entry, for protection against unscrupulous employers.
[49] A "law which was passed under James I. extended the power of the justices and town
magistrates to fix the wages of all kinds of labourers and workmen" (Lecky, *Eighteenth
Century*, 6:233).

246 vol 3 for crimes.[50]

Book 4, ch 27, Blackstone. Read it.[51]

Get Howard's "State Prisons"[52]

For any man or woman not rich or of noble rank, there was but an imaginary difference between England & hell ⟨a hundred⟩ ⟨75⟩ 100 years ago.

What was called English "liberty" was for gentlemen only. See vol 6; 262[53]

Price shall be either $8,500 or $9,000, but not *below* either of these, because the Farnham royalties have to come out of it.

⟨Se[-]⟩Sept. 17 '88. Sent Chatto's notes to Bissell, due 27th Feb & 27th March ',89, for £300 & £270.12.2.

In P & P 160 pages out of 400 are represented by pictures & blank backs, & about 20 more by Indices &c.

Good 180—or

$$\frac{400}{72,000}$$ words

Douglas Taylor belongs to the Typothetæ, & there are 510 members in the National organization. Ask him for their addresses.[54] [#]

---

[50] On this page Lecky discusses the immunities from prosecution and arrest enjoyed by members of Parliament. He also notes "the claim of the House of Commons to constitute itself a tribunal for the trial and punishment of private injuries done to its members," a power "altogether unknown to the law of England, and . . . as inequitable as it was anomalous." These parliamentary privileges were modified or fell into disuse in the second half of the eighteenth century.

[51] This chapter, "Of Trial and Conviction," in Sir William Blackstone's *Commentaries on the Laws of England* deals with various methods of determining guilt and innocence, including trial by ordeal, battle, and jury.

[52] *The State of the Prisons in England and Wales*, by John Howard (Warrington: W. Eyres, 1777–1780), an examination into the horrid conditions suffered by prisoners and a call for their reform.

[53] Possibly a reference to Lecky's discussion of Game Laws by which no one "was permitted to shoot or fish even on his own grounds, unless he possessed a freehold estate of at least 100*l.* a year, or a leasehold of at least 150*l.*"

[54] Douglas Taylor was the senior member of the New York printing firm of Douglas

The institution⟨s⟩ of royalty, in any form, is an insult to the human race.

The man who ⟨say⟩ believes there is a man in the world who is better than himself merely because he was born "royal" or "noble" is a dog, with the ⟨heart⟩ soul of a dog—& at bottom is a liar.

Arthur slept much. Kings & snakes are always best when asleep.

4323. = $662. T. W. Crane. Sept. 24, '88.
Farm, from June 23 to Sept. 24, 13 weeks & 2 days.
6 persons, $40 per week, ... ⟨$535⟩$532.
2 ponies, ($3 per week each) 80
Washing, 10 weeks at $5 50
                                                            ‾‾‾‾‾
                                                            $662.

William, ...$25;
His wife 12;
Liddy. 5
Oscar 12
Washerwoman, ... 5
⟨Doyle, ... 6⟩
Mr. Rice 5
Mothers ⎫
            ⎬ each, ... 2
people ⎭
Doyle. 6

Moderate but steady walk, & no stops, it is *40 minutes* from Farm to D. L. W.[55]

And 1 hour to mother's house.[56]

Wells Fargo takes the ponies *through to Hartford* from here for ⟨$[4-] each⟩——⟨[---]⟩.[#]

Taylor & Company. He was a member of the New York Typothetae. Clemens may have hoped to recruit support for the Paige typesetter among working printers. In October 1889 he would again seek Taylor's intervention with the printers' association, on that occasion to enlist their support for pending international copyright legislation.

[55] The Delaware, Lackawanna and Western Railroad.

[56] The Elmira home of Livy's mother, Mrs. Jervis Langdon.

If the master⟨s⟩ of a kingdom is so important that God will not
entrust his appointment to men but appoints him himself, it then
follows that the master OF that master is a still more important
officer, & so this one must *especially* be divinely appointed.
Therefore one is logically compelled to say Nell Gwynne by the
grace of God Monarch of Great Britain, &c.

Now name the other grace-of-God monarchs of European history.

In that far day the Eng will hunt a helpless fox with horses &
afterward with artillery; & tame chickens.

"The ex-empress Eugenie[57] has declined publicly to notice &c"—
It is an error. She has merely declined *to* PUBLICLY notice.
Declined publicly, & publicly declined, mean the same thing;
declined *to* PUBLICLY notice, means another thing.

Repeat "Consistency" (with a year's later comments) before the
Club.[58]

⟨Repub⟩ GOP. This political Lazarus sunk so low that even us
Mugwump dogs are forced in pity to lick his sores.[59]

Edison's gasoline, rhigoline, & caustic soda, for destructive of
yellow fever germs.[60] A coat sleeve (with thermometer in it)
saturated with the first, fell 30° in 3 min; with the second, fell 60°
in 20 minutes & was stiff with ice & frost.

People seem ⟨to think⟩ to ⟨p⟩think they are citizens of the

---

[57] Eugénie Marie de Montijo de Guzmán, wife of Napoleon III and formerly empress
of France.

[58] Clemens had read this paper to the Hartford Monday Evening Club on 5 December
1887. He never presented the revised version noted here.

[59] Clemens here compares the Republican party to the diseased beggar of Luke
16:19–31. In November 1888, when the Republicans would unseat Democratic presidential incumbent Grover Cleveland with Benjamin Harrison, a more apt comparison
might be to the resurrected Lazarus of John 11:1–44. Clemens' mugwump sympathies
were well known (see for example p. 436, note 95).

[60] Through the fall and early winter of 1888, a yellow fever epidemic raged in Jackson-
ville, Florida, and several other southern cities. In the middle of September the disease
was brought to New York by Richard A. Proctor, a prominent astronomer, who was fatally

Republican party & that that is patriotism ⟨o⟩& sufficiently good
patriotism. I prefer to be a citizen of the United States.[61]

⟨Ink. + Envelops.
Wood basket.
Paper-packets⟩
Easy shoes   Pipe & cigars & tobacco.
⟨*All MSS.* & books
A *filler.*⟩

Autographs.

Keene Valley storekeeper who didn't keep turkey red.[62] [#]

---

infected. Health officials assured the public that there was no occasion for alarm, but
Clemens evidently decided to be prepared to take action along lines suggested by Thomas
Edison. On 27 September 1888, the New York *Tribune* reported the following advice
from Edison:

> The only way to stop the spread of the disease is to put a cordon of gasoline around
> the infected place. If that don't stop it, nothing can. It would cost $24 to sprinkle a
> street 250 feet long by 60 feet broad with gasoline, and that would kill everything in
> the soil. Caustic soda should be used in damp places. A square yard could be covered
> with caustic soda to a depth of one-eighth of an inch for 1½ cents, and no organism
> could possibly survive it. In a room heated to 82 degrees Fahrenheit a coat was dipped
> in rhigolene [a petroleum distillate], and in fifteen minutes the temperature of the
> coat fell to 28 degrees and the coat was covered with hoar frost. Now, as cold weather
> is known effectually to destroy the fever microbes, this would prove an effective way
> of disinfecting clothing, as the rhigolene will evaporate within half an hour.

[61] In the presidential campaign of 1888, the Republican party made a patriotic issue of
Grover Cleveland's desire to reduce customs duties. An enormous budgetary surplus had
convinced Cleveland that taxes were too severe and he believed that existing tariff rates
showed unfair favoritism to protected industries. Although his proposed reforms were
mild, the Republicans claimed they were pro-British and would ruin American industry
and the American worker.

[62] On 30 September 1888, Clemens wrote to Theodore Crane about Harmony
Twichell's "adventure in the little village of Keene Valley" in the Adirondack Mountains. Mrs. Twichell asked the storekeeper there if he minded explaining why he did not
stock the common fabric known as turkey red:

> Something like the reminiscence of an ancient pain swept across the man's solemn
> face, & he said:
> "No'm, I'd just as soon tell you. It's this away. I *did* lay in a piece of that truck, once,
> & before I could seem to turn around, blamed if 'twarn't all sold! Well, I thought it
> over, & by 'm by I yielded, & laid in another piece. Well, just think! Before I could shet
> the door, *it* was all sold, every inch of it! That let me out. There ain't no use to fool with
> turkey red—you can't keep the dern truck in stock."

The Berlin Das Echo[63] (July, '88) says there are now 621 newspapers & periodicals published there.

Henrik Cavling.[64]

C. T. Christensen, Manager of Drexel, Morgan & Co.

The London Times has 12, 16, & 20 pages—but usually 16. '88. Blowitz.[65]

No more honesty than the Girard College Trustees, who swindle the dead in the name of the Lord.[66]

Will Sage's small son who started down a tree with a bird's-⟨eye⟩egg in his mouth, & it hatched!
(Sage's neat way of getting confession out of his boy at dinner)

N O T A.
Ein Todt-Bezeichniss anstellen lassen, in N.Y.[67]

und viele electriche Lichte auf meinem Hof aufheben lassen.[68]

October 15/88. Special officer Heise goes on duty to-day noon at $2.73 a day, regular policemen's wages, as he says, & as Mr. Smith told me last night. He will patrol the yard & frontage in uniform from 7 every evening & discourage the tramps—& is to stay until I get up my electric street-lamp. Let go ⟨No[v]⟩Oct. 27.

---

[63] A weekly newspaper of politics, literature, art, and science.

[64] Henrik Cavling was a Danish journalist visiting the United States to report on the presidential election of 1888. On 8 October 1888, Christen Thomsen Christensen, manager of the New York office of Drexel, Morgan & Company, the noted banking firm, and a former Danish consul in New York, wrote to Clemens asking him to grant Cavling "the honor of shaking you by the hand" and being "face to face with an author, who . . . has proven a benefactor to civilized mankind, scarcely less appreciated outside of, than in his own country." Clemens replied affirmatively on the following day. He received Cavling in Hartford on the evening of 22 October.

[65] Henri Georges Stephan Adolphe de Blowitz, foreign correspondent of the London *Times*. The manner in which de Blowitz became Clemens' source for this information has not been established.

[66] The Girard College controversy is discussed on page 407, note 24.

[67] *Have the death notice prepared in N.Y.* Clemens may have been expecting the death of Theodore Crane, who was seriously ill at this time. Crane did not die until 3 July 1889.

[68] *And have many electric lights set up in my courtyard.*

I found, yesterday, that Brer Franklin Chamberlin[69] (who has two skunk-friends on the Street-Board,) had at last succeeded in getting the light moved from the Gillette street corner to the mouth of Forest street, thus leaving our gates smothered in Egyptian darkness. The City government has done me many a mean trick, in 16 years, ⟨but⟩ & I stood the strain & kept the peace; but, to frightfully inconvenience me in order to accommodate a rectum like Franklin Chamberlin, was a little too much. So I went down last night & contracted for electric light at my own cost, & police protection at my own cost, & took measures to transfer my citizenship to some other town. So, after next June I shall have the satisfaction of paying a (possibly) very large tax every year to some town in which I do *not* live, ⟨& I shall⟩ & paying not a cent in Hartford any more forever, except on the house & grounds.

Jno P Foley,[70] 626, E. 137th.

2

Shave & tel in hous[e]

Henrik Cavling.

⟨Ask at office & at Alexander's for Livy's shoes (10 days ago.)⟩

⟨Telegraph the Children.⟩

Frau B. sagte "Dear Lil—Can't be home to dinner"—then dear Lil mopes."

Must divide the partnership into thirds, & stop unearned ⟨w⟩salaries

See about syndicating the Tale⟨.⟩, for $45,000.[71] [#]

---

[69] A Hartford lawyer whose property, at the corner of Farmington Avenue and Forest Street, adjoined Clemens'. Clemens had originally purchased his lot from Chamberlin and increased its dimensions with subsequent purchases. He had been protesting this alteration of the neighborhood's lighting since July 1888 (see p. 404, note 16).

[70] The author of a series of articles on the "Outdoor Life of the Presidents" which began appearing in *Outing*, a magazine of sport and recreation, in November 1888. Clemens' business with Foley is not known, but it may have been in connection with possible authorship of a book for Charles L. Webster & Company.

[71] Clemens discussed possible syndication of *A Connecticut Yankee* with Charles A.

Want to get part of debt returned to me, then have the $75,000 clause knocked out, so I can give away the property to some damned fool.[72]

Ask about my dues at the "Players"[73]

⟨George—stop the billiards.⟩

Scribner gives us no credit. Why?[74]

2 tin boxes the size of this book & twice as thick—for cigars.

1. Sell to ⟨Stedman⟩ ⟨Mch 1⟩ *now* for ⟨$25,000⟩$45,000, Nov. 15, & leave the rest to go on as it is. This will pay me $40 or

---

Dana, owner of the New York *Sun*. On 1 November, Dana mentioned this conversation to S. S. McClure, who immediately wrote to Clemens: "I would like to see you and negotiate, if possible, for the publication of your serial." Clemens noted "Let this wait a while" on the envelope of McClure's letter. There is no indication that he actually pursued the matter with McClure.

[72] The chaotic state of Webster & Company affairs in the fall of 1888 inspired the notions of withdrawal recorded here and at 429.8–431.5. On 23 October 1888 the company bookkeeper, Arthur H. Wright, sent Clemens a biannual statement which indicated a loss of $16,455.66 during the past six months. Wright's accounting showed the firm's indebtedness to Clemens to be $72,942.10, approaching the maximum of $75,000 capital he was obliged to provide by the contract of 1 April 1887. On 5 November, Frederick J. Hall would dispatch to Clemens a complex and desperate treatise which corrected some oversights in Wright's statement and predicted a solid future for the company if Clemens approved a new and radical organization of its procedures and personnel. Hall responded then to Clemens' desire to withdraw some of his capital by noting: "Properly managed $30,000 ought to be *ample* capital to run the business on, unless it should grow to great proportions." But, he hastened to add as an afterthought: "This capital could be increased as necessary."

[73] Clemens was a charter member of the Players Club, having attended the organizational meeting convened by Edwin Booth at Delmonico's on 6 January 1888. A printed letter of 9 June 1888 formally notified Clemens of his election to the club and an enclosed card requested payment of his initiation fee of $100 and semiannual dues of $20 on or before 1 November 1888. On the envelope that brought these notices Clemens wrote "Won't pay it." He was successful in securing a reduction of these fees, perhaps in his capacity as founder, for receipts dated 13 November show that he paid half the requested amounts.

[74] In August 1888, after extensive negotiations, Webster & Company had agreed to allow excerpts from the *Personal Memoirs of P. H. Sheridan* to appear in *Scribner's Magazine* (see p. 387, note 294). The magazine promised to include a footnote stating: "This article will be incorporated in the 'Personal Memoirs of P. H. Sheridan,'" (CLW & Co. to SLC, 3 August 1888). The footnote was not printed when the Sheridan material appeared in the November 1888 number.

$50000 & yet not impair my $75,000 capital, for all the *Baar* would be a dividend & leave them still in debt to me 60 or 70,000[75]

2. Rerserve Sheri but sell evrything else to them for 6% on capital & a share of possible profit. They assuming my responsibilities & my slavery to a lunatic.[76]

3. *Wait* until this other matter determines itself successfully; then collect what comes in from Sher, make my capital intact, let the old regime return Apl. 1 & go unassisted to destruction.[77]

I prefer No. 3.

1. If by Dec. 31 Sher proves to be unprofitable,[78] demand a reconstruction of contract placing power in my hands where it belongs. Refusal? Go into court.

2. Demand dissolution. Go into Court. [#]

---

[75] Probably a plan to sell Webster & Company rights in the *Library of American Literature* to Edmund C. Stedman. On 26 October 1888 Stedman wrote Clemens a long letter demonstrating the value of this work, assuring him that "You have made no 'losses', & will make none," on it and warning him to "Look *elsewhere* for the causes of an adverse balance-sheet." A week later he wrote again, reminding Clemens that the *Library of American Literature* "is the most valuable & *substantial* property the firm possesses" and asserting that "there is no limit to the profit from it. Thus far, we have scarcely *scratched* the end of the buying elephant's nose." Unconvinced of the work's possibilities, Clemens evidently thought Stedman might reinforce his lofty opinion of it with his purse. "*Baar*" is Clemens' German for "cash."

[76] The lunatic was probably Charles L. Webster. The work in question was the *Personal Memoirs of P. H. Sheridan.*

[77] This "other matter" cannot be precisely identified but was probably related to Arthur H. Wright's unfavorable financial report of 23 October 1888 (see note 72). On 29 October and again on 30 October, Hall asked for a meeting with Clemens and Daniel Whitford, Webster & Company's lawyer, apparently to discuss, among other matters, the status of Charles L. Webster, who on 1 April 1889 was due to end a temporary retirement occasioned by poor health. In fact, Webster was persuaded to retire permanently in December 1888 (see p. 374, note 239).

[78] Webster & Company hopes for the *Personal Memoirs of P. H. Sheridan* had been dampened by Frederick J. Hall's conclusions after recent consultations with book agents in Cleveland, Chicago, Omaha, Denver, and Saint Louis. On 15 October 1888 Hall reported to Clemens: "There is one thing this trip has convinced me of viz: *war literature of any kind and no matter by whom written is played out.* We have got to hustle everlastingly to get rid of 75,000 sets of Sheridan. I had set my mind on 100,000 sets but am forced to lessen this figure. There is not a man today who could write another book on the war and sell 5000 in the whole country."

Can I be held for debts made beyond the capital?

I will buy out or sell out.

Since the spring of '86, the thing has gone straight downhill toward sure destruction. It must be brought to an end Feb. 1 at all hazards. This is final.

Nov. 1, 1888. I have just seen the drawings & description of an electrical machine lately patented by a Mr. ⟨Teska⟩Tesla, & sold to the Westinghouse Company, which will revolutionize the whole electric business of the world. It is the most valuable patent since the telephone. The drawings & description show that this is the *very* machine, in every detail which Paige invented nearly 4 years ago. I furnished $1,000 for the experiments, & was to have half of the invention. We tried a direct current—& failed. We wanted to try an alternating current, but we lacked the apparatus. The $1000 was exhausted, & I would furnish nothing more because I was burdened in the 3 succeeding years with vast expenses on the Paige type-setting machine. ⟨Teska⟩Tesla (& Thompson?) tried everything that we tried, as the drawings & descriptions prove; & he tried one thing more—a thing which we had canvassed—the *alternating* current. *That* solved the difficulty & achieved success.[79]

Clarence *must* give market report—American heiressess buying up rotten dukes. *Charactr* as well as title considered in the market, & discounted accordingly.
Who the duke married first—next—& so on—causes of divorce. Disease—but can't name it.

⟨Buy hearts co[unt]ers⟩

(Jerusalem) "Well, the Savior's been here once!")

⟨To start with, 5 m.—no orders. 1 m sh at 5 each 5000,000.

---

[79] Nikola Tesla invented his first alternating current motor in 1883. On 1 May 1888 he received patents on such a motor. He soon sold his rights to George Westinghouse for one million dollars. Elihu Thomson, who had been instrumental in the perfection of arc-light systems, in the mid-1880s also developed a type of alternating current motor. Clemens' investment in an electromagnetic motor developed by James W. Paige, evidently initiated in 1887 and not "nearly 4 years ago," is discussed on page 338, note 111.

Each 1000th is worth \$5. After 500 orders, \$10—aftr 1000 15
after ⟨10,000

$$\begin{array}{r} 500 \\ \hline 5\ 000\ 000⟩ \end{array}$$

Ich werde Ihnen ⟨ein⟩ $\frac{1}{500}$ von den Ganzen um \$10,000
verkaufen.[80] (basis, \$5,000,000.

Nach ⟨[5]oo⟩⟨1000⟩ 500 ⟨orders⟩ Bestellen, um
⟨\$20,000⟩\$15,000.[81] (Grund, 10,000,000.

Nach 1000, um \$20,000. (Gr. 15,000,000)
"   1500   "   25,000   ("   20,000,000
"   2000   "   30,000   ("   25,00,000⟩

Einbildungs Hauptpreise von 100,000 Theilen.[82]
Um \$50 pro Theil es ist . . . . 5,000,000[83]

"	100	 10	500	Bestellen
"	150	 15	1000	"
"	200	 20	1500	"
"	250	 25	2000	"
"	300	 30	2500	"

Ein $\frac{1}{1000}$ int. oder ⟨[2]oo⟩100 Theilen.[84]

100 at 50	. . . . .is.	5,000
" 100	. . . .	10,000
" 150	. . . .	15,000
" 200	. . . .	20,000
" 250	. . . .	25,000
" 300	. . . .	30,000

⟨40,000⟩20,000 Bestellen erwartete. Wann wir nur 1500 erhalten
haben, wird $\frac{1}{20}$ eine ⟨millione⟩Millione werth.[85]

As deaf as a spider. [#]

---

[80] *I will sell them $\frac{1}{500}$th of the whole for \$10,000.*
[81] *Afterwards 500 Orders for \$15,000. (Basis, 10,000,000.*
[82] *Imaginary top price for 100,000 shares.*
[83] *At \$50 per share it is 5,000,000.*
[84] *A $\frac{1}{1000}$ interest or 100 shares.*
[85] *20,000 orders expected. When we've secured only 1500, it will be worth $\frac{1}{20}$ of a
million.*

There are two times in a man's life when he should not speculate: when he can afford it, & when he can't.[86]

P̲H̲IL-A̲-d̲el-p̲h̲i̲a̲fer

HOW
PLANTS
GROW
GRAY.[87]

The mash. will reduce the value of a million dollars or so of electros now kept in stock to one-seventh of that value.

Twichell's *Friday*.

Send Lib of Humor to Howells, 330 East 17[th.]

Nation

Box of Guns.
Interviewer.
Golden Arm.
Whistling Yarn.
Christening Story.
My Duel.
Lucerne girl
Jumping Frog.
European ⟨Guil⟩Guides.
UNCLE REMUS.
Huck Finn—71 & 109.[88]

Up at a Villa.⎫
                ⎬ Browning [#]
Horse-Race.   ⎭

---

[86] One of Mark Twain's favorite unheeded maxims. He used a version of it as the epigraph to chapter 56 of *Following the Equator*. The same sentiment is given a different form in one of the epigraphs to chapter 13 of *Pudd'nhead Wilson*.

[87] *Botany for Young People and Common Schools. How Plants Grow: A Simple Introduction to Structural Botany*. This book by Asa Gray was first published in 1858 and re-issued many times.

[88] Probably references to pages in the first edition of *Huckleberry Finn*. The first, toward the end of chapter 8, begins Huck's and Jim's comical discussion of Jim's invest-

Nov. 23, '88. At noon, was coming up a back street; 2 poorly
dressed girls, one about 10 the other 12 or 13 years old, were just
behind me; was attracted by the musical voice of the elder one, &
slowed down my gait to listen; by & by the younger said, "Yonder
they are?" "Where?" "Way down the street—don't you see?" The
elder threw back her head ⟨& p[our]ed⟩ ⟨g⟩ & gushed out a liquid
"Hoo-*oo-oo-ooh!*"—the most melodious note that ever issued from
human lips, it seemed to me. Nothing has equaled it, in my
hearing, but the rich note of the wood-thrush. I resolved to track
that child home—& did. She entered a poor frame dwelling next
to & north of a frame building that had a sign "Sigourney Tool
Company" on its front. Then I followed the ⟨e⟩younger girl home;
at least to a house in John Hooker's grounds.[89] So I shall be able to
find one or the other, by & by. I mean to educate that girl's voice.
She'll make a stir in the world, sure.

D^r· Rice—⟨pipe-box.⟩pipe-tray.

London Times—"consisted of the usual 16 pages," (96 columns)
(6 columns to the page). 50,000 ems to the page?

Sue *must* come for Thanksgivg. If she *doesn't*, then tell her Miss
King will pass through, Wednes^y,—& will lunch with her—& can
Oscar help her to the ferry at 2 or haf-past, with her bags?[90]

Read King Arthur & Yank 6th of December? Yes.—10 a.m.
129 Washington street—Edith Wilder Smith.[91] [#]

---

ments. The second, the initial page of chapter 14, leads into their conversation about
"ole King Sollermun." Clemens frequently included these passages in his readings.

[89] Hooker, a Hartford lawyer, was one of the founding residents of the Nook Farm
community.

[90] Grace King had come to Hartford on 10 October 1888 to visit with the Clemens
family. She stayed with them until 12 November when she moved to the home of the
Charles Dudley Warners. In this entry, made around 23 November, Clemens refers to a
plan for Grace King to lunch with Susan Crane in New York City and be assisted by Oscar,
one of the Crane servants, if Mrs. Crane could not be in Hartford for the Thanksgiving
holiday. The Cranes had been staying at the Murray Hill Hotel since 25 October, probably so that Theodore could receive medical treatment. Although they did go to Hartford
for Thanksgiving, Grace King was no longer there, having departed for Baltimore on
Wednesday, 28 November 1888.

[91] The wife of Wilder Smith, a clergyman living in Hartford, was active in local charitable organizations.

Introduce in King A, a battle of cats & other tame game & let
the nobility "bag" 2,000 "pieces"—tame fawns, kids, lambs &c

Rock-it (rocket)
Phan-tom.
Rail-road
Falls (false)-alarm
An-eck-dote
Mew-sick (music)
Court-house
Book-⟨agent.⟩ (agent)/keeper (of animals)
Cash-year (cashier)
Ball-loon (balloon)
Par-a/eh?-chute

Smith College:[92]
    Brer Rabbit: 2 or 3
    Up at a Villa: 25 Lucerne girl
    Golden Arm ⟨25⟩10 Tale of Fishwife
    Whistling story.
    Christening story.
    Browning's Horse-race.
    Phil'-d[e]-day-a-l'-pay-haitch i a fer
Print on small cards that can't be made to rattle.

Abby S. Richardson, 132 W 44[th][93] [#]

---

[92] On 26 November 1888 Grace King accompanied Clemens on a visit to Smith College, where he evidently read the pieces in the following program. Grace King described
their picturesque trip to the railroad station in a letter the following day, reporting that
"Patrick the coachman, enveloped in furs" resembled "one of Tolstoi's Russians, with his
big cap and shaggy tippet" while "Mr. Clemens was all sealskin except the tip end of a
very red nose. I thought I would freeze in my seat as the open carriage dashed at full trot
through the icy streets" (Grace King to Nan King, 27 November 1888, Grace King Papers,
Louisiana State University, Baton Rouge). Clemens' plan for printed programs that
would not rattle (435.22) was originally conceived before his 1884/1885 lecture tour with
George Washington Cable.
[93] Abby Sage Richardson, minor historian, literary editor, and Shakespearean actress,
wrote to Clemens on 4 December 1888 recalling The Prince and the Pauper as "one of
the most beautiful stories and most exquisite in treatment of anything I had ever read"
and asking his permission to dramatize it. "I can scarcely hope that an author of your
reputation and experience would accept even the assistance of a collaborateur," Mrs.

"Who the h—l sat down on that hat, Mrs. O'Hooligan?"

Der Grossherzog Hellandamnationowski[94]

"Mugwumps are despised in New York." C. D. Warner.[95]

Get 1000 orders on these terms; no payment till delivery. Then borrow at 10 or 15%, the money necessary to make them.

Thomas F. Reddy, Room 10,
   61 Court st. Boston.
Dramatized Prince & Pauper.[96]

Northampton, Jan. 21.[97]

Lost Leader
Tray
Andrea del Sarto
Mulèykeh (Dram. Idyls).
Love in a Ruin
Spanish Cloister

Richardson wrote. Five days later she was able to write again, thanking him "for your *very kind* letter received yesterday. Since you give me permission I am going to make the attempt." On 3 January 1889 Clemens and Mrs. Richardson signed a contract for this dramatization. Its terms are alluded to later in this notebook (p. 453).

[94] *The Grand Duke* Hellandamnationowski.

[95] While visiting Hartford in late 1888, Grace King noted with approval Clemens' "most exquisite delight" in maintaining his mugwump status by again voting for the Democratic presidential candidate, Grover Cleveland, as he had done in 1884. She reported that the Warners "are very indignant over Mr Clemens conversion—that is the women part of the family. Mr W, does not say any thing—in his secret heart he wants to do the same; but he has been whipped into line by his wife and Gen. [Joseph R.] Hawley" (Grace King to Sarah Ann Miller King, 6 November 1888, quoted in Robert Bush, "Grace King and Mark Twain," *American Literature*, March 1972, p. 41).

[96] On 25 January 1889, Reddy, a Boston attorney, informed Clemens that he had "nearly finished" a dramatization of *The Prince and the Pauper*. Reddy asked Clemens' permission to arrange for a production of the play by the Boston Museum Company and in return offered Clemens seventy-five per cent of the proceeds. Clemens replied, the following day, that he had already given such permission elsewhere, but Reddy politely pressed him, to no effect, for the "name & address of party who has agreed to dramatize work" so that "perhaps we together might be able to produce a creditable play" (Thomas F. Reddy to SLC, 28 January 1889).

[97] The following program of platform pieces was for an 1889 return engagement at Smith College in Northampton, Massachusetts. Clemens had last appeared there on 26 November 1888.

Up at a Villa.
My Duel.
Blue-jay
Golden Arm
Since Little Wesley's Dead.[98]

⟨In⟩The World averages about 10 pages a day, taking in the big Sunday issue. If half of this is leaded, we have this result:

1,000 ems in each column consists of leads; 7,000 pure leads to the page; 35,000 ems of leads per day; so that in a week's issue, about 250,000 ems ($125) are represented by leads (& dashes between the "Wants.")

At $4 for a man's day's work, this would fall not far short of paying the wages of 5 men for a week on 5 machines. Each of these would set 40,000 solid a day, & the whole would set 1,400,000 in a week. Lead half of it, & it becomes ⟨1,54[-00]—⟩1,540,000—all of which you get for nothing; & at present rates you would pay more than $750 for it.

The mach. makes no errors; ⟨the⟩ but the average operator will himself make about 1 error per 1000 ems—say 35 to a World or Tribune page⟨.⟩—say a couple of hundred in 6 pages of a daily newspaper. They should be very simple errors, & one individual ought to correct the 6 pages in 30 or 40 minutes. Good authorities assert that it takes 7 Mergenthaler machines & 7 men to correct the Tribune's proof.

The Merg's price is $1000; if ours were the same it would earn its price 6 times a year.

The price of the Thorne[99] is $2000; if ours were the same, it would earn its price 3 times a year.

For every man deprived of work by the M, 10 will *get* work, through it. [#]

---

[98] James Whitcomb Riley's poem, "The Absence of Little Wesley," a grandfather's lament for his dead grandson, appeared in the *Century* magazine in May 1888.

[99] A typesetting machine developed by Joseph Thorne in 1880 and manufactured in Hartford. The Thorne machine, which composed but did not justify automatically, was widely used by printing firms and newspapers in the late 1880s.

The Peckster Professorship.[100]

⟨Send Sheridan & Pope's book to Joe.

Mrs. E. L. Sluyter, $15.⟩[101]

⟨4 of each of my books.⟩

Sir Francis De Winton
President Emin ⟨B⟩Relief Committee, London.[102]

⟨Write Gerhardt.⟩

⟨Thank Jo Lane & Enders.⟩[103]

⟨Charge⟩ alarm battery

⟨Write Fuller⟩[104] [#]

---

[100] *The Peckster Professorship: An Episode in the History of Psychical Research* (Boston and New York: Houghton, Mifflin and Co., 1888), a novel by Josiah Phillips Quincy.

[101] Mrs. Elizabeth L. Sluyter was superintendent of the Union for Home Work which had been organized in 1872 "by women of Hartford, irrespective of religious denomination, for the purpose of improving the condition and, in particular, the home life of the poorer women and children of the city." The union supported "reading-rooms for boys and girls, a day-nursery, sewing and cooking schools, a clothing-club, lending library," and made an "effort to provide good and cheap tenements under thorough supervision" (J. Hammond Trumbull, *The Memorial History of Hartford County, Connecticut, 1633–1884*, 2 vols. [Boston: Edward L. Osgood, 1886], 1:538–539).

[102] Clemens had met Colonel Francis de Winton in May 1883 in Ottawa where de Winton was secretary to the marquis of Lorne, governor general of Canada. In 1887 de Winton was secretary of the Emin Pasha Relief Committee and assisted Henry M. Stanley's preparations for an African expedition to rescue Emin Pasha, governor of Equatorial Province, from the challenge of a Mahdist uprising. Clemens, who hoped to coax a book from Stanley for Charles L. Webster & Company, probably wished to consult de Winton about the expedition's progress. In the spring of 1890 he would enlist de Winton's help in an unsuccessful attempt to secure Stanley's narrative of the Emin Pasha mission (see p. 494, note 39, and p. 551, note 206).

[103] Joseph G. Lane was a Hartford "Importer and Wholesale Dealer in Groceries and Liquors" (*Geer's*[1889], p. 404) regularly patronized by the Clemens family. Thomas O. Enders was president of the United States Bank in Hartford where the Clemenses maintained an account. Clemens probably wished to acknowledge Christmas or New Year's greetings from these men.

[104] On 29 December 1888, Clemens wrote to Frank Fuller: "Thank you ever so much for the razor strop. When I strop I shall always think of you; and that will be three times a week." Fuller had evidently suggested a book for Charles L. Webster & Company, for Clemens advised him: "We can't take any more books for a long time yet. We are overcrowded and must wait till we work the list down" (TS in MTP).

⟨Ida—Hudibras.⟩[105]

"Travelers & Outlaws"—Higginson.[106]

The Peckster Professorship
Story of an African Farm.[107]

⟨Express package.

Send 2ᵈ Vol to Ida.⟩[108]

To Mrs. S. L. Clemens.
  Happy New Year!
The machine is finished, & this is the first work done on it.

SL Clemens
Hartford, Dec. 1888.

(Furnished to Van, Dec. 29, to be used as his first "copy.")[109]

The Heathwood,
  345 W. 58ᵗʰ
    Elsie Leslie[110] [#]

---

[105] Clemens apparently intended to send a copy of Samuel Butler's work to Charles J. Langdon's wife, Ida.

[106] Thomas W. Higginson, *Travellers and Outlaws: Episodes in American History* (Boston: Lee and Shepard, 1888).

[107] *The Peckster Professorship* is noted on page 438. *The Story of an African Farm*, by Olive Schreiner, who used the pen name Ralph Iron, was published in London by Chapman & Hall in 1883 and in Boston by Roberts Brothers in 1888. In his "Editor's Study" in the January 1889 *Harper's* magazine, Howells compared this novel favorably to Edgar W. Howe's *The Story of a Country Town*, which he and Clemens had read enthusiastically in 1884 (see *MTHL*, pp. 491–492). Howells noted that *The Story of an African Farm* "makes a most distinct impression of originality and authenticity." Olive Schreiner "naturalizes us to the Southern sky and the distant land among the Boers, the Kaffir serfs, the English emigrants, and adventurers; and we do not find the business of raising ostriches much odder than poultry farming."

[108] Evidently the second volume of the *Personal Memoirs of P. H. Sheridan*, which had not been sent to Charles and Ida Langdon (see note 111).

[109] Since the summer of 1888, completion of the Paige typesetter had repeatedly been pronounced close at hand. Nevertheless, despite the triumph registered on page 441, Paige's invention was not finished either in December 1888 or January 1889. Tinkering continued through the first part of 1889 until by mid-August the machine had been completely disassembled for repair.

[110] The child actress recommended by Abby Sage Richardson for the dual role in a dramatization of *The Prince and the Pauper*. In early December 1888, Elsie Leslie had

Send *us* 2—1$^{s.}$

Speak to W. & Co about our 2—2^{d} vols & Ch's 2—1$^{s\,111}$

Always charge & *pay* copyright on all books given away ⟨as pr⟩ to friends & to the firm BY the firm.

Geo. Standring
    7 & 9 Finsbury st E C^{112}

Magazine edited by Marion Harland, contains something by Annie Trumbull.^{113}

Elsie Leslie.
⟨Howells.⟩
Powder-puff (small.)
⟨Jean—glasses.⟩
⟨Booth   Clara. Players⟩
⟨Hair-cut⟩ [#]

---

begun a long and popular run at the Broadway Theatre in a play based on Frances Hodgson Burnett's *Little Lord Fauntleroy.*

^{111} Clemens wished to redress an error by which he had received two copies of volume two and the Charles J. Langdons had received two copies of volume one of a Webster & Company publication, probably the *Personal Memoirs of P. H. Sheridan.*

^{112} Clemens' reminder to write to his English printer friend who was interested in progress on the Paige typesetter. On 5 January 1889, Clemens sent Standring word of the typesetter's success noted on page 441. Standring passed Clemens' letter on to the *Pall Mall Gazette,* which reported on 18 January that "the genial humourist who is famous throughout the civilized world as 'Mark Twain' is a mechanician of no ordinary kind. For several years he has been engaged in perfecting a type-setting machine of his own invention, and at last his patient toil has been, as he declares, crowned with success." On 28 January, Clemens wrote to the paper's editor to set the record straight. "I did not invent that typesetting machine," he admitted. "I did speak of it as 'my' machine. . . . When I own part of a piece of property I always speak of it as 'mine.' This is merely for grandeur. I ignore the other proprietors. On the same principle, I always speak of America as my country. It is a misleading expression. Some think I own it all, others think I invented it. These are errors, but they do no particular harm, and I allow them to pass. But in the case of this machine it doesn't seem quite fair to let it pass. Mr. J. W. Paige invented it, and has spent eighteen toilsome years upon it. . . . I have built this machine at my private expense, and have been three formidable years at it. I do claim a good deal of credit for that—I don't know any particular reason why, yet I do—but I stop there" (*Pall Mall Gazette,* 16 February 1889).

^{113} Mary Virginia Hawes Terhune, whose pseudonym was Marion Harland, wrote more than sixty books during her lifetime. These included sentimental novels, works

Balt. Thur. 17^{th. 114}

Howells *Fri 18th*. If I find anything forbids this, write H & say so.¹¹⁵

2^d vol Sheridan.

Elsie Leslie.

Dr. Rice. (Giv[e -] Lie[be])

EUREKA!¹¹⁶

Saturday, January 5, 1889—12.20 p.m. At this moment I have seen a line of movable type ⟨justi⟩ ⟨spaced⟩ *spaced & justified* BY MACHINERY! ⟨for the first⟩ This is the first time in the history of the world that this amazing thing has ever been done. Present:

J. W. Paige, the inventor;

Charles Davis ⎫
Earll, ⎬ Mathematical assistants
Grohman ⎭ & mechanical experts.

Bates, foreman; and

S. L. Clemens.

This record is made immediately after the prodigious event.

SL Clemens [#]

---

concerned with domestic affairs and homemaking, biographies, colonial histories, and accounts of travel. In 1888 she established, and for two years edited, the *Home-Maker*. Annie Eliot Trumbull was a Hartford friend of the Clemens family. Her story, "Mary A. Twining," appeared in the *Home-Maker* in December 1888.

¹¹⁴ Clemens was to appear in Baltimore on 17 January 1889 in a public reading with Richard Malcolm Johnston. He was replacing Thomas Nelson Page who had withdrawn after the sudden death of his wife. This entry was probably made on 4 January 1889, shortly after Clemens informed Johnston that "in an emergency like this I am cheerfully ready to break all the promises I have made that I would infest the public platform no more" (Enoch Pratt Free Library, Baltimore, Md.). Clemens refused his share of the proceeds from this appearance, insisting that Johnston accept it instead (see *MTB*, pp. 877–878).

¹¹⁵ Clemens planned to return from the Baltimore reading with Richard Malcolm Johnston in time to attend one of the dinners of Howells' literary circle regularly held at Moretti's, a New York restaurant.

¹¹⁶ What appears to be part of a newspaper galley sheet set on the Paige compositor was inserted in the notebook at this point (see the illustration on page 442). Clemens' penciled notes on both sides of the sheet include calculations of the number of ems in the typeset passage. The canceled inscription above the first line of the heading remains unrecovered.

Sets solid matter at the rate of 10,000 ems per hour.

THE FOLLOWING IS ONE THOUSAND SOLID "EMS", STANDARD NONPARIEL, SET ON THE PAIGE COMPOSITOR IN SIX MINUTES:

Meanwhile the two ladies should be received in Minneapolis with distinguished consideration notwithstanding their natural deficiencies in the line of cigars, wine bibing, shouting, bulldozing, or helping to paint the Flour City red after the nominations are made. The convention should give them a choice place as the original pioneers of what may yet come to be a familiar occurrence. The women of Minneapolis also in their capacity as individuals or as women's clubs, Browning societies, fortnightlies, King's Daughters, or whatever other shape they may assume in the aggregate, should accord them an enthusiastic reception and see that they have a good time during their stay. It will be politic for all to treat them with conspicuous distinction, for now that the old barrier of prejudice has been so far weakened that two women have found their way into a National convention there is no telling what may happen in the future. The tyrant man must face coming possibilities with such resolution as he may.

LORD SALISBURY'S TACTICS.

Lord Salisbury is preparing his party for a general election. It probably will be timed for the middle of July, immediately succeeding the Orange demonstration in Ireland, and when the agricultural laborers will be busy with the hay harvest in England. The general election of six years ago was held at the same time of the year, and the Tories found it to their advantage. They gained two seats in Ireland as a result of the prejudice and passion growing out of the so-called loyalist demonstrations. It profited them also in Scotland, while in England the Liberals lost a score of seats through the action of the Tory landlords and squires in holding their laborers in the hay fields while the polling was going on.

Mt. Vernon Hotel
Baltimore[117]

Accept no courtesies of the Twilight Club; it thinks itself better
than Jews.[118]

Use Curtin's letter in Tribune, Jan. 18.[119]

H. H. Boyesen
48 W 45[th.]

Monday, Jan. 7—4.45 p.m. The first proper name ever set by this
new key-board was *William Shakspeare.* I set it, at the above hour;
& I perceive, now that I see the name written, that I either
mis-spelled it then or I've mis-spelled it now.

The space-bar did its duty, aided by the electric connections &
steam, & separated the two words ⟨&⟩preparatory to reception of
the space. [#]

---

[117] Clemens informed Richard Malcolm Johnston on 9 January 1889 that he would
"sneak down to Baltimore on *Wednesday,* 16th, (by the best train from New York that
morning), & go into hiding from all save you. The trip will tire me most to death, & I
must have a whole day's rest. Don't let anybody know I am to be there before *Thursday*
afternoon. I mustn't put my name on the hotel register until Thursday" (Enoch Pratt
Free Library, Baltimore, Md.). Johnston, grateful for Clemens' willingness to participate
in a joint reading (see note 114), modified this plan on 10 January, promising: "I will
meet you at Union Station, take you to my house, and keep you as hid treasure safely
from all inquisitions."

[118] "The Twilight Club exists, or does not exist, just as the president decides. Its
dinners are noted for the social and economic questions discussed thereat. To dine simply
and early is the motto of the club, whose whole chart of sailing is comprised in the following: No dues, no debts, no by-laws, no president, no constitution, no conventionality,
no salaries, no initiation fee, no full dress, no late hours, no gambling, no dudes" (James
Grant Wilson, ed. *The Memorial History of the City of New-York,* 4 vols. [New York:
New-York History Co., 1893], 4:254). Restrictive membership was evidently one of the
unwritten rules of this whimsical society.

[119] On this date the New York *Daily Tribune* printed a 15 January 1889 letter to
Mrs. P. H. Sheridan from Andrew G. Curtin, governor of Pennsylvania during the Civil
War. Curtin reported "how greatly I have enjoyed the perusal of the 'Personal Memoirs'
of your illustrious husband; a book which ought to be in the hands, not only of every
surviving soldier of the War of the Rebellion on both sides, but of every American who
loves his country and is proud of her heroes. . . . Every page is of absorbing interest,
and, in my opinion, it is destined to take its place among the fortunate books that mankind delights to read and cherish."

Leave 4.40. get to Sp. ⟨5.45.⟩5.42. Leave Spr. 6.15—get to North 6.55.

Leave here 2 20—get to S 3.02—Le Spr 3.15. get there 3.57.

Return.

Leave ⟨Hol⟩ ⟨10.38⟩10.15;
    Rech Spr. 11.
Lve. Sprin 11.45;
    rch Htfd,—12.24[120]

Miss Porter's[121] ⎞
Bryn Mawr   ⎬ Write for alogues.
Boston University ⎠

Jan. 21, Smith College.
Read:

	m.
Lucerne girl	20 or ⟨30⟩25
Andrea del Sarto	25
German lesson	20
Tar Baby	10
Interviewer	20
⟨J⟩Blue-jay	12
(Told) Baker's Cat	10
Golden Arm	6

⟨o⟩A full half hour too much. [#]

---

[120] Clemens' travel plans for his 21 January 1889 reading at Smith College in North-ampton, Massachusetts, included stops at Springfield, Massachusetts, and possibly, on the return trip, at Holyoke. This was one of Clemens' many charitable appearances of the period, raising $200.59 for the school's gymnasium fund.

[121] Around 1843, Sarah Porter established the Farmington, Connecticut, boarding school for girls which became one of the best known institutions of its kind in the United States. Although not directed toward college preparation, Miss Porter's School offered instruction in Latin, German, French, natural philosophy, rhetoric, mathematics, chemistry, geography, history, and music in a noncompetitive fashion that dispensed with grades and examinations and allowed each student to progress at her own pace. Clemens was interested in acquiring information from Miss Porter, as well as from Bryn Mawr and Boston University, on behalf of his daughters Susy and Clara, whose basic education

Mr. Backnumber.[122]

Johnson & I leave for Wash^n Jan. 31st (Thurday) 10. a.m.[123]

⟨*March 4.*⟩ Feb. 28. Introduce Riley & Nye in Boston[124]

Take the "prospectus" to Washington.[125]

⟨Read for Rev. Kittredge Wheeler in South Baptist Church Feb. 9—at   p.m.⟩[126]

⟨Feb. 6, 6.30 p. m. Yale dinner Armory Hall.⟩[127] [#]

---

had been accomplished almost exclusively at home. Susy enrolled in Bryn Mawr in October 1890.

[122] Frequent repetition of his favorite platform pieces, some of them in the preceding list, may have caused Clemens to conceive of this epithet for himself.

[123] Clemens had agreed to accompany Robert Underwood Johnson of the *Century* magazine to Washington on 31 January 1889 to assist in lobbying on behalf of international copyright interests. The House of Representatives was expected to vote on a motion to take up a copyright bill on 4 February. A filibuster by opponents of another bill prevented this vote and effectively killed the proposed international copyright legislation.

[124] On this date, Clemens introduced Bill Nye and James Whitcomb Riley to their audience at the Tremont Temple in Boston. James B. Pond, who was managing the Nye-Riley team, later claimed that Clemens' appearance was mere happenstance (see the account in *MTB*, pp. 876–877), but this note, made about a month before the event, indicates that it was well planned. In thanking Clemens on 6 March 1889, Pond noted that it was Mark Twain's "great name as presiding officer" that had gotten "the right kind of people out."

[125] Probably promotional matter for the Paige typesetter. The prospectus for *A Connecticut Yankee* would not be ready until October 1889.

[126] Kittridge Wheeler, pastor of the South Baptist Church of Hartford, wrote to Clemens on 12 February 1889, thanking him for initiating "The People's Lecture Course, with your name, your presence, your influence, your popularity, and your reading. . . . Your *name* gave us a prestige—a place to begin and something to begin with."

[127] The annual banquet of the Hartford Yale Alumni Association took place at Foot Guard Armory Hall on 6 February 1889. Mark Twain gave an apparently impromptu talk about his recent trip to Washington on behalf of international copyright (see note 123) and also recalled his first meeting with General Grant. He claimed to have prepared "two speeches, both of which had been condemned and remain at home" (Hartford *Courant*, 7 February 1889). Fragments of a speech or speeches in which, on the authority of the Master of Arts degree conferred upon him by Yale in 1888, Clemens offers comic advice on curriculum and administration occur on pages 456–457 and 472 of this notebook. They may have been drafted for the Hartford alumni dinner, which was attended by two potentially disapproving critics of such a speech, Olivia Clemens and Susan Crane.

Snuffling, butter-mouthed, Christian-for-cash, J W.[128]

Apl 2. Read at Lib Hamersley's—put in Interviewer &c.

For this reading—& the 9th:
The Skinned Man.
Huck Finn & (several selec)
Jumping Frog.
9th (only) all of Lucerne girl—
The Mate & Gov. Gardiner (sure)

Surely the test of a novel's characters is that you feel a strong
interest in them & their affairs,—the good to be successful, the bad
to suffer failure. Well in John Ward, you feel no divided interest,
no discriminating interest—you want them all to land in hell
together, & right away[129]

As the cow & the Christian think—I mean that process
⟨w[i]th⟩⟨wich⟩ which the cow & the Christian regard as thinking,
when the subject is religion & the "evidences."

⟨Mrs. President Cleveland.⟩[130]
⟨Gen. Hawley.⟩[131] ⟨Hawley 2030 I⟩—1
⟨Mrs. Ralph Cross Johnson⟩[132] 1735 I.   2

---

[128] A reference to John Wanamaker, who had angered Clemens in 1886 by retail
discounting of the Grant *Memoirs* (see p. 271, note 151). The occasion for the present
entry has not been determined. Wanamaker was frequently in the news in early 1889
because of his impending appointment as postmaster general in the cabinet of Benjamin
Harrison.

[129] Margaret Deland's controversial first novel, *John Ward, Preacher*, was published
in 1888 by Houghton, Mifflin and Company. The novel deals with the difficult love of a
strict Calvinist minister and the wife who does not share his beliefs. Its prolific author
has been compared to Jane Austen and William Dean Howells.

[130] Clemens evidently planned to call on Mrs. Grover Cleveland while in Washington
on international copyright business in the first week of February 1889 (see note 123). He
had previously met her in March 1888 when he was in the capital on similar business.

[131] On 3 February 1889, Hawley left a note at Clemens' Washington hotel, proposing
that they "get up a little party" for dinner before Clemens left for Hartford the next day.
The numbers 1 through 9 which Clemens added beside names and addresses here probably indicate the order in which he planned to pay visits.

[132] Clemens had called on Mrs. Ralph Cross Johnson in the spring of 1888 (see p. 380,

⟨Sent painted calendar Xmas—want her to visit us.⟩
⟨Mrs. Cabell.⟩
⟨Mrs.⟩ ⟨Secretary Whitney⟩ I. ⟨⟨17[- -]⟩1731-odd⟩ 3
⟨W^m. D. Cabell, 1407 Mass ave⟩ Sat Eve. 8.30. 9
Mrs. Hearst. 1435 Mass. Ave 6
   ″ Hitt—1507 K. cor 15th 5
   ″ Hay
    John Hay 8
Mr. S. G. Ward ⟨171[o]⟩ 1608 K st—4 & Miss Howard.
Z. C. Robbins, 1226 (or 0?) 15th ⟨7⟩

⟨H⟩Dried herrings—"They eat 'em guts & all."

Wed. Feb. 27. Athenæum—afternoon. Begin at 3—close at 5.[133]

Next day, Boston, 28th.[134]

A ⟨serene⟩ ⟨adventurous⟩ rapt joy/exalted contentment
lights/glows in/burns in the divine voyager's eye, the lips part, one
seems to almost hear the words—

Hark, hear you not the joy, the gratitude, the anticipation that
bursts from the old father's lips— ———
⟨& so eloquently⟩
& pleading seems to say— [#]

---

[133] note 263). From its position on the page, it is unclear whether the canceled passage
"Sent . . . us." (447.1) refers to Mrs. Johnson or to the unidentified Mrs. Cabell. The
phrase "Sat Eve. 8.30.9" (447.4) may have been meant to accompany the Hearst address
on the following line. Among the people Clemens was to see socially in February 1889
were: William C. Whitney, secretary of the navy; Mrs. Phoebe Apperson Hearst, wife
of George Hearst, Democratic senator from California; Mrs. Robert R. Hitt, wife of
the Republican representative from Illinois; and Mrs. John Hay. Hay held no official
position at this time, but was a supporter of the international copyright movement.

[133] Clemens planned an appearance at the Wadsworth Atheneum in Hartford which
housed, among other cultural organizations, the city's art society. On 28 February 1889,
the corresponding secretary of the society thanked Clemens for his "great kindness.
. . . The barren treasury is one hundred and seventy dollars richer than before, which
delights all hearts" (Harriet D. Andrews to SLC).

[134] Clemens was to present Bill Nye and James Whitcomb Riley at Boston's Tremont
Temple on 28 February 1889 (see note 124).

James S. Metcalfe, manager,
104 Temple Court,
   Cor Beekman & Nassau.
machines.[135]

Take the limited Tuesday a. m. at 9.50 arrive at Albany
1.10 p.m.[136]

"That's jist the main wonder of it—the *laws of gravitation* was
peetrified."

The 2 Mary Murphys. They go to the hospital, the one to have
a tooth pulled, the other to illustrate "Malformation of the
⟨vagina⟩" in a lecture before the students. ⟨They⟩ Each gets into
the room which the other ought to have gotten into. Tableau.

Rose Terry Cooke,
   Pittsfield, Mass.
Read there March 6.[137]

A dynamo creates ⟨or collects force or⟩ or generates power, but

---

[135] James S. Metcalfe was manager of the American Newspaper Publishers' Association. On 31 January 1889 he inquired if the Paige typesetter would be exhibited "at our
Convention on the 13th proximo?" On 13 February, however, the Paige typesetter was
not ready. Although that day it managed to *"perfectly"* set and justify *"by power* one
line of type," Franklin G. Whitmore estimated that "at least one week" was required
before exhibition "because the operators . . . are not well or hardly at all acquainted
with the key board on the machine when the machine is running by power. . . . Then
again, the machine . . . ought to be worked several days by power to permit the oil to
run freely, & to limber up all parts." Two days later Whitmore hedged on that prognosis
of completion: "There are several small matters to fix about the machine, before it
would be wise to give an exhibition. . . . In my opinion it will take from 2 to 3 weeks
more before the machine will be entirely done." Months later the Paige typesetter was
still being perfected.

[136] Clemens and his wife planned to go to New York City on Monday, 11 February
1889, and on to Albany the following day "to make the Sages a little visit, that is we shall
stay with them two days" (OLC to Mrs. Jervis Langdon, 10 February 1889, MTM). On
1 February, Dean Sage had written Clemens of an "Electro-matrix type machine" on
exhibit in Albany which, it was thought, would supersede "all other machines—sure.
You probably know all about it, its advantages & defects, & I write this merely to let you
know, in the remote case of your not already knowing, that there is a possible rival in the
field."

[137] Rose Terry Cooke, the poet, novelist, and short story writer, had solicited this

cannot exert it; a motor does not create power, but can receive it from a dynamo & communicate to machinery & make the machinery go.

Iron Hat.
Tannhäuser tickets—4.[138]
White cravats.
Century—Nelson's name. and who is Miss Phelps, at the White House[139]
Webster's—talk.

Chromos for the Ships. Come to Christ—& look in at Wanamaker Emporium on the way.[140]

For the forecastle: God bless our hole

⟨9.45⟩ 10.20—3.25
4.05—7.30 pm

Madame Fogarty (new address) 38 East 22ᵈ.[141]

There is no difference between Wit & humor, except that Wit

---

reading at the Academy of Music in Pittsfield, Massachusetts, "to assist a really excellent charity, the combined Old Ladies' Home and Union for Home Work." She promised Clemens: "There shall be lemons, hot water, and sugar galore; as to the fourth ingredient I am afraid I am not connoisseur enough to promise that I can suit you, but I will do my best" (Rose Terry Cooke to SLC, 26 January 1889).

[138] Wagner's opera was presented a number of times in February 1889 at the Metropolitan Opera House in New York. After their visit to the Dean Sages in Albany (see note 136), the Clemenses stayed in New York City from 14 to 17 February 1889. They probably attended the matinee of *Tannhäuser* given on Saturday, 16 February. This might explain the "White cravats" of the following line and the reminder to have his opera hat ironed.

[139] Henry Loomis Nelson was an author, editor, and newspaperman, who was involved in the international copyright movement. Nelson's editorial on "Filibustering Run Mad," in which he discussed the recent failure of Congress to act on international copyright (see note 123), appeared in the New York *Times* on 14 February 1889. Nelson sent Clemens a copy of it, along with a covering letter, that same day. The present entry evidently antedates receipt of this communication from Nelson since, presumably wanting to get in touch with him, Clemens intended to inquire about his full name at the *Century* magazine office. Miss Phelps has not been identified.

[140] Another of Clemens' recurrent jibes at John Wanamaker's propensity for combining piety and publicity.

[141] The exclusive New York City dressmaker patronized by Mrs. Clemens.

⟨entirely⟩ can ⟨entirely⟩ succeed without any pretence of being
unconscious, but humor can't.[142]

Wit

Instances: The mot about Metternich & X X X—The one always
deceived but never lied, the other always lied but never deceived.

The little pretending to be the big. Say it's like a cat letting on
to be a cataract.

Killaloe.[143]

Lannigan's Ball.

Sir Walter Scott's Diary—David Douglas, Edinburgh[144]

Phonograph story.[145]

Lowells "My Study Windows"[146]

England 600 yrs ago

Great Captains—Dodge—Ticknor[147]

Ask Howells about the Boston Authors' Reading for Mch 1.[148] [#]

---

[142] The central point of Mark Twain's "How to Tell a Story," which was not published
until 1895. A more elaborate comparison between wit and humor can be found on
pages 162 and 163.

[143] Clemens noted this title repeatedly and quoted verses and miscellaneous lines
from this song in Notebook 29 (pp. 492, 496, 511, 513, 569). The music for "Killaloe" was
composed by Robert J. Martin; no extant published version of the song has been discovered. The following title refers to an anonymous Irish street ballad, "Lanigan's Ball,"
included in The Oxford Book of Light Verse, ed. W. H. Auden, 2d rev. ed. (Oxford:
Oxford University Press, 1939).

[144] Clemens was evidently anticipating publication of The Journal of Sir Walter Scott:
From the Original Manuscript at Abbotsford. The work did not appear until 1890 (2 vols.
[Edinburgh: David Douglas]).

[145] Possibly a reference to a contemplated work about the future in which the phonograph was to figure prominently (see p. 347).

[146] James Russell Lowell's My Study Windows, originally published in 1871 by J. R.
Osgood and Company, was in its twenty-eighth American edition in 1889.

[147] Theodore Ayrault Dodge, Great Captains: A Course of Six Lectures Showing the
Influence on the Art of War of the Campaigns of Alexander, Hannibal, Cæsar, Gustavus
Adolphus, Frederick, and Napoleon (Boston: Ticknor and Co., 1889).

[148] On 12 February 1889, Clemens was asked to participate in an authors' reading
in Boston "for the benefit of the copyright cause. Dr. Oliver Wendell Holmes and other
people prominent in literature have agreed to take part in the reading. The date is still

Doctor, shall we remain over?

Write the dramatist[149] to correspond with W., I take no interest in it.

Yes, admit none without ticket.

Write Laffan to come & talk tonight or tomorrow on *Colt* project.

Call at bookstore.

Webster & Co.

Diary of Scott (Douglas)

5,000 of 1000 — ($\frac{1}{1000}$ is \$1000

$\langle\frac{25}{[1000]}\rangle$25 000

$\underline{\qquad 200}$ (a 200th interest)

5000,000

A test: set 100 lines with an error in every line. Then time the corrections.

Whitmore is to call on $\langle[\&]\rangle$Mrs. A. P. Lambrecht, (Tommy Russell's mother) 134 W 29$^{\text{th. 150}}$ [#]

---

left open in the hope that you will not only agree to come, but will let me know what date you would prefer. It might well be the 1st. day of March, being the day following your engagement at Tremont Temple" (Alex. P. Browne to SLC, 12 February 1889). Clemens evidently did not wish to remain in Boston after his 28 February introduction of Bill Nye and James Whitcomb Riley (see p. 445, note 124). This authors' reading was finally set for the Boston Museum on 7 March 1889, following Clemens' appearance in Pittsfield, Massachusetts, the preceding day (see notes 137 and 153). His contribution was a talk on "The New England Weather" (Hartford *Courant*, 8 March 1889), probably a version of the speech noted at 412.14. No correspondence with Howells about this event is extant.

[149] Possibly Thomas F. Reddy, who on 8 February 1889 again wrote to Clemens asking for "the name & address of the person to whom you gave authority to dramatize & produce the 'Prince & the Pauper'" (see p. 436, note 96). Clemens had now decided to refer Reddy either to Franklin Whitmore, who had vague responsibilities in connection with dramatization of the novel (see the entry at 451.16–17 and p. 514, note 112), or to Daniel Whitford, Webster & Company's New York lawyer, who handled many of the legal details concerning Abby Sage Richardson's *Prince and the Pauper* play.

[150] Tommy Russell was a popular boy actor. In late 1888 he sometimes substituted for Elsie Leslie in a dramatization of *Little Lord Fauntleroy*. Clemens may have considered using both child actors together in a stage version of *The Prince and the Pauper* (see

132 W 44th Abby S. Richardson

Monday evening, 25th, Trinity Dinner at Delmonico's.[151]

Stop with Frank Fuller, next time, at Windsor Hotel, 46th & 5th ave.[152]

—there's a vacuum in some diocese again, & nobody but D$^{r.}$ Smith can fill it.

You call it an innocent dinner party; you are ⟨trying to pass yourselves off for⟩ ostensibly only a band of Trinity alumni; whereas ⟨it is⟩*I* think you are a Consistory in disguise.

diocesan electoral college

Author's Readings—
Boston Museum (Thursday) March 7—if I can get there from Pittsfield in time. I'm to be 2^{d} or 3^{d} on the list.[153]

COSPIRACY.⃞NOW I KAN'T YOU KNOW.⃞The MOMENT

Can't imagine what there was to disagree about.

---

his entry at 453.22–24). In October 1890, Tommy Russell would appear in a brief run of Edward H. House's *Prince and the Pauper* play.

[151] The annual alumni dinner of Trinity College was held on 25 February 1889. Clemens gave a speech about his friend the Reverend George Williamson Smith, president of the college, whose near departure to accept an Ohio bishopric he had opposed in November 1888. "There's a vacuum in some diocese again, I reckon," he told the Trinity alumni, "an nobody but Dr. Smith can fill it. You are letting on that this is merely an innocent dinner party; ostensibly you are only a larking band of Trinity alumni, and without guile, whereas in my opinion you are a diocesan electoral college in disguise" (Hartford *Courant*, 26 February 1889).

[152] Clemens must have written to Fuller about this plan, for on 3 March 1889 Fuller responded encouragingly: "All right, old boy! come on, nexttime or the time after, only come, & no indefinite postponements." Fuller invited Clemens to accompany him to the opening night of *The County Fair*, a comedy by Charles Barnard, on 5 March 1889. Clemens was interested in this play (see p. 409, note 27), but probably did not join Fuller since he had to travel to Pittsfield, Massachusetts, the following day (see p. 448, note 137).

[153] This benefit on behalf of international copyright was scheduled to suit Clemens' convenience (see note 148) "since your co-operation is deemed *absolutely essential* to the success of the Reading" (Dana Estes, secretary of the International Copyright Association, to SLC, 23 February 1889). On 24 February, Clemens informed Estes of the condition noted here and three days later Estes sent him a railroad timetable and suggestions for convenient trains. Clemens' appearance in Pittsfield is explained on page 448, note 137.

There was but *one* thing to talk about—the *first condition*—not any other thing whatever.[154]

Conditions.

1. Procuring 〈Lestie〉Leslie.

After that:

2. Dramatize piece—necessarily in a reasonable length of time.
3. Concession—a year if necessary, in which to write it after contract with Leslie's manager. It is cover extraordinary emergencies.
4. To have my approval. Nothing of hardship about that. An essential. One could *never* 〈[w]〉part with that right. It is not a *concession* granted me, but a natural right.
5. ½ profits. A concession from *me*—it is worth no more than 10 per cent.
6. You make any terms you please with manager. I can't even protest. Here is a partnership in which one partner has no voice in the main question. Isn't that a concession?

Every point is on your side but just one—the first condition.

If *it* be delayed a year it enlarges itself to a 3-year limit because actors are usually hired for 3, & I would have to wait 2 more years to get this one. This would not be fair to me.

I never have required that it be for 2 people, nor ever said I would disapprove if it wasn't. I desire, but don't require. I combatted this with House.[155] [#]

---

[154] Clemens' notes through "Isn't that a concession?" (453.17) roughly summarize the terms of his 3 January 1889 contract with Abby Sage Richardson for the writing and production of a *Prince and the Pauper* play. Mrs. Richardson was evidently having difficulty in meeting the first condition, the securing of Elsie Leslie for the title roles (see note 156).

[155] In December 1886, through an informal exchange of letters, Clemens had authorized Edward H. House to dramatize *The Prince and the Pauper*. House's protest of the subsequent contract with Abby Sage Richardson led to legal proceedings (discussed in detail in Notebooks 29 and 30) and ended the friendship between the two men. The present entry indicates that Clemens had consistently opposed the use of one actor in the roles of Tom Canty and the Prince of Wales. In February 1889 he evidently explored the possibility of securing two prominent child actors, Elsie Leslie and Tommy Russell, for the parts.

Reasonables.

10 days to get a writing from manager & mother.[156] ⟨If it could be done⟩ You seemed to have no doubt when you wrote me. Then 10 would have been enough.

3 or 4 weeks ⟨(including the [--)]⟩ for writing the play (*with the scissors*, which I prefer, should be ample.

Take till March 10 to get those writings, or I shall consider the contract null & proceed accordingly. I will do nothing with other people till then.

In the meantime you can see Wood, or Frohman, or both[157]—you are not limited to Frohman, for that would limit *me* to him, & that would be hardly fair.

House seems to have a claim—I will go & see what it. I can't imagine, myself.[158] [#]

---

[156] G. W. Lynch, an advisor to Elsie Leslie's mother, wrote to Clemens on 24 February: "Have you sold the right of the Prince and the Pauper or would you sell the said right for a play for Elsie Leslie. Mrs Leslie requested me to write you in regards to it, a local manager called on Mrs Leslie yesterday and asked her to sign a paper stating that he the manager, could have Elsie Leslie for the Prince and the Pauper for next season. I told her not to sign any paper. . . . I would like Elsie to have an interest or own the next play herself as she [is] getting very little out of Lord Fauntleroy and is drawing packed houses to the theatre." Such a desire on the part of Elsie Leslie's representatives was naturally making it difficult for Abby Sage Richardson to produce the "writing" Clemens requested here.

[157] Daniel Frohman managed the production of Abby Sage Richardson's dramatization of *The Prince and the Pauper*, which opened at New York's Broadway Theatre on 20 January 1890. Allen H. Wood was the name used by twenty-two-year-old Charles F. Hahr in the spring of 1889 while promoting his proposed West End Theatre in Harlem which was to be "a palatial edifice and an ornament to the amusement temples of the metropolis" (New York *Dramatic Mirror*, 30 March 1889). Wood's grandiose scheme came to grief in the summer of 1889 when his pretense of being a millionaire and his juvenile record as a forger were discovered. The West End Theatre was never built.

[158] Having heard of Clemens' agreement with Abby Sage Richardson, in February 1889 Edward H. House wrote to Clemens reminding him of their earlier arrangement (see note 155). On 26 February Clemens replied: "I remembered that you started once to map out the framework [of a *Prince and the Pauper* play] for me to fill in, and I suggested to this lady that possibly you would collaborate with her, but she thought she could do the work alone. However, I never thought of such a thing as your being willing to undertake the dramatization itself—I mean the whole thing. I will look in when I come down" (quoted in Paul Fatout, "Mark Twain, Litigant," *American Literature*, March 1959, pp. 36–37). This was the opening exchange in a long legal battle over dramatic rights to *The Prince and the Pauper*.

Densmore did it in 2 weeks with the scissors & charged $200 a week. R & I divided $140,000.[159]

D was an *old* experienced dramatist.

Shall I give *you* $200 if you try & 3 times if it succeeds.

[Leave] the rest to me.

aspect
When I see it. Its *just* another
   conspiracy—that is what
     I see in this thing. I
       may be
         mistaken; & if
           I am, I

Ambitions. *SUCH A MAN.*

To Pitts—12.05, by Springfld, gets there shortly after 4. Preferable train.

10.15 a. m.—reach Pat 2.25. Conn Western & Housatonic. Poor train.[160]

INVITE.[161]

Gen. Franklin, Geo. Warner, Chas. Warner, Chas. Clark, A. E. Burr, Newton Case,

---

Hutchins? Reid?

Boston Herald; Globe; Adver. & others. [#]

---

[159] In 1874 Clemens paid Gilbert B. Densmore, drama critic of the San Francisco *Golden Era,* two hundred dollars for an unauthorized dramatization of *The Gilded Age.* He agreed to pay another two hundred dollars if his own rewriting of Densmore's play proved commercially successful. John T. Raymond played the featured role of Colonel Sellers. (See *MTHL*, pp. 372, 861–863.)

[160] Clemens copied the arrival and departure times in this and the previous entry from a 26 February 1889 letter from Rose Terry Cooke, who was organizing the 6 March reading in Pittsfield, Massachusetts (see p. 448, note 137). At 455.16 Clemens inadvertently wrote "Pat" instead of "Pitts."

[161] Clemens wished to invite the men noted here to a demonstration of the Paige typesetter. William B. Franklin, former vice-president and general manager of Colt's Patent

I have never had an honor which was more embarrassing to me than this one has been.[162] This is because of my not knowing just what authorities & privileges belonged to the title, & ⟨my⟩ trying to guess them out for myself, instead of asking somebody who knew. But to ask, would have been to expose the fact that I was not college-bred; & you know it strictly human nature to go & expose the same thing just as effectually in that other way. But that is ⟨all right⟩ no matter; I would rather be human than right⟨.⟩, any time. (Propositions to help govern the college declined; balked every time I tried to help; the same sort of thing a few months ago in the case of Johns Hopkins University. I was told they ⟨were going to give⟩ had given me a degree;[163] I naturally supposed that this constituted me a member of the faculty, & so I started in to help what I could, there, too. I told them I believed they were perfectly competent to run a college, as far as the higher branches of education are concerned, but what they needed was a little help here & there from a practical commercial mind. I said ⟨it⟩ the public are sensitive to little things, & they wouldn't ever have full/solid confidence in a college that didn't know how to spell John.

(However, *one* thing seemed certain enough, anyway—the degree

---

Fire-Arms Manufacturing Company in Hartford, had been appointed commissioner general of the United States exhibit at the World's Fair or Universal Exposition which was to begin in Paris on 6 May 1889. Clemens may have hoped to persuade Franklin to make the Paige typesetter part of the large United States exhibit in the fair's Palace of Industries. George Warner had recently advised Clemens on a plan for selling typesetter stock. Charles Dudley Warner and Charles H. Clark were associates on the Hartford *Courant*. Alfred E. Burr was editor and publisher of the Hartford *Times*. Newton Case was president of the Case, Lockwood & Brainard Company, Hartford printers and publishers, and a director of the American Publishing Company. Stilson Hutchins, a founder of the Mergenthaler Linotype Company, had only recently sold his newspaper, the Washington *Post*. Whitelaw Reid's New York *Tribune* had been using the Mergenthaler Linotype in its composing room since 1886.

[162] This extended entry is a partial draft of a speech Mark Twain intended for a Hartford Yale Alumni Association dinner of 6 February 1889 (see p. 445, note 127, and p. 472, note 230).

[163] Clemens was never awarded a degree by Johns Hopkins University. He evidently worked in mention of that school in this fashion in order to prepare for the joke at 456.20. Clemens used the joke to good effect on 26 June 1889 at a Yale alumni banquet in New Haven also attended by Daniel C. Gilman, president of Johns Hopkins.

constituted me a member of the ⟨corp⟩ governing body, &
doubtless the head of it; so I proceeded upon that.

matriculation, clinic, or whatever you call it.

Dine at Youngs, Mch 7, with Chas. H. Taylor.[164]

⟨Ha⟩Hearst and Jones.[165]

Toward the end of Feb. '89, I offered Charley Langdon a
one-hundredth interest in the U. S. business of the Paige
Compositor for $25,000, or a lesser share at the same rate; same
offer to Theodore Crane. Mr. Crane ⟨[-]⟩declined. Charley declined
also, but thought maybe his mother or his wife might conclude to
invest. I said I would keep the offer open till March 10th.[166] It is
now March ⟨[5]⟩6.

In the revised edition of the Koran it is asserted that no man
can ---- literature; but this is disproven by David Ker's travel-papers
in the Cosmopolitan. Pity to put that flatulence between the same
leaves with that charming Chinese story.[167] [#]

---

[164] Taylor, publisher of the Boston *Globe*, was interested in the Paige typesetter.
Throughout the spring of 1889 he kept other newspapermen interested as well and also
provided Clemens with information pertinent to the development and marketing of the
machine. On 2 March 1889, he wrote to Clemens acknowledging notice of a canceled
Paige exhibition and reminding him: "I am expecting to see you next Thursday evening
at Young's after the Authors' reading [see p. 450, note 148]. The dinner party will be
informal and you will not necessarily be required to wear a dress suit, but can go right
from the plow." Young's Hotel was one of Boston's most elegant establishments, famous
for its cuisine and a favorite dining place of businessmen.

[165] Probably wealthy senators George Hearst of California and John P. Jones of
Nevada. Clemens may have spoken to them about the Paige typesetter while in Washington in early February 1889 (see p. 445, note 123). He entered their names here as additions to the list of men he wished to invite to a typesetter exhibition (see note 161).

[166] Clemens had probably estimated that the typesetter would be perfected on 10
March 1889 on the basis of Franklin G. Whitmore's 15 February "opinion" that two to
three weeks were necessary for final small adjustments (see p. 448, note 135). On 12
October 1889 Susan Crane would invest $5,000 in the Paige typesetter in return for a
promised royalty of five dollars on each machine sold. Five days later, Charles J. Langdon
would secure a promised royalty of three dollars on each machine sold with an investment
of $3,000. Neither Ida Langdon, Charles' wife, nor Mrs. Jervis Langdon, his mother,
became typesetter investors.

[167] David Ker's "Over the Cossack Steppes" appeared in the February 1889 number
of the *Cosmopolitan*. The first installment of his "From the Sea to the Desert," an

Never carry a book onto the stage at an Author's reading. Hunt out 2 or 3 anecdotes like "Ben Holiday'd a fetched 'em through in 36 days"—the Christening Story, & others to be found in Innocents & other books.

Make a little lecture on "Anecdotes"—& illustrate with specimens.

Call "A True Story" an Anecdote, & put it in.

Also Golden Arm, Whistling Sotry &c.

"I wish to ⟨[-]⟩God it was in the old primeval forest yet."

Hayes the Arctic man & the Jones family interruptions.

Joe's Bermuda Girl.

Make the lecture 2 nights long.
Then add two nights of Readings.

"Well done, good & faithful servant."

Get things out of the old Innocents & S. Island lectures.

And the anecdotes out of the lecture on Artemus Ward.

"I hae my doubts aboot John"

I want Mr. R— to take a 1-100th & D half as much. To others I will part with twice as much & get it back from P. This will enable me to make all first payment & then collect from R or the Trust Co on the *vouchers*—they will represent not money to *be* paid out but money which has BEEN paid out.[168] [#]

---

account of travel across North Africa, was published the following month. Each issue of the magazine also printed a portion of "Wu Chih Tien, The Celestial Empress." The illustrations which accompanied this "Chinese Historical Novel" introduced Clemens to the work of Dan Beard who was to illustrate *A Connecticut Yankee.*

[168] The men referred to here are James W. Paige and, probably, Henry C. Robinson and Samuel G. Dunham, Clemens' Hartford friends. In a list of potential typesetter investors made in late 1887 (see p. 336), Clemens had included Robinson for a $10,000 contribution and Dunham for $3,000. Now, in March 1889, he wished Robinson to invest $25,000 and Dunham $12,500.

Then go up to Albany. ⎫
Next, *write* Elmira.[169] ⎭

Afterwards L write & sell that mortgage.[170]

I want the Feb. 6 contract & P & W.'s estimates.[171]

Brusnahan[172]
See Pond,[173] Mrs. Richardson[174] [#]

---

[169] Clemens intended to approach Dean Sage, of Albany, and Charles J. Langdon, of Elmira, about investment in the typesetter. Initially opposed, Langdon eventually invested in the machine, although less significantly than Clemens wished (see note 166). Sage planned to come to Hartford on 5 March 1889 to inspect the typesetter. He was never persuaded to take an interest in the machine, however (see p. 527, note 144).

[170] Clemens was thinking of raising typesetter money through the sale of one of the mortgages Livy held as part of her personal fortune. On 23 January 1889 Charles J. Langdon had reported on mortgages she might wish to sell, the most likely ones being in the amounts of $5,000, $5,500, and $2,000. Langdon thought that "perhaps if you dispose of the $5.500⁰⁰ & 2.000⁰⁰ that would be all you would want to realize," although he advised that if "as much as $20.000" was wanted Livy should sell both of the larger mortgages.

[171] A reference to the agreement of 6 February 1886 by which Clemens became the chief backer of the Paige typesetter. The agreement included Pratt & Whitney's "Summary of Cost of Machines, Tools, Fixtures and Gauges" to be used in building typesetters and their statement, dated 18 January 1886, guaranteeing the cost for a sample machine "not to be over twenty thousand dollars ($20,000), and time in building it not to exceed six months after the drawings are furnished us."

[172] John Brusnahan, the New York *Herald* compositor interested in the development of the Paige machine. Clemens had prematurely informed Brusnahan of the completion of the machine, probably in early January 1889. Brusnahan called it "without doubt, the greatest achievement of the age," and predicted that the "whole civilized world is your oyster now." He anticipated being sent for by Clemens so that "we can talk more in detail" (Brusnahan to SLC, 8 January 1889). Clemens evidently now wished to notify Brusnahan of the unfinished state of the machine.

[173] Clemens' business with James B. Pond probably concerned the recent Boston appearance with Bill Nye and James Whitcomb Riley (see p. 445, note 124). Pond may have proposed a regular return to the lecture platform. In June 1889 he would suggest that Clemens "enter into a little enterprise with me for a few Cities, say New York, Boston, and all of the large Cities—fifteen or twenty" (Pond to SLC, 28 June 1889). The program would require only that Mark Twain repeat his introduction of Nye and Riley and the pay would be handsome. Clemens refused Pond's proposition.

[174] Clemens had proposed to allow Abby Sage Richardson until 10 March to produce written proof of Elsie Leslie's commitment to the *Prince and the Pauper* play (see p. 454). Now, as that deadline approached, he may have intended to sound Mrs. Richardson on her progress.

Tell Mr. Hall to do his own preference in the matter of the Expert.[175]

I will sign that judgment in New York.[176]

Go & see Howells.

⟨⟨Feb.⟩ March 8. Offered Badlam a one-hundredth interest in the American business for $25,000 provided he takes me up before Apl. 15; also offered him the *same* share (this offer *begins* June 15) provided he takes me up before July 15.)⟩[177]

Hearst, Walters.[178]

March 9/89.
No more experiments. Definite work alone left to do.

---

[175] On 25 February 1889, Charles L. Webster & Company had sent Clemens a copy of a report from a firm of public accountants and auditors which had recently completed a full review and renovation of company bookkeeping procedures. These experts offered, "for the sum of $400.00 per annum," to "act as accountant and auditor permanently" to Webster & Company, assuming duties at which "all your Bookkeepers in the past have failed, and exhibited an utter lack of knowledge" and at which the present bookkeeper "is hardly to be expected" to succeed. "We are entirely unable to make up our minds with reference to this," Webster & Company's covering letter noted, "or to offer any suggestion as to whether it is advisable or not. Would be glad to have you think it over and give us your opinion." The publishing house had to prompt Clemens twice, on 28 February and on 6 March, before eliciting the response noted here.

[176] Webster & Company's lawyers had accepted an offer of $9,000 in settlement of a $30,000 claim against R. T. Root, an Iowa book agent (see p. 390, note 306). This entry was made after the firm passed along notification on 6 March that "the assignment of judgment" would soon be ready for Clemens' signature.

[177] Alexander Badlam of San Francisco, a former California state legislator (1863–1864), was president of the Bankers and Merchants Mutual Life Association of the United States. In "'White Man Mighty Onsartain,'" part of a January 1866 letter to the Virginia City *Territorial Enterprise*, Mark Twain had described Badlam's alleged promotion of a new swimming bath with a carefully manipulated shark scare (see *Mark Twain: San Francisco Correspondent*, ed. Henry Nash Smith and Frederick Anderson [San Francisco: Book Club of California, 1957], pp. 54–59). In 1889 and 1890 Clemens and Badlam corresponded, but no communications about the typesetter are known to have survived.

[178] Probably William Thompson Walters. In 1887 the proposed publication by Webster & Company of a catalog of Walters' extensive art collection had caused considerable friction between Clemens and Charles L. Webster. Clemens apparently now

4 months, sure, that is, July 10.[179]

No new ⟨defi⟩devices—or inventions.

J. W. Paige showed me to-day (⟨Feb.⟩ March 9, 1889,) a steel punch g, & a brass type g made with it. He completed these things this morning. This is the first brass type ever made for ⟨ordin⟩ composition no doubt.[180]

I want age[181] to take 12,500 now, & 12,500 conditioned upon the result of July 10.

And I want Stanchfield to come to the Murray Hill about Mch 15. Will write him.[182]

I verlange dass S 12,500 nehmen werde, und noch 12,500 ⟨und⟩unter dieselbe Bedingung die vorher erwähnt ist.[183]

Examine "The Siege of Berlin," & perhaps publish it in the Century.[184] [#]

---

wished to approach Walters, and California senator George Hearst (see p. 457, note 165), about investment in the Paige typesetter.

[179] Clemens had presumably been informed that the typesetter, which was to have been ready for public exhibition in early March 1889, would not be ready until July. He would have been particularly exasperated by this delay because of recent expressions of interest from newspapermen anxious to see the machine in operation.

[180] Type was generally made of lead, tin, and antimony, although brass type, cast for bookbinders and cigar box makers, was available.

[181] Clemens intended to write "Sage." He was attempting to convince his friend Dean Sage to become a backer of the Paige typesetter.

[182] Clemens was taking his family to New York City "for a couple of days" on Friday, 15 March 1889 (SLC to Augustin Daly, 13 March 1889, Houghton Library, Harvard University, Cambridge, Mass.). They were to stay at the Murray Hill Hotel where he planned to meet John B. Stanchfield, who had married Clara Spaulding, probably to discuss an investment in the Paige typesetter. In September 1889 Clara Spaulding Stanchfield would invest $5,000 in the machine.

[183] *I want S to take 12,500 and another 12,500 under the same condition previously mentioned.* At 461.7–8 Clemens noted his wish to have Dean Sage invest these amounts in the typesetter, the second installment to be conditional upon the machine's completion, currently scheduled for 10 July 1889. The present entry may be a restatement of the plan for Sage's investment or it may refer to a possible investment by John B. Stanchfield.

[184] Evidently a reference to a play about the Franco-German war which Clemens planned at an earlier point in this notebook (see pp. 403–405). No such work appeared in the *Century* magazine.

Can you talk half an hour with me at the depot in Al
⟨to-morrow⟩ about one to-morrow afternoon?[185]

For Apl. 2[186]

Muleykeh. 2. sure
Interviewer—1.
Christening
Scriptural Panorama—
Rabbi Ben Ezra sure
Isaac & Prophets of Baal.[187]
Up at a Villa.
Uncle Remus.
Quarrel of the raftsmen.
In armor 190—*12 m*
Sandy arrives—166K—22[188]
Skinned Man.
A True STORY.—
St. Stylites—450—11 m
77—Drilling the King (& for magazine.) down to where the K
gets that shot. [#]

---

[185] Possibly the draft of a telegram to Dean Sage. Clemens apparently wished to see
him about the typesetter while passing through Albany on 10 March 1889.

[186] Clemens was considering the following program, including selections from
Browning, Joel Chandler Harris, and his own material, as well as two of Edgar Wakeman's
anecdotes (462.9 and 463.1–5), for his reading at the Hartford home of Elizabeth
Hamersley (see p. 446). When he made these notes on 9 March 1889 he had not received
a letter of the previous day in which Ellen T. Johnson changed the date of his appearance
to 1 April and promised to "see you before the date fixed—as some of your friends and
admirers have petitioned for certain of their Especial favorite pieces." On page 464
Clemens noted the change in schedule.

[187] Clemens had used this ancedote by Edgar Wakeman in the second installment of
"Some Rambling Notes of an Idle Excursion" (*Atlantic Monthly*, November 1877).

[188] Here and below (462.17–19) Clemens refers to pages in the manuscript of *A
Connecticut Yankee* and, with one exception, notes the number of minutes required to
read each selection. "*In armor*" probably signifies chapter 12 of the book, in which the
Yankee's sufferings in armor are described. Sandy's arrival occurs in chapter 11. Saint
Simeon Stylites is parodied in chapter 22. The drilling of King Arthur in the mannerisms
of a peasant takes place in chapter 28. (The manuscript of *A Connecticut Yankee* is in
two separately numbered sections and "Drilling the king" appears around page 77 of the
second section.) In chapter 29 the king receives an accusatory "accidental home-shot"
from a dying peasant woman. Clemens evidently thought this last selection particularly
suitable for magazine publication.

Dan'l in the Den.

"He kep' them lions loaded up with lamb chops—jes' kep' 'em
stuff'd up with lamb chops, tell the mere sight o' Dan'l jes gagged
'em. Miracle! Twan't no miracle—they couldn't a et him *no* way—
twould a *busted* 'em.

"Well, the Savior's been here once."

Gadsby's Hotel.[189]

"*One* 'o them prophets—St. Paul, mebbe,—but *might* o' ben
Minneapolis."

"Git to the masthead you son of a ——" (Wakeman as a
sailor-boy—first day.)[190]

Here it is March 9, & the first condition of Mrs. Richardson's
contract unfulfuled.[191]

Send a photo of me to Theodore.

March 11. Made this proposition to Mrs. Richardson to-day:
That in lieu of the present contract, she dramatise the Prince &
Pauper for *me;* I to pay her $500 upon delivery of the MS to me,
June 1 or July 1, be her work good or bad. If the play *succeeds,*
I to pay her another $500 (this to be the *first* $500 received by me
as ⟨prophet⟩profits. After that, I to pay her $5 every time the piece
is played.
She will answer Thursday.[192] [#]

---

[189] An anecdote about a man who grows old lodging at this Washington hotel while
trying to obtain an appointment to the San Francisco postmastership. It appears in
chapter 26 of *A Tramp Abroad.*

[190] A version of this anecdote appears in chapter 2 of *The Log of an Ancient Mariner,
Being the Life and Adventures of Captain Edgar Wakeman,* edited by Minnie
Wakeman-Curtis (San Francisco: A. L. Bancroft & Co., 1878). Clemens heard this story,
the one alluded to in the previous entry, and those noted at 462.9 and 463.1–5 directly
from Wakeman.

[191] Clemens remarked in detail upon this unfulfilled condition for Abby Sage
Richardson's dramatization of *The Prince and the Pauper* on pages 453 and 454.

[192] Abby Sage Richardson did not accept this proposal, similar to an arrangement
Clemens had made with Gilbert B. Densmore for a dramatization of *The Gilded Age*
(see p. 455, note 159).

We double every 13 years.

We had 4,000 papers & periodicals in 1860; we had 8,000 in 1873, 16,000 in ⟨1888⟩1886; we ⟨shall⟩ should have 32,000 in 1899, without the Paige; with it we shall have—what? 40,000? or will it be 50,000?

Go & talk with a man who uses a patent outside—see what it costs him. Does he get it for nothing by letting the ads go in free?

Read at Miss Hamersley's 61 La Fayette st, Apl 1. They will tell me the hour.

March 30(?) Saturday, Daly's supper to Booth.[193]

See W. G.,[194] & Whtfd.
   (Paper I gave her.)
= My office:
   ⎰ Steadman,[195]
   ⎱ Cox, photographer
   Shall want $2,000 Apl 1, & about the same per month.[196] [#]

---

[193] Augustin Daly wrote to Clemens on 9 March 1889, inviting him to attend "a rousing Banquet" for Edwin Booth on Saturday, 30 March 1889. The dinner at Delmonico's was to honor Booth for his gift to the Players Club of the house at 16 Gramercy Park in New York which became its headquarters. Clemens attended and delivered a speech about an indigestible, insomnia-producing "Long Clam," which he included in an Autobiographical Dictation of 28 December 1906.

[194] On 12 March 1889, in response to a telegram from Clemens, William Gillette offered to arbitrate the complicated negotiations concerning the *Prince and the Pauper* dramatization which involved Daniel Whitford (Clemens' lawyer), Abby Sage Richardson, Daniel Frohman, and representatives of Elsie Leslie. Clemens' dissatisfaction with Mrs. Richardson's progress on the play is recorded in entries on pages 453–454 and 463.

[195] Edmund C. Stedman had appealed to Frederick J. Hall for an increase from three to five per cent in the royalties he and Ellen M. Hutchinson were to receive for the *Library of American Literature.* Hall passed the request on to Clemens on 12 March 1889, noting: "Of course if the book is a success we can afford to give this royalty, if it is not a success there will be very little royalty to pay any way." Clemens also wished to see Stedman about choosing a photograph for the engraving to accompany his selections in the *Library of American Literature,* the "Jumping Frog" story and excerpts from *Huckleberry Finn* and *The Prince and the Pauper.* On 10 March, Stedman had recommended that "you sit to [C. C.] Cox for the portrait . . . as it is quite time it sh^d reach the engraver." On page 465 Clemens reminded himself to inform Stedman about some photographs taken by Teddy Hewitt, a friend of Dora Wheeler's.

[196] Clemens probably wished to withdraw these amounts from Charles L. Webster &

Howells

Laffan

Telegraph W to send Mrs. R's letter to me.[197]

F. T. Merrill & Harley. But M is the one.[198]

"Sis, don't you drink a drop of water in this tavern—⟨I've --'d in the spring!"⟩

The Sage jokes

They have plowed a gutter round the whole globe stealing bases on their bellies. The new equator, you see. It has fooled many people.[199]

The "cork" anecdote.

Speak to Mr. Hall about Miss Northrop, D^r· Rice's frind. And tell Steadman about Mr. Hewitt's photos of me.

Write in 3 books for Mr. Hewitt. [#]

Company to help defray expenses on the Paige typesetter. The state of the business did not permit him to do so, however. In May 1889 even a reduced request for $1,000 brought an appeal for restraint. "As you know the dull season is upon us," Hall explained on the twenty-first of that month, "and while I hope to make this dull season a very much better one than it has been heretofore, it is hardly possible to do much more than enough business to keep the office going, so I think it would be well for you, if you could, not to count on getting any money from us until Fall, as it might embarrass us somewhat."

[197] A communication from Abby Sage Richardson in the hands of Daniel Whitford, Clemens' attorney. The letter has not survived.

[198] Clemens was considering possible illustrators for *A Connecticut Yankee*. F. T. Merrill and John J. Harley were two of the artists who had illustrated *The Prince and the Pauper*.

[199] On the evening of 8 April 1889, Mark Twain attended an elaborate dinner at Delmonico's in honor of two world-touring baseball teams. Responding to a toast to the Sandwich Islands, which the players had visited, Mark Twain poked fun at Hawaiian customs and then delivered his famous "Prose Poem" about the "deep strong charm" of that "alien land" (see N&J1, p. 105). He concluded by congratulating the teams for doing "a service to the great science of geography" by replacing the old "dim" equator with a visible one: "And so I drink long life to the boys who ploughed a new equator round the globe stealing bases on their bellies!" (account of speech in New York *Sun*, 9 April 1889, reprinted in Walter Francis Frear, *Mark Twain and Hawaii* [Chicago: Lakeside Press, 1947], pp. 501–503). The "'cork' anecdote" noted here appears neither in the manuscript nor the published versions of this speech.

Hall, write Anthony.[200]

Speak to Sue about violets & custard.

⟨The quarrel⟩
Wed. eve, Apl. 3, Boston Symphony Concert, Armory Hall.[201]

1. That is *enough* for *you,* but I want the contract altered to give me authority, then I will raise the terms in *my* favor if I can, —if I can't, leave it as it is. (⟨[th]⟩My project is, ½, after expenses.)[202]

If it is to stand as it is I want it altered, thus:

1. The idiotic *time*-limit reduced to 60 days;[203]

2. Payments made direct to my representative by *manager*—no quarrels with women

3. Payment every *week* instead of 2 months.[204]

---

[200] Andrew Varick Stout Anthony was an engraver employed by the Boston publishers Ticknor & Company. Around 19 March, Hall wrote to Anthony, who had assisted James R. Osgood in preparing *The Prince and the Pauper* for publication, to find out the addresses of the illustrators of that book, now being considered for *A Connecticut Yankee* (see note 198). Anthony provided the desired information immediately, also offering his own services.

[201] The Boston Symphony performed in Hartford's Foot Guard Armory Hall on 3 April 1889.

[202] On behalf of Clemens, Daniel Whitford was attempting to work out a new *Prince and the Pauper* play agreement that would include producer Daniel Frohman as well as Abby Sage Richardson. Clemens evidently wished the new contract to award him half the profits from the play as did his original agreement of 3 January 1889 with Mrs. Richardson. On 25 March 1889 Whitford forwarded to Clemens a draft of a new contract. It would allow Clemens and Mrs. Richardson half-shares of the following amounts: five per cent of the first $4,000 of receipts, ten per cent of the next $1,000, fifteen per cent of the next $1,000, and twenty per cent thereafter. Whitford noted that it was impossible "to make a more advantageous agreement. I am satisfied that can not be done. I have tried every way I could think of but the parties are on the alert." This new contract went into effect on 13 May 1889.

[203] Clemens' original contract with Mrs. Richardson had allowed her one year, that is, until 3 January 1890, for completion of the *Prince and the Pauper* play. Clemens thought two months or less sufficient for the work, but Daniel Frohman objected, insisting that "he would not take a play which she could write in sixty days" (Daniel Whitford to SLC, 25 March 1889). The new agreement of 13 May 1889 gave Mrs. Richardson until 1 October 1889, as Frohman wished, to prepare her dramatization.

[204] Provision for royalty payments at the end of each week's run of the *Prince and the Pauper* play was part of the 13 May 1889 contract between Clemens, Mrs. Richardson, and producer Daniel Frohman.

Explain this contract to me. The YEAR doesn't end it?[205]

Matthew & Mark, both of whom were members of Christ's Cabinet—

Wanamaker thinks *he* is one of them, too.[206]

of profound repose, & soft indolence & dreamy solitude,—[207]

The sublimes & the mightiest of all the centuries.

its remote summits floating serene.

Englishmen on America: Lepel Griffin, Matthew Arnold, Dickens, Trollope, &c: An Englishman on England: George ---[208]

Publish *simutaneously* a chapter in every magazine 1 month before issue, & after the main subscriptions have been taken. *Tell the Mags I am doing this deliberately as an ad.*[209] [#]

---

[205] Clemens' original contract with Mrs. Richardson clearly limited her exclusive right to dramatize *The Prince and the Pauper* to a period of one year. By its terms she had no authorization after 3 January 1890. The new contract Whitford proposed on 25 March gave Daniel Frohman "the right to the play for five years provided he play it seventy five times a year."

[206] A reference to John Wanamaker's recent appointment to the office of postmaster general in Benjamin Harrison's cabinet.

[207] The phrases in this entry and the following two were drafted for the speech Mark Twain was to deliver at Delmonico's on 8 April 1889 (see note 199) in which he called Hawaii "that far off home of profound repose, and soft indolence, and dreamy solitude," alluded to the might of "the raging, tearing, booming nineteenth century," and remembered Hawaii's "remote summits floating like islands above the cloud rack" (Frear, *Mark Twain and Hawaii*, pp. 501–502).

[208] Lepel Henry Griffin's aspersions on America in *The Great Republic* (1884) were noted by Matthew Arnold in his own recent critical piece, "Civilisation in the United States" (*Nineteenth Century*, April 1888). Charles Dickens' unfavorable *American Notes for General Circulation* (1842) and *Martin Chuzzlewit* (1844) had aroused angry reaction in the United States as had Frances Trollope's witty denunciations in *Domestic Manners of the Americans* (1832). Although Clemens was familiar with Mrs. Trollope's work, quoting from it in chapter 27 of *Life on the Mississippi*, he may here have intended Anthony Trollope's *North America* (1862), an often critical but more generally tolerant account of a visit to the United States. Clemens saw George Standring's *People's History of the English Aristocracy* (1887), a formative influence on *A Connecticut Yankee*, as a compendium of British disgraces to which English critics of America might have profitably directed their energy.

[209] This entry and the following one comprise an unconsummated scheme for serial publication of *A Connecticut Yankee*. Excerpts from the book were published in the

Harper's, 18th November; Scribner's 25th November; Century, Dec 1; publish Dec. 10. This make a live canvass from Nov. 18 to Dec. ⟨21⟩ 18—a full month.

Carry down George - -'s Exposure of English society & publish at 25 cents.

& Lepel Griffin in the same covers—& Arnold.[210]

Send up 2 or $3000 about this time

Mch 27/89. Wrote Laffan, offering 5 one-hundredths (one ninth of my ownership in *American* business, or one-eighteenth of the whole) at $100,000 cash (less $10,000 commission to *him*) payable upon view of the machine in *Hartford*—purchaser to be satisfied, or no trade. Or, one, or two, or ⟨3⟩three of the 5 at $25,000 cash each, payable as above, & commission 10 per cent.

Mch. 28/89. Told Paige of my talk with Hamersley, & he expressed his hearty willingness to let us raise the capital by selling the English patents for $10,000,000—either outright, or we to retain $4/10$ of the English stock.

Miss Brown's, (reading) 13th April, 715—5th ave.[211]

⟨Interviewer—15⟩
⟨Raftsmen⟩   True Story
?/ Skinned Man   Uncle Remus.
?/ Isaac—10 m
Muleykeh—20
Interviewer—15–20

May 7. Charity Ball, Union for House Work.[212] [#]

Century magazine in November 1889. *A Connecticut Yankee* was issued in England on 6 December 1889 and in the United States four days later.

[210] A plan to publish in a single volume works by two of the most severe English critics of America and a study by a dedicated English critic of British society (see note 208).

[211] Annie Brown wrote to Clemens on 25 March 1889 asking him to read at her New York City home on 13 April on behalf of the Society of Collegiate Alumnae, which was "interested in establishing a society for the lower Class of working women in the city." She acknowledged his affirmative response on 28 March.

[212] The Clemenses attended this ball at Foot Guard Armory Hall for the Hartford Union for Home Work. Clemens was on the reception committee, along with the gover-

Apl. 13.

1. King Arthur .... 40 m.
3. Muléykeh 20
2. Mate & Gov. Gardner 10
5 Christening Story 7
4 ⟨German Lesson⟩............................... 12
4. One Uncle Remus.

Engage room for Centennial.
Try Players Club & Lotos Club[213]

Go to German Theatre with Howells.[214]

Thursday, 8 to 10, 2 to 3.30. Dr Johnson's.[215]

He called the attention of the nation to the[216]

$100 to Joe.

Write Perkins about that goose.

Write Miss Hamersley about the roses.[217]

Talk to Mr. Hall about additions to the Pope's Life.[218] [#]

---

nor of Connecticut and numerous Hartford luminaries. The purposes of the Union for Home Work are discussed on page 438, note 101.

[213] In early April 1889 plans were being made for three days of festivities in New York City to celebrate the centennial of George Washington's inauguration. The 29 April–1 May celebration included elaborate naval and military parades, church services, and a banquet at the Metropolitan Opera House on 30 April, all attended by President Benjamin Harrison and other government officials. On 8 April Clemens accepted an invitation to attend the banquet, and arrangements were made for him to view the main parade the same day from the offices of Webster & Company. On 28 April he withdrew from his planned appearance at the banquet when he found himself "obliged to remain at home" (SLC to Clarence W. Bowen).

[214] The Amberg Theatre in New York City, recently opened by impresario Gustav Amberg. Amberg had previously been associated with the Thalia, another New York theater where Clemens saw German plays.

[215] Marcus M. Johnson, a Hartford physician with whom Clemens made an appointment for Tuesday, 2 April 1889.

[216] Clemens possibly began to draft remarks here for delivery at the Washington centennial banquet.

[217] Probably a gift from Elizabeth Hamersley in gratitude for Clemens' recent reading at her home.

[218] On 27 March 1889 Bernard O'Reilly, author of the *Life of Leo XIII*, sent Frederick Hall additional biographical information about the pope. "The Pope has entered on his

⟨S⟩Go to Dr. Roosa Tuesday.[219]

Let Mr. Hall ask Gen Agents whether to bring out K. Arthur. A gird at royalty & nobility.[220]

"Great Western"
Pleasant Valley Wine Co.
    Rheims, N.Y.
Champagne.

Game of Authors for Jean.

#4830. Apl. 12. $40.—2,000 miles.

June 1. Julie valedictorian[221]—Susie & I invited. Best weather. Bad weather up to 6.

See Dora Wheeler, & speak of Mr. Hewitt's kind offer.[222]

Prisoner sent up for 25 years for murder, stepping manacled from train:

"Auburn! ⟨7⟩25 years for refreshments!" [#]

80th year," O'Reilly explained, "& WE MUST BE READY with a 'complete' Life in case any accident should suddenly befall the aged & not very robust Pontiff." He urged Hall to "lose not a moment in printing the new matter, & having your *Second & complete* edition bound & ready for sale, in the event of ill tidings from Rome." Webster & Company forwarded O'Reilly's letter to Clemens on 6 April, soliciting his opinion about a revised edition. Clemens evidently approved, for Charles L. Webster & Company published an expanded version of O'Reilly's work in 1889. The pope did not die until 1903.

[219] Clemens periodically consulted Daniel Bennett St. John Roosa, a prominent New York physician. The occasion for this visit has not been determined.

[220] Although the wording of this entry remains puzzling, Clemens evidently wished to have the opinions of Webster & Company book agents about publicity for, not publication of, *A Connecticut Yankee*. On 18 April 1889, Webster & Company asked him to allow the New York *Tribune* to "make a very brief mention of it not more than fifteen or twenty lines giving a general idea of the book. . . . We think it might be well, as early as possible to get into circulation the fact that the book was a keen satire on the royalty and nobility of England all through, and to emphasize this fact whenever and wherever we could."

[221] Julie Langdon, oldest daughter of Charles J. Langdon, had been chosen valedictorian of her high school class.

[222] Dora Wheeler's photographer friend, Teddy Hewitt, had taken some photographs of Clemens. On 16 April 1889, Dora Wheeler told Clemens that "Teddy says he will make over any plates you want to you." In fact, Hewitt turned all his negatives of Clemens over to C. C. Cox, the photographer Edmund C. Stedman had engaged to work on the *Library of American Literature*.

Gov. Tod (& God)[223]

Wager of Battle. about ⟨114⟩ 117[224]

"Herr doctor, ich bin gestern bei eine Holzbeinigerin geschlafen!"[225] (which accounts for the splinter).

Cox, 12th &   photo.[226]

Send Charley Clark Men of the Time Biog slip.[227]

Laffan's address till June 5:
Office N.Y. Sun, Victoria Hotel, Northumberland ave, London.
Cable: Brisbane, London

This is very nearly the equivalent of saying that the M is not ⟨capable of⟩ ⟨saying⟩ ⟨doing⟩ able to do fine book-work at all. That is what it is intended to say.[228] [#]

---

[223] Clemens alludes here to an anecdote about David Tod, Civil War governor of Ohio. One evening while the governor was visiting the White House, "Mr. Lincoln said, 'Look here, Tod, how is it that you spell your name with only one *d*. I married a Todd, but she spelled her name with two *d*'s. All of her relations do the same. You are the first Tod I ever knew who spelled his name with so few letters.' Mr. Tod, smiling, replied, 'Mr. President, God spells His name with only one *d*, and what is good enough for God, is good enough for me'" (George B. Wright, "Hon. David Tod: Biography and Personal Recollections," *Ohio Archaeological and Historical Quarterly*, July 1899, p. 119).

[224] Henry William Herbert's *Wager of Battle: A Tale of Saxon Slavery in Sherwood Forest* (New York: Mason Brothers, 1855). Clemens' approximate reference is to a section describing a Norman noblewoman's realization that the Saxon serfs in fact despise their slavery and are as capable of devotion and self-sacrifice as any free man.

[225] *Doctor, yesterday I slept with a woman with a wooden leg!*

[226] Possibly a reference to two photographs, the twelfth and the second, in a series prepared by C. C. Cox, which Clemens thought acceptable for the *Library of American Literature*.

[227] A brief biography of Clemens appeared in *Men of the Time: A Dictionary of Contemporaries, Containing Biographical Notices of Eminent Characters of Both Sexes*, edited by Thompson Cooper and published by G. Routledge and Sons, most recently in 1887. Clemens owned several editions of this work and supplied information to keep his biography up to date.

[228] During the late 1880s, Clemens drafted many pages of promotional material for the Paige typesetter, usually elaborating its virtues while ridiculing its competition. In this note, evidently for such a piece, he claims the superiority of the Paige typesetter over the Mergenthaler Linotype. The Mergenthaler had already been used in printing a book, however, *The Tribune Book of Open Air Sports*, which appeared in 1887.

Saturday May ⟨1[2]⟩11, 10.30, our house ⟨[--]⟩ read to our Club
girls[229]

I told the Greek prof I had concluded to drop the use of the
Greek written character because it is so hard to spell ⟨[--]⟩with, &
so impossible to read after you get it spelt. I perceived by what
followed, that nothing but early neglect saved him from being a
very profane man. I ordered the prof. of mathematics to simplify
the whole system, because the way it was, I couldn't understand it,
& I didn't want things going on in the College in a clandestine
fashion (in what was practically a) ⟨I told him to knock out some
of the logarithms & see if he couldn't insert some lighter timber.⟩
He reception of this, bordered upon insubordination; insomuch that
I felt obliged to take his number & report him. I found the
astronomer of the University gadding around after comets (&
things?) instead of attending to business. I told him pretty plainly
that we couldn't have that. I told him ⟨that⟩ it was no economy
to go on piling up & piling up raw material in the way of new
stars & comets & trash that we couldn't ever have any use for till
we had worked up the old stock. I said if I caught him scouring
around after any more ⟨of⟩ asteroids, especially, I should have to
scour him out of the place. Privately, prejudice got the best of me
there, I ought to confess it. I don't mind comets, so much, but
⟨from my earliest⟩ somehow I have always been down on/never
could stand asteroids. To my mind ⟨theyre only just⟩ there's
nothing mature about them—only just pups/whelps out of some
planet. Well, then, of course it annoyed me to hear him say he
preferred asteroids to anything else,/they were just pie to him. &
I said it was pretty degraded taste. ⟨He said there was more money
in it than in any other (line?) of the business, because, he said
astronomical real estate has its fluctu.⟩ And I requested him to not
talk back. I said it was pretty low-down business for great
universities to be in—Rochester always raking the deeps of space
for comet-spawn & trading it to Yale for ⟨asteroids⟩
planet-pups.[230] [#]

---

[229] A meeting of the Saturday Morning Club.
[230] A partial draft of a belated acceptance speech for the honorary Master of Arts

Colored ⟨fold⟩folk, May 22.[231]

Skinned Man 12

Mate & Gov. Gardiner 10

Interviewer 20

Whistling story. 5

A World "Want" page contains 46,000 ems. The 13 (Sunday)
Want pages could be set by 13 good men in 7½ hours.

Tribune page, smallest type, 36,000.

World reading page, 35,000

Miss Chaese[232]
    59 Belleview st
        N. Main st

Ology Club
    Jarvis Hall, Trinity
        Wed. May 15
            7.⁴⁵ pm
Explosions.[233] [#]

---

degree conferred upon Clemens by Yale University in June 1888. Unable to accept the
degree in person then (see the headnote to Notebook 27), Clemens planned, but did not
use, a speech such as this for a Hartford alumni dinner in February 1889 (see pp. 445,
456–457), at which time he may have made these notes. Clemens was to appear at a Yale
alumni banquet in New Haven on 26 June 1889 and with that occasion in mind probably
reconsidered the rejected comic speech. He did not use these remarks, although he
spoke in the same mode, explaining: "Ever since Yale promoted me to a place among its
learned honoraries I have felt it a duty to scrutinize things more searchingly than I used
to in order to apply my new acquirements to the uses of the university. So I bought a dictionary and resolved to do what I could to help the college along in science and in everything I could." Clemens then "gave his opinions and observations upon the progress of
medical science and its condition now in contrast to what it used to be," closing with
the promise that "as long as he was permitted to appear with the faculty he would take
especial pains to pick up all the science he could for the college" (New Haven *Daily
Morning Journal and Courier*, 27 June 1889).

    [231] A tentative program for a reading in Hartford's Unity Hall, part of a benefit for
the Talcott Street Congregational Church (see pp. 486 and 489).

    [232] Emilie Chaese, an artist, resided at 59 Bellevue Street in Hartford. Clemens'
business with her has not been determined.

    [233] Since January 1889 New York City had been suffering a series of subway explosions,
caused by leaks of illuminating gas, which blew manhole covers high into the air and tore

Unitype Printing Co. 22 Spruce st. J. RISLEY[234]

The Berlin Das Echo (July '88) say there are now 621 newspapers & periodicals published in that city.

Douglas Taylor belongs to the Typothetæ, & there are 510 members in the national organization. Get their address.

⟨The book-house equipped will pay 5½ to 6^c; unequipped, 43; morning paper 7½ or 8—now 50. Formidable competition.⟩

Stilson Hutchins, 1603 Mass^{ts} av

The London Standard (88) says there are now 13,600 periodicals in Europe.

970 dailies in U.S.—⟨'88.⟩ '87.
12000 periodicals.
617 towns in US of 4,000 & upwards.

It will cost the same to set a page of a N.Y. daily on the M that it now costs to set a column by hand.

We have a youth who sets   ooo an hour & an old printer who sets 1000 by hand & 8,000 on the M.[235]

If an 8-page N.Y. daily will put itself all in one-size type, 8 men can do all of its composition on 8 of our M's. ⟨& 36 the Sunday World.⟩

Ck 4313 Aug 13 TW Crane $30.[236] [#]

---

up pavement. There was much discussion of the problem and some suggestion of remedies in the spring of the year, but since the gas companies involved balked at the cost of repairing or replacing old pipes no practical steps toward alleviation were taken. Clemens may have wished to address the issue before the Ology Club of Trinity College.

[234] On 16 October 1888, the New York *Times* reported that a "working model of a machine for justifying type composition automatically was on exhibition yesterday at 22 Spruce-street [in New York City]. It is the invention of Messrs. [Isaac] Risley and [V. F.] Lake." This entry is squeezed into the top margin of a notebook page. The entries which follow it, completing the notebook, all seem to have been made in 1888 and occasionally repeat earlier entries from this notebook and Notebook 27.

[235] Fred Whitmore, son of Franklin G. Whitmore, had begun his training on the Paige typesetter in early 1888. The old printer was Charles G. Van Schuyver.

[236] This check, probably in part payment of Quarry Farm expenses, was written in 1888. Theodore Crane died on 3 July 1889.

Appendix with liberal extracts covering all.[237]

Visit a kingdom where they sell commissions in the army; 4 generations of nobility required; nobility must have whore blood in it—one duke couldn't prove it; kingship always under foreigners, as now in Eng. Called the Cuckoo Monarchy, because always a foreigner on the nest. Harrying a Jew. Benjamin of Tudela, ancestor of the travler [238]

$$\left\{\begin{array}{l} \text{Hermit gulch.} \quad \text{(White Slaves of Wales.)} \\ \text{Monastery.} \\ \text{Foundling hospital;} \\ \text{Nunnery.} \end{array}\right\} \text{they propagate}$$

Sell advowsons & reversions; horse-jockeys & highwaymen [draw] them; has an Episcopal Estab Ch; have the Test Act.[239]

Women slaves stripped & whipped. A slave gets 500 & dies Families sold on auction block. Procession of 50 yoked with chains traveling—with a trader. Freedom speeches by buyers.

Forces vaccination—no missionarying so effective as the sword—force.

Stops the soap knight & washes all the hermits—they die. Simon Stylites.

July	5.	T.[240]	9.	. . . .	C. 36.	414
"	6	"	4	. . . .	" 20	276
"	9	"	12	. . . .	" 33	
"	11	"	11	. . . .	" 37	
"	13	"	13	. . . .	" 14	

---

[237] The following notes for *A Connecticut Yankee* were made in 1888.

[238] Benjamin of Tudela was a twelfth century Spanish Jew who traveled in the Middle East, the Orient, and parts of Europe. In 1877 Clemens acquired a copy of Thomas Wright's *Early Travels in Palestine* (London: Henry G. Bohn, 1848) which included Benjamin of Tudela's narrative of his travels.

[239] Test Acts passed in 1661 and 1672 required all candidates for public office in England to receive Holy Communion according to the rites of the Church of England. These acts were ameliorated by legislation passed in the late 1820s and were repealed some forty years later.

[240] Theodore Crane was probably the other party to the unidentified summer pastime suggested by Clemens' table of scores. Clemens made this record in 1888.

		T		C	
July 14	T.	15	....	C.	30
" —	"	23	....	"	16
" —	"	18	....	"	23
" —	"	12	....	"	35
" —	"	10	....	"	18
" —	"	33	....	"	17
" —	"	28	....	"	26
" —	"	16	....	"	24
" —	"	22	....		24
" —		20	....		34
—		30	....		27
—⟨380⟩		23	....		29
—		13	.... ⟨567⟩		13
		16	....		34
		12	....		22
		19	....		23
	380	21	 567		31
	108	21	 137		32
	146	30	 211		39
	634	36	 915		32
	108	21	.... ⟨137⟩ ...		34
		18	....		36
		17	....		53
		30	....		29
		30	....		22
		⟨3[-]	.... 22⟩		
		29	....		32
		T		C	
		⟨39⟩22	.... ⟨22⟩39		
		146	⟨2[20]⟩211—		
		30	....		26
		32	....		29
		28	....		21
		41	....		35
		14	....		37
Sept 5.		15	....		25 [#]

4310 Carl Schoenhof, July 25. books, $3.20.[241]

4311, D⁻ C C Rice, Aug. 3, ⟨$100⟩$105.

TW Crane ditto, $100. (4312)

4317 Aug 20 Twichell, $135

4314 Geo. Elmendorf Sept. 1 $48.75.

4318, Aug. 24 MacDonald $30.

4319 Patrick, Sept. 1, $100.

4320—John Sept 1 $120.

4315, Sep. 19 $100. Mrs. Ellen Trabue Smith.

4322, Sep. 21 $100—JL & Co.

⟨4324 Sept 24 $44, ponies, Wells Fargo.⟩

---

[241] The checks listed here were written in 1888 and include payments to: Carl Schoenhof, a Boston book importer and publisher (see p. 391); Dr. Clarence C. Rice, for professional services to Clemens, Livy, and Susy; Patrick McAleer, the Clemens family coachman; Mary C. MacDonald, a struggling artist whose career Clemens had tried to advance (see p. 387, note 296); John O'Neil, the Clemenses' gardener; Mrs. Ella Trabue Smith, who wrote to Clemens from Eureka Springs, Arkansas, on 26 September 1888, addressing him as "Dear Cousin" and thanking him for the "'nest egg' from you" which she promised to use to remove her ailing son from "all malarial influences"; J. Langdon & Company, for an undetermined reason; and Wells, Fargo & Company, for shipment of the children's ponies from Elmira to Hartford.

XXIX

"One of the Vanderbilt Gang"

(May 1889–August 1890)

THE CLEMENSES went to Quarry Farm in mid-June 1889 as usual, but the summer visit was an unhappy one because of the lingering, painful illness of Theodore Crane. On 3 July Crane died. Clemens stayed on at the farm for only a week after Crane's death before returning alone to Hartford. He had received momentous news: on 2 July Paige had telegraphed, "The machine is finished; come & see it work" (p. 498).

The miraculous machine did indeed appear to be perfected; all that remained was for the typesetter apprentices to acquire enough speed and dexterity on the machine to permit a public exhibition. Clemens came back to Quarry Farm within two weeks in an optimistic mood. He kept himself posted on the apprentices' progress and turned to other matters.

Several days were spent making selections from the manuscript of *A Connecticut Yankee* for publication in the *Century* magazine of November 1889. Then in mid-August Clemens began receiving proof of the book from Charles L. Webster & Company. Frederick J. Hall had never handled the publication of one of Clemens' own books and he confessed to feeling "nervous" about his "ability to properly place it on the market and give it the circulation it deserves" (Hall to SLC, 8 May 1889). Clemens, too, was nervous about his new

478

book. It was his first important work since the publication of *Huckleberry Finn* in 1885, and in theme and intent it differed radically from his previous work. E. C. Stedman read the *Yankee* in manuscript early in July 1889 and found it a great and stirring attack on "servility & flunkeyism & tyranny," of Clemens' books the "most original, most imaginative,—certainly the most effective and sustained." Stedman acknowledged that it was in some ways an "extension" of *The Prince and the Pauper* but, he added, "'tis very much else besides. The little book was checkers: this is chess" (Stedman to SLC, 7 July 1889). He felt sure the book would "make a great noise" but, like Clemens, he anticipated some critical disapproval. *The Prince and the Pauper*, despite its condemnation of certain injustices, was primarily a pleasing and quaint romance; in *A Connecticut Yankee* Clemens' indictments of aristocratic privilege and of the Church were uncomfortably explicit. Clemens took a firm stance with his English publishers Chatto & Windus. He wrote to Andrew Chatto on 16 July that the book was intended "to pry up the English nation to a little higher level of manhood" and warned that he would brook no changing of his manuscript (*MTL*, pp. 524–525).

But for Clemens the role of social reformer was necessarily secondary. As an established popular author and his own publisher, he might brave the critics but he could not afford to antagonize his reading public. In fact, he had "taken laborious pains" to "trim this book of offence" (SLC to Chatto, 16 July 1889, *MTL*, p. 524) and had expunged all that might "repel instead of persuade" (SLC to William Dean Howells, 5 August 1889, *MTHL*, p. 609). "I'm not writing for those parties who miscal themselves critics," he wrote to Howells on 24 August, "& I don't care to have them paw the book at all. It's my swan-song, my retirement from literature permanently, & I wish to pass to the cemetery unclodded" (*MTHL*, pp. 610–611).

Clemens' hopes of retirement undoubtedly hinged on the promise of the Paige typesetter. But the machine was disastrously capricious. Clemens was dismayed when he learned belatedly in mid-August 1889 that it had broken down and that Paige now hoped for completion by 1 September. He requested daily reports on the machine from Paige: "*Whatever* his daily reply is from now till the finish, no matter how far off that may be, I can live on it—& I am pretty hungry" (SLC to Franklin G. Whitmore, 27 August 1889).

In mid-September the machine was once more pronounced ready for testing and on 26 September Clemens obtained from Paige the right to a five hundred dollar royalty on each machine which was sold. Clemens promptly sold a number of shares in his royalty to friends and family in order to relieve the immediate financial burden of the typesetter.

Clemens was jubilant. He invited Howells to come and see the typesetter. "After patiently & contentedly spending more than $3,000 a month on it for 44 consecutive months, I've got it done at last, & it's a daisy! You & I have imagined that *we* knew how to set type—we shabby poor bunglers. Come & see the Master do it! Come & see this sublime magician of iron & steel work his enchantments" (SLC to Howells, 21 October 1889, *MTHL*, p. 615).

At the same time Clemens wrote to his old friend Joseph T. Goodman, now residing in Fresno, California, with a proposition to sell more shares of his royalty: "I want you to run over here, roost over the machine a week & satisfy yourself, & then go to John P. Jones or to whom you please, & sell me a hundred thousand dollars' worth of this property, & take ten per cent in cash or the 'property' for your trouble—the latter, if you are wise, because the price I ask is a long way short of the value." For one thousand dollars investors could purchase the right to a one-dollar royalty on each typesetter sold. "It is my purpose to sell two hundred dollars of my royalties at the above price during the next two months," explained Clemens, "& keep the other $300" (SLC to Goodman, 7 October 1889, Yale). Thus Clemens would retain three-fifths of the five hundred dollar royalty he obtained from Paige in September 1889 while realizing two hundred thousand dollars in ready cash. Goodman apparently accepted the proposition for he was in New York City early in November 1889 attempting to interest investors in the machine. On 16 November 1889 Clemens introduced a new plan: instead of merely selling royalties on the machine, Goodman was to interest Senator Jones and a few other wealthy men in undertaking the full capitalization of a typesetter factory. Goodman spent the next fourteen months commuting between Fresno, San Francisco, New York City, and Washington, D.C., in pursuit of Jones and other capitalists.

On 10 December 1889 *A Connecticut Yankee in King Arthur's Court* was published in the United States. Clemens had made certain that review copies were sent out selectively to assure favorable report. The earliest American reviews were those of Sylvester Baxter of the Boston *Herald* (15 December 1889) and William Dean Howells in the January 1890 *Harper's Monthly* (available 20 December 1889). Baxter and Howells were highly partisan in their enthusiasm for the book. Baxter praised its "abundant fun," "rich humor," and "earnest purpose"; Howells spoke of the "delicious satire, the marvellous wit, the wild, free, fantastic humor" mixed with the "force of right feeling and clear thinking" (*Mark Twain: The Critical Heritage*, ed. Frederick Anderson [New York: Barnes & Noble, 1971], pp. 148, 149, 153, 156). Later reviewers, in both the American and the English press, were less encomiastic. The book was condemned for its length, for its dubious historical framework, and for its forced humor and occasional tastelessness.

After six months Hall was able to report a sale of only about twenty-four thousand books—a disappointing showing, particularly in view of Clemens' belief that "the publisher who sells less than 50,000 copies of a book for me has merely injured me" (*MTLP*, p. 165). According to the company's July statement, the gross profits amounted to about twelve thousand dollars—and Webster & Company's financial situation made it impossible for Hall to forward any of Clemens' share to him. Hall, too, was crestfallen. The sales figures were "not satisfactory," he admitted on 8 August 1890. "I can only say, however, what I have already said, that it has been a very expensive book to make and a very expensive book to push. Its sale had to be forced all the time. . . . As the expense on the book is practically over with, from now on the sales will be nearly clear profit." A year after publication, however, the sales were only just over thirty-two thousand books and falling sharply.

Clemens' other affairs were no less disappointing. The typesetter defied deadlines; Paige continually introduced refinements and modifications. Completion was announced once again in May 1890 and Clemens, though crippled by typesetter bills, was still so dazzled by the machine that he could write to Goodman: "I am resolved to stick tight to the thing till I haven't any money left; & then I will hand it back to Paige & keep my royalties. Now here is a queer fact: I am one of the wealthiest grandees in America—one of the Vanderbilt gang, in fact—& yet if you asked me to lend you a couple of dollars I would have to ask you to take my note instead" (SLC to Goodman, 23 June 1890, Yale). Bonanza kings John P. Jones and John W. Mackay finally witnessed a performance of the typesetter in July 1890, but their financial response was tepid: they would personally commit themselves to no more than $5,000 apiece. Clemens and Goodman were crushed. "God damn this going round hat in hand and begging pennies!" raged Goodman in a letter to Clemens on 26 July 1890.

During 1889 and 1890 Clemens was also involved in two unhappy theatrical ventures. Early in 1889 he entered into a contract with Abby Sage Richardson and Daniel Frohman to produce a dramatization of *The Prince and the Pauper*. This agreement precipitated a bitter fight with Clemens' old friend Edward H. House over dramatic rights, which resulted in a lawsuit and a temporary injunction against Mrs. Richardson's play. Manager Frohman was able to obtain House's permission to continue performances of the play, but Clemens' share of the royalties was impounded in the process. Clemens emerged from the fray almost as irate with Frohman and Mrs. Richardson as he was with House. The play itself, a sentimental costume piece surviving through the attractions of child actress Elsie Leslie, was no less the object of Clemens' irritation. It was performed in New York City from 20 January 1890 until 1

March 1890, when it went on tour. An English dramatization of *The Prince and the Pauper* opened on 12 April 1890 at the Gaiety Theatre in London, but it fared no better than Mrs. Richardson's version. The English critics pointed out the play's obvious historical fallacy in both plot and language, and the use of a double for the main role was deemed awkward (*Illustrated London News*, 19 April 1890, p. 483; *Athenaeum*, 19 April 1890, p. 509). "As an exhibition, however, in the nature of what Mr. Barnum would call a 'side show,'" concluded the London *Times* of 14 April 1890, "the performance is curious and may prove attractive."

Clemens also commissioned a dramatization of *A Connecticut Yankee* which proved equally unfortunate. The play was prepared by the playwright Howard P. Taylor, one of Clemens' western friends. Taylor read the finished dramatization to Clemens in July 1890 and Clemens could only report that he bore the "awful ordeal" of several hours "in misery" (SLC to Clara Clemens, 20 July 1890, *LLMT*, pp. 257–258).

The Clemens family, after abandoning plans to go to Europe, spent the summer of 1890 at Onteora, New York, in the Catskills. The summer, usually Clemens' most productive literary season, provided no respite from business importunities. He spent the summer months shuttling between New York City, Hartford, Philadelphia, and Washington, D.C., on business matters.

Notebook 29 is one of a new group of twelve custom-made tabbed notebooks which Clemens ordered through Franklin G. Whitmore in July 1888 (see p. 390, note 307). Of the group, the eight known to survive (Notebooks 29 through 36) were used through March 1896. They differ only slightly from Notebooks 22 through 28: they have fewer leaves than the earlier notebooks, they are made of thinner paper with a different watermark, their pages are slightly larger, and the leather covers are a little redder and of a slightly finer grain. The new notebooks have remained in better condition than many of their predecessors, no doubt partly because the smaller number of pages and the thinner paper put less strain on the spines, but also because they were made of somewhat better materials and were more strongly constructed.

Notebook 29 originally contained eighty leaves of unlined white wove paper watermarked "Scotch Linen Ledger" and tinted red on the edges. The leaves measure $6\frac{3}{4}$ by $3\frac{13}{16}$ inches (17.2 by 9.7 centimeters) exclusive of the tabs, which measure $1\frac{3}{16}$ by $\frac{1}{4}$ inches (3.1 by .6 centimeters). As in the earlier notebooks, the endpapers and outer sides of the flyleaves are marbled red, blue, cream, orange, and green (but with the colors combed vertically rather than horizontally); the inner sides of the flyleaves are lined with the same paper used in the body of the notebook; the covers are pliable, reddish brown leather with blind-tooled borders; and the front cover is stamped in gold (though in a slightly different typeface), "MARK TWAIN, Hartford, Conn."

Notebook 29 now contains 154 pages, nineteen of them blank. Of the five leaves that have been torn out, three are missing and the other two remain in place in the notebook. One of these latter leaves is loose probably only because its conjugate half was torn out. The other, which must have been torn out deliberately, is discussed in note 159 (p. 534). Most of the entries in Notebook 29 are in black pencil, though there are a number in brownish black ink and one in purple pencil. Use marks in black pencil, probably by Paine, appear throughout but have not been reproduced.

A half-dozen miscellaneous pieces of material accompany the notebook. Some were undoubtedly tucked in the notebook by Clemens, but others may have found their way between its covers by chance. An English newspaper clipping that was pinned to a notebook page is discussed in note 83 (p. 505). Two clippings from New York newspapers were not attached to the notebook but lay interleaved in it for so long that they have stained pairs of facing pages. They are discussed in notes 222 and 252 (pp. 555, 562). A sheet of Clemens' random calculations of savings to be realized by users of the Paige compositor bears a broad resemblance to several passages in this notebook but no clear connection to any particular entry. It is not reproduced here. A flyer arguing the merits of the Paige compositor is reproduced at page 528 and discussed in note 146. Finally there is an empty envelope from Oliver Wendell Holmes addressed to "Mark Twain Esq. (Care of Samuel L. Clemens)" at the American Publishing Company in Hartford. The envelope, postmarked "Jan. 11," was probably mailed in 1870. There is no evidence to explain how the envelope came to be placed in this notebook or whether it was Clemens who put it there.

119 E 28[1]

562, 8th st Oakland, Moffett.

Laffan, 335 Lexington ave.

Fogarty, 38 E. 22^d [2]

Howells, Mt. Auburn Station,
    Cambridge, Mass.[3]

Frank Finlay, % H. R. Finlay, Box 2082.[4] Member & Hon. Sec.
of the Reform Club, London—Member of Arts Club; & is a
journalist. 61 E 73^{d.}

B. F. Underwood, P.O. Drawer 134, Chicago.[5]

Unalterable Laws.
No theatre & RR journey the same day.
No matinee & theatre the same day.
2 rooms ALWAYS.

Elsie Leslie Lyde, The Percival, 232 W. 42^d [6]

J. Niemeczek Very, 9, Strand.[7] [#]

---

[1] As usual, the initial entries in Clemens' notebook are primarily names and addresses written at various times during the notebook's use and grouped here for easy reference. Later entries in the body of the notebook reveal more specifically the relation of the persons mentioned to Clemens' current affairs.

[2] Clemens noted this "new address" for Livy's New York City dressmaker Madame Fogarty on page 449.

[3] William Dean Howells and his family were summering outside of Cambridge, Massachusetts, not far from Mount Auburn Station, in 1889.

[4] See page 511, note 104. In his letter of 29 July 1889 Finlay informed Clemens that he could be reached through his brother H. R. Finlay at the New York City post office box noted here.

[5] Possibly Benjamin Franklin Underwood, journalist, editor, and controversial lecturer.

[6] Child actress Elsie Leslie [Lyde] and family were staying at the Percival, a residential hotel in New York City, in the fall of 1889.

[7] Joseph N. Verey was the efficient and versatile courier of the Clemenses' 1878/1879 European trip; Clemens praised him in *A Tramp Abroad* (chapter 32). On 10 November 1889 Clemens wrote to young Julie Langdon, his wife's niece, thanking her for her description of the Langdons' European travels and for the "vivid glimpse you gave us of our mightily-prized & gratefully remembered guide, Joseph Very. I have entered his address

61 E. ⟨26th⟩25th % Care Mrs Hatch—Goodman

Daniel Whitford, 71 Madison ave

617 towns of 4000 & upwards in U. S. 12000 periodicals.[8]

Mary L. Bates
  Charleston
    Bradley Co. Tenn

Howard P. Taylor[9]
  % Actor's Fund
    145-5th ave.

Geo. T. Stevens, 33 W 33^{d}.[10]

Miss M. C. Thomas, Dean.[11]

Dr. Geo. T. Stevens,
33 W. 33^{d}. oculists

Ga Nun & Parsons, 5 W. 42^{d} Oculists [#]

---

in my note-book; for your Aunt Livy expects to take me & the rest of the children to Europe in the spring, & if her project holds good we shall want our wanderings . . . engineered by Joseph & none other." Verey wrote to Clemens on 28 March 1890 offering his services to the Clemens family or their friends should they come to Europe.

[8] Clemens was estimating the possible market for Paige typesetters in the United States. Among his miscellaneous notes about the Paige machine there is a list noting the names of over 200 American cities with populations over 10,000 and an estimate of the number of typesetters required by each city, with a resulting total of 2,173 typesetters.

[9] Dramatist Howard P. Taylor wrote to Clemens from this New York City address on 3 November 1889, reminding him of their friendship while on the staff of the Virginia City *Territorial Enterprise* and suggesting a possible collaboration on a dramatization of one of Clemens' works. Clemens responded amicably to Taylor's letter, the friendship was resumed, and at Clemens' suggestion Taylor began a dramatization of the forthcoming *Connecticut Yankee.*

[10] George T. Stevens was a New York City oculist who prescribed special "prismatic glasses" for Livy. The glasses were to be made by GaNun & Parsons, opticians, whose address Clemens noted below. Clemens had informed Mrs. William Dean Howells in December 1889 that Livy was "still blind, after a nine months' struggle with the oculist. To read a page or write one gives her a two-days' headache" (*MTHL*, p. 623). The prismatic glasses were evidently prescribed for this eye ailment.

[11] M. Carey Thomas was the first dean of Bryn Mawr College, where in 1890 Susy Clemens would apply for admission (see p. 556, note 226).

Gardiner G. Howland, Genl Manager. N. Y. H.[12]

⟨[-]⟩Howells, 184 Commonwealth ave[13]

⟨69⟩65. E. 59th—⟨H. H.⟩F. J. Hall.[14]

P. A. Moffett, Centennial House Oakland, Cal[15]

Fräulein Therese Reichenberger, Rüsterstrasse 10 Frankfurt a. M.[16]

Frau M. F. Kapp, 84 Elm st.

South Place Chapel & Institute,
  (South Place Ethical Society)
    Finsbury, E. C.
W. Sheawring, Hon. Sec. Inst. Com.

Ology Club. Jarvis Hall, Trinity, Wed, May 15, 7.45.[17]

Colored folk, Unity Hall, May 22[18]
⟨Skinned Man.⟩—boyhood.
⟨Mate & Gov Gardner

---

[12] Howland was general manager of the New York *Herald*. Through John Brusnahan, foreman of the *Herald* composing room, Clemens sounded Howland's interest in the Paige typesetter, hoping to get an early order from the newspaper. Unfortunately, despite Brusnahan's representations, the long delay in perfecting the Paige machine led Howland to regard the typesetter as a perpetual possibility rather than a reality.

[13] William Dean Howells and family lived at this Boston address from December 1889 until the end of 1891. Howells sent the address to Clemens on 15 December 1889.

[14] This address appears on a letter of 4 January 1890 from Frederick J. Hall to Clemens.

[15] Clemens' sister Pamela Moffett was in California visiting her son Samuel Erasmus Moffett, a reporter on the San Francisco *Examiner*. A letter of 31 December 1890 from Pamela to Sam Moffett bears this Oakland address; on an earlier visit ending in May 1889 Pamela Moffett had lived at the Oakland address noted at the beginning of this notebook.

[16] Nineteen-year-old Fräulein Reichenberger, apparently one of Clemens' admirers, wrote to him in German on 1 May 1889 thanking him for his kind response to a previous letter. Clemens reminded himself to "write her by & by" on the first page of the letter.

[17] Jarvis Hall was one of the buildings of Hartford's Trinity College. There is no record of Clemens' attendance at this meeting of the "Ology Club."

[18] Clemens' reading at Unity Hall in Hartford was part of the benefit for the organ fund of the 'Talcott Street Congregational Church. The Hartford *Courant* of 23 May 1889 pronounced the entertainment a "rich treat," noting that Mark Twain made an unexpected appearance and provided "no end of fun by reading an essay on 'Lying,' and an account of a dueling experience." (See also Clemens' comment on p. 489).

Interviewer
Whistling⟩
"Lying"
Duel.
⟨Artemus Ward & the "lone hand"
Christening.⟩

CLW,[19] send me $1000 end of May.

Laffan, N. Y. Sun,
Victoria Hotel,
Northumberland ave.[20]

Since she can't take care of me, I must take care of mysellf. After $2000 weekly, I want 10 per cent.
Otherwise, ⟨s⟩leave open till October[21]

Hair-cut.

Deceased Wife's Sister's Bill: 24 Bishops in House of Lords & 27 majority against the bill. Without the Established Church the bill would have had a majority.[22] [#]

---

[19] Charles L. Webster & Company.

[20] In Notebook 28 (p. 471) Clemens noted that William Mackay Laffan, publisher and owner of the New York *Sun*, was to be at the *Sun's* London office until 5 June 1889.

[21] On 3 January 1889 Clemens had signed an agreement with the lecturer and author Abby Sage Richardson regarding her projected dramatization of *The Prince and the Pauper*. The contract stipulated that Clemens was to receive half of any royalties earned by Mrs. Richardson's adaptation. Mrs. Richardson soon obtained a commitment from her longtime friend, the theatrical producer Daniel Frohman of the Lyceum Theatre in New York City. A new contract, dated 13 May 1889, was drawn up between the three parties (see p. 466, note 202, for details of the new royalty terms). Clemens' notebook entry indicates that the royalty terms in the May 1889 contract were not wholly to his liking and that he had considered delaying signing the contract until 1 October 1889, the date when Mrs. Richardson's dramatization was to be completed.

[22] The bill legalizing marriage between a widower and his deceased wife's sister had passed in the House of Commons, but was then defeated by a majority of twenty-seven in the House of Lords on 9 May 1889. Of the 267 voting peers only fifteen were spiritual peers so that, as the London *Times* commented, "it cannot be alleged that the measure is rejected by ecclesiastical bigotry, an argument which, though intrinsically absurd, has been heard on previous occasions." The *Times* also expressed the hope that this "decisive verdict" would forestall further attempts "to legislate on this wearisome and slightly nauseous subject" (10 May 1889). A much amended version of the bill was finally passed in both houses of Parliament in August 1907 amid another flurry of indignation.

I have never asked one of them a question yet without getting more information than I expected.

When in doubt, ask a student.[23]

In the matter of pensions, England has never made any distinction between public service & private shame⟨.⟩—except to pay highest for the latter. Consider the Dukes of Grafton & Richmond & ⟨Nell Gwy[---]'s⟩ progeny & Nelson's.[24] England pensions the rich whore with millions, the poor private with a shilling a month. She was always shabby & a humbug.

(May 22/89.

Mother[25] said, to Livy, "What ⟨was⟩ is the name of the sister of"—

"Mrs. Corning?"

"Yes, Mrs. Erastus Corning."

I was present. ⟨They ex⟩ Livy exclaimed that *this* was genuine mental telegraphy, for no mention had been made of the Cornings. Last week—4 or 5 days ago—occurred some talk about Mrs. Pruyn of Albany, the sister under consideration.[26]

---

[23] In this entry and the previous one, Clemens was planning his speech for the Yale alumni banquet of 26 June 1889 (see p. 472, note 230). On that occasion he poked fun at "the students of Trinity up in Hartford," noting: "They have been trying to befriend me ever since I got a degree. They give me all the advice I want. I don't have to go to them for it either" (New Haven *Daily Morning Journal and Courier*, 27 June 1889).

[24] Clemens' indignation about the privileges accorded England's nobility was fed by his reading of George Standring's *People's History of the English Aristocracy*, first published in 1887, and by a book he evidently acquired in 1879, Howard Evans' *Our Old Nobility* (see N&J2, p. 339). The aim of both authors was to reveal the absurdity and injustice of continuing to maintain an incompetent hereditary ruling class whose privileges and exemptions were the legacy of a handful of treacherous and self-serving voluptuaries. The dukedoms of Grafton and Richmond and the preferment accorded Nell Gwyn's son were all the result of Charles II's amorous liaisons. Histories of these families figure in both Standring's and Evans' books. Evans includes a history of the Nelson peerage, with details of the various pensions awarded the illustrious admiral and his descendants.

[25] Livy's mother, Mrs. Jervis Langdon, visited the Clemens family in Hartford in the late spring of 1889.

[26] Mrs. John Van Schaick Lansing Pruyn was the former Anna Fenn Parker; her sister Mary was the wife of Erastus Corning, Jr., of Albany. The Pruyns and the Cornings were prominent Albany families.

I proposed to take down the 3 sentences immediately, &
doubted if even immediately would be soon enough to get them
exactly, so unsure a thing is human testimony. It is agreed that
this report is *exact.* ⟨[*four? words*]⟩

Trib mach sets 120,000 a week for $30, & *saves* $30. We, 230,000
for $30, & save $85. ⟨[$- - -]⟩

May 22/89, I read to the colored people "An Essay on the Decay
of the Art of Lying" (first time in public) which went exceedingly
well—unexpectedly so. Also read the "Duel."

Wed. 29th. Train leaves at 5.10. Diner at 6. Return train at 10

And as concerns the Trinity,—that curious combination of
⟨spectre,⟩ thug, theological student & ⟨Thug—⟩ spectre.

F. E. Church about Coffee.[27]

Hartford, The Sepulchre City

⟨20⟩

You know how absent-minded Twichell (Rev. J. H.) is, & how
desolate his face is when he is in that frame. At such times he
passes the word with a friend on the street & is not aware of the
meeting at all. Twice in a week our Clara (aged 16) had this latter
experience with him within the past Month. But the second
instance was too much for her, & she woke him up, in his tracks,
with a reproach. ⟨she⟩She said:

"Uncle Joe, *why* do you always look as if you were just going
down into the grave, when you meet a person on the street?"—&
then went on to reveal to him the funeral spectacle which he
presented on such occasions. Well, she has met Twichell three

---

[27] Clemens and his wife had first visited Olana, the Hudson River home of landscape
painter Frederick E. Church, in June 1887. The visit was a memorable one and the Clemenses planned a return visit for May 1889 but were unable to go. Church had written to
Clemens on 10 November 1888: "Mrs. Clemens, who was kind enough to approve of our
coffee, was desirous to know where it could be procured." He enclosed a bag of "Colima
(Mexico) Coffee," a type which he believed to be "the best . . . that is grown" and
expressed a willingness to forward future orders for "the genuine berry" to a friend in
Mexico.

times since then, & would swim the Connecticut to avoid meeting
him the fourth. As soon as he sights her, no matter how public the
⟨place⟩ place nor how far off she is, he makes a bound into the
⟨air, flings⟩ air, hurls arms & legs into all sorts of frantic gestures of
delight, & so comes prancing, skipping & pirouetting for her like a
drunken Indian entering heaven. She feels as embarrassed as the
Almighty.[28]

Send Cable one of those old New Haven pamphlet novels.[29]

Killaloe[30]
Lanigan's Ball.

⟨[12]⟩ 10 pcs to Elmira.
         2 ″ ″ N. Y.[31]

   No. 6
   1.21 pm
arr. 8.43 Hoboken

lv. 9.40 a.m.
arr. 6.   Hoboken.

#4923. C. J. L. $200 June 15[32] [#]

---

[28] Clemens sent a copy of this anecdote to Susan Crane in a letter of 28 May 1889 for
the amusement of Theodore Crane who was gravely ill (see *MTL*, p. 509).

[29] See page 47, note 107. Clemens was apparently unable to locate his several copies
of S. Watson Royston's short novel *The Enemy Conquered; or, Love Triumphant*, for
he wrote to Cable on 11 June 1889: "They are lost! I have searched everywhere & cannot
find a vestige of that pamphlet. I possess not a single book which I would not sooner have
parted with" (Guy A. Cardwell, *Twins of Genius* [East Lansing: Michigan State College
Press, 1953], p. 110).

[30] See page 450, note 143. Clemens noted this title and quoted several verses and miscellaneous lines from the song elsewhere in this notebook (pp. 492, 496, 511, 513, 569).
The entry on page 569, which includes directions for gestures to accompany the lyric,
indicates that Clemens may have planned to perform "Killaloe."

[31] The Clemens family left for their summer stay at Quarry Farm around 11 June 1889,
probably stopping off in New York City for a short time on the way.

[32] An extensive list of numbered checks drawn on Clemens' Hartford account at
George P. Bissell & Company follows this entry almost immediately. The checks date
from the summer of 1889 and cover expenditures at Elmira and Hartford. Of the persons mentioned several are identifiable: Charles J. Langdon, Clemens' brother-in-law;
Otto B. Schlutter, German teacher to the Clemens family; Franklin G. Whitmore, Clem-

Leave $150 with him & bring $50.

Dispose of that mortgage.

#4973. Otto B. Schlutter., $22.^{50} June 18.

#4974. Whitmo, $125,   June 28.

#4975. F. G. Warner, $9.   "   "

4354. EL Holbrook, $15, July 31.

4388. A.H.H. Dawson, $10, Aug. 9.

4389. Langdon & Co. $100. Aug. 9

4390. Mrs. S. A. Quarles, $10, Aug. 10.

Patrick $50, John $60, for August.

4387. Twichell—$140. Aug. 19.

4395⟨. P⟩& 6. Patrick 50 & John, 60, Aug. 20

4406   WH Frost, Aug. 30 $16.

4417. Meyrowitz Bros. Aug. 31—81 cents.

4407   Dr Darby, Sept 1—$25

4415   Bosleman, $23, Sept. 7.

4416. Mrs. Crane,   Sept. 10, $640.

4411   Patrick (ponies)   "   24   65

4409—Patrik (ponies) $20 Sept 7.

4412. "Cash" Arnot, $300, Sept. 14.

---

ens' Hartford business agent; Frank G. Warner, son of the Clemenses' neighbor George H. Warner; Andrew H. H. Dawson, a New York City lawyer who had recently written to invite Clemens to an unspecified banquet and to solicit a contribution; J. Langdon & Company of Elmira; John O'Neil, the Clemenses' Hartford gardener; Joseph Hopkins Twichell; Meyrowitz Brothers, New York City opticians; Frank B. Darby, an Elmira physician; John Bostelmann, the Clemens children's piano teacher; Susan Crane (the payment probably represents the Clemenses' share of summer expenses at Quarry Farm); Patrick McAleer, the Clemenses' coachman; Matthias Hollenback Arnot, director of the extensive Arnot mercantile holdings in Elmira; Mme Cécile Freese, French teacher to the Clemens family. E. L. Holbrook, W. H. Frost, and Miller have not been identified. Mrs. S. A. Quarles may be a Clemens family connection through Clemens' uncle John A. Quarles but genealogical records fail to identify her.

4410   RR. fares, Sept. 16, $33.
4413, Miller (wood) Sept 24—$107.[50]
4414, Mad. Freese, Sept. 28 = $25.

Well I happen'd to be born
At the time they cut the corn
   Quite contagious to the town of Killaloe;
Where to tache us they'd a schame
And a Frinch mossoo he came
   To instruct us in the game of parley-voo.

I've wan father, that I swear,
But he said I had a "pair,"
   And he sthruck me whin I said it wasn't true;
And the Irish for a "jint"
And the Frinch for "half a pint"
   Faith we lairnt it in the school at Killaloe.

———————

"Mais oui" mosso would cry;
"Well ⟨[o]f [c]⟩uv coorse ye can," says I;
"Non." "No? I *know*," says I with some surprise;
   Whin a boy straight up from Clare
   Hard his mother called a "mare"
He gave mossoo his fist betune his eyes.

Ye may talk of Boneyparty,
Ye may talk about ecairte,
Or anny other pairty and "comment vous pairley-vous,"
We lairn't to sing it aisy,
That song the Marseillaisy,
Boolong, Toolong, the Continong
   We lairnt at Killaloe.

We make simply this broad claim: that ⟨in whatever
circumstances⟩ with wages above $2 a day, wherever *any other*
machine ⟨s⟩can save one dollar ⟨[we]⟩ours can ⟨in the same
circumstances⟩ save ⟨two.⟩ a dollar & a half.

We hope that the proprietors ⟨of other machines will not be
backward in requiring us to prove this.⟩ [#]

We make this broad claim: that wherever wages are \$2 & upwards per operator, our machine will save \$150 for every hundred saved by any other machine.

As soon as we shall have trained a third operator We shall also make this claim: that in a steady run of seven consecutive days & nights, (or 50, if preferred,) ⟨our machine shall show two ems⟩ in a competition with the other ⟨machine⟩machines now before the public, our machine shall show, at the end of the race, 2,000 ems of corrected matter for every 1,000 of corrected matter produced by the swiftest of the others. This is the only way to test the staying qualities of a machine; half-hour spurts prove nothing, & have no value.

The above ⟨cla⟩ statements are intended as challenges.[33] =

June 19, 1889, ⟨[gave]⟩ Susie L. Crane a paper agreeing (upon surrender ⟨to me⟩ of said paper) to deliver to her paid-up stock representing a *One Five Hundredth* of the whole of the capital stock "of the company which is to be organized to manufacture, & sell or rent Paige Compositors under the (American) patents, so soon as such company shall be formed & begin the issue of stock.

After some remarks of F W,[34] concluded to say nothing about this project & let it drop.

X-₁[35]

Papa's ben in the Legislature—there, now!
That ain't anything; *I*'ve got an uncle in hell. [#]

---

[33] With the relatively inexpensive Mergenthaler Linotype already in use on three major American newspapers—the New York *Tribune,* the Chicago *Daily News,* and the Louisville *Courier-Journal*—Clemens felt that his best selling points for the expensive Paige typesetter would be its promise of long-term savings and its speed in sustained operation. In May 1889 Clemens prepared a form letter, apparently intended for the editors of the major newspapers, announcing the completion of the Paige typesetter for 15 July 1889 and proposing to test the machine's speed, over many hours, against all others. As usual, Clemens was disappointed: the completion date of the typesetter was repeatedly postponed and Clemens' form letter remained unmailed.

[34] Clemens' Hartford business agent, Franklin G. Whitmore, kept Clemens posted during the summer of 1889 about progress on the Paige typesetter.

[35] Clemens made this notation in the upper left corner of the page, apparently as part of an intended indexing system such as he would use in Notebook 30 for marking entries of potential literary use. However, the index for this notebook is limited to the reference to this entry at 567.12.

Bring Chopin & Beethoven—in drawing-room—□ square, red-bound.[36]

Bring home ELSIE'S SLIPPER.[37]

Order suit of clothes.

⟨George spread coffee over kitchen inch deep.⟩

Beecher; Bon[d]s; Andrew Langdon.[38] Theodore.

Long-distance-telephone the farm.

Tell Chatto to telegraph Stanley.[39] [#]

---

[36] Clemens evidently left Quarry Farm and returned to Hartford briefly in late June 1889. The following several entries are memoranda of errands to be accomplished in Hartford.

[37] In the spring of 1889 Clemens and actor William Gillette had begun work on a surprise gift—a pair of embroidered slippers—for child actress Elsie Leslie. The two amateur needlemen finally presented their offering to Elsie on 5 October 1889, accompanied by a letter from Clemens explaining the intricacies of the embroidered designs. Elsie responded with a charming letter of appreciation. On 22 November 1889 Elsie's mother wrote to Clemens that the *St. Nicholas* children's magazine would like to reproduce the two letters. "A Wonderful Pair of Slippers" appeared in *St. Nicholas* in February 1890 and was later collected in *Europe and Elsewhere* (New York: Harper & Brothers, 1923).

[38] Livy's cousin Andrew Langdon was a wealthy Buffalo businessman. In 1887 Clemens had made him the subject of an uncomplimentary sketch, "Letter from the Recording Angel" (see *What Is Man? and Other Philosophical Writings*, ed. Paul Baender [Berkeley, Los Angeles, London: University of California Press, 1973], pp. 65–70).

[39] In January 1887 Henry Morton Stanley had sailed for Zanzibar in command of the Emin Pasha Relief Expedition. His mission was to locate and aid Emin Pasha, governor of the beleaguered Equatorial Province of Egypt, who had been forced to retreat before the Mahdist forces and had urgently requested support from the British government. Stanley's ill-fated mission was now almost at an end: he would return to Zanzibar from the interior in December 1889. Frederick J. Hall, recalling that in 1886 Stanley had promised Charles L. Webster a book, was anxious to secure a commitment from Stanley for an account of the two-year trek of the Relief Expedition. He wrote to Clemens on 13 June 1889: "[Stanley's] book is infinitely the largest thing in the wind at present. Would it not be a good idea as soon as his position is located so that a letter would reach him without fail, for you to write him a personal letter reminding him of his partial promise to write a book for us." On 19 June, Hall said he was willing to go in person to meet Stanley and added, "I am glad you wrote through Chatto a letter to Stanley and I hope Chatto will realize the importance of getting it into Stanley's hands at *the earliest possible moment.*" He suggested that Clemens also send a telegram to Stanley through Chatto. Intercepting Stanley proved impossible, but Hall did sail to England in January 1890 in an unsuccessful

"Beginnings of New England." Fisk.[40]

In 3 days at the case ⟨va⟩Van[41] averaged 865 ems solid brevier per hour for 6½ hours, & distributed 6,000 in 2 hours.

$$865$$
$$6$$
$$\overline{5190}$$
$$432$$
$$\overline{5{,}622} \text{ in } 6\tfrac{1}{2} \text{ hours}$$

Write Howells about Harrigan & Thompson ⟨& my book⟩.[42]

Book.

Long-distance Carey[43]

---

attempt to secure the American rights to Stanley's account of the expedition. *In Darkest Africa* was published in 1890 in England by Sampson Low, Marston, Searle and Rivington and in the United States by Charles Scribner's Sons.

[40] John Fiske's *The Beginnings of New England; or, The Puritan Theocracy in its Relations to Civil and Religious Liberty* was published by Houghton, Mifflin and Company in 1889.

[41] Typesetter Charles G. Van Schuyver.

[42] Edward Harrigan had written, produced, and starred in numerous immensely popular Irish plays at his Park Theatre in New York City. Denman Thompson built a career around the starring role in *The Old Homestead*, an expanded version of a play which Thompson had first presented in 1875. In the "Editor's Study" for July 1889 in *Harper's* magazine (pp. 314–319), William Dean Howells commented on the theatrical works of Harrigan and Thompson. The playwrights' works delighted their uncritical audiences, but, Howells felt, they also deserved serious consideration as harbingers of a distinctly American "national drama" (p. 315). "We like to speak of Mr. Harrigan and Mr. Thompson together," said Howells, "because we find them in their different ways working to the same effect of refinement and truth. Mr. Thompson has taken the old mask of Yankee life as Mr. Harrigan took the old mask of New York life, and through his study of nature has produced a series of pictures as true to Swanzy, New Hampshire, as Mr. Harrigan's work is true to the Bowery, to Mott Street, and the Mulberry Bend" (p. 316). Clemens probably shared Howells' high opinion of Harrigan and Thompson.

[43] Possibly William Carey of the *Century* magazine—"a very clever young man who died in his early forties—more than clever; Mark Twain called him the wittiest man he ever knew. . . . He had charge of proofs, sending them back and forth between author and printer, and seeing that the forms of The Century went to press on the proper date" (William Webster Ellsworth, *A Golden Age of Authors* [Boston and New York: Houghton Mifflin Co., 1919], p. 31). Clemens apparently agreed in May 1889 to publish extracts of his forthcoming *Connecticut Yankee* in the *Century*. Presumably Carey was to send him a tentative schedule for the work and details about the length of the extracted material.

$15 in bills & $5 in silver

Mend spectacles.

Buy "Nation"[44]

Ask for Carey's telegram.

Instruct Whitmo ⟨as⟩ to ⟨[co]⟩telegraph me when he hears
from Carey

Get Killaloe—another one

Telegram to Jean: Satan takes no care of her kittens. Have I your
permission to drown her? *Papa.*
(Jean refused.)

June 25/89. Offered William Gillette stock at ⟨[-]⟩ *one-2500*[th]
for $1000. This offer has also been made heretofore to Dean Sage,
Ned Bunce, H. C. Robinson, Mr. Parsons, Charley Langdon,
Theodore Crane & George Griffin.[45] I had the hope that they
would decline, & they did. The stock is worth either ten times that
or it is worth nothing; maybe the latter, though I think otherwise.

F. J. Griffith
D L & W.[46]

Copy summer-payments at the farm from last year's note-book.[47]

⟨Put Jimmy McAleer on.⟩[48]

A fez for Jean.

Give the thief's photos to Mr. Hall[49] [#]

---

[44] E. L. Godkin's liberal weekly review of politics, literature, and art.

[45] Clemens' friend Edward M. Bunce was the cashier at the Phoenix National Bank in
Hartford. Lawyer Henry C. Robinson was a former mayor of Hartford. Albany printer
John Davis Parsons was a friend of Dean Sage's. George Griffin was the Clemenses' butler.

[46] F. J. Griffith was assistant superintendent of the Delaware, Lackawanna and Western
Railroad in Hoboken, New Jersey.

[47] Clemens had listed the summer expenses at Quarry Farm for 1888 in Notebook 28
(p. 424).

[48] Jimmy McAleer was the son of the Clemens family's Hartford coachman Patrick
McAleer.

[49] The "thief" was Frank M. Scott, the Webster company bookkeeper who in April
1887 was sentenced to six years imprisonment for embezzling twenty-five thousand dol-

Crocheted lace that Marie made—in the bureau in our room.
Mail it home—and

Livy's Testament too

12 or 13 chapters of Grant, vol 1.[50]

All foreign for 10m. cash.
Eng for 7m cash.
 " " 3 " " & ¼ of the whole stock.
 " " 2 " "   ⁴⁄₁₀   "   "

Sell Sage or Dana, or Jones, or Taylor or Holmes, Case,[51] a
royalty of ⟨$5⟩$4.50 on every one that goes out of the factory, for
$30,000 cash—a perpetual lien⟨,⟩ on the patents, no matter into
whose hands they may fall; or $7.50 royalty for ⟨$60,000⟩$45,000
cash. We shall always turn out 1000 a year, & pretty soon[,] 2,000.

Sell to L[52] the first 15 at cost, $3,500 apiece.

or $1 per mach in the same proportion
Reduce this royalty by one-half.
This *only* for use in the U.S.

Let L offer Standard Oil ⟨$[-]5⟩ $25 per mach for $100,000. [#]

---

lars from the company. Clemens received a letter dated 4 July 1889 from a James W.
Housel, appealing to Clemens to use his influence to obtain a pardon for Scott. Housel
enclosed some photographs of Scott's family and tried to arouse Clemens' sympathy
by describing "the Wife & Children depending upon the charity of others, and whose
cry is constantly ringing in her weary Ears when is my Pa Pa coming home." Housel's
letter merely roused Clemens' scorn: he noted on the envelope that the letter was "un-
answered" and reminded himself to "preserve this sentimental rubbish." In November
1890, however, both Clemens and Charles L. Webster wrote to Governor David Hill of
New York urging that Scott be pardoned.

[50] See 509.10–11.

[51] These potential investors in the Paige typesetter are businessman Dean Sage;
Charles A. Dana, editor of the New York *Sun*; George Jones, publisher and manager
of the New York *Times*; Charles Henry Taylor, publisher of the Boston *Globe*; John
H. Holmes, editor of the Boston *Herald*. Newton Case, who already had a substantial
interest in the typesetter, was president of the Hartford printing company of Case, Lockwood & Brainard.

[52] William Mackay Laffan, since 1884 publisher of the New York *Sun*.

5:7 *p. m., July 2, 1889.* Theodore Crane believed to be dying.[53] Telegram this moment received (through telephone by Clara Clemens) dated Hartford to-day: "The machine is finished; come & see it work. J. W. P."

See D^r. Bacon[54]

Chatto's note £182.9.3. due Jan. 11/⟨8⟩90.
    ″   note for £182.9.3. due Feb. 11/90. Bissell & Co[55]

⟨53[-],432⟩538,432 ems. Yank.[56]

Mrs. Cabell's[57] old darkey with 9 ⟨kno[tt]s⟩knots in his whip, who married (No. 9) a *'fined* gal, 'an fo' God, arter I's married to her, D^r. Mason he happened to come 'long 'gin, an' he say he nuvver said nuff'n 'bout *'fined*, he say she de *sicklies'* gal in Albermarle Co. [#]

---

[53] Theodore Crane, husband of Livy's foster sister Susan, had suffered a stroke in September 1888. His condition worsened over the succeeding months: he "was a half wreck, physically, & suffered a good deal of pain of a bodily sort, together with a mental depression & hopelessness that made him yearn for death every day" (SLC to Mrs. Fairbanks, 13 September 1889, *MTMF*, p. 264). Crane was a partner in the Langdon family coal firm, J. Langdon & Company, where his position was that of "head clerk and superintendent of the subordinate clerks" (*MTA*, 2:136). Clemens later described him as "good and upright and indestructibly honest and honorable, but he had neither desire nor ambition to be anything above chief clerk. He was much too timid for larger work or larger responsibilities" (*MTA*, 2:136). Crane's death on 3 July 1889 evidently forestalled Clemens' departure for Hartford to view the perfected Paige typesetter. It was a week or more before Clemens arrived there, alone, to remain almost two weeks.

[54] Probably William T. Bacon, a Hartford physician. Livy had been under the care of Dr. Bacon in April 1889.

[55] These sums represent royalties from Clemens' English publisher, Chatto & Windus. The royalties were in the form of delayed payments deposited with George P. Bissell & Company of Hartford, Clemens' bankers.

[56] On 16 April 1889 Fred Hall had reported that two typewritten copies of the manuscript of *A Connecticut Yankee* were finished and on 17 July he sent Clemens an estimate of "Ems, Pages &c. of your new book."

[57] Clemens wrote to his daughter Clara from Hartford on 15 July 1889: "I dined with the Charley-Warnerses this evening, & they had just received a letter from Mrs. Cabell" (TS in MTP). Isa Carrington Cabell of Virginia was a friend of the Warners' and had been their houseguest in the winter of 1888. In 1893 her *Seen from the Saddle*, a whimsical ramble through Hartford and its environs, was published by Harper & Brothers.

July, 1889.[58]

July 20.

	V. 1.⟨[h]⟩32.	2678.	F. 2.55,	2851.
22ᵈ:	V. 2.10,	2144.	F. 4.25,	3166.
23ᵈ:	V. 3..	2289.	F. 4.10:	3298.
24ᵗʰ:	V. 2.37;	2415.	F. 3.20:	3539.
25ᵗʰ:	V. 1:40;	2543.	F. 4.05;	3862.

⟨Write Col. Taylor⟩[59]

| 26ᵗʰ. | V. 2.20; | 2777. | F. 1. | 4,374. |

— — — —

| 29ᵗʰ. | V. sick. . . . . .F. 4.35.—3741. |
| 30. . . . . 3.45. 3334. Sent to O.[60] |
| 31. . . . . .F. 4.10 3946. |

F   *August, '89.*

Fred:

1. a.m. 2.25—4168; p.m. 2.50—4050.

    average, 4109.

---

[58] Clemens received frequent reports on the progress of his two typesetter apprentices in mastering the keyboard of the Paige machine. The following list records the average number of ems set over several hours on successive days. "F." in this list is Fred Whitmore, young son of Clemens' Hartford business agent Franklin G. Whitmore, who had begun his apprenticeship on the Paige machine early in 1888 (see p. 382). "V." is the older typesetter Charles G. Van Schuyver, usually referred to as "Van" in correspondence about the machine. The goal of the compositors was an average hourly rate of five to six thousand ems, a speed which would assure the Paige machine supremacy in its field.

[59] Charles Henry Taylor, publisher of the Boston *Globe,* had written to Clemens on 18 April 1889 mentioning the recent interest in the Mergenthaler Linotype in Boston newspaper circles and requesting news of the completion of the Paige machine. Taylor continued to correspond with Clemens throughout the spring of 1889, often enclosing information about the operating expenses and problems of the Mergenthaler machine. Clemens probably intended to assure Taylor of the Paige machine's imminent perfection by sending him some of the recent statistics of the compositors' performances.

[60] Clemens sent some of these statistics on the performance of compositor Fred Whitmore to his brother Orion Clemens in a letter of 2 August 1889. The letter explains the disappearance of Charles G. Van Schuyver from Clemens' record after 29 July 1889: "Our veteran—63 years old—made such poor progress that he got discouraged & sick, & we have given him a vacation." Clemens added: "All of this letter is strictly private. Not 5 person in the country know that the machine is done, & no more will know it for a month

2 a.m. 1.35. 4382. p.m., 3.35.—4187
average for the day, 4249. (Shut down 10 days.)[61]

Sept. 19. 2.50—3600.
" 20 3.30—4112   F.
Send Yankee to—
Geo. W. Cable;
George Standring.
Pond   Ozias Pond[62]
Riley
Nye
Howells
Stedman
Twichell
Whitmo
Paige & the rest
⟨Charley Clark⟩
⟨Lilly Warner⟩[63]
Burdette
Grace King
Sue[64]

---

yet, if we can help it." Clemens calculated that in the next month young Whitmore might be able to bring his speed up to five thousand or more ems per hour.

[61] Franklin G. Whitmore wrote to Clemens on 16 August 1889 expressing surprise that Clemens had not been informed of the recent breakdown of the Paige machine. "They shut down two weeks ago today, & the machine is a good deal to pieces, with quite a number of things to fix & to apply. You will have to take M^r. Paige's word . . . that the machine will be finished Sept 1st." Despite Paige's assurances, the machine was not in working order again until the third week in September.

[62] Ozias W. Pond, the brother of lyceum entrepreneur Major James B. Pond, had been associated with Major Pond in his lecture agency and had accompanied Clemens and George Washington Cable on part of the 1884/1885 lecture tour. He was now operating his own lyceum agency for "Musical and Literary Celebrities."

This entire list of names through "John T. Lewis" (504.16), as well as the references to *A Connecticut Yankee* that interrupt it, are crowded onto a single notebook page. Apparently Clemens added to the lists of names and page references over a period of time.

[63] Clemens' Nook Farm neighbor Elizabeth Gillette Warner, wife of George H. Warner, and sister of actor and dramatist William Gillette.

[64] Susan Crane. William A. Goodrich, whose name appears next in this list, was an employee of the Cranes at Quarry Farm. The following entry ("Mother") probably refers to Livy's mother, Mrs. Jervis Langdon.

Wm Goodrich
Mother
Mrs. Laffan[65]
Mrs. Aldrich
   Atlantic
   Cosmopolitan
   Harper
   Century
   Scribner
Buck Stanchfield[66]
Charley Clark.
    ″   Warner.
Mrs. Cabell
Burdette.
Fred. Grant.
John T. Lewis.[67]
T. B. Aldrich.
Twichell

⟨⟨17[-]⟩174 Chas. Ball.[68]
     175   ″   ″
     176   ″   ″

---

[65] Publisher William Mackay Laffan's wife was the former Georgianna Ratcliffe. Further along in this list (504.8) Clemens also noted the name of Mrs. Laffan's mother, Mrs. Mary F. Ratcliffe. Mrs. Ratcliffe evidently visited the Clemens family at Hartford in the spring of 1889.

[66] Probably lawyer John Barry Stanchfield, who in 1886 married Livy's close friend Clara Spaulding.

[67] Clemens sent Lewis, a former slave and presently tenant farmer at Quarry Farm, a copy of *A Connecticut Yankee* for Christmas. Lewis thanked Clemens in a letter of 2 January 1890: "For a gentleman whos buisness cols him to move in the heigher circuls of life to paus and think of makeing one in my humble caulling happy on Christmas, is surley some thing to be proud of."

[68] The page numbers in this list probably refer to the no longer extant typescript of the manuscript of *A Connecticut Yankee* (see p. 498, note 56). Clemens later made a more complete and orderly list of references and sources (see pp. 505–506). Charles Ball's *Slavery in the United States; A Narrative of the Life and Adventures of Charles Ball, . . . a Slave* was first published in 1836; later editions bore the title *Fifty Years in Chains; or, the Life of an American Slave*. Ball's book furnished Clemens with some graphic details of slave life for chapters 21 and 34 of *A Connecticut Yankee*.

St. Stylites, 191.⟩[69]
204 2ᵈ—beginning of Century article.[70]
⟨226 Insert royal grant.⟩[71]
257. Ophelia's burial.
257. Recite the curse of Rome—⟨cyclopedia⟩Cyclopedia.[72]

Sheridan Children
Mrs. Custer
Gerhardt
Fred Grant
Whitford[73]

---

[69] Clemens' description of the "strange menagerie" of hermits, particularly Saint Simeon Stylites, in the Valley of Holiness (A Connecticut Yankee, chapter 22) derives from William Edward Hartpole Lecky's History of European Morals from Augustus to Charlemagne (2 vols. [New York: D. Appleton and Co., 1870], 2:115–119).

[70] Robert Underwood Johnson of the Century magazine wrote to Clemens on 26 July 1889 reminding him of his promise to allow the Century to publish excerpts from his forthcoming book. In order to insure publication in the November issue, the excerpts from A Connecticut Yankee had to be forwarded to the Century early in August. Clemens made selections from chapters 7, 10, and 39 of the book, included some introductory material, and provided explanatory passages between the selections. This notebook entry indicates that he originally planned to begin the excerpts for the Century with the account of the monks' first bath in the waters of the holy fountain (A Connecticut Yankee, chapter 24). Clemens finally decided, however, to avoid any mention of the book's attitudes toward the Church and religion, and the passages in the Century were carefully pruned of such references. Similar care was taken with the prospectus for the book and with advance reviews.

[71] Clemens' discussion of royal grants, the exorbitant incomes awarded in perpetuity to members of the royal family, occurs in chapter 25 of A Connecticut Yankee. In the original manuscript of the book, chapter 25 concludes with the words "The king was charmed with the idea"; the discussion of royal grants in the last three paragraphs of the chapter was apparently added on the lost typescript.

[72] Clemens is referring to the Anathema, the Church's solemn formula for major excommunication. Clemens was understandably tempted to quote this most elaborate and thorough curse (a particularly vivid version is recorded in book 3 of Sterne's Tristram Shandy). In chapter 29 of A Connecticut Yankee Hank Morgan and the king encounter a family dying of smallpox who have incurred the Church's curse. They are denied the sacraments and the society of other Christians in life; in death they are denied burial in consecrated ground. Clemens' previous notebook entry regarding "Ophelia's burial" suggests that the incident in A Connecticut Yankee was influenced by the funeral scene in Hamlet (act v, scene 1). There Ophelia, because of her noble birth, is allowed Christian burial even though suicide is an excommunicable offense.

[73] Clemens' lawyer Daniel Whitford of the New York City firm of Alexander & Green.

Mrs. Cleveland.[74]
Gilder.
Walt Whitman
Sylvester Baxter Bos. Herald[75]

292 297 Ancient prices—Atlantic Vol. 24[76]
⟨309.⟩ 310 Proofs that ye are freemen. Richard II[s] time, &
Chas Ball.[77]
315. The woman burnt. Hist 18th C.[78]

---

[74] Clemens had first met President Cleveland's young wife, the former Frances Folsom, on 19 March 1888 at the Authors' Reception at the White House. From 1889 to 1892, between his two presidential terms, Cleveland resided mainly in New York City and was associated with a major law firm there.

[75] Clemens met Sylvester Baxter in June 1880 when the young journalist came to Hartford, bearing a letter of introduction from Howells, to interview him for the Boston *Herald*. His initial impression of Baxter was unfavorable. "A kind-hearted, well-meaning corpse was this Boston young man," he wrote to Howells on 9 June 1880, "but lawsy bless me, horribly dull company" (*MTHL*, p. 311). Nevertheless, Clemens' acquaintance with Baxter survived, and in 1889 there was an exchange of friendly letters relating to the publication of *A Connecticut Yankee* and certain mutual political enthusiasms, chiefly their shared admiration for Edward Bellamy's utopian romance *Looking Backward*. Baxter was able to arrange a meeting between the two authors in January 1890, but he was unsuccessful in his attempts to draw Clemens into the Nationalist movement inspired by *Looking Backward*.

[76] Clemens culled statistics for his chapter on "Sixth Century Political Economy" (*A Connecticut Yankee*, chapter 33) from Edward Jarvis' article "The Increase of Human Life" which appeared in the *Atlantic* from October through December 1869. Clemens' debt to Jarvis' article is examined in James D. Williams' "The Use of History in Mark Twain's *A Connecticut Yankee*" (*PMLA*, March 1965, pp. 108–109). A few pages later in this notebook, Clemens again included Jarvis' article in a list of sources for *A Connecticut Yankee* (p. 506).

[77] In chapter 34 of *A Connecticut Yankee* Hank Morgan and King Arthur are captured and required to prove that they are freemen in order to escape being sold as slaves. Charles Ball describes a similar situation in his autobiography, where, like Clemens' characters, he argues "that it would appear more consonant to reason that my master should prove me to be a slave" (*Fifty Years in Chains; or, The Life of an American Slave* [New York: H. Dayton, 1860], p. 395). Clemens found another illustration of the precariousness of the freeman's personal rights in John Richard Green's *History of the English People*: during the last quarter of the fourteenth century, a period of political and social unrest, the "landlords were . . . forcing men who looked on themselves as free to prove they were no villeins by law" (4 vols. [Chicago: Belford, Clarke & Co., 1883], 1:446).

[78] This and the following entry refer to two episodes in chapter 35 of *A Connecticut Yankee*: the burning of a woman for witchcraft by irate villagers and the hanging of a young woman for theft. Clemens based the episodes on accounts in W. E. H. Lecky's

319. Lecky, Hist. 18th ⟨320⟩321.
324. Boiling in oil.[79]
331. The Roman law.[80]

For Century, ch. 39—revolver.

361. Interdict. Cyclopedia & Dean Stanley, Memorials of Westminster Abbey.[81]

⟨Char⟩
Mrs. Ratcliffe
Dana.
Grace King   Library
Buck Stanchfield
Bob Ingersoll.
Elsie Leslie
Clara Stanchfield Xmas
Mrs. Cleveland.
John T. Lewis.

For Century.
Type-writer as follows:
Begin page 9, with the heading, "The Stranger's History, & copy the rest of that page & the 10th & 11th pages. (2 pages.)
The skip to page 50, & copy the whole of Chapter 7. (7 pages
Skip to page 71 & begin with "I was pretty well satisfied &c" & copy all that follows thence to middle of page 75, ending with the words "either by matter or flavor." (about 3 pages.)

History of England in the Eighteenth Century (8 vols. [New York: D. Appleton and Co., 1878–1890], 2:88–90, 3:582–583, and 6:251).

[79] In chapter 36 of *A Connecticut Yankee* Hank Morgan witnesses a man being boiled in oil for counterfeiting pennies. Clemens found historical precedent for this extreme punishment in J. Hammond Trumbull's *The True-Blue Laws of Connecticut and New Haven and the False Blue-Laws* (Hartford: American Publishing Co., 1876, p. 13).

[80] "An atrocious law . . . provided that if a master were murdered, all the slaves in his house, who were not in chains or absolutely helpless through illness, should be put to death" (Lecky, *History of European Morals*, 1:320). Clemens mentions the Roman law in chapter 37 of *A Connecticut Yankee*.

[81] Clemens evidently based his account of the interdict imposed on King Arthur's kingdom (chapter 41) on accounts of the interdict of 1208 which resulted from King John's defiance of Pope Innocent III. In Notebook 24 (167.5) Clemens gives his source as the *Encyclopaedia Britannica*.

Then go to page 337 & copy the whole of Chapter 39. (11 pages).—23 in all.

$$\frac{300}{6900}$$

7,000 words in all.

⟨7⟩ say 8 Century pages.

Then go to page 238 & copy the whole of Chapter 27. (nearly 14 pages)[82]

Total 37 pages.

$$\overline{\quad\; 300\quad\;}$$

⟨1[-,-]oo⟩11,100—⟨11,[2]oo⟩11,100—14 Century pages.

Make ⟨appendix⟩Appendix without a reference to it except in preface.[83]

Chap. Page.

18	144	Lettres de cachet; Carlyle, Taine, duBarry.[84]
18 —	147.	Castle d'If. Du Barry Memoirs.
20 —	160.	From an English paper of '85.

---

[82] Clemens drew a line from this entry to a caret placed before "Then go to page 337 . . ." (505.1) to indicate that chapter 27 should be typed before chapter 39. Clemens ultimately changed his mind: the excerpts which appeared in the *Century* followed the scheme outlined here, except for chapter 27 ("The Yankee and the King Travel Incognito") which was not included.

[83] In the appendix Clemens planned to cite various histories and memoirs "in support of the assertion that there were no real gentlemen & ladies before our century" (from notes included with the manuscript of *A Connecticut Yankee*, Berg). Presumably the appendix would have served two purposes: like the section of "Notes" appended to *The Prince and the Pauper*, it would allow Clemens to present the historical sources for his book; in addition, it would allow him to state more explicitly his own views on monarchical and hierarchical systems. Nonetheless, the projected appendix was abandoned and *A Connecticut Yankee* appeared with only a brief preface. In it Clemens assured his readers that "the ungentle laws and customs touched upon in this tale are historical" and added that certain other discussions proved too "difficult to work into the scheme." Clemens later admitted to Howells that "if it were only to write over again there wouldn't be so many things left out" (22 September 1889, *MTHL*, p. 613).

A clipping from an English newspaper was pinned to the top of the page that begins with this entry. The clipping shows three classified advertisements of advowsons for sale. Someone signing himself "H J [or "I"] Smith" has written "Funny aint they" in ink at the top of the clipping.

[84] Carlyle's *French Revolution*, Hippolyte Taine's *Ancient Régime*, and Madame Du Barry's *Memoirs* provided Clemens with details for his description of conditions in Morgan le Fay's dungeons in chapter 18 of *A Connecticut Yankee*.

Say 6 men set (1200⟨o⟩ per hour) 43,200 in 6 hours, & distribute it in 2 hours. Fred must set ⟨[-]⟩5,400 an hour for 8 hours to tie them.[89]

By the 20th of August he will reach that figure. Let the contest be appointed for the 12th or 15th of Sept. [#]

---

[85] The history of the funding of London's Mansion House in chapter 25 of *A Connecticut Yankee* is based on Lecky's account in *A History of England in the Eighteenth Century* (3:538). Clemens entered Lecky's information in some detail in Notebook 28 (pp. 416–417).

[86] Both Taine and Carlyle point out that before the French Revolution it was necessary to prove four generations of nobility to be eligible for rank as lieutenant or captain in the army (Taine, *Ancient Régime* [book 1, chapter 4]; Carlyle, *French Revolution* [part 2 ("The Constitution"), book 2, chapter 2]).

[87] Clemens' source was probably the *American Cyclopaedia*, published in sixteen volumes with a supplement in each volume between 1873 and 1883 by D. Appleton and Company.

[88] Clemens' source for the account of the ceremony of the "King's evil" in chapter 26 of *A Connecticut Yankee* was probably Lecky's *History of European Morals* (1:386–388).

[89] By the end of July 1889 Clemens was confident that a public test of the Paige typesetter could be arranged for September. The following several entries outline his plans to test the machine against the compositors of the Hartford *Courant*. At this time type for the Hartford *Courant* was still set and distributed by hand. In the beginning of August Clemens would learn that the machine had broken down and plans for the public trial had to be canceled (see p. 500, note 61).

The Courant time to be taken & kept & matter measured by Rogers, Whitmore, Van, Kinney & Col. Taylor—2 hours each.[90]

Ours by Holmes, A. E. Burr, Laffan, & people from the World, Herald, Times, Post (& Tribune?), Harpers, Trow's, & Associated Press & reporters; & old Houghton. The Gov. & Lt. Gov. to help watch both gangs. Also Howells & Stedman.

These to go back & forth from one place to the other, issue bulletins of the state of the game every hour—naming our distribution as well as our setting.

Courant to ⟨n[---]⟩name their men, & make no changes in them before the day nor *on* the day without our consent.

We to pay the Courant men 50ᶜ for setting & 20ᶜ for distribution if they lose; & divide $100 among them if they win. If our man wins (this is private) he is to have $100; & an addition of $50 per 1000 for all he sets above 43,200 ems.

⟨The contest to be⟩
At the noon hour of rest, somebody to take 3 proofs of all the matter set by both gangs, so that when the Courant boys are done setting, they can begin to distribute their morning's work without any delay. When their afternoon setting is finished, 3 proofs of *that* to be taken by somebody at ⟨the⟩ once & the matter released so that they can distribute it⟨[.]⟩, without delay.

Every proof to be marked with the man's name who set it & the contents of it.

Our dead matter to be measured when it is put into the machine, & strict record kept of the amount distributed by the machine in the 8 hours.

⟨T⟩*All* the proofs to be read by Laffan & audited & passed by experts to be appointed by both gangs. But the proofs need not

---

[90] Clemens proposed to have two teams of judges, listed here and in the following entry. Among those listed are John C. Kinney, city editor of the Hartford *Courant;* Charles Henry Taylor, publisher of the Boston *Globe;* John H. Holmes, editor of the Boston *Herald;* Alfred E. Burr, editor and publisher of the Hartford *Times;* Henry Oscar Houghton of Houghton, Mifflin & Company. The governor and lieutenant governor of Connecticut were Morgan G. Bulkeley and Samuel E. Merwin. Trow's Printing and Bookbinding Company was the publisher of the New York City directory.

be corrected. Or, if corrected, it shall be done by appointees of the two gangs, & the time occupied strictly kept & recorded *on* the proofs.

Nobody to be allowed *in* the rooms where the men are, except ⟨such as shall be⟩ Laffan at the Courant & such one or two as ⟨[h]e⟩ may be needed for proof-taking supplying sorts, &c; & none allowed in ours but A. S. Hubbard[91] & one or two to tend the machine & strike proofs & sort-up.

Presidents of the several Typothetae & the government printer to be invited.[92]
Also Stilson Hutchings & the backer of the MacMillan.[93]
Also, Dean Sage & Parsons.[94]
Also, London Master printers.
Also[n] John Brusnahan.[95]
Also, Mr. Trow.[96]
    "   " Pulitzer.

---

[91] Clemens is probably referring to Stephen A. Hubbard, managing editor and part owner of the Hartford *Courant.*

[92] The various Typothetae societies in major American cities were associations of master printers and employer-printers. Frank W. Palmer succeeded Thomas E. Benedict as public printer, head of the Government Printing Office, in May 1889.

[93] Stilson Hutchins was editor and publisher of the Washington *Post* until 1889 and was one of the founders and principal backers of the Mergenthaler Linotype Company. John Loudon McMillan's popular typesetter, first used in 1884, was manufactured in Ilion, New York, by the McMillan Typesetting Machine Company.

[94] John Davis Parsons was one of the partners in Weed & Parsons, a large and successful printing company in Albany, New York. Clemens' friend Dean Sage, also of Albany, mentioned Parsons in a letter to Clemens as "an old printer who put $30,000 in the Page machine years ago, & lost it" (Sage to SLC, 1 February 1889). Subsequently Sage arranged to bring Parsons to Hartford to see the machine and was able to report that they were both "charmed" with it (Sage to SLC, 8 November 1889), although they also admitted certain serious reservations about the financing of the typesetter enterprise.

[95] John Brusnahan, foreman in the New York *Herald's* composing room, had been corresponding with Clemens since 1887, frequently expressing his enthusiasm for the Paige typesetter. He inspected the Mergenthaler Linotypes being used in the New York *Tribune* composing room and reported on them to Clemens. He eventually invested in the Paige typesetter.

[96] Clemens was unaware that printer and publisher John Fowler Trow of Trow's Printing and Bookbinding Company had died in August 1886. (See also p. 187, note 25.)

President of No. 6?[97]

Publishers of Hartford Post[98] & other Hartford papers.

Also, Laffan's locomotive works man.

No, invite none of them; they could see nothing, & would be in the way & get mad.

All parties to begin at 8 (watches to be set in unison & assisted by telephone) stop at 12. Begin again at 1 & stop at 5.

Both gangs to set up the same copy, & set it solid. Plain matter, without italics, small caps, dialect, figure-work, or other troublesome composition; for instance, the first 12 or 13 chapters of Grant's Memoirs.

Copy to be in the hands of the contestants at 7.45 a. m.

⟨The men to be⟩ *Luncheon.*

Blank check for $100 to be placed in the Courant office when contest begins.

Each to distrib his own matter, & when that is exhausted, take dead matter that has been in the paper.

$30,000. cash.

I will make him this offer & not depart from it: $5 per Comp for all sold or rented under U. S. patent; 1,000 a year to the death of the patent, ⟨[if]⟩ 15 years 15,000—$75,000. Or this: royalties aggregating $60,000. These to be collected from the first 2,000 sold or rented under the U. S. patents.

July 31, '89. By the late compromise, weekly wages in N. Y. ⟨⟩⟩(morning papers) are $27 per week. In the Tribune's celebrated Linotypetable, they pay their men a much lower average⟨.⟩, & hence make Linotype *itself* seem an economy.

There are 100 men in the Times office.—Eve Post, July 29. [#]

---

[97] William E. Boselly was the president of New York Typographical Union No. 6 from January 1889 until April 1890.

[98] The Hartford *Evening Post* was published by the Evening Post Association headed by H. T. Sperry.

Mergens at 25 cents a pair cannot compete with Paige
Compositors at $12,000 apiece.

Lampman's   Poems[99]
C.H. Webb's   ″

P. bringen das Erste Woche Octobers bei uns zu.[100]

Schicke Gelt an Ehrwürdige Herrn T— um die Unterrict seiner
Tochter zu bezahlen[101]

At 4,000, 32,000 in 8 hours.
Hand: 5 men 5000, 30,000 in 6 hours.
   Fight Aug. 30.
Add a sixth man & fight Sept. 30.
Add a seventh & fight Oct 30 in N. Y.

Get 2 months' leave of absence for Will Whitmore?[102] [#]

---

[99] Canadian nature poet Archibald Lampman's first collection of poetry, *Among the Millet*, was issued in 1888 (Ottawa: J. Durie & Son). William Dean Howells reviewed the volume in the "Editor's Study" of *Harper's* magazine for April 1889, characterizing it as "mainly descriptive; but descriptive after a new fashion, most delicately pictorial and subtly thoughtful, with a high courage for the unhackneyed features and aspects of the great life around us" (p. 822). In the same article Howells reviewed Charles Henry Webb's *Vagrom Verse* (Boston: Ticknor and Co., 1889) in which he found "a dry wit and a dry wisdom" (p. 821). Clemens and Webb had been fellow journalists in San Francisco in the 1860s and Webb had published Clemens' first book, *The Celebrated Jumping Frog of Calaveras County, and Other Sketches.*

[100] *P. is to spend the first week of October with us.* Clemens extended the invitation to his sister Pamela Moffett in a letter of 1 July 1889.

[101] *Send money to the Reverend Mr. T— for payment of his daughter's tuition.* Clemens may have been contributing to the educational expenses of one of Joseph Hopkins Twichell's three eldest daughters—Julia, Susan, or Harmony.

[102] In August 1886 Clemens had offered Franklin G. Whitmore's son William a position as an apprentice typesetter on the Paige machine. Young Whitmore apparently did not keep the position very long as there are no further references to him as a compositor. Clemens' notebook entry suggests that Whitmore was now employed elsewhere and that Clemens was considering impressing him into service again as a typesetter. Clemens may have hoped that Whitmore could refresh his knowledge of the Paige keyboard sufficiently to compete in the projected typesetting contest. Clemens' best typesetter at the moment was Fred Whitmore, Will's brother.

Erzahlungen aus der Deutchen Geschichte—Schrakamp⟨f⟩.[103]

Finlay & daughter invited for Oct 10 (Thursday) for 2 days.[104]

2
"Mais, *oui*, mos*su* w'd *cry*,[105]
==
Says Mos*su* wid much alairm.

3
Oh *by*es there was the fun—
==
Thin he swore an awful oath
    For he found it wouldn't do—

4
If disguise ye'd loike to try,
==
The Frinch language may be foine—

5
Now I'm glad to find 'tis true,
==
We're all *I*rish tinants there.

Elmira, *Aug. 18/89.* We have been here 2 months; in which time Brer W has written me some 3 meagre notes about the machine. I wrote once & asked him to tell me anything there was to tell from time to time. No answer. Wrote him & asked him to keep Fred in practice while the machine is stopped. No answer. The mach. stopped Aug 2 ⟨& has⟩—not a line from him to say why, or how

---

[103] Josepha Schrakamp's compilation of tales from German history, a children's book, was published in 1888 (New York: H. Holt and Co.).

[104] Francis D. Finlay, former owner of the Belfast *Northern Whig*, had become acquainted with the Clemenses during their 1873 trip to Great Britain. He wrote to Clemens on 29 July 1889 informing him that he and his daughter Mary would be arriving in the United States in August for an extended tour and would be glad of a chance to visit Clemens. Clemens received the letter after some delay and replied on 17 August, proposing that the Finlays visit Hartford on 10 and 11 October. (Additional information about Finlay is in the *Twainian*, October 1944, pp. 1–6.)

[105] These are evidently some additional lines from the song "Killaloe" which was recorded at greater length on page 492.

much is to be done on it. Suppose it were a sick child of mine? Would he give me any news about it? I suppose it is merely my own disposition—to depend upon Davis or somebody else to do the thing & save you the trouble. How many times I have hopefully opened those envelops in the last 3 years & found not a scratch in them but checks to be signed for the damned household Expenses![106]

S. E. Dawson take it to England.[107]

Order shirts.

Tell them to issue a few $6 copies of the book on very fine paper.

Send pictures between boards.[108]

Telegraph W & Co & Paige & Whitmore.

Call & see Laffan. & propose to offer $50 in London for 25,000, corrected matter on one machine in 8 hours.

Send the next proofs to (?)[109] [#]

---

[106] See page 500, note 61. This exasperated entry is a reaction to Whitmore's letter of 16 August 1889 which informed Clemens of the machine's breakdown. Charles E. Davis was a draftsman and mechanical engineer who was assigned to work on perfecting the Paige machine.

[107] Samuel E. Dawson of Dawson Brothers, Montreal booksellers and publishers, had been instrumental in securing Canadian copyrights on Clemens' books since 1881. Charles L. Webster & Company assumed that Dawson would be handling Canadian publication of A Connecticut Yankee, but Dawson's letter of 9 August 1889 revealed that he had retired from the book business. He recommended the Rose Publishing Company of Toronto. Fred Hall made a brief trip to Canada in the last week of August to draw the contract for the book with George M. and Daniel A. Rose. Dawson advised Hall about the language of the contract and about copyright details. Clemens' notebook entry suggests that he may have considered asking Dawson to carry the proofs of A Connecticut Yankee to Chatto & Windus in London.

[108] Clemens began receiving proofs of Daniel Beard's illustrations for A Connecticut Yankee in mid-August 1889.

[109] On 21 August 1889 Charles L. Webster & Company reported: "We mail you today the first batch of page proofs. Our proof reader is now revising these with the galley proofs and we will send you a revised set as soon as ready." Clemens received these first proofs at Quarry Farm on 24 August. In addition, the cover design and proofs for Daniel Beard's illustrations were being forwarded to the farm. Since the Clemenses were planning to return to Hartford by way of New York City in September, Clemens was concerned that

⟨2⟩ 3 Erl-Königs[110]

Er hat zwelf cents postage auf ein Packet envelops bezahlt![111]

Aber er hat die Gerhardt muddle vernünftig gehandelt. (Later: *Nothing of the kind.*

Er ist nich begnügt *"it"* ⟨[to]⟩zu sagen, sondern telegraphirt *"die Machine"* wird nict, ⟨s⟩Sept. 1ᵉ vollgebracht werden.

Er hat mir nie Zeit genug gegeben um Gelt zu versorgen, sondern am letzten Augenblick hat er mir erkundigt dass das Geltbeutel ungefahr Leer sei.

Killaloo.
Larboard Watch.
Lorelei.
Lang Syne.
Swing Low.
Gospel Train.
Grave of Napoleon.
Old Folks at Home.
My Ain Countree
Golden Slippers
Die Wacht am Rhein
Der Feldmarschall.
Treu und herzinniglich
Blau ist das Blümelein
Lily of the Valley
Go Down Moses
Go chain de lion
Roll Jordan [#]

---

subsequent batches of proofs would not reach him quickly unless he gave careful mailing instructions.

[110] Clemens is probably referring to Goethe's famous poem about the elf king.

[111] This and the following three entries concern the business conduct of Clemens' Hartford agent Franklin G. Whitmore. The German reads: *He paid twelve cents postage on a Packet of envelopes! But he handled the Gerhardt muddle cleverly. He is not content to say "it" but telegraphed "the machine" won't be completed by Sept. 1. He has never given me enough time to procure money, but has instead told me at the last moment that the till is almost empty.*

Er wollte/wurde die autographie-Briefen in einem Buche Kleben.[112]

Auch mir wöchentlich die Zustand meiner Bank-Rechnung schicken. Es gibt jetz 10 Wochen dass diese Nachricht gefehlt ist.

Er hat aus Frau Richardson eine Enragē gemacht.

(Copy.)[113]

Elmira, Aug. 31/89.

Dear Hamersley—

You didn't holler early enough to save me. A warning voice would have been a lucky thing for us all. The ten-day stoppage, Aug. 2^d, disturbed my plans, but not seriously, because I was prepared for a brief stoppage & was expecting it. I was blown to the moon, tho', when the sudden news came that we should not get done the 1st of Sept. I was to get the money from my brother-in-law this time, but as it was conditioned on an actual & final finish within this month, so that he could know the fact before sailing for Europe, that trade is now off. I had one more consultation with him this morning after I got Whitmore's letter & yours, but I accomplished nothing. He says he has talked with me every summer for three years & that I have always been mistaken about when the machine was going to be finished; & that when I

---

[112] In this entry and the following two entries Clemens continues his list of grievances against Franklin G. Whitmore: *He wanted to glue the autograph letter in a book. Also to send me weekly the standing of my bank account. This information has been neglected for 10 weeks now. He has enraged Mrs. Richardson.*

[113] Clemens copied this letter into his notebook in brownish black ink on four successive right-hand pages. He wrote *"over"* at the bottom of the last page of the letter; the related telegram (p. 516) appears on the verso of that leaf. Both letter and telegram are addressed to Hartford lawyer William Hamersley, one of the original investors in the Paige typesetter. Hamersley was involved with Clemens in efforts to capitalize the manufacture of the Paige machine and also drew up the various contracts between Paige and Clemens. In late 1890 Clemens reviewed his involvement with the Paige typesetter in a manuscript entitled "The Machine Episode," which reveals that he was less than satisfied with Hamersley: "I have no feeling about him; I have no harsh words to say about him. He is a great, fat, good-natured, kind-hearted, chicken-livered slave; with no more pride than a tramp, no more sand than a rabbit, no more moral sense than a wax figure, and no more sex than a tapeworm" (*MTA*, 1:75).

visited Hartford last month I came back here & said it *was*
finished, & once more I was mistaken; that I promised another
finish for Aug. 12, & another for Sept. 1 & failed twice more; that
on a *finished* machine he would take the chances & help me if he
were going to be here, but as he is leaving for a year's stay in
Europe he can't afford the risk. I offered to get a big royalty
saddled on the machine's American business, the same to remain
until the money & interest should be repaid. That seemed to strike
him, & I came away & left it to work. If he fails me I do not
know of any way to raise the money we shall need Sept. 20 when
we square with P & W. I shall keep away from him until I hear
from you. He will leave here Tuesday noon. If you & Paige
approve of a royalty as security, put your⟨s⟩ heads together & name
as big a one as you can. Then you or Paige telegraph me thus:

"It will be *considered* (insert date.) He shall have (insert the
sum) on each American for each & every error exposed."

That cipher is to mean to me—

"The machine will be *finished* (such-&-such a date—insert it in
the telegram. He shall have for each $1000 lent, (such-&-such a
sum—name it in the telegram) on each & every machine rented or
sold under the American patents until the loan & interest are
repaid.

(Signed) Ham or Paige.

_____

You see I suggest a distinct royalty for each thousand dollars
lent, & fasten said royalty on each American-marketed machine. I
could name a lump sum, & have a royalty on that, but I might
name too small a one to meet the occasion, & on the other hand
I don't want to borrow a dollar more than is necessary.

Name a sum that he can't possibly find fault with, for time is
short & the corner I am in is distressedly tight.[114] Last night is the
&c &c.

— — — till I arrive Sept. 14 or 15.

Sin'y S L C [#]

_____

[114] Clemens was hard pressed to raise money for a payment of six thousand dollars due
to Pratt & Whitney on 20 September 1889. As indicated in this letter, he offered his

(Telegram.)

Elmira, Sept 1/89.

Wᵐ M Hamersley—
    Hartford, Conn—
He drove up this morning to talk. Was surprised at my
proposition when I re-stated it. He wouldn't touch it. Said he
supposed I was proposing to sell a perpetual lean, parting with it
out & out, a stipulated sum for each thousand dollars cash. Of
course that is what I did mean, but in trying to write it out I got
it turned into a loan. In telegraphing me now, leave off the last
seven words of the form mailed to you, & I will understand. ⟨it.⟩
⟨to be⟩

S L Clemens

Paid.

B. L. Westervelt,[115]
    D L & W, Hoboken.

Hire Herr Schlutter[116] to come before breakfast for ½ hour; noon
for ½ hour, daily. & Sundays. He to *confine* himself strictly to
asking questions, & I to confine myself to answering them. *No
disquisitions.* Take one part of speech & stick to it & to nothing
else until it will *use itself.* Then pass to the next; & so with the
whole ten.

12 Hartford checks.
Drawing-room seats—7 ⎱ [#]

---

brother-in-law Charles J. Langdon a substantial royalty on the Paige machine in return
for the needed funds, but Langdon refused the proposition. Langdon and his family left
Elmira on 3 September for a year-long tour of Europe. Fortunately, at about this time
Clemens received $15,000 from J. Langdon & Company, in partial repayment of a sum
loaned to the company by Livy. He wrote to Franklin G. Whitmore on 13 September
1889: "I have sent $15,000 to the U.S. Bank to-day. Make no mention of it to anybody.
You will use from it to square up with P & W the 20th if Paige wishes it done. . . . When
I come I will transfer a considerable part of the $15,000 to Bissell's bank for to live on." In
October 1889 Langdon decided to make a small investment in the typesetter and he sent
Clemens three thousand dollars in exchange for a three-dollar royalty.

[115] Probably an official of the Delaware, Lackawanna & Western Railroad whom
Clemens contacted to arrange his family's railway accommodations from Quarry Farm
to New York City in September 1889.

[116] Otto B. Schlutter was Clemens' German instructor in Hartford.

⟨Sept. 1. Fragt mir an, soll er P's Sold am 10ten, [wie-g--]
bezahlen? Ich [er----]⟩[117]

Sept. 1. Er "weisst nicht" wie viel wird "dass grosse
Bezahlung⟨"⟩" am 20 Sept. Always ignorant, and never otherwise
than behindhand with statements, bank accounts & so on.

Man hat mir versprochen dass die Rechnung Bissels—aber ich
habe dass ⟨⟨scho[-]⟩schon⟩ schon bemerkt.

Laf. or Sage. I will sell $360 commissions for $230, & Laf ⟨ta⟩ or
S take the $30.

Will sell a permanent royalty (American) ⟨f[--]⟩ of 50 cents on
the $1000; this would be a permanent income of not less than 50
per cent on the investment. No, not a good idea.

Will sell $1,000,000 on the first 2,000 American ($500 on each)
for $250,000 cash—Laf to get better terms & pocket the difference.

P. give me permanent royalty of $1000 on each American as
security. This to be *relinquished* when I get my stock. I to give
H.[118] a royalty of ⟨$[5]o⟩$100 on each American as security—this
also to be relinquished when he gets his stock.

Want a permanent roy of ⟨$100⟩ $2 on the $1000 on each
American; this to be sold from until all borrowed money has been
returned, with interest—what is left unsold to be then relinquished.

The $1000 per American is mere *security*, unless the capital
should not be made up.

Final.

I want none of the foregoing. What I want is ⟨$250⟩$200 on

---

[117] In this entry and the following one Clemens makes additional complaints about
Franklin G. Whitmore. The first two paragraphs are reactions to a letter from Whitmore
of 1 September 1889. The German reads: *He asks me, should he pay P's salary on the 10th?
He "doesn't know" how much "that big payment" of 20 Sept. will be.* The "big payment"
referred to by Whitmore in his letter is the upcoming payment due to Pratt & Whitney.
The third German passage reads: *He has promised me that the Bissell account—but I
have already noted that.* Clemens had previously noted Whitmore's failure to send him
a weekly statement of the account at his Hartford bank, George P. Bissell & Company
(see 514.3–4).
[118] William Hamersley.

each American ($20 to Ham), permanent. I ⟨s⟩to be allowed to sell
from this until past & future loans ⟨shall b⟩& interest shall be
satisfied. Whatever remains of it when we get our stock, we
relinquish. *But,* ⟨[no]⟩*none* of it to be sold until we shall have
tried & failed to get the money on sales of royalties on the first
2,000 Americans.

Thus, if we sold $50 in permanent royalties & finally failed to
organize & get capital, we would still have a $150 permanent
interest in the thing, no matter who procured the capital & got up
the company. P. can always protect *himself* in this way with any
new company, but we are without protection.[119]

Schumann's "Musical Criticism."

Hawley's fine story of General Patterson ⟨(85 or⟩ ⟨κκ yr
old/nearly 90 yrs old—20 at Lundy's Lane) at a soldiers' re-union in
Philadelphia in 1880. He was born in ⟨1790 or 95 or along
there.⟩1792)[120] "Good-morning General" (military salute)—returns
it. (Civil war.) "Good morning Colonel"—(Mexican war.) "Good ·
morning ⟨Major⟩ Captain"—shake hands—Black Hawk war of
1833. ⟨"Goo⟩ Shake hands & take a glass of beer. Tottering bald
veteran in piping treble—"Good morning ⟨Captain⟩ Lieutenant"—
⟨both⟩ ⟨(Lundy's Lane & New Orleans)⟩ Bonjour, M. le Capitaine!
(Waterloo!)—embraces him—snatches him home in a carriage,
"& by God we smash a bottle of champaign!" [#]

---

[119] The preceding several entries reflect Clemens' attempts to draft a contract proposal
to be presented to James W. Paige. The final contract, drawn by William Hamersley, was
signed on 26 September 1889. Clemens was assigned a five hundred dollar royalty on each
machine manufactured "in consideration of one hundred thousand dollars in hand paid
to the said James W. Paige by the said Samuel L. Clemens, the receipt whereof is hereby
acknowledged." The title to all the machine patents remained with Paige. Presumably
Clemens' payment of one hundred thousand dollars represents the sum of his expenditures on the machine since 1886, rather than an additional outlay of funds.

[120] General Joseph R. Hawley, United States senator and former governor of Connecticut, was one of the owners of the Hartford *Courant*. General Robert Patterson
was born in 1792 and served in the War of 1812, the Mexican War, and the Civil War.
He died in Philadelphia in 1881. Lundy's Lane, near Niagara Falls, was the site of a battle
between American and British troops on 25 July 1814.

⟨Shirts.[121] 2. Patent⟩ leathers.

⟨3. Players card for⟩ Frank Finlay. Laffan. & Lotos.[122]

4. ⟨Money from⟩ hotel.

5. ⟨Telegraph⟩ home.

⟨6. Barber. 7. Hamersley.⟩

8. ⟨Century Office.⟩ ⟨9. Harpers.⟩

10. Laffan. 11. Whitford 3 p.m.[123]

12. Phonograph.

Diffusion. "That man (a writer) would be competent to inflate a balloon with a single ————"

The train-boy who sold me a September Harper.

The farmer with a bloodshot eye who discussed buckwheat with me. His words were gentle, but the lurid eye seemed to ⟨seemed to⟩ volley forth profanity all around them. I will detail that conversation, giving alternately his kindly remarks, & that eye's awful ⟨comment⟨s⟩⟩comments upon each of them.

The adventure at 2 a. m. ⟨with⟩ ⟨w⟩clothed with night-shirt & ⟨check⟩ checkered summer parasol when I chased the dog Bruce

---

[121] The following numbered list of errands dates from Clemens' brief stay in New York City on 11 and 12 September 1889. The Clemens family had planned to return to Hartford from Quarry Farm by way of New York City, staying there at the Murray Hill Hotel from 10 to 12 September, but Clemens apparently made the trip to New York alone and returned to the farm for a few days before removing the family.

[122] In expectation of Frank Finlay's visit in October (see p. 511, note 104), Clemens arranged temporary memberships for him in two New York City clubs—the Lotos Club and the Players. Clemens apparently asked William Mackay Laffan who, like Clemens, was one of the founding members of the club, to secure the membership in the Players. In addition, in a letter of 5 October 1889 Clemens asked Richard Watson Gilder for permission to bring Finlay to a meeting of the Fellowcraft Club (see note 132), describing him as an "old English-Irish friend of mine in London 17 years ago, when he was editor & proprietor of the principal daily in the North of Ireland (the Belfast Whig)—visiting member of the Players & the Lotos, here, & Hon. Sec. of the Reform Club on the other side, & a rattling good fellow withal, & bright."

[123] Clemens had a three o'clock appointment on 11 September 1889 with his lawyer Daniel Whitford of the New York City law firm of Alexander & Green. The purpose of the meeting was to decide what action, if any, should be taken against a theatrical manager named Jacobs who was illegally presenting a dramatization of *Tom Sawyer* in Buffalo.

over the hills, & finally encountered the colored preacher who was afraid of ghosts & took me for one.

Charles Giblin's wife & children. Address World.[124]

1

We Americans worship the Almighty Dollar⟨, do we⟩? Well it is a worthier god than Hereditary Privilege. The Dollar has no contempt for you but the other has. It is amazing—what a European can stand, in the way of the contempt of his "betters." ⟨Better the Almighty Dollar than a tub of rancid guts labeled king, noble, & so on.⟩[125]

Write John P. Jones, & go & see him.[126]

Silver screw bottle

See ⟨st⟩Strong & show George's letter—at Frost's, cor. Lake & Water. Receipt.

Send telegram to Patrick about horses.

Pay telegraph & book bills.

Pay Mr. Rice & Doyle.[127]

Livy pay the gardener & [#]

---

[124] The New York *World* had focused public interest and sympathy on the case of young Charles Giblin, who had been convicted of murder in 1888 and was awaiting death in the Tombs prison in New York City (see p. 374, note 235). The prisoner was granted a reprieve of several months in order to allow the evidence to be reviewed, and as a result of the review his sentence was commuted to life imprisonment. The *World* started a fund for Giblin's needy wife and children.

[125] Clemens scrawled a number of lines across the notebook's hinge between the canceled final sentence of this paragraph numbered "1" and the paragraph numbered "2" beginning "Better a ⟨D[e]ity⟩deity" (521.2) which stands on the facing page, perhaps intending to replace the canceled sentence with the second paragraph.

[126] Clemens hoped to interest the wealthy senator from Nevada in forming a corporation to manufacture the Paige machine. His efforts to fix Jones's interest would continue throughout 1889 and 1890. Clemens' old newspaper friend Joseph T. Goodman usually acted as intermediary between Jones and Clemens during the negotiations.

[127] Clemens had previously noted money due to Rice and Doyle in a list of summer expenses at Quarry Farm (see p. 424).

2

Better a ⟨D[e]ity⟩deity that represents labor of your hands & your contribution to the world's wealth than a deity which represents not a contribution but a robbery; for no king or noble has ever lived who was not a robber & the ⟨success of⟩successor of robbers, since no kingship or nobility was ever yet conferred by the one & only authority entitled to confer it—the mass of a nation.

2

It's as if the British Lion itself, with head up & mane flung back, were roaring innocent joy & delight over the cheap miracles of a gang of 3-card monte sharps.

1. Mr. Gladstone should not have been degraded to an advertisement for ⟨a quack⟩ such a thing. ⟨The disproportion between the⟩

Sept. 16, '89, received of Clara L. Stanchfield, check for $5,000, for which I am to assign to her a royalty of $5 on every Paige Compositor marketed under the American patent during the life of said patent.

S L Clemens

Fulfilled Sept. 28, 1889.[128]

I intend to add a one-dollar royalty to these, to take the place of a twenty-five-dollar share in the old K. Co., which I gave to Clara years ago, & which never came to anything. This must not be forgotten, but attended to by others if I forget—that is the reason I am making this entry in my note-book.

S L Clemens

Fulfilled Sept. 28, 1889. [#]

---

[128] Clemens wrote to Clara Stanchfield on 29 September in a mood of confidence, assuring her that she could purchase additional royalties in the typesetter and adding: "You will not need to know anything about the printing business in order to understand the grin on this machine's face when it is thinking about this world's other type-setting machines. Dear me, those others—they are bound straight for the junk-shop; every one of them" (original owned by Stanchfield Wright, Earleville, Md.). Clemens enclosed six royalty certificates with the letter—five representing Clara Stanchfield's five thousand dollar investment, and one extra royalty, as Clemens notes in the following entry, to replace her share in Clemens' unsuccessful Kaolatype Engraving Company.

Als ich begehrte dass Paige ein⟨e⟩ ¹⁄₄₀₀ Theil Laffan geben wollen,
und seine zustimmen dazu erwarb, W. versaumte mehrere Wochen
ehe er konnte die Muth kriegen die Document vor P. zu legen
seiner Unterscrift zu bekommen.[129]

Wann ich eine royalty auf jeder Amerikanische Machine haben
wollen lag ich meine Vorschlag P. vor *selbst*.

At 12.15, Sept. 24, a man went along my sidewalk on a low
bicycle; Jo Lane & Hough[130] were in a buggy; I stopped them &
pointed the man out, who was now on the sidewalk beyond the
bridge, & asked them to get his name, so I could report him to
the police.

Paige, make me a perpetual calendar.[131]

Fellowcraft—be at 32 W 28ᵗʰ 7 p. m. Oct. 16. Wednesday.[132] [#]

---

[129] *When I requested that Paige give a ¹⁄₄₀₀ share to Laffan, and he agreed to it,
W[hitmore] went several weeks before he could get up the courage to lay the document
in front of P. to get his signature.* The following entry reads: *If I want to have a* royalty
for every American Machine *I'll put my proposal to P. myself.*

[130] Probably Hartford grocer Joseph G. Lane and former banker and broker Niles P.
Hough, like Clemens a resident of Farmington Avenue.

[131] In 1884 and 1885 Clemens had prodded Charles L. Webster to perfect and patent
a portable perpetual calendar, despite Webster's negative opinion of its market value.
In October 1889 an inquiry from a man who had seen an advertisement for the calendar
recalled it to Clemens' mind and he noted: "I remember it now, but had long ago forgotten it. I never manufactured it because matters of greater moment intruded and
obliterated my interest in it; in fact, swept it wholly out of my memory" (written on the
envelope of [Q.] J. Drake to SLC, 16 October 1889).

[132] In a letter of 5 October 1889 Clemens informed Richard Watson Gilder of his
willingness to attend the 16 October dinner at the Fellowcraft Club. Clemens, however,
was sick in bed with a cold on the appointed date and it is unlikely that he attended.
Gilder renewed his invitation to Clemens the following month (see p. 530, note 148).
Gilder had been president of the Fellowcraft Club since its founding in 1888. The club
had a large membership mainly of journalists and illustrators employed on the New York
City dailies. "One of the principal features," according to Gilder, "is a monthly dinner,
which begins with a little informal speech-making, and goes on into music, story-telling,
etc. A peculiar point of this dinner is its informality, and the fact that although the room
is full of reporters the speeches are not reported" (*Letters of Richard Watson Gilder*,
ed. Rosamond Gilder [Boston and New York: Houghton Mifflin Co., 1916], p. 185).

Read Tar-Baby at tail-end of Authors' Reading in Brooklyn Dec. 16, '89, Academy of Music.[133]

Oct. 13 '89. Proposed ⟨[-]⟩my idea (of buying the remains of Columbus & bringing them over to the Fair of '92,) to the N.Y. World "Committee on Ideas"—but shan't *name* the idea till I hear from them.[134]

See Mr. Hall & put this in ⟨circulars⟩ as a foot-note or in Appendix.

Write to Standring for particulars. of this

Earl of Galloway rape-case. Oct. '89. Scotland.[135] [#]

---

[133] R. R. Bowker, owner and editor of *Publishers' Weekly* and a member of the executive committee of the American Copyright League, wrote to Clemens on 8 October 1889 inviting him to read at the authors' benefit for copyright at the Brooklyn Academy of Music on 16 December 1889. Notwithstanding the assent expressed in this notebook entry, Clemens wrote Bowker promptly on 9 October and declined to appear at the reading. Clemens' amusing letter explained at length his distaste for such readings. "We can't point to a single one of them," he argued, "& say it was rationally conducted." The programs were too long, and the "small-fry" readers tended to exceed their time limits. The result was inevitably "an experience to be forever remembered with bitterness by the audience" (New York Public Library). Bowker responded on 10 October 1889 with a playful threat: "I addressed S. L. Clemens, Esq., and I have a reply from Mark Twain, in his most exageratin mood. Tell Mr. C. that if he don't come, we'll read M. T's letter at the audience." Clemens was adamant and the 16 December reading took place without him. Clemens' letter was read at the start of the program and was printed in full in the New York *Times*'s coverage of the event (17 December 1889).

[134] On 13 October 1889 the New York *World* announced a "contest of ideas," offering a first prize of one thousand dollars. The entries were to be judged by the *World's* "Committee on Ideas" and the winners announced on Christmas morning. There is no record of any response to Clemens from the *World*. Plans for the Columbian Exposition of 1892/1893 were well under way, although there still was controversy over the site of the fair—New York City and Chicago vying for the honor. In April 1890 Congress approved Chicago as the site. The exposition included an exhibition of various Columbian relics, but the explorer's remains—resting temporarily in Havana after a number of relocations —were not disturbed.

[135] Presumably the previous two entries refer to the Galloway case. Clemens probably saw the article in the New York *World* of 15 October 1889 which announced the acquittal of Alan Plantagenet Stewart, earl of Galloway. The New York *World*, always quick to stress the sensational elements of a story, implied that the earl won acquittal by virtue of

I dropped a strong phrase, in the presence of manager K (some others present.) He rebuked me. I was surprised out of my self-possession for two or three awkward moments; then I said, seriously: "I ought to explain. I have often used profane language in the presence of God. ⟨He⟩As he has always put up with it, I had an idea that maybe a damned theatre manager could stand it."

✳ It caught him unexpectedly, & his sudden explosion of laughter shot his false teeth across the corner of his desk, & they fell at my feet like a trophy.

Oct. ⟨21 or⟩ 22, offered Bunce at the Stanchfield &c price. To Robinson, Oct. 26.[136]

Satanville.
Ounalaska

Call on Gilder & talk Chicago.[137]

Write Frohman[138] [#]

---

his power and wealth. Clemens apparently wished to contact his friendly correspondent George Standring, a London journalist and printer, for more information about the case with the idea of using it in *A Connecticut Yankee* as an indictment of aristocratic privilege. According to the London *Times*, the earl's trial and acquittal took place on 14 October, the charge being "using lewd, indecent, and libidinous behavior" toward a ten-year-old girl. The testimony showed that there was no evidence of a physical assault on the child. The earl argued that he merely "put his hand under the petticoats of the small child and patted her knee. He had no intention of doing anything indecent towards the child, but was merely showing kindness" (London *Times*, 15 October 1889). The London *Times* of 16 October 1889 added: "The Sheriff substitute, in his summing up, stated that he had never . . . known a case in which such a charge was brought where the circumstances attending it were of so slight a nature."

[136] Clemens' Hartford friend Edward Bunce was cashier of the Phoenix National Bank. Robinson is probably lawyer Henry C. Robinson, former mayor of Hartford and a member of the Monday Evening Club. There is no evidence that either Bunce or Robinson bought shares of Clemens' Paige typesetter royalty.

[137] Richard Watson Gilder of the *Century* was one of the most influential members of the American Copyright League. Clemens apparently wished to discuss with Gilder the projected authors' reading for copyright in Chicago (see note 139).

[138] Daniel Frohman, manager of the Lyceum Theatre, wrote to Clemens through Daniel Whitford on 2 October 1889 announcing that a new version of Mrs. Richardson's dramatization of *The Prince and the Pauper*, "embodying some recent changes," would

Condition. I am not to go to Chicago to read unless the Authors secure Bellamy, Kennan, Roosevelt, Warner, Riley, Nye, Stockton Wrote this to Johnson Oct. 27[139]

Ennoble all the tramps

Go for these wretched American women who buy titles (& noble tramps) with their money. Give them a foul nickname. (Mongrel-breeders; have a bench-show of their children.)

The Eagle, the scavenger bird, bird of prey—the proper symbol of royalty & nobility. But the unicorn Yank turned into a donkey to represent the people. But ours should be our native bird, the turkey. True, he *is* ⟨the⟩ one of the biggest fools in featherdom, ⟨but [-]⟩ that is a merit—the majority of all peoples are fools.

Add a chapter & confer nobility by sentence upon *all* thieves, upon conviction.

Seedless Muscat (raisin)

"Brave" knights—whereas his steel defence was the very symbol of personal cowardice—no, not quite that, but of ⟨un[-]⟩unmagnanimous willingness to take advantage; he rode down the battalions of unpanoplied militia, & thought it a daring thing to do. [#]

---

be forwarded to Clemens "within two weeks." By the terms of her contract of 13 May 1889 Mrs. Richardson was to have completed the play by 1 October 1889. Within the next few weeks, however, Frohman apparently requested another postponement of the deadline. Clemens probably wished to contact him about the repeated delays.

[139] Robert Underwood Johnson of the *Century* was a member of the executive committee of the American Copyright League. He wrote to Clemens on 26 October 1889 with a proposal: "We are organizing Authors' Readings for Copyright at Chicago (for the third or fourth week in November, most probably) the idea being to charter a car and take the Eastern readers out and back without personal expense. May we count on you?" Johnson explained that Chicago and the Chicago newspapers were "the heart of the opposition" to copyright legislation. Clemens' acceptance of the reading engagement, Johnson added, would "capture" other readers such as Edward Bellamy, George Kennan, Theodore Roosevelt, Charles Dudley Warner, William Dean Howells, James Whitcomb Riley, Bill Nye, and Frank Stockton. Johnson took Clemens' response of 27 October to be a refusal.

Latest quotations, ⟨[£]⟩$2,000—what Miss Huntington paid for
her Sauer-kraut Prince Hatzfeld. Give his history (imaginary)
beginning with a highwayman.)[140]

Give Badlam's letter to C L W.[141]

Describe the terms offered for Joe's book⟨.⟩; sale of 7,000 or
10,000 copies—after that, divide equally.

Began "Looking Backward" Nov. ⟨[-]⟩ 5, 1889, on the train.
A fascinating book.[142] [#]

---

[140] In an earlier note Clemens had reminded himself to "go for these wretched American women who buy titles" (525.5). Clemens' indignation had been aroused by recent
newspaper rumors of the impending marriage of Clara Huntington, adopted daughter of
California railroad tycoon Collis Potter Huntington, to Prince Francis Hatzfeldt, nephew
of the German ambassador to England. The New York *World* announced on 27 October
1889: "Millionaire Huntington's purchase of a Prince as the husband of his daughter for
$10,000,000 or thereabouts in settlement of debts and dowry is more and more the sub-
ject of drawing-room gossip in London, Paris and Berlin as the date of the nuptials ap-
proaches." In the same issue, the *World* traced the unsavory history of the Hatzfeldt
family and characterized Miss Huntington's fiancé as a middle-aged profligate, enjoying
"a reckless career of extravagance and dissipation." The wedding took place in London
on 28 October 1889. The New York *World* followed up with a long, illustrated article on
3 November 1889 chronicling the lives of "American heiresses who have speculated in
the foreign matrimonial market." Clemens apparently did not write a sketch about such
title-hungry heiresses, although on 20 November 1889 he was still fulminating against
"these bastard Americans" who offered "cash, encumbered by themselves, for rotten
carcases and stolen titles" (SLC to Sylvester Baxter, *MTL*, p. 520).

[141] Alexander Badlam, formerly a member of the California legislature and assessor
of San Francisco, was currently president of the Bankers and Merchants Mutual Life
Association of the United States based in San Francisco. He had been friendly with
Clemens in the 1860s and had been the subject of a humorous article by Clemens in the
Virginia City *Territorial Enterprise* of 8 January 1866 (published in *Mark Twain: San
Francisco Correspondent*, ed. Henry Nash Smith and Frederick Anderson [San Fran-
cisco: Book Club of California, 1957], pp. 54–59). Through Clemens, Badlam offered
his book, *The Wonders of Alaska*, to Charles L. Webster & Company, probably at the
time of this notebook entry. In the following entry, Clemens outlined the terms of a possible contract, evidently based on terms offered to either Joseph T. Goodman or Joseph
Hopkins Twichell for an unidentified work. Badlam's book was refused by Webster
& Company but he secured publication through the Bancroft Company in 1890 and
promptly sent Clemens a copy in June 1890.

[142] Clemens went to New York City on 5 November with William Dean Howells and
returned to Hartford the next day. Edward Bellamy's *Looking Backward: 2000–1887* was
first published in 1888 (Boston: Ticknor and Co.). Clemens admired the book and was

The Curious Repub of Gondomar.

Mr. Skunkington, railroad thief,—daughter marries Prince Hatfeldt.[143]

"What have *oi* to do wid his ammoors?"

Carry 1601 to the Players.

Nov. 9 '/89. Offered to D. S.[144] by letter, to sell him a 1-45th of my future stock at $25,000, & put up 50 royalties as security; or two 1-45^{ths} for $50,000, & put up 100 royalties as security.

Will offer at double these figures hereafter.

Don't need to pay anybody a commission on orders & collections —the Trust ⟨c⟩Co will collect & charge a commission for it.[145]

Will sell a 1-20th (future stock) (5 one-hundredths) for $250,000, & put up 250 royalties as security. [#]

---

glad of a chance in January 1890 to "meet the man who has made the accepted heaven paltry by inventing a better one on earth" (SLC to Sylvester Baxter, [24 November 1889], Berg; see p. 503, note 75). In the following notebook entry Clemens apparently refers to his own utopian sketch, "The Curious Republic of Gondour," first published in the *Atlantic* in October 1875. Unlike Bellamy's socialistic utopia, in the enlightened society of Gondour "brains and property managed the state."

[143] See note 140.

[144] Albany businessman Dean Sage, a friend and occasional financial advisor to Clemens, came to Hartford around 6 November to view the Paige typesetter. Sage was inclined to be dubious about Clemens' plan for capitalizing the machine's manufacture and his visit to Hartford only confirmed his doubts. The investment scheme mentioned in this notebook entry elicited a frank response from Sage on 19 November 1889. He warned that the outlay of almost two million dollars to capitalize a typesetter factory before any machines could be produced was unjustifiable; he suggested instead that the first several hundred machines could be jobbed out to a reputable machine shop. "You have either got a great bonanza or nothing," he cautioned, "& until you have a good number of the machines actually turning out successfully the work they are expected to do this is a question. . . . To tell the truth I feel anxious about *you*—as I understand it, *you* are the man who will have to furnish the capital, so large in amount that a failure in the business might sweep away all you have, or very seriously embarrass you."

[145] In a letter of 16 November 1889 to Joseph T. Goodman, Clemens suggested that money raised to finance the typesetter factory should "not pass through our hands at all, but through the Chemical Bank or Drexel Morgan & Co., (who must assume the trust & be responsible); they to pay it out only on vouchers for plant & manufacture; the trust to also deliver the machines & collect the money."

SOME COMPARATIVES.

A glance at the following object lesson will enable one to realize the difference between the PAIGE COMPOSITOR and the other type-setting machines. Each bar represents AN HOUR'S OUTPUT of uncorrected matter, PER INDIVIDUAL CONCERNED IN CREATING THAT OUTPUT. Explanation: Instead of calling the output of the several "gravity" machines 4,000 ems for the hour, we call it 1,333, because it takes 3 persons (a setter, a justifier, and a distributor), to create the 4,000 ems. The important thing to know, is, how much money a machine SAVES. When a "gravity" machine produces 4,000 ems an hour, and pays wages to 3 men to do it, we know that that machine is able to save ONE MAN'S WAGES. When the Mergenthaler produces 2,500 ems an hour, and pays wages to one man to do it, we know that that machine is (apparently) saving the wages of one man and a half,—and would really be doing it if the operator's wages constituted the only expense connected with the output. It costs as much to set 2,500 ems on the Mergenthaler as it costs to set 2,000 by hand. What the Mergenthaler actually SAVES is, merely THE HALF OF ONE MAN'S WAGES. When the PAIGE COMPOSITOR is producing 7,000 ems an hour, and paying wages to one man to do it, we know that the machine is SAVING SIX MEN'S WAGES.

The estimate of the capacity of the "gravity" machines is taken from the official report of Mr. Pasko, made to the Newspaper Publishers' Convention in New York, Feb. 13, 1889.

The estimate of the Mergenthaler average and "full capacity," are taken from statistics published by the Mergenthaler officials:

Bar No. 1—Mergenthaler operator's average output,	. . . . .	2,500 ems.
Bar No. 2—Full capacity of Mergenthaler machine,	. . . . .	3,000 ems.
Bar No. 3—Output of the "Gravity" machines,	. . . . .	4,000 ems.
Bar No. 4—PAIGE COMPOSITOR—three months' apprentice,	. . . . .	7,000 ems.
Bar No. 5—PAIGE COMPOSITOR—veteran extraordinary expert—probably	. . . . .	12,000 ems.
Bar No. 6—PAIGE COMPOSITOR—full capacity of the machine,	. . . . .	24,000 ems.

1.
2.
3.
4.
5.
6.

All machines LIMIT THE OPERATOR, except the PAIGE COMPOSITOR. It is twice as swift as any operator can possibly become. It seems safe to guess that the most extraordinary expert will never accomplish more than 12,000 ems an hour on it; yet the machine's setting-capacity is demonstrably 24,000 ems an hour.

MONEY-SAVING CAPACITIES.

When the several machines are producing the average outputs above specified, the Mergenthaler is saving one-half of one man's wages; the gravity machines are saving one man's wages, and the PAIGE COMPOSITOR is saving six men's wages. A glance at the object lesson below will make these proportions clear.

The Mergenthaler saves 1-2 man.
Gravity machines save 1 man.
PAIGE COMPOSITOR saves 6 men.

–	Hand Composition[146]
——	Grav
=====	MᶜMillan
——	Thorne
——	Matrix
——— Rogers	
——	Mergenthaler
————— Paige.	

—	possible
——	capacity
——— possible Paige	

$$
\begin{array}{r}
95 \\
96 \\
80 \\
84 \\
\underline{84} \\
439 \;[\#]
\end{array}
$$

---

[146] On 29 September 1889 Clemens informed Clara Stanchfield: "I am writing up my statistics, now, for issue in pamphlet form" (original owned by Stanchfield Wright, Earleville, Md.). Discarded notes and incomplete pamphlet drafts in the Mark Twain Papers contain some of Clemens' extensive and complicated calculations proving the Paige typesetter's superiority over other machines. The bar graphs in this notebook entry formed the basis for a printed sheet titled "Some Comparatives," evidently set on the Paige compositor, that was revised by Clemens and tucked inside the notebook (reduced one-fourth in the illustration on page 528).

Over the notebook passage that follows, Clemens drew a heavy inverted V extending downward from "Grav" to "Matrix," probably to indicate that the McMillan, Thorne, and Matrix machines should all be included in the category of "gravity" machines. In fact, the "gravity" principle for moving type was a feature of almost every major typesetting invention, including the Mergenthaler Linotype. The rival typesetters in Clemens' list, unlike the Paige machine, were already in use on American and British newspapers. John L. McMillan's typesetter, invented in 1883, was the first machine to justify automatically; the compact Thorne typesetter, invented in 1880 by Joseph Thorne, combined a setter and a distributor; John R. Rogers' Typograph, invented in 1888, was a slug-casting machine manufactured in Cleveland but sold abroad because of patent conflicts with the Mergenthaler Linotype. The "Matrix" machine to which Clemens refers was probably an "Electro-matrix type machine" which Clemens heard about from Dean Sage in February 1889. The column of figures which follows Clemens' list of typesetters shows the average number of pages in the New York City daily newspapers (see note 147).

No of mach required to set up H. S. W. T. for a week, in one
size of type. ⟨[5]⟩⟨8⟩⟨6⟩7 hours a day,—⟨1[6]⟩13 of ours
(⟨[--]⟩⟨[7]⟩ 13 pages a day by each, ⟨[90] pages a day,⟩ 91 pages a
week

H. 95 a week, W. 96, Trib 80, S., (?) Times (?)—all, say 439 p a
week, 63 of ours would do it, 157 Merg., 150 Rogers.[147]

$$⟨61⟩63 \text{ m. set } 61 \text{ p a day}$$

$$
\begin{array}{r}
7 \\
⟨4[9]7⟩⟨427⟩\overline{441}
\end{array}
$$

$$
\begin{array}{r}
⟨36 \\
7 \\
\hline
252⟩
\end{array}
$$

Fellow-craft, 32 W. 28
7 pm, Nov. 16.[148]

Saturday, Dec. ⟨7,⟩ 14 West Point
    Col. Jno. M. Wilson, Supt.[149] [#]

---

[147] Clemens is computing the number of Paige typesetters, Mergenthaler Linotypes,
and Rogers Typographs which would be required to set the complete weekly editions of
the New York *Herald, World, Tribune, Sun,* and *Times.* He has noted the total weekly
number of pages issued by each newspaper (the missing page calculations for the *Sun* and
the *Times* are evidently shown in the column of figures at 529.12–16) and totaled these
to arrive at the figure of 439 pages.

[148] On 6 November 1889 Richard Watson Gilder, president of the Fellowcraft Club,
wrote to Clemens naming 15 November as the date of the club dinner. Clemens attended
and with the aid of Major James B. Pond contrived to surprise and amuse the party. Pond
asked Gilder to be allowed to present an unknown speaker—a Samuel Langhorne—who
had a "scheme for teaching impromptu oratory." The club members protested until they
discovered the speaker was Clemens. Clemens agreed to construct, extemporaneously, a
speech on any subject of the club's choice. His method was to use the supposed subject of
the speech merely as a hook upon which to hang "three first-rate anecdotes" which would
so delight the audience that they would not notice that the anecdotes were "dragged in
by the scruff of the neck and had no relation to the subject which the speaker was pretending to talk about" (Autobiographical Dictation, 28 August 1906). Brander Matthews, a
Fellowcraft member, recalled the evening and Clemens' speech and observed that it became "very difficult for those who had to speak after him to employ their customary
formulas" (Brander Matthews, *The Tocsin of Revolt and Other Essays* [New York:
Charles Scribner's Sons, 1922], p. 275).

[149] John Moulder Wilson, superintendent of West Point from 1889 to 1893, wrote
to Clemens in November inviting him to address the cadets. Clemens accepted and

Miss M. C. Thomas, (Dean).[150]

Don't drive to old Belmont house, but to Mt. Auburn Station &
ask for me.[151]

9 a.m. limited express—telegraph save 2 seats.

10 a.m. is good—2 h & 25 m.

11 am goes in 2 h & 20.

Returning, leav Phil at 4 pm—a 2 h & 20.
                              4.50 gets in at 7—2 h & 10,
                              5—gets in at ⟨2⟩7.20 (2 h & 20)

P Gilbert Hamerton "French & English." Roberts
Bros. Boston.[152] [#]

---

named the date of 14 December, but was forced to cancel because of illness. The
reading was postponed until 11 January 1890 (see p. 536) and Clemens tried, unsuccessfully, to convince Howells to go with him: "Can't you go with me? It's great fun. I'm
going to read the passages in the 'Yankee' in which the Yankee's West Point cadets figure
—& shall covertly work in a lecture on aristocracy to those boys. I am to be the guest of
the Superintendent, but if you will go I will shake him & we will go to the hotel. He is a
splendid fellow, & I know him well enough to take that liberty" (SLC to William Dean
Howells, 23 December 1889, *MTHL*, p. 625).

[150] M. Carey Thomas was dean and professor of English at Bryn Mawr College from
its opening in 1885 until 1894 when she became president of the college. Clemens probably noted her name in connection with the plans for enrolling Susy at Bryn Mawr the
following year.

[151] Clemens visited William Dean Howells on 12 and 13 November 1889 in Mount
Auburn, Massachusetts, where the Howells family had temporarily sublet a home. Howells had written Clemens on 10 November inviting him to come up and see a dramatization of *A Foregone Conclusion* in Boston. He gave him careful directions for the trip—
evidently preserved in this entry—and asked that Clemens telegraph him at Belmont,
Massachusetts, to confirm his arrival. The Howells family had lived in Belmont several
years earlier, but the use of the address at this time is mysterious.

[152] Philip Gilbert Hamerton's *French and English: A Comparison*, based on a series
of articles which appeared in the *Atlantic Monthly* in 1886 and 1887, was published in
1889. The following title, *The Foes of the French Revolution*, written by Hermann Lieb,
also appeared in 1889. Clemens' view of the French Revolution had changed with time,
and during the period of his work on *A Connecticut Yankee* he identified himself as a
"Sansculotte!—And not a pale, characterless Sansculotte, but a Marat" (*MTHL*, p. 595).
Clemens would have been particularly interested in Lieb's opinion that the French Revo-
luction was a result "of the inexorable law of evolution which impels humanity . . .
toward a better condition, and that the crash which came was but a manifestation of this
law" (quoted in the New York *Times*, 12 August 1889).

"The Foes of the Fr. Revolution" NY, Belford Clark & Co.

Speak of Frohman's propositions to W & Co.[153]

Put Gill & the circular together & they might accomplish something out of the 4 week's engagement in Phila.[154]

Send 2 sets sheets to ⟨McEw[an]⟩McEwen, 2 to Sam Moffett, (& Goodman?) about Dec. 1. Wait till I hear from Baxter.[155]

M. Huc's Thibet, Mongolia & China.[156] [#]

---

[153] Fred Hall wrote to Clemens on 29 November 1889: "I have made Frohman a definite offer regarding his advertising plan. He wanted us to stand half the expense & let *him say* just what would be in the circular, which would mean all to his benefit. He wanted 50000 circulars & they would cost just $310.00. The circular to be 8 pages. I told him we would print & make the circular; allow him 6 pages of the 8. . . . He to pay ⅔ & we ⅓ the cost." Frohman's proposed circular was evidently for use in advertising the dramatization of *The Prince and the Pauper.*

[154] This entry appears to be related to Frohman's advertising circular plan, but Clemens' meaning is not clear. Watson Gill of Syracuse was one of Charles L. Webster & Company's most successful general agents. He had recently contracted with Fred Hall to canvass for *A Connecticut Yankee* in the western New York territory. *The Prince and the Pauper* would open in Philadelphia on 24 December 1889 for an engagement of about four weeks before the play's 20 January 1890 New York City opening.

[155] Fred Hall wrote to Clemens on 29 November 1889. "You left three names with me sometime ago saying that the parties were to have copies of your book for review as soon as it was ready. . . . The names were, Mr. McEwen, Mr. Goodman, and Mr. Sam Moffat." Arthur McEwen, long a prominent California journalist and Joseph Goodman's friend, was chief editorial writer on the San Francisco *Examiner.* Clemens wrote to his nephew Samuel Erasmus Moffett, also employed on the *Examiner,* on 28 November 1889: "I will have sheets of my book sent to you. If you review it, or cause a review to be prepared, keep it out of print till as late as Sunday, DEC. 8." Joseph Goodman had been a journalist in the 1860s but was currently owner of a "grape ranch" in Fresno, California. He still contributed occasionally to journals. Sylvester Baxter of the Boston *Herald* had requested advance sheets of *A Connecticut Yankee* on 13 November 1889 in order to write a review of the book for the *Herald.* Clemens complied with Baxter's request but stipulated that the review should not appear until about 20 December when Howells' review would be published in *Harper's* magazine. He explained: "The book itself will issue 8 days earlier (Dec. 12) but there will be no reviews of it in the month of December except yours & Howells's, & possibly another from some other friend & sympathizer, for no copies will be sent to the press until the book has been out a few weeks & its canvass completed" (SLC to Baxter, 14 November 1889, Berg). Baxter acknowledged receipt of the advance sheets on 22 November 1889.

[156] Evariste Régis Huc's *Recollections of a Journey Through Tartary, Thibet, and China, During the Years 1844, 1845, and 1846,* first published in French in 1850, was published in New York by D. Appleton & Company in 1852.

1st class, 10 per centers.

2^n "   5   "   "

No. 2 can at any time join No. 1 & take its place at bottom of list.[157]

Invite gov't printer[⟨.⟩]—thro' Hawley (?)

Cheap edition with strong linen-envelop ⟨ba⟩ cover.

8.30.   9.50—2h 10m.

Proposition to Jo Goodman, Nov. 1/89. He to get Jones et al to put up all the capital required & take all profits until it is paid back & $500,000 over. After that, recive ⅓ of the profits permanently. Jo to receive $500,000 of the profits before we get anything.[158]

Telephoned at 6 for a carriage to be at M. F.'s at 6.30. ⟨At 20 min to 7 telephoned again;⟩ Tele at 7.30 they said the carriage was gone long ago. ⟨Telephoned at 7.30 & they said the order was for 8.30 (then **X** why did they say it had gone long ago.⟩ The young lady arrived ⟨at⟩ by car. at 7.40; tele & they said order was for 8.30. **X** Telephoned for the carriage to be here at 9.30; Telephoned at 9.40 to know why it wasn't here; got same old answer "gone long ago." ⟨at 10 it was not here.⟩ Just starting in car at 10 when it arrived. Telephoned & got it; when the young lady had just got away in it, ⟨(10)⟩ her mother arrived in the car (10.20) badly frightened.

Please bring suit for your bill.

---

[157] Clemens' miscellaneous notes on Paige affairs include two drafts of a proposed schedule of payments by typesetter purchasers. The selling price of the machine was to be twelve thousand dollars. In his schedules Clemens proposes that "Class A" purchasers pay ten per cent as a down payment with payments of ten per cent in the two succeeding years and an additional ten per cent on delivery in 1892. Thereafter the payment would be two hundred dollars per month for three years. "Class B" purchasers would pay six thousand dollars three months after delivery and the same amount a year later. Five lesser classes are listed with varying payment schedules. Clemens adds that "an order in a minor class may be changed at any time to the bottom place in a higher or lower class after 300 in Class A have been accepted."

[158] This proposition is stated in Clemens' letter to Goodman of 16 November 1889.

An hour later than the order a carriage arrived & Miss Reardon went up—Mrs. F. said she had ordered none.[159]

Nov. 19 '/89, 10.25, p.m. To Mr. Lewis: Tele at ⟨6.[2]o⟩6.30 for carriage to

8.03 am—⟨get to Spr. at 9⟩ leaves Spr. 9.50—get to Buf 8.35 pm

Pay us 37½ per M.
  " Op. 8   "   "   } In effect you pay 7½ & save 5^c per
Save ½^c per M for leads. } M—or $2 a day per Mch.

At 6 M per hour, 7 hours per day, you pay us $16.80 per day 50^c daily paper
365 days, ⟨$5,[5-]o⟩$6,132 (6,132)
You save 5^c per M, 30^c per hour say $2.00 per day—say $730 per year—total, $6,862
The mach pays for itself in considerably less than 2 years, out of its own savings.[160]

With orders for 250 & four 10 p.c. advances—1 down, 1 in 6 mos, 1 in 12, & 1 on delivery, ⟨[&]⟩we go to work.
When orders for 500 reached, knock out ⟨third⟩ advance No. 3.
When 750 reached, knock out No. 4.
When 1000   "   "   "   " 2.

Offer ⟨a⟩ the ⟨sole⟩exclusive right to MANUFACTURE in a State & the further tho' not exclusive right *sell* anywhere in ⟨the U.S.⟩ the Continent of America.[161] [#]

---

[159] Clemens filled one side of a leaf with notes about the late carriage (533.13–534.2) and tore the leaf out of his notebook, perhaps intending to use it as the draft of a letter, although no letter on the incident is known to exist. The leaf may for a time have been removed from the notebook, but it is now in place.

[160] Clemens is calculating the cost to a purchaser of a Paige typesetter per thousand ems of set matter, taking into account wages paid to the operator and costs for leaded matter. He compares the result with the cost for hand composition, currently averaging fifty cents per thousand ems.

[161] Clemens' miscellaneous papers on the typesetter include a draft of a proposition to be offered by Clemens' lawyer, Daniel Whitford of Alexander & Green, to American typefounders. This and the following several notebook entries refer to this proposition. Clemens offered for sale a process "which will make a *homogeneous* type—*not porous*—& which will be about as hard & durable as *steel*, & as clean-cut & sharp-faced & beautiful."

Offer the exclusive right to *manufacture* in a State, & the further tho' *not* exclusive right to *sell & vend* anywhere within the U.S.

Offer the exclusive right to manufacture sell & vend in the U.S.

Offer ditto for U S & Europe.

Plant will cost but ¾ of present.

"Metal as hard as hardened brass"—⟨practically indestructible.⟩
Headings of paper are brass.
(Last like brass rules.)
Can be made & sold for less money than type-metal type.
Fewer operators & fewer *operations* required.
Quicker made than the present.
The whole process is almost entirely automatic. No hand-finishing required. Picking is entirely done away with.

⟨⟨May use our nicks, but⟩ May use our nicks, but must furnish our machine-users at ⟨a slightly cheaper rate than⟩ as cheap a rate as to other people.⟩

We will show, in 6 months, that it can be done, as we say, & that the application for patent has been made. ⟨You⟩ If satisfied, you are then to pay us the cash payment down & secure us one-fourth of all future profits.

See how the various foundrymen, & tackle in the several cities the one with the most money.

We have a process which will make a homogeneous type & not porous, which will be as hard, & sharp-faced as steel & about as durable.
It is nothing *resembling* the so-called hardened type, but is infinitely superior to it.

Pulish in England the 6th. Must be in Canada that day.[162]

Stole McCarthy's teeth. [#]

---

[162] Fred Hall wrote to Clemens on 23 November 1889 confirming that copyright laws required that Clemens "be on Canadian soil the day the book is published *in England, viz: December 6th.*"

Used to take ⟨his⟩their glass eyes out to play marbles with, then get them mixed & have a quarrel. Both of them color blind, anyway

The Journal of a Young Artist. Cassell.[163]

Rose Publishing Co, Toronto.

Cable Chatto & Windus.

Hartford, Dec. 14/89.

Mem. of Agreement.

Dec. 9/89, I sold to Mr. M. H. Arnot[164] fifty Royalty Deeds of the Paige Compositor for fifty thousand dollars, this money to be paid to me in instalments as required by me. And we mutually agreed & bound ourselves as follows:

That when the royalties shall have repaid Mr. Arnot the fifty thousand dollars he shall then restore to me the fifty Deeds & receive in lieu thereof Fifty Thousand Dollars of my stock in the company formed to manufacture & sell the Paige-Compositor machines under the American patents.

Witness: S L Clemens
Olivia L. Clemens[165]

P. S. was added: I not to draw for any large proportion of the whole at one time, & not to draw at all without giving a month's notice.

West Point ⟨Dec.⟩ Jan 11[166]

Eggleston, Author's Club, midnight, Dec. ⟨2⟩31.[167] [#]

---

[163] Clemens acquired a copy of *Marie Bashkirtseff: The Journal of a Young Artist*, translated by Mary J. Serrano, published by Cassell & Company in 1889.

[164] Elmira businessman Matthias Hollenback Arnot.

[165] The signature is in Clemens' hand.

[166] See page 530, note 149.

[167] Author and journalist George Cary Eggleston, currently editorial writer on the New York *World*, wrote to Clemens on 19 December 1889 inviting him to the Authors Club "watch night meeting." In his *Recollections of a Varied Life* Eggleston recalled

Victor Pagels,
  143 Collins st.[168]

                              (Copy.)
                         Elmira, N. Y. Dec. 19/89.
S. L. Clemens—
  My Dear Sir:
    Yours of 14th inst., also mem° of agreement has been recv[d].
So far as my recollection serves me, your statement is correct.
                                        Yrs M. H. Arnot.

Send $40 for 2060 miles. Dec. 28

Send full Morocco to Daly & write in it.

4399. Dec. 28. Ticket office RR, for 2000 miles, $40.

Milly Cheney[169]
% Mr. Rianhard
  264—4th ave.

  New England road.
  So. Manch: 5.10; 6.30.

"He said he would rather sleep with ⟨Adelini⟩Adelina Patti
without a stitch of clothes on than with General Grant in full
uniform."[170] [#]

---

the occasion. The club festivities were patterned after "the old custom of the Methodists
who held 'Watch Night' meetings, seeing the old year out and the new year in with rejoic-
ing and fervent singing. . . . Fortunately, Mark Twain was called upon to begin the
story telling, and he put formality completely out of countenance at the very outset.
Instead of standing as if to address the company, he seized a chair, straddled it, and with
his arms folded across its back, proceeded to tell one of the most humorous of all his
stories" (New York: Henry Holt and Co., 1910, p. 281).

[168] Victor Pagels was a draftsman employed at the Pratt & Whitney Company in
Hartford and was presumably engaged in work on the Paige typesetter.

[169] Emily Cheney was the daughter of Mary Bushnell Cheney and Frank Woodbridge
Cheney, one of the directors of the Cheney silk mills of South Manchester, Connecticut.
The Clemens family occasionally attended dinners and social functions given by the
Cheney family.

[170] James Montgomery Flagg recorded this anecdote, told to him by a friend, in his
autobiography Roses and Buckshot: "Mark and Howells were in the front row at the old

Dying man couldn't make up his mind which place to go to—both have their ⟨advances⟩advantages, "heaven for climate, hell for company!" [171]

Flush the first of the month.

Feb. 1/90. Sir W^m. Gull is just dead. He nursed the P. of W. back to life in '71, & ⟨f⟩apparently it was for this that Mr. Gull was granted knighthood, that doormat at the threshhold of nobility.[172] "When the Prince seemed dead Mr. Gull dealt blow after blow between the shoulders, breathed into his nostrils, & literally cheated Death." It startlingly reminds us of the earliest incident in the history of the human race.⟨—& look at Gull's reward!⟩ If the Prince had been Adam & Gull had been God, I believe the Queen would have considered His aristocratic position & made Him a duke. But Sir is good enough for a commoner. Contrast this with rewards conferred upon royal bastards.

Coat of arms—half lion & half cur.

Viele antworten sind besser LANG als KURZ[173]

ich bin g ven[n] dass [we]ter gut ist
[un]d w[enn] wohl sei GUT.—

Wenn ich das glück andre gang verderben kann

Das wort zubring has nicht ⟨ges⟩ das rechte Geschlect. [#]

Academy hearing Adelina Patti in some opera. Howells noticed the wicked leer in Mark's eye and questioned him. Mark, heaving a big sigh, said through his teeth in Howell's ear: 'I would rather sleep with that woman *stark naked*, than with General Grant in full uniform!'" (New York: G. P. Putnam's Sons, 1946, p. 169).

[171] Clemens included this anecdote in a political speech of 1901 (*MTS*[1910], p. 117).

[172] Sir William Withey Gull, physician to Queen Victoria and the Prince of Wales, died on 29 January 1890. Both the New York *Times* and the London *Times* reported Gull's death on 30 January and sketched his career. Gull's professional success was partially attributed to his attendance on the Prince of Wales through a severe bout of typhoid fever in December 1871. "He was given chief credit for the Prince's recovery," stated the New York *Times*, "and as a mark of the esteem and confidence in which he was held by the Queen was the next year created a baronet."

[173] *Many answers are better long than short.* The following three entries are badly written and can be translated only approximately: *I am g when the weather is good and well if it would be good. If I can completely spoil another's luck. The word zubring doesn't have the right gender.*

H BREI
VIELE.
Nat[--] – – – – – – Kochin ⟨ALS GUT⟩als gut[174]

Title:
Monarchy
"by the Grace of God".

We admit martyrs but not fools.

Margaretta Hohndorf
% Mr. Joseph Haight
210 E. 15th st

Gardiner's Elixir of Hypophosphites of Lime & soda. 3
teaspoonfuls in water after each meal.

& 1 2-gr quinine pill daily before breakfast & dinner

Hot water gargle for 2 days.

Do a deal of resting.[175]

Monarchical govt is a system invented to secure the comfort,
safety & prosperity of the few; ⟨a⟩ republiclican govt is a system
invented to secure the liberty, comfort, safety & prosperity of the
many.
England's coat of arms should be a lion's head & shoulders
welded onto a cur's hindquarters.

"On the 8-hour scheme public" (capitalist-employer) "opinion is
almost unanimous" (if this were true, there'd be no argument)
"that it should be left to voluntary action." That is, no legislation.
The English laws don't allow a man to shoot himself, but you see
these people don't want to make a law to prevent a man's

---

[174] This entry may involve a play on *viele Köche verderben den Brei*—"too many cooks
spoil the broth."

[175] This course of treatment was probably prescribed for Livy Clemens, who was
stricken with quinsy during a stay in New York City in mid-February 1890. In a letter to
Grace King of 25 February, Livy wrote that she was "just getting well from an attack of
Quinzy," having been bedridden for "nearly a week in New York with Mr Clemens as
nurse" (Grace King Papers, Louisiana State University, Baton Rouge).

committing half-suicide & being other-half murdered by overwork—
& his family left destitute. No legislation to strengthen the hands
of these despised strugglers. Why doesn't the Church (which is a
part of aristocracy) leave tithes & other robberies to "voluntary
action"?[176]

Monarchy? Why it is out of date. It belongs to the stage of
culture that admires a ring in your nose, a head full of feathers, &
your belly painted blue.

Assassination of a crowned head whenever & wherever
opportunity offers, should be the first article of all subjects' religion.

⟨[-]⟩Always (of course) Saviors have come in the costume of the
time. Pictures of our Second Advent are going to lose something by
this, unless clawhammer coats go out, meantime.

It was that kind of so-called "housekeeping" where they have six
Bibles to one cork-screw.

Feb. 1890.
It has always been a Cleveland-street aristocracy, the British.[177] [#]

---

[176] In the United States labor union agitation for shorter hours resulted in some unsatisfactory eight-hour day legislation in a few states in 1867. Strikes and demonstrations
in 1886 and the demonstrations of 1 May 1890 resulted in more substantial gains. In
1892 Congress legitimized the eight-hour movement by approving a bill establishing the
eight-hour day for laborers employed on government-sponsored public works. In England
progress was slower: interest in the eight-hour movement became widespread in 1889
and 1890, but the shorter day did not become a reality for the great mass of workers until
after World War I.

[177] The private club at 19 Cleveland Street in London, catering to the homosexual and
perverse tastes of a number of titled personages, was discovered by the police in the summer of 1889. The police investigation, however, was impeded by the Home Office and by
the Prince of Wales, whose profligate son Albert Victor, duke of Clarence, was implicated. Some of the implicated nobles were allowed to escape to the Continent and attempts were made to remove crucial witnesses. Apparently no report of the case appeared
in London newspapers until November 1889 when Henry Labouchere, editor of the
London weekly *Truth*, aroused public indignation with his revelation of the cover-up.
Clemens probably read of the affair in the columns of the New York *Times* in November
1889. Official and royal efforts to suppress the scandal were successful. The dossier on
the case, comprising documents dating from 1882 until 1889, was not made available to
the public by the English government until March 1975.

⟨"I have a suspicion⟩ "Ich hege die Verdacht dass Sie den unrechter Mench geshneidet habe." [178]

"Den Hund hat seinen *Tag* gefressen." (chewed off).
(—abgekauert.)

Write "Eleven thousand eleven hundred & eleven" in figures.

Prairie dog.

All governments begin with election by majority.

If heredity is good, it should be extended to judgeships, doctors, & all—otherwise its logic won't wash.

Englishman came to my town & criticised.
So have a thousand in books.

Dickens, Marryatt, [179] Mrs. Trollope, Sir Griffin (?) & Arnold.

But all failed to dectect our chiefest advantage, & its meaning.

That govt is not best which best secures mere life & property—there is a more valuable thing—Manhood.

Rolfe's Shakspeare for Elsie Leslie.—See Harpers. [180]

⟨Watch, at Tiffany's.⟩

⟨Cheap-book scheme. [181] [#]

---

[178] *I have a suspicion that they've cut the wrong person.* The following entry reads: *The dog has chewed off his* Tag.

[179] Frederick Marryat had criticized American institutions and society in his *Diary in America* (1839). Clemens had previously noted the other English critics of America in Notebook 28 (see p. 467, note 208).

[180] William James Rolfe was editor of a twenty-volume edition of Shakespeare's works published by Harper & Brothers from 1871 to 1884. The complete set sold for thirty to sixty dollars, depending on the quality of the binding.

[181] Fred Hall wrote to Clemens on 25 February 1890 with an advertising scheme primarily intended to bolster the publishing company's sales during the sluggish summer season. "I thought of getting up a little pamphlet, such as would sell for five or ten cents on

Mrs. Ratcliffe.[182]

Grant pictures⟩

For some centuries your laws have been made by the King, Cleveland-street & the Commons.

5,000-em, $12,000.
6,000　"　15,000
7,000　"　18,000
8,000　"　20,000

Had I best appeal, or sit still & let the others do the fighting?[183] Here are the points:

1. My letter of Dec 17 & H's response of Dec 24, 1886, constitute a contract.

2. Then is it anywhere claimed that H is to pay *me* a share of the proceeds? Isn't it always I that am to pay *him*? I think so.

a. Then if this injunction is made permanent, ⟨[h]e cannot [co]⟩—

b. He cannot contract with Frohman for *his* piece, ⟨but⟩ without my first-secured consent;　?

c. And Froh, H. & Richardson cannot compromise on the present play without my consent?

d. If I am *compelled* to make a contract for the production of H.'s piece, I can make the terms as ridiculous as I please, provided I give him half? Ten dollars a year, say? [#]

---

news stands, elevated stands, etc. . . . The inside cover of each book and half a page of each book to be devoted to the advertising of our works, and half the pages to reading matter. . . . It strikes me to be the best kind of advertising. This would also pave the way and assist the sale of any cheap edition of your works."

[182] See page 501, note 65. Livy wrote to her mother Mrs. Jervis Langdon on 2 February 1890: "I hope to have Mrs. Ratcliffe here sometime during the next two months. I should like very much to do it while you & Sue [Crane] are here" (MTM).

[183] Clemens' several entries at this point in the notebook are a response to legal developments in March 1890 in the case of *Edward H. House* v. *Clemens, Richardson, and Frohman.* House had initiated injunction proceedings in January 1890 against Mrs. Richardson's dramatization of *The Prince and the Pauper.* The suit was largely based on two letters: on 17 December 1886 Clemens had suggested that House attempt a dramatization of *The Prince and the Pauper* and on 24 December House had expressed

B.

The Judge's decision seems to say Mr. H. cannot get damages—has no recourse of that kind.

a. Then ⟨his⟩ Frohman's stopping my royalties by the strong hand & without command or suggestion from any court, is his own private act, & a deliberate annulment of our contract⟨?⟩—if I see fit to enforce that clause? (THIS IS WHAT I DEARLY WANT TO DO.) I want to kill that contract & stop the ⟨piece⟩ present piece, & also I want to prevent House from reinstating the present piece or playing his own.

MY NOTION

is, that I ought to immediately terminate my Frohman contract if it be possible—

(That would be joy!) [184]

Then lay for the firm of Frohman, House & Co., & defeat their every attempt to get up a satisfactory ⟨attempt⟩ contract for a resumption of business. [#]

---

his willingness. When in February 1889 House heard rumors of Mrs. Richardson's play he wrote reminding Clemens of his prior claim. Clemens' reply on 19 March, while apparently cordial, was guarded. "If you have a previous [contract]," he wrote, "I beg you to send me a copy. & I will come as near setting things exactly right as possible" (Clifton Waller Barrett Library, University. of Virginia, Charlottesville). Clemens stubbornly held to his own definition of "contract" as a formal, notarized document—a definition which unfortunately had no legal validity. House responded by initiating legal proceedings. All friendly communication with Clemens ceased. Mrs. Richardson's play, produced by theatrical manager Daniel Frohman, opened in Philadelphia on 24 December 1889 and in New York City on 20 January 1890. After examining the numerous affidavits filed by the various parties in the case, Judge Joseph F. Daly of the Court of Common Pleas on 8 March 1890 decided that the two December 1886 letters constituted a legal contract and granted a temporary injunction which prohibited performance of the play unless House's consent was obtained. On 12 March 1890 Daniel Frohman's attorneys notified Clemens' lawyer Daniel Whitford that Frohman had "been compelled in order to obtain [House's] consent, to arrange with the plaintiff for a deposit with his attorneys for the royalties accruing to Mr. Clemens." Clemens' weekly royalty checks, received from 1 January through 10 March 1890, ceased henceforth. The complete history of the lawsuit and its aftermath is the subject of Paul Fatout's "Mark Twain, Litigant" (*American Literature*, March 1959, pp. 30–45).

[184] Clemens welcomed the idea of preventing performances of Mrs. Richardson's play and had attempted to do so shortly before this entry was written. The entire Clemens family had gone to New York City for the opening night of the play and, as Livy noted,

Then finally, let Mrs. Richardson proceed against me. I should not mind that. She has been my enemy from the start, but she has been an honorable one, & frank & open. That kind would sit at the right hand of God, if ⟨merit⟩Merit ⟨& ⟨gol⟩god⟩ & ⟨godliness⟩Godliness were placed according to right values up yonder.

⟨Her suit would b[e] [against a man] who made a contract with her, [⟨not⟩] supposing she had a right [to do it]⟩

Gillette has a prior & stronger contract. Let *him* bring suit.[185] [#]

---

they had initially been "uncritical," being "carried along" by the enthusiastic audience (OLC to Sam and Mary Moffett, 30 January 1890). Livy wrote to her friend Grace King on 25 February that the family found the play a "real disappointment." "In the main it is poor," she added, "and does not in the least do the book, we think, justice. Such inferior English is put into the mouths of the actors in many places" (Grace King Papers, Louisiana State University, Baton Rouge). Clemens reacted with a characteristically vitriolic letter to Daniel Frohman on 2 February 1890, which, however, he never mailed. He had been "bewitched" by Elsie Leslie's performance at first, but later he realized that the play was a mere "burlesque" whose language was "ludicrous" (Doheny). Clemens immediately made extensive revisions of Mrs. Richardson's play, intending to use his version for the English production. Frohman later recalled that "though Mr. Clemens's work was admirable, it was not so suited to acting requirements as the adaptation I was using; so I returned it to the author with my very adequate but, to him, unconvincing reasons for its rejection" (Daniel Frohman, *Memories of a Manager* [London: William Heinemann, 1911], pp. 51–52). Within a few days Clemens discovered that he had no authority over the English production since the rights lay with his English publisher Chatto & Windus, and he abandoned plans for supplanting Mrs. Richardson's play with his own version.

[185] Clemens' affidavit of 23 January 1890, one of the documents in the lawsuit over *The Prince and the Pauper*, mentioned that actor and playwright William Gillette had "done some work in shaping" a dramatization of the novel. "I do not know how much he did to put a play together," declared Clemens, "but he did not complete it or make any arrangement about putting it upon the stage." Presumably, Clemens is referring to the dramatization which he attempted early in 1884 and which he asked Gillette to read. Gillette felt that Clemens' version had "the backbone of a good piece—very striking and interesting" but that "a considerable amount of dressing up and rearranging" would be needed "to bring out the points" (Gillette to SLC, 27 May 1884). He offered to suggest revisions of the play, or to collaborate with Clemens on it, but there is no evidence that he did so. Moreover it is clear that Gillette did not consider that he had any rights over the dramatization. Clemens hoped that by emphasizing Gillette's early involvement with the play he would discredit House's later claim on it. It is exceedingly unlikely, however, that Gillette could have been persuaded to bring a countersuit merely to forestall House's injunction.

Can the General Term ⟨knock me entirely in the head by⟩ try⟨ing⟩ the case over again & admit⟨ting⟩ additional evidence?[186]

—& can I admit evidence that H is an habitual liar?

—& can that court decide wholly against me & give H specific damages?

Der Knabe muss täglich 7 Bücher um 25^c verkaufen, dann bekommt er $1 täglich. Für jeden Buch mehr als 7, bekommt er 10^c per Exemplar.

Für 50^c Bücher bekommt er $1 für 4. Für jeden mehr als 4, bekommt er 20^c.

Für irgendeiner 10^c Buch bekommt er $1 für 15, und 5^c für ein jeder mehr als 15 täglich.[187]

House didn't write Arrah na Pogue.[188] [#]

----

[186] Daniel Whitford assumed that Clemens would wish to appeal Judge Daly's decision. "You will see that the decision rests entirely upon the two letters of December 1886, which he construes to be a valid contract. If he is wrong in this his whole decision falls," wrote Whitford on 11 March 1890. "There are two appellate tribunals that can pass upon this question—the General Term of the Court of Common Pleas and the Court of Appeals." Whitford warned Clemens, however, that although Daly's opinion might be appealed, there was nothing to be gained in retrying the case or admitting new evidence, since the whole matter turned upon one legal issue—the contractual validity of the two 1886 letters.

[187] The preceding three entries read: *The boy has to sell 7 books a day for 25^c, then he will get $1 a day. For every book over 7 he will get 10^c a copy. For 50^c books he'll receive $1 for 4. For every one more than 4, he gets 20^c. For any 10^c book he'll get $1 for 15, and 5^c for each one above 15 a day.*

[188] Dion Boucicault's Irish play *Arrah-na-Pogue; or, The Wicklow Wedding* opened in Dublin in November 1864 and in London and New York City in 1865. Edward H. House had apparently been involved in theatrical work in the mid-1860s, but his purported collaboration with Boucicault has not been fully substantiated. In an unfinished manuscript titled "Concerning the Scoundrel Edward H. House" written in March 1890 Clemens explains that he suggested that House dramatize *The Prince and the Pauper* "because he had told me more than once that he wrote the bulk of 'Arrah na Pogue.'" "I have been laughed at for believing Mr. House's statement," added Clemens, "but I did believe it, all the same. He told me that his share of the proceeds was $25,000. A theatre manager assures me that Mr. House merely wrote a few lines in 'Arrah no Pogue' to protect Mr. Boucicault's rights here against pirates." In a later recollection, which, however, contains so many errors and embroideries that it is unreliable, Clemens states

John B. Carson (New York?)

Hearst & Hitt.[189]

It is 3,500 an hour, utmost—Mch '90.[190]

This sordid soul. Centred solely in himself.

Belle Shreve Nuñez 9 am to-morrow.

& U. S. Grant[191] same hour.

Maid below, no extra charge, electric bell—right below. Or in our room no extra charge.

Optician
⟨Dʳ⟩ Crosse, 16 W 23 [#]

---

that Boucicault when he heard House's claim about *Arrah-na-Pogue* "laughed at it and said it was a straight lie, with not a vestige of truth in it" (Autobiographical Dictation, 28 August 1907). House did secure American copyright for *Arrah-na-Pogue* in December 1891 and is named as co-author with Boucicault of "The Wearing of the Green," a popular song from the play.

[189] George F. Hearst was the influential California mining millionaire and United States senator. Robert R. Hitt, whom Clemens had met in Paris in 1879 when Hitt was secretary of the American legation, was currently a congressman from Illinois and chairman of the Committee on Foreign Affairs. The New York *Tribune* noted the arrival of Hearst in New York City on 8 March 1890, and of Hitt on 12 March 1890. Clemens' arrival at the Murray Hill Hotel was reported on 12 March and again on 28 March. Presumably Clemens hoped to see Hearst and Hitt in connection with his efforts to finance the Paige typesetter.

[190] Clemens wrote to Joseph T. Goodman on 31 March 1890: "There's an improved Mergenthaler in New York; Paige and [Charles E.] Davis and I watched it two whole afternoons" (*MTL*, p. 531). This was the Simplex Linotype (Model 1), the culmination of Ottmar Mergenthaler's years of experimentation. The Simplex was destined to surpass and supplant all other typesetters, but Clemens, after viewing it in action, was unimpressed. He did realize, however, that the successful performance of the Simplex would dampen interest in the Paige machine. He wrote Goodman on 18 April: "The Mergenthaler, which was dead, has come to life again. In this way: they've got a new machine on a changed plan; it is the customary gravity machine like all the others, except that matrices instead of type flow down the grooves & channels & form a line. Paige, Davis & I have watched it work, & think it is both better & worse than the old machine. We saw an expert turn out 2,250 ems in 30 minutes, with only 3 typographical errors & one bad face. . . . We considered it liberal to call it a 3500-em machine, (corrected matter.) But they talk as glibly as they've always done, & make as prodigious claims as they used to when the old machine was a new wonder" (Yale).

[191] Presumably Grant's son, lawyer Ulysses S. Grant, Jr.

Champagne ⎫
                  ⎬ these are the choice boats.
Bretagne ⎭

Majestic & Teutonic, und White Star.[192]

9th Apl. Navy Club

27th Apl (Sunday) Everett House, Max O'Rell[193]

Apl. 7/90. Marty[194] corrected 23 errors (some of them bad ones,) in $6\frac{1}{2}$ minutes. About 4 errors to the minute. Linotype corrects about 1 error per minute (& loses the whole line)—that is, sets it twice, pays for it twice, & double or ⟨quad⟩ treble price for the second setting.

Roget's Thesaurus.

Mrs. Cleveland.

Mr. Barnum.[195] [#]

---

[192] Livy wrote to her mother on 10 March 1890 of their plans to spend the summer in Europe rather than at Quarry Farm: "We are not entirely certain yet whether we can go or not, it will depend somewhat upon Mr Clemens business. It may be that it will be necessary for him to go to England on account of the machine, and then of course we should be with him. Then we want to have the children settle in France for a little while on account of their French. If Susy enters Bryn Mawr next year she must get more French during the Summer & this seems the best way to do it" (MTM). Clemens made inquiries as to accommodations on various steamship lines. *La Champagne* and *La Bretagne* were ships of the Compagnie Générale Transatlantique; the *Majestic* and the *Teutonic* were ships of the White Star Line. Clemens booked staterooms on the Inman Line's *City of New York* sailing on 4 June 1890, then apparently canceled these reservations. He wrote to his sister Pamela Moffett on 13 May: "We sail for the Pyrennees either June 7 or July 5, I reckon" (*MTBus*, p. 393). The Clemenses ultimately decided against the European trip and spent the summer instead in the Catskills.

[193] French author and lecturer Paul Blouet (known as Max O'Rell) was in America from January through April 1890 on a lecture tour under the management of Major James B. Pond. Pond arranged a farewell breakfast for Blouet at his headquarters in the Everett House hotel in New York City on 27 April 1890. The guests included Clemens, George Kennan, E. C. Stedman, Richard Watson Gilder, Augustin Daly, General Horace Porter, and Lloyd Stephens Bryce.

[194] Printer Martin J. Slattery was involved in perfecting the Paige typesetter.

[195] The New York *Tribune* announced the arrival of P. T. Barnum at the Murray Hill Hotel in New York City on 24 March 1890. Barnum had just completed a highly success-ful English tour. Clemens arrived at the Murray Hill Hotel a few days later and presum-ably met with Barnum whom he had known for many years.

Andrew Carnegie, 12 Broad.

Whitford—if I go on business can I be stopped?[196]

Do you know, & can you *swear* you can defer it to October?

About Carnegie Books[197]

Edison—Lathrop.[198] [#]

---

[196] Edward House's lawsuit over the dramatization of *The Prince and the Pauper* had been only temporarily resolved by Judge Daly's injunction. House's lawyers intended to appeal for a permanent injunction either in June or in the fall of 1890. Clemens' attorney Daniel Whitford wrote on 8 April 1890 warning Clemens that his projected trip to Europe might cause difficulties. "If you were to be in the country," he explained, "[House's attorneys] would probably make no serious objection to its going over until [the fall] but as they understand you are going they will push it as hard as they can and perhaps try to detain you by subpoenaing you as a witness." The issue was resolved by 20 May when Whitford informed Clemens: "The House case is over until October so you need fear no annoyance. I suppose before that time you will be home again." In any event, Clemens ultimately canceled his planned European trip.

[197] Andrew Carnegie had written two popular books of travel, published in 1883 and 1884. His controversial and highly personal *Triumphant Democracy*, a paean to the democratic system and to America's material wealth, appeared in 1886. Frederick J. Hall wrote to Clemens on 13 March 1890: "I have sent you by express a set of Carnegies works to which he referred in the letter which I sent you. You will notice he has turned down certain pages and written on the title page. . . . Carnegie seems inclined to consider giving us his next book and as his works sell well it is wise to keep on the right side of him." Clemens sent Carnegie a short note of thanks for the books on 17 March, in which he wrote: "The Triumphant Republic is a favorite of mine, & helped to fire me up for my last book. I am reading it again, now" (Carnegie Collection, New York Public Library). Fred Hall was able to report to Clemens on 15 May: "Received a letter from Carnegie yesterday, in which he said that his book was not yet far enough advanced to say anything definite, but that when it was he would not forget our '*enterprising firm*.'" Carnegie's next book-length work, *The Gospel of Wealth and Other Timely Essays*, would not appear until 1900.

[198] George Parsons Lathrop's article "Talks with Edison" appeared in the February 1890 *Harper's* and probably caught Clemens' attention. In July 1888 Charles L. Webster & Company had been interested in publishing Thomas A. Edison's autobiography, a book apparently suggested to them by Lathrop. The autobiographical work did not materialize but neither Hall nor Clemens completely gave up the idea of capitalizing on the public's interest in Edison. On 7 October 1890 Hall wrote to Clemens suggesting that a book by Edison on electricity—"written with the idea of bringing within the comprehension of ordinary intelligent people who are not electricians the developements that have been made in the use of electricity during the past two years"—would be more profitable than an autobiography. Clemens' response was tepid but he added: "Still, if

Brusnahan.

Mrs. Grant's Memoirs.[199]

Gen. Butler's book.[200]

Take from the time he touches the bolt that sends the line away from before his face till that line of matrices have been elevated to the top preparatory to being distributed. This tells how long it takes to *cast*.

Leave us ⟨[1]o⟩20 pc, you can have them for ⟨6⟩3 m., ⟨15 pc⟩ 15, p.c. 4,500 m, 10 pc, 6 m, or the whole for 8½ m ⟨Sck⟩ Agt, to have: 1, 100,000; 2, 200,000; 3, 300,000; 4, 500,000. Sck to have: 1, ⟨10,000⟩20,000; 2, ⟨20,000⟩40,000; 3, ⟨30,000⟩60,000; 4, ⟨50,000⟩100,000.[201] [#]

---

you will remind me next time I am down, I will send Geo. Lathrop to ask him if he will dictate a book for us into the phonograph" (SLC to Frederick J. Hall, 15 October 1890, *MTLP*, p. 262).

[199] Julia Dent Grant had begun dictating her memoirs as early as 1886 or 1887, but the agreement with Charles L. Webster & Company prohibited her from publishing any work which might compete with the *Personal Memoirs of U. S. Grant* until May 1889. Mrs. Grant's memoirs remained unpublished, despite her high hopes for the book, until 1975 (see *The Personal Memoirs of Julia Dent Grant*, ed. John Y. Simon [New York: G. P. Putnam's Sons, 1975], pp. 18–19, 22–23).

[200] The controversial Civil War commander and politician produced a weighty one-volume memoir, *Autobiography and Personal Reminiscences of Major-General Benj. F. Butler; Butler's Book* (Boston: A. M. Thayer & Co., 1892), which was sold by subscription. Clemens probably heard rumors of Butler's literary work and hoped to secure it for his publishing house's series of military memoirs.

[201] William Hamersley wrote to Clemens on 3 May 1890 with long-awaited news: Paige had finally pronounced the typesetter complete and ready for exhibition, and he was urging Clemens to find advance orders for the machine as an "inducement to capital." Paige's announcement came opportunely: Clemens' funds had been drained by the machine and he had notified Paige that he would "scrape together $6,000 to meet the March and April expenses" but that unless he found some outside "financial relief" he would be forced to withdraw his backing at the end of April (SLC to Joseph T. Goodman, 31 March 1890, *MTL*, p. 531). In the letter of 3 May, Hamersley enclosed a draft of a statement to be sent to the newspapers announcing the completion of the machine and the imminent formation of a joint stock company "with a capital stock of at least $10,000,000, and with at least $3,000,000 of the capital stock paid in cash at the time of the organization." The statement solicited orders for the first 500 machines. Clemens' several notebook entries at this point, dealing with plans for capitalization and also testing of the machine, are apparently a response to Hamersley's news.

⟨25⟩30 p.c. 2 m; ⟨33⅓⟩40 pc., 1 m.

They can have ⅓ of Amer for 6 m⟨.⟩—the cap to be 39 m; 6 m to be sold but not below par; they to receive of all divids 90 pc till 6 m paid back.

3 Can't turn out	6,000 cor. m. in 1 h.		
⟨3.⟩4. " " "	5,500 " " " "		
⟨4.⟩5. " " "	5,000 " " " "		
⟨5.⟩6 " " "	4,500 " " " "		
⟨6.⟩7. " " "	4,000 " " " "		
⟨7.⟩8. " " "	7,500 " " " 2 h.		
⟨8⟩9 " " "	⟨13,000⟩⟨14,000⟩28,000 cor. m. in ⟨4⟩8 h.		

1. " " "	2,500 " " " ¼ "		
2. " " "	⟨5,000⟩2,000 cor. m. in ¼ h.		

Can't do No. 9 six successive days.
    "   "   "   " 12   "   "

Proof to be corrected, then REVISED *twice or 3 times*

In each instance, he shall set during the full time stipulated; then ⟨the time taken to correct the proof shall be subtracted from the result. Z. B.[202] If he set 6000 in an hour & it take 10 minutes to correct the proof, ⟨he⟩⟩ ⟨the lines containing errors & unpassable faces shall be subtracted as being non-existent⟩ the time taken to correct the proof shall be subtracted from the result. Z. B. If he set 6000 in an hour & it take 10 minutes to correct the proof, he has then taken 70 min to produce 6,000, & the rate is *so-much* per hour, but isn't 6,000⟨.⟩; it is only 5,160.

Copy to be N.Y. editorials of *that morning*. Begin at top of 2ᵈ column & set the rest of the page *except* poetry & tabular work.

Both Mergs, 8 men, to our one P & 4 ⟨[men—]⟩apprentices. 6 days & nights without stop. Then correct the mass, & revise & correct until no errors left. Time to be kept, & a watch. Ignore *words* left out or doubled.

It is *all* preferred stock till the capital [#]

---

[202] The abbreviation for the German phrase *zum Beispiel* meaning "for example."

⟨⟨3¼⟩ All of ⟨their⟩ ⟨our⟩ their stock & ¼ of ours to be preferred stock until the capital is returned.⟩

Ballyhooly.[203]
Hall, give me sheets 495–507 inclusive.[204]

Conway,
8 Delamere Terrace[205]
  Bayswater,
    London W

Stanley, Sir Francis de Winton, Dawson.[206]

Read something from Col. Sellers. Turnips[207]

Talk to Sat. Morning Club here May 10.[208]

McDowell's Origin of the Irish.

"Save him, save him, he's got de bait!" [#]

---

[203] Clemens may be referring to the song "Ballyhooly" by Robert Martin, whose composition "Killaloe" he cited earlier (see p. 450, note 143).

[204] These pages of *A Connecticut Yankee* contain the complete text of chapter 39, "The Yankee's Fight with the Knights."

[205] Moncure Conway, a preacher and author well known in literary circles in England and America, had formerly acted as Clemens' English agent in literary matters. The two men saw each other rarely yet kept up a cordial friendship. Clemens probably made a note of Conway's English address with the intention of answering his letter of 12 April 1890, which contains a detailed and laudatory description of the opening night of the English production of *The Prince and the Pauper*.

[206] See page 494, note 39. Henry M. Stanley had lingered in Africa and on the Continent for several months after disbanding his Emin Pasha Relief Expedition in December 1889. He finally arrived in England on 26 April 1890. News of his arrival may have occasioned Clemens' notebook entry: presumably Clemens wished to approach him, possibly through the medium of the two men whose names he notes here. Clemens had met Sir Francis de Winton in May 1883 in Ottawa where de Winton was acting as secretary to the marquis of Lorne, governor general of Canada. In 1884 de Winton had succeeded Stanley as coadjutor of the Congo and was thenceforth his close associate and friend. Samuel E. Dawson, retired Montreal publisher, had until recently acted as Clemens' Canadian publisher.

[207] The account of the Sellers family's frugal repast of turnips and water occurs in chapter 11 of *The Gilded Age*.

[208] There is no record that Clemens made any formal address to the young girls of Hartford's Saturday Morning Club between 1888 and 1907.

"When I catch the one I'm after & two more, I'll have 3."

Public Printer come.[209]

1. Verbesserung der Document
a. $25,000 ausgestricken.
b. Actien-Co stiftet *sogleich.*[210]

1. Vortrag beim Connery—brass^{t.}[211]

Der Engländer?

Herr Case?

Muss nach N. York gehen Ausstellung zu führen.[212]

Donnerstag, nach Washington[213]

Auf Rückkehr, Laffan sehen[214]

Hearst, 1400 N. H. Ave.[215]

And make it so that Herr J. can buy my whole interest out
& out.[216] [#]

---

[209] Clemens intended to invite the head of the Government Printing Office, Public Printer Frank W. Palmer, to the planned test exhibition of the Paige typesetter.

[210] *1. Improvement of the document a. $25,000 deleted. b. joint-stock co established immediately.* The same unspecified document is the subject of three entries beginning with "And make it so" (552.13) on the facing notebook page. The relationship between the entries is indicated by an arrow and a hand pointing across the hinge of the notebook.

[211] *Report from Connery*—brass^{t.} This entry may refer to the improved brass type which Clemens had been attempting to market (see p. 534, note 161). Thomas B. J. Connery, formerly managing editor of the New York *Herald*, was now editor of the New York *Truth.*

[212] *Must go to N. York to manage the drawing up of the contract.*

[213] *Thursday, to Washington.* Clemens went to Washington, D.C., around 8 May 1890 for a few days.

[214] *On return trip, see Laffan.*

[215] R. U. Johnson wrote to Clemens at the Arlington Hotel in Washington, D.C., on 10 May 1890 from the Hearst home, forwarding a dinner invitation from Mrs. George Hearst (see note 255).

[216] This entry and the two German entries that follow it concern the document referred to at 552.3–5 (see note 210). The German reads: *Or, a new contract without Conditions. Take out the foreign patents and collect the sum total in all five countries—*$1/5$ *in France,* $1/5$ *in Germany,* $2/5$ *in England,* &c. $1/5$ *or* $2/5$ *here.*

Oder, eine neues Document ohne *Conditions*.

Hinsetzen die Fremden patente, & die Hauptsumne in alle fünf Ländern sammeln—⅕ in Frankreich, ⅕ in Deutchland, ⅖ in England, &c. ⅕ oder ⅖ hier.

10 gals whisky in an 8-gal keg. Strained it.

Bill Nye's bald-headed brother.

Pretend to get Arba Langton's views on all great subjects.[217]

When one-dollar men order *more*, they must stand the raise.

"Man don't get his *Same* back."

Take German idioms from Adler.[218]

French from — — ——

May 19
Cheney, train 4.50, return 10.15.[219]

Wide spacing costs the Trib. ⟨24⟩25 lines in a column of small type, ⟨leaded⟩ solid. Thus they pay for 5,000 ems on each page which they don't *get*. It is more than 300,000 ems a week.

They pay 20^c per 1000. So they pay more than $60 a week unnecessarily.

$$\frac{52}{\$3,220 \text{ a year.}} \quad [\#]$$

---

[217] The Hartford directory contains a full-page advertisement for the nostrums of Arba Lankton, "Practical Helminthologist" (*Geer's* [1890], p. 424I). Lankton's "Tape Worm Expeller," "Corn Salve," "Pile Ointment," and "Worm Syrup" are described and testimonials from grateful users are quoted. Lankton is also listed as a manufacturer of popcorn and the president of the Arba Lankton Total Abstinence Society.

[218] George J. Adler compiled a much-reprinted *Dictionary of the German and English Languages*, first published by D. Appleton & Company in 1849.

[219] The next meeting of the Monday Evening Club was to be on 19 May at the home of Frank W. Cheney in South Manchester, Connecticut. Although Clemens noted the train schedule for the trip to South Manchester, on the envelope of his invitation he instructed Franklin Whitmore to inform the club that he would be away in New York City at the time of the meeting.

The World would lose 235 lines in ⟨a⟩2 pages & a half of "Wants (20 cols.) by Rogers spacing.[220]

It would take 3⟨½⟩ Roges' to set up one of those pages in 7 hours—which would cost ⟨$1[4]⟩$12 for composition on ⟨$7-wo⟩$7,000-worth of machines; the lost lines are worth $6 to the paper: total cost, ⟨$20⟩$18 for the page—& somebody must put in the brass rules besides, & get paid for it.

We would ⟨come within an hour & a half of⟩ do⟨ing⟩ the page, brass rules & all, on one machine in 8½ hours—total cost, $4.75. Saving, $13.   365

$$\begin{array}{r} 365 \\ 13 \\ \hline 1095 \\ 365 \text{ a year} \\ \hline \$4{,}745 \end{array}$$

Rogers is a 2500-em per hour, corrected matter. Composition on it must cost 25^c. Composition on ours cannot cost more than 7^c. They reduce $150,000 a year to $75,000. We reduce it to below $20,000.

Prendergast—Appleton.[221] [#]

---

[220] John R. Rogers obtained a patent on a preliminary version of his Typograph in September 1888 and the following year improved and modified the machine. The final Typograph was a practical, small-sized, slug-casting machine quite similar in concept to the Mergenthaler Linotype. Rogers and his partner Fred E. Bright filed for patents on their Typograph in February and April 1890 and the patent rights were granted on 23 September 1890. Hundreds of advance orders were secured and manufacture of the machine was begun, but the Rogers Typograph Company was balked early in 1891 by an injunction for infringement of patent brought against it by the Mergenthaler company. The Mergenthaler company eventually bought out Rogers' company and all its patents, and Rogers became one of the most valuable members of the Mergenthaler staff. Clemens' notebook entries, written in the spring of 1890 when Rogers' patents were still pending, indicate that he had advance information about the Typograph. Spacing and justification on the Rogers machine were accomplished by adjustable rotating disks and the copy produced was comparatively open in appearance.

[221] Thomas Prendergast's "mastery series" of language instruction books was published by D. Appleton and Company of New York.

Care Jno Monroe & Co[222]
7 rue Scribe,
M. Pouchere, ⟨guide⟩ courier £5 a day

W W Pasko[223]
19 Park Place
Typothetæ
From 9 a.m. to 5 p.m.

Geo. W. Childs[224]
Bryn Mawr.

Philip S. Garrett

Francis R Cope

Jas. Whittall.[225]

Edw. Bettle, Jr.
2007 Ches^{nt}
512 Walnut

1104 Spruce st Hon. Cor. Sec.
Mary McMurtry [#]

---

[222] The Clemenses had used the office of Munroe & Company, bankers, as their mailing address while in Paris in 1879. Presumably Clemens noted the name here in connection with his still unsettled plans for a European trip in the summer of 1890.

A clipping from a New York newspaper was interleaved between the facing pages that bear this and the following entries (555.1–556.6). The clipping, headed "JEALOUSY'S CRIME. Jacob Epstein Shoots His Wife and Himself," tells a story that was printed in the New York *Herald, Times, Tribune,* and *World* for 30 May 1890, although this clipping came from none of those newspapers. Clemens' reason for saving the story is unknown, but it is interesting that in April 1888 he had written in his notebook "'He shot his wife & then himself'" (p. 382.7).

[223] Wesley Washington Pasko was recording secretary of the New York Typothetae, the association of master printers with offices at 19 Park Place in New York City.

[224] Philadelphia publisher George W. Childs had a large country residence at Bryn Mawr, Pennsylvania.

[225] Philip Cresson Garrett was president of the board of trustees of Bryn Mawr College. Francis R. Cope and James Whitall were both members of the board.

1

Can one get carriage at Station B.M. all hours?[226]

2

Can get lunch there, or must carry it out?

3

Any hotel or place a body can stay the long day?

Bets, Atterbury & Bets. 120 B'way.

19 Park Place.

Wenn Sie Eine Grösse mache, Eine ⟨millione⟩Millionen ist genug; aber wenn man 6 machen will, wird 3 Millionen unentbehrlich.[227]

Derr Herr Mackay sagt; "— — kann so viel Gelt nicht verschaffen."

Erstens, wird von das *Ausfuhrung* gesprochen.

Zweitens, Bericht machen über die Zusammenbrechung des Fairchildischen Entwurfs.[228] [#]

---

[226] Livy reminded Clemens on 21 May 1890: "Next week we must take the children to Bryn Mawr for their examinations." Susy Clemens took entrance examinations in several subjects and was accepted to the college with the provision that she pursue her studies during the summer so as to pass additional examinations before admission in the fall of 1890. Livy's remark suggests that Clara Clemens may have taken the Bryn Mawr examinations as well.

[227] At this point in his notebook Clemens wrote a number of entries in German outlining various propositions to be put to Senator John P. Jones regarding the projected joint-stock company and American and foreign rights to the machine. His figures and proposals, however, can hardly be taken seriously since they involve a capitalization of thirty million dollars. This first entry and the following two read: *If you make a big amount, a million is enough; but if one wants to make* 6, *3 million will be indispensable. Mr. Mackay says; "— — so much money can't be raised." First, exportation will be spoken about.*

[228] *Second, make a report about the collapse of Fairchild's plan.* Clemens may be referring to Charles Fairchild, a broker with the Boston firm of Lee, Higginson & Company, who was acquainted with Clemens through William Dean Howells. Fairchild apparently brought two potential investors—identified only as Ludlam and Livermore— to view the Paige typesetter. The two men came away feeling "that the wise thing to do now is to build a few machines and put them into actual use, and wait until they are fairly tested before putting up any large factory for building these machines." Fairchild

Drittens, dreissig Tagen Warnung geben.[229]

John M und die Telegraphische Erfindung.[230]

Wir müssen still bleiben drei Monate, bis die Leute vom Sommer Ferien zurückkommen dürfen.[231]

Verkaufen das Vortrag an Herr J. auf dass wir stark und unanhänglich werden.

Col (Joe's friend)

Carnegie & (Fuller's friend) Delamater.[232]

Ich will nicht gestehen dass unser Ausgabe ist beinahe drei Tausend ⟨monatlick.⟩monatlich.[233]

Das Buch des Herrn Jowens.

Col. Forsythe, Fresno.

Die Nebenbühler sind in Streit ⟨gereethen⟩geriethen.[234]

Hamersley wird nicht bezahlt werden.[235] [#]

---

added: "If I can do anything further for you at this stage of the proceedings, please command me" (Fairchild to SLC, 3 June 1890).

[229] *Third, give thirty days warning.*

[230] *John M and the telegraphic invention.* In 1883 John Mackay and James Gordon Bennett, Jr., of the New York *Herald,* formed the Commercial Cable Company in order to break Jay Gould's Atlantic cable monopoly. Mackay supplied seventy per cent of the capital. The rival cable was successfully completed in 1884 and became the chief among Mackay's financial interests.

[231] *We have to stay quiet for three months, until the people can return from summer vacation.* The following entry reads: *In the presentation to Mr. J. sell the idea that we will become strong and independent.*

[232] Probably Cornelius H. Delamater, president of the Delamater Iron Works of New York City. Clemens may not have been aware that Delamater had died in February 1889.

[233] *I don't want to confess that our expenditure is almost three thousand a month.*

[234] *The rivals had a dispute.*

[235] *Hamersley will not be paid.* Clemens had applied to Hartford attorney William Hamersley, his partner in the Paige typesetter enterprise, for a temporary loan to relieve the burden of the typesetter expenses. Hamersley responded on 3 April 1890 with a check for $2,500, stressing the fact that he could not risk anything more on the typesetter and that the loan should be considered a personal one payable by 1 July 1890. Clemens' continued financial distress, however, made repayment inconvenient and he had Franklin G. Whitmore inform Hamersley of that fact on 9 June 1890.

190 revolutions.

Actien-Gesellschafft von 30,000,000, 6,000,000 barr Gelt, und
$⟨1[-],000,000⟩⟨1[5],000,000⟩ $14,0,00⟨0⟩ ⟨[-]⟩ Theilen bekommen
dafür.[236]

300,000 Theilen.
Barr Gelt, ⟨1[3]0,000⟩⟨1[7]0,000⟩140,000 Theilen.
Wir, ⟨1[-]0,000⟩⟨180,000⟩ ⟨1[-]0,000⟩ 150,000 Theilen.
⟨G, [20,000] Theilen⟩
Wir müssen G. [--],000/10,000 Theilen geben.[237]
⟨Ich werde J. oder er und seinen Freunden ein Dritte der
Europaischen Eigenthum geben.⟩
Nein, diese muss in die Handel enthällt sein.
Endlich will ich die ⟨vollmacht⟩Vollmacht ersetz, durch proxy.
Wir werden ⁹⁄₁₀ geben bis die 6,000,000 bezahlt sei.

⟨300,000.00⟩

Oder, ⅓ für 2,000,000, *ohne* Europe.
Und ich die Vollmacht ersetz durch proxy.

Sie müssen die Vorrect verlangen, die Beherrscher zu nennen.
Auch die Staat wo die Actien ⟨anstifften⟩angestifft sein sollen.

Make the offer & keep it open 90 days.

Bates—viellicht wird ein gut Herrscher machen.[238]

Oder, ich will ⅓ Europe zu ihm verkaufen um $200,000, als *ein
Theil der Handel.*[239] [#]

---

[236] The last three words of this rather confusing entry mean: *get shares for it.*

[237] This and the following German sentences read: *We must give G. 10,000 shares. I
will give J. or he and his friends a third of the European property. No, these have to be
included in the dealings. Finally, I want to give full power, by* proxy. *We will give ⁹⁄₁₀ until
the 6,000,000 is paid. Or, ⅓ for 2,000,000* <u>without</u> *Europe. And I will give full power by*
proxy. *They must demand the right to name the directors. Also the state where the company shall be established.*

[238] George A. Bates was foreman in charge of the Paige typesetter's construction at
the Pratt & Whitney shop in Hartford. The German reads: *Perhaps he will make a good
boss.*

[239] *Or, I will sell him ⅓ Europe for $200,000, as* <u>a share of the business.</u>

¼ inter⟨set⟩

$2,000,000 zum $20,000,000 ausgebreitet, und also getheilt:

$3,000,000 (Theilen) zur Anstiftern;

$12,000,000 (″) Unsereins;

8,000,000 bei Seite gelegen, um grösser capital zu leisten.[240]

He was to bring Wilkin(or *er*)son. Well, let him come; & go from here with statistics (of speed, interruptions, proof-correcting, &c.,) to the Merg, & take *theirs* & compare.

Die erste 100 müssen *genau wie dieses* gemacht.[241]

Mr. Hitt 15th & K.[242]

⟨200,000 shs.⟩

Was the F. stocked for $150,000 to build the first & manufac-*other* M^s?[243]

And the money didn't quite build the *one*. Lacked $25,000.

Then $500,000 was wanted to build ⟨[$]⟩ 2,000.[244]

---

[240] *$2,000,000 to $20,000,000 extended and apportioned; $3,000,000 (shares) to the backers; $12,000,000 for us; 8,000,000 set aside to form a larger capital.*

[241] *The first 100 must be done exactly like this.*

[242] See page 546, note 189. Clemens was in Washington, D.C., in mid-June with Joseph T. Goodman in an unsuccessful effort to secure a firm commitment from Senator Jones.

[243] According to the Hartford city directories the Farnham Type-Setter Manufacturing Company was organized in 1872 and chartered in 1875. Its capital in 1880 was $125,000; by 1890 its capital was listed as $199,900. The company had originally undertaken to perfect and manufacture the Farnham typesetter and a separate distributor but in 1877 it began to work with James W. Paige toward the development of a combined typesetter and distributor ("Private Circular to the Stockholders of the Farnham Type-Setter Manufacturing Company," dated 26 January 1891). According to the Farnham company's circular, the company's resources were exhausted by 1883: almost $90,000 had been spent on the Paige typesetter alone in addition to the capital expended on the previous machines. Because of these unanticipated expenses and the difficulty of obtaining any new capital, the Farnham company withdrew from the enterprise and accepted a royalty of $150 on future sales in return for its investment. This notebook entry and those that follow reflect Clemens' dismay about the ever-increasing estimates of production costs for the typesetter.

[244] In the fall of 1881 William Hamersley, director of the Farnham company, asked Clemens if he would undertake to find $300,000 to capitalize the manufacture of the experimental typesetter. Clemens later recalled that the sum named was $500,000 (see *MTA*, 1:71). Presumably Clemens' notebook entry refers to this early effort to attract

By estimate it appeared that $1,900,000 was required for 1 a day,
& it would cost $1,600.[245]

⟨It now app⟩

$12,000 would build this one.

When $30,000 had been spent, $4,000 would finish it—& for
$10,000 would *guarantee* to finish & exhibit in N.Y.

It has cost much more than $100,000 since then.

Now $2,000,000 are requird to build *100*.

And they will cost $6,000 instead of $1,600.

Did the royalties of $50 to Coit & Sturges *add* to the F.'s
$150,000?[246]

Where & who made your gauges? Could they have made these
instead of galleys?

If J. wants *details* of what plant will cost, where will he find the
proper disinterested expert to furnish them? His relative Wheeler?

Shall we lay the above facts before J. as an argument that we
know how to manage?

You two built the old M & so you must have know that
$500,000 would build 2,000 of them. If so, you know that that
amount will build 200 of these.

I am well satisfied that 1000000 is twice what is needed—in
economical hands & to start in a modest way. I will not be a party
to starting in any other way.

I ⟨t[-]⟩started in to finish this M, & I have done it. I retire, now,
& ⟨p⟩die Bezahlung must stop to-day.[247]

---

capital for the machine. The estimated manufacturing cost per machine would appear
to have been $250 at that time.

[245] The original agreement of 6 February 1886, whereby Clemens undertook to finance
the development of the Paige typesetter, includes a "Summary of Cost of Machines,
Tools, Fixtures and Gauges" supplied by the Pratt & Whitney Company. Pratt &
Whitney estimated that to equip a plant capable of manufacturing one machine a day
would cost $1,781,167 and that the cost per machine would be $1,526.69.

[246] James W. Paige had granted a typesetter royalty of ten dollars to "Buck and
Steljes" on 18 January 1875 and a royalty of forty dollars to Samuel Coit on 7 May 1883.
Since the royalties were assigned in return for capital invested in the machine, Clemens
is reasonable in expecting that there should have been a corresponding increase in the
working capital of the Farnham company.

[247] Clemens' distress over his financial situation was allayed by an afternoon spent in
awed contemplation of the machine in action. He wrote to Joe Goodman on 23 June

If 1000000 would answer, & J & M[248] & Carnegie would
subscribe 100,000 apiece, we might raise it—but I would not be of
the party unless an approved man were going to manage. Some one
chosen by Carnegie.

Make C an offer?

Aufforderungen von —
Er wird die Actien verschaffen wenn sie nicht Eine Millionen
über geht;
Connecticut muss ausgezogen werden.
Herr --- Gebieter sein muss.
Verwechsel: According to ⟨specifications now existing.⟩ ⟨the
present one—no changes till 10 [dozen] made?⟩ existing specifi &
drawings. (or first 100).
Er will durch experts die Actien ausfinden.[249]

Rub simple glycerine into the scalp & it will keep the head clear
from dandruff. It can be immediately washed away with plain
water, & will leave no grease behind or stickiness.

Wenn Batterson es unternehmen will, wird Herr J. 100,000 der
Actien unterschreiben?[250]

Und Herr Case?[251] [#]

1890 that he felt renewed confidence that "the machine's market (abroad & here
together), is to-day worth $150,000,000, without saying anything about the doubling &
trebling of this sum that will follow within the life of the patents. . . . And so I am
resolved to stick tight to the thing till I haven't any money left" (Yale).

[248] Clemens' reluctant capitalists John P. Jones and John W. Mackay.

[249] The preceding German passages read: *Invitations from — he will back the company if it doesn't go over a million; Connecticut has to be taken out. Mr. --- has to be
the director. Exchange. . . . He wants to find* [find out about?] *the stock through
experts.*

[250] *If Batterson will undertake it, will Mr. J. subscribe to $100,000 worth of stock?*
James G. Batterson was founder and president of the Travelers Insurance Company of
Hartford and president of the New England Granite Works. Presumably Clemens hoped
that if Batterson would agree to direct the Paige typesetter company Jones would be less
reluctant to invest in it. Franklin G. Whitmore wrote to Clemens on 8 July that he would
arrange for Batterson to see the machine as Clemens had instructed.

[251] Newton Case, president of the well-known Hartford printing house of Case,
Lockwood & Brainard, had a seventy thousand dollar interest in the Paige typesetter.
Clemens apparently hoped to interest Case in an additional subscription.

Clarence C. Wheeler.

Mother at Moodus.

Brother, Frank (photographer?) Meriden.

Palenville.[252]

Leave foot of W. 42^d st at ⟨9.50⟩9.40 a.m. Weehawken 10.30, (?) get to Catskill at ⟨1.37⟩1.40 pm.

Leave Katersville Junction at 4.56 pm, arr. at Ktsville at 5.34.

Joe, 111 W. 25th st.[253]

2 pks cards.
Rubber ball for Jean
New game   ″   ″
White flannel suit
Jumping Frog.

204 W. 23^d, Howard Taylor.[254] [#]

---

[252] Palenville was one of the stations of the Catskill Mountain Railroad along the route to Tannersville, New York. The following two entries and the entries at 564.1–4 also refer to the trip to Tannersville and suggest various possible routes requiring transfers between the West Shore Railroad, the Ulster & Delaware Railroad, the Catskill Mountain Railroad, and the Kaaterskill Railroad. Clemens and his family went to Onteora Park near Tannersville in the first week of July 1890. Onteora Park was founded by the decorative artist Mrs. Candace Wheeler and her brother Francis B. Thurber, a wealthy merchant. The Clemenses had enjoyed a short visit there in August 1885, and now they returned for a stay of almost three months, renting one of the picturesque cottages in the colony of artists and literary people.

A classified advertisement for "Day Line Steamers" operating between New York City and Albany was torn from a New York newspaper and placed between the facing pages that bear this and the surrounding entries (561.15–562.14).

[253] Joseph T. Goodman wrote to Clemens at Onteora from this New York City address on 11 July 1890. His recent meeting with John W. Mackay had been unsatisfactory, reported Goodman, for "Mackay appeared to be in rather a querulous mood" and "spoke almost petulantly" about the machine and the excessive amount of capital required to manufacture it. Goodman blamed the "fatal delays" in perfecting the typesetter for having "sicklied over the bloom of original enthusiasm." Goodman added: "Come down to the city, and let's get our war paint on. I am never at my best until the situation is desperate." Clemens responded to the call and was in New York City at the Hoffman House hotel by 12 July. He spent the remainder of the month shuttling between New York City and Hartford on typesetter business and did not return to Onteora until 30 July.

[254] See page 485, note 9. Howard P. Taylor wrote to Clemens on 15 July 1890 from this New York City address to announce that he had "just put the finishing touches to

Let all matter, whether you lead it or not, be *considered* leaded, & pay us 50^c per M for the leads alone, & we will set the matter for nothing. Twenty-eight lines nonpareil of the Sun become 38 when leaded—the leads add a full $\frac{1}{4}$ to the bulk; 7,000 ems an hour ⟨w⟩for 23 hours (all day & all night) would pay us ⟨87½^c⟩ $1.15 per hour:

⟨87½	115
23	23
251	345
174	230
1991	$26.45
43½	
$20.34½⟩	

We pay each compositor *one-half* of the sum we get for his string.

If he sets 8,000, he gets 50^c.

Set 150,000 & lead it, it becomes 200,000, & $25 is due us for the leads. This is but 6,750 an hour *solid*.

Add 50,000 & lead it & it becomes 66,000, & $8 is due us for the leads.

We can earn $33 a day & pay the boys $16.50⟨.⟩ of it

This is less than 8,000 ems *solid* per hour for 24 hours. [#]

---

the first copy" of his dramatization of *A Connecticut Yankee*. Within a few days Taylor came to Hartford and read the play draft to Clemens. Clemens wrote to his daughter Clara on 20 July: "It's a secret that isn't to be breathed outside of the family—the new play, the Yankee in Arthur's Court, has bored the very soul out of me. Four level hours I listened, today, in misery." While he found Taylor's play "rattling, stirring, & spectacular," he thought the language "dreadful." Taylor's Yankee was "a mere boisterous clown, & oozes slang from every pore." "However, the awful ordeal is over," added Clemens, "& Taylor is gone. He is a very old friend of mine, & a good fellow; so I was careful to say nothing harsh about his work. . . . This is the very last play that I ever mean to have anything to do with" (*LLMT*, pp. 257–258). Taylor revised the play somewhat and submitted it to almost all the theatrical producers in New York City over the next several months with no success. There was a flurry of interest in the play early in 1891: Clemens tentatively agreed to transform his Connecticut Yankee into a Jew to meet the requirements of an interested performer, but a more conventional offer from theatrical managers Randall & Dickson was accepted before this bizarre revision was attempted. Apparently the play never reached production and no further correspondence on the subject with Taylor survives.

Leave   Weehawken ⟨4.0[4]⟩4.05
⟨Arr.⟩ Leave Kingston   6.35
        ″   Phenica   7.50
Arr.   Tannersville 8.52

⟨Go up & call Joe⟩ Ask J. if I better employ Wall to place a lot
at $1000 to 5000.
⟨Lotos⟩ Players, bkfast, 8.
Hearst,[255]. . . . . 9.30.
Office about fruit[256]. . . 10.30
⟨Joe, hotel⟩
Mackay's office,[257] to POST JONES, 11.
Ask if Hall can copy the play.[258]

⟨280 lines is 10,000 an hour when leaded⟩ 37   8,000 solid
                                                          8
                                                       ——
                                                       296 lines
                365   75 lines are 2,000 ems.
                 19
                ——
              3 295
                365
         —— ——
         280 6,945

---

[255] In March, Clemens had noted the name of California senator George F. Hearst,
probably as a potential investor in the Paige typesetter (see p. 546, note 189). Clemens
improved his acquaintance with the Hearst family on at least one occasion in May 1890,
dining at the Hearst home in Washington, D.C. In his letter to Clemens of 11 July,
Joseph Goodman mentioned that he "saw young Hearst on the street to-day" and added:
"If we have to advance upon the publishers, he would be a good hostage to push in front
of us." Young William Randolph Hearst had been proprietor and editor of the San
Francisco *Daily Examiner* since 1887, and his sensational journalistic methods were
beginning to earn him a national reputation. Clemens and Goodman apparently were
considering approaching some of the publishing moguls for typesetter funds and had
some hopes of benefiting from Hearst's influence.

[256] The Clemenses were evidently having baskets of fruit delivered to them at Onteora
from a New York City merchant. Clemens wrote to Fred Hall on 3 September from
Onteora: "At first the fruit was rotten, mainly. I complained to you & it greatly improved.
And the basket grew *larger*" (Berg). But Clemens had not authorized the additional fruit
and he refused to pay for it. The dealer could "sue for the balance," he told Hall.

[257] The offices of Mackay's Postal Telegraph-Cable Company in New York City.

[258] In his letter of 23 July 1890 Howard Taylor informed Clemens that he had revised
his dramatization of *A Connecticut Yankee* but that the manuscript was "pretty well
marked up." He suggested that four typed copies be made. "Have you not type-writers

```
 37        56
  8         6
───       ───
296       336
           15
          ───
          3.51
 365
24.50
─────
 1460
 730.
─────
 8760
  175
─────
8,935
```

D B Davidson
Agency of The Nevad Bk of San F[259]

⟨Put 50 royalties in the safe at Webster & Co, July 29, '90.⟩[260]

John W. Mackay, July 29/90, deposited $5,000 ⟨fo⟩ to my credit in above Bank. When Co is formed, I shall give him its equivalent in stock.

Also, Jno. P. Jones deposited $5000 in above bank to my credit on the same terms.[261] [#]

---

in your publishing house here who could do the work. On the outside it would cost perhaps $30 or $40, and just at present I don't feel as though I could stand it all myself."

[259] Davidson, New York City agent of the Nevada Bank of San Francisco, wrote to Clemens on 2 August 1890 assuring him that his "signature (specimens)" had been verified by the bank. The signature verification undoubtedly related to the ten thousand dollars deposited in the bank by Jones and Mackay (see note 261).

[260] Franklin G. Whitmore wrote to Clemens on 25 July 1890: "I also forward as requested 50 blank royalties." Clemens apparently expected a flurry of investment interest in his typesetter once Jones and Mackay had made a commitment.

[261] Clemens' and Goodman's expectations about John P. Jones and John W. Mackay suffered a crushing blow in July 1890. After months of hesitation and indifference, Jones and Mackay finally came to Hartford on 23 July and saw the Paige typesetter at work. They then returned to New York City and within a few days Goodman reported to Clemens the proposition presented by the two capitalists. Instead of the large capitalization Clemens hoped for, Jones proposed "that six of them put in $5,000 apiece—or $30,000 in all—to give the machine a trial—Mackay to find two and Jones two" (Joseph T. Goodman to SLC, 26 July 1890). Goodman confessed that he was "a good deal disgusted with the cowardliness and stinginess of their course," but Clemens' financial embarrassment made it imperative that even this modest offer be accepted.

(Copy—to Mr. Arnot.)[262]
_____

Tannersville, Aug. 9/90.

My dear Sir:

This enclosed letter is from Mr. Goodman, an old & particular
friend of Senator Jones's & mine. I enclose it to let you see that I
have fulfilled all the obligations laid upon me by my conversation
with you last December. I produced Senator Jones in the flesh in
Hartford after keeping the machine waiting for him 6 months &
upwards at great expense; & he did not merely "approve" the
machine, he sat over it a long time pretty nearly tongue-tied with
astonishment & admiration. He has found his tongue since, & is
using it with energy. I told you I would show Jones a 6,000-em
machine; I did better than that; he saw a youth of 36 days'
apprenticeship set 7,000 ems in an hour, which is more than twice
as much as any other type-setting machine can do.

I am moving the machine from the factory to quarters of my
own, now,[263] & taking this opportunity to improve it with a device
which will increase its speed. I expect it to go to work again 3
weeks hence, & within 2 months thereafter I count upon its
proving itself 3 times as fast as any other machine. It will then
establish the fact that it can set type at one-ninth of present cost
of composition instead of one-sixth as claimed by me when I talked
with you in December last.

_____

[262] In December 1889 Matthias H. Arnot had agreed to underwrite expenses on the
Paige typesetter to the extent of fifty thousand dollars in return for a fifty dollar royalty
on future sales. Arnot was to advance the fifty thousand dollars in installments of five
thousand dollars as needed. He sent a first installment on 28 March 1890 with a cautioning
note to Clemens: "Now you know that in reality I am going it blind in this matter, having
never seen the machine and even if I had, it would be about the same, as I know little or
nothing of mechanism—so dont get me in any deeper unless you are mighty certain that
some time or other I can draw something out." Clemens responded with a rather loftily
worded letter, returning Arnot's five thousand dollars and explaining that he "could not
think of taking it, with you unsatisfied" (SLC to Arnot, n.d. [between 29 March and 3
April 1890]). Clemens' letter had what may have been the intended effect: Arnot posted
the money draft back immediately with an apology for his uncertainty. The following
letter to Arnot copied into Clemens' notebook was written to assure Arnot of Jones's
financial commitment to the machine and to request a resumption of Arnot's payments.

[263] Clemens cabled Whitmore on 24 July 1890 that the typesetter should be moved
immediately from the Pratt & Whitney workshop to 42 Union Place, Paige's Hartford

John Mackay was also converted when he saw the machine at work; & his last word to John Russell Young of the N.Y. Herald[264] when he sailed for Europe a few days ago was, "do everything you can for Sam & his machine. So Young writes me.

I have been for many months ashamed of my failure to perform my promises with regard to Senator Jone & the machine & am more than glad to know that that score is cleared off at last.

Truly Yours
SL Clemens

The above is formal notice that it is now in order for Mr. Arnot to resume payments on that $50,000.

X-1. Remark[265]

Fred.[266]

Sept. 23.		3.	4401.			
" 24		2.	5040.			
Sep. 25.	F.	3.57 = 4620.		J. (first attempt)[267]	1.	1485.
26	"	3.45 = 4793.		"	0.20.	1377
27	"	2.10 = 4614				
28	"	3.55 ⟨4680⟩4584 J.			1.07.	1908
30	"	⟨4.18⟩			4.18	2325

---

workshop. The association with Pratt & Whitney was at an end and the machine was to be tested for a month at Union Place before the major test in New York City.

[264] Clemens' journalist friend John Russell Young had come to Hartford and seen the typesetter on 19 July 1890 and was instrumental in influencing Jones and Mackay to make the trip to Hartford a few days later.

[265] See page 493, note 35. This entry appears at the top of a page which is otherwise blank and is followed by five blank pages. The remaining entries in the notebook apparently date from 1889, except for the final entry dated 19 March 1890.

[266] Clemens continues the daily record of ems set by his typesetter apprentices in the fall of 1889 (see pp. 499–500, notes 58, 60, and 61).

[267] On 29 September 1889 Clemens wrote to Clara Stanchfield, an interested investor in the Paige typesetter: "Our new apprentice 'J,' is a practical printer. He hasn't had a show, yet, that would enable us to guess the rate of speed he is going to make eventually, because his chances at the machine have been so very brief. But we'll give him the best part of the day, tomorrow, & an hour a day the rest of the week, & if he shows up pretty fairly, we shall hire him permanently" (original owned by Stanchfield Wright, Earleville, Md.). Clemens added that the new apprentice's knowledge of typesetting was proving a liability and that he seemed "to have most too much unlearning to do."

Sep. 30 M^{c}N, 1st H. r. 648 ⎫
               2^d "   " 810 ⎬ first time he ever saw M or K. b.[268]
               3 "   " 918 ⎭

Oct. 1.   3.52. = 4,992. F.   4.37. = 2,352. J.
      2.   4.21 = 4,926 "   3.52 = 2,506 "

Book to Collins, station agent.[269]

C. M. Underhill, Buffalo[270]

Sept 30
H. McNeilly, 314 B'way.

Oct. 3 & 4. Slattery[271] in his third hour (he had never seen the machine or its keyboard before) set 1593 ems. He sets 1500 an hour at the case.

Gen. Sherman.
Players & Lotos.
⟨Mrs. Custer⟩
⟨Catholic. Sheridan's boy⟩
J. S. Quin, station[272]
Mr. Collins   "

---

[268] In the fall of 1889 Clemens intended to hire three additional "cub" apprentices for the Paige typesetter—"a type writer, a stenographer, and perhaps a shoemaker, to show that no special gifts or training are required with this machine. We shall train these beginners two or three months—or until some one of them gets up to 7,000 an hour—then we will show up in New York and run the machine 24 hours a day 7 days in the week, for several months" (SLC to Joseph T. Goodman, 7 October 1889, *MTL*, p. 517). H. McNeilly of New York City was one of the intended apprentices. He saw and tried the typesetter on 30 September 1889 in Hartford but wrote to Clemens the following day that he had decided against moving to Hartford to pursue his apprenticeship on the machine. He asked instead if Clemens would send him "one of your pasteboard copies of the key board" to study in anticipation of the machine's arrival in New York City. "M" and "K. b." in this entry stand for machine and keyboard; "H. r." probably stands for hourly rate.

[269] Clemens usually sent copies of his new books to the Hartford stationmaster William H. Collins.

[270] Charles M. Underhill of Buffalo, New York, was a partner in J. Langdon & Company and also "Western Manager" of the company.

[271] Martin J. Slattery.

[272] J. Scrugham Quin was the Hartford ticket agent for the New York, New Haven & Hartford Railroad.

Edward Bellamy
    Chicopee Falls.[273]

You may TALK (quadruple time) (both hands down) o' *Bon*
(right) APARTE (both) you may TALK (2) a*boot* (right) e-CARTE (2)[274]

⟨M. H. Anot, [E]⟩ M. H. Arnot, Elmira.
Dumbrowski of J. L & Co Buf.
⟨Dʳ⟩

$$
\begin{array}{l}
3 \\
\langle26\rangle \\
\underline{3} \\
78{,}000 \\
\underline{4} \\
31.2
\end{array}
$$

```
        3
 ⟨26⟩
        3
 ─────
 78,000        2
     4        $1.
 ─────        4.56
 31.2         2350
        35
         8
       ─────
       28.0
              18
               4
             ───
              72
                 [3]6
                  28
```

⟨[----]⟩ 1 to & including 6[275]
Six one-dollar royalties sent to Clara Stanchfield, Sep. '28/89.
2 & 3, Oct. 3. One to Orion Clemens; the other to Mrs. P. A.
Moffett.
⟨17ᵗʰ⟩12ᵗʰ Oct., Mrs. Susan L. Crane,   *five.*
17ᵗʰ   " Gen. Chas. J. Langdon, *three*
Nov. 27. S. E. Moffett, ... one

---

[273] Novelist Edward Bellamy was a resident of Chicopee Falls, Massachusetts.
[274] See page 490, note 30.
[275] Clemens is referring to the six royalties assigned to Clara Stanchfield in September
1889. Mrs. Stanchfield purchased five royalties and Clemens gave her an additional royalty
to reimburse her for a previous investment in the unsuccessful Kaolatype Engraving
Company. This and the remaining entries were written over the preceding miscellaneous
numbers, probably over a period of time, on the back flyleaf of Clemens' notebook.

Dec. 9. M. H. Arnot .... ⟨one hundred.⟩ 50
″   18 Karl Gerhardt .... one
Mch. 19, '90, Chas. Hopkins Clark ... one—
    (as trustee for Hartford Free Library).[276]

---

[276] Charles Hopkins Clark, associate editor of the Hartford *Courant,* was treasurer
of the Hartford Library Association.

XXX

"I Am Out in the Cold"

(August 1890–June 1891)

IN MID-AUGUST 1890, when the entries in this notebook begin, Clemens had left Onteora, near Tannersville, New York, where the family was spending the summer, on one of his increasingly frequent business trips to New York City and Washington, D.C., to promote the Paige typesetter. While in New York City on 13 August, Clemens signed a contract drawn up by James W. Paige, in which the inventor agreed to sell all his rights in the machine for a quarter of a million dollars. This was a dangerous arrangement for Clemens, who was obliged by the terms of the contract to pay Paige this sum within six months. Franklin G. Whitmore, Clemens' Hartford business agent, feared that Clemens had been "deceived with promises" and was not sufficiently protected under the new contract (Whitmore to SLC, 19 August 1890), but Clemens was nonetheless sanguine. That same month he visited Senator John P. Jones of Nevada, the "Silver King," in Washington, D.C., and was able to win his backing in the enterprise. Jones accepted a six-month option to form a stock company to capitalize the typesetter, and Clemens began to rely on Jones's influence and connections to carry his plans to fruition.

August 1890 was a trying month, for, in addition to business anxieties, both Clemens and his wife had to face the ordeal of parental illness. On the fourteenth of the month, the same day that Livy traveled to Elmira to be at her

571

mother's bedside, Clemens was summoned from Washington, D.C., to Keokuk, Iowa, to be present at what was expected to be Jane Clemens' deathbed. His mother had recently suffered a stroke but appeared to recuperate during his visit, and he spent a few days with her and with Orion and Mollie Clemens before returning East on business. At the end of August he rejoined Livy in Onteora.

The Clemenses spent the remainder of the summer of 1890 in the congenial company of friends in Onteora. The family returned to Hartford toward the end of September, and Susy was accompanied by her parents to Bryn Mawr, where she began her freshman year. On 27 October 1890, Jane Clemens died at the age of eighty-seven. Clemens attended the funeral, which took place at the Mount Olivet Cemetery in Hannibal, where Jane Clemens' husband and son Henry were buried. The family's grief at the death of Clemens' mother was still fresh when word of Mrs. Jervis Langdon's serious illness brought Clemens and Livy to Elmira in late November. Clemens rushed back to Hartford a few days later at the news of his daughter Jean's illness. It is possible that Jean suffered her first epileptic seizure at this time. While in Hartford, expecting at any moment to receive notice of Mrs. Langdon's death, Clemens wrote William Dean Howells a troubled letter which closed: "I have fed so full on sorrows, these last weeks that I seem to have become hardened to them—benumbed" (27 November 1890, *MTHL*, p. 633). Livy's eighty-year-old mother died on 28 November.

In addition to these personal sorrows, Clemens and his family were burdened with the financial difficulties of Charles L. Webster & Company, which was in debt to the Mount Morris Bank for nearly $25,000. Clemens allowed his royalties and profits for 1890 to be turned back into the company in order to avoid draining it of badly needed capital. The firm's major problem was in trying to promote the *Library of American Literature*. The slow receipt of installment payments from subscribers could not offset the firm's expenses in producing and distributing the books. In November 1890 Livy made a personal loan of $10,000 to Charles L. Webster & Company, which helped to subsidize its installment department for a few months, but Frederick J. Hall soon urged Clemens to furnish the company with even more capital. Clemens was unable to do so and, in the spring of 1891, Hall borrowed $15,000 from personal friends and used the money to pay off some of the Mount Morris Bank notes.

During the winter of 1890/1891, the Paige typesetter again appeared to be near completion, and Clemens was anxiously awaiting news from Senator Jones about the formation of a stock company. But Jones was unable to show prospective backers a finished and reliable machine. Paige was once again "tinkering" with the typesetter and as 13 February 1891 drew near (the date Jones's option was to expire), the machine was still in Hartford undergoing last-minute repairs. From the entries made in his notebook at this time, Clemens' irritation with Paige and his mechanics is evident. "These frauds & liars!" he noted after Paige announced the machine's completion "for certainly the half dozenth time in the past twelvemonth" (p. 596). He was distressed by his continuing responsibility for Paige's huge bills, especially since he had already expended about $150,000 in developing the machine and had only a conditional guarentee of ownership to show for it.

The final blow came with a letter from Jones on 11 February 1891 reporting that prospective investors were either uninterested or, worse, backers of the Mergenthaler Linotype. "For a whole year you have breathed the word of promise to my ear to break it to my hope at last," Clemens began in an unmailed, undated letter to Jones. "It is stupefying, it is unbelievable." In a letter of 22 February to Joseph Goodman, Clemens raged over Jones's perfidy, calling him a "penny-worshiping humbug & shuffler . . . a very good sage-brush imitation of the Deity" (Doheny). Clemens' attachment to the typesetter appears finally to have broken under this crushing disappointment. "I've shook the machine," he wrote Orion on 25 February, "& never wish to see it or hear it mentioned again. It is superb, it is perfect, it can do 10 men's work. It is worth billions; & when the pig-headed lunatic, its inventor, dies, it will instantly be capitalized & make the Clemens children rich." Clemens was still entitled to collect a $500 royalty on each machine sold or marketed in the United States, but from this point on would return Paige's bills unpaid.

Now that the typesetter fiasco had left him "out in the cold" (SLC to Joseph Goodman, April 1891, *MTL*, p. 546), Clemens was forced into a practical appraisal of his financial situation. Intent on rebuilding his wasted fortune, he set himself the task of doing enough literary work within three months to ensure him an income of $75,000 for the year. He turned to projects put aside years before. The history game, which he had invented in 1883, once again engaged his interest, and he set Fred Hall to work on perfecting a dummy board of the game. Of greater importance, he decided to transform the play *Colonel Sellers as a Scientist*, written in collaboration with William Dean Howells in 1883, into a novel—*The American Claimant*. In adapting the play, Clemens altered it substantially, but he still retained the farcical situations which had finally made the piece an embarrassment to Howells. After finishing the fourth chapter of the novel, Clemens was thoroughly pleased with the results: "I think it will simply howl with fun," he wrote Orion on 25 February 1891. "I wake up in the night laughing at its ridiculous situations." When rheumatism threatened to reduce his output, Clemens tried using a recording device to dictate a portion of the novel, a process he subsequently described as "so awkward for me and so irritating that I not only curse and swear all the time I am dictating, but am impatient and dissatisfied because God has given me only one tongue to curse and swear with" (SLC to Mary M. Fairbanks, 29 May 1891, *MTMF*, p. 267). The book was completed on 2 May 1891 and sold to the McClure Syndicate for $12,000. After its syndication in various American newspapers and in the *Idler* magazine in England, the story was published for retail sale by Charles L. Webster & Company in May 1892. One of Clemens' most disjointed literary productions, *The American Claimant* had a meager sale.

In the spring of 1891, Clemens also revived two pieces that had been pigeonholed years earlier. His short sketch "Luck," written in 1886, was published in *Harper's* magazine in August 1891, and "Mental Telegraphy" appeared in *Harper's* in December of that year. The latter half of this notebook is filled with ideas for potential literary use, some of which would later be worked into books and sketches, but Clemens produced no other writing for publication during the period covered by this notebook.

As summer approached, the Clemenses were making preparations to leave Hartford for an indefinite stay in Europe. Doctors had recommended that Livy try the European baths, for she had been showing signs of heart strain; and it was hoped the waters would relieve Clemens' rheumatism. Financial pressures were also a large consideration in their plans, for Clemens' expenses on the typesetter had placed the family in straitened circumstances and made the upkeep of the Hartford house a burden. "I don't know how long we shall be in Europe," Clemens wrote Howells on 20 May 1891, "I have a vote, but I don't cast it. I'm going to do whatever the others desire, with leave to change their mind, without prejudice, whenever they want to. Travel has no longer any charm for me. I have seen all the foreign countries I want to see except heaven & hell, & I have only a vague curiosity as concerns one of those" (*MTHL*, p. 645). On 6 June the entire family, accompanied by Susan Crane, left for France, and the last dated entry in this notebook records their arrival at Le Havre on 14 June 1891. For Clemens and his wife the European trip would lengthen into an almost unbroken nine years of exile.

Notebook 30 is identical to Notebook 29 in design and format. It now contains 158 pages, as one leaf has been torn out and is missing. Torn-out portions of three other leaves are also missing. Sixteen pages are blank. The notebook is inscribed in black pencil except for scattered entries in brownish black ink and purple pencil. Clemens employed a series of numbered Xs in this notebook to identify entries for possible literary use. The marked entries correspond to a list near the end of the notebook (pp. 645–646). In the present text, these numbered Xs precede the entries they designate, although Clemens indifferently placed them before, after, or directly across passages he wished to index. Like Notebook 29, Notebook 30 is much less worn than the other notebooks included in this volume. A short clipping pinned to a notebook page is discussed in note 82, page 596. Use marks in black pencil, probably by Paine, appear throughout but have not been reproduced.

Send George down to summon P first thing in the morning—or Patrick.[1]

Telegraph Livy to go on to Elmira.[2]

John Brusnahan[3]
154 S. 8th st. Brooklyn, E. D.

First, put in 3 blanks—sum to be paid, length of time,

---

[1] Clemens was expecting James W. Paige to come from Hartford and join him in New York City on 14 August 1890. Together they would travel to Washington, D.C., to discuss with Senator John P. Jones the organization of a corporation to manufacture and market the typesetter. Apparently Clemens intended George Griffin, his butler, or Patrick McAleer, his coachman, to notify Paige that he was expected in New York.

[2] Livy left the Onteora Club in the Catskills, where the Clemens family had been spending the summer, and traveled to Elmira on 14 August 1890 to spend a week with her ailing mother.

[3] The printing foreman at the New York *Herald*, who was eager to see the Paige typesetter completed and installed in his newspaper's composing department. On 17 August 1890 he wrote Clemens an anxious letter urging him to "make a move" because the *Herald* office was considering a trial installation of the Mergenthaler Linotype.

proportion of gross proceeds (to be not less than $\frac{1}{10}$ on first 200, & not more than $\frac{1}{8}$ afterward.) Or, re-assign.[4]

& $\langle^{19}\!/_{20}\rangle^{9}\!/_{20}$ of foreign & domestic in case of failure.

⟨Put in a clause restoring my foreign interest in case of failure.⟩

Reduce the 250,000 to ⟨5[000?]⟩ 12,000 a year for 5 years.

⟨Resurrect the escrow contract & make it good by inserting 5000 salary; for my honor is at stake here.⟩[5]

⟨None of these being satisfactory, I re-assign, now, reserving $^{9}\!/_{20}$ in any future foreign & domestic company.⟩

Failing to see F, I take copy of new contract to Washington as a proposed contract, & if it is not satisfactory, restore [the] 10,000 & stop negotiations.[6]

---

[4] In August 1890 James W. Paige framed a new typesetter contract which was forwarded to Clemens in New York City. In this entry Clemens seems to have been formulating tentative proposals for changing the terms of the contract, although none of these proposals is to be found in the final agreement which became effective 13 August 1890. The agreement transferred all Paige's right, title, and interest in the typesetter to Clemens for the sum of $250,000, to be paid within six months of the date of the contract. In addition, Paige was to receive one-quarter of the gross income to be made from the sale and rental of the machines. Should Clemens fail to pay Paige $250,000 by 13 February 1891, his ownership in the typesetter would be forfeited to Paige, and Clemens would receive instead a $500 royalty on each machine sold or rented in the United States, in accordance with their agreement of 26 September 1889. An unsigned copy of the 13 August 1890 contract is in the Mark Twain Papers.

[5] The escrow contract had been drawn up in May 1890; there is, however, no known copy extant. Years later Clemens would write that this particular contract was the only "good & rational one" he ever made with Paige, for it gave him an unconditional ninetwentieths ownership in the invention. According to Clemens, Paige reneged on this agreement, claiming that the document was not a "real contract, because it had a blank in it (for his salary)." Clemens' recollections are drawn from an undated manuscript in the Mark Twain Papers (DV 274) which was probably written in the lates 1890s.

[6] Clemens evidently regarded the new typesetter contract as tentative until he was assured of Senator Jones's backing. While in Washington, D.C., during the last week of August, Clemens offered the senator a six-month option to form a corporation and to acquire, through issue of stock, $950,000 in capital to construct a plant for the manufacture of the typesetters. Clemens was prepared to call a halt to negotiations with Paige if Jones proved unwilling to enter into the agreement, probably because his chances of buying out Paige's interest in the invention within six months seemed highly unlikely without the senator's support. In that case, Clemens was ready to return to Jones and John W. Mackay the $5,000 deposit each had already made toward purchase of stock in the still unformed corporation (see p. 565). By the end of August, however, Senator

Get North's assignment & Hamersley's consent.[7]

F. J. Hall, 275 Madison ave (near 40th)
D. Whitford, 24 E. 32[d].[8]

You said you would fill out & re-date the escrow contract—well, do it.

Geo. S. Coe, Pres.
⟨National⟩ American Exchange Bank
128 Broadway.[9]
St. Johnsbury Scale Works
Fairbanks (Schweine)[10]

Geo. E. Spencer[11]
Austin, Nevada.
$7 ⟨p⟩& carriage paid
Grant, cloth.
Send by Mail. [#]

Jones had agreed to undertake the responsibility of forming a stock company. The identity of "F" in this entry remains obscure.

[7] Charles R. North was a machinist in Paige's employ who had invented an automatic justifier for the Paige compositor. North's assignment for his contribution to the typesetter was not included in the 13 August 1890 contract, but was handled as a separate transaction between the two inventors. William T. Hamersley was a Hartford lawyer who had invested in the typesetter during the early stages of its development. The 13 August contract provided him with one-tenth of the net profits which would accrue to Clemens.

[8] These two addresses were written several months after the surrounding entries had been made. On Sunday, 30 November 1890, Clemens wrote to Fred Hall asking for his home address and also that of Daniel Whitford, the New York attorney handling Charles L. Webster & Company's legal affairs, for he had been unable to reach either man by telegram that weekend. Hall furnished the information on 2 December 1890.

[9] Coe was also a director of the Commercial Cable Company and the Postal Telegraph-Cable Company. Both corporations had been organized and were largely controlled by John W. Mackay, the Comstock Lode millionaire, whom Clemens hoped would become a major backer of the Paige typesetter. Coe's business affiliation with Mackay may have prompted Clemens to approach him with a proposal for investing in the typesetter, although there is no evidence of Clemens' having done so.

[10] Henry Fairbanks was a clergyman and inventor who manufactured scales and other machinery in Saint Johnsbury, Vermont.

[11] Clemens was evidently planning to send Spencer a copy of the *Personal Memoirs of U. S. Grant*. A former senator from Alabama, Spencer had turned to Nevada mining and ranching interests in the early 1880s.

No control till 250,000 furnished.[12]

No consideration.

Can withhold patents.—no date stated.

Ham must have $\frac{1}{20}$ of your portion & $\frac{1}{20}$ of mine. $\frac{2}{20}$ of the whole would be prodigious.[13]

(Paige)

Geo. Robinson[14]
Thorne T.S. Machine[15]

Bohunkus.

Andrew Mellon,
    Pittsburgh
Recom. by Alex MacKenzie
Bismarck Dak.
Thos. Mellon & Sons
    Bankers.[16]

9,000 an hour reduces composition to $\frac{1}{9}$ of present cost. If you lead one half of the matter, it reduces it to $\frac{1}{10}$ of present cost.

Work the machine 10 hours a day—90,000—lead half, which adds 20,000—110,000—saving $50 per day—350 a week—$18,200 a year—the machine earns its cost in 8 months.[17] [#]

---

[12] In this and the two entries which follow, Clemens evinced doubt about the new contract made with Paige. He was to have no rights to the invention until Paige was paid $250,000, nor would his financial responsibility for the typesetter's manufacture cease until a corporation was formed. Also, as Clemens notes, Paige was not obligated to effect a transfer of patents to Clemens' name by any specific date.

[13] This is the first of many entries in which Clemens insists on reducing William Hamersley's interest in the typesetter.

[14] Robinson, Clemens' long-time friend and billiards partner, was a furniture manufacturer in Elmira, New York. Clemens joined Livy in Elmira about the twentieth or twenty-first of August, and may have planned to solicit Robinson's interest in the typesetter.

[15] Thorne typesetters were manufactured in Hartford and were used successfully by various United States and English newspapers.

[16] Thomas Mellon & Sons was a well-known Pittsburgh banking firm. Alexander McKenzie, an influential political leader in North Dakota and a successful businessman, had large investments in North Dakota real estate and securities.

[17] In calculating the benefits to be derived from using the Paige machine, Clemens was

P. to take $1 per mach till ⟨[-]⟩500 have been made & sold—after that, ¼ of the gross.[18]

⟨Separate [the] foreign ent[i-]⟩
Then J. & the caps. have %10 of the full stock. & Joe, Ham & I 4/10.[19]

Separate the foreign entirely[20] & give ½ to Jns & the other half to Joe Ham, P & me. *No ¼ gross. Strike it out.*

Write P. to have Ham deed half his interest to me in foreign & domestic, I to pay him the 2500 as soon as I can.[21]

Strike out the lump sum & substitute $12,000 a year.[22]

Quite willing to return capital when it was to be furnished by 2 men—but not when furnished to a crowd, at $2 in stock for $1 in cash.

If organize under Conn. law, go back to half-&-half contract?[23] [#]

---

assuming that the hand compositor set approximately 1,000 ems an hour and received an hourly wage of fifty cents—the prevailing rate for compositors employed by major New York City newspapers. Clemens' estimate of 9,000 ems an hour on the Paige typesetter anticipated a marked improvement in the proficiency of its operators, who at this time were producing no more than 6,500 ems.

[18] Clemens intended to reduce the initial share of Paige's profits. The August contract provided Paige with one-quarter of the gross profits starting with the sale of the first machines manufactured.

[19] The people to whom Clemens refers are Senator Jones, other capitalists who might invest in the typesetter, Joseph T. Goodman (who had not received any assignment of interest in the 13 August 1890 contract), William T. Hamersley, and Clemens himself.

[20] The August 1890 contract treated domestic and foreign sales of the machine as a single entity.

[21] In April 1890 William Hamersley had loaned Clemens $2,500 to help him meet typesetter expenses. The loan was to have been repaid within three months, but Clemens' debt was still outstanding more than a year later.

[22] Clemens is referring to the $250,000 due Paige in accordance with the August contract.

[23] Clemens and Paige had drawn up a contract in December 1889 which gave them equal shares in profits from typesetter sales, but it appears that this contract was never ratified. A rough draft of the August 1890 contract in the Mark Twain Papers states that Paige and Clemens' last outstanding agreement was that of September 1889 according to which Clemens was to receive a $500 royalty on each machine marketed; the subsequent contract of December 1889 is not mentioned.

$600,000,000.

"Americans, b'God!"

"Oh *hell*-yes!"

"I'm the ⟨last⟩ first that's riz, anyway!"

Chewed off his tag.

"Sinclair! Sinclair, ye G— d—d heathen, work'n on the Sabberday."

"The ⟨Bashaw⟩ Begum of Bengal 116 days out from ⟨Hong Kong,⟩Hong *Kong,*/Can*ton*, homeward *bound*. What vessel's that?"²⁴

X-1

Thos. Donaldson²⁵
326 N. 39ᵗʰ Phila
Indian book.

As eloquent as God when he created light, or an Englishman when he is talking about something to eat.²⁶

Miss Pinney is a "Confused Christian." ²⁷ [#]

---

²⁴ The entry refers to a story told in chapter 35 of Richard Henry Dana's *Two Years Before the Mast* (see p. 378, note 256). The "X-1" that follows is the first in a series of numbered Xs that appear throughout the notebook. They were intended for use as indexing devices and correspond to a numbered list near the end of the notebook (pp. 645–646). If this mark was intended to identify the "Begum of Bengal" entry, it was either overlooked or rejected when Clemens compiled his index list, which begins with a reference to the entry marked "X1" at 589.1–3.

²⁵ Donaldson, a Philadelphia lawyer and agent for the Smithsonian Institution, was a collector of North American Indian artifacts and in 1890 was in charge of taking a census of North American Indians. Clemens may have considered asking him for advice regarding a book about Indians to be published by Charles L. Webster & Company.

²⁶ Clemens later considered using this sentence in *The American Claimant*, which he would begin in February 1891. In a working note which Clemens decided not to use in the novel, young Lord Berkeley, upon arriving in the United States, quotes this remark in his journal as an example of the "national habit" of being "unconsciously extravagant in language."

²⁷ The Clemenses met Jessie Pinney (later Baldwin) during their summer stay at Onteora. A pianist who had studied under Franz Liszt, Miss Pinney had taken an interest in Clara Clemens and agreed to give her lessons twice a month in New York.

Conf. Agnostic

dâk-bungalow[28]
lakh
rupee
walee
syce
ayah
sahib
memsahib
khansamah (inn-keeper?)
doolie (man)
doolie-bearers
anna (money)

['I] W Arthur[29]
  Bryn Mawr

5. ⟨R. I.⟩ Tramp Ab. = Miss.; Yank.
  Wh. El. H. Finn(?)
Write in them.[30] [#]

---

[28] The Hindi vocabulary list reflects Clemens' reading of Rudyard Kipling. Clemens had met the young author, whose work was then unknown to him, during the summer of 1889 at Elmira (see *MTE*, pp. 309–312). Kipling had been touring the world as a correspondent for the Allahabad *Pioneer* and made a special effort to visit Elmira and pay homage to the man he "had learned to love and admire fourteen thousand miles away." Kipling's account of the visit was printed in the New York *Herald* on 17 August 1890 and was later included in his letters of travel, *From Sea to Sea* (1899). About a year later George Warner introduced Clemens to Kipling's work by handing him a copy of *Plain Tales from the Hills*. By September 1890 Clemens was rereading Kipling's tales: "I have just found out," he wrote a Hartford neighbor, "that whereas Kipling's stories are plenty good enough on a first reading they very greatly improve on a second" (SLC to Mrs. George Keller, 12 September 1890, MTM).

[29] J. W. Arthur was the proprietor of the Summit Grove House in Bryn Mawr, Pennsylvania, where Clemens, Livy, and Susy lodged during the first week of October. Susy Clemens was starting her freshman year at Bryn Mawr College, but the dormitory to which she had been assigned was still under construction, so the Clemenses stayed at the hotel until Susy was given a room at Radnor Hall on campus.

[30] On 1 October 1890, Charles Warren Stoddard wrote Clemens a letter of thanks for "all those lovely books that now make my set complete." Stoddard had begun his collection of autographed copies of Clemens' books in 1877 when Clemens presented him with signed copies of his work up to that date.

Wie geht's die L A L mit?[31]

House auch.
    "   new Schauspiel
    "   alte[32]

Sorry to have missed you, but welcome you heartily home.

The C[s. 33]

James M. Dodge[34]
    Cor. M[c]Kean & Clapier [sts]
    Germantown
    Phila

Taxes. [#]

---

[31] *How's it going with the LAL?* The *Library of American Literature* is discussed in the headnote to this notebook and on page 612, note 141.

[32] Clemens wonders about the status of Edward House's suit against the Richardson/Frohman production of *The Prince and the Pauper* (see p. 542, note 183, and p. 548, note 196). In October 1890 House produced his own dramatization of *The Prince and the Pauper*. This "new play," as Clemens refers to it here, opened on 6 October at the Amphion Academy in Brooklyn under the management of H. A. D'Arcy. Daniel Frohman immediately requested that D'Arcy's production be enjoined and on 9 October 1890 an injunction was granted. House's play was closed on 18 October 1890.

The case of *House* v. *Clemens et al.* never did come to trial. Daniel Whitford claimed that when he wanted to put the case on the calendar in February 1891, Clemens instructed him to "do nothing" (Whitford to Frederick J. Hall, 7 August 1891). The matter was left unattended until Whitford moved for a dismissal, which was granted in January 1894, and the temporary injunction was removed. In February of that year Clemens ordered that suit be brought against Frohman to collect his share of the royalties, which he estimated came to "only five or six thousand dollars" (SLC to OLC, 7 February 1894); and in 1896, he again considered taking legal action against Frohman. In an Autobiographical Dictation of 28 August 1907, Clemens recalled that his lawyers neglected to attend to the matter and that he never received his share of the royalties.

[33] This note may have been sent as a telegram to the Charles Langdon family, returning to Elmira after a summer abroad.

[34] An inventor and mechanical engineer, Dodge visited the Onteora colony during the summer of 1890 when the Clemens family was staying there. His mother, Mary Mapes Dodge, had been among the first to establish a home in the Onteora community of artists and writers. Dodge was known for his talent as a raconteur and Clemens pronounced him "the greatest story-teller in America" (Candace Wheeler, *Yesterdays in a Busy Life* [New York: Harper & Brothers, 1918], p. 311).

See Whitford about Bat^{n}. selling 200,000 for 25 p.c.[35]

Get new Royal Baking Powder.

Carry Brusnahan's Report to Jns.[36]

Inquire about letter of credit.

W., start your famous pile-driver[37]

See ⟨H[earst]⟩ again.

Sir James Kitson.[38]

Kann Mann diese typen machen beim schmelzen?[39] [#]

---

[35] Clemens had asked Daniel Whitford, his New York attorney, to approach James G. Batterson with a proposal for investing in the Paige typesetter (see p. 561, note 250). On 24 September 1890 Whitford wrote Clemens that Batterson had seen the machine and had been favorably impressed but that he was not "so situated that he could take any financial interest in it now as his legitimate business requires all his time."

[36] Clemens was in Washington, D.C., on 1 October 1890 to visit Senator Jones and probably took with him a report written by John Brusnahan of the New York *Herald*. There is no known copy, but Brusnahan's 7 September 1890 letter to Clemens makes it evident that the report was designed to convince the general manager of the *Herald*, Gardiner Howland, that the Paige compositor was superior to the Mergenthaler Linotype. The *Herald* office was at this time favorably disposed toward installing a Linotype on a trial basis.

[37] The note is probably a sarcastic jab at Daniel Whitford for a lack of assertiveness in representing Clemens in his legal entanglements with Edward House and Daniel Frohman. Whitford's "theory" for handling the case was "to keep perfectly quiet until the proper time comes—then move forward utterly independent of everyone and we can probably force a satisfactory settlement" (Whitford to SLC, 17 July 1890).

[38] Kitson, a British iron and steel manufacturer, arrived in New York on 28 September 1890 to preside at the International Congress of the Iron and Steel Institute. The English delegation had sailed to New York on the steamship *Servia*, in the company of Clemens' friend Andrew Carnegie, chairman of the American reception committee. On 4 October, after the close of the convention, foreign delegates began their train tour of the United States with a four-day visit to Philadelphia. Clemens was in Bryn Mawr at the time and may have considered calling on Kitson.

[39] *Can these types by made by melting?* Since 1889 Clemens had been interested in Paige's scheme to manufacture type of hardened brass, which would be more durable than standard type (see p. 461 and p. 534, note 161). His plans to market the process were never realized.

Wie lange muss Mann warten, bis eine diese Machinen gebaut sein können?[40]

Ich will zu A. C. gehen, auf keine andere Verstand als diese: Ein Viertel bezahlte Actien-Theilen; oder ein fünfte des Grossen nach drei Millionen erhalten gevesen ⟨s[ein]⟩sind.

Oder, besser, Hundert Tausend baar Gelt, und Ein Vierte bezahlte Actien.

Or of my proceeds therefrom. Then let the Rogers flicker.[41]

North, $25
Fred,— 15
Earl,— 35—$25 later.
$R^{l\cdot}$ &c 25
———
100
P---- 50
———
150—$600.[42]

Prop. to Nelson.

Give me a deed, consideration $1, halb Theil in alle Electriche und Messing-type Entdeckungen, damit ich zum Connery und Arnot gehe.[43] [#]

---

[40] *How long does a person have to wait until one of these machines can be built?*

I want to go to A. C. [Andrew Carnegie] *on no understanding but this: One fourth of the stock shares paid for; or one fifth of the whole after three million have been obtained.*

Or, better, a hundred thousand cash, and a quarter of paid-up shares.

[41] The Rogers Typograph was a successful slug-casting machine in use at the New York *World* office.

[42] This list accounts for a portion of Clemens' typesetter expenses. Those to be paid are machinist Charles R. North; Fred Whitmore, Franklin Whitmore's son, who was learning to operate the compositor; and Charles Earll, a draftsman. The notation "$R^{l\cdot}$ &c" probably represents one week's rent plus incidentals (monthly rent at 42 Union Place, Hartford, where the typesetter was housed, came to $83.33), and "P" probably stands for Paige.

[43] This and the preceding entry appear to be connected with Clemens' plans to promote the manufacture of hardened type. The sentence reads: Give me a deed, consideration $1, *a half share in all electric and brass-type discoveries, with which I'll go to Connery and Arnot.* The proposition may have been directed at Robert W. Nelson, president of the Thorne Type-setting Machine Company of Hartford. Thomas B. J. Connery, for-

Nach ein Jahr bekomme ich $30,000 jährlich beim N.Y. Hause.[44]

⅙ of their body of machines are to correct proof on.[45]

60 machines means 10 proof-correctors, 45 operators, & 5 machines standing still.

The 45 turn out 90,000 (corrected matter) per hour—
⟨5[0,]⟩540,000 in 6 hours. The 10 men correct it.

Wages of the 55 per day, $220.
Rent of 60 mach   "   "   60
Metal, gas & attendance   25
     Total $305
        365
     ⟨1725⟩1525
     ⟨2[1]30⟩1830
        915
   Per year $111,325

Our machine, to do the same work.
10 to work, 2 to stand idle.
10 operators, 3 correctors.
Wages of the 13 per day $52
     Attendance   5
     Total $57

          P. Comp.
          365
           57
          2555
         1825
         20,805

Original cost of the machines, $144,000. [#]

---

merly managing editor of the New York *Herald*, was now editor of the New York *Truth*, and Matthias H. Arnot was the Elmira banker and merchant who had already purchased an interest in Clemens' future royalties on the Paige typesetter.

[44] *After a year I'll receive $30,000 annually from the N.Y. house.*

[45] The calculations which follow probably concern the Mergenthaler Linotypes at the New York *Tribune* office.

In 10 years *they* cost:

per year

⟨11⟩   111,325
_____
10
_____
10 years $1,113,250

& they own nothing.

In 10 years we pay out

20,805
_____
10
_____
⟨20,8050⟩208,050
Cost of mach?—   144,000
_____
$352,050

& they own 12 machines worth *more* than they originally cost.

Ask Mr. Thomas (at Wama's)[46] if he has received the creton Mrs. C. sent him for the cushions.

Ask him about the $5 rocking chair which was to come C.O.D.— why hasn't it come?

Ask him when the cot bed & mattrass are coming.

Want the Mahog Secretary (Keller's, 216 S. 9th) TO-DAY.[47]

Solution Triple Hydroiodates
Reutz & Henry Drugs
Louisville, Ky.

"Shadow of Dante" by Miss Rossetti.

"Dante & his Circle" by Dante Rosetti.

"A Boy's Town"[48] [#]

---

[46] Wanamaker's department store in Philadelphia.

[47] The secretary was intended as a gift to Susy in Bryn Mawr from her grandmother, Mrs. Jervis Langdon, and her aunt, Susan Crane. Keller's furniture store was in Philadelphia.

[48] William Dean Howells' account of his boyhood in Ohio was published on 11 October 1890 and drew the following response from Clemens: "'A Boy's Town' is perfect—perfect as the perfectest photograph the sun ever made" (SLC to Howells, 27 November 1890, *MTHL*, p. 633).

⟨Creton has not arrived—cushions are ⟨w⟩ready & waiting.

Chair will go to-morrow.

Cot & mattrass will go to-morrow.⟩

Stanley, Henry M[49]
2 Richmond Terrace
  Whitehall
  London
Hamilton Aïdé[50]

Rent   83.⎫
4 Comps. 300 ⎬ 700.
      317 ⎭

Invs. to be assigned to *me*—you to have ½.

⟨Or give⟩ You to assign to me ½ what you may get out of mach, for[n] & domestic.

Little's lawsuit goes against us, possibly.[51]

3½ ys ago Sie wurden fertig machen für 4,000.[52] [#]

---

[49] Stanley was scheduled to begin a five-month lecture tour of the United States in November 1890. When Clemens received news of the forthcoming tour from his friend James B. Pond, who was acting as Stanley's agent, he invited the explorer and his wife to visit with him in Hartford. The Stanleys probably made their visit in the first half of December 1890.

[50] Aïdé, a London society figure, was a playwright, poet, and composer of drawing room ballads. He was a cousin of Henry Stanley's mother-in-law, Gertrude Tennant, and accompanied Stanley on his American lecture tour.

[51] In April 1885, Charles L. Webster & Company had contracted with J. J. Little & Company for the printing of the *Personal Memoirs of U. S. Grant*. After about half the volumes were printed, Webster & Company sent the remainder to other printers in order to expedite the work. Little & Company brought suit against the publishing firm for breach of contract and in the summer of 1887 won a judgment in the amount of $1,950, with interest from 1 April 1886, and costs. Webster & Company's appeal was denied. On 5 January 1891 Fred Hall wrote Clemens that he had paid the Little judgment of some $2,900 but that he had not yet received the bill for legal fees.

[52] This entry concerns the sum quoted by Paige in 1886 as necessary to complete the typesetter and may roughly be translated as: 3½ ys ago *you would have finished for 4,000.* The following entry reads: *I don't want to reveal to anyone that my outlay is so much.* Clemens had voiced similar embarrassment about typesetter expenses in June 1890 (p. 557, note 233).

Ich wollte zu Keiner entdecken das mein Ausgab so viel ist.

Ich habe zwei grosse disappointments gelitten.[53]

Davis . . . .   10 . . . .   10.
4 Comps . . . . $85 . . . . . . ⟨1[0]⟩14. Fred. 21.50. 50/8[5]
Van   25
Watchman   21
Rent   21   2 com. 50
                                                       —   Watch 21
                                                       162   Tucker 22
                                                            4   Rent 21
                                                       —   Power &c . . . . ⟨[3 -]⟩8
                                                       648   Sundries 15
                                                                                                             —
                                                                                                             137
                                                                                                                4
                                                                                                             —
                                                                                                             648[54]

Begin (?)
Perfect Wednesday or Thursday. Oct.

Stanley's book at Scribner's.[55]

I always come to X to introduce Stanley every time he goes off
to hunt up some mislaid person in Africa & gets forgotten.[56] [#]

---

[53] *I have suffered two great disappointments.*

[54] Included in this list of expenses, which have been broken down into weekly payments, are the salaries of machinists Charles E. Davis and Charles H. Tucker and compositors Fred Whitmore and Charles G. Van Schuyver.

[55] Henry Stanley's book, *In Darkest Africa; or, The Quest, Rescue, and Retreat of
Emin, Governor of Equatoria*, was published by Charles Scribner's Sons in July 1890. On
26 October Livy wrote her mother: "Mr Clemens is reading aloud to me Mr Stanley's
new book which we are enjoying very much indeed" (MTM).

[56] Clemens had been asked to introduce Henry Stanley in Boston on 18 November,
and this is the first of several notes written in preparation for his speech. Clemens had
introduced Stanley in Boston once before, on 9 December 1886, when Stanley was beginning his first American lecture tour. That tour had come to an abrupt halt after a few
lectures when Stanley was called to England to head the Emin Pasha Relief Expedition.
After spending almost three years in Africa, he returned to England in the spring of 1890
and agreed to fulfill his original contract with Major James B. Pond. Clemens' introductory speech was never delivered; after the death of his mother on 27 October, he canceled
the engagement.

X1 A schoolgirl once told me that the only way to learn the German language was to divide it into 24 parts & learn 1 part at a time.[57]

single act—epitome—so that you can see at a glance the whole character of the man, the whole circumference of his greatness—

—& delivered his humble black friends to the arms of their waiting wives & children. This noble sacrifice of self, this splendid self-abnegation, is the most heroic thing that even S ever did.

Write H M Whitney, S. I & Pub. German Prince & Pauper[58]

X-2 I said Why its perfectly easy. Look at me; I've been lecturing for years. All you've got to do is to just stand up & speak the truth. He smiled a smile which I judged he had imported from Africa. I had never seen anything just like it in this country. I wonder why you laugh at that. Why it's perfectly true.

Wm Penn achieved the deathless gratitude of the savages by merely dealing in a square way with them—well, kind of a square way, anyhow—more rectangular that the *savage* was used to, at any rate. He bought the whole State of Pa from them & paid for it like a man. ⟨[at]⟩ ⟨Paid⟩ ⟨Bt the whole State for⟩ Paid $40 worth of glass beads & a couple of second-hand ⟨army⟩ blankets. Bought the whole State for that. Why you can't buy its *legislature* for twice the money now.

chin driven back in between shoulders
—spine projected far out behind like a ramrod. It gave him a very warlike aspect. [#]

---

[57] The numbered X that Clemens imposed on the following entry is the first in a series that correspond to the items in a numbered list near the end of the notebook (pp. 645–646). This indexing device is discussed on page 575.

[58] Henry M. Whitney was a newspaper publisher whom Clemens had met during his four-month stay in the Sandwich Islands in 1866. On 26 August 1890 Whitney had written Clemens that he would be sending him a copy of his new publication, *The Tourists' Guide Through the Hawaiian Islands*, the preface of which contained Clemens' "prose poem" tribute to Hawaii (see N&J1, p. 105).

A German translation of *The Prince and the Pauper* was published by J. Ricker of Giessen, Germany, in 1890; there is, however, no surviving correspondence between Clemens and Ricker or any other German publisher during this period.

I said it'll be no trouble to him; he can find Emin Bey ⟨or any other Bey⟩ ⟨easier than ⟨you or⟩ I could find the Gulf of Mexico.⟩
⟨I could find the commonest ordinary bay on a map.⟩
a peninsula.
    Hudson Bay.

    Medals, decorations.
    He hunts people, of course; but he travels there largely for his complexion.

    I don't know—that is, I don't know any ⟨r[- -]⟩reason that would fit in between your intellectual horizons,—but I will say this much, in the strictest confidence: that if he goes there for his complexion⟨[s]⟩ he's making the biggest mistake he ever made⟨[-]⟩ in his life.

    Is supposed to be grim & uncompanionable. Nothing of the kind; he is as sociable as a fly.
    It is said that in every illustrious man's ⟨character⟩ history can be found some one act which will itself epitomise the man's character.

    6,293 lines by patient actual count. Which is—157,275 ems solid.
    ⟨6⟩   ⟨6⟩
    They paid $67.50 in wages for this. But they forgot that the time represented was fifteen working days. They must add $15 for rent of machine; which makes it $82.50. Whereas it ⟨was⟩would cost by hand ⟨only⟩ just $82.65. It appears that that machine is able to save a cent a day—if you can get metal & gas for nothing.[59] [#]

-----

[59] Clemens' calculations concern the Rogers Typograph which was in use at the New York *World* office. An eight-page section of the *World's* Sunday edition of 28 September was set on the Rogers Typograph, and Clemens has counted up the number of lines actually set on the machine. In an article of 19 October, the *World* gave a highly complimentary account of the Rogers machine and furnished information about compositor's wages and the time it took to set the matter printed in its 28 September issue. "If we can't set up & correct that amount in one-sixth of the time, we'll go hang ourselves," wrote Clemens, concluding that the Rogers "has nothing but certain death before it" (SLC to Joseph T. Goodman, 23 October 1890, Yale).

We put into 23 ems what Boston Herald puts into 27 nonpareil.
Into 24 nonpareil what World puts into 27 nonp.[60]
The same in nonp that N.Y. Times puts into agate.
The same into 22 ems that Boston Herald puts into 20 agate.
We put into 26½ nonp. what World puts into 25 agate.

7
9 –26
58

We make 15 errors in 3,500 ems, & correct them in 5 minutes.
One man can correct for 6 machines when turning out 7,000 per
hour.

Oct. 24, '90. Took 12.24 train, Hartford. Waited 10 minutes at
New Haven, changed to shore line. No further change of *car* or
cars, thence to Phila. Fine large parlor smoker. Very few passengers
—the other ⟨[one]⟩line crowded. Check baggage *through*. Arrive
Phila 6.50 p.m. 1½ hours sailing around N.Y. Dinner during that
time.[61]

57		19
26		33
31		52

"Lesson 4." [62]

Spacing & difference of face considered, what they actually set
was ⟨1[24],000⟩⟨13[2],000⟩⟨131,000⟩ 131,000 in Herald non. in
119½^{h}

You have Lesson 4 set up in Herald non & see what it makes.

Tom Donaldson, 3722 Lancaster ave. [#]

---

[60] Clemens canceled this paragraph and then restored it with the instructions "STET"
written beside it and ".*stet.*" written below it.

[61] Clemens, accompanied by Clara, left Hartford on 24 October for a three-day visit
with Susy in Bryn Mawr.

[62] "Lesson 4" was part of an essay in nine lessons on horseback-riding instruction for
women. The text had been set on the Rogers Typograph and printed in the New York
World on 28 September 1890 (see note 59).

Ask Stilson Hutchins[63]

Forgot about Batterson.

Forgot about Nelson, too, & the brass.[64]

1 man, 856 ems per hour; 3 men, 2,550 ⟨ems per hour⟩ per hour. saves 2 men's wages. There is not another machine that can do that much.

Ours does 7,500 an hour, & saves 8 men's wages. This in the hands of an apprentice.

Mr. Iddings, Eve P [65]

Halstead, Murat—[66]

Oct. 28. Left at 8.03 a.m. Left Springfield at 10.32 a.m. Should have reached Chicago at 10.10 next a.m. Really got there 6.45 p.m. Took C. B. & Q at 10.30 p.m. Due at Quincy without change at 8.30 next morning. Hannibal at 9.55.[67]

Slee. At Farm?[68]

Car 106—down 6th ave—11.45[69] [#]

---

[63] Former editor and publisher of the Washington *Post* and one of the principal founders of the Mergenthaler Linotype Company.

[64] Clemens had planned to visit James G. Batterson at his Hartford office on 28 October, probably to discuss typesetter investments. He also may have intended to approach Robert W. Nelson, president of the Thorne Type-setting Machine Company of Hartford, with his plans to promote the manufacture of hardened brass type.

[65] Lewis M. Iddings was on the staff of the New York *Evening Post*. A letter from Iddings to Clemens on 16 November 1890 reveals that Clemens had declined an invitation from Iddings, the nature of which is unclear—perhaps to be Iddings' guest at the University Club of New York. Clemens evidently excused himself on account of his mother's death.

[66] Murat Halstead was editor of the Brooklyn *Standard-Union*.

[67] Jane Lampton Clemens died at the age of eighty-seven on 27 October 1890. Clemens arrived in Hannibal on 30 October for the funeral, which took place in the afternoon, and probably began his return trip to Hartford that same evening.

[68] There is no information that J. D. F. Slee (manager of J. Langdon & Company, the coal firm founded by Livy's father) was at Quarry Farm.

[69] Clemens took note of this New York City streetcar with the intention of reporting the conductor's behavior to the railway company. Not finding a responsive ear at the

Mary Mapes Dodge
170 W. 59th.

Van 100	
Fred 84	
Marty........................ 100	
Steve 80	
Rent......................... 83	
Power........................ 35	$482⁷⁰

"They've taken My Lord away—where have they laid him."[71]

"I know ⟨I know⟩ that my Redeemer Lives"

"Steal Away"⎫
Lord's Prayer⎭ chant

Talk by Sheldon.

One is going to Africa.

There's a Meeting here to-night.

Walk together Children.

De old Ark's a Moving [#]

---

superintendent's office, he wrote a letter to the press describing how, after arriving in New York the morning of 8 November, he boarded the crowded streetcar and had no choice but to stand in the doorway. He claimed that the conductor, when attempting to pass him, took him by the lapel and said, "with that winning courtesy and politeness which New Yorkers are so accustomed to: 'Jesus Christ! what you want to load up the door for? Git back here out of the way!'" (New York *World*, 10 November 1890). As a result of Clemens' complaint, the conductor was fired.

[70] Some monthly expenses connected with the typesetter. To be paid are: Charles G. Van Schuyver, printer; Fred Whitmore, apprentice on the Paige compositor; Martin J. Slattery, printer; and Steven Rogers, machinist.

[71] On 16 November Clemens attended a concert given by the Fisk University Jubilee Singers in Hartford's Asylum Hill Congregational Church. The songs were interspersed with brief speeches by the Reverend C. W. Shelton, a secretary of the American Missionary Association who was traveling with the choir, the Reverend Joseph Twichell, and several of the singers. The group hoped to raise enough money on their concert tour to establish a theological seminary for southern Negroes.

It Causes me to tremble.
(Beautiful)

Little David David play *on* yo' Harp.

Thos. F. Shields[72]
    317 East ⟨14^(th.)⟩34^(th.)

Go to my firm, W & Co 3 East 14^(th), tell them to see President
Curtiss personally, do the best they can & write me the result.
Your letter went to Norwich & is 3 days old.

Dr. C L Dana[73]
50 W. 46^(th)—Gicht.

It degrades D^(r.) Koch to kinship with the hereditary aristocratic
⟨([&] royal) line of⟩ Europe.[74]

⟨Stratford Hotel⟩Hotel Stratford, Philada.

W. H. Jenner
    190—11^(th) st.
    Brooklyn

Tom muss die rôle Medicine Man spielen.[75] [#]

---

[72] The streetcar conductor whose behavior had drawn Clemens' ire (see note 69).
Shields had written Clemens a letter on 15 November 1890 (incorrectly addressed to
"Mr Geo Clemens (Mark Twain)" in "Norwich Conn") in which he apologized for his
conduct and asked Clemens to intervene on his behalf. The notebook entry which follows
was sent as a telegram to Shields on 18 November. Shortly afterwards, Fred Hall wrote
to Frank Curtiss, president of the Sixth Avenue Railroad Company, and Shields was
subsequently reinstated.

[73] A neurologist residing in New York City. In the months to follow, Clemens would
complain not of gout, as the notation in German reads, but of rheumatism.

[74] Robert Koch, the German bacteriologist, received widespread attention in November 1890 for his discovery of tuberculin, which was erroneously hailed as a cure for tuberculosis. As a reward for his scientific research, Emperor William II conferred upon Koch
the Grand Cross of the Order of the Red Eagle.

[75] *Tom must play the role of a* Medicine Man. Clemens may have considered incorporating this idea into "Huck Finn and Tom Sawyer Among the Indians," begun in 1884
and never completed (published in *HH&T*, pp. 92–140).

1

H. to have ⟨[19]⁄₂₀⟩¹⁄₂₀ of P's & mine.
P & I to have, each, ⁹⁄₂₀ of H's interest.

2.

Restore the foreign interest

Restore the clause wh requires H. to pay back half of outlay.[76]

Or clause requiring him to pay ¹⁄₅ of the whole.

The Crime of Sylvester Bonar.[77]

The Abbè Constantine.[78]

Dec. 13, '90. Went to N.Y. with Clara in 8.29 a.m. train.
Henry C. & Mrs. Robinson also. Erkundigt Herr. R. dass die
Machine und fünfzig ⟨Th⟩ Tausend Thaler ⟨v⟩Wert von
Machinery gehört Herr P. und steht heute in seinem Name.[79]

It was Saturday. We caught 4. p.m. train & returned.

The apparently hard conditions are J's own suggestion.
Do not extend the time. That is not our affair.
The royalties must be left unembarrassed, or whence are funds to
come for continuance till expiration?

Dec. 18. Framing new contract with Robinson & Whitmore.[80] [#]

---

[76] In an earlier contract regarding the typesetter, dated 6 February 1886, Hamersley had agreed to reimburse Clemens for half the expenses incurred in obtaining capital to manufacture the machines. This clause was dropped from the 13 August 1890 contract.

[77] About one month after making this entry, while spending several days in Washington, D.C., waiting to see Senator Jones, Clemens wrote Livy that he had found "a charming book" for her to read, Anatole France's novel, *The Crime of Sylvestre Bonnard* (SLC to OLC, 13 January 1891, TS in MTP).

[78] Ludovic Halévy's novel, *L'Abbé Constantin*, first published in 1882.

[79] *According to Mr. R. the Machine and fifty thousand dollars worth of Machinery belongs to Mr. P. and is still in his name.* Clemens requested further legal advice from Robinson, a Hartford attorney, when attempting to frame a new contract with Paige late in December 1890.

[80] The contract was undoubtedly drawn up to guarantee Clemens a nine-tenths interest in the typesetter even if he failed to buy out Paige by 13 February 1891. Paige refused to sign the proposed contract. In writing to Clemens on 30 December 1890, he

Send for Slee.

Don't see any mention of the foreign.

Dec. ⟨1[8]⟩19/90. Take the 9th Ave. Elevated, every time.
Passes within 1 block of both the Xstopher st & Desbrosses ferries.
Take West shore car to 9th Ave. station. From hotel door to the
ferry stations ½ hour is plenty of time. Came to N.Y. in early train
with Beecher.[81]

Dec. 20/90. About 3 weeks ago, the machine was pronounced
"finished," by Paige, ⟨s[ince] f[or perhaps] the⟩ for certainly the
half dozenth time in the past twelvemonth. Then it transpired—I
mean it was discovered—that North had failed to inspect the
period, & *it* sometimes refused to perform properly. But to correct
that error would take just one day & *only* one day—the "merest
trifle in the world." I said this sort of mere trifle had interfered
often before & had always cost ten times as much time & money
as their loose calculations promised. P. & Davis *knew* (they always
"know," never guess) that this correction would cost but one single
day. Well, the best part of 2 weeks went by. I dropped in (last
Monday noon) & they were still tinkering. Still tinkering, but just
one hour, now, would see the machine at work, blemishless, & never
stop again for a generation: the hoary old song that has been sung
to weariness in my ears by these frauds & liars! Four days & a half
elapsed, & still that "one hour's" work was still going on, & another
hour's work still to be done. I have not heard how things stand,
to-day. I wish they would get down to where one minute's work
would make a finish. In that case we should see the end, certainly,
in, say, 15 years.[82] [#]

---

did not specify his objections, but only protested that "its legal effect would prove suicidal
for us both."

[81] The Reverend Thomas K. Beecher, pastor of the First Congregational Church of
Elmira, New York, and an intimate friend of the Langdon family. The purpose of their
trip is not known.

[82] A clipping from an unidentified newspaper, which has been pinned to the page and
covers a small portion of the preceding entry, reads: "Mrs. Bloomfield Moore has notified
the directors of the Keely Company that 'the modern Prometheus' will have to make his
motor mote without any more cash from her."

Dec 22

Let Ham drop his indebtedness & $\frac{1}{20}$.

Dec. 29. The "one hour" lasted till last Thursday; it was reported
to me by Whitmore that it got to work again that day. The next
day I sent down the new (proposed) contract prepared by
Robinson.

The machine broke down again *that* day! Remains so, still.

To-day Davis writes that the insurance agent wants his money.[83]
Also can I let him (Davis) have $200. According to my verbal
agreement, he reminds. In the first place there was nothing said
about $200, but only $100. And he forgets the verbal agreement of
the same time, that all future money was to come from royalties &
that Paige was to sell them. They never remember *their* agreements
of any kind.

⟨Dr⟩⟨Op⟩   Opera.

"They stole, they stole, they stole me child away."

Reduce your & O.'s salary.[84]

How many notes?[85]

Also your legal costs.

Who made the execrable estimates on the Yank. Show them
to me.

If W. disapproved of the Little suit, why did he consent to
appeal it? To get a compromise?[86] [#]

---

[83] Charles E. Davis was a draftsman and mechanic in Paige's employ. The money was
for fire insurance on the machine.

[84] Clemens is referring to Fred Hall's annual salary of $3,800 and Orion Clemens'
monthly pension of $200.

[85] Charles L. Webster & Company's indebtedness to the Mount Morris Bank now
amounted to $23,666.68.

[86] These queries concern Daniel Whitford, who represented Charles L. Webster &
Company when the publishing firm was sued by printers J. J. Little & Company for breach
of contract in printing Grant's *Memoirs* (see p. 587, note 51). On 26 December 1890,

Why don't you apply for Mrs G's book on $\frac{1}{2}$?[87]

The business cannot afford your salary (which is $\frac{2}{5}$ more than Slee's) nor Whit's.[88]

"Reality is the limitation of absolute substance by the this-&-the-thatity"—Duns Scotus.

Hair pillow, left by Mrs. Warner in 307 M. Hill.[89]

1

Ham must yield $\frac{1}{20}$. to me or to Joe.[90]
2. That responsibility must be removed from me.

Concern is about 10,000 in debt.
Will require 15,000 to properly go to N.Y. 25,000.
I will not accept this & apply it on a "private" show.
I will spend *nothing* until a permanent $\frac{9}{20}$ ownership, free of further expense is conferred in writing.

My claim is good & I will contest it against any corporation.

Jan. 8—Joe, in his 14th day (nearly complete) set in $1\frac{3}{4}$ hours at the rate of 7,482. [#]

Fred Hall informed Clemens that Little had won the suit and commented: "At the beginning of the suit Little offered to compromise for $800.00, and Mr. Whitford advised Mr. Webster to accept the compromise, but Mr. Webster thought it best not to."

[87] See page 549, note 199. Clemens' suggestion that Fred Hall consider publishing Julia Dent Grant's memoirs led to preliminary negotiations between Hall and Mrs. Grant in April 1891 but never resulted in a contract, possibly because Mrs. Grant expected too high a percentage of the profits.

[88] Upon learning that the Little lawsuit had been decided against Charles L. Webster & Company, Clemens voiced his irritation with Whitford in a letter to Fred Hall: "He is simply a damned fool—in Court—and will infallibly lose every suit you put into his hands. . . . If I were you I would ask Whitford to present a modified bill—or better still, present it to the parties he won the case for" (27 December 1890, *MTLP*, p. 265).

[89] Clemens evidently had been asked to retrieve a pillow left at the Murray Hill Hotel in New York by Susan Warner. The Charles D. Warners had left New York on 10 December 1890 for a year's stay in Europe.

[90] William T. Hamersley and Joseph T. Goodman.

In ⟨his⟩ the previous day he set during 3 hours at rate of 7,380 per hour.

In Fred's 42^d day he set 58,913 ems in 8 hours. Rate, 7,364 per hour.

Same day, during a three-hour stretch, he set at rate of 7,737 per hour.

Whatever amount the Rogers can do for $25 ⟨(on rental of $1⟩ (on machines hired at a rental of $1 per day) we can do $4. That is to say, we will take the same matter which they set on 5 machines in a given number of hours, & reproduce it on our machine in the same number of hours.

Washington, Jan. 14/91. Paige says Hamersley says he is given more than he is entitled to, in the contract, in proportion to mine. And he will give one of the two twentieths to me⟨.⟩, under certain conditions.

S L Clemens
James W. Paige.

The $2500 & apology.[91] [#]

---

[91] Since the signing of the 13 August 1890 contract, Clemens had been irritated over an assignment of one-tenth interest in the typesetter to William Hamersley, thinking it too generous. The assignment had originally been made in 1886 in return for Hamersley's legal advice and for his purchase of stock in the Farnham Type-Setter Manufacturing Company early in the 1880s. The notebook entry, to which Paige has appended his signature, suggests that a transfer of interest was imminent, but Clemens did not repay his debt of $2,500 to Hamersley for at least another six months. The apology which Hamersley demanded of Clemens stemmed from an argument about typesetter finances which erupted in July 1890 when Clemens was expected to repay his debt. Clemens, pressed for money and anticipating "another heavy bill" from Pratt & Whitney, wrote Hamersley that he could no longer "carry the whole burden of expense" and henceforth wanted Hamersley to pay one-fifth of all future typesetter bills (SLC to Hamersley, 11 July 1890). "I can hardly believe that you realized what you were writing," responded Hamersley in a letter of 15 July, "as you have perfectly well understood all along that I could not and was not expected to invest a dollar in this matter." Hamersley nonetheless offered to surrender a portion of his interest "for the sake of success" if Clemens retracted his letter of 11 July. There is no record of an apology from Clemens, and Hamersley retained his full interest in the typesetter.

Alex. Graham Bell.[92]
Andrew Carnegie.
   17 Broad. st.   5 W 51st
Thos. L. James.
W. J. Arkell
Depew, Vander

Make price 13, ½ cash⟨,⟩ (to cover all royalties) on delivery & ½
in ⟨6⟩3 mos.; ⟨or⟩ $16, ¼ down & ⟨⟨¼⟩ ⟨the rest⟩ ⟨[¼]⟩ in 6, 12
& 18 mos;⟩in 6, & the rest in 12 mos., ⟨or⟩ $20, with nothing
down & 40^c per M. on N.Y dailies⟨,⟩ & books offices, & 30^c
elsewhere.

N.Y. daily would pay 5½ per M. & the leads would reduce it to
5. Books would pay 4½^c per M & the leads would reduce it to
⟨3.⟩4. The proprietor would pay us not less than $3.50 per hour,
⟨[48]⟩56 hours per week, about $9,000 a year. ⟨She⟩ ⟨earns⟩
⟨would pay the proprietor $2^{000} in⟩ would pay the proprietor 45^c
per hour at the same time.

The ⟨[rate]⟩ rate to us could be reduced to 35^c per M. Then she
would buy herself entirely.

The Courting of Dinah Shadd[93] (heavily leaded, contains 135,750
ems solid, & 181,000 leaded. Composition cost $72.50. We would
do it for $6.50 (5 cents per 1000.)

Fresh-Air Fund Children checked to all points.

Letters to a Dog.
⟨Explaining⟩
About Man, & explaining his Ways.[94] [#]

---

[92] Clemens may have been considering these men as potential investors in the typesetter. Included in the list are: Thomas L. James, president of the Lincoln National Bank
in New York City; William J. Arkell, a subscription book publisher and proprietor of the
New York newspapers *Judge* and *Frank Leslie's Illustrated Newspaper;* Chauncey Depew;
and Cornelius Vanderbilt who, since the death of his father in 1885, was acting as head of
the Vanderbilt family.

[93] Rudyard Kipling's *The Courting of Dinah Shadd and Other Stories* was published
in the United States by Harper & Brothers in the fall of 1890.

[94] An unfinished, undated manuscript of thirty-two pages, bearing the cumbersome

This old stallion is always lying about something.

There are really no rational people but the suicides.

326 N. 39th
Tom Donaldson.

& Ike Bromley (get address from Depew.
Hall see both[95]

In 4 weeks, the Herald paid the Mergenthaler ⟨operators⟩ force
(2 at $27 each per week of 6 days, 10 hours a day & $20 to
attendant,) $396; & the type they set was worth $265 at 50^c per
thousand. Didn't earn wages.—Sometimes it took about as long to
correct the proof as it did to set it.

Grant, Chicago, locomotives

Saturday night, 10 o'clock
Feb. 7. '91. ⟨Sent⟩Wrote a note to Paige saying I had seen &
talked with Batterson but had not seemed to convince him that the
proposed plan was the best & safest. Had done my best to sow
fruitful seed with him, aware that this was to be my last appearance
upon any stage in the character of negociator & promoter of
commercial enterprises—& made an appointment with him for
⟨to-night⟩ Sunday night with Paige.

(This was ⟨my la⟩ quite plain notice, that, having earned my ⁹⁄₂₀
interest & paid for it many times over (as often heretofore
confessed by Paige), ⟨[that]⟩ I now hold myself as released from all

---

title "Letters from a Dog to Another Dog Explaining & Accounting for Man," was
probably written by Clemens about this time. The piece, never published, is an abusive
criticism of man's character and culminates in a denunciation of the institutions of kingship and nobility. "All things considered," the canine author muses, "a Man is as good as
a Dog. . . . Give a Man freedom of conscience, freedom of speech, freedom of action,
& he is a Dog; take them from a Dog & he is a Man."

[95] On 2 February 1891 Fred Hall wrote that he had received "a pleasant letter from Mr.
Donaldson this morning asking me to come to Philadelphia some Sunday and talk the
matter over with him." Clemens and Hall were considering publishing a cheap trade book
about Indians and may have wished to consult with Donaldson, whose knowledge of
Indian life and culture was extensive (see p. 580, note 25). In the same letter, Hall wrote
that he had been "unable to get track of Mr. [Isaac] Bromley," the journalist, who at that
time was serving as an assistant to the president of the Union Pacific Railroad.

or any further effort or expense on behalf of the machine. I told him ⟨yesterday [------]⟩ to-day that this was going to be my last negotiation, & then I was done; that I should not renew the insurance or pay out any more money.⟩

(Copy).—in substance.

Feb. 9/91.

My Dear Senator Jones:

In the pressure of your duties & occupations it may have slipped from your mind that my option under the contract of Aug. 13th will expire 4 days hence. Therefore won't you please send me a note or a telegram to tell me what I may count on?

Y truly
SLC.

After the above was mailed to-day, came a letter from Paige saying Mr. Jones ought to receive notice—or something to that effect. But that is all right. I had already written him.

(Copy.

Feb. 10/91.

My Dear Paige—

I had already attended to it by mail (although as far as our machine was concerned it seemed but a form & pallidly perfunctory), reminding ⟨him⟩Senator Jones of the Expiring date & asking him to write or wire me what to count upon. There is no answer yet.[96]

Yours sincerely
S L Clemens [#]

---

[96] Senator Jones's answer would arrive the next day. On 11 February he wrote Clemens: "I have received your note of 9th and telegraphed you today that within the time named it is impossible to accomplish anything, and that even with time, so far as my investigations had gone, the difficulties seemed almost insurmountable." Jones went on to say that he had discussed the enterprise with various senators only to find that Senator J. Donald Cameron and ex-Secretary of the Navy William Whitney were large stockholders in the Mergenthaler Linotype company. "I shall be glad to do anything I can to help you," he wrote, but closed his letter with the equivocal comment that "there cannot be a doubt as to the future of the machine."

Edmund W. Ballentine
Central Music Hall
Chicago,
Feb. 18—$1000 to lecture.[97]

Feb. 20. It is more than 2 weeks since I have seen Paige or the machine. Am deep in work—the Date & Fact Game, Col. Sellers, &c.[98]

D^r C C Rice[99] 123 E 19th

Mary Mapes Dodge,[100]
170 W. 59th.

Bryn Mawr, Prest. J. R. Rhoads. ⟨offered⟩ to read ⟨Friday⟩ Monday, 4 p.m., ⟨Apl. 10.⟩ March 23.[101]

McClane, Simsbury, 21.[102] [#]

---

[97] There is no record of any arrangement made by Clemens to lecture in Chicago during this period.

[98] Having failed to promote the typesetter, Clemens returned to projects which had lain dormant for years. The history game had been patented in August 1885, but no further effort had been made to perfect and manufacture the board. Clemens now assigned Fred Hall the task of finding someone to construct a dummy of the game.

The idea of basing a novel on the play *Colonel Sellers as a Scientist* had occurred to Clemens in the summer of 1884. He decided to postpone work on the novel until after his 1884/1885 lecture tour, but failed to pursue the matter. It appears that Clemens' original intention was to write a novel that closely paralleled the Colonel Sellers play, but the new story, which became *The American Claimant*, was developed along substantially different lines.

[99] The Clemenses' family physician who resided in New York.

[100] Mrs. Dodge invited Clemens and Livy to dinner at her New York City residence on 23 February 1891. Clemens may have declined the invitation since Livy was "sick abed" at this time (SLC to William Dean Howells, 24 February 1891, *MTHL*, p. 636).

[101] James E. Rhoads, president of Bryn Mawr College, where Susy was enrolled, had invited Clemens to give a reading for the students. Evangeline Walker (Mrs. Charles M. Andrews), then a sophomore, recalled that Susy had initially been excited at the idea, but became increasingly nervous as the date for the reading grew near. "Apparently there were some of his stories—especially the 'Ghost Story'—that she did not like and felt were not suitable for what she called 'the sophisticated group at Bryn Mawr College'" (*S&MT*, p. 287). Despite his reassurances that he would not tell "The Golden Arm," Clemens, much to Susy's distress, used this ghost story to close his reading.

[102] Later notebook entries (609.1–2 and 609.13–14) reveal that Clemens was planning to give a reading at Simsbury, Connecticut, on 21 March 1891.

The Boylston Phonograph Co of N. Eng.[103]

Wrote Chapter I of Col. Mulberry Sellers Feb. ⟨24⟩20, 1891.

Wrote Chap. IV Feb. 24. These 60 pages contain 9,000 words.

New Eng Phno Co, in the Boylston Building

Fac-simile of check.
$1000. Pay to largest
list of subscribers for
Sellers. CL W & Co.

Ad. in magazines. & $100 for largest list in *each* general agency.[104]

Bryn Mawr.[105]

Whistling Story   3
Christening "   7
Golden Arm.   3
⟨Gov. Gardner (sailor yarn)   7⟩
Lesson in German   10
Tar-Baby.—⟨15⟩10
⟨Joe's Bermuda Girl—15   *Sally Jane*⟩
Blue-jay⟨.⟩—15.

---

[103] On 28 February Clemens asked Howells to visit the Boston agency of the New England Phonograph Company to determine if a phonograph would prove practical for literary dictation. "My right arm is nearly disabled by rheumatism, but I am bound to write this book [*The American Claimant*] (& sell 100,000 copies of it—no, I mean a million—next fall.) I feel sure I can dictate the book into a phonograph if I don't have to yell. I write 2,000 words a day; I think I can dictate twice as many" (*MTHL*, p. 637). After testing the machine, Howells wrote back: "If you have the cheek to dictate the story into the fonograf, all the rest is perfectly easy" (3 March 1891, *MTHL*, p. 638).

[104] This statement and the preceding "Fac-simile of check" concern promotional schemes to increase subscription sales for *The American Claimant*. Instead of being sold by subscription, however, the story would first be serialized in various United States and foreign newspapers, then published for retail sale in May 1892.

[105] The items that follow are selections Clemens considered using in his reading at Bryn Mawr; following each is a figure representing the number of minutes required to deliver the piece. The program Clemens actually delivered will be found on pages 616–617.

From the New book (end on p. 58)[106]
Gunga Din
Clive[107]
Files on parade?
Tommy Atkins?—(8)?[108]
(Description of Gwendolen, page 70.)[109]
Possibly ⟨[d-]⟩Mrs. S.'s description of S.[110]
Interviewer

"Impressions of America"   Tittle
Being a Diary ⟨Stolen from an Englishman⟩ of a visiting
Englishman found in a room in a hotel. (Sojourn of 2 weeks).
Information obtained from 2 sources—personal observation &
⟨some⟩ *other* flitting Englishmen.[111]

Hall, try one little Red-Cap boy.

Arabian Nights in 25ᶜ parts.

Rob. Crusoe, ditto. [#]

---

[106] The end of page 58 of *The American Claimant* manuscript is near the close of chapter 4. The manuscript page concludes with a description of neighborhood reaction to the new hatchments, bearing the Rossmore arms and motto, which Colonel Sellers has nailed to the front of his house.

[107] The poem by Robert Browning.

[108] "Gunga Din" and "Tommy" were included in the first American edition of Rudyard Kipling's *Departmental Ditties, Barrack-Room Ballads, and Other Verses* (New York: United States Book Co., 1890). "Files on Parade" is Clemens' notation for the poem "Danny Deever," which appeared in the same volume.

[109] "Lady Gwendolyn" is the title Colonel Mulberry Sellers bestows on his daughter Sally when he lays claim to being the rightful Earl of Rossmore. Gwendolyn's extraordinary beauty is described in chapter 5 of *The American Claimant*. Clemens' page reference is to the manuscript of the book.

[110] Mrs. Sellers' description of that "same old scheming, generous, good-hearted, moonshiny, hopeful, no-account failure," Colonel Mulberry Sellers, constitutes the first half of chapter 3 of *The American Claimant*.

[111] "Impressions of America" became the title of the journal kept by Lord Berkeley in *The American Claimant*. Chapter 7 of the novel opens with Berkeley having just settled into his hotel in Washington, D.C., and making "preparations for that first and last and all-the-time duty of the visiting Englishman—the jotting down in his diary of his 'impressions' to date."

Memory-Builder. ⟨Sharpener⟩
⟨A Date-&-Fact Game⟩
A Game
For acquiring & retaining all sorts of
Facts & Dates.
(Freeman Clark's remark about linking together study &
amusement.)[112]
securing impressing.

Huck comes back, 60 years old, from nobody knows where—&
crazy. Thinks he is a boy again, & ⟨seeks⟩ scans always every face
for Tom & Becky &c.

X3 Tom comes, at last, 60 from wandering the world & tends
Huck, & together they talk the old times; both are desolate, life
has been a failure, all that was lovable, all that was beautiful is
under the mould. They die together.

X4 Only "birth" makes noble. So it follows indisputably that if
Adam was noble, ⟨we⟩ all are; & if he wasn't, none are.

⟨⟨If an⟩ So long as an insane patient's hair remains dry & harsh
& refuses to relent, his case is not curable. Examine Darwin again
about this.⟩[113]

⟨Foundation-stone Layer—*proper* title of an English prince, &
his only useful vocation.⟩

⟨Hens lay eggs, *he*, stones.⟩ [#]

----

[112] James Freeman Clarke, a Unitarian clergyman, devoted a chapter in his book *Self-Culture* (Boston: James R. Osgood and Co., 1880) to "Education by Means of Amusement." "Why not," asks Clarke, "introduce into schools games of history, of biography, of geography, of chronology, of arithmetic. . . . What could be better discipline than this?" (p. 385). Clarke's remarks no doubt struck Clemens as a useful endorsement of his own history game.

[113] Darwin correlated hair condition and states of mind, making specific mention of the "dryness and harshness" of an insane patient's hair and noting that if "the bristling of the hair is extreme, the disease is generally permanent and mortal" (Charles Darwin, *The Expression of the Emotions in Man and Animals* [New York: D. Appleton and Co., 1886], pp. 296–297). Clemens owned a copy of the edition cited.

Sherman delivering diplomas at West Point.

Dry & harsh as a crazy man's hair.

Monkeys emit a low chuckling laugh when you tickle them under the armpits.[114]

Of Yamersley. "About ⅔ of him is knave & the other ⁹⁄₁₀ is fool."

Mr. Hall see Arnot.[115]

Capt. Burns's (?") full account of Campaigning with Crook. *Get it*. But he is a crank & must be ingeniously approached, Howells says. Reduction & pacification of *all* Indian tribes. The Scribner one *is only an episode*.[116]

Cheap edition of Huck. Talk with Mr. Hall.[117]

Got the phonograph March 11/91, Howells present—& McDonald.[118] [#]

---

[114] This information, like that about "a crazy man's hair," is drawn from Darwin's *Expression of the Emotions in Man and Animals:* "If a young chimpanzee be tickled— and the armpits are particularly sensitive to tickling, as in the case of our children,—a more decided chuckling or laughing sound is uttered; though the laughter is sometimes noiseless" (p. 131).

[115] In December 1889, Matthias H. Arnot, an Elmira merchant, had agreed to purchase a substantial interest in Clemens' future royalties on the typesetter for $50,000. He made an initial payment of $5,000 in the spring of 1890 and gave Clemens a note for the remaining sum. Fred Hall and Clemens, worried about the possibility of a financial panic, were now considering the idea of raising money on Arnot's note to pay Charles L. Webster & Company's debt to the Mount Morris Bank and obtain more working capital for the firm. There is no evidence that Clemens or Hall pursued this idea.

[116] In early February 1891, Howells had passed on to Clemens a recommendation made by Webb Hayes, son of Rutherford B. Hayes, that Charles L. Webster & Company consider publishing Captain John G. Bourke's account of his service in the Indian campaigns under General George Crook. But Bourke had already made arrangements with Charles Scribner, who published the work as *On the Border with Crook* in October 1891 (see *MTHL*, pp. 634–635). The "episode" to which Clemens refers was an article on Crook which Bourke had published in the March 1891 issue of the *Century* magazine— not, as Clemens mistakenly notes, in *Scribner's Magazine*.

[117] Fred Hall visited Clemens in Hartford the weekend of 14 and 15 March to discuss, along with other business matters, the idea of issuing a cheap edition of Clemens' books for trade publication, starting with *Huckleberry Finn*.

[118] Both Elinor and William Dean Howells were visiting the Clemenses in Hartford at this time. T. H. Macdonald was an agent of the New England Phonograph Company who visited Clemens' home to set up the phonograph.

Berkeley diaries his opinion of the shabby White House.
Call one of the boys the Missing Link.

Bryn Mawr.

⟨M

4.	Tar-Baby	12
4.12	Blue-Jay	19–15
4.27	Christening Yarn	7
4.34	Drilling King[119]	17
4.51	Whistling Yarn	5
[4.]56	Golden Arm	5

$\overline{61}$⟩

⟨M.

⟨Blue-jay	19	15⟩
⟨Drilling King		15⟩
⟨German Lesson		10⟩

Tar-Baby		4.12	4.12
⟨Drilling the⟩			
Blue-jay	19 ⟨—⟩4.27	15	4.27
Christening Yarn	⟨—⟩4.34	7	4.34
Drilling the King	4.49.	15	4.49
⟨G⟩Whistling Yarn		5	
Golden Arm		5	

$\overline{59}$⟩

Huck & Hare-Lip.[120]

Finds Mary Jane Crying over her trunk

Sends her to Lothrop's

Explains about the Mumps to Hare-lip [#]

---

[119] From chapter 28 of *A Connecticut Yankee,* in which Hank Morgan tries to teach the king how to comport himself with humility.

[120] This selection is from chapter 26 of *Huckleberry Finn,* and the three that follow are from chapter 28.

Add ⟨German Lesson⟩ *Clive* at Simsbury & ⟨Gov. Gardiner.⟩ CLIVE.

"You git busted—in health or in money—⟨[-]⟩ land, but its long work & up-hill to git back again—& you scacely *ever* do."

"The Americans are a patient people—put up with everything—"
"No—they don't put up with royalties & ⟨[putrefied]⟩ nobilities."
"Look at your ⟨Vanders⟩ Goulds & Rockef"
"⟨They⟩Their own work & talent gave them money—& its the work & the talent that are respect-worthy, not the money. The money merely *represents* the money & the talent, as paper represents gold.[121]

Simsbury, Saturday 21st. Train leaves Central N.E. depot at 3.25 p.m.

Always talking about "When I was at College"—turns out to be Girard.[122]

First day, 6 cylinders in 1½ h.
2d   " 22   "   " 5   "
200 words on a cylinder[123]

"Revelations-View. St. John in Patterson's Island."[124] [#]

---

[121] The dialogue may have been intended for inclusion in *The American Claimant*, but was never incorporated into the manuscript.

[122] Girard College, in Philadelphia, was founded to provide a free primary and secondary education for poor white orphan boys.

[123] Clemens dictated chapters 12 and 13 and part of chapter 14 of *The American Claimant* on the phonograph. He finally decided he couldn't "write literature with it, because it hasn't any ideas & it hasn't any gift for elaboration, or smartness of talk, or vigor of action, or felicity of expression, but is just matter-of-fact, compressive, unornamental, & as grave & unsmiling as the devil" (SLC to William Dean Howells, 4 April 1891, *MTHL*, p. 641).

[124] In chapter 16 of *A Tramp Abroad*, Clemens makes note of the "happy" English which "distinguishes an inscription upon a certain picture in Rome,—to wit: 'Revelations-View. St. John in Patterson's Island.'" Clemens mentions this bizarre misrendering of the Isle of Patmos in closing his chapter on the comical effects caused by faulty translations.

PAMPHLET PINACOTEK. "It is not permitted to make use of the work in question to a publication of the same contents as well as to the pirated edition of it." [125]

The book will issue ⟨⟨[5]⟩2⟩ 3 months ⟨[---]⟩ from the day the ⟨first⟩ canvassing books are finished & ready for delivery. [126]

German Water-Cure book. [127]

SEE NEXT PAGE: Notes.

You borrow through a N.Y. broker. [128]

I want all *my* notes withdrawn & *firm* notes with my endorsement substituted. If I should die, I ⟨should⟩would seem to owe the *firm!* [129]

How can you put *those* in as ⟨an asset⟩ a liability *of the firm?*

Ask Wallace Peck,
     124 Water st. N.Y.,
who made the pictures for "How to Run a Railroad." Want him for my book. [130] [#]

---

[125] This quotation is printed in chapter 16 of *A Tramp Abroad* as one of a number of curiously worded extracts from a small pamphlet entitled "A Catalogue of Pictures in the Old Pinacotek," brought to Clemens' attention while traveling in Germany.

[126] Clemens later changed his mind about issuing *The American Claimant* by subscription. By May 1891, he and Hall had plans to print the story in serial form, to be followed by a volume for trade publication in 1892.

[127] Charles L. Webster & Company was interested in obtaining American rights to Sebastian Kneipp's *Meine Wasser-Kur*, a popular German work, but never made arrangements to publish the book.

[128] Fred Hall had written to Clemens on 17 March 1891 about raising money to pay off Webster & Company's bank debts: "I have been seeing what I could do among my friends—in a quiet way of course—and I think I can promise positively to raise $15,000 on our notes properly endorsed." Hall secured $15,000 on 1 May from personal friends, the George Barrow family, and the money was used to take up three Mount Morris Bank notes of $5,000 each.

[129] Charles L. Webster & Company had evidently borrowed money from the Mount Morris Bank by discounting notes Clemens wrote to the firm. This entry records Clemens' concern that these notes not be interpreted as representing an actual indebtedness on his part.

[130] Wallace Peck was an American humorist who had published several ephemeral works by 1891. "How to Run a Railroad" has not been identified. *The American Claimant* was illustrated by Dan Beard, who had done the illustrations for *A Connecticut Yankee.*

Otto Schlutter.[131]

⟨[-]⟩ The descriptions of scenery in this book are patented, under ⟨Section/Chapter 44,368 Revised⟩ the Statute⟨s⟩ Extra-hazardous ⟨of the United States, which provide⟨s⟩ for the⟩ "protection of improvements in the mechanic arts." [132]

48 Park Ave. N.Y.
Miss Annie B. Jennings
⟨Thursday⟩Wed'sday, Apl. ⟨23.⟩22
Author's Readings.
7 East 15th (afternoon. 3. p.m.)

Conditions: I am to be No. 3 if there are 4 or 5 readers; & No. 4 if there should be *more* than 5.[133]

Readings.
Huck's "sand" remark about Mary.[134]

Lev N.Y. at 11, arr 1.20.
⟨Leave N.Y. 12.20.⟩ SHAVE
" Phil. 8.20, arr. ⟨12.40⟩10.40[135]

Add to readings, A. Ward's "Lone-hand baptism" & "Adam? what was his other name?" [136] [#]

---

[131] Otto B. Schlutter was the Clemenses' German instructor, who resided in Hartford. Clemens was planning to have Schlutter translate Sebastian Kneipp's *Meine Wasser-Kur* into English, but the idea was eventually discarded.

[132] Evidently a draft of a humorous proviso for *The American Claimant*. Clemens did not use it, however, deciding instead to poke fun at "persistent intrusions of weather" in "fictitious literature" by borrowing "such weather as is necessary for the book from qualified and recognized experts" and relegating it to an appendix.

[133] On 20 March Annie B. Jennings invited Clemens to participate in authors' readings for the benefit of the Young Women's Christian Association. Also appearing were H. H. Boyesen, Robert Underwood Johnson, Frank R. Stockton, Will Carleton, and John Kendrick Bangs. The New York *Tribune* of 23 April 1891 reported that the event was attended by a "large and sympathetic audience. . . . Mr. Clemens told the story of 'A Scotch-Irish Christening' with such effect that he was forced to tell another story to satisfy his hearers."

[134] Huck's comment that Mary Jane Wilks "had more sand in her than any girl I ever see" occurs in chapter 28 of *Huckleberry Finn*.

[135] Clemens' schedule for travel to and from Bryn Mawr, where he appeared on the afternoon of 23 March 1891.

[136] Both these anecdotes have been identified on page 69, note 8.

Cash collections in Jan. '91, $18,000.

Sent out, in Oct to & including Jan. '91, 49,214 books. Subtract that big batch of Sheridans, it is 45,000 in 5 months. Say 100,000 in a year. The profit (nett) ⟨[--]⟩should be $95,000.

Your best chance is to prospect the Game, & if it promises well, out with it. $10,000.[137]

Next, the cheap Huck—rush it out. $10,000[138]

⟨A cheap G[-]⟩[139]

Goes the Admiral into the War Library?[140]

We issue 50,000 general books & 24000 sets LAL a year, & still no dividends & no reduction of debt. How many of the two *are* required to produce a result?[141] [#]

---

[137] "Mark Twain's Memory-Builder" did not promise well. On 6 May 1891, after a dummy board had been made, Fred Hall wrote to Clemens: "I have talked with one or two toy stores. They are willing to take any reasonable quantity we want to send them on sale, but they will not buy very many of them to start with; they say they want to see how the public take it up." It is not known how many were actually manufactured. In 1892, acknowledging that "the trade see no promise in the Game," Clemens advised Hall to "put it aside," and expressed regret that he had attached his name to it (8 March 1892, *MTLP*, p. 307).

[138] The one-dollar cloth edition of *Huckleberry Finn* appeared in the fall of 1891.

[139] Possibly a reference to the *Personal Memoirs of U. S. Grant*. On 10 April Fred Hall acquired Mrs. Grant's consent to "our taking the Grant sheets we have on hand, binding two volumes in one and selling it for $2.00" (Hall to SLC, 11 April 1891). For reasons which are not clear, Charles L. Webster & Company did not publish the one-volume edition of the *Memoirs* until 1894.

[140] Fred Hall had been approached by a representative of Admiral David Dixon Porter's family, who were interested in publishing his biography. Porter, who had risen to prominence during the Civil War, died on 13 February 1891. Hall doubted the book would sell except in "army and naval circles," and the proposed volume was not accepted (Hall to SLC, 25 March 1891). Charles L. Webster & Company's "Great War Library" was a uniformly bound collection of works by or about Grant, Sherman, Sheridan, McClellan, Crawford, Hancock, and Custer, offered on the installment plan. With the exception of William T. Sherman's memoirs, the original editions of these works had been individually published by Webster & Company.

[141] *Library of American Literature* sales had been steadily increasing, but Charles L. Webster & Company's growing deficit was a direct function of the *Library's* success. The eleven-volume set was sold for $33 and could be purchased with monthly payments of $3. A set was sent to the subscriber upon receipt of the first payment, and the canvasser who

You have a cash income of $7,000 a month & no dividends. How much *is* required?

Why not follow Huck, 2 months later with $1 Yankee? $10,000.

And both a few months later With White Elephant (using the *present* plates) at 50ᶜ in paper. $5,000.

Except these, let us make no new books except the authors advance the money for the plates, paper & *printing*, (not the binding.)

Shall we, or can we, *sell* a ⅓ interest in the business for $100,000?

And follow the above, a few months later with $1 *P. & P.* $10,000.

The weekly reports have ceased from coming, lately.

We have no monthly reports for July & Aug. '90.

What said the Am. Pub. Co.?[142]

Got all the monthly statements in my pocket.

I would not re-set the Pope. Can't you make a cheap edition with these plates?[143] [#]

---

had made the sale was entitled to his $12.24 commission immediately. Thus, between production costs and commission payments, the installment method necessitated "the locking up of a good deal" of the firm's capital for a substantial period of time (Frederick J. Hall to SLC, 20 March 1891). By March 1891 over $30,000 was due in outstanding payments, and Hall estimated that the firm would eventually need to borrow at least $100,000 to keep its installment department afloat.

[142] The American Publishing Company had been notified of Charles L. Webster & Company's plans to issue a one-dollar edition of *Huckleberry Finn*. Frank E. Bliss wrote Clemens on 3 April 1891 that he thought the move a "mistake" for it would be liable to interfere with the sale of Clemens' books by the American Publishing Company. Fred Hall considered Bliss's letter "the strongest argument possible in favor of the cheap edition. . . . They know if we get out cheap editions of our book that it will make a demand for a cheap edition of the books that they publish, and I think it will force them into making some arrangement with us whereby we can get out a uniform edition of your books" (Hall to SLC, 8 April 1891).

[143] Bernard O'Reilly's *Life of Leo XIII* was originally published by Charles L. Webster & Company in 1887 and reissued in expanded form in 1889. No cheap edition was published.

How many L A L so far this month?

How many other books so far this month?

Compare this March '91, with March '90 on L A L.—& '89.[144]
Compare the year '90 with '89, all through.

We issued only Vol. 11 in '90.[145] Where did our heavy expense
fall?

What ⟨is⟩ are your *cash* collections from L A L *per month* from
Jan. '89 till & including the present month?

Cash collections for the *whole* business per month from Jan. '89
till to-day?

If there is money in a cheap Sherman, why not in a cheap Grant
& Sheridan? Or is the War Library likely to be more profitable?[146]

When was the first effort made on the instalment plan?[147]

And did W. begin it?

What month did W. begin?

Come up to Hartford with me & talk the rest. [#]

---

[144] Charles L. Webster & Company sold 1,379 volumes of the *Library of American
Literature* in March 1889, 1,923 volumes in March 1890, and 3,961 volumes in March
1891.

[145] Charles L. Webster & Company distributed the eleventh and last volume of the
Library of American Literature to subscribers in mid-July 1890.

[146] After General W. T. Sherman's death on 14 February 1891, his family proposed
that Charles L. Webster & Company issue a cheap edition of the general's memoirs and
agreed to pay for its manufacture. Fred Hall calculated that a cheap edition would not
injure the sales of the costlier two-volume set of the work which the firm had been selling
since September 1890, as the latter was sold primarily in connection with the "Great War
Library" series. The new two-dollar volume, which was ready for distribution in April
1891, was sold by subscription and through bookstores simultaneously. A similar cheap
edition of Sheridan's *Personal Memoirs* was issued later that year. The one-volume Grant
Personal Memoirs published in 1894 (see note 139) was evidently also an inexpensive
edition.

[147] Charles L. Webster & Company's first efforts to sell books on the installment plan
began with the sale of the *Library of American Literature* in the last week of December
1887, when Webster's active involvement with the firm was drawing to a close.

Or, you write & ask Bunce[148] for a date.

⟨I don't really see that L. A. L. has climbed fast. Don't feel strongly [encoura]ged.⟩

How long would it take to try one boy with a basket?[149]

Is the Sherman all printed?

Are the canvassing books out, or shall you use any?

When shall you issue?

Get the $15,000 & let the rest wait till we get the L A L higher. We can't show a steady & large monthly increase on L A L.[150]

With your collections as large as now, do you really need more capital?

Your monthly cash must now reach $8,000. Do you need more?

What *is* the average monthly out-go, now that L A L is complete & 3,000 all printed?

I had the idea that the Extra $1800 of your salary was undrawn & went to the purchas of your ⅓. Webster was to have it till his (stolen) $4000 was made good, then go back to $3000. Why not pay it on the ⅓ till we reach dividends?[151] [#]

---

[148] Clemens' friend, Edward M. Bunce, was the cashier of the Phoenix National Bank in Hartford. Clemens may have wished Fred Hall to confer with Bunce about Charles L. Webster & Company's financial affairs.

[149] Clemens had previously noted a plan for boys to sell very cheap editions of Webster & Company books (see p. 545, note 187).

[150] In his letter of 25 March 1891, Fred Hall had proposed that Charles L. Webster & Company raise $45,000 immediately. Hall had already arranged to borrow one-third of this amount (see p. 610, note 128) and asked Clemens to raise the remaining $30,000 "on the firm's notes."

[151] In 1887 Clemens had agreed to increase Charles L. Webster's $3,000 annual salary by $800 for a period of five years, to make up for the $4,000 loss Webster claimed he suffered after Frank M. Scott's embezzlement of company funds (see p. 315, note 46). When Webster retired from the partnership in December 1888, Fred Hall, who had been earning $2,000 a year, became heir to this inflated salary and agreed to purchase Webster's one-third interest in the firm for $12,000. Webster was paid this sum by the company, and Hall was gradually paying off his indebtedness to the firm by turning his share of the profits back into the company.

I have cut Orion down $100 a month.

Does 111 L A L pay the *entire* working expense, or ½ of it?

Bismarck's book.[152]

We made Vols. 7, 8, 9, 10, & part of 11 in '89. What heavy Expense had we in ⟨'8⟩'90?

Sell a ⅓ to Stanley for $100,000.

Or preferably ⅙.

Or to Chatto.[153]

What we want to know *exactly*, is this:—& is this so?
1. Up to 200 subs. a month, we can take care of ourselves.
2. On every 50 added, per month, we need to borrow what?—⟨[bo]th the [money *and*]⟩ the canvasser's $12.24? Say $600 per 50?
3. Or *half* the gross money coming in—⟨[sa]y⟩ which is $35 per set. Borrow $17.50 per set?[154]

Where is Jones?

What will the check-ad cost in Century & Harpers kept standing all the time? $50 prize & $1000.

On 3,200 sets per year (1600 sets in 6 mos., near 270 per month,) there is a clear profit over *every* expense, of ⟨3⟩$32,000, a year. The rest of the business clears $25,000 a year over *every* expense.

At Bryn Mawr—[155]
Tar-Baby—

---

[152] Early in 1891 Prince Otto von Bismarck was preparing his memoirs for publication. After having guided Prussian and German policy for twenty-eight years, Bismarck had resigned the chancellorship and his other offices in March 1890 owing to a series of political clashes with Emperor William II. His recollections were published posthumously in 1898.

[153] That is, sell a one-third or one-sixth interest in Charles L. Webster & Company to Henry M. Stanley or to Andrew Chatto, Clemens' English publisher.

[154] Charles L. Webster & Company's difficulty in subsidizing the *Library of American Literature* is discussed in note 141, page 612.

[155] Clemens performed at Bryn Mawr on 23 March 1891.

Christening.
True Story
Whistling
Golden Arm.
And left out Blue-Jay—an immense mistake.

Gen. Sherman, 75 W 71st [156]

Metcalf. [157]

"Don't shake the ancestral tree. You won't find the proportion of ripe fruit to rotten satisfactory."

Put the Mind Telegraphy in the book as an Appendix. [158]

Insert chapters of Visit to Heaven—from crazy man in an Asylum at Geneva. [159]

Carry the Scrap-book to Europe.

Scrap-book the "Adoration" 842–3 April Century, 1891. [160]

X5 Spectacled girl in Boston asked Nasby, "Do you believe Aristotle was a teleologist?" "Carry me home to-die." [#]

---

[156] Clemens had been corresponding with Thomas E. Sherman, son of William T. Sherman, about problems in issuing a cheap edition of his late father's *Personal Memoirs*. The exchange of letters, which took place in the last week of March, concerned James G. Blaine's tardiness in preparing an appendix to the book which would briefly cover the final years of the general's life. Charles L. Webster & Company had hoped to rush the volume out before other "cheap lives" appeared on the market at the end of March. The anxious flurry of correspondence between Fred Hall, Clemens, and the Sherman family subsided when Blaine's material reached Hall's office on 30 March, and the firm was able to distribute the book during the second week of April.

[157] On 31 March 1891 Clemens wrote to Lorettus S. Metcalf, founder of the *Forum*, offering him the manuscript of "Mental Telegraphy," an article written in 1878. Metcalf, however, had resigned the editorship of the *Forum* earlier that month. On 3 April 1891 Walter H. Page, Metcalf's successor, offered to read "Mental Telegraphy," but the following day Clemens decided to send it to *Harper's* magazine (see note 168).

[158] A plan to publish "Mental Telegraphy" as part of *The American Claimant*.

[159] Clemens evidently planned to make use of unidentified extracts from the unpublished "Captain Stormfield's Visit to Heaven" in *The American Claimant*.

[160] These pages in the April 1891 *Century* magazine contain Timothy Cole's engraving of a detail from Leonardo da Vinci's *Adoration of the Magi*, accompanied by a note describing the picture.

The Story of the Rat in the Trap. Told by her mother.

From a letter from London to Howells, March, '91: "Mark Twain, you know, is more valuable on the continent⟨,⟩ than any writer, English or American. He sells in Persia & Samarcand & the Grecian Archipelago."[161]

The Extrordinary Crowninshield Case—as related by Miss Hesse. Annette LaNeaugan. (Ann Lannigan.)

Inferior to the tug in grandeur of conception & breadth of design. Washtub & tug.

DIARY.
Like the telephone—one of the very most useful of all inventions, but rendered almost worthless & a cold & deliberate theft & swindle by the black scoundrelism & selfishness of the companies of chartered robbers who conduct it.

Electric light Co's permitted to murder men & horses unrebuked.[162]

Barrow[163]—"You pick out our manners, & things which are none of your business—why don't you talk of our infernal telephone & electric light system.

And *we* go over yonder & criticise trivialities & leave your aristocratic adulteries unmentioned.

In fact *no* American traveler has dared to criticise England as you have us.

"Lay low, cover the child."[164] [#]

---

[161] The compliment was from Charles Wolcott Balestier, an American novelist who had just established a publishing firm in London and wished to add Clemens to its list of authors. Howells had enclosed Balestier's letter in his own to Clemens of 3 April 1891 (*MTHL*, pp. 640–641).

[162] Clemens nursed a longstanding grievance with the Electric Light Company of Hartford (see p. 404, note 16).

[163] The egalitarian chairmaker in *The American Claimant* who befriends Lord Berkeley.

[164] The quotation is from a melodramatic episode in chapter 54 of George W. Cable's

Publish the Bermuda girl.

And the Christening

So big it takes only 11 of 'em to make a dozen

Life-prisoner that saw the moon the first time in 9 years.

Story of the Vanderbilt of the Esquimaux—13 gunflints.[165]

Paige the Microbe

X6 *Stranger*—Observing the nymphs in Hans Makart's "Hunting Party"[166]—I wonder what they are hunting.
Another Stranger. Don't know. But it would be a good time to hunt fleas.

Edw. W. Bok—Women's Home Journal? Phila[167]

The Baby's Diary.

⟨[-]⟩The gentleman said he carried his hdkf in his breast pocket

---

novel, *Dr. Sevier* (1884), in which Mary Richling crosses the battle lines during the Civil War to reach the bedside of her dying husband. "Mary's Night Ride" had been a staple in Cable's repertoire of readings during his 1884/1885 lecture tour with Clemens.

[165] In "The Esquimau Maiden's Romance" (*Cosmopolitan*, November 1893), Clemens depicted a "polar Vanderbilt," whose fortune of twenty-two fish hooks made him the envy of his tribe.

[166] Makart was a celebrated nineteenth century Austrian painter whose hastily executed paintings were grandiloquent portrayals of historical or mythological subjects. *Diana's Hunting Party* (1880), a painting of immense size, depicts the goddess Diana surrounded by nymphs and hunting dogs. She is standing on the shore of a lake ready to hurl a dart at a stag swimming across the water, and in the immediate foreground are several nymphs bathing.

[167] Bok, editor of the *Ladies' Home Journal*, paid a visit to Fred Hall on 25 April 1891 to discuss the possibility of purchasing the serial rights to Clemens' new novel, *The American Claimant*. The interview "in a measure" persuaded Hall that "with a trade book, publication in periodical form first would not injure its sale so much as I imagine," and he helped Bok arrange a visit to Clemens in Hartford on 30 April or 1 May to learn "something of the character of the book" before making any definite offer (Hall to SLC, 25 April 1891). The meeting with Clemens was followed by a further discussion of financial arrangements between Bok and Hall on 2 May and culminated in Bok's offer of $4,000 to serialize the story in the *Ladies' Home Journal*. Clemens thought the price too low, and negotiations with Bok and others continued until late May (see p. 625, notes 191 and 192).

sometimes, sometimes in his ⟨[h]⟩side-coat pocket. "Everybody has has own notions, I said—I sit on mine."

⟨THHITT⟩
Carry Mental Telegraphy to Century.[168]

Ask Mr. Hall what "Collections" followed by "⟨S⟩CLW & Co" means.

Remind that they don't *yet* signify in weekly report how many *new* subscriptions to LAL.

Want them to keep my US bank account recruited while I am gone.[169]

Sergius Stepniak[170]
Alvorton, Tremont st

Collections $4,500 in 6 days, Apl. 13 to 18 inclusive. $5,500 before. $10,000 in 18 days of Apl. '91.

Don't copyright game or book till after July 1.

Mr. Hall, sell my story, but not to a Syndicate [#]

---

[168] Clemens actually submitted "Mental Telegraphy" to *Harper's* magazine around 4 April 1891 (see note 157). He let editor Henry M. Alden set the price, and on 1 May 1891 was sent $500 for the piece. The article was published in *Harper's* in December 1891.

[169] The Clemenses were planning to leave Hartford in early June 1891 for an indefinite stay in Europe (see the headnote).

[170] The Russian revolutionary, Sergei Mikhailovich Kravchinski, who had taken the name Stepnyak ("Son of the Steppe") as his pseudonym. He wrote Clemens from the Alvorton Hotel in Boston and asked if he might call upon him when passing through Hartford in the middle of April 1891. His letter of 12 April was accompanied by a brief note of introduction from William Dean Howells, who was sure that Stepnyak and Clemens would "not fail to be great friends" (*MTHL*, p. 643). Howells admired Stepnyak immensely and, in writing to his father of the Russian Nihilist, described Stepnyak as "a most interesting and important man; one of those wonderful clear heads that seem to belong to other races than ours" (*Life in Letters of William Dean Howells*, ed. Mildred Howells, 2 vols. [New York: Doubleday, Doran & Co., 1928], 2:12). After his visit to the Clemens household, Stepnyak sent Clemens a copy of his *Underground Russia* (Eng. trans., 1883) and wrote Livy expressing his delight at "having had the opportunity of knowing all your family and Mr Clemens whose work, I understand now finer better than before" (Stepnyak to OLC, 19 April 1891, TS in MTP).

Stop street sprinkling.

And electric lights.

And publications.

And clubs, 3 yrs.

And pensions.

Hall, geben Sie mir Geld[171]

Marshall H. Mallory[172]
47 Lafayette Place

Prof. Tappan
2ᵈ Advent[173]

Send the Feather-duster man to Harpers—have it told on Shipboard.

Write several & call them Tales ⟨to⟩Told in the Smoking Cabin"

Take daily notes.

Remember Bayard Taylor in the Holsatia[174]

May 2. Finished the book which I began to write Feb. 20. 71 days.[175] [#]

---

[171] Hall, *give me money.*

[172] Mallory was the publisher of the *Churchman,* a religious weekly issued in New York City. At the end of April 1891, he agreed to try to organize a company for the manufacture of Paige typesetters and anticipated buying out Clemens' interest in the machine for $250,000; his attempts to establish a company, however, met with no success.

[173] "The Second Advent," a manuscript of eighty-four pages, was probably drafted by Clemens in 1881. On the title page of the manuscript, Albert Bigelow Paine termed the piece a "semi burlesque of a new Christ, born in Arkansas," and dismissed it as "hardly usable." The story has been published in *Mark Twain's Fables of Man,* ed. John S. Tuckey (Berkeley, Los Angeles, London: University of California Press, 1972), pages 53–68. The professor to whom Clemens evidently intended to send a copy of "The Second Advent" has not been identified.

[174] Taylor and Clemens had been fellow passengers while crossing from New York to Germany on the S.S. *Holsatia* in April 1878. Taylor, who had been traveling to Berlin to take up his new post as United States minister to Germany, died eight months later.

[175] *The American Claimant.*

Frascati's, Havre—good—& the best in Havre[176]

Madame Thekla de Soto
    Jena

Steamer chairs

Pipes & tobacco (quantity)

"Giessen Sie kaltes Wasser drüben".[177]

    1   2   3
Wills. Executrix. Visit him.[178]

Give easier terms if part of proceeds come to me.

X7 In writing to thank hosts who have been entertaining you a day or more, your letter *must* have one or the other of these 2 essentials,—*length* or *strength*; but both or not necessary. Mrs. S.'s had the former, & a deal of pleasant appreciation & real kindness— a model letter, 4⟨,⟩ pages, flowingly said.

His was ⟨[--]⟩40 or 50 words, but said with a satisfying vigor that made up for the brevity, & wound up with a kind of sudden, swift strong, something as unexpected & as gratifying as a snatched kiss— when both are willing.[179]

X8 S.[180] walked 15 miles in the Alps one day, with his girl, *determined* to offer himself that day if *any* even momentary chance

---

[176] The Clemens family, accompanied by Susan Crane and Katy Leary, would sail for Europe on 6 June, arriving in Le Havre on the fourteenth. The Hôtel Frascati was on the beach in Le Havre, outside the center of town.

[177] *"Pour cold water over it."*

[178] Clemens drew up his will on 9 May, and Livy prepared hers early in June 1891 ("Contents of Safety Deposit, Hartford, June 5, 1891"). Neither of these documents is extant.

[179] William Milligan Sloane, professor of history at Princeton University, and his wife had visited the Clemenses in Hartford in late April or early May 1891. Mrs. Sloane's letter of thanks has not survived, but Professor Sloane's brief letter of 5 May closed with the following words: "We appreciate better than we can acknowledge the great kindness of yours and you in our visit. The oriental model of hospitality gives his house and his salt and all his belongings to his guest—you give yourselves."

[180] Probably William Milligan Sloane.

was left open by the rest of the party. When he undressed that night he found 18 *wax matches in one of his shoes!*

The thing that reminded him of this was my sitting down on the curbstone & saying "there's been something in my shoe the last 2 minutes, & *that* I can't & *won't* stand"—& I emptied out a nearly ⟨nearly⟩ invisible object made of some soft substance.

See if the Altman bill was paid twice.[181]

Ask about return passage for Katie[182]

Stop the telephone.
And
La Gascoigne will sail from Havre July 25.

Put a gas-metre in

W.[183] sell the piano. Cost ⟨[$900.]⟩$1000.

9**X** Bret Harte's story.

An Uncomfortable Companion

Black cat's maintenance charged upon an estate in England—cat to be kept by one particular family—been going on 300 years— can't prove it ain't the same old original cat. The cat-feeder lives fine.[184]

10**X** Man left huge sum for housing & maintaining cats—"& when they shall have increased to 1,500,000"—tell what happened then— region deserted by people; heirs bought the estates for a song & reduced the output to 3 percent [#]

---

[181] The Clemenses often made purchases at B. Altman & Company, the New York City department store.

[182] Katy Leary, who had come to Hartford in 1880 to work as Livy's personal maid, was the only member of the household staff to travel with the Clemenses to Europe. Although Clemens considered booking a return passage for Katy on 25 July from Le Havre, she remained with the family until the beginning of October 1891, at which time the Clemenses settled in Berlin for the winter and Katy returned to Elmira, New York, her home town.

[183] Franklin G. Whitmore.

[184] Clemens would later write a short tale based on this theme, entitling it "The Black Prince's Cat." Albert Bigelow Paine dated the seven-page manuscript "Probably 1896."

11**X** Man starting out to commit suicide with bottle of whisky & strichnia ⟨[&]⟩is assauted by a robber—fatally injures latter &ccc.[185]

⟨Sell the pew & give half the result to Mrs. Warner for Miss Foote.⟩[186]

Let W & Co send John O'Neil ⟨$6⟩ $70 from & including June 1.[187]

Send money to ⟨J⟩Chas J. Langdon just before we leave.[188]

How do you like Chicago![189]

Want Ch W & Co to presently begin to pay 6% half-yearly on $74,000, & copyrights & due & money lent.[190] [#]

---

[185] The germ of an anecdote Clemens worked into one of his European travel letters, "Marienbad, a Health Factory," written in the fall of 1891. Clemens noted it at somewhat greater length in Notebook 23, page 92.

[186] The sale of the Clemens family's pew in the Asylum Hill Congregational Church was handled by Franklin G. Whitmore after the Clemenses left for Europe. In an undated letter written about this time, Clemens noted that the money from the sale of the pew, seventy-five dollars, had been promised to a "bedridden permanent invalid"—probably a relative of Mrs. George H. Warner's.

[187] O'Neil, the Clemenses' gardener, acted as caretaker of the Hartford house during their stay in Europe. His wages, commencing on 1 July 1891, were paid through Charles L. Webster & Company.

[188] On 13 May Clemens sent Charles Langdon a check for $3,000 to be deposited to Livy's credit. The Clemenses expected to draw upon this money while in Europe.

[189] In 1890 Clemens used this bellowed punch line from an old anecdote (see p. 268, note 137) to "subdue" a large Onteora dinner party at which simultaneous conversations produced an "intolerable volume of noise." He began telling the story to the woman next to him, purposefully mumbling so as to draw the attention of everyone else at the table. By the time he screamed the punch line about Chicago, the "dining-room was so silent, so breathlessly still, that if you had dropped a thought anywhere in it you could have heard it smack the floor. When I delivered that yell the entire dinner company jumped as one person, and punched their heads through the ceiling, damaging it, for it was only lath & plaster. . . . Then I explained why it was that I had played that game" (*North American Review*, September 1907, pp. 8–10).

[190] Clemens' capital investment in Charles L. Webster & Company at the beginning of 1891 totaled $74,087.35. Despite his desire to collect his royalties and receive interest on his and Livy's investment in the firm, miscellaneous royalty payments ($9,071.17), interest ($377.05), and his two-thirds share of the 1891 profits ($11,162.19) were turned back in to the company.

John, ⟨[at]⟩ to Mrs. Harriett Beecher Stowe—*"tried* to!"

Mr. Hall, why not issue Claimant, at $1 in cloth, or 50ᶜ, & Huck, contracting the editions to the big syndicates?

Game—let it on a 10% royalty

Or offer it to the big syndicates.

Send for a notary, Whit.

No news from Cockerill?[191]

Have you no record of my copyright account? Get it up again from your books.

Try for $10,000—if declined, make no offer for less than $7,000 cash. We don't want their pictures.[192]

Webster left this dying injunction—that upon his monument be this inscription after his name:
"Publisher of Gen. Grant's Memoirs & Knighted by the Pope." His wife is troubled about it.[193] [#]

---

[191] After receiving Edward Bok's offer of $4,000 for *The American Claimant* (see p. 619, note 167), which he did not "think very much of," Clemens instructed Fred Hall to "appoint a meeting with Col. Cockerill managing editor of the World, and see if you can sell him the use of this 70 or 75,000-word story for $10,000" (4 May 1891, *MTLP*, p. 273). John Cockerill, however, had resigned from his post at the New York *World* that month.

[192] As part of his offer for serial rights to *The American Claimant*, Edward Bok promised "to have the story illustrated by Kemble or Frost and to sell us electrotypes at one-third the original cost. So we save at least a thousand or twelve hundred dollars in this way on the illustrating and at the same time get good illustrations" (Frederick J. Hall to SLC, 2 May 1891). After Bok's employer Cyrus Curtis, proprietor of the *Ladies' Home Journal*, increased the offer from four to six thousand dollars on 12 May, Clemens accepted, but problems arose about coordination of English and American installments of the story. Clemens then instructed Hall to see Samuel S. McClure of the McClure Syndicate. Hall's 21 May conference with McClure produced an offer of $12,000 for the right to syndicate the story both in the United States and abroad. A week later Hall withdrew from the earlier agreement with the *Ladies' Home Journal* and began formal arrangements with McClure. The final contract provided McClure with world serial rights to the novel, publication to commence on 1 January 1892, the story to run about three months. Clemens would hold the copyright and was permitted to publish the story in book form as early as 15 March 1892.

[193] Charles L. Webster had died on 26 April 1891 at the age of forty. Ill health had

Print Dr. Martin & the Etchings.[194]

Mr. Hall, begin John O'Neils check *July* 1 instead of June.

12**X** Sloane's story of the man defeated in a duel who ⟨was
[-]⟩became reconciled to his antagonists ⟨daughter, m⟩ married his
daughter, took her a few miles away; stripped her to the waist,
cowhided her nearly to death & deserted her on a country road at
night. She crawled home to her father's house & finally recovered.
The husband was not heard of again, but a son was born to him,
grew up, hunted his father over the world (giving him notice that
he was on his track to kill him) & in the fourth year of the chase
caught him in the desert of Sahara & killed him.[195] [#]

---

forced him to withdraw from Charles L. Webster & Company in 1887, and he had since
been living a quiet life in Fredonia, New York. Clemens did not attend Webster's funeral
but sent Orion Clemens in his place. "Your aunt Livy is invalided, & I am debarred from
travel by rheumatism. Otherwise we should go to you at once," he told his niece Annie
(SLC to Annie Moffett Webster, 26 April 1891, TS in MTP). Webster had been made a
Knight of the Order of Pius in 1887 for his work in publishing the *Life of Leo XIII*. The
Fredonia newspaper always referred to him as Sir Charles Webster; he never used the title
himself, but he did on one or two occasions appear in town wearing the sumptuous uniform and decoration which accompanied his title.

[194] Dr. Benjamin E. Martin, a surgeon during the Civil War and later an author of
travel books, had visited Onteora during the summer of 1890 while the Clemens family
were staying there. Clemens himself was absent during Martin's visit, but Livy met him
and invited him to call in Hartford. When Martin did pay a visit several months later,
Clemens took a brief look at the unfamiliar name on the calling card, assumed Martin
was some sort of salesman, and determined to be rid of him. He entered the parlor and
found Martin seated amidst a collection of etchings which lay at his feet. Not realizing
that Livy had placed the etchings there with the intention of rehanging them, Clemens
concluded Martin was peddling them. After asking after Mrs. Clemens and the children,
Martin, to make conversation, pointed to one of the etchings and said, "This is pretty."
"We've got that one," was Clemens' curt reply. It was not until after Martin had been
ushered out the door that a conversation with Livy disclosed his identity and sent Clemens scampering after him to make amends. The story was printed in an article by Brander
Matthews, entitled "Mark Twain as Speech Maker and Story Teller" (*Mentor*, May
1924, pp. 24–28), and was also recounted by Paine, with some variations (*MTB*, pp.
679–681).

[195] The tale was apparently told to Clemens by William Milligan Sloane, who had
recently paid a visit to Clemens in Hartford (see p. 622, note 179). It would serve as the
foundation for "A Double-Barrelled Detective Story," a heavy-handed burlesque of
Sherlock Holmes, written in 1901 and published in two installments in *Harper's* magazine (January and February 1902).

Add picture of the Claimant's Coat of arms.

The 2 old-maid twins, ⟨Spit f[ire]⟩ "Soft Soap" & "Hellfire", aged 58, who ⟨take⟩ take their pug-dogs solemnly out exercising, walking them just so many turns on their own block—& leave their maniac mother to the sole care of a tired-out Irishwoman, from whom she escapes daily & suddenly appears softly in people's houses letting off her hideous gobblings in their ears—a terror to women great with child. (This maniac is Mrs. Harriet Beecher Stowe.)[196]

A Father Tillou who uses an occasional big word just for the sound of it when it means nothing in that connection.[197]

One called popularly the Changeling or the Weather-Vane, because like Orion ⟨w⟩he is always trying new things, religion, politics, &c & sticks to nothing.

An inventor (snuffling hypocrite & liar) & his pal, an obese, goose-voiced lawyer who can't earn a living.

A Captain Sluyter.[198]

---

[196] Following the death of her husband in 1886, Harriet Beecher Stowe lapsed into a state of reverie; she died a decade later, never having recovered her presence of mind. In his autobiographical dictations, Clemens recalled how Mrs. Stowe "wandered about all the day long in the care of a muscular Irishwoman," assigned to her as a guardian. "Among the colonists of our neighborhood the doors always stood open in pleasant weather. Mrs. Stowe entered them at her own free will, and as she was always softly slippered and generally full of animal spirits, she was able to deal in surprises, and she liked to do it. She would slip up behind a person who was deep in dreams and musings and fetch a war whoop that would jump that person out of his clothes" (*MTA*, 2:242–243).

[197] Cornbury S. Tillou is fictionally portrayed in chapters 27–33 of *Roughing It* as "old Mr. Ballou," the kindhearted blacksmith whose malapropisms befuddle his companions. Tillou was a Frenchman, a veteran miner and jack-of-all-trades, whom Clemens had met in Nevada in 1861.

[198] The purpose of Clemens' list is not clear, and the identity of some of these persons remains obscure. Included in the list are: Jones, the senator from Nevada, who had recently disappointed Clemens in the Paige typesetting venture; Warner, a Hartford neighbor; Isabella Beecher Hooker, the eccentric feminist who also resided in Nook Farm; Charles J. Langdon and his wife Ida; Susan L. Crane; Matthias H. Arnot, an Elmira merchant who had purchased an interest in Clemens' future typesetter royalties; Karl Gerhardt; Mr. and Mrs. Dean Sage; and the Reverend Nathaniel J. Burton, one of Hartford's liberal Congregational clergymen, who had died in 1887.

A John P. Jones.
A Joe Goodman
Mrs. Lilly
Mrs. Jones
Alice
Col. Corcoran
  "   Churchill
Geo. Warner
Mrs. Hooker
Ida
Charley
Sue.
Matt Arnot
Gerhardt & wife & child
Hirsch the handsome.
Joe Twichell
Dean & his wife
D^r· Burton

Send Harper & Century to Annecy, & Pop. Science[199]

That squab who is conducting his Empire with so much fuss & squawk.[200]

The Story of the Californian. Wife been dead 22 years.[201] [#]

---

[199] Clemens planned to pass most of the summer of 1891 at Annecy, "recommended as a pleasant resting-place, though in itself it has little of interest" (Karl Baedeker, *Southern France* [Leipsic: Karl Baedeker, 1891], p. 290). In fact he and Livy spent part of June and almost all of July at the sulphur springs at Aix-les-Bains before going on to Germany in August.

[200] Probably a reference to William II who in 1888 became emperor of Germany and king of Prussia at the age of twenty-nine.

[201] "The Californian's Tale" is Clemens' story about a man who for nineteen years deludes himself into believing that his wife, captured by Indians, is merely away visiting relatives. Clemens first made note of the situation in a notebook kept in 1865 (see *N&J1*, p. 77). A later entry in the present notebook (633.12) indicates that Clemens gave a manuscript of the story to Fred Hall early in June 1891, before leaving for Europe, to have it typed and held in the Webster & Company office. In October 1892 he sent Hall a manuscript of the story from Florence for use in a proposed book "suitable for railroad and summer reading and such-like" (*MTLP*, p. 322). He evidently postdated this manuscript "Florence, Jan. '93" so that, when published, the piece would have the appearance of

Jo ⟨– – –⟩Lawrence Golden Era & Mr. Flower on a journey.[202]

The Englander who read a book of mine all the way to London & gave no sign.[203]

"Well, Christ has been here once."

"Did you go to West^r Abbey?"
"No, stopped at the Langham."[204]

Bret Harte's tale of the sailor[205]

The 2 glasseyed sweethearts.

Dean Sage, Twichell & the tapeworm.[206]

⟨Commodore Vanderbilt & the Memphis man—[Bivouac].⟩

The £1,000,000 note.[207]

Bloody raid to release a milliner's dummy from imprisonment. [#]

---

fresh work (MS at University of Wisconsin). In December 1892 Clemens instructed Arthur Stedman to secure the manuscript from Hall for inclusion in *The First Book of the Authors Club; Liber Scriptorum* (New York, 1893). "The Californian's Tale" was subsequently republished in the March 1902 issue of *Harper's* magazine.

[202] An obscure reference to Joseph E. Lawrence, former editor of the San Francisco *Golden Era*, and Charles E. Flower, mayor of Stratford-on-Avon when Clemens was in England in 1879.

[203] The incident occurred during Clemens' first visit to England in 1872, while taking the train from Liverpool to London. Clemens' initial feeling of gratification at seeing a fellow passenger absorbed in reading *The Innocents Abroad* was soon replaced with a growing uneasiness, for the man never laughed or even smiled once during his hours of reading (*MTB*, p. 459).

[204] Clemens playfully assumed ignorance of Westminster Abbey when parrying the foolish questions of a youth on board the *Parthia* during his crossing from Liverpool to Boston in January 1874. Shortly after his return home, Clemens gave an account of this ludicrous conversation when called upon to speak at a dinner given by the Massachusetts Press Association on 17 February 1874 in honor of Charles Kingsley, canon of Westminster.

[205] The story is identified in *N&J2*, page 509, note 256.

[206] Dean Sage's practical joke on Joseph Twichell is described in *N&J2*, page 379, note 67.

[207] Twelve years earlier, Clemens had entered in his journal: "Case of a tramp who was loaned a £1000,000 note for 30 days & he got rich on it because nobody could change it" (*N&J2*, p. 297). The story was completed in October 1892 and appeared in the January 1893 *Century*.

Robbery in the Russian church[208]

X13 She who keeps 5 horses, (pets) 5 cats & 20 dogs (all of them old—one of the cats 14) here & many cages of different kinds of birds (including macaws, parrots & other noisy ones⟨[)]⟩) & in addition keeps duplicates on her farm & 30 cats there, lost her first & only child when it was near 2 years old, & her husband a week later. Dͬ Skaife is the family physician (the pets are the family), & he is kept humping himself all the time, for the pets are all bloated & diseased with pampering & old age. He is called by telephone at all hours of the night. The other night one of his patients died in her arms at 2.30 a.m. she crying bitterly all the time & he administering faint hopes & stimulants. "Oh, Doctor, he has never been himself since the fire crackers frightened him 4th of July 9 years ago." (Change her to Lilly Warner.)[209]

The young couple next door in Charley Warner's house—charming young people.[210]

X14 Miss Griswold told Mr. Higginson's father quite frankly that she didn't like him. She had gone up there to get acquainted with her future relatives. She is a most strange mixture of fine-fibred, pure-minded, utterly truthful, sincere affectionless Woman, & brusque (even rude) plain-spoken, consequence-scorning, straight-hitting, intrepid, go-ahead, obstruction-smashing, have-my-own-way-whatever-it-costs, practical, matter-of-fact, uncaressing Man. Her intended would make the more eligible wife.

This girl & her two sisters, her mother & her mother's sister are

---

208 Clemens included this incident, which occurred during his *Quaker City* excursion in 1867, in chapter 47 of *A Tramp Abroad*. After giving a French gold piece to an old and blind beggar-woman in an Odessa church, Clemens realized he did not have enough money to cover his night's lodgings. He reapproached the old woman and, feeling "unspeakably mean," snatched the gold piece from out of her palm and quickly replaced it with a Turkish penny. Two later entries in this notebook (634.9–10 and 646.16) record Clemens' futile attempt to find the anecdote in *The Innocents Abroad*.

209 The wife of George H. Warner, Clemens' Hartford neighbor.

210 Charles and Susan Warner had left Hartford in December 1890 to spend the year abroad and had rented their Nook Farm home to the banker Francis R. Cooley and his wife.

all elaborately educated, accomplished & widely traveled, & they quarrel all the time, even in the presence of a guest. The girls say "oh do shut up!" to mother & aunt; if asked to do something they say "I cahn't—find somebody else." In their quarrels they rage & scream. Miss G. was at work on her trousseau when Mrs. Ivins called. The mother sat idle. Mrs. I said, "Don't it make you want to take hold & help?" Mrs. G. said reproachfully, "I furnish all the money—I'm allowed to do that—but when I want to take hold I'm not wanted." Miss G. said, "Well, you're *not*, so there's no use in mincing it."

A close examination of Susy Corey's history, character, cultivation & ambitions makes a curious study.[211]

Borrowing Hopkinson Smith's overcoat after the burglary.[212]

How we made an honest woman of the English servant girl.[213]

Zodiac- Whittier & "drown them."

15**X** Z. Man that bought a fire-horse & always went to fires instead of to weddings & funerals.
Milk-route horse.—being some one's answering tale.

Old Siphylis Hawkins hoped & expected to live till the words "Christian & should cease to be synonymous."

Jan. 23, Note of SLC for $1,666. paid by CLW?

May 16, 1890, 25,211? [#]

---

[211] Susan Corey, a family friend, had been Susy Clemens' piano teacher during the 1880s.

[212] Clemens used this story, in which a policeman suspects him of being a shady character, in a section of "Down the Rhône," published in *Europe and Elsewhere* (1923).

[213] During the summer of 1877, while the family was at Quarry Farm, Clemens went to Hartford to investigate rumors of a prowler around the Hartford house. The suspect turned out to be a jobless mechanic who was spending his nights in the house with Lizzie, the Clemens' housemaid. Despite the reluctance of Lizzie's lover, Clemens saw to it that the couple married immediately. The entire incident is vividly narrated by Clemens in a series of letters which kept Livy posted on all the details of the story as they emerged (see *LLMT*, pp. 197–201) and is also recounted by Paine (*MTB*, pp. 600–602). In 1898 Clemens wrote about this episode in an unpublished piece titled "Wapping Alice," giving the story a peculiar twist by having the housemaid Alice turn out to be a man.

May 29/91, 1.30 p.m. tried to send a telegram through telephone & couldn't. They charge you for the use of this deaf & dumb thing.

From Mr. Hall, May 28/91.

"In re your letters from the other side. For all letters containing not less than 3,500 words, McClure is to pay you $1,000,⟨[o]oo⟩ per letter. If they contain more than 3,500 words, so much the better. If the letters contain less than 3,500 words he is to pay you at the rate of $300 per thousand words."

I telegraphed Hall to accept these terms for me.[214]

P.S. Changed, June 3. Letters to contain 5,000 to 6,000 words. $1,000 per letter.

Usable.

Mrs. C.	$12,500
" "	2,500
Mr. C.	10,000[215]
" " (Mallory, 15th,	5 000[216]
	$30,000

If the third sum ($10,000) comes in, pay at once to Hamersley .... $2,500.[217]

---

[214] The McClure Syndicate had submitted this offer for any European travel letters Clemens might wish to write while abroad. Clemens finally agreed to write six letters, for $1,000 apiece, which were syndicated in both the United States and Europe in 1891 and 1892. Two of the letters, "Playing Courier" and "The German Chicago," were later published in *The £1,000,000 Bank-Note and Other New Stories* (1893); another two, "At the Shrine of St. Wagner" and "Switzerland, the Cradle of Liberty," are included in *What Is Man? and Other Essays* (1917); and the remaining articles, "Aix, the Paradise of the Rheumatics" and "Marienbad—a Health Factory," were first collected in *Europe and Elsewhere* (1923).

[215] McClure's Syndicate was to pay Clemens $10,000 upon receipt of the manuscript of *The American Claimant*, then to pay him the final $2,000 when the story had been half published. Instead, Clemens received $2,500 from McClure's on 11 June 1891 as an initial payment on the story, $2,500 more upon publication of the first installment, another $2,500 upon publication of the fourth installment, and $4,500 when the story was half published.

[216] Clemens was expecting Marshall H. Mallory to make his first payment of $5,000 on 15 June 1891 toward the purchase of Clemens' interest in the typesetter (see p. 621, note 172, and p. 633, note 218).

[217] Clemens' old debt of $2,500 to William Hamersley (see p. 579, note 21).

Let Hall have
$2,500 in June &
$2,500 in July 5,000

Apply Mrs. C.'s $2,500 on the letter of credit & ⟨invest⟩ ⟨lend⟩ invest the Mallory $5,000 & Mrs. C.'s $12,500. in safe securities & keep them to back Hall's bank account against a panic until the Mallory matter is decided 1ˢᵗ of Aug one way or the other.[218]

Why, I'd just as lives be in a Presbyterian heaven.

Ingersolls[219] story of the man that went down from heaven on a reduced-rate excursion ticket good for 30 days—& ⟨r⟩tried to sell his return ticket.

Gave Mr. Hall "The Californian's Story" to be t-p'd & kept.

Also gave him the Wheeler dectective story.[220]

Aries the Ra̽m.
Pisces " Fishes
Aqua̽rius the Prohibitionist
Capricornus.

---

[218] On 15 June Mallory wrote that "the change in the money market, due to gold shipments, etc." had made it impossible for him "to make any progress in organizing a company" to market the Paige typesetter (Marshall H. Mallory to Henry C. Robinson, 15 June 1891). As the notebook entry makes clear, Clemens had been planning to use Mallory's $5,000 as well as other money to secure Charles L. Webster & Company against any crisis. Clemens received notice of Mallory's inability to make the $5,000 payment upon his arrival in Paris in mid-June. The collapse of this business transaction, combined with McClure's changes in the payment schedule for *The American Claimant*, necessitated a 17 June letter from Clemens warning Fred Hall to "modify your instalment system to meet the emergency of a constipated purse; for if you should need to borrow any more money I would not know how or where to raise it" (*MTLP*, p. 277).

[219] Robert G. Ingersoll, lawyer and lecturer on agnosticism.

[220] "Cap'n Simon Wheeler, the Amateur Detective." Clemens had begun turning the play into a novel in 1877 and probably wrote the bulk of the story within a few months. He returned to the manuscript periodically over the next twenty years, making minor revisions, but never brought the story to completion. The incomplete manuscript with Clemens' working notes on a projected conclusion has been published in *Mark Twain's Satires & Burlesques*, ed. Franklin R. Rogers (Berkeley and Los Angeles: University of California Press, 1967), pages 312–454.

Sagitarius the Cent**ᵡ**aur.

ᵡ
Scorpio Clark

Libra the Scales Shipman

Virgo the Virgin Warner

Leo the Lion Burton

ᵡ
Cancer the Crab Perkins

Gemini the Twins (I.)

ᵡ
Taurus the Bull. Hamersley

X16 Robbery of the blind woman in the Odessa Church is not in the Innocents. Use it.

San Galmier (water) (Source Badois.)[221] This is the breed you want,—there are *two* "sources."

Telegram, June 3/91, 9.30 a.m Mrs. O. B. Gleason, Elmira.
If you & Zippie feel that the voyage is a risk to Sue, I beg that you will persuade her to give it up. Olivia L. Clemens[222]

Hall—1.

If my letters are syndicated in Europe they will be robbed of freedom—better not do that. I want to speak of certain things in a which *they* would not print.[223]

How MANY letters are wanted? [#]

---

[221] The mineral water of Saint-Galmier, France, near Lyons, was widely exported.

[222] Rachel Brooks Gleason, with her husband Dr. Silas O. Gleason, had for many years directed the Gleason Sanitarium, the water cure establishment near Elmira, New York. Zippie Brooks (presumably a relative of Mrs. Gleason's) was formerly Livy's personal physician. Susan Crane's health was apparently not so uncertain that it required a change in plan, for she was able to accompany the Clemens family on their European trip. She met the Clemens party at the Murray Hill Hotel in New York City and left with them on 6 June aboard the French steamship *La Gascogne.*

[223] Clemens' wariness of the European press was apparently justified. All of his travel letters were printed in the *Illustrated London News* with the exception of "Switzerland, the Cradle of Liberty," which contained a paragraph contrasting Switzerland's praiseworthy political history to "the purposes and objects of the Crusades, the siege of York, the War of Roses, and other historic comedies of that sort and size."

⟨Some I shall doubtless make very long. Now if they *split* them they should pay ⟨for⟩ accordingly. If they *don't* split them I don't require anything more than the $1000 per letter.⟩

By new contract, the letters are to be 5,000 to 6,000 words long. (June 3.)

Hall, save ⟨2 copies⟩1 copy of my Harper's & syndicate things & scrap-book them in ⟨2⟩ one of my scrap-books—*not* on both sides of a page, but on only *one* side of the page.

In this book is the "Open Court" notice.[224]

In this book Talmage Brown's obituaries—⟨tell⟩ Who does *ever* know a man? Did we know B., or was it these people? Tell Millet's graveyard story.[225]

Occupations of the nobility, adultery & cheating at baccarat. [#]

---

[224] The *Open Court* was a weekly magazine, published in Chicago, "devoted to the work of conciliating religion with science." The "notice" to which Clemens refers in this entry has been lost, but, on an envelope bearing the return address of the *Open Court* and a 2 June 1891 Chicago postmark, Clemens noted "Text for first letter & T. E. Brown." The unidentified *Open Court* clipping (possibly an amusing short article on health habits and contradictory prescriptions for longevity on page 2825 of the 28 May 1891 number) apparently struck Clemens as good material for his first European travel letter for McClure's Syndicate.

[225] Clemens saved three clippings about the death and funeral of Talmage E. Brown, an Iowa lawyer and real estate developer, with the intention, indicated in this entry, of using them in his first syndicated letter (see also the envelope notation quoted in note 224). The clippings all eulogized Brown as a generous and high-principled citizen and business man, and a devoted family man—"one of nature's noblemen." Clemens, who was evidently acquainted with Brown, seemingly disagreed with these obituary delineations of Brown's character. "Millet's graveyard story" is included in an undated and unpublished Autobiographical Dictation. According to Clemens, artist and journalist Francis D. Millet told the story of the chance encounter of two men in a cemetery: one was searching for the grave of "the dearest soul, the sweetest nature, the lovingest friend and the faithfulest, a man ever had"; the other man sought "the hatefulest scoundrel the human race has ever produced" in order to "curse his ashes." After a long search "together they scraped the moss from a gravestone and revealed the inscription: both had been seeking the same man!" Clemens added: "Of course the moral of the story is that there is a good side and a bad side to most people, and in accordance with your own character and disposition you will bring out one of them and the other will remain a sealed book to you."

Let one of the gang tell Harte's story of the life buoy? Or has Harte told it himself?

Members pretend to have met & interviewed sovereigns & Bismarck

⟨Pay Patrick $25.⟩

John bank the money he collects.

Paint roofs—John make bargain for it.

Does John want Patrick to help him a few days.[226]

Pearl ⟨street⟩Street Congrega¹ Church & Episcopal in Elmira— infernal bells.

Bill Styles,[227] lobbying in behalf of a candidate for U. S. Senator, —in the legislature. Spoke of the low grade of legislative morals.
"Kind of discouraging. You see, it's so hard to find men of ⟨that⟩ a so high type of ⟨honesty⟩ morals that'⟨ll⟩ they'll *stay bought.*"

At the time we are ready to sail, the Heir Apparent's trade (baccarat dealer) has been interrupted by the trial & he has been ⟨preven⟩unable to earn his livelihood this week.[228]

---

[226] John O'Neil was the Clemenses' gardener, and Patrick McAleer their coachman.

[227] Possibly the late lawyer and congressman William Henry Stiles of Georgia.

[228] On 1 June 1891 the sensational baccarat scandal trial began in London. The plaintiff, Sir William Gordon-Cumming, an army officer and an intimate friend of the Prince of Wales, brought charges of libel against five persons who had accused him of cheating at baccarat during a stay at a country residence, Tranby Croft, in September 1890. The Tranby Croft houseguests included Edward, Prince of Wales, and a number of his sporting friends. The prince was the pivotal figure in the drama: the game of baccarat had been introduced at Tranby Croft at his suggestion and was played with his own counters, himself acting as banker. Upon learning that several of the houseguests had witnessed Gordon-Cumming's cheating, the prince had agreed to suppress the affair to avoid scandal, requiring only that Gordon-Cumming sign a statement admitting his guilt and promising never to play cards again. Despite the vow of silence, the affair was soon common knowledge and Gordon-Cumming initiated the libel suit in an effort to clear himself. The trial and the Prince of Wales's appearance on the witness stand occasioned unprecedented public interest. On 9 June the jury decided against the plaintiff; Gordon-Cumming was immediately cashiered from the army and socially blackballed.

I carry my baccarat chips around too, like the P. of W.
Everybody does, now, just as one carries ⟨his⟩ one's jug & Bible
into a strange country—there may not be any there.

June. Woman suffrage failed by a very close vote in Ill.
legislature[229]—& w^d have won but for a protest from "the women
of Illinois'—that is, some of them. It was a narrow escape; for the
ballot, which is useful only when it is in the hands of the
intelligent, would have gone into the hands of those very women.

We are going to a world where are no watermelons—& not
much other food or cookery.

Wills made when you are expecting to be drowned at sea should
be made with a *pencil.*

Get pair rubbers

The West Point cadets become gentlemen the first year &
remain so the rest of their lives.

How common it is to pass an old street corner beggar, then
slacken your pace for 2 blocks, stop, turn, go back & settle with
your conscience.

$8 or $8.50.
Meyrowitz bill OK[230]

Remarks Overheard.
June 6. 10.30 a.m. (first breakfast)—went to it—⟨b[u]t⟩been
kindly put down for second breakfast 12.30. Before these hours—6

The English, American, and European newspapers were unanimous in denouncing
Edward's role in the scandal: he was severely criticized for associating with "frivolous"
persons, for encouraging gambling, and for failing to report the dishonorable conduct of
an officer.

[229] On 2 June 1891, the Illinois legislature moved to reconsider the vote by which a
municipal woman suffrage bill had recently been defeated. The bill again failed to receive
the necessary number of votes, being defeated in the House by a vote of 63 to 44 (Springfield [Ill.] *State Capital,* 6 June 1891).

[230] Meyrowitz Brothers in New York City, opticians and dealers in surgical instru-
ments.

to 9—you can have coffee tea & an egg or chop to stay your
stomach.

1 deck steward to 200,000 passengers.

Began at 9 to hunt for him & pray to him—got the order to him
at 10.15; at 10.30 he has not appeared & I have retreated from
the sight of the starving family.

Remarks Overheard.

The facts of the ship resemble the diagram as the facts of the
circus resemble the circus bill.

A took ⟨an inside⟩ a particular room because it had a long
(diagram) sofa. ⟨The⟩ The (fact) sofa was scant 4 feet. You can bed
a telegraph pole on a diagram sofa; but ⟨to⟩ you can't ⟨bed⟩ bed a
cat on a fact sofa—I mean a long cat.

Electric stateroom light, all night.

Sea almost level. At breakfast not aware of motion of any kind.

Fermez la porte—the only sentence I could recal—seldom usable.

Full rigged vessel framed in the port-hole—just like a Kodak.

Very narrow gangways

Stewards (bedroom) speak but little English.

Cork life-preservers in a rack over upper berth—acquirable
with an axe.

Good smoking quarters—several swarthy San Domingans.

"By the humping jumping J[es]
What the 'l is that to you?"[231] [#]

---

[231] Clara Clemens later recalled the occasion for this verse:

Once, in the middle of a careful description of a very devout clergyman that Mother
was reading aloud, Father sprang to his feet and danced a kind of hornpipe while he
sang, "By the humping, jumping Jesus, what the hell is that to you?"
Never shall I forget the strange sound that burst from Mother's lips. It could hardly
be called a laugh and yet it certainly was not a sob. It contained mirth and horror, so
Father was triumphant. But I noticed that the next time he repeated this gem from

Sorrowful looking cat came down forward companionway about 11 p.m., evidently on business not play.

Papers should have printed "Clive" during this P.W. episode[232]

7[th.] Glassy sea—no wind—everybody on deck—overcoats not needed.

X17 Formerly editor of magazine could tell by the handwriting whether the paper of a new contributor was valuable or not. Now, the type-writer has abolished that warning.

However, he formerly lost his temper over an illegible article & returned it when it was *good*. Type-writer prevents that disaster now.

If Jane Eyre was written in that woman's customary hand—500 words to the square inch & a microscope required—no wonder no publisher accepted it. To-day, in clean t-w, it wouldn't get by the first publishers.[233]

T.W. soon suits one's eye & understanding better than his own hand.

Delicious breakfasts, 12.30. Lie abed till 10.30: they bring you a cup of coffee & a biscuit about 8.30 if you want it—& you do. [#]

---

the literature of song, the words had been altered to, "By the humping, jumping Jackson, what the yell is that to you?" (Clara Clemens, *My Father, Mark Twain* [New York: Harper & Brothers, 1931], p. 26)

[232] In Robert Browning's "Clive" the hero of the Indian campaigns recalls an incident of his early life when as a poor clerk he gambles with a set of military men and discovers one of them to be cheating. The accusation leads to a duel; young Clive misfires and finds himself at the mercy of the infuriated soldier; but he braves it out and the officer admits to cheating. The other gentlemen are shocked and indignant at the officer's dishonorable conduct and demand public disclosure, but Clive convinces them to remain silent. Clemens was struck by the parallel to the current baccarat scandal (see note 228).

[233] Mrs. Gaskell described Charlotte Brontë's hand as "clear, legible, delicate traced writing, almost as easy to read as print" (E. C. Gaskell, *The Life of Charlotte Brontë*, 2 vols. in 1 [New York: D. Appleton and Co., 1880], 2:9). Charlotte Brontë's handwriting, while admittedly fine and delicate, was so minute that a magnifying glass was required to decipher many of her early manuscripts. There is no evidence, however, that the manuscript of *Jane Eyre* tried the patience or the eyesight of Miss Brontë's publishers: it was accepted for publication by Smith, Elder and Company of London almost immediately upon receipt.

Good barber shop—with pictures (in the French taste) & things
to sell.

In big drawing-room, deck steward has books to sell.

A company rents chairs & has somebody to place them & take
care of them.

X18 Life in the old Batavia.[234]

A woman springs a sudden hot reproof upon you, which provokes
a hot retort—& then she will presently ask *you* to apologize.

What is it that moves people to preserve their home-time all
through a European absence & be always losing trains in
consequence?

20 young wheelmen, paying a specific sum apiece, in charge of a
personal conductor who wheels them all over Europe & relieves
them of all care & expense.

With such seas as this they could practice on these long decks
⟨[b-]⟩ all day if they chose.

Our man says they do practice 2 hours after midnight & spin
along ⟨l⟩silently like ghosts.

This ship seems to be about the same length as the City of New
York.[235]

The strenuous, insistent muffled burr or buzz of the propeler
flanges, like the humming-birds buzz—lulling & not unpleasant.

Time I borrowed Hopkinson Smith's overcoat.

Describe with rapture pictures in the Louvre—God the Father
Embarrassed by a German prayer—or trying to understand it.
&c&c&c [#]

---

[234] Clemens traveled on the S.S. *Batavia* in 1872 and 1873.

[235] Clemens had booked, then canceled, passage on the Inman Line's *City of New York* in the spring of 1890 (see p. 547, note 192).

```
                        ⟨[--]
   [--]                  84
   N[a]                 [--]
   [Sl]                 8[8]
   [--]                 8[/3]o
   P[-]      [—]        3[8]
   ────────────────────────
                        [---]2⟩
```

June 8. Certainly the sunniest & most beautiful day the Atlantic
ever saw. But little sea—though what there is would be seriously
felt on a smaller vessel⟨l⟩. This one has no motion.

The phosphorescent waves at night are very intense on the black
surface.

Square blocks of cork—Nicholson pavement—over my head
supported on slats.[236]

I have often yearned to know how you get them down & how
you use them, & I think it a mark of ⟨[p]⟩the perfection of my
native procrastination that I continually put it off. Are there 10 in
our 300 who have done differently?

Open fire place & big mantelepiece in great salon—imitation,
not real; but a cosy & perfect counterfeit.

The haggard perplexity in the face of the All-Knowing is
admirably brought out.

The perfect cleanliness of the rest of the ship is realized to you
when you happen suddenly upon the violent contrast afforded by
the ⟨smoking-cavern⟩smoking-cabin of the 1[er] classe, whose oil-cloth
carpet has apparently never been washed or swept, & is littered
with the burnt matches of a bygone generation.

The Lodge of Sorrow or the Towers of Silence—divans all around
a great square salon occupied by silent folk in the squalmish stage.
A piano in there—hated by the above. [#]

---

[236] "Nicholson pavement was composed of wood blocks laid on tarred plank flooring,
with the chinks filled with gravel and the whole surface covered with hot coal tar. It came
into general use in the United States during the 1860s" (*Roughing It*, ed. Franklin R.
Rogers [Berkeley, Los Angeles, London: University of California Press, 1972], p. 554).

Contrasts between the menu here & that of the old Cunarders, with the candles out at 11—without notice.

No life-rafts. visible.

Ships arranged at bow & stern for the mounting of cannon

The polite commssaire—ditto maitre d'hotel

Baggage checked from N.Y to Paris.

Man that coughed his false teeth into the brook.

June 9. Brilliant sun, but good deal of sea. Breakfast table rather deserted. It is a good, easy-riding sea-boat.

Stealing money from Odessa beggar has been published.

Young chap in barber shop covered my hat up on sofa with his various coats.

Little rack & watch pocket over each berth—convenient.

Blow whistle for noon—can't hear the bell far.

Seen the whole length of the gangway, people at dinner are diminished to children

⟨Any idiot⟩A sour deck steward who makes all calls upon him a reluctant & uncomfortable thing.

June 10. Rough sea.
Il est défense d'apporter du petit pain et du vin blanc a la chambre.[237]

Mrs. Franklin advised to get immediately the habits of smoking, drinking, coffee, chewing, snuffing & swearing—then leave them all off for a week & be cured. She had no habits to change when she got sick—therefore was in a helpless & perilous situation.

June 11. The loneliness of a ship at 4 a. m. Saw just one person for an instant flit through the gray of yesterday's dawn. Very

---

[237] *It is forbidden to take rolls and white wine to the rooms.*

rough—winds singing—first wet deck. Electrics seemed to burn dim. Smoking sty stunk unendurably.

Susy: "Their gesticulations are so out of proportion to what they are saying.

Smooth sea again.

Jean, positively comfortable,
Clara, compara   "
Susy, superlatively un"   "

Know a new voyager because he don't re-set his watch.

Makes a body uncomfortable to see a string of men along a foot-rope & their bellies over the reeling yard furling a sail.

1ˢᵗ & 2ᵈ *captain*—good idea.

Every kind of *cap* worn.

Savior's been here once!

Kodak.

Baggage checked thro' from N. Y. to Paris & tickets by special train.[238]

June 12. Very smoothe sea.

Dʳ Martin & the Etchings

Saturday, 13. Concert.
Sunday 14. Arrived.

Smith & overcoat.
⟨Dʳ⟩*Sir* Wᵐ· Martin & etchings.
Savior's been here once.
Stealing from blind woman.
Seed—don't get it back. [#]

---

[238] *La Gascogne* arrived in Le Havre on 14 June 1891; the Clemens party then went to Paris where they remained until 18 June.

Fitch & Gould—
  W-where's the savior?
  B-buy the rat.[239]
——Bermuda Girl.
  Feather-duster
  Fink I can follow that.
  Advantages—h. & hell.[240]
  Ach Gott—God-dam.
  Acquitment.

      Amen!
G.   Ach Gott
      Guts & all.
      Gravitation petrified.
      Gagg'ed 'em—lions.
D.   Dog—long dog.
      Drink—don't, Sir.
      Dundreary dogs.
      Depew.
M.—   Moncoon.
      Martyrs, not fools.

---

[239] The entry contains the punch lines to two anecdotes concerning William R. Travers, the Wall Street magnate who delivered his sarcastic witticisms in a stammer. The first story tells of Travers' visit on board one of the magnificent steamboats owned by stock market speculators James Fisk and Jay Gould. Not without some vanity, Fisk showed Travers and his other guests through the boat's lavish quarters. Stopping in front of two large portraits, one of himself and one of Gould, which hung across from each other on a stairway landing, Fisk asked Travers if he didn't think they were good. Travers thought the portraits very good, but that to complete the effect, "th-there sh-sh-should b-b-be a p-p-picture of our S-S-S-Saviour in th-th-the m-middle."

The second anecdote relates Travers' attempt to purchase a dog that was a good rat catcher. One dog owner offered to put his animal in a bin with three rats to prove its ability. After a ferocious struggle the dog dispatched two of the rats, but a prolonged fight with the third rat finally ended in a draw. Turning to the dog owner, Travers declined to purchase the dog but offered instead to "b-b-b-buy the r-rat." Both anecdotes are printed in Henry Clews, *Fifty Years in Wall Street* (New York: Irving Publishing Company, 1908), pages 411, 421.

[240] The story tells of a dying man who sent for a clergyman and asked him, "Where is the best place to go to?" The minister replied that "each place had its advantages— heaven for climate, and hell for society" (*MTS*[1910], p. 117).

E— embarrassed.

⟨H⟩O. ⟨Hostler⟩Ostler.

Feather Duster

F— follow that.—ft.

Frog, jumping

T.— tag chewed off.

teeth lost.

B.— buy the rat.

christening.

C.— chilluns, no place.

chastity—Harte.[241]

H.— hat, O'hooligan.

⟨T.— teeth lost.⟩

W— whistling.

Morot—German cavalry fleeing before a charge of F cavalry. Imaginary incident of the Franco-Prussian war.

Bonnat. Seems to be St Jerome ⟨dy⟩ about to die in desert. Skiny & wrinkled—naked—looks like a frog. Overdue Wonderfully painted.

X.1. To learn German[242]

2. Introducing Stanley.

3. Tom & Huck die

4. Noble birth

The story of the Rat in the Trap. Told by her mother.

X5. Boston girl & Nasby.

Joe's Bermuda girl

---

[241] When Bret Harte was reading proof for a small local journal in Yreka, California, one of the items that crossed his desk was a flowery obituary notice containing the sentence: "Even in Yreka her chastity was conspicuous." Realizing that "chastity" was a misprint for "charity," Harte followed the usual proofreader's custom of indicating that the manuscript needed checking by underscoring the word in question and placing a question mark in parentheses in the margin. When he picked up the next morning's paper, Harte found the emended sentence printed in this form: "Even in Yreka her *chastity* was conspicuous(?)" (*MTE*, pp. 268–269).

[242] Clemens' index list is discussed in the headnote to this notebook and in note 24, p. 580.

So big it takes on 11 of them to make a dozen.

X-6. A peculiar hunt.

X7. The right way to do it.

  8. Courting adventure

  9. Bret Harte's story

10. A cat tale

11. Tell that robber tale

John. Beecher Stowe. "*Tried* to."

12. Effective Story. *(Scent)*

Tillou's big words.

X13. The woman with 30 pets

14 Queer girl Miss Griswold

English Mary.

Borrowing Hop Smith's coat

X15. Man bought a fire-horse & milk-route horse.

⟨16.⟩ **X**16 Robbing blind beggar woman is *not* in the Innocents.

X17. Effect of type-writer

18 The old Batavia.

$$
\begin{array}{r}
350 \\
52 \\
\hline
700 \\
1750 \\
\hline
18,200 \\
\end{array}
$$

$$
\begin{array}{r}
56 \\
3.50 \\
\hline
168 \\
26 \\
\hline
194 \\
\end{array}
$$

---

[243] The calculations that follow concern the number of ems per page set on typesetters used by the New York *World* and the New York *Herald* and were probably written before mid-February 1891, when Clemens' typesetting venture with Senator Jones failed to materialize. The notation "non" stands for nonpareil, or six-point, type.

$$\frac{25}{8}$$

World, 8 non ⟨ems⟩ lines wide, $\overline{200}$ ⟨lines⟩ ems;[243]

$$\frac{27}{\langle7\rangle6}$$

Herald, ⟨7⟩6 non   *"*   *"* $\overline{\langle189\rangle162}$ World (11 ems) wider.

World, 242 lines in non col.

Herald 251   *"*   *"*   *"*   *"*

$$\frac{\langle7\rangle6}{1506}$$ lines in a page

$$\frac{27}{10542}$$ Herald.

$$\frac{3012}{40{,}662}$$ ems on a page.

       Col—World, 242

$$\frac{8}{\text{page }1936}$$ lines

$$\frac{\langle[\text{-}]\rangle 25}{9680}$$

$$\frac{3872}{}$$

⟨H[era]⟩ ems on page $\overline{48{,}400}$ World

TEXTUAL
APPARATUS

Textual Introduction

Nine holograph notebooks are copy-text for this volume. Insofar as print can render the idiosyncrasies of inscription in private documents, this volume presents every entry that Clemens made in these notebooks in its original, often unfinished, form with his irregularities, inconsistencies, errors, and cancellations unemended.

The headnote to each notebook includes a physical description of the manuscript and a discussion of textual characteristics or problems peculiar to that notebook. Although the footnotes do not often contain textual information, they do discuss textual matters that significantly affect the meaning of the text. All textual details brought to the reader's attention in footnotes are fully treated in the Textual Apparatus.

The Textual Apparatus contains two lists for each notebook: Emendations and Doubtful Readings, and Details of Inscription. These lists report all recoverable significant facts about the manuscript not fully represented in the text itself and enable the reader to trace the course of a notebook's composition. Emendations and Doubtful Readings reports all departures from the language of the manuscript, except those points of holographic or typographic style described below, and records editorial conjectures about ambiguous and unrecovered passages. Details of Inscription records all readings that apparently were added by Clemens after the initial drafting of a passage, describes complex revisions, and reports other aspects of the manuscript that may bear on the evolution of the text.

The list of emendations includes editorial corrections of obvious author's errors in those few cases in which there is no doubt about the intended reading, in which the error is excessively distracting, and in which the emendation makes no appreciable change in the meaning of the text. In Notebook 24, for example, "stanidg" has been emended to "standing" at page 147.25.

Sometimes letters are missing because Clemens inadvertently wrote off the edge of a page or because part of a page has been torn away. When such a gap is very short and there can be little doubt what letters are missing, the probable reading is supplied in the text in square brackets and is reported as an emendation, as in the word "Brigg[s]" at page 52.18.

A few emendations report the substitution of words for ditto marks. The printed text follows Clemens' use of ditto marks, *ditto*, and *do* except when the vertical alignment of words is not naturally the same in print as in the manuscript notebooks. In such cases, to avoid awkward spacing of words or lines, the appropriate word is supplied in place of the abbreviation and the substitution is reported as an emendation.

The doubtful readings reported in the list include possible alternative versions of words whose manuscript form is unclear. For example, Clemens' habit of running words together when writing hastily and his inconsistent use of hyphens in compound words (usually *to-day* and *good-bye*, but occasionally *today* and *good bye*) sometimes make it difficult to say whether he intended to write two separate words, a hyphenated compound, or one solid word. Similarly, possible compounds hyphenated at the ends of lines in the manuscript could be transcribed either as hyphenated words or as solid words. Whenever the intended form of a compound word is in doubt, the form Clemens used most frequently at the time is printed in the text. If no authorial preference can be established, the conventional form according to dictionaries of the period appears in the text. In either case, the editorial decision is reported in Emendations and Doubtful Readings.

In most notebooks, a single writing material predominates; the Details of Inscription list for those notebooks opens with a statement of that writing material. All affirmable changes of writing material are reported. However, differences and similarities among ink colors are often indistinct. Apparent ink color may vary to a remarkable extent even within a passage evidently written with only one pen at one sitting. Conversely, the ink colors of passages written at widely different times under circumstances that all but guarantee the use of different inks may look so much alike that no useful distinction between them can be made. Therefore, the various inks are identified in Details of Inscription by color names that apply to more or less broad groups. This means that inks with different names are almost certainly different inks, but inks with the same name are not necessarily the same ink.

Vagaries of handwriting and the points in the text where manuscript pages begin and end are mentioned in Details of Inscription only when they cast light on the meaning of an entry or the sequence of composition. The lengths of lines and the position of words or lines on the manuscript page are not reproduced in the texts, except for headings, verse, addresses, and similar formal elements. In lists and tables Clemens often used a hodgepodge of organizing devices (such as spaced periods, broken lines, dashes of various lengths, and braces enclosing runover lines) to make his meaning clear in the cramped space of the manuscript page. However, on the wider and more orderly printed page such a profusion of different devices would be misleading. Therefore, where Clemens' intentions are clear, the spacing and alignment of items in lists and tables have been normalized, and leaders have been supplied where they are needed for clarity. Clemens' regular division of the text into entries has been followed, but no attempt has been made to reproduce the inconsistent means by which he separated entries. In particular, the horizontal lines or flourishes following many but not all entries have been omitted; the separation of entries is indicated here by extra space between lines or, when the end of a manuscript entry coincides with the end of a page of the printed text, by the symbol [#].

Uniform paragraph indentation has been imposed on the first lines of all entries except those that require special alignment, such as the formal elements mentioned above. Clemens indented most entries, but neither this fact nor his occasional failure to indent affects the meaning of the text. Moreover, the depth of indentation (which has been standardized in this text) varies widely throughout the notebooks, and in places it is difficult to tell which lines are indented and which are not. Indeed, occasionally when Clemens neglected to indent the first line he indicated paragraphs by indenting the second and succeeding lines instead. Since in such cases his intention to form paragraphs is clear, these are also presented in the conventional manner. When the separation of entries is in doubt or an ambiguity in paragraphing affects the meaning of the text, the problem is reported in the apparatus and if it is crucial is discussed in a footnote.

Clemens' grasp of the use of accent marks in foreign languages was never firm: he often omitted them, placed them over the wrong letter, or used the wrong mark. All Clemens' accent marks are retained in the text, whether they are right or wrong.

The occasional dots and lines under superscript letters, which Clemens tended to write indistinctly when he used them at all, have been silently omitted. Thus words which might at different times be interpreted as M^r, $M^r_{\cdot}$, M^r, or M^r are all rendered as M^r. However, a period following a superscript appears on or above the line as Clemens wrote it, thus: $M^r.$ or $M^{r.}$.

Although Clemens' cancellations are generally retained, most cancellations to repair such purely mechanical problems as misspellings and miswritten words or letters are omitted. However, every authorial change that might possibly provide a clue to anything more significant than a moment's inadvertence is included in the text. Thus, words originally written clearly and spelled correctly that nevertheless were canceled and then rewritten are retained in the text as evidence of possible authorial indecision. While most spelling errors corrected by Clemens are omitted, when he misspelled and then corrected a proper name, both the error and the correction are included in the text as evidence that Clemens may have been unfamiliar with the subject.

Clemens' occasional drawings and other illustrations related to the text are reproduced in positions that reflect as clearly as possible their relationship to the text. Scrawls and random marks are reproduced or described only if they may bear on the meaning of the text. When it has been necessary to reduce an illustration from its actual size in order to fit it on the printed page, the reduction is stated in terms of linear rather than square measure. Thus an illustration reduced "one-fifth" is four-fifths as wide as the original, although its area is only about two-thirds that of the original.

When Clemens, and later Paine, copied or adapted a passage for use in a work intended for publication, they frequently marked the passage with a simple stroke or two of pencil or pen. Most such use marks reveal nothing about the meaning of a passage or the use made of it, if any, and are omitted. However, when on a few occasions Clemens organized entries into recognizable and meaningful categories by marking them with sets of special symbols, the symbols are represented in the text and their implications discussed.

Clemens underlined words in the notebooks so unsystematically that it is often impossible to say whether he intended to convey different degrees of emphasis by single, double, and triple underlining. While no attempt has been made to impose a system where Clemens may have intended none, differences in the manuscript are reported by means of the normal typographic conventions: letters underlined once have been set in italic type, letters underlined twice in small capitals (with the rare exception noted below), and letters underlined three times in full capitals. Because the printed form of letters underlined two or three times does not reveal whether the letters were initially written as capital or lower case, all instances of double and triple underlining are recorded in Details of Inscription. Thus, if Clemens wrote "in," "In," or "IN" and underlined the word three times, the text reads "IN" and Details of Inscription gives the manuscript form. If Clemens underlined "in," "In," or "IN" twice, the text reads "ɪɴ" except in rare cases in which the editors feel that replacing Clemens' handwritten full capital with a printed small capital would probably violate his intention.

Most entries are presented in the physical order they follow in the manuscript notebooks, although that order is not necessarily the order in which they were written. Pages at either end of a notebook, in particular, often contain notes, calculations, lists, and addresses jotted at various times during a notebook's use. Since such short entries cannot usually be precisely dated and since their aggregation is typical of Clemens' practice, these groups of entries have been presented intact. Elsewhere in the notebooks, however, occasional entries or blocks of entries have been moved into chronological order when a reconstruction of the order of their inscription can be defended and the rearrangement does not separate passages deliberately juxtaposed by Clemens. When the order of entries has been changed, Details of Inscription describes the original manuscript sequence and any textual peculiarities bearing on the rearrangement. When the order of entries has been left unchanged because the chronology of their inscription cannot be firmly established, the list nevertheless reports aspects of the manuscript that suggest a chronological sequence different from the physical sequence, such as the fact that an entry was written with the notebook inverted. Footnotes explain the external evidence for moving or dating a passage.

Passages whose intended position Clemens did not clearly indicate and leaves that have come loose from the notebooks are placed in the text where the available evidence suggests they belong. Words that are written across another entry or in the margin but that have no syntactical function are usually placed following the entry with which they are associated. A special problem arises in parts of some notebooks where Clemens used only the right-hand pages for the main sequence of his remarks but wrote a few scattered entries on the otherwise blank left-hand pages. In such cases the context sometimes suggests that Clemens deliberately placed the isolated entry opposite a particular passage on the facing manuscript page, while at other times it seems more probable that he simply picked a convenient blank space to write in. In the present text an isolated entry of this kind normally is placed in a position that reflects as nearly as possible its manuscript location and its logical relationship to other entries, but it may be moved, to avoid interrupting a continuing sequence of entries. Problems of the appropriate sequence or placement of entries vary so widely from case to case that no general statement of editorial principles can cover them all. In each instance the situation in the manuscript is described in Details of Inscription and is discussed if necessary in a footnote.

Inscription not in Clemens' hand that is more or less contemporary with Clemens' use of a notebook (something that Clemens probably saw) is printed in the text and identified in a footnote and in Details of Inscription. Inscription not in Clemens' hand that postdates his use of a notebook is not printed in the text but is described in Details of Inscription (with the exception of the use marks made by Albert Bigelow Paine, which are mentioned in the headnotes but not individually reported). Clippings and notes not in Clemens' hand that are interleaved in the notebooks or attached to them are described or printed in full, according to their importance and length, in the footnotes.

Clemens occasionally wrote in his notebooks while in a moving vehicle or a crowd or in very bad light. Such passages may be chaotic scrawls. Even in passages written under more favorable conditions, minor lapses and inaccuracies sometimes produce puzzling ambiguities. These characteristics cannot be rendered in type, and some of them defy verbal description. But, except under unusual circumstances, Clemens' handwriting is clear, and a description of the occasional problems makes it appear more challenging than it is in fact. The sometimes confusing resemblance of *a* and *o*, *n* and *u*, and *w* and *m*, and Clemens' occasional crossing of an *l* mistaken for a *t* or dotting of part of an *n* or *u*, misread as an *i*, are typical of hasty and informal notes. (When writing in German, Clemens often distinguished *u* from *n* by placing a mark like a breve [˘] above the *u*; the practice is common in handwritten German, and the present text follows Clemens' intention but does not record his use of the mark.) Finally, a terminal *s* may be no more than a hook on the penultimate letter. Context easily resolves most of these problems. When a word is so badly written that it is impossible to tell whether it is spelled correctly or incorrectly but there is no question what word was intended, it is assumed that Clemens spelled the word correctly. When an obscurity cannot be resolved, the alternatives are registered in Emendations and Doubtful Readings and, if crucial to the understanding of an entry, are discussed in a footnote as well.

Clemens used both the exclamation point and the question mark as internal punctuation, and he frequently followed a terminal period with a dash. He also sometimes used a terminal dash in place of a period or extended a period so that it looks like a dash or a comma. Colons, semicolons, and commas sometimes resemble each other. These difficulties are often compounded by the similarity between the capital and lower-case forms of some of Clemens' letters such as *c*, *k*, *m*, *s*, and *t* and by his occasional use of *E* to start a word that he had no apparent reason for capitalizing. Not surprisingly in a handwritten document, the spacing of initials in the notebooks is inconsistent. For example, Clemens sometimes wrote "a. m." and sometimes "a.m." Problems caused by these characteristics of Clemens' handwriting and punctuation are resolved silently here on the basis of familiarity with his hand and practice and of any other information available. Cases in which doubt persists are reported in Emendations and Doubtful Readings.

To keep the text as uncluttered as the demands of completeness and clarity will allow, the number of special symbols used has been held to a minimum. Readings canceled by Clemens are enclosed in angle brackets, and the spacing following the closing angle bracket indicates how a cancellation was made. When Clemens canceled a word or word-ending simply by striking it out, a normal space follows the closing angle bracket, thus: "⟨American⟩ passengers" and "bell⟨s⟩ rang." When he canceled a word or word fragment by writing something else over it, the original reading is enclosed in angle brackets and the new reading follows the closing angle bracket without the customary intervening space. Thus, when Clemens wrote "organ" over "part" the text reads "⟨part⟩organ," and when he wrote "take" to cover and cancel the false start "s" the text reads "⟨s⟩take."

On the rare occasions when Clemens revised a word by writing over or striking out just a part of it (other than the terminal letters), the entire original reading is given within angle brackets, the entire revised reading follows the closing angle bracket without an intervening space, and an entry in Details of Inscription explains exactly how the change was made. Thus, when Clemens wrote "sen" (possibly intending originally to write "sent") and then changed it to "stayed" by writing "tayed" over "en," the text reads "⟨sen⟩stayed" and the revision is explained in Details of Inscription. Similarly, if he had written "t" over the "s" of "sake" the text would read "⟨sake⟩take," and if he had simply canceled the "t" of "stake" the text would read "⟨stake⟩sake." The process of revision in such cases is described in Details of Inscription. The same procedure applies to revised numerals: when the text reads "⟨10⟩30-ton rocks" Details of Inscription records that "3" was written over "1" (if Clemens had written "30" over "10," the text would read the same way but there would be no entry in Details of Inscription). For ease of reading, punctuation marks have been spaced normally even when they fall within or immediately follow a cancellation. Therefore, the lack of an extra space after the closing angle bracket in readings like "⟨"⟩How" and "I will ⟨not⟩!" does not necessarily mean that the canceled material was overwritten by what follows it. When a mark of punctuation is written over a word or letter, or when something is written over a mark of punctuation, Clemens' revision is explained in Details of

Inscription. Clemens' failure to cancel punctuation that accompanies canceled passages is assumed not to have been intentional but simply evidence of hasty revision; such punctuation appears within the angle brackets and is not identified in Details of Inscription.

Interlineations and other readings apparently added by Clemens after completion of the initial inscription appear in the text unaccompanied by special symbols except for one limited category. When Clemens interlined a reading as an alternative to a previously inscribed reading but canceled neither, both are printed in the text, separated by a diagonal line and with the earlier reading first, thus: "Turn/Flee."

All Clemens' identifiable additions are recorded in Details of Inscription, where they are enclosed within vertical arrows, thus: "↑innocently↓." To help the reader find the additions in the text, a word or two of context may be included in an entry in Details of Inscription, thus: "↑the↓ noted occasions." Similarly, for the reader's convenience, extra words, such as cancellations associated with additions, may be presented in an entry if doing so provides enough context to clarify the revision, thus: "⟨mighty⟩ ↑very↓" or "Hotel↑s↓ gouge⟨s⟩." (All cancellations, whether or not they are repeated in Details of Inscription, are enclosed in angle brackets in the text.)

Occasionally when revising a passage Clemens used proofreader's marks such as *stet* and ¶, or he indicated the placement of passages with lines, arrows, or written instructions. His intention is followed in each case. Passages canceled and then restored by Clemens appear twice, once enclosed within angle brackets and once without them, except that for convenience long passages canceled and then restored appear only without angle brackets and are discussed in a footnote. Details of Inscription describes the mechanism of revision for all canceled and restored passages.

Conjectural reconstructions of illegible readings and of letters where the manuscript is torn or words are written off the edge of the page are enclosed in square brackets in the text. Hyphens within square brackets stand for unreadable letters. Editorial explanations are in italics and within square brackets. Thus "[------]" stands for an illegible word of about six letters, and "[*three words*]" stands for three unrecovered words. (To preserve square brackets for editorial insertions, Clemens' square brackets, which he used interchangeably with parentheses, are rendered as parentheses.) In the apparatus a vertical rule is used when necessary to indicate a line-ending, thus: "to-|day." An asterisk in Emendations and Doubtful Readings refers the reader to the corresponding entry in Details of Inscription.

In descriptions of Clemens' revisions, a reading identified as written "above" another reading is interlined, while something written "over" something else is written in the same space, covering the reading it supplants. "Follows" and "followed by" are spatial, not necessarily temporal, descriptions. The word *endpaper* designates the pasted-down page inside either cover of a notebook and the word *flyleaf* refers to the leaf next to an endpaper.

Line numbers in the annotation and in the Textual Apparatus refer to Clemens' text only and do not count editorial language on the same page.

Key to Symbols

⟨word⟩	Clemens' cancellation
↑word↓	written later than the surrounding inscription
[word]	doubtful reading, marginally legible
w[--]d	illegible letters
[*page torn*]	editorial remarks
word/word	alternative readings proposed but never resolved by Clemens
word | word	end of a line
[#]	last line of text on the printed page is the end of an entry in the manuscript
*	cross-reference from Emendations and Doubtful Readings to Details of Inscription

Notebook 22

Emendations and Doubtful Readings

	MTP Reading	MS Reading
8.1	*Pays*	[*no column heading needed: middle of manuscript page*]
8.2	cost 105 7 p.c	['*cost' and 'p.c' replace ditto marks below preceding 'cost' and 'p.c'*]
*8.7	⟨1,4500⟩14,500	1,4,500
*8.9–10	5,000 | Conn.	5,000 | *Pays* | Conn.
*8.10	″ 142, 10 ″	cost 142, 10 p.c.
9.1	*Pays*	[*no column heading needed: middle of manuscript page*]
9.2	10 p.c.	['*p.c.' replaces ditto marks below preceding 'p.c.'; see Details of Inscription 8.9–10*]
*11.10–12	J H . . . MacDonald,	[*possibly canceled*]
*12.25	⟨bricabrac⟨c⟩⟩bricabrack	[*doubtful*]
13.2	B's	[*possibly 'B;'*]
13.8	grave-digger	grave-|digger
*14.3	⟨ma[in]⟩Maine	[*possibly '⟨ma⟩Maine'*]
14.13	redheaded	red-|headed
*14.24	⟨unwill⟩	[*possibly canceled 'unwitt'*]
*15.15	& then . . . late—	[*possibly '—& then . . . late'*]
*21.16–17	10 (also . . . reign; a battle	10; (also . . . reign a battle

*21.29	⟨B⟩ bg.	[*possibly* '⟨S⟩B bg.']
23.6	Con Journal	[*possibly* 'Cou Journal']
25.3	pinholes	pin-|holes
26.3	work-box	work-|box
*26.20	steam boat	[*possibly* 'steamboat']
27.28	far-away	far-|away
30.6	sour-grass	sour-|grass
30.6	hazel nuts	· [*possibly* 'hazelnuts']
30.10	Pater-rollers	Pater-|rollers
30.12	*fire*	[*possibly* '*fine*']
31.1	Tinner.	[*possibly* 'Turner.']
39.6	Farmer	[*possibly* 'Farmer⟨s⟩']
*43.7–12	Howells's. . . . sleep.⟩	[*order uncertain*]
*45.1	IN	[*possibly* 'in']
45.9	temperal	[*possibly* 'temperol']
46.9	interlines	inter-|lines
*48.1	W.	[*possibly* 'W.']
48.22	gilt	[*possibly* 'gibt']
49.14	straightway	straight-|way
52.18	Brigg[s]	[*page torn*]
54.26	Wawhawp	Waw-|hawp
55.4	⟨sad⟩	⟨sad-⟩|
57.19	down town	[*possibly* 'downtown']
59.5–6	school book house	[*possibly* 'schoolbook house']
60.6	gone out	[*ditto marks below preceding* 'gone out']
60.17	smallpox	[*possibly* 'small-pox' *or* 'small pox']

Details of Inscription

[Entries are in black pencil unless otherwise noted]

7.1	↑302 Beacon st.↓ *[written in the top margin of the page above 'Am. Bk. Note' (7.3)]*
7.2–9.11	*Pays*	Bk Note . . . ↑200 shs Beech . . . paid up.↓ *[written on pairs of facing pages; 'Am. Bk. . . . 5,000' (7.3–8.9), 'Conn. Fire Ins. . . . 2,500' (8.10–9.7), and '200 shs Beech . . . paid up.' (9.8–11), probably written first, are written in blue ink on the first, second, and third right-hand pages, respectively; 'Pays	Bk Note . . . 6 " ' (7.2–8.8) written in pencil on the verso of the front flyleaf, and 'Pays	Conn. Fire cost . . . Burr— " 100 ' (8.10–9.7) written in pencil on the first left-hand page (emended); '200 shs Beech . . . paid up.' written over 'Addresses.	CL. Webster, 418 W. 57ᵗʰ' (10.6–7) but moved to reflect its place in the list of stocks]*
7.9	⟨Adams . . . 5,000⟩ ⌊written in blue ink; canceled in pencil]
8.6–7	⟨Hartford . . . 14,500⟩ *[written in blue ink; canceled in pencil]*
8.7	⟨1,4500⟩14,500 *[originally '1,4500' written in blue ink; a comma added lightly in pencil following '4'; the comma following '1' not canceled; emended]*
8.9–10	5,000	Conn. Fire " 142, 10 " *['Conn. Fire cost 142, 10 p.c.' begins a manuscript page, with 'Pays' written above 'p.c.'; the headings 'Pays', 'cost', and 'p.c.' have been removed here, and 'Pays' and 'p.c.' have been reinserted where the table runs over to a new page of the printed text at 9.1–2; 'cost' has not been reinserted at 9.2 because Clemens did not write ditto marks in that line of the 'cost' column, instead rewriting 'cost' in the following line (9.6)]*
8.14–16	⟨Farnham . . . ⟨3⟩5,000⟩ *[written in blue ink; '5' written over '3'; canceled in pencil]*
8.21–24	⟨Ind. . . . 3,600⟩ *[written in blue ink; canceled in pencil]*

9.4 ⟨⟨½⟩ ↑all↓ paid up) [‘(½ paid up)’ *written in blue ink; altered in pencil*]

9.6 ↑(cost)↓ [*written in blue ink*]

9.12–14 ⟨Engineering . . . ↑($8,000)↓⟩ [*written on the verso of the front flyleaf following* ‘Pays | Bk Note . . . 6 ″ ’ *(7.2–8.8)*]

9.22 ⟨St[o]⟩Stechert [‘e’ *written over what appears to be* ‘o’]

10.3 House↑, W H Davis & Co↓ [*the addition may be related to* ‘Old china & things’ *(see 11.9)*]

10.5 ↑Hutton . . . 34th↓

10.6–7 Addresses. . . . 57th [*overwritten by* ‘200 shs Beech . . . paid up.’ *(9.8–11); see 7.2–9.11 above*]

11.7–8 214 . . . 66$^{\text{th.}}$ [*written in brownish black ink*]

11.9 ↑Old china & things↓ [*interlined with a caret above* ‘Parke 186 Front’; ‘W H Davis & Co’ *(10.3) on a left-hand page and* ‘Old china & things’ *on the facing right-hand page are closely aligned across the hinge of the notebook and may have been written at the same time*]

11.9 ⟨W⟩ ↑SW↓

11.10–12 J H . . . MacDonald, [*a grayish blue ink scrawl across these entries may have been intended as a use mark or a cancellation*]

12.7–9 ↑Orion | Ma | Pamela.↓ [*written in the available space to the right of* ‘Dean Sage’ *and* ‘Joe Goodman.’ *(12.5–6)*]

12.17 (⟨women⟩ ↑ladies↓)

12.21 another.” [*followed by one blank page*]

12.23 ⟨“Here’s another⟩ ↑Pedlar *brought* him an↓

12.25 ⟨bricabrac⟨c⟩⟩bricabrack [*sequence of revision uncertain;* ‘c’ *apparently canceled, then overwritten by* ‘k’]

14.3 ⟨ma[in]⟩Maine [*originally either* ‘main’ *or* ‘ma’; *then either* ‘Ma’ *written over* ‘ma’ *of* ‘main’ *and* ‘e’ *added or* ‘Maine’ *written over* ‘ma’]

14.9 ⟨reputations⟩ ↑lives↓

14.10–11 ⟨last⟩ ⟨↑final↓⟩↑charitable↓ & ⟨best⟩ ↑good↓ friend ↑yonder↓ ['final' *interlined above canceled* 'last'; 'charitable' *written over* 'final']

14.16 Col. x x x ↑in "Cromwell"↓

14.24 ⟨unwill⟩ innocent [*since the cancellation was made before the word was completed,* 'unwitt' *may have been intended*]

15.9 He invented [*someone, probably Paine, wrote* 'Speech?' *in the margin at the opening of this paragraph and rewrote* 'invented' *above Clemens' inscription of that word*]

15.11 ↑Could . . . kinds.↓

15.12 ↑he was . . . sin—↓

15.15 oppose it ↑& then . . . late↓—& ↑(↓experience shows↑)↓ that ↑that other fellow↓ he would ['& then . . . late' *interlined without a caret above* 'it—& (experience')]

15.19–16.1 ↑at least . . . meas↓

16.2 do it ↑at↓ all

16.2–3 time,↑—↓⟨in a measure⟩—or [*it is unclear whether the dash was added before or after the following words were canceled*]

16.6 something/↑body↓ ['body' *interlined above* 'thing']

16.11 ↑[I] reckon↓

17.1 ↑Arthur↓ Collins. [*the bottom three-quarters of the page is blank below this entry*]

17.7 cats. [*one leaf has been torn out following the page that ends here*]

17.17 ⟨5⟩352 [*followed by one blank page; the following leaf has been torn out; an unreadable trace of pencil inscription appears on the recto of the narrow surviving stub of the missing leaf*]

17.18   A . . . jury. [*written on the surviving stub of a leaf whose outer half was torn out before this phrase was written; the remainder of the page and the verso of the stub are blank*]

18.1–2   Louise . . . May./83 [*autograph in a brownish black ink unique in these notebooks; below the autograph Albert Bigelow Paine wrote in pencil, 'Signature of Princess Louise (Marquise of Lorne)'; the remainder of this page and the following page are blank; the next leaf has been torn out*]

18.7   ⟨Purchis⟩ ⟨↑Purkis↓⟩

19.5–6   the ⟨US⟩ ↑Gov't↓ Asylum for ↑(↓⟨impotent⟩ ⟨↑(homeless)↓⟩ ↑the nation's↓ paupers⟨.⟩↑)↓ [*the closing parenthesis written over the period*]

19.7   ⟨—↑The↓ *head*

20.5   between them. [*the bottom third of the page is blank below these words*]

20.6   ↑Historical↓

20.8   Memory-Improver [*a mark that may be a small capital T appears below* 'Improver']

21.1   ↑Beginning . . . Dynasties;↓

21.2   ↑introductions,↓

21.3   ↑& Memorable↓ Earthquakes . . . & ⟨⟨C[a]⟩Memorable⟩ ↑other↓ Calamities

21.5   ↑(it's . . . reign)↓

21.16   ↑or President's↓

21.16–17   10 ↑(also . . . reign↓; a battle ['(also . . . reign' *interlined with a caret inadvertently placed between the semicolon and* 'a'; *emended*]

21.17–19   a great citizen . . . ↑(death↓ ⟨6⟩5 ↑(when . . . date 1)↓ (but . . . counts as a King;) ↑(above a King)↓ minor ['(death' *interlined without a caret above* 'great citizen';

'(When . . . date 1)' *interlined without a caret above*
'(but . . . counts as a'; '(*above* a King)' *interlined with-*
out a caret above 'King;) minor']

21.20   ↑& introductions? & revolutions.↓

21.21   ⟨3⟩ ↑8↓ each.

21.22   ↑K.↓ Harold

21.24   ↑score-column↓

21.27   ⟨[S]⟩B↑g↓.

21.27   (begins ↑to reign↓)

21.27   ⟨E⟩C↑s↓

21.28   ⟨D[i]⟩D (died.) [*the opening parenthesis written over*
             what may be 'i']

21.29   ↑3↓ [*interlined with a caret above the broken line follow-*
             ing 'W^m· I b⟨o⟩.']

21.29   ⟨B⟩ b↑g↓. [*the line that appears to cancel* 'B' *may be*
             an S over which 'B', *uncanceled, is written; see Doubt-*
             ful Readings]

21.29   1066 ↑10↓. ['10' *added without a caret above* '1066.']

21.29   1087. 10. ['10.' *written in a superscript position following*
             '1087.']

21.30   ⟨1685⟩1688 ['8' *written over* '5']

22.12   ⟨13⟩1137 ['1' *written over* '3']

22.16   ⟨18⟩1285 ['2' *written over* '8']

22.17   ⟨12⟩1314 ['3' *written over* '2']

22.23   ⟨1370⟩1380 ['8' *written over* '7']

22.24   Chas. VI ↑ins↓

22.24   ⟨1378⟩1422 ['422' *written over* '378']

23.1–5   Louis XIII . . . 1848. [*written lengthwise in the margin*

of the page beside 'Philip I. . . . Henry IV . . . —21'
(22.10–33)]

23.1 ⟨[1515]⟩1610 ['6' and 'o' written over what look like '5'
and '5']

23.2–3 ⟨Louis XVII—1.⟩ ↑Louis XVII. 93.↓

23.14–15 ↑Use . . . copyright.↓ [written lengthwise on the page
across the preceding paragraph]

23.16 ⟨date⟩ ↑fact↓

24.16–20 hair | —— | —— | —— | —— [followed by one blank
page]

24.22–26 ⟨When he goes ⟨thither⟩ ↑to sth[1]↓, ⟨the⟩a Roman
Emp precedes him with a torch, ⟨the⟩a Grand Lama of
Thibet ⟨raises⟩ ↑lifts↓ up the, ↑whilst↓ a Pope of Rome
asks a blessing—& when⟩When he goes to sth[1], a
Roman Emp ↑carries the candle, Pope Alex VI↓ lifts
up the — ↑for him↓ & when [sequence of revision uncertain; apparently originally 'When he goes thither, the
Roman Emp precedes him with a torch, the Grand Lama
of Thibet raises up the, a Pope of Rome asks a blessing—
& when'; 'thither' canceled, and what appears to be 'to
sth[1]' written above it; 'a' written over 'the' before 'Roman'
and 'Grand'; 'raises' canceled, and 'lifts' written above it;
'whilst' interlined; 'precedes . . . Thibet' canceled, and
'carries . . . Alex VI' written above it; the comma and
'whilst . . . blessing' canceled; 'for him' interlined. In
the original inscription Clemens omitted a word following 'raises up the'; when Clemens canceled the comma
and 'whilst . . . blessing', he apparently intended the
dash to stand for an unspecified word following '⟨raises⟩
lifts up the']

25.2 house. [followed by one blank page]

25.6 once. [followed by one blank page]

25.11 ↑(fine opera glass)↓

25.14–15	↑(a single game)↓
25.19	⟨5⟩ ↑10↓
26.7	a N. Y. pub school/↑Smith College↓
26.12	↑Townsend MacCoun, Chicago.↓
26.19–20	↑railway, steam boat,↓
27.6	admirals, &c. [*the bottom quarter of the page is blank below this entry*]
27.22–26	4.25 . . . 7.25 [*possibly written by Olivia Clemens*]
27.27	⟨—⟩¶ [*Clemens' paragraph sign, inscribed backwards, written over the dash*]
28.3–6	Mail . . . Shoe store [*written on a leaf subsequently torn out and used for a letter; see note 48*]
28.7	↑Let . . . count 8?↓
28.9–10	↑see next page.↓ [*written below* 'a battle.']
28.15	↑Henry VI—1461↓
28.16	⟨Dis⟩Dethroned ['et' *written over* 'is']
29.14	↑(Tell . . . story)↓
30.1	⟨sie⟩Sie . . . ⟨sie⟩Sie ['S' *written over* 's' *twice*]
31.1	Nicodemus. . . . Tinner. [*written lengthwise in the margin beside the preceding paragraph*]
31.7–8	↑In costly ones↓ Each . . . matter [*boxed;* 'Each . . . matter' *canceled, then restored with the instruction* 'STET.'; 'In costly ones' *was probably added when* 'Each . . . matter' *was restored; to the right of* 'In costly ones' *Clemens wrote the instruction* 'OVER'; 'THIS . . . at all' (31.17–32.6) *is on the verso of the leaf*]
31.17	↑THIS . . . THING↓
31.19	↑(Put . . . board.)↓
31.21	↑& Length of Reign.↓ [*interlined below* 'Throne ascended'; *a caret after* 'ascended' *is canceled*]

32.5   ⟨marked . . . 5⟩ ↑put in italics↓

32.9   ⟨boards⟩ ↑games↓

32.11–12   ↑H reigned months↓ ↑2↓

32.14   ⟨11[-]00⟩1100. [*an illegible mark canceled after* '11']

32.14   ↑2↓ Descended

32.16   ↑Capt. S. finds that↓

33.9   greenbacks. [*the bottom four-fifths of the page is blank below this word*]

34.5–6   ⟨⟨Do not⟩ ↑Never↓ . . . ⟨but⟩ ↑(but always)↓ . . . ⟨↑exclusively↓⟩ . . . teeth.⟩

34.21   an ↑funny↓ anecdote [*originally* 'an anecdote'; 'an' *at the bottom of one page was not revised when* 'funny' *was interlined at the top of the next page*]

35.6   91½ [*followed by what appears to be a canceled flourish originally ending the entry here*]

35.12   ↑Sold . . . Apl. 18.↓ [*interlined above canceled* '86⅜']

35.14–15   ↑May 3 . . . 60½.↓ [*written lengthwise in the margin beside* 'Oct. 18 . . . 85⅝' (35.3–13)]

35.16   ↑RAZORS↓

37.4   ↑by or in↓ [*written lengthwise in the margin and connected to* 'an' *by a line*]

37.6   das↑s↓

37.14   Der Tag . . . gemacht. [*the bottom half of the page is blank below this line*]

37.19   ⟨fraid 'would disfigure⟩ fraid 'would/↑come near↓ disfigure⟨↑d↓⟩ [*sequence of revision uncertain; originally* 'fraid 'twould disfigure'; 'fraid 'twould' *canceled and later restored by stet marks; a terminal* 'd' *added to* 'disfigure', *then canceled;* 'come near' *interlined above* 'fraid 'twould']

38.1–2   Sel. Often . . . one. [*written in grayish blue ink; the bottom fifth of the page is blank below this entry*]

38.21   3 times a day. [*the bottom four-fifths of the page is blank below this line; followed by one blank page*]

38.23   company to luncheon [*the bottom two-thirds of the page is blank below this line*]

39.1–3   Due . . . 304.7.11. [*written in grayish blue ink*]

39.1   '84 [*underlined twice*]

39.9–12   What . . . before. [*a long bracket is drawn in the left margin beside these paragraphs*]

40.8   ↑prliminary↓

41.6   Schreiber. [*the bottom quarter of the page is blank below this word*]

41.11   ↑6 in. . . . white↓

41.13–42.15   Consistency . . . idiot. [*written in grayish blue ink*]

42.18   Paine's, 3 W 53^{d}. [*the bottom half of the page is blank below these words*]

43.5   80 Trumbull St [*the bottom half of the page is blank below these words*]

43.6   Send . . . cover. [*written in grayish blue ink*]

43.7–12   ↑Howells's.↓   ↑Aldrich↓ . . . ↑Need . . . second.↓ ⟨Worms.⟩ ↑Worms.↓ . . . ↑Murders . . . sleep.↓ ⟨↑Violence in sleep.↓⟩ [*the order of inscription is uncertain; 'Violence' appears to have been written earlier than any of the other words in the right-hand column and may originally have been placed to the right of 'Shock—' and 'Worms.' simply because that was the handiest available space; 'Need . . . second.' and 'Murders . . . sleep.' were interlined respectively above and below 'Violence'; 'Violence in sleep.' was written in the top margin above 'Send paper cover for' (43.6), probably after some, if not all, of the page had been filled, and has been placed here*]

to reflect its evident relationship to the notes on dreams;
the page ends with '& talk' (43.16)]

43.16   talk [*one leaf has been torn out following the left-hand page that ends here*]

44.13   you⟨?⟩! [*the question mark mended to an exclamation point*]

44.16   ⟨H[-]⟩ (Pause)— ['Pause' *written over* 'H' *and one other letter; the parentheses may have been added later; the closing parenthesis may have been intended to cancel the dash*]

45.1   —put Bonanza IN this [*written at the bottom of a right-hand page and followed by Clemens' instruction* 'OVER'; 'A stranger . . . year' *(45.2–7) is on the verso of the leaf*]

45.1   IN [*three lines below* 'in' *may have been intended as a general mark of emphasis for the whole line* '—put Bonanza in this']

45.12   prophet. [*the bottom quarter of the page is blank below this entry*]

46.5   Commodore ⟨Smith⟩ ↑Cyclone↓

46.10   temperance song. [*a strip about two lines deep has been torn from the bottom of the leaf below these words on the recto and below* 'with G.' *(48.3) on the verso*]

48.1   W. ['W.' *underlined twice; see Doubtful Readings*]

48.8   Les Bébés d'Hélène [*followed by about two lines of blank space, below which the bottom quarter of the leaf has been torn out; the gap follows* 'is easy . . . get' *(48.13) on the verso*]

49.16   Heine's works. [*the bottom third of the page is blank below these words*]

49.24   ↑Cucumber↓ Salat

50.8   ↑in N. Y.↓ [*interlined without a caret above* 'for a person']

50.12   ⟨Studies⟩ ↑Stories↓

50.21   Letters) [*followed by a flourish which may originally have ended the entry here*]

50.23   ↑Butler   Billings   Phillips↓ [*written in the top margin of two facing pages, 'Butler' and 'Billings' on the left-hand page above 'Constipation Smith' and 'Phillips' on the right-hand page above 'Neuralgia' (51.11)*]

50.25   ⟨↑Wheeler-Davis.↓⟩

51.3   ⟨Ba[- -]⟩Billings ['illings' *written over* 'a' *and one or two unrecovered letters*]

51.5   ⟨Consumption ⟨Hoyt.⟩ ↑Babcock↓⟩

51.12   ⟨Neuralgia ⟨Garth⟩ ↑Bliss↓⟩

51.13   ⟨Lumbago ⟨Haynes⟩ ⟨↑Anderson↓⟩ ↑St. Clair↓⟩

51.15   ⟨Apoplexy ⟨Holcomb⟩ ↑Anderson↓⟩

51.19   ↑160 . . . Root↓

51.21   ↑gesteckt↓

51.22   ↑Wart↓ [*written in the top margin of the page*]

51.25   ↑Convulsion↓

51.29   ⟨Chilblain ⟨Parker⟩ ↑Batterson↓⟩

52.1   ⟨Cuticle ⟨Plummer⟩ ↑Batterson↓⟩

52.3   ⟨↑Suffocation Billings↓⟩ ↑Loomis↓

52.6   ⟨Elephantiasis ⟨Aldrich⟩ ↑Addison↓⟩

52.7   ⟨↑Influenza Butler↓⟩

52.13–18   ↑Liver . . . Brigg[s]↓ [*written in the top margin of the page, probably at different times; the exact order of inscription is unclear*]

52.19   ⟨↑Rectum Jones↓⟩

52.27   ⟨Diaphram⟩ ⟨↑Influenza ⟨Briggs⟩ ↑Smith↓↓⟩

52.30 ↑Suffocation Billings/↑Briggs↓↓ [*written in the available space to the right of* '⟨General . . . Lewis⟩' *(52.21–22)*]

52.31–34 ↑Hemmorhage ↑Templeton↓ Belladonna Debility↓ [*written in the available space to the right of* '⟨Calomel | Borax⟩' *(52.24–25)*]

52.35–36 ⟨↑Paralysis Brown↓⟩ ↑Epilepsy Thompson↓ [*written diagonally below* 'Scrofula' *(52.29) in the otherwise blank bottom quarter of the page; followed by one blank page*]

53.1–31 Apoplexy . . . Augustine [*written on consecutive right-hand pages numbered* '1' *and* '2'; *the left-hand page facing* 'Apoplexy . . . Davis' *(53.1–16) is blank; the lines* 'Codliver . . . Ashcat' *(53.32–36) are on the top half of the otherwise blank left-hand page facing* 'Blister . . . St. Augustine' *(53.17–31) and may have been written before the surrounding right-hand pages were inscribed; the left-hand page following* 'St. Augustine' *is blank; the number* '28', *written near* 'Apoplexy Addison' *and circled, is the count of the names in the list, not including* 'Blister McManus' *(53.17) and* 'Dropsy Miller' *(53.19), which were added, and* 'Codliver . . . Ashcat'*]

53.17 ↑Blister McManus.↓

53.19 ↑Dropsy Miller↓

53.22 ⟨Addison⟩ ↑Templeton.↓

54.6 ⟨massacr⟩massaccers. ['c' *written over* 'r']

54.15 Perhaps [*one leaf has been torn out following the page that ends here*]

54.30 ↑⟨Ha⟩What . . . teach?↓

55.5 ⟨mochte⟩ ↑hätte↓

55.5 ⟨können⟩kön↑'↓ ['nen' *canceled and the apostrophe added*]

55.12 ⟨me⟩ ↑my legs↓

55.19 Xtopher st. N.Y. [*the bottom quarter of the page is blank below these words*]

56.1   ↑Plates for 3↓

56.3   ↑Cold↓

56.4   Tea ↑Oolong↓ ↑for↓ 1

56.9–10   thousand years [*one leaf has been torn out following the page that ends with* 'thousand']

56.25   Aug. 12. [*someone, probably Paine, interlined* '84' *following this date*]

56.28   not us. [*the bottom fifth of the page is blank below these words; the following leaf has been torn out*]

57.5   Black Ink [*the bottom fifth of the page is blank below these words*]

57.7–16   20. . . . 51,600 [*written by Olivia Clemens*]

57.20   ⟨$356.11⟩£356.11 ['£' *written over* '$'; *four-fifths of the page below this entry and the following 14 pages are blank, except for some grayish blue ink scrawls on one page, probably the result of testing a pen*]

57.21   ⟨Mch 29, 2055⟩ [*written in black pencil and canceled in grayish blue ink; presumably written on what was an otherwise blank page and then engulfed by the subsequent inscription of the list* 'People . . . Osgood, too.' (58.1–59.6), *within which it appears below* 'Whitford' (58.5)]

58.1–59.6   People . . . Osgood, too. [*written in grayish blue ink except for* 'of false rubber?' (59.2) *written in black pencil*]

58.2   ↑& 1,002.↓

59.1   ↑about *Huck Finn.*↓ ↑& 1,002.↓

59.2   ↑of false rubber?↓ [*interlined in black pencil*]

59.14   Spring . . . Chas W [*written in brownish black ink; the bottom third of the page below these words and the following two pages are blank*]

60.7   ⟨Izaac⟩Izaak ['k' *written over* 'c']

60.10   ↑disc of↓

60.10   ⟨↑all↓⟩ arts

60.14–61.14   1 & 2ᵈ . . . Huck). [*written on the recto of the back
                         flyleaf*]

60.19–22   ↑Bucking . . . Soliloquy.↓ [*interlined to the right of*
                         'C—10' *and* 'Mrs. C.—1   —1—2' (61.1–2)]

61.7   ⟨150⟩15[2] [*what may be '2' written over 'o'*]

Notebook 23

Emendations and Doubtful Readings

	MTP Reading	MS Reading
67.1–2	*Pays*	[*no column heading needed: middle of manuscript page*]
67.2	Eur	[*possibly* 'Eu.']
67.2	cost	[*ditto marks below preceding* 'cost']
71.12	left-handed	[*possibly* 'lefthanded' *or* 'left handed']
71.14	Adam Calf	[*possibly* 'Adam calf']
72.14	bat	[*possibly* 'hat']
*74.7	⟨Pets⟩Pete's	['Pets' *possibly* 'Pets' '; 'Pete's' *possibly* 'Pet's' *or* 'Petis']
75.6	Am	[*possibly* 'Ann']
76.17	er klingen	[*possibly* 'erklingen']
76.17	Hussa!	[*possibly* 'Hussa!,']
77.1	gemacht	[*possibly* 'gewacht']
77.6	ward	[*possibly* 'word']
*78.8	heart,	[*possibly* 'heart.']
*80.7	✖ ((Fisk	[*possibly* '✖ Fisk']
80.8	o[ne]	[*possibly* 'out' *or* 'our']
80.11	railroaded	rail-|roaded
80.19	railroad-honeymoon	railroad-honey-|moon
80.21	shamefaced	shame-|faced
80.22	bridegroom	bride-|groom

*80.27	of 15 years ago	[*placement uncertain*]
81.26	⟨[or] of⟩	[*possibly canceled* 'as of']
*82.2	myself⟨.⟩;	[*possibly* 'myself⟨,⟩;']
*83.15	⟨15⟩10	[*possibly* '⟨10⟩15']
*83.21	*princi*pal	[*possibly* 'principal']
*84.23–24	*Col. Sellers* | *Put up at Gadsby's*	[*possibly* 'Col. Sellers | Put up at Gadsby's']
86.12	Say	[*possibly* 'Spy']
*87.18–19	<u>15 m</u> | 25	[*underlines doubtful*]
88.16	nobody 'll	nobody | 'll
*89.9	⟨1[o]⟩15	[*possibly* '⟨15⟩⟨10⟩15']
89.24	⟨f[arm]er⟩	[*possibly canceled* 'former' *or* 'father']
90.2	sea-phrases	[*possibly* 'sea phrases' *or* ' 'sea' phrases']
90.3	brakeman	brake-|man
91.11	S[itu]	[*very doubtful*]
93.9	charm	[*possibly* 'charms']
93.9	⟨[(-]⟩	[*very doubtful; possibly* 'E']
94.9	bedrooms	bed-|rooms
*94.10	2 *other*	[*possibly* '2 *other*']
*94.10	2 *open fires.*	[*possibly* '2 open fires.']
96.8	See	[*possibly* 'Sec' *or* 'Sa']
96.11	medallion	[*possibly* 'Medallion']
*99.11	Sheridan 1632	1632 Sheridan
102.1	⟨l⟩Leide	[*possibly* '⟨L⟩leide']
103.7	Entzückend	[*possibly* 'entzückend']
103.8	Entblösst	[*possibly* 'entblösst']

103.16	fl[ü]ssend	[*possibly* 'fliessend']
104.4	Each	[*possibly* 'each']
104.11	⟨Uber⟩	[*possibly canceled* 'Meer']
104.16	Notenbuch	[*possibly* 'Noten buch']
105.2	windpipe	[*possibly* 'wind pipe']
*107.29	answer.)	[*possibly* 'answer.']
*108.6	*harm*	[*possibly* '*harm.*', '*harm*', or '*harm.*']
*108.16	Barrett's House	[*possibly* '*Barrett's House*' or *canceled*]
*109.7	*Genl*	[*possibly* 'Genl']
*111.3–4	Clover Club . . . Bellevue. C. R. Deacon . . . Continental Hotel	Clover Club C. R. Deacon . . . Continental Hotel . . . Bellevue.
113.7	Free Trade	[*possibly* 'Free-Trade']
*113.8	⟨Hab⟩Have	[*possibly* '⟨Hah⟩Have']
*114.18	(nigger)	[*position doubtful*]
114.19	Napolèon	[*possibly* 'Napolion']
115.1	Huck Finn	[*possibly* 'Huck Finns']
*115.10	⟨grandfather⟩father	[*possibly* '⟨grand⟩ father']
116.6	Coincide	[*possibly* 'coincide']
*119.14	use . . . ⟨No⟩	[*placement uncertain*]
*119.16	Tale.	[*possibly* 'Tale.']

Details of Inscription

[Entries are in black pencil unless otherwise noted]

66.1–6   Tip . . . ↑& 1885.↓ [*written on the verso of the front flyleaf; 'Tip . . . Centre.' written in blue ink; the bot-*

tom three-quarters of the page is blank below 'Centre.'
except for '1884 & 1885.' written at an angle in mid-page,
'1884' in black pencil and '& 1885.' in black ink]

66.7–67.26   Pays . . . 18,000⟩ [written on three consecutive right-
hand pages; the intervening left-hand pages are blank;
the next nine left-hand pages may also originally have
been left blank until after the inscription on the facing
right-hand pages had been begun; of the nine, only the
left-hand page 'Anything . . . boys.' (70.12–19) is completely filled; three blank and five partially blank left-
hand pages are mentioned below at 67.27–68.5, 68.15–
16, 69.8, 71.8–11, 72.5, 72.17–18, 73.6–8, and 73.17]

67.26   ⟨300 . . . 18,000⟩ [canceled in a black ink unlike that
used elsewhere in this notebook]

67.27–68.5   15 Grande . . . Boston [written on a left-hand page
the bottom quarter of which is blank; see 66.7–67.26]

68.3   ↑839 St Mark's ave↓ [interlined without a caret above
'Dean . . . Wall']

68.15–16   Brander . . . 18$^{th.}$ [written in purple pencil; followed
by one blank page; see 66.7–67.26]

68.18   ↑**X**↓ ['**X**' added here and at 69.2, 69.4, 71.6, 71.12, 71.13,
71.14, 73.1, 73.9, 73.12, 74.1, 74.3, 77.11, 78.10, 78.12,
78.13, and 80.1; related symbols are listed at 79.11 and
92.11–13; see the headnote discussion on pages 65–66]

69.1   ↑'84–5.↓

69.3   ↑What's her line?↓

69.8   Golden Arm [written at the top of an otherwise blank
left-hand page; see 66.7–67.26]

69.9   ↑1884?↓ [written in the top margin of the page, possibly
as an alternative to the unrecovered cancellation in the
next line]

69.10   ⟨[word]⟩ [heavily canceled]

70.12–19   Anything . . . boys. [written on a left-hand page that

	may originally have been left blank when the facing right-hand page was inscribed; see 66.7–67.26]
70.16–17	out early. Lost the bet. [*a line drawn across the page below these words originally ended the entry at* 'early.' *or possibly at* 'bet.'; *the line was disregarded when the entry was continued*]
70.19	↑I . . . boys.↓ [*squeezed into the margin beside* 'Found . . . driver.' (70.17–18)]
71.2	↑Ch↓ 33
71.8–11	Decided . . . humor—kill the tadpoles. [*written on a left-hand page the bottom half of which is blank; see 66.7–67.26*]
71.8	↑Decided it best to↓
71.9	⟨ju[- -]⟩judicious ['di' *written over two unrecovered letters*]
72.5	Heaven? [*followed by one blank page; see 66.7–67.26*]
72.12	⟨t[-]⟩thread ['h' *written over an unrecovered letter*]
72.17–18	There . . . away. [*written at the top of an otherwise blank left-hand page; see 66.7–67.26*]
73.1	Mrs. ↑B. W.↓ Jones
73.2	leg. [*a line originally ending the entry here was disregarded when the entry was continued*]
73.6–8	Paid . . . Doyle $6. [*written on a left-hand page the bottom half of which is blank; see 66.7–67.26*]
73.12–15	⟨we are⟩ ↑the worlds . . . space↓ are . . . blood of ⟨some . . . us.⟩ ↑God.↓ [*canceled* 'are' *restored with the instruction* 'stet']
73.17	sock [*followed by one blank page; see 66.7–67.26*]
74.3	no-'count⟨: "⟩; very [*the colon mended to a semicolon;* 'very' *written over the quotation marks*]
74.4	⟨upon⟩on ['up' *canceled*]

74.7   ⟨Pets⟩Pete's [*what appears to be 'e's' written over what appears to be 's'; see Doubtful Readings*]

75.5–9   ↑Patrick . . . Remus.↓

76.3   ⟨solch [ein]⟩⟨solche[- -]⟩solchen [*originally what looks like 'solch ein'; 'e' added to 'solch', perhaps in an attempt to form 'solchein'; 'en' written over 'e' and the letters that follow*]

76.7   Tausend [*Clemens drew a wavy line under 'ause'*]

76.10   ⟨Franzozen⟩Franzosen ['s' *written over* 'z']

76.14   w↑i↓e

76.16   ⟨we⟩wie ['ie' *written over* 'e']

76.20   ⟨Glüch⟩Glück ['k' *written over* 'h']

76.22   Feldmar↑s↓chal⟨[!]⟩. [*what appears to be an exclamation point altered to a period*]

76.27   TA⟨p⟩↑-ap-↓-fer-er ['ta' *underlined twice*]

76.27   ⟨D[a]gen⟩De↑-e-↓gen [*the first 'e' written over what appears to be 'a'; '-e-' interlined with a caret*]

78.1   Orleans [*the bottom third of the page is blank below this entry*]

78.5   English [*the bottom fifth of the page is blank below this entry*]

78.8   heart, [*the bottom third of the page is blank below this word; see Doubtful Readings*]

78.12   ages. [*following the page that ends here, two leaves were cut and torn out and used by Clemens for a letter to his wife dated 3 December 1884; presumably the leaves were removed before this entry was continued on the next surviving page*]

78.13   ↑X↓ Have . . . habits ['X' *written in the top margin of the page above 'habits', probably as a reminder that these words are a continuation of the entry begun with*

'Dream of being' *on the previous page, which is also marked with an* '**X**']

79.1–8   ↑Fall . . . SL C↓ [*written in brownish black ink lengthwise on the page across the preceding entry*]

79.10   ⟨'66⟩'86 ['8' *written in purple pencil over* '6']

79.11   ↑**XX**↓ ['**XX**' *added here and at* 80.4, 80.7, 80.11, 86.2, 86.13, 87.1, 87.5, 87.10, 88.19, 89.23, 90.9, 90.10, 91.1, 91.5, 92.15, 98.14, *and* 102.9; *related symbols are listed at* 68.18 *and* 92.11–13; *see the headnote discussion on pages* 65–66]

80.7   ↑**XX**↓ ((Fisk & graveyard. [*possibly written later than surrounding entries; written at the bottom of a right-hand page opposite* '**XX** Jim . . . dollar.'" (79.11–13) *on the facing page; what appear to be two opening parentheses may have been intended as pointers to indicate the relationship between this entry and the earlier one*]

80.11   years⟨.⟩, [*the comma written over the period*]

80.14   ⟨him,⟩ ↑her lovey-dove,↓

80.15   ⟨& ↑s↓he would⟩

80.18   ⟨at him⟩ ↑over his shirt collar↓

80.20   ↑in↓ the same

80.24   ↑must have↓ seemed

80.27   way ↑of 15 years ago↓, ['of . . . ago' *interlined without a caret above the beginning of the line* 'old soul-enchanting way,'; *possibly intended as a parenthetical explanation of* 'old' *rather than as a part of the sentence following* 'way']

80.30   sleep ⟨just⟩ [*a mark over* 'sl' *of* 'sleep' *appears to be the beginning of a cancellation which was not carried out*]

81.2–3   ⟨& won ↑back↓ your vanished⟩

81.7   railroading↑.↓ ⟨of mine.⟩ ['Railroading improvements' *is written in the top margin of the page above the canceled words, probably by Albert Bigelow Paine*]

81.13	way⟨,⟩;[*the semicolon written over the comma*]
81.16–17	↑in many cases↓
81.30	⟨down⟩done ['ne' *written over* 'wn']
82.2	myself⟨.⟩; [*the period mended to a semicolon; see Doubtful Readings*]
82.3	⟨missionary⟩ ↑man↓
82.15	↑Delay . . . 10↓
82.16	⟨1[-]⟩15. ['5' *written over one unrecovered figure*]
82.17	⟨1[-]⟩15 ['5' *written over one unrecovered figure*]
82.22	⟨95⟩105 & ⟨1[5]⟩10 ['o' *written over* '9'; 'o' *written over an incomplete* '5']
83.7	Gad'sby's [*apparently originally* 'Gad's'; *the apostrophe left standing when* 'by's' *was added*]
83.9	Fanshaw [*a vertical line drawn to the right of* 'Blue-jays. . . . DE-parted.' (83.4–8) *sets off a narrow blank space on the side of the page;* 'Fanshaw' *is written to the right of* 'Blue-jays.' *at the top of this space*]
83.11	⟨[12]⟩⟨14⟩10 ['o' *written over* '4', *which may be written over* '2']
83.13	⟨[10]⟩20 ['20' *written over what may be* '10']
83.15–19	Tragic Tale . . . Jumping Frog . . . 10 [*a line in the left margin connects* 'Tragic Tale' *with a caret below* 'Jumping Frog'; *these devices—together with the letters* 'a' *and* 'b' *beside* 'Tragic Tale' *and* 'Situation', *the short lines drawn in the space between those two selections, the brace beside them, the note* 'tr' *that follows* 'Jumping Frog . . . 20', *and the* '10' *connected to no title at the bottom of the list—apparently reflect Clemens' inconclusive efforts to vary the order of his readings*]
83.15	⟨15⟩10 ['o' *apparently written over* '5'; *see Doubtful Readings*]

83.20   ↑ony↓

83.21   principal [*a line under 'princi' may be a flourish at the
               end of the entry*]

83.21   GO ['go' *underlined twice*]

84.2   au↑dience↓ ['dience' *added in purple pencil*]

84.6   ↑(2 pieces, a & b)↓

84.10   107 [*the bottom two-fifths of the page is blank below
               this entry*]

84.13   15↑–17↓

84.21   ↑JUMPING FROG↓ [*written lengthwise in the right
               margin beside* 'Wait . . . 7' (84.11–16)]

84.22   ↑Call . . . sit.↓ [*written in the margin to the right of*
               '2ᵈ . . . 13' (84.17–18)]

84.23–24   ↑Col. . . . Gadsby's↓ [*written lengthwise on the page
               across* '1ˢᵗ Escape . . . 112' (84.15–20) *in printed rather
               than cursive letters, probably for legibility; underlining,
               here represented by italics, may also have been meant
               to set these lines off for clarity rather than to impart
               emphasis*]

86.1   ↑Chas. . . . lawyer.↓ [*written in the upper right corner
               of the page beside* 'Pipe . . . book.' (85.4–6) *and sep-
               arated from these entries by a curved line*]

86.12   ↑Say↓ [*interlined without a caret above* 'is a' (86.13)]

87.5–7   ↑✖↓ To one . . . had! ['To one . . . foot?' *is written
               at the bottom of a left-hand page; the remainder of the
               anecdote* ('The other . . . had!') *is written at the top
               of the facing page;* '✖', *written in the top margin of the
               page above* 'other man:', *has been placed at the beginning
               of the entry*]

87.5   ⟨"⟩O ['O' *written over quotation marks*]

87.9   crockery. [*a flourish originally ending the entry here was
               disregarded when the entry was continued*]

87.9   NEW ['new' *underlined twice*]

87.10   ↑**X**?↓ Describe . . . rout; ['Describe . . . so-& so's' *is
                written at the bottom of a right-hand page; the entry
                continues with 'rout;' on the verso of the leaf;* '**X**?',
                *written in the top margin of the page above 'rout;', has
                been placed at the beginning of the entry*]

87.12   daughter↑s↓

87.18–19   15 m | 25 [*it is unclear whether Clemens intended the
                lines below these figures to serve for emphasis or for
                totaling the figures above; the line below '25', here repre-
                sented by italics, is longer than that below '15 m'*]

88.1   ⟨20⟩ ↑15↓ m.

88.3   ⟨20⟩ ⟨↑15↓⟩ ↑20↓

88.4   ↑RAFTSMEN↓

88.6   ⟨↑GHOST↓⟩

88.14–15   ↑Cable . . . it.↓ [*written in purple pencil lengthwise in
                the margins on either side of '1*st*. . . . Ghost' (88.8–13)*]

88.14   ↑$550 to↓ $600

88.19   under foot.) [*the bottom two-thirds of the leaf below
                this entry has been torn out; the verso of the surviving
                third is blank; the following two leaves have also been
                torn out*]

89.2   brag. [*a flourish originally ending the entry here or
                possibly at 'hair' was disregarded when the entry was
                continued*]

89.4–5   ⟨Kelly⟩Riley . . . ↑pay him↓ . . . week⟨.⟩ & expenses.
                ['Ri' *written over 'Ke'; 'ey' written over 'ly'; '&' written
                over a period; alterations and additions are in purple
                pencil*]

89.9   ↑K.↓ Sol. ↑& bank↓

89.9   ⟨1[o]⟩15 ['5' *written over what looks like 'o'; '5' appears
                to have been traced over, but possibly the original read-*

ing was '15', 'o' was written over '5', and '5' was written
over 'o']

89.11   ↑or Escape↓ [*interlined without a caret below* 'K. . . .
             Sit']

89.12   ↑5↓ Du M.

89.19   ↑McClellan↓ [*written in the space to the right of* 'Es-
             cape | Gardiner' (89.15–16)]

89.21   daughter. [*a flourish originally ending the entry here was
             disregarded when the entry was continued*]

90.9   ↑✗ Tom . . . remark↓ [*written between the two preced-
             ing sentences*]

90.11   interrupting. [*two leaves have been torn out following
             the page that ends here*]

91.1–5   ↑✗?↓ Make . . . ↑✗?↓ Invent . . . [t]aking [*written
             in grayish blue ink except for* '✗?' *added twice in black
             pencil*]

91.2   boy⟨[—]⟩& ['&' *written over what may be a dash*]

91.8   ⟨(⟩⟨[E]⟩(Enc. [*sequence of revision unclear;* 'E' *written
             over a parenthesis and what looks like* 'E', *one of which
             had been written over the other; the surviving parenthesis
             and* 'nc.' *may or may not have been part of the original
             inscription*]

91.9   ⟨2.⟩4? ['4' *written over* '2'; *the period mended to a
             question mark*]

91.11   ⟨4.⟩2 ['4' *canceled;* '2' *written over the period*]

91.11   ↑Agricul Editor.↓ [*interlined without a caret above can-
             celed* 'S[itu] (Gov. Gardner?)']

91.12   Call this a gov't.? [*boxed; the bottom third of the page
             is blank below this entry*]

91.13   ↑1st n.↓

91.17   ↑Blue-jay? 3 & Duel 4.↓ [*written diagonally to the right
             of* '1. Agricul . . . Gardner.' (91.15–18)]

92.1   ↑1ˢᵗ night↓

92.11–13   ↑#↓ The only time Gen . . . ↑Genˡ. Spinner↓ ['#' writ-
                  ten in the top margin of the page above 'time'; 'Genˡ.
                  Spinner' written in the top margin of the page above
                  'time Gen'; the sequence in which the additions were
                  made is uncertain; '#' also added at 92.14, 92.23, 93.6,
                  110.6, 112.5, and 113.1; related symbols are listed at 68.18
                  and 79.11; see the headnote discussion on pages 65–66]

92.15–16   ↑✖↓ Man . . . desperate ['Man . . . Fright—' is writ-
                  ten at the bottom of a right-hand page; the entry con-
                  tinues with 'desperate' on the verso of the leaf; '✖',
                  written in the top margin of the page above 'desperate',
                  has been placed at the beginning of the entry]

92.17   ↑Kills robber.↓

93.4   ⟨the⟩ ↑its own↓

94.10   ↑2↓ other [the underlining below 'other' may have been
                  meant to apply also to '2']

94.10   2 open fires. [a line below 'open fires.' may have been
                  intended not to emphasize the words but to conclude
                  the entry; the bottom fifth of the page is blank below
                  this entry]

95.10   ↑Plaudern zu viel.↓ [written in the top margin of the page
                  above 'Extravagance:' (94.11)]

95.11   ↑Eure . . . bescheiden↓ [written lengthwise in the right
                  margin beside and partially covering 'Thick . . . book.'
                  (94.14–17)]

96.11   Grant↑.↓ ⟨& put on sale.⟩ [altered in purple pencil]

96.12   ↑Andrew↓

96.12   ⟨near⟩ ↑below↓

96.13–98.1   Feb. 26 . . . week [written in grayish blue ink, with
                  alterations in purple pencil at 97.11 and 97.18–19]

96.21   ⟨opposition⟩opposite ['e' written over 'i'; 'on' canceled]

97.2   ⟨his⟩ ↑the↓

97.11   ⟨I⟩ I made ↑to him↓ ['I' *underlined and* 'to him' *added in purple pencil*]

97.18–19   ↑that much↓ [*written in purple pencil*]

98.8–9   ⟨What . . . which⟩ | Bissell called for? ['What . . . which' *canceled in purple pencil at the bottom of a page;* 'Bissell called for?' *left uncanceled at the top of the following page*]

98.14   ↑✗↓ [*written in black ink*]

99.1   ↑Mr. Lincoln↓ [*written in the top margin of the page above* '312 C (Gen Hawley)']

99.7   President. [*the bottom half of the page is blank below this entry*]

99.11   ↑Sheridan↓ 1632 ['Sheridan' *interlined with a caret inadvertently placed after* '1632'; *emended*]

100.1   ⟨Gen.⟩General ['eral' *added;* 'e' *written over the period*]

100.9–10   ⟨divide . . . her.⟩ [*canceled in purple pencil*]

101.4–113.13   In N. Y. . . . made. [*written in purple pencil except for entries or additions in black ink and black pencil at* 102.9, 107.29, 109.7, 110.6, 111.1, 112.1–2, 112.5, 112.14, *and* 113.1]

102.3   ⟨die⟩dich ['ch' *written over* 'e']

102.7   ⟨W[e-]⟩Wir ['ir' *written over what may be* 'e' *and an unrecovered letter*]

102.9   ↑✗↓ [*written in black ink at the bottom of the page* 'Du . . . geworden."' (102.1–8)]

102.13–14   ↑Also O. W. Holmes.↓ [*squeezed in above* 'Station-Agenten']

102.15   recht.⟩ [*the bottom quarter of the page is blank below this entry*]

104.4   de luxe⟨.⟩—$50 [*the dash written over the period*]

104.5	↑—broad 1 foot margin↓ [*the intended position of this phrase is uncertain; interlined without a caret above* 'de luxe⟨.⟩—$50 apiece.']
104.11	⟨Uber⟩ ↑Vom↓
104.15	↑gütigst↓
104.18	↑dem . . . Grant↓
104.20	⟨groosmüthiges⟩grossmüthiges ['s' *written over* 'o']
105.10	↑& Jim↓
106.3	note. [*a line originally ending the entry here was overwritten when the entry was continued*]
106.10	⟨looked at⟩ ↑examined↓
106.12	it⟨, for⟩. [*the period written over the comma*]
107.1	⟨U. S.⟩ ↑General↓ Grant
107.5	⟨told you⟩ ↑was sure ⟨his⟩↓
107.25	⟨puzzles⟩puzzled ['d' *written over* 's']
107.26	years⟨."⟩, and [*the comma written over the period;* 'and' *written over the quotation marks*]
107.29	answer.↑)↓ [*the parenthesis is in black pencil and may have been added by Paine*]
108.2	"↑No *sir*—↓They was ['No *sir*—' *interlined without a caret above* '"They was']
108.4	it—lose grip— [*a line across the page below these words may originally have ended the entry at* 'it' *or* 'grip'; *the line was disregarded when the entry was continued*]
108.5	wher' they *fell*—They [*a line across the page below these words may originally have ended the entry at* 'fell'; *the line was disregarded when the entry was continued*]
108.5–6	was handsome & no *harm* [*a line across the page below these words may originally have ended the entry at* 'handsome' *or* 'harm'; *the passage was continued below the*

line with no indication that a new sentence, new paragraph, or new entry was beginning; nevertheless context
suggests that the line may still have been intended to
mark a hiatus within the entry; the underline below 'harm'
may have been meant as an extension of the longer line
across the page; 'harm' is written to the edge of the page;
a dot above the 'm' of 'harm' may have been intended
as a period; see Doubtful Readings]

108.8–9   denom | them times [a right-hand page ends with 'denom',
and the verso of the leaf begins with 'them times' with no
indication that a new sentence, new paragraph, or new
entry is beginning; nevertheless, the page break (like the
line across the page discussed above at 108.5–6) seems
to mark a hiatus within the entry]

108.10–11   the cellar.— | not [a line across the page below 'the cellar.
—', like the line reported at 108.5–6, may originally have
ended the entry at 'cellar.' and now apparently indicates
a hiatus within the entry; the words 'the cellar.—' fill
only half a line, the remainder of which is blank as though
a new paragraph were to follow, but the next line begins
without either a capital letter or paragraph indentation]

108.12   sight! [the line separating this from the following entry
is heavily traced over]

108.16   Barrett's House. [a line drawn across the page partly below and partly through these words may have been intended to emphasize or cancel them]

109.2   (⟨85⟩84) ['4' written over '5']

109.7   Genl [underlined in black pencil, possibly by Paine]

110.6   ↑#↓ [written in black ink]

111.1–4   Actor's . . . ↑J. W. Ryckman, Committee↓ ↑Clover
Club . . . Bellevue.↓ ↑C. R. Deacon . . . Continental
Hotel↓ ['Actor's . . . Music.' written in black pencil; the
additions written in purple pencil, in an order that remains uncertain; 'J. W. Ryckman, Committee' interlined
above 'afternoon of Apl. 9,'; 'Clover Club . . . Bellevue.'

interlined to the right of 'Acad Music.' *and* 'Send book to Life' (111.5); 'C. R. Deacon . . . Continental Hotel' *interlined above* 'Fund, Phila,' *and connected by a line to a caret following* 'Clover Club'; *emended*]

111.6–10   ⟨Hartford . . . Gerhardt.⟩   ['Hartford . . . received.' *written by Clemens; signature, almost certainly written by Gerhardt, canceled more heavily than usual*]

111.6   ⟨26⟩27 ['7' *written over* '6']

112.1–2   ⟨J. R. Randall . . . Chronicle.⟩ [*written in black pencil; canceled in purple pencil*]

112.5   ↑#↓ [*written in black ink*]

112.8   ⟨talked⟩talking ['ing' *written over* 'ed']

112.11   sit ↑up↓

112.14   Mad. Square . . . readings. [*written in black pencil*]

112.14   Apl. 28 ↑& 29↓

113.1   ↑#↓ [*written in black ink*]

113.6   INDEX ['index' *underlined three times*]

113.8   ⟨Hab⟩Have ['ve' *written over what looks like* 'b' *or* 'h']

113.12   Index ['ndex' *of* 'Index' *underlined twice*]

113.14–114.11   ⟨Boston . . . Cure.⟩ [*written in black pencil; first* 'Sollermun' (114.15) *and* '(went well.)' (114.2), *then the entire passage, canceled in purple pencil*]

114.12–118.4   What . . . moment. [*written in purple pencil except for an entry at* 117.11–12 *and a revision at* 117.15]

114.18   ↑(nigger)↓ [*intended position uncertain; interlined without a caret below* 'the god.' *and above* 'Carlyle; Napoleon']

115.10   ⟨grandfather⟩father ['grand' *canceled;* 'father' *not canceled;* 'grand' *may have been canceled before* 'father' *was written*]

116.5   ⟨my father's [*one leaf has been torn out preceding the page that begins here*]

116.7   ↑new↓

116.8   INDEX ['index' *underlined twice*]

117.11–12   Chatto's . . . ↑was↓ . . . $857.⁸⁴. [*written and revised in black pencil*]

117.15   ⟨[-]⟩ [*one or two unrecovered characters canceled in black pencil*]

118.4   moment. [*followed by five blank pages*]

118.14   Duel. [*the bottom quarter of the page is blank below this entry; two subsequent leaves were cut out; the first of these is missing; the second was used by Clemens for a letter to his wife dated 12 November 1884*]

118.16   ⟨Wa⟩What . . . brief? [*written in purple pencil; the bottom two-thirds of the page below this entry and the three following pages are blank*]

118.18   ⟨Capt.⟩ ↑Gov.↓

119.4–7   ⟨Jumping . . . Duel [*all of this inscription except 'Enc' is circled; 'Enc' is written to the left of the circle*]

119.9–121.18 1ˢᵗ . . . tadpoles. [*written on two facing pages, '1ˢᵗ . . . Tar Baby. +' (119.9–120.22) on the verso of the note-book's final page and 'En. . . . tadpoles.' (121.1–18) on the recto of the back flyleaf*]

119.12   Tale of Fishwife + + [*the crosses here and in the following lines (through 121.16) may have been written later than the lines they accompany; they are discussed in note 183*]

119.14   ↑Gov. . . . ⟨No⟩↓ [*written in the right margin so that 'Gov. Gardner' stands beside 'Enc. ⟨Hamlet.⟩'(119.14), 'use it in Boston too—' stands beside 'A Trying Situa-tion. +' and '2ᵈ.' (119.15 and 119.17), and '⟨No⟩' stands beside '⟨Telephone talk.⟩ +' (119.18); the intended posi-tion of 'use . . . ⟨No⟩' is uncertain; 'use . . . too—'*]

or 'use . . . too—⟨No⟩' *may have been meant to fol-*
low 'Situation. +'; '⟨No⟩' *may have been meant to fol-*
low 'talk.⟩ +']

119.16 ↑*Eng.* . . . TALE.↓ [*written in the right margin beside*
'1st . . . Story. + +' (119.9–13); 'Tale' *underlined twice*
by lines that may have been meant to indicate the end
of the entry rather than emphasis]

120.1–4 A Dazzling Achevmnt | ↑Gov. Gardner +↓ | ⟨↑Whis-
tling.↓⟩ | ⟨Eng.⟩Enc. ⟨*Whistling*⟩ ⟨↑Gov. Gardner,⟩ 41
W.E.↓ ↑Whis↓ [*the intended position of some of these*
items and the sequence of revision are uncertain; probably
originally 'A Dazzling Achevmnt | Eng. *Whistling*'; 'c'
written over 'g' *of* 'Eng.'; *possibly when* 'Telephone talk.'
(119.18) was canceled, 'Whistling' *was moved to the main*
part of the program and 'Gov. Gardner' *was added as an*
encore; possibly then 'Gov. Gardner' *and* 'Whistling'
were exchanged; as the passage now appears, 'Gov. Gardner +' *stands above canceled* 'Whistling.', *both of them*
to the left of 'Enc.' *and below* 'A Dazzling', *while can-*
celed 'Gov. Gardner,' *followed by* '41 W.E.' *stands above*
canceled 'Whistling', *both of them to the right of* 'Enc.'
and below 'Achevmnt'; 'Whis' *is squeezed in between*
'⟨*Whistling*⟩' *and* '⟨Gov. Gardner,⟩']

120.5–11 3^d | ↑Petroleum. 57 . . . Agricul Editor +↓ | 4th Day.
['4th Day.' *was written below* '3^d' *with no intervening*
space, and apparently the list below '4th Day.' *was be-*
gun before the two columns that now follow '3^d' *were*
squeezed into the remaining available space: 'Petroleum.
57 . . . Agri. Editor. + +' *to the left of* '3^d' *and* '4th
Day.', *and* 'Petroleum! . . . Agricul Editor +' *to the*
right; although the sequence of inscription and revision
is not certain, the right-hand column probably was written
first, originally beginning with a dash holding a place
for a title to be selected later; the dash was left standing
when 'Essay Lying' *was written beside it; probably* 'Essay
Lying' *was canceled when* 'Petroleum!' *was added; a caret*
below and to the right of '3^d' *seems to indicate the in-*
tended placement of the right-hand column; the column

on the left was probably written as a fair copy of that
on the right, including a replacement for canceled 'Dis-
cuticled Man']

120.14   ⟨My Duel⟩ ↑Tar Baby? + +↓

120.17–18   ↑Sizing . . . Soldiers, 83↓ [*written above* 'Guides.'
                    (120.19) and to the right of '5*th*']

120.22   ↑⟨C⟩⟨Eng.⟩Enc. Tar Baby. +↓ [*written in the right
                    margin beside* 'Bret . . . Fanshaw. + +'; 'E' *written
                    over* 'C' *and* 'c' *written over* 'g']

121.2   ↑Dying . . . Ele↓ [*written in the upper right corner of
                    the page beside* 'En.']

121.10   ↑The New Cimetery—37. Wh. E.↓

121.13   ↑Capt. Rounceville, 44 Wh. El.↓

Notebook 24

Emendations and Doubtful Readings

	MTP Reading	MS Reading
127.19	tonight	[*possibly* 'to-night']
129.6	bks years	[*possibly* 'bk 5 years']
129.6	families:	[*possibly* 'families;']
129.21	Scripture-oozing	[*possibly* 'scripture-oozing']
129.27	boot heel	[*possibly* 'boot-heel']
131.1	to-day	to-|day
132.3	knock-⟨down	knock-|down
132.15	steel-trap	steel-|trap
133.6	print it	[*possibly* 'print & ' *or* 'print—']
134.8	sie	[*possibly* 'Sie']
*135.11	Hochwürdig	[*possibly* '⟨Hochwürdig⟩Hoch-würdig']
*135.14	hauptsachliche	[*possibly* 'hauptsächliche']
135.17	ein-zehnte	ein-|zehnte
137.11	mayhap	may-|hap
*138.4	in *ages*—	[*placement uncertain*]
138.5	go—with	go | —with
139.7	Poli	[*possibly* 'Pole']
*139.14	(any . . . make)	[*possibly* 'any . . . make']
140.3	seine	[*possibly* 'seiner' *or* 'sine']
140.9	roof-pipe	roof-|pipe

*142.12	⟨$6[1]0,000⟩610,000	[*possibly* '⟨$6[1]0,000⟩$610,000']
142.24	*facsimile*	[*possibly* 'fac simile']
143.5	high school	[*possibly* 'highschool']
*143.11	⟨truly⟩ devoted?	[*possibly* '⟨truly?⟩ devoted']
147.8	type-setters	type-|setters
*147.10–11	*the other one wouldn't.*	[*possibly* 'the other one wouldn't.']
147.25	standing	stanidng
*147.25	rock	[*possibly* 'rhock']
*147.26	childer	[*possibly* 'childher']
149.18	Hairdresser	[*possibly* 'Hair dresser']
*153.12	President	Presi-|ident
*160.16	(June 9/85.)	[*possibly* '(June 9)/85.)']
160.17	to-day	[*possibly* 'today']
*161.4	hours;	hours;;
164.4	bed⟨stead⟩	bed-|⟨stead⟩
164.7	full page	[*possibly* 'full-page']
*166.3	I don't . . . not a word. ⟨"I⟩"I lay	[*possibly* '"I don't . . . not a word. ⟨"I⟩I lay']
170.7	to-night	[*possibly* 'tonight']
170.22	book stores	[*possibly* 'bookstores']
*170.22–171.2	idea. In . . . people. Otherwise	[*order uncertain*]
171.5	bookstores	book-|stores
*173.6	get all . . . you get .	[*placement uncertain*]
173.13	battlefields	[*possibly* 'battle fields' *or* 'battle-fields']

Details of Inscription

[*Most entries are in purple pencil or black pencil as noted*]

126.1–3   ⟨Webster . . . 30th [*written on the verso of the front flyleaf; the bottom three-quarters of the page is blank below these entries*]

126.1–2   ⟨Webster . . . 126. [*written in black pencil;* 'Webster . . . 125' *canceled in purple pencil*]

126.3–6   Stedman . . . Htfd. [*written in purple pencil; the bottom two-thirds of the page is blank below* 'Htfd.'; *followed by two blank pages*]

126.7–11   Ch Webster . . . Beacon [*written in black pencil; the bottom two-thirds of the page is blank below these entries*]

127.1–128.3   280 000 . . . Gillett. [*written in purple pencil*]

127.8   ⟨452⟩252 ['2' *written over* '4'; *the bottom half of the page is blank below this entry; followed by three blank pages*]

127.24   ⟨half⟩halb ['b' *written over* 'f']

128.1–2   ⟨Flehen, Flehen, Flehen⟩ ↑Beten, Beten, Beten↓

128.4–136.20   Donkey . . . pavement. [*written in black pencil except for entries or alterations in purple pencil at* 130.21–22, 134.2–10, 134.14, 135.11–13, *and* 135.16–19]

128.6   altogether) [*three-quarters of the page is blank below this entry*]

128.7–130.15   "Suspicion . . . forgotten him. [*eight leaves inscribed on right-hand pages only except for the entry at* 129.19 *written on a left-hand page*]

128.9   ↑in Chicago.↓

128.11   ↑A↓ Further

128.12   ⟨seduced⟩ ↑betrayed↓

128.13   ⟨important⟩ ↑pathetic↓

129.5   "A Society Man's Crime." [*Clemens originally left blank*
                    space following this entry, probably to permit the addi-
                    tion of new items; see 129.6–9]

129.6–9   It will . . . year.⟩ ↑but the W. gets . . . holy↓ ['It will
                    . . . year.⟩' *written at the bottom of the page below*
                    '"A . . . Crime"' (*129.5*) *and the blank space that orig-*
                    inally followed that entry; 'but the W. gets . . . holy'
                    written in the blank space with a line between 'but' *in*
                    the addition and 'but the W.' *in the original inscription*
                    indicating the intended position of the new passage; the
                    sequence of revision is unclear: either 'carries . . . pro-*
                    tection' *was written first and then canceled when* 'but
                    . . . ahead &' *was written above it, or* 'but . . . protec-*
                    tion' *was written and then* 'carries . . . protection' *was*
                    canceled; 'carries its' *may originally have been* 'carries it',
                    but if so the 's' *was probably added to* 'it' *before the line*
                    was continued; separate strokes cancel 'carries its' *and*
                    'high . . . protection', *and either phrase may have been*
                    canceled independently before another, longer stroke
                    was drawn through the whole line]

129.13   ↑¶↓

129.18   ↑home circle↓

129.19   4,000,000 . . . a year [*written on an otherwise blank left-*
                    hand page; 'further . . . newspaper.' (*129.15–18*) *and*
                    'There . . . preparations' (*129.20–21*) *fill the facing*
                    right-hand page; since most surrounding leaves (beginning
                    at 128.7) are inscribed on right-hand pages only, it is likely
                    that Clemens wrote these lines later than at least some of
                    the entries which follow 'a year']

129.21   ↑particularly pious & Scripture-oozing↓

129.24–25   ↑—don't . . . accuracy.↓

130.1   ↑—missed that man↓

130.1   ↑disinterested↓

130.9–10   ↑—with . . . details.↓ [*written in the top margin of the page above* '"Hacked himself . . . col.'; *a line drawn from* 'col.' *to the dash indicates the intended sequence*]

130.11   5 cols ↑a↓ in 1 issue. [*'a' interlined above* 'cols', *probably a misplaced false start on the interlineation* 'a week' (*130.11*) *which was completed two lines further down the notebook page*]

130.11   ⟨10 issues⟩ ↑a week↓

130.12–13   ↑—4,000,000 . . . say.↓

130.14   ⟨30,000,000⟩ 50,000,000 ['50' *written over* '30']

130.21–22   Dog show . . . see it. [*written in purple pencil*]

131.9–10   work in U. S.? [*a quarter of the page is blank below this entry*]

131.12   ⟨die⟩ ↑moderate↓

131.16   ⟨⅓⟩ ⅕ ['5' *written over* '3']

132.3–4   100 . . . knock-⟨down . . . canvassig.⟩ ['down . . . canvassig.' *canceled at the top of a page;* '100 . . . knock-' *left uncanceled on the preceding page*]

132.4   ⟨250⟩ ↑300↓

132.5   ↑(with 20 pp. MS)↓

133.16   ⟨$64,061.60⟩ $74,061.60 ['7' *written over* '6']

134.1   Send Pond $200 [*the bottom quarter of the page is blank below this entry*]

134.2–10   ⟨Welche . . . Zoll.⟩ [*written in black pencil; canceled in purple pencil;* '⟨Wi[s]⟩Wich . . . Zoll.' (*134.10*) *circled in purple pencil*]

134.2   ⟨gewöh[- - -]⟩gewöhnliche ['nl' *written over what appear to be three letters*]

134.3   Erlaubnis↑s↓

134.10   ⟨Wi[s]⟩Wich ['c' *written over what may be* 's']

134.12   ⟨ick⟩⟨ich⟩ ich ['h' *written over* 'k'; 'ich' *canceled and rewritten, probably for clarity*]

134.14   herum? ↑𝕏↓ ['𝕏' *written in purple pencil*]

135.1   ⟨Der⟩Des ['s' *written over* 'r']

135.1   ↑der Mench↓

135.3   ⟨Zeitungen⟩Zeitungist [*final* 'e' *dotted to serve as* 'i'; 'st' *written over* 'n']

135.6   MEIN ['mein' *underlined twice*]

135.6   ⟨were⟩wäre ['ä' *written over* 'e']

135.10   FEST ['fest' *underlined twice*]

135.11–13   Hochwürdig . . . mag. [*heavily boxed in purple pencil; a line below* 'Hochwürdig', *written and canceled in black pencil, may have been meant to lend emphasis to* 'Hochwürdig'; *however, since the underline resembles the line immediately above* 'Hochwürdig' *separating this entry from the previous one, it seems probable that it represents either an abandoned effort to end the entry at* 'Hochwürdig' *or a misplaced flourish between entries*]

135.12   ⟨him⟩ihm ['i' *added;* 'h' *rewritten, covering* 'hi']

135.12   wun↑s↓chen

135.14   hauptsachliche [*a mark above the second* 'a' *may have been intended as an umlaut*]

135.15   ⟨Sagen⟩Sagung ['ung' *written over* 'en']

135.16–19   ⟨Verkaufen . . . bleibenden⟩ Rechten . . . oben. [*written in purple pencil;* 'Verkaufen . . . bleibenden' *canceled in purple pencil at the bottom of a page;* 'Rechten . . . oben.' *left uncanceled on the following page; the bottom quarter of the page is blank below* 'oben.']

135.18   "⟨"⟩Jahrhundert" ['J' *written over quotation marks; another pair of opening quotation marks was added, probably when the closing quotation marks were written*]

136.10   ⟨Menshen⟩Menchen ['c' *written over* 's']

136.11	"⟨"[-]⟩Thrice ['T' *written over quotation marks and an unrecovered incomplete letter; another pair of opening quotation marks was added, possibly when the closing quotation marks were written following* 'again.']
136.21–142.9	Write . . . 17 tons. [*written in purple pencil*]
137.1	8 pm. [*the bottom third of the page is blank below this entry*]
137.3	⟨a⟩ ↑the↓
137.4	misfortune. [*what looks like a flourish originally ending the entry here was overwritten and the entry was continued*]
137.10–12	↑forlorn &↓ homeless, ⟨so forlorn & . . . it is,⟩
137.13	very nose. [*what looks like a flourish originally ending the entry here was overwritten and the entry was continued*]
137.16	Hendon—see next page. [*circled;* 'Confusion . . . chair' (138.7–11) *is on the following page*]
138.4	↑in ages—↓ [*apparently interlined without a caret above* 'here who']
138.7	↑I *will* enter!↓
138.8	way, ↑!↓ ⟨I say!⟩ [*the exclamation point after* 'way,' *was probably added when* 'I say!' *was canceled*]
138.8–9	⟨kidneys⟩ ↑gizzards↓
138.10	chair [*possibly not underlined like the rest of the sentence only because it is written very close to the bottom of the page*]
138.11	⟨Sue⟩Susie ['s' *written over* 'e']
139.1–2	↑Why dn't . . . cat?	Well,↓ A cat
139.7	⟨toast⟩ ↑text↓
139.8	⟨a very fruitful &⟩ ↑so↓ easy a subject. [*sequence of revision uncertain; the original inscription probably read*

'a very fruitful & easy subject.', *to which Clemens added* 'a' *before* 'subject' *when he interlined* 'so']

139.13 ⟨to conspire⟩conspiring ['to' *canceled;* 'ing' *written over* 'e']

139.14 (any . . . make) ['any . . . make' *originally followed* 'success,' *(139.15); the phrase was enclosed in parentheses and its new position indicated by a line from the opening parenthesis to a caret following* 'turn'; *the parentheses may have been intended merely to indicate the limits of the passage to be moved rather than to form part of the passage*]

140.1 ↑Sie↓

140.5 eine . . . verheisste [*possibly originally* 'ein . . . verheisst'; *the terminal* 'e' *of each word appears to have been added later*]

140.7 Fiskill⟨,⟩ ⟨10⟩ Landing [*originally* 'Fiskill, 10'; *the comma mended to a caret but there is no interlineation;* 'Landing' *written over* '10']

142.3 perhaps⟨.⟩— [*the dash written over the period*]

142.8 ⟨£[5]0,000⟩£20,000 ['2' *written over what may be* '5']

142.10–17 *April 15 . . . volumes.* [*written in brownish black ink, filling the bottom two-thirds of the page that was originally left blank below* '17 tons.']

142.12 ⟨$6[1]0,000⟩610,000 ['$' *canceled, apparently in bluish black ink and possibly by Paine;* '1', *written very heavily, appears merely to be traced over but may cover some other number*]

142.18–149.3 Canvassers . . . is it? [*written in purple pencil except for entries or alterations in black pencil at* 143.11, 144.7–9, 144.11–12, *and* 146.6]

142.19–20 ↑of the city↓

143.6 ⟨astrology⟩astronomy ['n' *interlined with a caret above canceled* 'l'; 'm' *written over* 'g']

143.11   ↑or Ihrer↓

143.11   ⟨truly⟩ ↑devoted↓? [*originally 'truly?'; altered in black
                    pencil; although not struck through by the line canceling
                    'truly', the question mark may also have been intended
                    for cancellation when 'devoted' was added*]

143.14   railroads. [*the bottom quarter of the leaf has been torn
                    out following this word on the recto and* 'Mary Bacons—'
                    (143.17) *on the verso*]

143.15   ⟨der⟩das ['as' *written over* 'er']

143.20   30,000. [*the bottom quarter of the page is blank below
                    this entry*]

144.3   ⟨he⟩his ['is' *written over* 'e']

144.6   May ↑11 or↓ 12

144.7–9   L. D. Haymond . . . fall. [*written in black pencil*]

144.11–12   Macaulay's . . . tons.) [*written in black pencil*]

144.13   ↑Teleg. . . . Watterson.↓

144.16   7,500/↑at cost↓

145.3–4   ↑(& take . . . thing)↓

145.6   ⟨12,000⟩12,500 ['5' *written over* 'o']

145.7   ⟨fails⟩ ↑wins, ⟨[I]⟩↓

145.8   OPTION ['option' *underlined twice*]

145.12   also. [*the bottom fifth of the page is blank below this
                    entry*]

145.24   between us. [*a line originally ending the entry here was
                    overwritten when the entry was continued*]

146.5   a test. [*the bottom fifth of the page is blank below this
                    entry*]

146.6   G↑erhardt↓ ['erhardt' *squeezed in in black pencil*]

146.11   ↑⟨400⟩100 . . . $400↓ ['1' *written over* '4']

146.15   ⟨400⟩200 ['2' *written over* '4']

146.18   Paris with. [*the bottom fifth of the page is blank below this entry*]

146.23   sold. [*the bottom two-fifths of the page is blank below this entry*]

147.10–11   *the other one wouldn't.* [*a line across the page below these words appears to be an underline, but may have been intended to end the entry here*]

147.21   *new.* [*the bottom fifth of the page is blank below this entry*]

147.25–26   rock⟨.⟩, ↑me childer.↓" [*originally* 'rock.'"; *the comma written over the period, and* 'me childer.' *squeezed in below* 'upon a rock' *at the bottom of the page; what looks like an* 'h', *interlined above the* 'e' *of* 'childer' *and below* 'ro' *of* 'rock', *may have been meant as a tentative addition to either word* ('rhock' *or* 'childher') *or to both*]

148.5   ⟨(   )ˢ⟩Garibaldiˢ / ↑(stone cutter)↓ studio [*sequence of revision uncertain; probably originally* '(   )ˢ stu-dio'; '(stone cutter)' *interlined below the parentheses;* 'Garibaldi' *written over the parentheses*]

148.13   ↑Dʳ· Porter.↓

148.17   ⟨Shakes⟩Shakers ['rs' *written over* 's']

149.1   ⟨Genˡ⟩General's ['e' *written over superscript* 'l']

149.4–160.19   If God . . . Tel Co, N. Y. [*written in black pencil except for entries or revisions in purple pencil at 152.22–153.2, 156.9–12, and 160.16*]

149.5   ↑, unceasingly,↓

150.2   men &c. [*the bottom fifth of the page is blank below this entry*]

150.5   ↑Gewiss ist↓

150.5   ↑noch↓

150.5   Jahre↑n↓

150.7	⟨geblieben⟩ ↑war↓
150.8	⟨ihres Mannes⟩ ⟨↑des Vaters↓⟩
150.8	Schwiegervaters⟨.⟩, [*the comma written over the period*]
150.9	⟨ziehmlich⟩ziemlich ['h' *canceled*]
150.9	wohlhaben↑d↓er
150.10	⟨Landsmann⟩Landmann ['s' *canceled*]
150.10	Rosa/↑die Ehepaar↓
150.11	⟨glüchlich⟩glücklich ['k' *written over* 'h']
150.12	Sommer↑en↓
150.13	⟨die⟩⟨der⟩ ↑der↓ ['er' *written over* 'ie'; 'der' *canceled and rewritten above the line, probably for clarity*]
150.14	⟨Die⟩D↑er↓ ['er' *interlined above canceled* 'ie']
150.17	⟨aber⟩ ↑denn↓
152.3	W^m A Paton, 15 W. 19. [*possibly added later*]
152.6	↑Charley↓
152.12	↑General . . . afterward.↓ [*written lengthwise in the margin beside the preceding paragraph*]
152.16	↑a short time ago↓
152.22–153.2	Mrs. . . . younger [*written in purple pencil*]
152.22	Mrs. ↑H. J.↓ Brooks
153.3	May 26 ↑'85.↓
153.12	President ['Presi-' *at the bottom of a page followed by* 'ident' *at the top of the next page; emended*]
153.15	⟨Wise's⟩Wises [*the apostrophe canceled*]
156.5	↑Begin . . . quiet.↓
156.5	IF ['if' *underlined twice*]
156.9–12	G. G.'s first . . . jealousies. [*written in purple pencil*]

158.8   ↑Pope mentions &c &c.↓

159.14   He↑a↓dley's

160.3   ↑"↓simplicity, naturalness & purity↑"↓ [*the quotation marks probably added later*]

160.7   Paige. [*a line originally ending the entry here was over-written and the entry was continued*]

160.13   ⟨6½⟩6⅓ ['3' *written over* '2']

160.16   (June 9/85.) [*a line in purple pencil between* '9' *and the diagonal line may be either a stray mark or a closing parenthesis*]

160.20–174.16   Make 1000 . . . sta Master, Htfd [*written in purple pencil except for cancellations in black pencil at* 171.8 *and* 171.10, *and entries in grayish blue ink at* 172.2–3 *and* 174.8–11]

160.21   ASK JOHN HAY. [*circled*]

161.4   ems ↑in 12¼ hours;↓ [*originally* 'ems;'; *the semicolon inadvertently repeated in the interlineation; emended*]

161.8   ⟨[40],000⟩50,000 ['50' *written over what appears to be* '40']

161.17   quieter? [*the bottom half of the leaf has been torn out following this word on the recto and* 'Shake!'" (161.20) *on the verso; the following leaf has also been torn out; the surviving stubs of the torn leaves bear traces of inscription in purple pencil*]

163.19   ⟨dis[a]⟩disgusted ['g' *written over what may be* 'a']

163.24   ↑Reginald↓

164.11   statue. [*possibly added later*]

165.14–20   4⟨↑½↓⟩ . . . reprint. [*all or parts of this passage may have been written later than surrounding entries; it appears to be squeezed into the space it occupies*]

165.19   ↑It . . . work[.]↓ [*squeezed in to the right of* '4⟨½⟩ . . . 3250' *and boxed*]

165.20   ↑Does . . . work.↓ ↑reprint.↓ [*squeezed in to the right of* '29250' (165.18) *and below* 'man's work[.]']

165.22   Telegraph Redpath [*the bottom fifth of the page is blank below this entry; the following leaf has been torn out*]

166.3   ↑I don't . . . not a word.↓ ⟨"I⟩ "I lay ['I don't . . . not a word.' *interlined without a caret above* 'lay . . . hand'; "'I' *written over* "'I'; 'I don't . . . not a word.' *may have been meant to follow the opening quotation marks*]

166.12   Munn & Co. ['Munn & Co.' *underlined twice; possibly added later*]

167.4   ⟨in⟩—[*the dash written over* 'in']

167.5   ↑papal↓

167.5   Cyclo. Britan. [*probably added later*]

167.18   ⟨—⟩(Memorials [*the parenthesis written over the dash*]

167.21–22   ↑(M of W. A.)↓

168.19   ↑a few pages—↓—Essay

168.22   ⟨pickwick⟩Pickwick ['P' *written over* 'p']

169.1   GET A DONKEY ['Get a Donkey' *underlined twice*]

169.9   ↑fire↓

170.8   ↑bank↓

170.12   exceptions—of course [*the dash possibly added later*]

170.22   idea. [*followed by the instruction* '—OVER'; 'Otherwise . . . otherwise.' (171.2–6) *fills the verso of the leaf; it is unclear whether Clemens meant to change the order of paragraphs or merely to call attention to the presence on the verso of an elaboration of his thoughts*]

171.8   ⟨Ask . . . stock.⟩ [*heavily canceled in black pencil*]

171.10   ⟨Go . . . scheme.⟩ [*heavily canceled in black pencil*]

172.2–3   Somebody . . . relation." [*written in grayish blue ink on the bottom fifth of the page below* 'Mt McGregor.'

(172.1); *possibly this space was left blank until the entry at* 174.8–11 *('Aug. 8. . . . 40*[th] *st.') was written in the same color ink*]

172.5   humorist) [*followed by about two lines of blank space, as though space were being provided for the forgotten name*]

172.10   Tale of 2 Cities. [*most of the leaf following the page that ends here has been torn out; the remnant is blank*]

173.1   ⟨French⟩ ↑Parisians↓

173.5   ⟨thrifty⟩ ↑volatile↓

173.6   ↑get all . . . you get↓ [*intended position uncertain; interlined without a caret above 'the thrifty nation.'*]

173.8   chaste women & [*the bottom third of the page is blank below this entry*]

173.20 $1,100,000 [*the first two numerals inscribed heavily, perhaps traced over; possibly originally '$100,000' to which '1,' was added*]

174.8–11   Aug. 8. . . . 40th st. [*written in grayish blue ink; the bottom half of the page is blank below this entry*]

174.12–16   Send Memoirs . . . Htfd [*written on the recto of the back flyleaf; the bottom two-thirds of the page is blank*]

Notebook 25

Emendations and Doubtful Readings

	MTP Reading	MS Reading
180.8	newspapers	news-|papers
180.9	every	[*possibly* 'Every']
181.8	estimate	[*possibly* 'Estimate']
182.13	⟨tender-hearted⟩	[*possibly canceled* 'tender hearted']
*182.15–18	plundered & impover-ished old war-chief . . . I had	[*possibly* 'I had plundered & impoverished our old war-chief']
184.1	bondsmen	bonds-|men
184.23	bawgunstrickter	bawgun-|strickter
*185.20	$145[6].54	[*possibly* '$1451.54']
187.5	⟨co⟩send	['co' *possibly* 'ca']
187.21	newspapers	news-|papers
187.22	*non*-printers	*non*-|printers
188.24	div,	[*possibly* 'div.']
189.5	stock,	[*possibly* 'stock.']
189.11	eiginen	[*possibly* 'eignien']
191.7	theilen	[*possibly* 'Theilen']
191.16	$6\frac{1}{4}^{c}$ per M,	[*possibly* '$6\frac{1}{4}^{c}$, per M']
191.16	work, &	[*possibly* 'work. &']
192.9	sweetheart	sweet-|heart
192.12	money-making	money-|making

709

*192.16	*it*	[*possibly* 'it']
193.2	type setter	[*possibly* 'typesetter']
*193.6	Typesetter	Type-|setter
196.26	distance.	[*possibly* 'distances.']
199.27	edgeways	edge-|ways
201.3	41	[*possibly* '4"']
201.13–14	early evening	[*possibly* 'Early Evening']
202.1	⟨Se⟩	[*possibly canceled* 'Sa']
203.4	*Boot*	[*possibly* '*Boat*']
*204.17	⟨26⟩21	[*possibly* '⟨21⟩26']
208.26	countermanded	counter-|manded
210.21	apprentice-work	apprentice|-work
211.4	ag*ain*	[*possibly* '*again*']
*211.16	& that	[*possibly* '⟨the⟩that']
215.5	Jos.	[*possibly* 'Jas.']
216.4	knight	[*possibly* 'Knight']
216.10	watermark	[*possibly* 'water mark']
*216.12	⟨[¶][T]h⟩	[*possibly canceled* 'th'; *possibly unindented*]
217.3	boatman	boat-|man
219.11	expense	[*possibly* 'Expense']
220.1	Fancheron	[*possibly* 'Faucheron']
220.3–4	Ladies school	[*possibly* 'Ladies School']
220.5	Mr. Prime's	Mr. Prine's
*220.11–12	upon delivery of the stock oder von aus Dividends	[*possibly* 'upon delivery of the stock/von aus Dividends']

220.14	Pottstausand!	[*possibly* 'Pottstausand:']
222.20	Tell-lie	Tell-|lie
*223.8	Ma['⟨-⟩]ss-a-saw-it.	[*apostrophe and canceled hyphen may be* 'it' *printed above* 'Mass']

Details of Inscription

[*Entries are in purple pencil unless otherwise noted*]

178.1–12	Draper . . . Wall st. [*written on the verso of the front flyleaf*]
178.1	↑Draper 19 E 47.↓ [*written in black pencil*]
178.2–8	Send Memoirs . . . in '84. [*written in grayish blue ink*]
178.11	Henry A. Taylor [*not in Clemens' hand*]
178.12	Wall st. [*the bottom fifth of the page is blank below this entry*]
179.1–180.1	R. G. Brooks . . . 9$^{\text{th.}}$ [*written in grayish blue ink except for cancellations in purple pencil at 179.2 and 179.7*]
179.2	⟨Webster . . . Co.⟩ [*canceled in purple pencil*]
179.5	↑& 142 . . . Wall.↓ [*interlined above* 'Dean . . . ave.'; *intended position designated by a line drawn from* '& 142' *to a caret below* 'Dean']
179.7	⟨Gerhardt . . . N. Y.⟩ [*canceled in purple pencil*]
180.1	9$^{\text{th.}}$ [*followed by one blank page*]
180.5	⟨$1[5]000⟩$16000 ['6' *written over what appears to be* '5']
180.6	↑Correct.↓ [*circled*]
180.7	↑Geo. P.↓
180.11–12	↑or ⟨27,000⟩25,000.↓ ['5' *written over* '7']
180.13	⟨12^{c}⟩10^{c} ['0' *written over* '2']
180.16	⟨$1085⟩$1095 ['9' *written over* '8']

180.18   ⟨60⟩ ↑30 or 60↓

180.24   ⟨daily⟩ ↑yearly↓

181.14–15   Send Mrs. . . . Cable's. [*boxed*]

182.3   ↑a good . . . business.↓ [*written in the top margin of
                  the page*]

182.6   ↑& he↓

182.8–10   ⟨pay⟩ ↑give↓ such ⟨[c]⟩a ⟨price[.]⟩ ↑figure[;]↓ I
                  ⟨would⟩should ⟨not have liked to venture it."⟩ ↑have
                  been ⟨[wary]⟩chary of venturing it myself."↓ ['sh' *written
                  over* 'w' *of* 'would'; 'not . . . it."' *canceled and replaced
                  by* 'have been . . . myself."' *as follows:* 'not' *canceled,*
                  'have been . . . it' *interlined,* 'myself."' *written over*
                  'have liked', *and* 'to venture it."' *canceled;* 'ch' *of* 'chary'
                  written over what looks like 'w', *and* 'y' *written over what
                  looks like* 'y']

182.12   One ['Grant' *is written in black pencil above this word
                  in the upper left corner of the page, almost certainly
                  by Paine*]

182.12   ↑of grief & shame↓

182.13   ⟨in some⟩by some ⟨tender-hearted⟩ ↑some↓ ['by' *written
                  over* 'in'; 'some' *canceled and then rewritten in the line;
                  another* 'some' *interlined below canceled* 'some' *and
                  above canceled* 'tender-hearted'; *see Doubtful Readings*]

182.14   ↑at that time↓ [*interlined by Clemens in purple pencil
                  without a caret above* 'correspondents that'; *someone,
                  probably Paine, marked the position of the interlineation
                  with a caret and connecting line in black pencil*]

182.14–17   persuading ⟨him⟩ ↑the ⟨robbed &⟩ ⟨abused⟩ ⟨hero of
                  the war⟩↓ ↑plundered &↓ ↑impoverished old ↑war-
                  chief↓ ⟨standard-bearer⟩↑flag↓-bearer of the vanished
                  ⟨[- - sts]⟩⟨[chil]⟩⟨hosts⟩ ↑children↓ of victory↓ to burn
                  ['the . . . war' *interlined above* 'persuading ⟨him⟩ to
                  burn'; *although originally intended to be read as one
                  phrase,* 'robbed &', 'abused', *and* 'hero of the war' *were*

canceled separately; 'impoverished old standard-bearer of
the vanished [- - sts] of victory' *written below* 'had' *(182.18)
in the closest available space, with a line between* 'abused'
and 'impoverished' *to indicate the intended position of
the phrase (see 182.15 below);* 'plundered &' *interlined
above* 'impoverished';* 'flag' *interlined above canceled*
'standard';* 'war-chief' *interlined with a caret before canceled* 'standard';* what looks like* 'chil' *written over an
earlier, partially illegible word, then canceled;* 'hosts'
written over both words, then canceled; then 'children'
written below the multiple cancellation; 'victory' *is followed by about four lines of space presumably left blank
for further revisions or additions*]

182.15   impoverished old ↑war-chief↓ [*someone, probably Paine,
interlined* 'our' *in black pencil with a caret before* 'old';
*apparently whoever made the addition ignored the line
connecting* 'impoverished' *with* 'abused' *above (see
182.14–17) and assumed that* 'plundered & impoverished'
was meant to follow 'I had' *syntactically, thus changing*
'in persuading the plundered & impoverished old war-
chief . . . to burn a contract . . . I had [*blank*]' *to* 'in
persuading the [*blank*] to burn a contract . . . I had
plundered & impoverished our old war-chief . . .'*]

182.17   ⟨promised⟩promised ['h' *canceled*]

182.19–20   that . . . whipped⟩ to [*written at the top of the right-
hand page that faces the page containing* 'One . . . I
had' *(182.12–18); followed by about two lines of blank
space*]

182.21   ⟨I was guilty of⟩ ↑I had done↓ . . . act. [*written below
the blank space that follows* 'that . . . whipped⟩ to'
*(182.19–20) on the right-hand page that faces the page
containing* 'One . . . I had' *(182.12–18); a line next to
canceled* 'I was' *may point to where the passage on the
facing page breaks off at* 'had' *(182.18); followed by one
line of blank space*]

183.1–2   If I . . . Boston Ad. [*written at the bottom of the page containing 'One . . . I had' (182.12–18), *following the four lines of blank space mentioned above at 182.14–17*]

183.9–11	↑I committed . . . since.↓
183.23	⟨very⟩ ↑movingly↓
183.26	⟨must⟩ ↑would↓
183.27	the↑se↓ breaking
184.4	⟨he had⟩the ['t' *added to* 'he' *and* 'had' *canceled*]
184.5	⟨now,⟩ ↑at that date,↓
184.7–9	⟨if ordinary . . . iron-clads.⟩ ↑& we did.↓
184.13	10 p c. [*possibly added later*]
184.18–20	↑Great fear . . . *at all*↓ [*heavily boxed*]
184.19	↑il↓logically ⟨discourage⟩encourage ['en' *interlined above canceled* 'dis']
185.1–2	Oct 7 . . . Secy. [*boxed*]
185.5	promises ↑n↓or
185.7	↑Patenting↓
185.8	4 years ['4' *underlined twice*]
185.18–21	Sept. 8 . . . 368.10.5. [*boxed heavily in black pencil*]
185.19	↑'86↓
185.19	↑paid Mch 25 ($145[8]↓ [*written in black pencil lengthwise in the right margin, with a line drawn to indicate placement*]
185.20	↑" Apl 10, $145[6].54↓ [*written in black pencil lengthwise in the right margin, with a line drawn to indicate placement*]
186.9	antennæ [*ligature indicated by a line above* 'ae']
186.22	↑2 cnts . . . power.↓
186.24–25	About . . . machine. [*possibly added later*]

187.8–9	Spin . . . hunting-dog. [*written on an otherwise blank right-hand page;* 'Bissell . . . distributing.' *(188.26–29) is on the facing page; the notation* '(Turn a page.)' *below* 'distributing.' *indicates that* 'Spin . . . hunting-dog.' *was written some time before* 'distributing.' *and was not meant to break the sequence of the long series of type-setter notes beginning with* 'Order' *(187.10)*]
187.14	↑1.a. Pay other $2000.↓
188.18–20	⟨& loss . . . per M.⟩ ⟨↑& $600 . . . (?)↓⟩ ↑(take away . . . used).↓
188.23–25	(Mem. . . . sooner.) [*possibly added later*]
188.26	Bissell . . . '85. [*boxed in black pencil*]
188.29	distributing. [*followed by the instruction* '(Turn a page.)'; *see 187.8–9*]
188.31	↑(2^d year)↓
189.8	EIN ⟨ZEHT⟩ZEHNTEN [*underlined twice;* 'n' *written over* 't']
189.9	⟨ist⟩ ↑wäre↓
189.10	⟨de⟩die ['i' *written over* 'e']
189.11	⟨[be]-⟩|
189.14	↑'85↓
189.15	⟨Deiner⟩Diener ['ie' *written over* 'ei']
189.16	Thaler⟨.⟩, [*the comma apparently intended to cancel the period*]
189.16	⟨have⟩habe ['b' *written over* 'v']
189.17	⟨Sieben⟩ ↑Fünf↓ Hundert ↑und 50↓
189.18	($550.) [*possibly added later*]
189.19–20	Lass . . . schicken. [*boxed*]
190.12	⟨fun[g]⟩funf ['f' *written over what may be* 'g']
190.17	⟨Half⟩Halb ['b' *written over* 'f']

190.18	⟨or⟩oder ['d' *written over* 'r']
191.1–2	27. Don't . . . way. [*boxed*]
191.12	⟨$15,000⟩$12,000 ['2' *written over* '5']
191.14–18	7½ . . . 6½?) ['7½ . . . 5½ per M' *on a right-hand page is boxed on the top and sides;* 'or $2.20 . . . 6½?)' *on the verso of the leaf is not boxed*]
191.17–18	↑(No, . . . 6½?)↓
191.25–26	If we can . . . year. [*boxed*]
192.11	↑stock speculator ⟨&⟩ &↓
192.16	*accomplishing it.* ['accomplishing' *underlined in purple pencil;* 'it' *underlined in black pencil, possibly by Paine*]
192.27	⟨2_⟩24 ['4' *written over a line apparently indicating a blank to be filled*]
193.6–13	Mr Clemens . . . James W. Paige. [*written by James W. Paige*]
193.8–14	⟨all⟩ . . . '85 [*the leaf bearing this passage on its recto and* 'Nelson . . . proportion.' (193.15–194.6) *on its verso is the only fully inscribed leaf in this notebook that retains its tab*]
194.3	⟨sell⟩ ↑rent↓
194.18	↑or 3↓
194.20	N.O. ↑2↓
194.21	⟨M⟩ ↑machine↓
194.22–23	↑⟨2,000 . . . $5,000,000 a year.↓ [*written lengthwise in the right margin beside the preceding list at* 194.7–20]
194.26	⟨$6,000⟩ ↑$2,500↓
194.27	⟨$60,000⟩$25,000 ['25' *written over* '60']
194.30	⟨2[6]⟩24 ['4' *written over what appears to be* '6']
195.1	⟨is⟩ ⟨↑just↓⟩ ↑is↓

195.2	↑rent↓

195.3   year⟨.⟩— [*the dash written over the period; a line origi-nally ending the entry here was disregarded when the entry was continued*]

195.19–196.3   Sept. 20 . . . Nov. 20. [*written in grayish blue ink*]

196.4–5   ↑(6th, no doubt)↓ Guest . . . Pittsfield, ['Guest . . . Pittsfield,' *written first in black pencil;* '(6th, no doubt)' *written in purple pencil in the top margin of the page above* 'Guest of Wm'; *a black pencil line across the page originally ending the entry at* 'Pittsfield,' *was overwritten when the entry was continued in purple pencil*]

196.5–6   ↑for the reading . . . 11 am.↓

196.7–11   Leave Hartford . . . do. [*order of inscription uncertain, but probably* 'L. Spr. . . . 3.02. p.m.' *was written first at the bottom of the page, leaving about half the page blank above* 'L. Spr.' *and below* '11 am.' (196.6); *probably then* 'Won't do.' *was added below* '3.02. p.m.', 'L. Spr. . . . 3.02. p.m.' *was canceled,* 'Leave Springfld . . . Albany.' *was written above* 'L. Spr.', *and* 'Leave Hartford . . . Haven' *was written above* 'Leave Springfld'; ⟨L. Spr. . . . do.' *is boxed on the top and sides; about two lines of blank space precede* 'Leave Hartford' *and a narrow line of blank space follows* 'New Haven']

196.23   No . . . for [*repeated heavy pencil-strokes above and beside this entry were apparently intended to set it off*]

196.24–25   ⟨make⟩ ↑reduce↓

196.28   ⟨cynchromatic⟩synchromatic ['s' *written over* 'c']

197.1–2   ↑5.60↓ ↑4.60↓

197.8   ⟨42⟩46 ['6' *written over* '2']

197.15   ⟨↑& one-twelfth↓⟩ ↑& a fraction↓

197.15   ⟨are⟩ ↑have been↓

197.19   ↑We get 18c↓

197.20	↑We get 12½↓
197.21	⟨8¾.⟩8½. ['1' *written over* '3' *and* '2.' *written over* '4.']
197.21	↑We get about 15ᶜ↓
197.22	Papers . . . 12. [*written at the top of an otherwise blank page*]
198.1	See Ross Winans. [*heavily circled*]
198.2	↑1↓ ↑2↓
198.4	↑3↓
198.5	↑Drive at 4.↓ [*heavily underlined*]
198.6	↑4↓ Hawley
198.7	↑(or Twichell)↓
198.8	↑5↓
198.9	Union Lines tel. [*boxed*]
198.16–17	hour. [*following this paragraph at the bottom of a right-hand page Clemens wrote the instruction* 'OVER'; 'This . . . 35.' (*198.18–199.3*) *is on the verso of the leaf*]
198.18	⟨12⟩ ↑11½↓
198.19	⟨48ᶜ⟩46ᶜ ['6' *written over* '8']
199.1	He makes 30. [*possibly added later*]
199.2	↑P. S. . . . ⟨36⟩35.↓ ['5' *written over* '6']
199.3	⟨9⟩ ↑8¾↓
199.29	⟨*none*⟩ ↑no other↓
200.23	↑—⟨4[o]⟩41 . . . it.↓ ['1' *written over what appears to be* 'o']
200.33–201.1	⟨150⟩ ↑75↓
201.11	⟨oc⟩of ['f' *written over* 'c']
201.14	⟨ca[p]⟩camped ['m' *written over what may be* 'p']
201.17	⟨then⟩ ↑immediately↓

201.20	⟨⟨[16]⟩18⟩ 18 ['8' *written over what may be* '6'; *then* '18' *canceled and rewritten for clarity*]
201.20	↑PLACE↓
202.9	⟨↑[c]↓⟩
203.7	⟨cases⟩Case↑'↓s ['C' *written over* 'c']
203.7	⟨gardiner⟩gardener ['e' *written over* 'i']
203.8	↑Dated↓ Tuesday ↑Oct↓ 27th 3 nos ↑come due↓ Jan. ⟨F⟩Jam. 29th. ['3 nos' *possibly added later;* 'come due' *interlined without a caret above* 'Jam. 29th.' *and below* '27th 3 nos']
203.9	⟨25⟩24 ['4' *written over* '5']
203.10	↑S. G. Dunham↓ ↑66 State st↓ ['S. G. Dunham' *interlined with a caret following* 'Telegraph'; '66 State st' *written lengthwise in the margin beside* 'Paper . . . we' (203.9–10)]
203.19	⟨one⟩ ↑2↓
204.3	↑notes↓
204.12	⟨band⟩bank ['k' *written over* 'd']
204.15	Oct. 26. ↑'85.↓
204.17	Oct. ⟨26⟩21 ↑'85↓ [*probably* '1' *written over* '6', *but possibly* '6' *written over* '1']
204.21	↑get↓ 37
205.2–3	↑I have read them;↓
206.8	Oct. 26. ↑'85↓
206.11	"⟨[O],⟩It ↑is↓ ['It' *written over what appears to be* 'O,']
207.1	Sep 5/84 [*the bottom third of the page is blank below this entry*]
207.6	Shirt man. [*the bottom third of the page is blank below this entry*]

207.7   ↑Hall . . . sht-hand?↓ [*written in the top margin of the page above* 'How . . . been' *and boxed*]

208.2   ⟨88⟩8? [*the question mark written over* '8']

208.29   (for Hall.) [*possibly added later*]

209.11   ⟨24th⟩20th ['o' *written over* '4']

209.15   ⟨ad⟩ahead ['h' *written over* 'd']

209.20   now⟨;⟩, [*the comma mended from a semicolon*]

209.25   ↑at↓ any cost

211.4–5   again in galleys. [*followed by one blank page; the follow-ing leaf has been torn out*]

211.16   & that ['that' *possibly originally* 'the'; 'at' *written over what may be* 'e']

212.2–3   General . . . Sheridan. [*originally a separate entry; then linked to the preceding entry by a line between* 'them.' *and* 'General'; *followed by one blank page*]

212.2   ⟨Lieut⟩ Lieut. [*probably rewritten for clarity*]

212.13   pay ⟨15^c.⟩ [*a line originally ending the entry at* '15^c.' *was disregarded when* '15^c.' *was canceled and the entry was continued*]

213 illustration   [*the Balkan map follows* 'Troy.' (212.5)]

214.6 $1500⟨.⟩, ↑at 15↓ [*the comma written over the period*]

214.12   ⟨is willing⟩ ↑is↓ ↑wishes↓ ['is' *interlined above* 'is willing', *possibly to replace the first* 'is' *which was badly written; interlined* 'is' *not canceled when* 'wishes' *was interlined above canceled* 'is willing']

214.12   ↑Stereopticon views.↓

215.1   not [*possibly added later*]

215.2   ↑Gainesville, Ga.↓

215.5–7   Jos. Casey . . . City [*not in Clemens' hand; written in black pencil; surrounded by the following entry*]

215.8–9   I left . . . M. T. [*written in grayish blue ink; this entry surrounds the previously inscribed entry at 215.5–7 but is spaced and interlined to avoid obscuring either entry*]

215.12–14   ⟨& became reconciled⟩ —as far . . . & ⟨then⟩ ↑so was reconciled . . . but↓ presently began to [*apparently* '& became reconciled' *was canceled before the entry was continued;* 'so . . . but' *interlined without a caret above* '⟨then⟩ presently began to']

216.6   ⟨Conneci[t]⟩Conneticut ['t' *written over* 'c' *and* 'c' *written over what looks like unfinished* 't']

216.7   ↑(Bring . . . book.↓

216.9   ↑(palimpsest)↓

216.12   ⟨[¶][T]h⟩Get them [*what may be* 'Th' *apparently indented to begin a new paragraph; overwritten by* 'Get'; *see Doubtful Readings*]

216.19–21   ↑He is also . . . arrive.↓ [*written lengthwise on the page across the preceding paragraph*]

217.15–19   ↑Twichell↓ . . . Hong Kong [*written in black pencil;* 'Twichell' *written diagonally in the left margin and across* 'Mrs.' (217.12)]

217.23   ⟨Smith College⟩ ↑Hatfield House↓

218.1   Prime . . . E 23 [*written in black pencil; the pencil line extends at one point across the purple pencil line of the preceding drawing but has been removed from the drawing as reproduced here*]

218.6   ↑Add negotiable paper.↓

219.2   ⟨If⟩ ↑When↓

219.2   HAS ['has' *underlined twice*]

219.20   ⟨Shinneat[e]es⟩S[k]inneat[e]es ['h' *apparently mended to* 'k']

220.8   ⅟₅₀↑th↓ [*superscript* 'th' *apparently added later*]

220.8   ⟨barre⟩baare ['a' *written over* 'r']

220.9   ↑½ in↓

220.11–12   ⟨von aus Dividends⟩ ↑upon . . . stock↓ ↑oder↓ von aus
                   Dividends ['upon . . . stock' *interlined above canceled*
                   'aus Dividends'; Clemens interlined 'oder stet' *('or stet')*
                   below canceled 'Dividends', *possibly because he was un-*
                   decided whether to retain both readings or to retain just
                   one (but was uncertain which); 'oder' *may not have been*
                   intended as part of the sentence]

220.15   horror!" [*the bottom third of the page is blank below*
                   this entry]

221.3   rebate checks? [*the bottom third of the page is blank be-*
                   low this entry]

221.4–5   Marsh-mallow. . . . Wheeler. [*written in purple pencil*
                   with the notebook inverted below Dora Wheeler's draw-
                   ing, which is in a black ink unique in this notebook; the
                   black pencil sketch on the facing notebook page may be
                   by Clemens]

222.1–223.17   Man . . . Prof. Sloan. [*written in black pencil and fol-*
                   lowed by 38 blank pages; the last page of the notebook
                   has been torn out]

222.3   baar↑es↓

222.17   Wm [*boxed on the sides and bottom below* 'Tell']

222.17–19   letter most used [*boxed on the sides and bottom below*
                   '-e-']

223.5   ↑'s!-indicate.↓ [*possibly added later*]

223.7   ↑(soit)↓

223.8   Ma↑['⟨-⟩]↓ss↑-↓a-saw-it. [*marks that look like an apos-*
                   trophe and a canceled hyphen interlined without a caret
                   above the ligature between 'a' *and* 's' *(see Doubtful Read-*
                   ings); a hyphen interlined with a caret between 's' *and* 'a']

Notebook 26

Emendations and Doubtful Readings

	MTP READING	MS READING
*227.3	⟨[E - -]⟩W 11th	⟨[E - -]⟩W 11th W 11th
229.6	"Personal."	[*possibly* ' "Personal!']
*230.2	gooseherder	[*possibly* 'goose herder']
*230.11	[⟨8⟩⟨7⟩8]	[*possibly* '⟨8⟩7']
*230.12	⟨5,000⟩	[',ooo' *uncanceled*]
*230.22	P.S.,	[*possibly* 'P.S;']
*230.22	⟨[-]⟩ 5,000	[*possibly* '⟨[-]5,000⟩5,000']
*233.10	warum	[*possibly* 'warüm']
234.14	Ad man	[*possibly* 'Adman' *or* 'Ad-man']
235.4	Club &	[*possibly* 'Club—']
235.11	blood-hound's	blood-|hound's
236.3	to-morrow	to-|morrow
240.13	Whitmo "get	[*possibly* 'Whitmo" get' *or* 'Whitmo' 'get']
*245.13	25 M . . . 1000	[*possibly canceled*]
*245.14–15	⟨4,500⟩ ⟨6,000⟩ 4,500 . . . ⟨5⟩ ⟨3¾⟩ 5	[*possibly* '⟨4,500⟩ 6,000 . . . ⟨5⟩ 3¾']
*245.16	22 M . . . 1000	[*possibly canceled*]
*245.17–18	⟨5½⟩ ⟨4⅝⟩4¾ 4¾ . . . ⟨4,000⟩4,700 . . . possibly 4,800	[*possibly* '⟨5½⟩ ⟨4⅝⟩ ⟨4¾ 4¾⟩ 5½ . . . ⟨4,000⟩ ⟨4,700⟩ 4,000 . . . ⟨possibly 4,800⟩']
*245.19	28 M . . . 1000	[*possibly canceled*]

*245.20–21	⟨6,300⟩ 8,000 . . . ⟨[3½]⟩2¾ . . . 2¾ (short . . . 1000	[*possibly* '⟨6,300⟩ ⟨8,000⟩ 6,300 . . . ⟨[3½]⟩⟨2¾⟩ [3½] . . . ⟨2¾ (short . . . 1000⟩']
246.16	Memoirs	[*possibly* 'Memoires']
247.5	clean-cut	clean-|cut
*248.32	⟨[2]22⟩[1]22	[*possibly* '⟨122⟩222']
*253.3	The	[*possibly* '⟨[-]⟩ The']
253.5	monment	[*possibly* 'Monment']
256.8	fac simile	[*possibly* 'facsimile']
257.6	orto	[*possibly* 'ortd']
257.9	Harvest Apple Trees.	['Apple Trees.' *replaces ditto marks below preceding* 'Apple Trees.']
257.15	overlookings	over-|lookings
258.12	(Mrs. C)	[*possibly* '(Mrs. Cl']
*258.20	11.³⁰	[*possibly* '11³⁰.']
*258.20	*in*	[*possibly* '—in', '⟨—⟩in', *or* '⟨—⟩*in*']
259.8	Christ;	[*possibly* 'Christ,']
*260.1	Brown	[*possibly* 'Brawn']
261.3	notebook	[*possibly* 'note book']
262.5	Desbrasses	[*possibly* 'Desbrosses']
*264.7	⟨[10.4]5.⟩12.15.	[*possibly* '⟨3.45.⟩12.15.']
264.12	Ac	[*possibly* 'AC']
265.10	drawing-room	drawing-|room
266.33	conceive	conceieve
268.2	[es].	[*possibly* 'e&.', 'ls.', 'l&.', *or* 'A.']

270.7	dumb show	dumb | show [*possibly* 'dumb-|show']
*270.15–271.1	binderies ⟨8⟩6; tons 1,000	binderies; ⟨8⟩6 | tons 1,000
271.1	1,000:	[*possibly* '1,000;']
271.4	Wanamake[r.]	[*written off the edge of the page*]
273.12	[deter]	[*possibly* 'dates']
*273.14	*BRING WITH* ME	[*possibly* 'BRING WITH ME']
274.1	candle-shade	candle-|shade
*277.8	Scheemann	[*possibly* 'Schiemann']
278.1	Holcombe	[*possibly* 'Halcombe']
278.11	[1]o[o,oo]o	[*possibly* '400,000' *or* '800,000']
*281.1	T J V up Wash	['J' *possibly* 'S'; 'V' *possibly* 'v'; 'Wash' *possibly* 'wash']
281.2	7 k a b k	['7' *possibly* 'T'; 'k' *possibly* 'K' *twice*]
*281.3	⟨Wash.⟩	[*possibly canceled* 'wash.']
281.6	⟨[1]⟩	[*possibly uncanceled* 't' *or* 'x']
*281.6	⟨[o]51⟩⟨O51⟩51	['o' *possibly* '5'; 'O' *possibly* 'o']
*281.6	⟨502102⟩5 21 2	['502102' *possibly* '5O21O2' *or* '502102']
281.6	014e1	[*possibly* 'O14e1' *or* '014e1']
*282.4	May J	[*possibly* 'May ⟨5⟩J']
283.17	alongside	along-|side
285.8	long-winded	long-|winded
289.2	type-setter	type-|setter

292.4	good night	[*possibly* 'goodnight']
292.7	good morning	[*possibly* 'goodmorning']
293.11	hain't	[*possibly* 'h'aint']

Details of Inscription

[*Entries are in black pencil unless otherwise noted*]

227.1–2   Eugen . . . 56th [*written at the top of the verso of the front flyleaf, which is otherwise blank*]

227.2   ⟨⟨[31]4⟩154, East 56th⟩ [*written in black pencil; canceled in brownish black ink;* '1' *written over what may be* '3', *and* '5' *written over what appears to be* '1']

227.3   ⟨[E --]⟩W 11th ['W 11th' *written over what appears to be* 'E' *and two or three figures, then rewritten for clarity above the line; emended*]

227.9   302 ⟨Beekman⟩ ↑Beacon↓

227.11   House . . . aves. [*written in brownish black ink*]

227.12   Mme . . . 16th⟨(?)⟩ [*written in black ink*]

228.4   Mch 27, ↑£300↓

228.5   May 10, $1,786.22⟩ [*the bottom half of the page is blank below this entry*]

228.10   WAHN . . . BILD ['Wahn' *and* 'bild' *underlined twice*]

228.10   ↑or erroneous↓

228.13   ↑Calvin . . . Cal.↓ [*written in pale brownish black ink*]

229.1–14   Mrs . . . ⟨46⟩48 [*written in brownish black ink*]

229.14   ⟨46⟩48 ['8' *written over* '6']

230.1   ↑M. Allen . . . 19$^{th.}$↓

230.2   gooseherd↑er.↓ ['gooseherd' *written in black pencil;* 'er.' *written in black ink*]

230.3   ↑(250 shs)↓ [*interlined without a caret above* '1/200 *interest*']

230.4   ⟨pay⟩ ↑keep↓

230.8   The P.S. [*follows a blank left-hand page*]

230.11   ⟨& [⟨8⟩⟨7⟩8] ⟨on⟩in book offices⟩ [*sequence of revision uncertain; either '8' written over '7' that had been written over '8', or '7' written over '8' that had been traced over (see Doubtful Readings)*]

230.11   ⟨5 ↑or⟩ 6↓ ['5' *underlined three times; 'or 6' interlined; '5 or' canceled*]

230.12   at ⟨5,000⟩ ↑4,500↓ ['5' *of '5,000' canceled; the comma and '000' left standing; emended*]

230.13 $2.50 now. [*followed at the bottom of a right-hand page by Clemens' instruction 'OVER.'; 'Whoso . . . 40.' (230.14–19) is on the verso of the leaf*]

230.14   ⟨24ᶜ⟩27ᶜ ['7' *written over '4'*]

230.15   paper↑;↓ ⟨& the same in⟩

230.22   P.S., [*the comma appears below the second period and may have been intended to change it to a semicolon*]

230.22   ⟨[-]⟩ 5,000. [*it is unclear whether the unrecovered cancellation was canceled before '5,000.' was written; it may have been the first digit of a five-digit number*]

230.23   ⟨1[2]ᶜ⟩10ᶜ ['o' *written over what appears to be '2'*]

230.25–26   ↑(& Washington & N. Orleans & Frisco)↓

231.8   ⟨By⟩Buy ['u' *written over 'y'*]

231.11–12   Hopkinson . . . 34ᵗʰ· [*written in grayish blue ink*]

232.3–4   ↑tr.↓ | Der . . . hear ['tr.' *written in the top margin of the page above 'Der'; a line between 'tr.' and 'hear' embraces the entry on the left side; see note 14*]

233.6   horse[-] ['horse' *followed by what may be either an apostrophe or an uncompleted letter*]

233.10   warum [*two curved marks above 'r' and 'u' could have been intended as an umlaut on 'u' but seem more likely to be misplaced and rewritten versions of the mark like a*]

breve, *often employed by Clemens, that distinguishes* 'u'
from 'n' *in handwritten German*]

233.11   ⟨du siehst so⟩ ↑du so↓ viel besser ⟨aus als⟩ fühlst

233.13   ⟨What⟩Which ['ich' *written over* 'at']

233.20   ⟨the[r]⟩that ['at' *written over* 'e' *and what appears to
              be* 'r']

234.7–10   He . . . admittance.) [*written in purple pencil*]

234.9   stairs. [*one leaf has been torn out following the page that
              ends here*]

234.11–13   Author's . . . 12 PM. [*written in grayish blue ink*]

234.14–19   Tell . . . or 10 [*written in purple pencil*]

234.16   ⟨Whst⟩Whist. ['st' *written over* 't' *and the original* 's'
              dotted to serve as 'i']

234.17   ↑in Italian,↓

235.4   ⟨the⟩that ['at' *written over* 'e']

235.8   ⟨Palla⟩Pilla ['i' *written over* 'a']

235.10   ⟨Wenn⟩Venn ['V' *written over* 'W']

235.13   scent. [*one leaf has been torn out following the page that
              ends here*]

236.6   ⟨[met]⟩ ↑surrounded↓

236.7   ↑by several hours↓

236.9–15   ⟨There was⟩ . . . will resign. [*written in purple pencil*]

236.9   ⟨There was⟩ ↑I↓ once ↑saw↓ a man ⟨who got⟩get up
              ['who' *canceled*; 'e' *written over* 'o' *of* 'got']

236.9–10   ↑weary &↓

236.10–12   ⟨make speech No. 22—just⟩ ↑add . . . program↓—
              uttered ['make . . . 22' *and* 'just' *canceled; the dash re-
              tained*]

236.13   ↑⟨—⟩so startled(?)—↓so deeply moved ['—so startled(?)—' *interlined with a caret; the first dash canceled; another caret following 'moved' is not accompanied by an interlineation*]

237.5   ↑9th or 10th st B'way—↓

237.9   ⟨↑Try that chair—↓⟩

237.11–12   (chair breaks down ↑under De Boon)↓ ↑or Hawkins.↓)

238.3   ↑Uncle Danl↓ [*interlined without a caret above 'Sarcasticises' (238.4)*]

238.6–7   ↑—You been gone a good while you know—↓ [*interlined with a caret following 'changes' (238.7); new placement indicated with a line to a caret following 'Ah well,'; 'you know—' may have been written later than the rest of the interlineation*]

238.9   ⟨S.⟩ ↑Uncle Danl.↓

238.10   ⟨S.⟩D. ['D' *written over* 'S']

238.10   a↑n↓ ⟨[a]⟩exhaustive fit

238.21–23   Go . . . Sutherl. [*written in purple pencil*]

239.4   ↑Cor. Madison ave.↓

239.7   See . . . Monitors [*the bottom third of the page is blank below this entry*]

239.8   Simon⟨.⟩; [*the period mended to a semicolon*]

241.1–2   ↑1 part . . . lard.↓

241.4   ↑—200 more to Elm.↓ [*written in purple pencil*]

241.7–8   ⟨Give . . . Bway.⟩ [*canceled in purple pencil*]

241.9   Show . . . pen. [*written in purple pencil*]

241.10–242.14   ⟨$583.³⁴⟩ . . . Co $5. [*written in blue ink*]

241.10   ⟨$583.³⁴⟩$583.³³ [*superscript '3' written over '4'*]

241.10   ⟨pay to Paige July 10.—as usual.⟩ ['—as usual.' *may have been added later, and 'July 10.' may have been canceled*

separately some time before the whole passage was can-
celed]

242.3   ⟨$500⟩$100 ['1' *written over* '5']

242.9   ⟨47.⁸⁵⟩45.⁸⁵ ['5' *written over* '7']

242.15–17   91 . . . 85. [*written in black ink; the bottom half of the*
                 page is blank below this entry]

242.18–243.13   2 pens . . . Shave. [*written in blue ink*]

243.14–24   Olives . . . House.) [*written in black ink*]

243.16   cherries, strawber ⟨↑or[a]↓⟩ [*what appears to be* 'ora'
                 written below 'cherries', *then canceled*]

243.18–19   187 West | 187 West NY. [*possibly originally* '87 West';
                 the first '1' *may have been miswritten, then blotted during*
                 correction; the phrase was probably rewritten for clarity]

244.1–12   Mrs. . . . committee. [*written in brownish black ink*]

244.1–7   Mrs. . . . see it. [*boxed in brownish black ink*]

244.8–12   *Thursday* . . . committee. [*boxed in brownish black ink*]

244.13–246.4   July 21 . . . week. [*written in black ink except for the*
                 changes in brownish black ink in lines 245.13–21 and the
                 word 'STET' *written in brownish black ink across the en-*
                 try '25 M . . . is 1000.' (245.13–15); *see 245.14–15*]

245.10   ↑Ghost Story.↓ [*written lengthwise in the right margin*
                 beside 'Mexican . . . Frog.' (245.6–8)]

245.12   Christening? ↑Mary Ann.↓ ['Mary Ann.' *interlined with-*
                 out a caret above 'Christening?'; *the bottom quarter of*
                 the page is blank below this entry]

245.13   ↑25 ↑M↓ . . . 1000↓ [*interlined in brownish black ink;*
                 the figures in this line apply equally well to both the origi-
                 nal and the revised figures in the paragraph that follows;
                 therefore, it seems unlikely that Clemens meant to delete
                 this line (or those at 245.16 and 245.19) when he wrote
                 'STET' *across the entry, apparently deleting the other*
                 changes in it and restoring the original readings, and pos-

sibly restoring as well the original readings in the related entries that follow at 245.16–18 and 245.19–21; see note 70 and Doubtful Readings]

245.14–15 ⟨4,500⟩ ⟨↑6,000↓⟩ 4,500 . . . ⟨5⟩ ⟨↑3¾↓⟩ 5 ['6,000' *and* '3¾' *interlined in brownish black ink above canceled* '4,500' *and* '5'; *then* 'STET' *written in brownish black ink across the entry* '25 M . . . is 1000.' *(245.13–15); since the entry had not been canceled,* 'STET' *apparently was intended to restore the original readings* '4,500' *and* '5' *and possibly to restore as well the original readings in the related entries that follow at 245.16–18 and 245.19–21; see note 70 and Doubtful Readings]*

245.16 ↑22 M . . . 1000↓ [*interlined in brownish black ink; see 245.13, note 70, and Doubtful Readings]*

245.17–18 ⟨5½⟩ ↑⟨4⅝⟩4¾ 4¾↓ . . . ⟨4,000⟩4,700 . . . ↑*possibly* 4,800↓ [*revised in brownish black ink;* '¾' *written over* '⅝'; '4¾' *repeated, probably for clarity;* '7' *written over* '0'; '*possibly 4,800' interlined without a caret above* 'solid in a column.'; *see 245.14–15, note 70, and Doubtful Readings]*

245.19 ↑28 M . . . 1000↓ [*interlined in brownish black ink; see 245.13, note 70, and Doubtful Readings]*

245.20–21 ⟨6,300⟩ ↑8,000↓ . . . ⟨[3½]⟩2¾ . . . ↑2¾ (*short* . . . 1000↓ [*revised in brownish black ink;* '2¾' *written over what may be* '3½', *then rewritten for clarity in the phrase* '2¾ (short . . . 1000' *which is interlined without a caret above* 'inches to the 1000.'; *see 245.14–15, note 70, and Doubtful Readings]*

245.24 ⟨[21],000⟩31,000 ['31' *written over what may be* '21']

245.29–246.2 ↑Add . . . day↓ [*written lengthwise in the right margin beside the preceding entries at 245.13–28]*

246.5–247.9 2 type . . . good. [*written in brownish black ink except for the entry at 246.10 written in black ink and the addition at 247.5 written in black pencil]*

246.8–9 5,000 . . . 1200. [*boxed]*

246.10   Alice, $28.16—3329. [*written in black ink*]

246.11   Mrs. Z. B. ⟨Barnes⟩ ↑Gustafson↓,

246.16   ↑—both vols.↓⟩ [*the bottom half of the page is blank below this entry*]

247.1   merely ↑the↓

247.3   ⟨&⟩⟨dis[s]⟩disease ['e' *written over what appears to be* 's']

247.5   Aug. 10 ↑'86↓. ["86' *added in black pencil, possibly by Paine*]

247.7   ↑almost↓

247.8   ↑(except 4 or 5 first lines)↓

247.9   good. [*the bottom half of the page is blank below this word*]

247.10–13   ↑58 . . . 1,500 | 1,500↓ [*squeezed into the top margin of the page above* 'Montreal']

247.15–249.22   Toronto . . . ↑6↓ . . . 86. . . . Berne . . . ↑20↓ . . . 44 [*these lines were originally written to form just two columns: the name of each city followed by its population (in thousands); all the numbers in the middle column from* '6' *to* '20' *were added later*]

247.18   ↑18↓ [*written lengthwise in the left margin beside* 'Halifax . . . Ottawa' (247.16–17)]

247.25   ↑12↓ [*written lengthwise in the left margin beside* 'Santiago' (247.22)]

248.8   ↑28↓ [*written lengthwise on the page across the lines* 'Christiania . . . Moscow' (248.1–5)]

248.10   Glasgow | ⟨20⟩25 ['5' *written over* 'o']

248.32   ⟨[2]22⟩[1]22 [*what appears to be* '1' *written over what appears to be* '2'; *see Doubtful Readings*]

250.12–13   1700 . . . US. [*written lengthwise in the right margin beside portions of the preceding entries* (249.26–250.12)]

250.13 ⟨2000⟩2200 ['2' *written over* 'o']

250.14–251.22 Prop. . . . later. [*written in brownish black ink*]

250.20 ↑Him?↓

251.17 ⟨their⟩there ['re' *written over* 'ir']

251.21–22 ⟨in⟩ ↑about↓ the first ⟨week⟩

252.1 L↑ivy↓ [*the addition possibly not in Clemens' hand; see note 81*]

252.3 harbor. [*a line originally ending the entry here was canceled and the entry was continued*]

252.14 ⟨↑"I . . . away."↓⟩

253.3 The Family Cat [*follows a mark that may be either a canceled letter or part of Clemens' drawing; it appears in front of the cat in the illustration on page 253*]

253.8 ↑GERHARDT.↓

254.1–2 Law . . . locomotives. [*boxed*]

254.3–5 Chatto's . . . March 27, '87. [*written and boxed in brownish black ink*]

254.4 due ⟨6 months later⟩ | ↑Feb. 27, '87↓.

254.16 brain [*the bottom third of the page is blank below this entry*]

255.1–2 ↑N. Y. . . . Apparatus.↓ [*written in brownish black ink over* 'Wise . . . harassments' (254.15)]

255.3 ↑⟨18⟩ 17 years practice↓

255.4–6 ⟨applying s[o]⟩⟨⟨a[p]⟩⟩assaulting so small a trouble with so large a⟩ ↑so large a remedy to so↓ so ↑apparently↓ small a trouble ⟨is⟩was [*originally* 'applying' *followed by what appears to be* 'so'; 'applying' *canceled and what appears to be* 'ap' *written over* 'so'; 'assaulting so small a trouble with so large a' *added* ('s' *of* 'assaulting' *written over what appears to be* 'p' *of* 'ap'); 'assaulting' *canceled,* 'so large a remedy to so' *interlined above* '⟨assaulting⟩

so small', 'with so large' *canceled, and* 'is' *written over*
'a'; 'apparently' *interlined below* 'so small' *in the only*
available space, and a caret added before 'small' *to indi-*
cate the placement of 'apparently'; 'was' *written over* 'is']

255.13   Your⟨s⟩ ↑confession↓

255.16   ↑(Bunco-steerer" for "Christ,"↓

256.1   ↑Pier 8 North river.↓

256.12   ⟨life⟩Life. ['L' *written over* 'l']

256.13   ⟨about 1870⟩1867 1867 [*originally* 'about 1870'; *order of*
              revision not certain; '1867' *interlined without a caret*
              above 'about'; 'about' *canceled;* '67' *written over* '70']

256.16–17   ⟨Pay ↑40 cents per piece↓ . . . Elmira.⟩ [*boxed, perhaps*
              simply to set the passage off for cancellation]

257.1   Drum. [*the bottom third of the page is blank below this*
              entry]

257.2–7   ⟨Mrs. . . . home.⟩ [*a heavy vertical line drawn across*
              these entries]

257.7   home.⟩ [*the bottom third of the page is blank below this*
              entry]

257.14–15   ↑(Add . . . overlookings.↓

258.5–8   Dr. . . . st [*written in brownish black ink*]

258.11   3360. . . . 93⁹⁰ [*written in brownish black ink*]

258.12   ↑(Mrs. C) will be glad this af or eve.↓ [*see Doubtful*
              Readings]

258.16   See House. [*four-fifths of the page is blank below this*
              entry]

258.17   E. ↑I.↓ Horsman

258.20   S & I . . . 11.³⁰ [*written in brownish black ink*]

258.20   in [*Clemens may have added* 'in' *above a dash, possibly*
              intending to retain the dash, to cancel the dash, or to use
              the dash as an underline; see Doubtful Readings]

258.20	11.^{30} [*superscript '30' possibly added later; see Doubtful Readings*]
259.4	↑Old . . . Speech.↓
259.5	"Experience-meeting [⟨"⟩]⟨"⟩↑"↓ [*Clemens apparently wrote opening quotation marks, then altered them to closing quotation marks, and finally canceled them and rewrote the closing quotation marks for clarity*]
259.6	conversion ↑with↓ | ↑:↓ "And
259.6	for ⟨one,⟩ ↑me,↓
259.7	⟨the⟩this ['i' *written over* 'e']
259.9	↑cease to↓ be ⟨no longer⟩
259.19–20	3381 . . . $25 [*written in grayish blue ink*]
259.24	Thalia? [*the bottom quarter of the page is blank below this entry*]
260.1–3	Anne . . . resumed. [*written in grayish blue ink*]
260.1	↑Anne Brown . . . av.↓ [*written in the top margin of the page, above the following paragraph; the comma and '715—5th av.' may have been added later; see Doubtful Readings*]
260.5	↑Charley—↓
261.9–10	The beads . . . audience. [*written in grayish blue ink*]
261.10	PRIVATE ['private' *underlined twice*]
262.1	Oct. . . . stock. [*written in brownish black ink*]
262.2	Saturday . . . 6$^{th.}$ [*written and boxed in grayish blue ink*]
262.13	⟨No probation⟩ ⟨↑Hell.↓⟩
263.16	countries. [*the bottom half of the page is blank below this entry*]
264.1	⟨Thursday⟩ ↑Friday↓
264.7	⟨[10.4]5.⟩12.15. ['12' *written over what appears to be*

'10'; '1' *written over what appears to be '4'; see Doubtful Readings*]

264.8–9   Get . . . Fry. ['Get spectacles.' *heavily boxed, and a heavy vertical line drawn to the right of these entries*]

264.10–11   Dr Snow.⟩ [*a leaf torn out of the notebook following the page that ends here was used by Clemens for a letter to his wife; see note 126*]

265.15   the parson ↑came↓

266.7   ↑Read . . . '86↓ [*written lengthwise in the margin beside* 'However . . . God had' (266.3–8)]

266.16   piousness↑,↓⟨ ⟩⟩

266.31–33   or did he . . . understood [*boxed with a light line that may indicate Clemens was considering the passage for cancellation*]

268.4–5   Stationers & . . . 7 p.m. [*written in pale brownish black ink and boxed on three sides by a wavy line in the same ink*]

268.6   ↑Henry B. Barnes↓ [*written diagonally in pale brownish black ink across the preceding paragraph*]

268.7   ↑Alexander Agar.↓ [*written diagonally in black pencil across the paragraph at 268.4–5; one leaf has been torn out following the leaf that ends here*]

268.8   CHICAGO ['Chicago' *underlined twice*]

268.11   ⟨novel[i]s⟩novels ['s' *written over what may be* 'i'; *the original* 's' *canceled*]

268.12   ⟨Susy⟩Susan ['a' *written over* 'y']

269.7–10   Send . . . New York [*not in Clemens' hand*]

269.13   ↑Livy says↓ [*interlined without a caret above* 'send that']

270.7   all.) [*the bottom quarter of the page is blank below this entry*]

270.8–14   ↑Badeau's Book (?)↓ ⟨Get . . . Courant. ['Get . . .

Courant.' *written in brownish black ink;* 'Get a sponge.' *canceled and* 'Badeau's Book (?)' *written in the top margin of the page, both in black pencil; in both side margins beside* 'Badeau's . . . business' *Clemens drew a pair of parallel lines in black pencil*]

270.15–271.1 Presses ↑41↓; binderies ↑⟨8⟩6↓; | tons ↑1,000↓: ['6' *written over* '8', *which was added in the margin to the right of* 'binderies;'; *emended*]

271.18 ↑Henry Clews's book.?↓ [*written in the top margin of the page above* 'How . . . selling?']

272.2 ↑Back.↓ [*written in the top left corner of the page above* 'How' (272.1) *and boxed; two parallel lines extending down from* 'Back.' *were apparently intended to link this word to* 'How . . . selling?' *and to refer back to the earlier entries at* 270.15–271.9 *about the sales of Grant's book*]

272.8–9 —↑(↓*he* . . . stuff↑)↓—

272.12 ↑(My "Sermon.")↓ [*written in the top margin of the page and boxed*]

273.3 ↑Col. Grant editing papers?↓

273.9–10 ⟨Why . . . Owen?⟩ ⟨↑Too . . . complaints.↓⟩ ['Too . . . complaints.' *interlined below* 'Why . . . Owen?'; *two lines run horizontally through* 'Too . . . complaints.': *one is clearly a cancellation; the other may originally have been a flourish ending the entry at* 'Owen?']

273.12–13 The Unitarian . . . autobi- [*possibly added later than surrounding entries;* 'autobi-' *falls at the foot of a page; the word is not continued on the next page, and no leaf is missing from the notebook at this point*]

273.14 ↑BRING WITH ME.↓ [*written in the top margin; a line across the page below* 'BRING WITH' *seems to have been intended for emphasis but also looks like the lines used elsewhere to separate entries;* 'ME.' *is squeezed in below* 'WITH' *and below the line*]

274.24   I ↑allays↓ 've [*originally 'I've'; 'allays' interlined with a caret following 'I'*]

275.12   ⟨Rice⟩Ryce ['y' *written over* 'i']

275.15   ↑*Grant & McClellans.*↓

276.9   Humor. [*the bottom quarter of the page is blank below this entry*]

276.14   Ar-chi-bald-⟨as⟩As-kin. ['A' *written over* 'as']

277.6   ↑Stewart's place↓

277.8   ↑Scheemann↓ [*see Doubtful Readings*]

279.7   ↑(Osgood.)↓ [*written above* 'dine March 17.']

280.1   ↑Old London street↓

280.5   ↑Loisette↓ [*written above* 'Meinz—']

280.13   Hartford↑'s↓ (?) [*the question mark in parentheses was written before 's' was interlined but was probably added after the initial inscription of the passage*]

280.21   9010. [*written at the beginning of a left-hand page, possibly as a heading to indicate that the subsequent paragraph is a continuation of the subject begun with the same heading on the preceding page (280.12)*]

281.1   ↑T J V up Wash↓ [*see Doubtful Readings*]

281.3   ⟨↑Wash.↓⟩ [*see Doubtful Readings*]

281.6   ⟨[0]51⟩⟨O51⟩51 [*what looks like 'O' written over what looks like 'o', then canceled; 'o' could be '5', and letter 'O' could be numeral 'o'; if the overwritten character is '5', '51' was probably added after 'O' was written*]

281.6   ⟨502102⟩5 21 2 [*what looks like letter 'o' canceled in two places; the canceled characters could be either letter 'O' or numeral 'o'*]

281.6   014e1. [*the bottom half of the page is blank below this entry*]

281.13   ↑In a hot↓

281.15	↑night↓
281.17	↑because cool weather.↓
281.18	↑In↓ Oct
281.20	⟨Se[p]⟩Same ['a' *written over* 'e' *and partially formed* 'p']
282.3	↑4↓
282.4	May ↑J↓ ['J' *may be written over* '5'; *but, if so, the place-ment of* '5' *almost certainly precludes the possibility that Clemens intended to associate* '5' *with* 'May' *as a date*]
282.8	⟨unbias↑s↓ed⟩unbiased ['s' *interlined, then canceled*]
282.9	shallow quality ['shallow' *possibly written in a space origi-nally left blank*]
282.14	Dinner . . . Apl. 13. [*written in brownish black ink*]
283.8–12	↑should have been↓ . . . ↑8,00000↓ . . . ↑16,000,000↓ . . . ↑32,0000↓
283.13	⟨1880⟩1881 ['1' *written over* 'o']
283.13	⟨28,000,000⟩38,000,000 ['3' *written over* '2']
284.13	publish it. [*a line across the page originally ended the entry here; a V-shaped mark through the line apparently cancels it and indicates that the entry continues with* '& add']
287.10	Go . . . return. [*heavily boxed*]
288.5–10	Article . . . year? [*written in brownish black ink*]
288.16–20	Tribune . . . true. [*heavily boxed*]
288.18	ALL ['all' *underlined twice*]
289.2	↑& Standring's letter.↓
290.4	↑May 17/82↓ [*squeezed in above* 'Greeley (Depew']
290.15	↑She . . . SLC↓ [*written lengthwise on the page in brownish black ink across the preceding paragraph*]
291.11	⟨we⟩ ↑you↓

291.19	↑the↓ ⟨G⟩Col.
292.4	O ⟨*sigh-ye-*⟩ ↑yas↓↑-me↓ no↑-↓*sigh*
292.8–15	Saml. . . . S L Clemens [*written in pale brownish black ink*]
292.10–12	Sa	Samuel L. Clemens	Samuel L. Clemens [*written by Clara L. Stanchfield*]
292.13	Samuel L. Clemens [*not in Clemens' hand*]
292.14	Lilly G. Warner. [*written by Lilly G. Warner*]
292.16	Publish . . . telephone. [*written in brownish black ink*]
293.3	↑F. E. Church↓
294.4	↑to Mrs. Higgins.↓
294.8	⟨Ain't⟩ ↑Don't↓
294.11–12	Moncoon. . . . Irish. [*written in brownish black ink*]
295.3	flints. [*a line originally ending the entry here was overwritten and the entry was continued*]
295.15–16	Add . . . Bayreuth. [*written diagonally across the preceding paragraph*]
296.7	same." [*followed by 19 blank pages*]
296.13	add 40—600 [*three-quarters of the page below this entry and the following page are filled by scrawls in brownish black ink, evidently the result of testing a pen; followed by three blank pages*]
296.14–18	1 Porter . . . charade) [*written on the recto of the back flyleaf; the bottom three-quarters of the page is blank*]
296.14–17	1 Porter . . . 1 " 1 [*written in black ink*]
296.14–15	↑1↓ Porter—2	↑2 . . . 1↓

Notebook 27

Emendations and Doubtful Readings

	MTP Reading	MS Reading
305.17	Sin	[*possibly* 'sin']
305.19	light-head	light-|head
*306.9	⟨2⟩⟨[3]⟩one	[*possibly* '⟨[3]⟩⟨2⟩one']
*306.13	116 ⟨over⟩over	116 ⟨over⟩ "
*306.27	⟨1[0]⟩15	[*possibly* '⟨16⟩15']
*307.3	⟨$[-].25⟩$3.25	[*possibly* '⟨$2.25⟩$3.25' or '⟨$3.25⟩$3.25']
307.6	Han 8,000 . . . 8,000	[*possibly* 'Han 8,100 . . . 5,000']
308.2	Gen¹ Agency.	[*possibly* 'Gen¹, Agency.']
308.9	estimate	[*possibly* 'Estimate']
308.22	*him*self	*him*-|self
309.15	Roll-call.	Roll-|call.
*310.22	⟨fust⟩⟨f[ir]st⟩fust	[*possibly* '⟨fust⟩⟨first⟩first']
315.1	exclusively[,]	[*possibly* 'exclusively)']
315.11	newspaper	news-|paper
316.6	⟨d⟩imagined	[*possibly* '⟨id⟩imagined']
316.14	Biography	[*possibly* 'Biographing']
316.14	[It]	[*possibly* 'Yr']
*317.7	⟨£2[3]5.[50]⟩	[*possibly canceled* '£255.50']
*317.17	spirit-stirring/crushing	spirit-|stirring/crushing
318.10	outpourings	[*possibly* 'out-pourings']

318.15	⟨filled⟩	[*possibly canceled* 'fabled']
*318.15	all-bracing	all-|bracing
*318.21	journalist	[*possibly* 'joournalist']
*319.1	[C]L W & Co	[*possibly* 'SL W & Co']
321.16	snuffling	[*possibly* 'smuffling']
324.15	[or]	[*possibly* '&']
325.18	near by	[*possibly* 'nearby']
326.24	*edition*	[*possibly* '*Edition*']
326.30	stage-plays	stage-|plays
327.1	secretive	[*possibly* 'Secretive']
327.8	sea-phrases	sea-|phrases
327.32	names	[*possibly* 'name']
328.11	some day	[*possibly* 'someday']
*329.11	⟨comet⟩ ⟨prominent⟩the Matterhorn.	⟨comet⟩. ⟨prominent⟩the Matterhorn
*330.2	⟨degree⟩degree	['de' *canceled;* 'gree' *left standing*]
330.17	ticket-seller	[*possibly* 'ticket seller' *or* 'ticketseller']
*330.29	quite—to	['quite' *possibly* 'quaint' *or* 'quiet']
330.30	bunco-steerers	bunco-|steerers
331.14	K:	[*possibly* 'R:']
331.16	⟨new⟩asks	[*possibly* 'asks' *written over* 'now']
332.1	Oct. Nov. Dec	[*possibly* 'Oct, Nov, Dec']
332.3	Pay	[*possibly* 'Pays']
*332.8–10	? —Heading . . . sentence.)	[*arrangement doubtful*]

*337.15	⟨P⟩between	be-|⟨P⟩tween
344.10	Brusnahan's	[*possibly* 'Brusnohon's']
347.8	newsp.	news-|p.
348.6	an appt.	[*possibly* 'my appt.']
348.9	callin'	[*possibly* 'cullin'']
350.8	case-harden	case-|harden
351.8	Hells-bells	Hells-|bells
*354.14	(See	[*possibly* '(*See*']
355.1	Isaa[c]	[*written off the edge of the page*]
355.10	Giving	[*possibly* 'Living']
*356.5	(Make	[*possibly* '(*Make*']
357.20	get	[*possibly* 'got']
358.5	I had	[*possibly* 'J had']
358.6	upward.	[*possibly* 'upwards']
359.2	night clothes	[*possibly* 'night-clothes' *or* 'nightclothes']
359.18	outlay	out-|lay
*362.7–8	facts. [*end of entry*] | 12860 48	[*possibly* 'facts. | 12860 48']
363.5	ne[w boo]ks	[*possibly* 'next bks']
363.11	copyrighted	copy-|righted
365.3	copyrighting	copy-|righting
365.5	Use . . . to.	[*possibly canceled*]
365.19	$21	[*possibly* '$2.']
*366.20	⟨Ass[-]⟩	⟨As-|s[-]⟩
368.1	copyrighted	[*possibly* 'copy righted']

*368.17	stage:	[*possibly* 'stage⟨:⟩.']
370.4	⟨u[s]s⟩*use*	[*possibly* '⟨u[s]s⟩*use*']
370.19	stove—coal stove	[*possibly* 'stove-coal stove' *or* 'stove—coalstove']
371.8	nonpareil	non-|pareil
*372.12	hell I	[*possibly* 'hell, I']
*372.12	wagon".	[*possibly* 'wagon'!']
*372.16	⟨[ag,]⟩	[*possibly canceled* '8,']
372.19	book work	[*possibly* 'bookwork']
379.6	to-day	[*possibly* 'today']
379.7	to-morrow	to-|morrow
*380.3	⟨T⟩X	['T' *possibly a cross*]
*382.6–7	working. [*end of entry*] | "He	[*possibly* 'working. "He']
382.18	B[low]	[*possibly* 'Btrn']
384.10	archangel	arch-|angel
385.16	sons	[*possibly* 'son,']
386.5	brook-bridge	brook-|bridge
*392.9	what[?]	what. [*page torn*]
393.5	Whis[k]	[*possibly* 'Whist']

Details of Inscription

[*Entries are in black pencil unless otherwise noted*]

300.1–301.8	A. P. Bur. . . . Mo.) [*written on the verso of the front flyleaf*]
300.1	A. P. Bur.—227 - E. 14. [*written in brownish black ink*]
300.4–6	Next . . . School. [*written in brownish black ink*]
301.5	↑Apl. . . . 26th↓

301.9   ↑562 . . . (Moffett)↓

302.1–304.5   Aus . . . Laffan. [*written in brownish black ink with cancellations in black pencil at* 303.2 *and* 304.1]

302.6   The↑y↓

302.10–11   ⟨Asks leave [to]⟩The widow explains ['The widow' *written over wiped-out* 'Asks leave'; 'explains' *written over what looks like wiped-out unfinished* 'to']

302.14   ⟨↑Hell!↓⟩

302.15   week! [*the bottom fifth of the page is blank below this entry*]

303.2   ⟨45. . . . 50.⟩ [*canceled in black pencil*]

304.1   ⟨Purchase . . . magazine?⟩ [*canceled in black pencil*]

304.4   Patrick—⟨.⟩(break.)⟨.⟩↑—on . . . carriage.↓ [*the opening parenthesis written over one period, the second dash written over another*]

304.6   ⟨Calico's⟩Kalico's ['K' *written over* 'C']

305.14–23   Rev. . . . Ghost. [*written in brownish black ink*]

305.16   Great God! . . . ⟨"⟩Great Scott ['Great' *written over ditto marks inscribed below the preceding* 'Great']

305.23–24   In . . . Christ. [*written below* '"Isaac . . . ball.)' (306.1); *a line between* 'In' *and* 'Ghost.' *indicates the intended position*]

306.1–22   "Isaac . . . ships. [*written in brownish black ink*]

306.4   ↑An admiral . . . spare.↓

306.9   ⟨2⟩⟨[3]⟩one [*sequence of revision uncertain;* 'one' *written over two wiped-out characters, a* '2' *and what may be a* '3', *one of which is written over the other*]

306.13   116 ⟨over⟩over [*originally* '116 over'; 'over' *wiped out and ditto marks written over the cancellation; emended*]

306.14   ↑the year↓

306.15   ⟨Admirals⟩Generals ↑Generals↓ ['Generals' *written over*

'Admirals' *almost illegibly;* 'Generals' *interlined, presumably for clarification, above two carets*]

306.21   ⟨335⟩332 ['2' *written over* '5']

306.24   ⟨[-]s⟩is ['i' *written over an unrecovered letter*]

306.24   ⟨20⟩ ↑100,000↓ miles

306.27   ⟨1[0]⟩15 ['5' *written over what appears to be* 'o'; *see Doubtful Readings*]

306.30   ↑his eye↓

306.30   ⟨dark⟩ ↑night↓

307.3–5   The Yank . . . Legends. [*written in brownish black ink*]

307.3   ⟨$[-].25⟩$3.25 ['3' *written over a wiped-out character that may be* '2' *or* '3']

307.6   Han ↑8,000↓ ⟨5,000⟩7,000 ↑8000↓ ⟨20,000⟩18,000 ['7' *written over* '5'; '18' *written over* '20'; *see Doubtful Readings*]

307.7   ↑14,000↓ 5,000 ↑7000↓

307.8   ↑10,000↓ 7,000 ↑Cox 6000↓

307.9   ↑6,000↓

307.11   ⟨[40],000⟩20,000 . . . or ⟨20,000⟩25,000 ['20' *written over what may be* '40'; '25' *written over* '20']

307.12   ↑13,000↓ 5,000 ↑13,000↓

307.14   ↑$81,000↓

307.17   Bills receivable? [*a flourish originally separating this line from the next was canceled*]

308.2   ↑N.Y. Gen¹ Agency.↓ [*written lengthwise in the right margin beside* 'Rip . . . parts.' (307.15–308.1)]

308.4   Rule . . . ready . . . issue. [*because of the relative narrowness of the manuscript page, the three italicized words fall at the beginning of successive lines; Clemens may have intended to emphasize the entire entry by under-*

lining the first word in each line, whatever it happened to be]

308.14–15   (Last   . . .   ↑$18   &↓   ⟨&   Ernest⟩Richard   . . .   ⟨$1[8]⟩$12 each ⟨&⟩.) [*'&' canceled and 'Richard' written over 'Ernest'; '2' written over what may have been '8'; the period and the closing parenthesis written over '&'; the parentheses may have been added*]

308.17   ↑Simplified . . . pony.↓ [*written lengthwise in the left margin beside 'copyrights . . . back.'" (308.7–16 and 308.18)*]

308.23   telling ↑me↓

308.24   ⟨humories⟩humorous stories [*'ous' written over 'ies'*]

308.27   ↑chaffingly↓

309.3   ⟨Ten or 15⟩Twenty minutes [*'Twenty' written over 'Ten'; 'minutes' written over 'or 15'*]

309.5   told it ↑to↓ me

309.25   ⟨you'll⟩You'll [*'Y' written over 'y'*]

310.9–26   Ole . . . at a-h. [*written in brownish black ink*]

310.10   Heave/↑Slap↓

310.15   OUT [*'out' underlined twice*]

310.19   (2^d Advent.) [*possibly added later*]

310.20   "↑Look here,↓

310.22   ⟨fust⟩⟨f[ir]st⟩fust [*revision unclear; 'fust' apparently changed to 'first' by the addition of a dot over the first upstroke of 'u', the second upstroke serving as 'r'; the dot was then canceled, apparently restoring 'fust'; a second mark near the cancellation may be another dot; see Doubtful Readings*]

310.23   ⟨Schütz⟩, & ⟨Fahrt⟩ ⟨& Konnt.⟩ [*heavily canceled*]

310.24   ⟨putting on frills⟩ [*circled*]

312.4–5   "You . . . hurry" [*opening quotation marks possibly added later*]

312.7	⟨Tha⟩The ['e' *written over* 'a']
313.7	The money-borrowing [*a double line running across the hinge of the notebook connects these words and* 'interest!' *(312.22) on the facing page, apparently to indicate the relationship between the two paragraphs*]
313.7	⟨bac[k]⟩pages ['p' *written over* 'b' *and* 'g' *over* 'c'; 'k' *left unfinished;* 'es' *added*]
314.3	↑George Herbert:↓
314.18	⟨that⟩the ['e' *written over* 'at']
314.19	⟨'87⟩'86 ['6' *written over* '7']
314.24	⟨the⟩this ['is' *written over* 'e']
316.3	⟨see⟩sell ['ll' *written over* 'e']
316.5	"would . . . if" [*the opening quotation marks possibly added later*]
316.9	↑Sept. 13,↓
317.6	↑2 notes. . . . pocket-book.↓
317.7	⟨£2[3]5.[50]⟩£200. ['oo' *written over what appears to be* '35'; *what may be* '50' *canceled; see Doubtful Readings*]
317.16–17	to add . . . occasion. [*possibly added later; written at the bottom of a left-hand page in a space that may originally have been left blank when the paragraph* 'I am called . . . sir.' *(317.18–318.17) was begun at the top of the facing page*]
317.16	weak/↑broken↓
317.16	jubilations/↑lamentations↓
317.17	spirit-stirring/↑crushing↓
317.19	⟨↑to ad↓⟩
317.20	↑after all but↓
317.20–21	↑political↓/↑spiritual↓
317.21	economically/↑spiritually↓

318.1   our being/↑—our ending↓

318.1   ↑political↓

318.2   short/↑long↓

318.2–3   manifold ills/↑vicissitudes↓/↑curses↓ ['vicissitudes' *inter-*
               lined above 'manifold ills'; 'curses' *interlined below* 'man-*
               ifold ills']

318.5   must ↑continue to↓ have

318.6   purest/↑saddest↓

318.6   elevating/↑depressing↓

318.7   activities/↑potentialites↓

318.7   glorious/↑sorrowful↓

318.7–8   Agriculture/↑Death↓

318.11   precious gift/↑profitable monitor↓/↑[b]oon↓ [*what ap-*
               pears to be 'boon' *is written on the facing notebook page,*
               immediately across the hinge from 'precious . . . moni-*
               tor'; *Clemens wrote this word and, below it,* 'Post-prandial
               oratory' *(318.18) in what was then apparently the blank*
               bottom half of the page; when 'Only . . . journalist.'
               (318.19–21) was written on the same half of the page, it
               was indented to fit around the earlier inscription]

318.12   bodies/↑morals↓/↑intelligences↓ ['morals' *interlined*
               above 'bodies'; 'intelligences' *interlined below* 'bodies']

318.13   nourished/↑modified↓

318.13–14   our ↑otherwise sterile↓/↑sinful↓ lives ['otherwise sterile'
               interlined above 'our lives'; 'sinful' *squeezed in above*
               'lives' *and below* 'sterile'; *it is not clear whether the alter-*
               native to 'our otherwise sterile lives' *was intended to be*
               'our otherwise sinful lives' *or* 'our sinful lives']

318.14   grand, ↑&↓ aspiring

318.15   ⟨filled⟩ ↑are↓

318.15   all-bracing ['all-' *falls at the end of a line; presumably it*

was an inadvertent elision that produced 'bracing' instead
of 'embracing' at the beginning of the next line]

318.18–21   Post-prandial . . . journalist. [see 318.11 above]

318.21   journalist [originally written so awkwardly that 'j' and 's'
                 were traced over for clarity; a second 'o' was interlined
                 with a caret, either to assure correct spelling or to produce
                 'joournalist']

319.1   ↑[C]L↓ W & Co [see Doubtful Readings]

319.5   Jean—Central Park [boxed]

319.6   tickets [the bottom fifth of the page is blank below this
                 entry]

319.8   NOTE ['note' underlined twice]

321.11   ⟨so⟩ ↑right↓ soon

321.13–14   ↑& Burdette's . . . Burdette.↓

321.15   ⟨spoons,⟩ ↑soup,↓

322.7   ⟨is⟩it ['t' written over 's']

323.1   ↑3,814↓ ↑Sept 22 H M & Co $100↓ [interlined in brown-
                 ish black ink below and to the right of 'Sell . . . house.'
                 (322.16); 'Sept . . . $100' may have been written earlier
                 than '3,814']

323.3   ↑Aug 10↓

323.16   (B.R.) [parentheses possibly added later]

323.17   ⟨13,1[2]8.42⟩⟨13,178.42⟩13,108.42 ['7' written over what
                 appears to be '2'; 'o' written over '7']

325.3 $11,000 [the bottom half of the page is blank below this
                 entry]

325.4   ⟨Protestant . . . that.⟩ [possibly added later]

325.11   ⟨in ⟨17⟩1610⟩ ['6' written over '7']

325.21   at 16; [the semicolon possibly mended from a period]

326.6   ⟨register⟩Register ['R' written over 'r']

326.17	"⟨*a life of mere*⟩ a life of mere DREAM ['a . . . mere' *underlined; the underline canceled;* 'dream' *underlined twice*]
326.24	⟨The f⟩His ['His' *written over* 'The f']
326.32	1634. [*probably added later*]
326.33	↑at Ludlow Castle.↓
327.23	⟨Delect[i]ble⟩Delectable ['a' *may be written over* 'i']
327.26	↑still↓
327.37	↑—16 months↓
328.6	⟨were⟩was ↑just↓ ['as' *written over* 'ere']
328.8	↑sublime↓
329.2–3	⟨most likely⟩ ↑of course↓
329.5	turned ↑up↓
329.11	a ⟨comet⟩ ↑⟨prominent⟩the Matterhorn↓. [*originally* 'a comet.'; 'comet' *canceled and* 'prominent' *interlined with a caret inadvertently placed after, instead of before, the period;* 'the Matterhorn' *written over* 'prominent'; *emended*]
329.16–17	He looked . . . situation. [*written below* 'CLW & Co."' (329.21); *a line in the margin connects* 'He looked' *and* 'you were out.' (329.15), *indicating the relationship of this sentence to the earlier paragraph; the bottom fifth of the page is blank below this entry*]
329.22–23	Whereas, ↑his ⟨[d]⟩Divine Hiness, ↑the↓ Deputy↓ First Assistant ⟨↑God↓ Almighty⟩ ⟨God⟩ ↑Sup. B.↓
330.2	⟨degree⟩degree ↑& character,↓ ['de' *of* 'degree' *canceled, but* 'gree' *left standing; the effort at cancellation may have been abandoned when* '& character,' *was interlined*]
330.3	⟨invidual⟩ ↑citizen↓
330.3	⟨↑all↓⟩
330.4	can ⟨[¶] [1].⟩ Have [*originally what appears to be* '1.

Have' *began a new paragraph; what appears to be* '1.' *was canceled, a caret was added before* 'Have', *and a line was drawn from* 'Have' *to* 'can' *at the end of the preceding line, apparently to indicate that the passage should run on without a paragraph break*]

330.5   ↑either with or↓ without

330.7   ↑cash↓ purchase

330.10   ⟨in the world⟩ ↑divinable↓,

330.11–12   Gen Franklin, ↑& CD. Warner↓ & the Bishop of Hart-
                         ford, ↑the President of Trinity—↓ ['& CD. Warner' *inter-
                         lined without a caret above* 'Franklin'; 'the President of
                         Trinity—' *interlined without a caret above* 'Bishop of
                         Hartford,']

330.14   slaves ⟨↑subjects↓⟩ [*Clemens first wrote* 'slaves', *then
                         interlined* 'subjects' *without canceling* 'slaves', *and then
                         canceled* 'subjects']

330.16   ↑a shade↓

330.21   ⟨God Almighty⟩ ↑S. B.↓,

330.24–25   reported⟨—⟩ ↑as . . . consideration—↓

330.28   ↑quite↓ manly

330.28–29   ⟨godly⟩ ↑plucky↓—⟨B & A⟩ ⟨godly⟩ ⟨↑style &↓⟩
                         ↑quite↓— [*sequence of revision uncertain*]

330.33   donkeyish/↑asinine↓/↑kittenish↓,

330.36–37   ⟨⟨ignorant⟩ small-souled & the⟩ ↑stuck-up↓ childish.
                         ['stuck-up' *interlined without a caret above* 'small-
                         souled']

331.3   ↑fine . . . sublime↓ [*written lengthwise in the left mar-
                         gin beside* 'alone. . . . Holy' (330.34–331.1); *the addition
                         begins beside* 'Holy' *and may have been intended as an
                         interlineation to precede that word*]

331.4–7   Call & . . . expense. [*written in brownish black ink*]

331.10   Frau Peeve an. [*one leaf was torn out following the page that ends here, evidently before the next entry was written*]

332.8–10   ? ↑—Heading.↓ | Have we a *Whelker.* among us? ↑(Translation . . . sentence.)↓ [*the order of inscription and intended placement are unclear; probably 'Whelker.' was written first, indented to begin a paragraph; 'Have we a' is written to the right of and slightly above 'Whelker.', and 'among us?' is written below 'Whelker.'; these phrases were probably added; the centered question mark, heavily and deliberately inscribed following 'Whelker.' in what would have been the only available space at the top center of the entry, was probably added; '—Heading.' is interlined following the question mark and above 'Have'; '(Translation . . . sentence.)' is squeezed in to the right of and below 'among us?', apparently after the following entry had been started*]

332.12   pickpocket⟨;⟩— [*the dash written over the semicolon*]

332.12–13   ⟨for . . . living/↑do battle with the↓⟩ ↑at risk↓

332.13–14   ⟨a careful . . . ↑friendless↓ dead⟩

332.16   ta↑l↓k

333.10   ⟨their cost⟩ ↑24,0000↓

333.13   Mail these letters [*written at the top of an otherwise blank left-hand page*]

334.1   Burbank [*the bottom fifth of the page is blank below this entry*]

334.2–14   Dress . . . this. [*written in brownish black ink*]

334.19–23   ⟨Sep⟩ . . . enough. [*written in brownish black ink*]

334.19   ↑⟨Sep⟩ . . . 1887.↓

334.26   people. [*the bottom fifth of the page is blank below this entry*]

335.5   ↑& squirrel↓

335.12   ↑CHALEY CLARK↓ [*written diagonally in the right margin beside 'See . . . ⟨Ammunition⟩' (335.10–11)*]

335.13 ↑or Chly.↓

335.17 "Will pay you⟨["]⟩ ↑15 to↓ ⟨["]⟩17½ [*sequence of re-vision uncertain; '15' and '17½' appear to be written over closing quotation marks*]

336.1–337.1 List . . . [Mr.] Hall . . . 1,000 [*written in brownish black ink except for additions at 336.4, 336.6, 336.13, and 336.19–21, and the cancellation at 336.22 in black pencil*]

336.3 Ch↑s↓. H. Clark

336.4 Twichell . . . 1,000 ↑G↓ ['G' *written in black pencil*]

336.5 WD ⟨[-]⟩H↑owells↓

336.6 Sourmash ↑Stan↓ . . . 1,000 ↑G↓ ['G' *written in black pencil*]

336.13 ↑½G↓ [*written in black pencil*]

336.13 —24 hours' notice—. [*written lengthwise in the right margin beside 'Whitmo' . . . [Mr.] Hall . . . 1,000' (336.13–337.1)*]

336.19–21 S. E. Moffett . . . O. ⟨C.⟩Cl . . . 1,000 ↑[brace] G↓ [*the brace and 'G' written in black pencil*]

336.21 ⟨C.⟩Cl ['l' *written over a period*]

336.22 ⟨C L W. . . . 10,000⟩ [*canceled in black pencil*]

337.5–10 ↑George . . . 25,000↓ [*written in the available space to the right of 'C.D. Warner . . . (preferred) 5,000' (336.2–8)*]

337.11–12 ↑Gov't . . . machinery↓

337.15 ⟨P⟩between ['be-' *at the end of a line followed by* 'tween' *written over* 'P' *at the beginning of the next line*]

337.17 Skip . . . 344. [*followed by about one line of blank space*]

337.19 Lane [*the bottom fifth of the page is blank below this entry*]

338.3–8 Tuesday . . . results. [*written in brownish black ink*]

339.1   ⟨[St]⟩Have [*what appears to be 'St' mended to 'H'*]

340.10   ⟨dabe[u]⟩dabei ['i' *written over what may be* 'u']

342.15   ↑**X**↓ Gerhardt's check. ['**X**' *written following* 'check.' *in the only available space*]

342.18   ↑**X**↓ . . . canvasser yet? ['**X**' *written over* 'canvasser']

343.2   ↑**O**↓ Laffan . . . me. ['**O**' *written following* 'me.' *in the only available space*]

343.16   ⟨build⟩ ↑create &↓ build ['build' *canceled, then restored with stet marks*]

344.7   ⟨Oct. 31⟩ ↑Nov 1↓,

344.9   Uncle Remus, & [*followed by about one line of blank space*]

345.10   ↑in order↓

346.5   ⟨punishment⟩punished ['ed' *written over* 'm'; 'ent' *canceled*]

346.6   ↑public↓ exposure

346.7   Death/↑Gallows↓

346.9   ↑"1988."↓ [*centered in the top margin of the page with a caret indicating placement*]

346.14   ⟨changing⟩changed ['ed' *written over* 'ing']

347.8   ↑printed↓

348.7   ↑noon,↓

348.10   ⟨s[aw]⟩sees ['ees' *written over what may be* 'aw']

349.9   Belle↑s↓—↑Susie . . . Julie↓

349.10   Dumb-Bell↑s↓

351.1   ⟨$5⟩$4.50 ['4' *written over* '5']

351.6   NOW. ['now.' *underlined twice; following the page that ends here, one leaf was torn out about 19 November 1887 and used by Clemens for an undated note to Bram Stoker*]

351.16   ↑IN-DIG-NAY-SHUN.↓

352.12   IN-DIE-JEST-SHUN. [*written at the top of a right-hand
                    page opposite* 'PAR-(pa) SIGH-MONY.' (351.15) *at the
                    top of the facing page; possibly written later than* 'Him
                    a marksman!' (352.13)]

352.18   pay/↑paid↓

352.19–20   They charge 40 . . . now. [*a line that apparently origi-
                    nally ended the entry below* 'They charge 40 . . . it.' *and
                    another below* 'They charge 88 . . . now.' *were disre-
                    garded when the entry was continued*]

353.1   ⟨9,6[1]1.12⟩9,591.12 ['59' *written over* '6' *and what may
                    be* '1']

353.6   Nov. 26⟨.⟩— [*the dash written over the period*]

353.17   ↑Get . . . P.↓ [*written lengthwise on the page to the
                    right of* 'Mary . . . Twichell.' (353.7–14); *boxed*]

353.21   ↑12 . . . anyway.↓ [*written in the top margin of the page
                    above* 'Clara . . . Tiffany's' (353.20)]

354.13   Twichell's 2 sets of soldiers. [*written in a small hand at
                    the top of the page; possibly squeezed in above* 'Martin
                    . . . **X**' (354.14)]

354.14   ↑(See **X**↓ ['See **X**' *embraced on the left by a bracket that
                    extends under* 'See' *and may also have been intended as
                    an underline*]

354.17   IF ['if' *underlined twice*]

354.19   ↑The *only* . . . nations, the↓ ⟨The⟩

355.16   ↑(Banquet-Management)↓ [*written diagonally across the
                    preceding paragraph*]

356.5   (Make ['Make' *embraced on the left by a bracket that
                    extends under the word and may also have been intended
                    as an underline*]

356.7   ↑|Moncoon↓

356.11   Tom⟨["]⟩? [*the question mark may be written over quo-*
                  tation marks]

357.6   ⟨16,198.78⟩16,196.78 ['6' *written over* '8']

357.9   ↑ADJU↑S↓TABLE Speech.↓ ['ADJUTABLE Speech'
                  written diagonally across the left side of the preceding
                  paragraph; 'S' *added to* 'ADJUTABLE' *with a caret*]

357.10   ↑ALSO . . . pocket.↓ [*written diagonally across the right*
                  side of 'For . . . Yarn.' *and* 'Chilblains.' *(357.8 and*
                  357.12)]

357.13   ↑& McDonald.↓ [*interlined without a caret above* 'Call
                  on Mr.']

357.14   apple-wood ['wood' *underlined twice*]

357 illustration [*the lines enclosing the* X *extend to the top edge of the*
                  page]

358.17   ↑—Prophesy—↓ [*possibly written by Paine; interlined*
                  without a caret above '1910. In']

359.14   ⟨deserted⟩deserting ['ing' *written over* 'ed']

359.20   ⟨bo⟩bk ['k' *written over* 'o']

361.7   discharged 3 in fall ['3' *written in a space that may*
                  originally have been left blank]

361.13–14   ↑or . . . better.↓ [*interlined without a caret above* 'in-
                  side . . . ⟨Union⟩']

362.7   facts. [*it is unclear whether a line below this word was in-*
                  tended for emphasis or to conclude the entry]

362.9   to Chatto. [*the bottom quarter of the page is blank below*
                  these words]

363.3   ⟨1880⟩1878 ['78' *written over* '80']

363.7–8   ↑Century protects them↓ Cable . . . Howells. [*em-*
                  braced by a line running down the right margin and part
                  way across the page below 'Howells.'; 'Howells.' *may have*
                  been added later]

363.11 copyrighted. there. [*the bottom third of the page is blank below these words*]

364.3 ⟨10 or ⟨a⟩12⟩ ↑15 or 16↓

364.17 ⟨Miss [- - - - -]⟩ [*the unrecovered word is heavily canceled*]

365.5 ↑Use . . . to.↓ [*interlined without a caret above 'London pub—'; the line canceling 'A great . . . don't' (365.4) may also have been intended to cancel these words*]

366.15 ⟨Simpson⟩Simpkins ['*kins' written over 'son'*]

366.19–21 ↑He . . . pay."↓ ↑They . . . pirates.↓ ['They . . . pirates.' *squeezed in following* 'mistake.' (366.22); *a line from* 'They' *to* 'pay."' *indicates the intended sequence*]

366.20 ⟨Ass[-]⟩What have ['What' *written over* 'As-' *at the end of a line;* 'have' *written over* 's' *and an unrecovered letter at the beginning of the next line*]

367.3 ↑T & Co↓

367.5 ⟨⁵⁄₆⟩5/6 [*the original* '6' *canceled and* '6' *rewritten in a different position, apparently to make it clear that shillings-and-pence rather than a fraction is what is meant*]

367.5–6 ⟨T &⟩Ticknor & Co. ['i' *written over* '&']

367.26–27 ⟨the⟩ ↑a↓ shadow

368.7 ↑SHAVE.↓ [*written in the top margin of the page; a line connects this word and* 'SHAVE. . . . Book.' (368.12)]

368.12 SHAVE. . . . Book. [*set off from other entries by heavy retraced lines above and below the entry; a line connects this entry and* 'SHAVE.' (368.7)]

368.17 stage: [*the colon possibly mended to a period*]

369.14 Lucerne⟨.⟩ girl. ['g' *written over the period*]

370.1 ↑No SEAT↓ ['No seat' *underlined twice*]

370.2–12 Jan. 25 . . . in 8 hours. . . . (8 hours.) ['Jan. 25 . . . in

8 hours.' (370.2–6), *written on the bottom half of a left-hand page, is followed by the note* '(Skip a page)' *and an asterisk;* 'Knock . . . (8 hours.)' *(370.7–12), which occupies the top half of the next left-hand page and is preceded by an asterisk, has been moved to reflect the intended sequence;* 'Jan. 21 . . . dull.' *(370.13–21) is on the right-hand page following* 'in 8 hours.', *and immediately below* '(8 hours.)' *the entries continue with* 'Miss' *(370.22) and the symbol that precedes it*]

370.4   ⟨u[s]s⟩use ['s' *written over what appears to be* 's'; 'e' *written over* 's'; *the original inscription may have been underlined*]

371.20   My Duel. [*written in black ink*]

372.12–19   wagon".   ↑"Adam . . . name?↓   Jean . . . leaded. ['wagon".' *was originally followed by about two lines of blank space;* 'Jean . . . thing."' *was written following* 'leaded.' *(372.19) but its intended position is indicated by a line in the margin between* 'Jean' *and a caret added in that blank space;* '"Adam . . . name?' *was added later at the top of the blank space and above the caret*]

372.12   hell I . . . wagon". [*punctuation uncertain; it is possible that the first of these quotation marks is a comma between* 'hell' *and* 'I' *in the manuscript line immediately above and that the second quotation mark and the period form an exclamation point following* 'wagon'*]

372.15   KIND ['kind' *underlined three times*]

372.16   set ⟨↑[ag,]↓⟩ 997 [*see Doubtful Readings*]

373.3   See Pond. [*boxed heavily*]

374.2   55$^{th.}$ [*followed by about two lines of blank space*]

374.15   vast canvass [*the bottom third of the page is blank below these words*]

375.1   ↑Theodore↓ Roosevelt

376.5   ↑Howells, 46 W. 9$^{th.}$↓

376.6	Dinner . . . 7.30 p.m. [*written in blue ink*]
376.8	↑April↓
377.13	March 26, ↑(88)↓ ['(88)' *possibly not in Clemens' hand*]
378.8	BEECHER ['Beecher' *underlined three times*]
378.10	↑W↓ 9th.
379.2	⟨11th⟩10th ['o' *written over* '1']
379.2	—↑to↓ dinner
379.4	⟨b[u]zzard⟩blizzard [*what looks like* 'u' *mended to* 'li']
379.8	↑nor a telephone↓
379.18	↑Derby (Doesticks)↓
380.2	↑MARCH, 1888.↓
380.3	Mrs. Ralph ⟨X⟩ ⟨T⟩X Johnson [*Johnson's middle name was 'Cross'; the 'T' overwritten by 'X' may have been intended to serve as a cross*]
380.5	9↑½↓ pm.
380.7–9	⟨Fortnightly . . . 1600 I st⟩ [*boxed*]
380.7	pm. [*a line originally ending the entry here was overwritten and the entry was continued*]
380.13	Thursday night [*the line separating this from the following entry is heavily traced over*]
381.1	↑Miss↓ Clymer
381.6	Ck . . . 110.²⁰ [*written in grayish blue ink*]
381.11	G⟨.⟩— ⟨G⟩D— [*the dash written over the period*]
381.15–382.4	Rabbi . . . ⟨A . . . $100,000.⟩ [*boxed*; 'A . . . $100,-000.' *may have been added in a space originally left blank for additions to the list* 'Rabbi . . . Gondola.']
382.5–6	⟨his . . . working.⟩ ⟨↑he . . . morals.↓⟩ his . . . working. [*a line originally ending the entry with 'working.' was disregarded when 'his working.' was canceled and the*

entry was continued with 'he . . . morals.' *written below the line; then* 'he . . . morals.' *was canceled and* 'his . . . working.' *was restored with the instruction* 'stet']

382.7   "He . . . himself." [*because the line originally separating this from the preceding entry was disregarded when that entry was continued (see 382.5–6), it is possible to read this as an extension of the preceding entry*]

382.10   ↑Sept. 8 . . . hour.↓ [*two leaves have been torn out following the page that ends here*]

382.11   ↑Fowle's trial, page 112.↓

382.17–18 ↑Unfair . . . cathedrals.↓ [*written diagonally in the corner of the page to the right of* 'Fowle's . . . one.' *(382.11–15)*]

382.18   ⟨Advowson's⟩Advowsons [*the apostrophe canceled*]

382.19   ↑Telegraph Charley Lang↓ [*written lengthwise across the preceding entries,* 'Fowle's . . . Tales.' *(382.11–16)*]

383.1   No . . . week. [*heavily boxed*]

383.14   7⟨—⟩yrs ['yrs' *written over the dash*]

384.5   ⟨45,000⟩45,500 ['5' *written over* 'o']

384.11   ↑& friendly↓

384.15   100 men. [*a line originally ending the entry here was disregarded when the entry was continued*]

385.1   in US. [*the bottom fifth of the page is blank below these words*]

385.15   apiece⟨. All⟩; 3 & upwards [*originally* 'apiece.' *ended one line and* 'All' *began the next; the period was mended to a semicolon,* 'All' *was canceled, and the sentence was continued with* '3' *added at the end of the line following the semicolon and* '& upwards' *following canceled* 'All']

385.16–17 4143 . . . $80.20. [*written in grayish blue ink*]

386.8   dropped . . . returned [*a line across the page below*

these words may originally have ended the entry at
'Miss!'"]

386.9–13   4144 . . . 1868. [*written in blue ink*]

386.13   ↑Their . . . 1868.↓ [*squeezed in above* 'Army of the
                 Cumberland,' (386.10)]

387.3   ⟨[H]s⟩As ['A' *written over what may be* 'H']

389.2   4145 . . . House. [*written in grayish blue ink*]

389.8   ↑purposely↓

391.9   115 E. 18th C. C. [*superscript* 'C. C.' *underlined twice*]

391.12   4146 . . . $2.25. [*written in grayish blue ink*]

391.14   Chicago. [*a line originally ending the entry here was can-
                 celed and the entry was continued*]

392.6   ↑famlies↓

392.9   what[?] [*the tab on the corner of the page has been torn
                 off immediately following this word; only a period and a
                 faint mark on the torn edge survive of what must once
                 have been a question mark; emended*]

392.17–19   4147 . . . 25.00. [*written in blue ink*]

393.2   in America. [*the bottom four-fifths of the page is blank
                 below these words*]

393.4   try it. [*the bottom four-fifths of the page is blank below
                 these words; followed by two blank pages*]

393.9   Brer Whitmore [*the bottom three-quarters of the page
                 is blank below these words*]

393.10–30   My Duel . . . years. [*written on the recto of the back
                 flyleaf*]

393.13–24   151 . . . 1475 [*written in brownish black ink*]

393.13–19   151 . . . 2249 [*bordered by a pattern of faint wavy pen-
                 cil marks*]

393.16   ⟨115⟩151 ['51' *written over* '15']

393.17   ⟨2905⟩2265 ['26' *written over* '90']

Notebook 28

Emendations and Doubtful Readings

	MTP Reading	MS Reading
*398.2	operative;	[*possibly* 'operative⟨.⟩;']
400.3	to-day	[*possibly* 'today']
401.12	⟨than yours⟩;	[*possibly* '⟨than yours;⟩']
401.21	upstarts	up-|starts
*402.1	Magna Charta⟨!—haha⟩	[*possibly* 'Magna Charta⟨!⟩. ⟨—haha⟩']
403.17	playbill	[*possibly* 'play bill']
403.18	bad man	[*possibly* 'badman']
405.13	monseiur	[*possibly* 'monseur']
*405.24	speech	[*possibly* '*speech*']
405.25	Trade-Mark	Trade-|Mark
406.13	bulldog	[*possibly* 'bull dog']
*406.20	⟨[outer]⟩	[*possibly* '⟨other⟩']
406.24	Jee[m]s	[*possibly* 'Jeews']
407.5	blatherskite	blather-|skite
*407.5	[-----]/arouse	[*the unrecovered word possibly canceled* 'awake' *or* 'evoke']
408.20	proofreader	[*possibly* 'proof reader']
*410.4	one⟨.⟩,	[*possibly* 'one,']
410.22	ferry boat	[*possibly* 'ferryboat']
410.22	sea.	[*possibly* 'sea,']

*410.26	nearly ⟨1400⟩1600	[*possibly* '⟨1400⟩1600 nearly']
410.27	sea.	[*ditto marks below preceding* 'sea.']
*411.13	royalty or other fraud,	[*possibly* 'royalty, or other fraud']
*412.4	land⟨.⟩;	[*possibly* 'land⟨.⟩,']
412.4	to-day	to-|day
*413.14	⟨"Lance"—⟩"Lance|" lot—	[*revision doubtful*]
413.27	church	[*possibly* 'Church']
414.4	bell	[*possibly* 'hell']
415.15	overthrows	over-|throws
416.19	everywhere	[*possibly* 'every where']
417.1	bedridden	bed-|ridden
417.10	I[ts]	[*possibly* 'I p.']
*417.15	584 vol 3—18th cent.	[*possibly* '584 vol 3—18th cent.']
*418.5–6	The bicycle. [*end of entry*] | Journal	[*possibly* '*The bicycle.* | Journal']
*418.10–11	Search expeditions. [*end of entry*] | Journal	[*possibly* '*Search expeditions.* | Journal']
422.10	alongside	along-|side
425.3	the master	[*possibly* 'the Master']
425.17	Mugwump	Mug-|wump
427.2	newspapers	news-|papers
427.19	street-lamp	street-|lamp
*428.17	hous[e]	[*page torn*]
431.3	downhill	[*possibly* 'down hill']

434.9	wood-thrush	wood-|thrush
434.20	Wednes^y,—	[*possibly* 'Wednes 27']
438.9	Charge	[*possibly* 'Change']
440.3	copyright	copy-|right
445.1	Mr. Backnumber	[*possibly* 'Mr. Back number']
446.16	evidences	[*possibly* 'Evidences']
447.2	Mrs.	[*ditto marks below preceding* 'Mrs.']
*447.4–5	ave⟩ Sat . . . 9 | Mrs. . . . 6	[*possibly* 'ave⟩ | Mrs. . . . 6 Sat . . . 9']
451.5	tonight	[*possibly* 'to-night']
451.5	tomorrow	[*possibly* 'to-morrow']
452.2	evening	[*possibly* 'Evening']
453.11	essential	[*possibly* 'Essential']
453.14	per cent	[*possibly* 'percent']
455.13	Ambitions	[*possibly* 'Ambitious']
456.6	college-bred	college-|bred
462.2	⟨to-morrow⟩	[*possibly canceled* 'tomorrow']
462.2	to-morrow	[*possibly* 'tomorrow']
464.3	1873	[*possibly* '1875']
465.5	Sis	[*possibly* 'Sir']
465.9	equator	[*possibly* 'Equator']
468.13	per cent	[*possibly* 'percent']
468.16	outright	out-|right
*468.20–24	⟨Raftsmen⟩ True Story | ? Skinned Man Uncle Remus. . . . Interviewer—15–20	[*possibly* '⟨Raftsmen⟩ | ? Skinned Man . . . Interviewer—15–20 | True Story | Uncle Remus.']

471.5	photo.	[*possibly* 'photos']
472.9	College	[*possibly* 'college']
472.33	comet-spawn	comet-|spawn
475.2	kingdom	[*possibly* 'Kingdom']
475.12	highwaymen	[*possibly* 'highway men']
476.1	July . . . T. . . . C.	[*ditto marks below preceding* 'July', 'T.', *and* 'C.']

Details of Inscription

[*Entries are in black pencil unless otherwise noted*]

397.1–398.16	Eugen . . . ant.) [*written on the verso of the front flyleaf*]
397.1	↑Eugen . . . ave↓ [*written in the top margin of the page*]
397.2	↑562 . . . Moffett↓ [*written in brownish black ink in the space between* 'Prices.' *and* 'First . . . each' (397.3–4)]
397.10	↑we↓
398.1	↑to be . . . hours,↓
398.2	↑or 7↓
398.2	operative; [*possibly originally* 'operative.'; *a comma may have been added below a period*]
398.6	⟨earn⟩ ↑save↓
398.11	↑on a . . . day,↓ [*interlined without a caret above* 'it saves . . . months']
398.15–16	↑Here is . . . ant.)↓ [*written lengthwise near the right margin of the page across portions of the preceding entries,* '562 . . . Randolph st.' (397.2–398.14)]
398.17–18	↑from . . . English-German↓ [*written in the top margin of the page with a line indicating placement*]

398.21   ↑(Darwin)↓

398.22   ⟨which⟩ ⟨makes . . . hand⟩ ['makes . . . hand' *prob-
                    ably canceled before* 'which']

398.24   shabby/↑mean↓

399.25–400.1   at all. . . . —but if [*a line, possibly drawn by Paine, runs
                    from* 'at all.' *to* '—but if' *to indicate the sequence of
                    the passage*]

400.1–413.13   To this . . . lion.⟩ [23 *leaves are inscribed on right-hand
                    pages only, except for entries at* 401.2–18, 403.12–16,
                    406.16–23, 407.10–14, 409.1–2, 409.9–20, 410.16–21,
                    410.30–31, 411.1–7, *and* 412.9–413.1 *written on left-hand
                    pages*]

400.4   ↑the memory of↓

400.4   ⟨Quin⟩Gwin ['Gw' *written over* 'Qu']

400.5   envy↑.↓ ⟨of her⟩

400.6–7   a ⟨⟨pet⟩ ↑darling↓ of fortune.⟩ ↑one of the peculiarly
                    fortunate of this world.↓ [*originally* 'a pet of fortune.';
                    'pet' *canceled, and* 'darling' *interlined; then* 'darling' *and*
                    'of' *canceled,* 'one of the peculiarly' *interlined,* 'fortune.'
                    altered to 'fortunate', *and* 'of this world.' *interlined*]

400.12   ⟨is⟩ ↑⟨wo⟩wd. be↓ ['d' *written over* 'o']

400.13   ⟨pissed on.⟩ ↑used.↓ ['pissed on.' *canceled in brownish
                    black ink;* 'used.' *interlined in pencil; the bottom quarter
                    of the page is blank below these words*]

400.15–16   ⟨Pr of W.⟩ ↑Queen↓,

400.16   ↑—female—↓ [*interlined without a caret above* 'have no']

400.17–18   bless ⟨↑enchant↓⟩

400.18   ⟨[-]⟩ ↑worshiping↓

400.18   ⟨glimpse⟩ ↑view↓

400.25   judgment day ⟨↑&↓⟩ ['&' *interlined without a caret*
              above 'judgment', *then canceled*]

401.2–3   ⟨the system ⟨degrades⟩ ↑does not↓ degrade the . . .
              few,⟩ ['s' *of* 'degrades' *canceled, presumably when* 'does
              not' *was interlined*]

401.3–4   ⟨few⟩ ↑many↓

401.7–11   ↑⟨You⟩ There . . . faces.↓ [*written on an otherwise
              blank left-hand page opposite* '⟨the system . . . with a
              fac-|' (401.2–18) *on the facing page; since most of the
              surrounding leaves are inscribed on right-hand pages only,
              it is likely that Clemens added this entry at some time
              after he completed the entry at* 400.24–401.6 ('Ours . . .
              idleness.')]

401.9   ⟨monarch[i]s⟩monarchs ['s' *written over what may be* 'is']

401.19   ⟨other factions, &⟩ ⟨↑dissent↓⟩ ⟨↑[of]↓⟩ ['dissent' *inter-
              lined with a caret before canceled* 'other factions, &',
              then canceled; what may be 'of' *interlined without a caret
              after canceled* 'other factions, &', *then canceled*]

401.22   ↑—he erects . . . nobility—↓

401.24   ⟨invasion⟩ ↑surprise↓

402.1   Magna Charta⟨!—haha⟩ [*altered in brownish black ink;
              the cancellation strikes through the top mark of the
              exclamation point but not the period, suggesting that
              Clemens may have intended the period to remain stand-
              ing*]

402.3   authority. [*the bottom fifth of the page is blank below
              this entry*]

402.4   ⟨queer⟩ ↑curious↓

402.5   ⟨assumed⟩assumes ['s' *written over* 'd']

402.13   ↑Now,↓ By

402.23   bee⟨s⟩↑.↓

403.12–16 ↑Picture . . . square.↓ [*written lengthwise on a left-hand page opposite '⟨his⟩the crown . . . bureau.' (403.9–11) and 'Publish . . . (Scribner)' (403.17–404.3) on the facing page; since most of the surrounding leaves are inscribed on right-hand pages only, it is likely that Clemens added this entry at some time after he completed the entry at 403.3–11 ('Father . . . bureau.') and at least some of the following entries about the Franco-German War play*]

403.15 ⟨killed⟩ ↑losses↓,

404.8 Congress escutcheon [*half-circled; possibly added later (see the illustration on page 404)*]

405.5 ↑Last . . . parlor.↓

405.19–20 ⟨no taxes/↑heavy taxes↓ meantime.⟩

405.24 ↑Arrogance.↓

405.24 ↑Chicago speech.↓ [*written diagonally in the top right corner of the page that begins with 'Arrogance.'; it is unclear whether a line below 'speech.' was intended for emphasis or to separate these words from other inscription*]

405.26 ↑A↓ Buffon

405.26 ⟨s[a]⟩skeletons ['k' *written over what may be* 'a']

406.3 ⟨Vanity (effeminate)⟩ ↑nastiness;↓ ↑&c↓

406.6 ↑Chicago speech↓ [*squeezed into the top margin of the page*]

406.10 ↑social↓

406.13 ⟨lion⟩ ↑bulldog↓

406.15 ⟨sheep?⟩Wombat ['sheep' *canceled;* 'W' *written over the question mark*]

406.16–23 insolent . . . Evangeline [*written on a left-hand page opposite 'They would . . . England.' (406.24–407.9) on*

the facing page; since most of the surrounding leaves
are inscribed on right-hand pages only, it is possible that
Clemens added these entries at some time after he completed the entry on the facing page; the bottom fifth of
the page is blank below 'Evangeline.']

406.16   ↑insolent↓   ↑Russian—wombat.↓ [squeezed into the
              top margin of the page, 'insolent' directly above 'Bull-dog'
              (406.17)]

406.20   ⟨[outer]⟩ outer ['outer' follows a canceled word that
              looks like miswritten 'outer'; see Doubtful Readings]

406.24   would ⟨[notice] a⟩ ['would' followed by a caret with no
              interlineation]

406.25   ⟨of⟩if ['i' written over 'o']

407.1   ↑noble↓

407.2   ⟨should⟩could ['c' written over 'sh']

407.2–3   ↑that . . . for↓ four generations↑.↓ ⟨of . . . tribe.⟩

407.5–8   ⟨⟨[--]⟩& ⟨⟨get⟩ ↑[-----]↓/↑arouse↓ no⟩ more ⟨[----
              tion] ⟨[----]⟩& get no⟩ ⟨↑excitement &↓⟩ ⟨↑pow[---]↓⟩
              ↑attention, rouse no↓/get no more ⟨[homage]⟩ ↑enthu-
              siasm↓ than would a⟩ [sequence of revision uncertain;
              the second '& get' is written over an unrecovered word;
              'attention, rouse no' was interlined below canceled
              '[----tion] ⟨[----]⟩& get no', probably some time after
              'get no more [homage] than would a' was written; finally
              '⟨[--]⟩& . . . enthusiasm than would a' was boxed and
              canceled as a unit; see Doubtful Readings]

407.8   ↑& get no more attention/↑homage↓ than would a↓
              ['homage' written in brownish black ink]

407.10–14   ⟨Bert⟩ . . . there. [written on a left-hand page opposite
              'Andover . . . charging a' (407.11–408.7) on the facing
              page; since most of the surrounding leaves are inscribed
              on right-hand pages only, it is possible that Clemens
              added these entries at some time after he completed the

entry at 408.3–8 ('Let us . . . ditto)'); the bottom third of the page is blank below 'there.']

407.11   ⟨↑those unsp↓⟩ [*interlined without a caret above* 'of Girard College']

407.12   ⟨the⟩ ⟨great⟩ ↑their↓

408.3   ⟨↑in fancy↓⟩

408.3   ↑male↓

408.4   naked⟨; also⟩⟨↑.↓⟩↑;↓ [*originally* 'naked; also'; *the semicolon and* 'also' *canceled and a period added following* 'naked'; *the period canceled and a semicolon added after canceled* 'also'}

408.5–6 ⟨↑50 dancing masters, 50 quack doctors↓ & then march the whole⟩['50 dancing . . . doctors' *added below* '& then . . . whole' *with an arrow indicating placement*]

408.8   ↑(Nobles, ditto)↓

408.9–10 The new . . . transmitted. [*circled*]

408.14   ⟨Do⟩ ↑These↓

408.19   ⟨j[ec]t[e]d⟩ [*follows a blank space within the line, as though space were being left for later addition of a prefix or some other word*]

408.20   ⟨cold shudders.⟩ ↑dry gripes.↓ [*altered in brownish black ink*]

409.1–2 ↑When we . . . castrated peoples—↓ [*written on an otherwise blank left-hand page opposite* 'the European . . . play.' *(408.9–409.8) on the facing page; since most of the surrounding leaves are inscribed on right-hand pages only, it is likely that Clemens added this entry at some time after he had completed at least the first paragraph of the second entry on the facing page,* 'London . . . G. W. S.' *(409.3–6)*]

409.8   play. [*a fifth of the page is blank below this word*]

409.9–20   You take . . . $140 [*written on a left-hand page opposite* 'But you . . . military office in' *(410.1–12) on the facing page; since most of the surrounding leaves are inscribed on right-hand pages only, it is possible that Clemens added these entries at some time after he completed the entry at* 410.10–13 *(*'By Catholic . . . terms.'*);* '3.75 . . . $140' *is written lengthwise on the otherwise blank bottom half of the page*]

409.12   ⟨solemnly⟩ ↑gravely↓

410.4   ↑why↓

410.4–5   one⟨.⟩, ⟨⟨if⟩You don't know what y⟩ [*the comma apparently written over a period; see Doubtful Readings*]

410.8   ⟨He [w]⟩A ['He' *canceled;* 'A' *written over what appears to be* 'w']

410.11   generations of [*followed by a caret with no interlineation*]

410.16–21   ↑But I . . . through it."↓ [*written on a left-hand page opposite* 'France . . . cases.' *(410.12–15) and* 'On ferry . . . Scranton ⟨1700⟩ 1700' *(410.22–29) on the facing pages;* 'A little . . . high' *(410.30–31) is also on the left-hand page, immediately below* 'But I . . . through it."'; *since most of the surrounding leaves are inscribed on right-hand pages only, it is likely that Clemens added these entries after he completed at least some of the entries on the facing page*]

410.16   ↑ever↓

410.17   ↑perhaps↓

410.26   Pocono⟨[es]⟩ ↑summit↓ ↑nearly↓ ⟨1400⟩1600 ⟨odd⟩ ⟨↑(ab[--t])↓⟩ ['16' *written over* '14'; 'nearly' *was added later than the illegible word in parentheses and may have been intended to follow* '1600']

410.30–31   ↑A little . . . high↓ [*see 410.16–21 above*]

411.1–7   quiet. . . . machine [*written on a left-hand page opposite* 'What is . . . live.' *(411.8–11) on the facing page; since*

most of the surrounding leaves are inscribed on right-
hand pages only, it is possible that Clemens added these
fragmentary paragraphs at some time after he completed
the entry on the facing page; a fifth of the page is blank
below 'machine']

411.6   ↑impudent↓

411.10   ⟨usurpation⟩ [the remainder of the line following this
             word is blank]

411.12–13   ⟨No god,⟩ ⟨no religion,⟩ no ↑political↓ church ['No god,'
             was apparently canceled later than 'no religion,']

411.13   royalty ↑or other fraud↓, ['or other fraud' interlined with-
             out a caret; the comma may have been intended to follow
             'royalty']

411.14   ⟨confront⟩ ↑face↓

411.18   ⟨dumb⟩ ↑dull↓

411.19   throw/↑chuck↓

412.2   Death-rate. [possibly added later]

412.4   land⟨.⟩; [apparently·originally 'land.'; a comma added,
             probably mending the period to a semicolon, but possibly
             canceling the period]

412.9–413.1 Speech introducing . . . Adjustable Speech. [written on
             the top half of an otherwise blank left-hand page opposite
             'If the Honi . . . lion.⟩' (413.2–13) on the facing page;
             since most of the preceding leaves are inscribed on right-
             hand pages only, it is possible that Clemens added these
             entries at some time after he completed the entry on the
             facing page]

412.15   ⟨Ne[-]⟩N. E. dinner [the first period and 'E' written over
             'e' and an illegible letter]

413.3–4   ⟨This⟩ ↑A woman's↓

413.6   indelicate⟨,"⟩. [the period probably added when the can-
             cellation was made]

413.8–9   ↑to keep it in mind,↓

413.10–11   ↑It is observable that↓ It

413.12–13   ↑motto of the↓

413.14   ⟨"Lance"—⟩"Lance↑|↓"↑lot↓— [*intended revision un-
                   clear; 'lot' is written below the closing quotation marks
                   and the dash and may have been intended to cancel one
                   or both of them; Clemens may have intended to place
                   'lot' within the closing quotation marks*]

413.21   ↑timber & clothes↓ [*interlined without a caret below
                   'salt & medicines', possibly as an alternative to 'salt &
                   medicines'*]

414.23   ⟨made a slave⟩ ↑have his liberty debauched—↓

414.26–27   ↑Marinel—the leech hermit↓ very . . . world. ['Mari-
                   nel . . . hermit' *possibly added after the list had been
                   written as far as* 'Gander, an expert' (415.29); 'very . . .
                   world.' *is written below* 'Gander, an expert' *with a line
                   drawn to* 'Marinel' *to indicate the intended sequence*]

415.28   Artigal, The Bastard. ⟨one Expert⟩ . . . washed. ['The
                   Bastard.' *written on the line following* 'washed.' *as a
                   separate item in the sequence* 'Brunor . . . Artigal . . .
                   The Bastard. . . . Gander'; *a line connecting* 'Artigal'
                   and 'The Bastard.' *apparently indicates the intended
                   placement of* 'The Bastard.']

416.12–13   there⟨.⟩↑; but I remitted the baptism.↓ [*the period
                   mended to a semicolon when* 'but . . . baptism.' *added*]

416.17   ⟨Congregat⟩Congrega &c. ['Congrega-' *falls at the end
                   of a line;* 't' *at the beginning of the next line overwritten
                   by* '&c.']

417.9   ↑in↓ impressment

417.15   ↑584 vol 3—18ᵗʰ cent.↓ [*squeezed into the top margin
                   of the page above* 'the press is necessary' (417.5); *it is un-
                   clear whether a line below* '584 . . . cent.' *was intended
                   for emphasis or to set the phrase off from the text below it*]

418.1–2	↑Hello . . . Shalott.↓
418.5	The bicycle. [*it is unclear whether a line below these words was intended for emphasis or to conclude the entry*]
418.10	Search expeditions. [*it is unclear whether a line below these words was intended for emphasis or to conclude the entry*]
418.12	Light. [*the bottom fifth of the page is blank below this entry*]
418.13	↑Ck! & take a ride!↓
419.3	as abjectly ['as' *possibly added later*]
420.2	↑(↓to . . . Queen⟨()↑)↓ [*the closing parenthesis written over an opening parenthesis*]
420.7	out. [*the bottom fifth of the page is blank below this entry*]
420.24	remember [*the bottom half of the page is blank below this entry*]
421.16	⟨not⟩now ['w' *written over* 't']
421.19	⟨[irr]esponsiveness⟩unresponsiveness ['unr' *interlined above canceled letters that appear to be* 'irr']
421.20	⟨irresponsiveness⟩unresponsiveness ['un' *interlined above canceled* 'ir']
421.21	⟨irresponsiveness⟩unresponsiveness ['un' *interlined above canceled* 'ir']
422.10	Arkwright↑,↓ ⟨↑Eli Whitney↓⟩
422.11	Stephenson. ⟨↑Daguerre↓⟩
422.14–16	The book-house . . . Yes! [*Clemens drew three heavy horizontal lines across the page above and below this entry*]
423.5–6	⟨a hundred⟩ ⟨↑75↓⟩ ↑100↓
423.11	⟨Se[-]⟩Sept. ['p' *written over an illegible letter*]

423.18	Typothetæ [*ligature indicated by a line above 'ae'*]
424.5	⟨heart⟩ ↑soul↓
424.7–23	4323. = $662 . . . Doyle . . . 6 [*written in a pale green-ish black ink apparently unique in the notebooks in this volume*]
424.9	↑$↓40
424.9	⟨$535⟩$532 ['2' *written over* '5']
424.24–26	Moderate . . . house. [*written and boxed in black pen-cil to the right of the ink inscriptions* 'William . . . Doyle, . . . 6⟩' (424.13–23)]
425.1	important that ['that' *probably added later*]
425.11	PUBLICLY ['publicly' *underlined three times*]
425.13	PUBLICLY ['publicly' *underlined twice*]
425.21	frost. [*the bottom fifth of the page is blank below this entry*]
426.6	↑Pipe & cigars & tobacco.↓
426.9	↑Autographs.↓ [*written lengthwise in the right margin beside* 'Paper . . . filler.⟩' (426.5–8)]
427.10	bird's-⟨eye⟩egg ['egg' *written over* 'eye']
427.11	dinner) [*the bottom two-thirds of the page is blank below this entry*]
427.14	lassen. [*the bottom three-quarters of the page is blank below this entry*]
427.15–428.15	October . . . E. 137[th.] [*written in blue ink except for interlineations at 427.19 and 428.12 and the clarification at 428.7 written in black pencil*]
427.19	↑Let go ⟨No[v]⟩Oct. 27.↓ [*written in black pencil;* 'Oct' *written over what appears to be* 'Nov']
428.7	rectum ['rectum' *rewritten in black pencil, apparently*

for clarity and possibly by Paine, above 'rectum' written
somewhat awkwardly in blue ink]

428.12	↑(possibly)↓ [written in black pencil]
428.12	↑every year↓
428.16–17	↑2 . . . tel . . . hous[e]↓ [added to the right of 'E. 137th.'; 'tel' and 'hous[e]' run off the torn edge of the page]
428.21	↑dear↓
428.25	Tale⟨.⟩, [the period mended to a comma]
429.8	⟨$25,000⟩$45,000 ['4' written over '2']
431.7	⟨Teska⟩Tesla ['l' written over 'k']
431.17	⟨Teska⟩Tesla ['l' written over 'k']
431.17	↑(& Thompson?)↓
431.24–25	↑Who . . . name it.↓ [written lengthwise on the page across the preceding paragraph]
431.28	↑1 m sh at 5 each↓
432.7	⟨[5]00⟩⟨1000⟩ ↑500↓ ['10' written over what may be '5']
432.8	⟨$20,000⟩$15,000 ['15' written over '20']
432.11	25,00,000⟩ [followed by Clemens' instruction 'OVER' written in the otherwise blank bottom third of the page; 'As . . . spider.' (432.28) is on the otherwise blank verso of the leaf; 'Einbildungs . . . werth.' (432.12–27) is on the following recto]
432.26	⟨40,000⟩20,000 ['2' written over '4']
432.27	⟨millione⟩Millione ['M' written over 'm']
432.28	As . . . spider. [written at the top of an otherwise blank page]
433.7	GRAY. [the bottom half of the page is blank below this entry]

433.12   Nation [*the bottom fifth of the page is blank below this entry*]

433.21   ⟨Guil⟩Guides ['des' *written over* 'l']

433.22   UNCLE REMUS ['Uncle Remus' *underlined three times*]

433.24–26   Up . . . Browning | Horse-Race. [*boxed; one leaf has been torn out following the page that ends here*]

434.15   sure. [*the bottom quarter of the page is blank below this word*]

434.16   ⟨pipe-box.⟩pipe-↑tray.↓ ['tray.' *interlined above canceled* 'box.']

434.22   Yes.—10 [*a line across the page originally ended the entry at* 'Yes.'; *another line, connecting* 'Yes.' *and* '—10' *indicates the continuation of the entry*]

435.10   Book-⟨agent.⟩ ↑(agent)↓/keeper (of animals) ['agent.' *canceled and* '(agent)' *interlined without a caret above the hyphen;* 'keeper' *follows canceled* 'agent'; '(of animals)' *written lengthwise in the margin following* 'keeper']

435.13   Par-a/↑eh?↓-chute

435.16   Villa: ↑25↓ ↑Lucerne girl↓ ['25' *apparently added after* 'Lucerne girl']

435.17   Arm ↑⟨25⟩10↓ ↑Tale of Fishwife↓ [*the numbers apparently added after* 'Tale of Fishwife']

435.21   ↑Phil'- . . . fer↓

435.22   rattle. [*the bottom third of the page is blank below this word*]

435.23   ↑Abby . . . 132 W 44ᵗʰ↓

436.6–8   ↑Thomas . . . Pauper.↓ [*written in brownish black ink; the dates of Reddy's correspondence with Clemens suggest that this entry was written later than the list of readings that follows (see note 96)*]

436.9	↑Northampton, Jan. 21.↓
437.5	Dead. [*the bottom third of the page is blank below this word*]
437.8	↑pure leads↓
437.9	↑of leads↓
437.13	↑of these↓
437.14	↑solid↓
437.15	⟨1,54[-00]—⟩1,540,000 ['0,000' *written over an unrecovered character and what looks like* '00—']
437.20	page⟨.⟩— [*the dash written over the period*]
438.1	↑The . . . Professorship.↓ [*written and boxed in the top margin of the page* 'The mach. . . . through it.' (437.18–30)]
439.2–4	"Travelers . . . Farm. [*heavily bracketed in the right margin*]
439.6	Ida. [*the bottom half of the page is blank below this word*]
440.1	↑Send . . . 1ˢ·↓ [*written in the top margin of the page*]
440.4	BY ['by' *underlined twice*]
441.6	Lie[be]) [*the bottom three-fifths of the page is blank below this word*]
441.7–22	↑EUREKA!↓ . . . SL Clemens [*written in brownish black ink;* 'EUREKA!' *written in the top margin of the page and underlined with a wavy line*]
441.10	BY MACHINERY ['by machinery' *underlined three times*]
443.7	48 W 45ᵗʰ [*the bottom quarter of the page is blank below this entry*]
443.8–14	Monday . . . space. [*written in brownish black ink*]
443.12	by ↑the↓

443.14	space. [*following this entry, the bottom quarter of the page and the following page are blank*]
444.1	⟨5.45.⟩5.42. ['2.' *written over* '5.']
444.5	⟨10.38⟩10.15 ['15' *written over* '38']
444.10	alogues. [*the bottom three-quarters of the page is blank below this entry*]
445.1	Mr. Backnumber. [*the bottom fifth of the page is blank below this entry*]
445.2	Johnson . . . ⟨March 4.⟩ ↑Feb. 28.↓ . . . Boston [*written in brownish black ink; altered in black pencil*]
445.5–6	⟨Read . . . p.m.⟩ [*written in brownish black ink; canceled in black pencil*]
445.7	↑6.30 p. m.↓ [*interlined without a caret above* 'Feb. 6,']
445.7	↑Armory Hall.↓ [*interlined without a caret above* 'Yale dinner'; *the bottom quarter of the page is blank below this entry*]
446.2	Apl. 2 . . . &c. [*written in brownish black ink*]
446.5	(several selec) [*probably added later*]
446.8	(sure) [*the bottom third of the page is blank below this word*]
446.15	⟨w[i]th⟩⟨wich⟩ which ['ich' *written over what appears to be* 'ith'; 'wich' *canceled and rewritten as* 'which']
446.18	⟨↑Hawley 2030 I⟩—1↓
446.19	↑Ralph Cross↓
446.19	1735 I. ↑2↓ [*a line in the margin connects* '1735 I' *and* '1731-odd' (447.3)]
447.1	⟨↑Sent . . . ↑Xmas↓ . . . us.↓⟩
447.3	⟨Mrs.⟩ ⟨Secretary Whitney⟩ ↑I.↓ ⟨⟨17[--]⟩1731-odd⟩ ↑3↓ ['31' *written over two unrecovered figures*; 'I.' *interlined with a caret*; '3' *interlined without a caret above*

'1731'; 'Mrs.' *canceled; then* 'Secretary Whitney 1731-
odd' *canceled but* 'I.' *and* '3' *left standing*]

447.4   ↑Sat Eve. 8.30. 9↓ [*interlined without a caret below* '1407
Mass ave' *and above* '1435 Mass. Ave 6'; *although the
addition appears to have been intended to follow the
former phrase (which was canceled), it may have been
meant to accompany the latter;* '9' *may have been added
later than* 'Sat Eve. 8.30.']

447.5   ↑1435↓ Mass. Ave ↑6↓ ['6' *interlined without a caret above*
'Mass.' *and circled; a line connects* '6' *with the circled
numbers* '5' (447.6) *and* '4' (447.9) *below*]

447.6   ↑5↓ [*interlined without a caret below* 'cor' *and circled;
see 447.5 above*]

447.8   ↑↑John↓ Hay 8↓ ['Hay 8' *written in the otherwise blank
bottom third of the page below* 'Z. C. . . . ⟨7⟩' (447.10);
'John' *written above* 'Hay 8'; 'John Hay 8' *circled and
connected by a line to* 'Hay' (447.7)]

447.9   ↑S. G.↓ Ward ↑⟨171[0]⟩ ↑1608↓ K st↓↑—4↓ ['4' *circled;
see 447.5 above*]

447.12   Athenæum [*ligature indicated by a line above* 'ae']

447.14   ⟨serene⟩ ⟨↑adventurous↓⟩ ↑rapt↓ joy/↑exalted content-
ment↓

447.15   lights/↑glows in↓/↑burns in↓

447.17   ↑hear you not↓

447.17   ↑the gratitude,↓

447.20   say— [*two leaves have been torn out following the page
that ends here*]

448.1–4   James . . . machines. [*written in brownish black ink*]

448.11   ⟨vagina⟩ [*canceled in brownish black ink*]

448.16   dynamo creates ⟨or collects force or⟩ ↑or generates↓
power

449.7–8 ↑and who . . . House↓ [*squeezed in above and below* 'Nelson's name.'; *Clemens drew a double wavy vertical line in the right margin beside this paragraph*]

449.9 Webster's—talk. [*followed by about two lines of blank space, probably to allow the list to be extended*]

449.12 hole [*two widely spaced lines separate this from the following entry (a single line usually separates entries in this notebook)*]

450.1 ⟨↑entirely↓⟩ can ⟨↑entirely↓⟩ ['entirely' *is interlined above* 'can'; *a caret before* 'can' *is canceled; a caret following* 'can' *is not canceled*]

450.3 ↑Wit↓

450.10 ↑David↓

451.1–9 Doctor . . . (Douglas) [*each of these entries is followed not by Clemens' usual single line separating entries but by relatively short double lines near the left margin; the effect is to set these entries off as a group among surrounding entries*]

451.11 ⟨²⁵/₍₁₀₀₀₎⟩25 ↑000↓ [*the denominator of the original fraction canceled; the numerator mended from* '25' *to* '25 000' *and incorporated in the subsequent computation*]

452.9 ⟨it is⟩I think ['*I think*' *written over* 'it is']

452.14 KAN'T ['KAN'T' *underlined twice*]

452.14 The MOMENT ['moment' *underlined twice; the bottom half of the page is blank below these words*]

453.2 whatever. [*the bottom two-thirds of the page is blank below this word*]

453.4 ⟨Lestie⟩Leslie ['l' *written over* 't']

455.6 ↑aspect↓

455.7–12 When . . . I am, I [*except for* 'may be', *all these lines end at the right edge of the page*]

455.13	MAN. [*the bottom quarter of the page is blank below this word*]
455.22	others. [*the bottom quarter of the page is blank below this word*]
456.8	than right⟨.⟩, [*the comma written over the period*]
456.12	⟨were . . . to give⟩ ↑had↓ give↑n↓ ['were . . . to' *canceled;* 'had' *interlined;* 'n' *added to* 'give']
456.19	full/↑solid↓
457.3	matriculation . . . it. [*written at the top of a right-hand page opposite* 'a few . . . University.' (456.10–11) *on the facing page; followed by about two lines of blank space*]
457.5	⟨Ha⟩Hearst ['e' *written over* 'a']
458.8	So↑t↓ry [*originally* 'Sory'; 't' *misplaced*]
458.22	BEEN ['been' *underlined twice*]
459.4	estimates. [*the bottom fifth of the page is blank below this word*]
459.5	↑Brusnahan↓
460.5–8	⟨⟨Feb⟩ ↑March↓ . . . July 15.)⟩ [*written and revised in brownish black ink; canceled in black pencil; the bottom fifth of the page is blank below this entry*]
460.10	↑March 9/89.↓ [*written in brownish black ink*]
461.1	↑4 months . . . July 10.↓ [*written in brownish black ink*]
461.2	⟨defi⟩devices ['vi' *written over* 'fi']
461.3–6	J. W. Paige . . . doubt. [*written in brownish black ink*]
461.3	⟨Feb.⟩ ↑March↓
461.12	⟨und⟩unter ['t' *written over* 'd']
462.4	*Muleykeh.* 2. ↑sure↓ ['sure' *interlined without a caret above* '*Muleykeh*']

462.8   *Rabbi Ben Ezra* ↑sure↓ ['sure' *interlined without a caret above 'Rabbi Ben'*]

462.10–19   ↑Up . . . shot.↓ [*written at different times in the available space to the right of 'For Apl. 2 . . . Baal.' (462.3–9); the exact order of inscription is unclear; probably written later than at least some of the entries at 463.1–11 ('Dan'l . . . day.)'), which follow 'Baal.' on the same page*]

462.12   Quarrel . . . raftsmen [*boxed*]

462.13–14   *In armor . . . 22* [*written in brownish black ink*]

462.18–19   77—Drilling . . . shot. [*written in brownish black ink*]

463.1   ↑Dan'l . . . Den.↓

463.12–13   ↑Here . . . unfulfuled.↓ [*squeezed into the top margin of the page in brownish black ink*]

463.20   ⟨prophet⟩profits ['fits' *written over* 'phe' *and the final* 't' *of* 'prophet' *canceled*]

464.1   ↑We . . . years.↓

464.2–3   ↑8,000 in 1873,↓

464.3   ⟨1888⟩1886 ['6' *written over* '8']

464.3   ⟨shall⟩ ↑should↓

464.10   Booth. [*the bottom fifth of the page is blank below this word*]

464.11   See W. G. [*follows about one line of blank space at the top of the page*]

464.15   month. [*Clemens left some blank space following this entry and following 'Howells' (465.1) and 'Laffan' (465.2), probably to permit additions*]

465.5–6   ⟨I've . . . spring!"⟩ [*written in black pencil; canceled in brownish black ink*]

465.12   frind. [*a flourish originally ending the entry here was overwritten when the entry was continued*]

466.1   Hall . . . Anthony. [*circled*]

466.2   custard. [*the bottom fifth of the page is blank below this word; the following leaf has been torn out*]

467.1   YEAR ['*year*' *underlined twice*]

467.7   serene. [*the bottom fifth of the page is blank below this word*]

468.6   Arnold. [*the line separating this from the following entry is heavily traced over*]

468.8–13   Mch . . . per cent. [*written in brownish black ink*]

468.20–21   True Story | Uncle Remus. [*Clemens may have written these titles beside '⟨Raftsmen⟩' and 'Skinned Man' to indicate a relationship among the titles, or he may have added them later as a continuation of the list, writing them in the available space and separating them with a vertical line from the earlier titles*]

469.11   ↑the↓ attention

470.4–7   ↑Great . . . Champagne. [*written in brownish black ink*]

470.9   #4830 . . . miles. [*written in brownish black ink; the ink line separating this from the following entry is very heavily traced over in black pencil*]

470.11   to 6. [*the bottom fifth of the page is blank below this entry*]

471.2   ⟨114⟩ ↑117↓

472.1   May ⟨1[2]⟩11 ['*11*' *written over what may be* '*12*']

472.3   ↑use of the↓

472.9   ↑in the College↓ [*interlined without a caret above* 'going on in a' (472.9)]

472.23   ⟨from my earliest⟩ ↑somehow↓

472.23–24   have . . . down on/↑never could stand↓

472.24–26	↑To my . . . planet.↓ ['To my mind they're only just' *interlined with a caret; then* 'they're only just' *canceled by a line that extends onto the facing right-hand page where, in what must have been the closest available space,* 'there's . . . planet.' *is written lengthwise along the left side of that page*]
472.25	pups/↑whelps↓
472.25–26	he preferred . . . else,/↑they were . . . him.↓ ['he' *is partly canceled;* 'they were . . . him.' *interlined without a caret above* 'he preferred asteroids']
472.31	↑to be in↓
472.33	planet-pups. [*the bottom four-fifths of the page is blank below these words except for the inscription along the side of the page, described above at* 472.24–26]
473.1	⟨fold⟩folk ['k' *written over* 'd']
473.5	Whistling story. . . . 5 [*the bottom three-quarters of the page is blank below this entry*]
474.1	↑Unitype . . . J. RISLEY↓ [*squeezed into the top margin of the page above* 'The Berlin Das Echo']
474.4	Typothetæ [*ligature indicated by a line above* 'ae']
474.11	⟨'88.⟩ ↑'87.↓
474.18	↑N.Y.↓
474.20	World.⟩ [*the bottom quarter of the page is blank below this word*]
474.21	Ck . . . $30. [*written in brownish black ink in the upper right corner of the page*]
475.1	↑Appendix . . . all.↓ [*squeezed into the top margin of the page beside* 'Ck . . . $30.' (474.21) *and above* 'Visit a kingdom' (475.2); *written in brownish black ink*]
475.6–7	↑Harrying . . . travler↓ [*interlined in brownish black ink above* 'because . . . nest.' (475.5–6)]

475.8   ↑(White . . . Wales.)↓ [*written in brownish black ink; squeezed into the available space to the right of 'gulch.'*]

475.10   ↑Foundling hospital;↓ [*written in brownish black ink*]

475.21–477.11   July 5 . . . Fargo.⟩ [*written on the recto of the back flyleaf; the table of scores through '108 . . . 34' (476.21) apparently written first, filling all of the page except the margins; next probably the first items in the list of checks, through 'TW Crane . . . (4312)' (477.3), squeezed into the right margin; then probably the table of scores, through 'Sept . . . 25' (476.36), completed below 'TW Crane . . . (4312)' in the right margin; then probably the remaining items in the list of checks written at different times across portions of the table of scores; the table of scores written in black pencil except for entries in brownish black ink at 475.19 and 476.32; the list of checks written in brownish black ink except for the cancellation in black pencil at 477.11*]

475.21–22   414 | 276 [*written in the upper right corner of the page*]

475.19   30 . . . 39 [*written in brownish black ink; the intervening calculation ('567 . . . 915') is in black pencil*]

476.29   ⟨39⟩22 . . . ⟨22⟩39 ['39' *and* '22' *canceled, and* '22' *and* '39' *written heavily over the canceled figures*]

476.30   ⟨2[20]⟩211 ['11' *written over what may be* '20']

476.32   32 . . . 29 [*written in brownish black ink*]

477.1–11   4310 . . . Fargo.⟩ [*written in brownish black ink except for the cancellation in black pencil at 477.11; see 475.21–477.11 above*]

477.2   ⟨$100⟩$105 ['5' *written over* '0']

477.11   ⟨4324 . . . Fargo.⟩ [*written in brownish black ink; canceled in pencil*]

Notebook 29

Emendations and Doubtful Readings

	MTP Reading	MS Reading
486.12	folk,	[*possibly* 'folk.']
*486.13	—boyhood.	[*possibly canceled*]
*487.3–6	"Lying" . . . Christening.	[*order uncertain*]
488.7	progeny	[*possibly* 'progeney']
489.20	Month	[*possibly* 'month']
*490.13–492.3	No. 6 . . . $25.	[*placement uncertain*]
492.18	"Non."	[*possibly* '"Non".']
*492.22–28	Ye . . . Killaloe.	[*placement uncertain*]
492.22	Boneyparty	[*possibly* 'Boney party']
492.24	pairley-vous	[*possibly* 'pairlez-vous']
492.27	Continong	[*possibly* 'continong']
*493.1–13	We . . . challenges. =	[*placement uncertain*]
498.13	Albermarle Co.	[*possibly* 'Albermarle co.']
500.1	a.m.	[*ditto marks below preceding* 'a.m.']
506.1	*Chap. Page.*	[*no column headings needed: middle of manuscript page*]
509.9	figure-work	figure-|work
513.2	envelops	[*possibly* 'Envelops']
514.5	eine	[*possibly* 'Eine']
517.1	10ten	[*possibly* '18ten']

518.7	royalties	['royaltes' *with the* 'e' *dotted*]
518.21	Bonjour	[*possibly* 'Bon jour']
519.12	buckwheat	buck-|wheat
519.17	a. m.	a. | m.
*520.9–521.7	⟨Better . . . on.⟩ | Write . . . gardener & | 2 | Better . . . nation.	[*possibly* '⟨Better . . . on.⟩ | 2 | Better . . . nation. | Write . . . gardener &']
522.7	sidewalk	side-|walk
527.2	railroad	rail-|road
*529.2	Grav	[*possibly canceled*]
*529.3	McMillan	[*possibly canceled*]
*529.4	Thorne	[*possibly canceled*]
*529.5	Matrix	[*possibly canceled*]
530.2	⟨[5]⟩⟨8⟩⟨6⟩7	[*order of inscription uncertain*]
530.6	Rogers.	[*possibly* 'Rogers,']
*533.5	Invite gov't printer	[*possibly* 'Invite gov't printer']
534.21	exclusive	[*possibly* 'Exclusive']
*535.14–16	⟨⟨May . . . people.⟩	[*the cancellation possibly restored*]
*536.24	⟨2⟩31	[*possibly* '⟨21⟩31']
*537.18	⟨Adelini⟩Adelina	[*possibly* '⟨Adelina⟩Adelini']
538.18	[we]ter	[*possibly* 'vocter' *or* 'voeter']
*538.19	GUT.—	[*the period possibly canceled*].
538.20	gang	[*possibly* 'ganz']
*539.3	⟨ALS GUT⟩als gut	[*possibly* 'ALS GUT']
541.7	election	[*possibly* 'Election']

542.11	Dec 24	['Dec' *replaces ditto marks below preceding* 'Dec']
544.8	[⟨not⟩]	[*possibly canceled* 'but']
545.11	irgendeiner	[*possibly* 'irgend einer']
546.5	to-morrow	[*possibly* 'tomorrow']
546.7	our	[*possibly* 'one']
*549.12	⟨50,000⟩100,000	[*possibly* '⟨150,000⟩100,000']
550.11	cor. m. in ⟨4⟩8 h.	['cor. m. in' *replaces ditto marks below ditto marks in preceding line;* 'h.' *replaces ditto marks below* 'h.' *in preceding line*]
550.13	cor. m. in ¼ h.	['cor. m. in' *and* 'h.' *replace ditto marks below ditto marks in preceding line*]
550.21	.non-existent	non-|existent
*556.9	Eine Grösse	['Eine' *possibly* 'eine' *and possibly italic*]
556.9	Eine ⟨millione⟩Millionen	['Eine' *possibly* 'eine']
*556.12	sagt;	[*possibly* 'sagt⟨.⟩,' *or* 'sagt⟨.⟩;']
557.8	Delamater	[*possibly* 'Delameter']
*557.13	⟨gereethen⟩geriethen	[*possibly* '⟨gereethen⟩gereiethen']
*558.3	$14,0,00⟨0⟩	[*the second comma possibly canceled*]
559.12	manufac-	manufac-|
559.13	Mˢ	[*possibly* ' 'Mˢ']
564.2	⟨Arr.⟩ Leave	['Leave' *replaces ditto marks below preceding* 'Leave']

568.1   Sep.   [*blank space below preceding* 'Sep.']

Details of Inscription

[*Entries are in black pencil unless otherwise noted*]

484.1–485.2   119 E 28 . . . Madison ave [*written on the verso of the front flyleaf*]

484.1   ↑119 E 28↓ [*written in brownish black ink*]

484.11–14   ↑*Unalterable* . . . ALWAYS.↓ [*written in brownish black ink lengthwise along the left margin of the page across portions of the two preceding entries*]

484.14   ALWAYS ['*always*' *underlined five times*]

485.1   ⟨26ᵗʰ⟩25ᵗʰ ['5' *written over* '6']

485.11   Miss . . . Dean. [*written in brownish black ink*]

485.12–13   ↑↑Dr.↓ Geo. T. . . . oculists↓ [*written in the available space to the right of* 'Miss . . . Dean.' (485.11); 'Dr.' *written above* 'Stevens,'; '*oculists*' *possibly added later*]

485.14   ↑Oculists↓ [*written above* 'Nun & Parsons']

486.1   ↑N. Y. H.↓

486.3   ⟨69⟩65. ['5' *written over* '9']

486.3   ⟨H. H.⟩F. J. Hall ['F.' *written over* 'H.' *and* 'J.' *written over* 'H.']

486.6–10   Frau . . . Com. [*written in brownish black ink*]

486.10   Inst. Com. [*the bottom three-fifths of the page is blank below this entry*]

486.13–487.2   ⟨Skinned Man.⟩↑—boyhood.↓ | ⟨Mate . . . Whistling⟩ ['Skinned Man.' *and* 'Mate . . . Whistling' *canceled by a single* 'X'; *the cancellation possibly intended to include* '—boyhood.']

487.3–4   ↑"Lying"↓ | ↑Duel.↓ [*written to the right of* 'Interviewer' *and* 'Whistling' (487.1–2) *respectively; possibly written*

later than 'Artemus . . . Christening.' *(487.5–6);* 'Duel.'
circled, then '"Lying"' *enclosed by a line joined at both
ends to the circle around* 'Duel.']

487.5–6   ⟨↑Artemus . . . Christening.↓⟩ [*written lengthwise in
the margin to the right of* '⟨Skinned . . . Duel.' (486.13–
487.4)]

488.5   shame⟨.⟩— [*the dash written over the period*]

488.9   humbug. [*followed by one blank left-hand page*]

488.10   ↑(May 22/89.↓

488.11   ↑to Livy,↓

489.4   ⟨[*four? words*]⟩ [*the bottom two-fifths of the page is blank
below these unrecovered words*]

489.11   Trinity,↑—↓

489.12   ⟨spectre,⟩ ↑thug,↓

489.14   ↑Hartford,↓

489.14–15   Sepulchre City | ⟨20⟩ [*two-thirds of the page is blank
below* 'Sepulchre City' *except for the number* '20' *which
is written and canceled in brownish black ink in the center
of the blank space*]

489.15–492.28   ⟨20⟩ . . . Killaloe. [*written in brownish black ink except
for the entries at 490.11–491.2 written in black pencil*]

489.16–493.21   You . . . drop. [*probably originally inscribed on right-
hand pages only; when the text of the right-hand page
* 'You . . . no' *(489.16–490.2) was run over to the next
right-hand page,* 'matter . . . N. Y.' *(490.2–12), the intervening left-hand page,* 'No. 6 . . . $25.' *(490.13–492.3),
was presumably blank; similarly when the text of the
right-hand page* 'Well . . . eyes.' *and* 'We . . . proprietors' *(492.3–21 and 492.29–33) was run over to the
next right-hand page,* '⟨of other . . . this.⟩' *and* 'June
. . . drop.' *(492.33–34 and 493.14–21), the intervening
left-hand page* 'We . . . challenges. =' *(493.1–13) was
presumably blank; in view of this pattern, it seems likely*

*that the left-hand page in the middle of this sequence, 'Ye
. . . Killaloe.' (492.22–28), was also inscribed after the
facing right-hand page (492.3–21 and 492.29–33) had
been begun]*

489.22   ⟨she⟩She ['S' *written over* 's']

490.3   ⟨place⟩ place ['place' *canceled and rewritten, apparently
                for clarity*]

490.12   N. Y. [*followed by about two lines of blank space at the
                bottom of the page*]

490.13–492.3   No. 6 . . . $25. [*written on a left-hand page; probably
                written later than at least part of the text of the facing
                right-hand page,* 'matter . . . N. Y.' *(490.2–12); see
                489.16–493.21*]

490.13   No. 6 [*possibly added later; written in the top margin of
                the page*]

491.12   4395⟨. P⟩& 6. ['&' *written over the period and wiped-out*
                'P']

491.19–492.3   4409 . . . $25. [*written lengthwise along the left side of
                the page across* 'No. 6 . . . mortgage.' *(490.13–491.2)*]

492.15   school at Killaloe. [*the flourish that follows may originally
                have ended the entry here or may be Clemens' indication
                that stanzas are missing at this point*]

492.17   ⟨[o]f [c]⟩uv coorse ['uv' *written over what looks like* 'of c']

492.22–28   Ye . . . Killaloe. [*written on a left-hand page, the bot-
                tom two-thirds of which is blank; probably written later
                than at least part of the text of the facing right-hand
                page, which includes* 'Well . . . eyes.' *(492.3–21) and*
                'We . . . proprietors' *(492.29–33); see 489.16–493.21*]

492.23   eca↑i↓rte

492.29–30   ⟨in . . . circumstances⟩ ↑with . . . wherever↓

492.32   ⟨two.⟩ ↑a dollar & a half.↓

492.33–34   We . . . proprietors ⟨of . . . this.⟩ ['proprietors' *ends*

	a right-hand page in the manuscript; Clemens probably intended to cancel the entire passage but neglected the portion on the earlier page; see 489.16–493.21 and 493.1–13]
493.1–13	We . . . challenges. = [*written on a left-hand page; probably written later than at least part of the text of the facing right-hand page, which includes* '⟨of . . . this.⟩' *(492.33–34) and* 'June . . . drop.' *(493.14–21);* '⟨of . . . this.⟩' *was probably canceled when* 'We . . . challenges. =' *was written; see 489.16–493.21]*
493.4	↑As soon . . . oprator↓ We ↑shall↓
493.6	↑(or 50, if preferred,)↓
493.7	⟨machine⟩machines ['es' *written over* 'e']
493.14–21	June 19 . . . drop. [*written in brownish black ink; a quarter of the page is blank below this passage*]
493.20–21	↑After . . . drop.↓ [*written diagonally across the preceding paragraph*]
493.22	↑**X**-1↓ [*written diagonally in the upper left corner of the page*]
494.3	ELSIE'S SLIPPER ['Elsie's slipper' *underlined twice*]
494.6	Theodore. [*followed by about two lines of blank space at the bottom of the page*]
496.7	another one [*the bottom quarter of the page is blank below this entry*]
496.10	↑(Jean refused.)↓
496.13	↑Ned Bunce, H. C. Robinson,↓
497.8	⁴/₁₀ [*possibly mended from* '⅓', '⅕', *or* '⅘']
497.9	↑or Dana . . . Case,↓
497.10	⟨$5⟩$4↑.50↓ ['4' *written over* '5'; '.50' *added*]
497.12	⟨$60,000⟩$45,000 ['45' *written over* '60']

497.15–17   ↑or $1 . . . the U.S.↓ [*written lengthwise on the page across the two preceding entries*]

497.18   ⟨$[-]5⟩ ↑$25↓

498.1–4   5:7 p. m., . . . J. W. P." [*written in brownish black ink; followed by one blank left-hand page*]

498.6–7   Chatto's . . . Co [*written in brownish black ink*]

498.8   ⟨53[-],432⟩538,432 ['8' *written over an unrecovered figure*]

498.9   ⟨kno[tt]s⟩knots ['ts' *written over what appears to be* 'tts']

499.1–500.4   July, 1889. . . . 4112 [*written in brownish black ink (except for the overwritten line at 499.8 written in black pencil) on a left-hand page, the bottom quarter of which is blank; apparently the page was bypassed, probably after the first three lines had been written, and then filled in a line at a time in the ensuing weeks*]

499.3   1.⟨[h]⟩32 ['3' *written over what looks like a canceled* 'h']

499.8   ⟨Write Col. Taylor⟩ [*written faintly in black pencil, presumably some time after the list beginning at 499.1 had been begun in ink; overwritten by* '26th . . . 4,374.' (499.9)]

499.11   ↑Sent to O.↓

500.2   ↑(Shut down 10 days.)↓

500.5–504.16   Send . . . Lewis. [*squeezed onto one page; order of inscription uncertain; the basic arrangement is of two columns:* 'Send . . . Twichell' (500.5–501.18) *and* '⟨⟨17[-]⟩174 . . . Lewis.' (501.19–504.16); *the lines* 'Charley . . . Twichell' (501.11–18), 'Mrs. Cleveland. . . . Herald' (503.1–4), *and* 'John T. Lewis.' (504.16) *were squeezed in around the earlier inscription wherever space could be found for them*]

500.8   ↑Ozias Pond↓ [*written in the available space to the right of* 'Pond' *and* 'Riley' (500.8–9); *boxed*]

500.16–17   ⟨Charley Clark⟩ | ⟨Lilly Warner⟩ [*separately canceled in brownish black ink*]

501.11–13   ↑Charley . . . Cabell↓ [*written in brownish black ink in the top margin of the page above* 'Send Yankee to—' (*500.5*)]

501.14–16   ↑Burdette. . . . Lewis.↓ [*written in brownish black ink to the right of* 'Nye' (*500.10*)]

501.17   ↑T. B. Aldrich.↓ [*written lengthwise on the page in brownish black ink to the right of* 'Howells . . . Whitmo' (*500.11–14*)]

501.18   ↑Twichell↓ [*written lengthwise on the page to the right of* 'Mrs. Aldrich . . . Century' (*501.4–8*)]

501.19   ⟨17[-]⟩174 ['4' *written over an unrecovered figure*]

502.2   204 ↑2ᵈ↓—

502.5   ⟨cyclopedia⟩Cyclopedia ['C' *written over* 'c']

503.1–4   ↑Mrs. Cleveland. . . . Herald↓ [*written to the right of* 'Mrs. Custer . . . Whitford' (*502.7–10*); 'Mrs. Cleveland. . . . Whitman' *in brownish black ink,* 'Sylvester . . . Herald' *in black pencil*]

503.5–504.7 292 . . . ⟨Char⟩ [*written in brownish black ink*]

503.5   ↑292 297↓ Ancient prices—Atlantic ↑Vol. 24↓ ['292' *interlined above* 'Ancient', '297' *above* 'prices', *and* 'Vol. 24' *above* 'Atlantic']

503.6   ⟨309.⟩ ↑310↓ Proofs ['310' *interlined without a caret above* 'Proofs']

504.1   ⟨320⟩321 ['1' *written over* '0']

504.9   Dana. [*written in brownish black ink*]

504.14   Clara Stan↑ch↓field

504.16   ↑John T. Lewis.↓ [*written lengthwise on the page in brownish black ink to the right of* '319 . . . law.' (*504.1–3*)]

504.17–506.16   For Century. . . . Abbey. [*written in brownish black ink*]

504.18   Begin ↑page 9,↓

505.7   Then . . . Chapter 27.) [*a line from this sentence to a caret placed before 'Then go to page 337' (505.1) indicates the final order of the excerpts Clemens wanted typed*]

505.11   ⟨1[-,-]oo⟩11,100—⟨11,[2]oo⟩11,100—   [*in the first '11,100' the second and third digits are written so heavily that the figures they cover are unreadable; in the second '11,100' the third digit may be written over '2'*]

505.12–13   Make . . . preface. [*a clipping from an English newspaper was pinned to the top of the page that begins here; see note 83*]

505.12   ⟨appendix⟩Appendix ['A' *written over* 'a']

506.16   the Abbey. [*the bottom quarter of the page is blank below this entry*]

506.16   (1200⟨o⟩ per hour) [*the parentheses may have been added later*]

507.1   ↑& matter measured↓ [*the intended position of this phrase is uncertain; interlined without a caret above* 'time to be taken &']

507.2   ↑Whitmore↓

507.5–6   The Gov. . . . Stedman. [*probably added later in space originally left blank between* 'Houghton.' *and* 'These to go']

507.10   ⟨n[---]⟩name ['ame' *written over unrecovered letters*]

507.22   it⟨[.]⟩, without delay. ['without delay.' *may have been added later and the comma written over a period*]

507.25   measured ['meas-' *ends one right-hand page and* 'ured' *begins the next; the intervening left-hand page is blank*]

508.4   room↑s↓

508.6   ↑supplying sorts,↓

508.7   two ↑to↓ tend

508.9–509.5   Presidents . . . mad. [*written on a left-hand page, pos-*
                   sibly later than at least part of 'All . . . paper.' (509.6–
                   17) *on the facing right-hand page; the bottom quarter of
                   the page is blank*]

509.18   ↑$30,000. cash.↓ [*written in the top margin of the page*]

509.21   ↑15 years↓

509.25   ⟨)⟩⟨morning [*the opening parenthesis and* 'm' *written
                   over the closing parenthesis*]

509.26   average⟨.⟩, [*the period mended to a comma; a line orig-
                   inally ending the entry here was disregarded when the
                   entry was continued*]

511.2   for 2 days. [*the bottom half of the page is blank below
                   this entry*]

511.3–15   2 . . . there. [*written on a right-hand page, the bottom
                   quarter of which is blank; a blank left-hand page follows*]

511.16   ↑Elmira↓ [*written in the top margin of the page above*
                   'Aug. 18']

512.2   about it? [*the entry may originally have ended here, near
                   the bottom of a right-hand page;* 'I suppose . . . trouble.'
                   (512.2–4) *is squeezed in below these words; and* 'How
                   many . . . Expenses!' (512.4–7) *is written on the follow-
                   ing, otherwise blank, left-hand page*]

512.8   S. E. Dawson . . . England. [*written in brownish black
                   ink*]

512.14–15   ↑& propose . . . 8 hours.↓

513.1   Erl-Königs [*the lines separating this from the preceding
                   entry and from the blank space that follows are heavily
                   traced over; the bottom fifth of the page is blank below
                   this entry*]

513.5   ⟨[to]⟩zu ['z' *written over what appears to be* 'to']

513.24–27   ↑Lily of . . . Jordan↓ [*written to the right of 'Lorelei. . . . Swing Low.' (513.12–14)*]

514.1   wollte/↑wurde↓

514.4   die↑se↓

514.5   gemacht. [*the bottom half of the page is blank below this entry*]

514.6–516.14 (Copy.) . . . Paid. [*written in brownish black ink; '(Copy.) . . . S L C' is written on four consecutive right-hand pages (the three intervening left-hand pages are blank); the direction 'over' is written below 'S L C' at the bottom of the fourth right-hand page, and '(Telegram.) . . . Paid.' (516.1–14) is on the verso of the leaf*]

515.5   here, but ['*here,' falls in the middle of a line, the last part of which is blank; the next line begins at the left margin with 'but'; the blank space, apparently without function, may indicate a pause in the inscription*]

516.11–12   understand. ⟨it.⟩ ⟨to be⟩ [*sequence of revision uncertain*]

516.18   daily. ↑& Sundays.↓

516.24   seats—7 [*the bottom quarter of the page is blank below this entry*]

517.7   ⟨⟨scho[-]⟩schon⟩ schon ['n' *written over an unrecovered letter; then the whole word canceled and rewritten, presumably for clarity*]

517.7   bemerkt. [*followed by about three lines of blank space at the bottom of the page*]

517.12   No, . . . idea. [*possibly added later*]

517.14   difference. [*two-thirds of the line following this word is blank but is boxed as though to reserve space for a short additional note*]

517.17   ⟨$[5]0⟩$100 ['100' *written over what appears to be* '50']

517.18   stock. [*followed at the bottom of a right-hand page by*

	the boxed instruction 'OVER'; 'Want . . . sales' *(517.19–518.5) is on the verso of the leaf*]
517.19	⟨$100⟩ ↑$2 on the $1000↓
517.25	⟨$250⟩$200 ['2' *rewritten*; 'o' *written over* '5']
518.2	⟨shall b⟩& ['shall' *canceled*; '&' *written over* 'b']
518.4	⟨[no]⟩*none* [*possibly originally* 'no'; 'one' *written over what appears to be a terminal* 'o', *and* 'none' *underlined*]
518.12	Criticism." [*followed by about three lines of blank space at the bottom of the page*]
518.13–14	⟨(85 or⟩ ↑(↓88 yr old/↑nearly 90 yrs. old—20 at Lundy's Lane↓) [*apparently originally* '(85 or 88 yr old)'; 'nearly . . . Lane' *interlined without a caret above* '88 . . . soldiers*'', presumably before* '(85 or' *was canceled and a new opening parenthesis was added before* '88']
518.15–16	⟨1790 or 95 . . . there.⟩1792↑)↓ ['or 95 . . . there.' *canceled*; '2' *written over* 'o' *of* '1790', *and the closing parenthesis written over* 'o' *of canceled* 'or']
518.17–18	"Good morning ⟨Major⟩ ↑Captain↓"
518.21–22	⟨both⟩	⟨(Lundy's . . . New Orleans)⟩ ↑Bonjour . . . (Waterloo!)↓ ['both' *canceled at the bottom of a page, and* '(Lundy's . . . Orleans)' *canceled at the top of the next page*; 'Bonjour . . . (Waterloo!)' *written in the margin above* '⟨(Lundy's . . . Orleans)⟩']
519.1–4	⟨Shirts . . . home. [*Clemens may have intended to fully cancel these items; the lines partially crossing them out may be of merely random lengths*]
519.2	Finlay. ↑Laffan.↓ ↑& Lotos.↓ ['Laffan.' *written below* 'Finlay.' *and partially boxed*; '& Lotos.' *written in brownish black ink below* 'Laffan.']
519.5	⟨6. . . . Hamersley.⟩ [*canceled in brownish black ink*]
519.8	12. Phonograph. [*the bottom third of the page is blank below this entry*]

519.16	⟨comment⟨s⟩⟩comments ['s' *of* 'comments' *canceled, then rewritten*]
519.18	⟨check⟩ checkered ['check' *awkwardly written; probably abandoned as a false start and rewritten to insure legibility*]
520.4	↑1↓ [*partially circled*]
520.5	We ↑Americans↓
520.6	Hereditary Privilege ['h' *of* 'hereditary' *underlined three times*]
520.9–10	⟨Better . . . on.⟩ [*many lines scrawled across the hinge of the notebook between this canceled final sentence of the paragraph numbered '1' and the paragraph numbered '2' on the facing right-hand page,* 'Better . . . nation' *(521.2–7), may have been intended simply to underscore the connection between the passages, or they may indicate Clemens' intention to replace the canceled sentence with the second paragraph*]
520.11	see him. [*followed by about two lines of blank space at the bottom of the page*]
520.12	↑Silver screw bottle↓ [*written in the top margin of the page above* '⟨st⟩Strong & show'; *circled*]
521.1–7	↑2↓	Better . . . nation. [*see* 520.9–10]
521.2	⟨D[e]ity⟩deity ['d' *written over* 'D'; 'e' *written over what was probably a badly written* 'e']
521.5	⟨success of⟩successor ['or' *added to* 'success' *and written over* 'of']
521.8	↑2↓
521.14	between the⟩ [*the bottom half of the page is blank below these words*]
521.20	Fulfilled . . . 1889. [*written lengthwise on the page in brownish black ink across the preceding paragraph*]
521.27	Fulfilled . . . 1889. [*written lengthwise on the page in brownish black ink across the preceding paragraph*]

522.1   Als ich [*follows a blank left-hand page*]

522.12   calendar. [*the bottom three-fifths of the page is blank below this word*]

522.13   Fellowcraft . . . Oct. 16. ↑Wednesday.↓ ['Fellowcraft . . . Oct. 16.' *written and circled in brownish black ink;* 'Wednesday.' *added in black pencil within the encircling line*]

523.3–4   idea ↑(↓of buying . . . of '92,↑)↓

523.10   ↑Oct. '89. Scotland.↓

525.1–3   Condition. . . . 27 [*written in brownish black ink*]

525.9–10   ↑But . . . people.↓

525.18   ⟨un[-]⟩unmagnanimous ['m' *written over an unrecovered letter*]

526.5   book⟨.⟩; [*the period mended to a semicolon*]

527.6–9   *Nov.* . . . hereafter. [*written in brownish black ink*]

527.12   ↑(future stock)↓

529.1   ↑– Hand Composition↓

529.2–5   Grav . . . Matrix [*overwritten by an inverted V drawn heavily through all four words, probably to connect but possibly to cancel them; see note 146*]

529.9–11   ↑— possible . . . Paige↓ [*written lengthwise on the page to the right of '– Hand . . . Rogers' (529.1–6); probably written later than '95 . . . 439' (529.12–17)*]

529.12–17   95 . . . 439 [*written to the right of '– Hand . . . Rogers' (529.1–6) and '— possible . . . Paige' (529.9–11)*]

530.2   ⟨1[6]⟩13 ['3' *written over what looks like '6'*]

530.3   ⟨[--]⟩⟨[7]⟩ ↑13↓ [*what looks like '7' written over one or more smudged numbers, which may in turn be written over others*]

530.4–6   week [¶] H. 95 . . . Rogers. [*the paragraph ending 'week'*
                   is at the bottom of a left-hand page; 'H. 95 . . . Rogers.'
                   follows '⟨61⟩63 . . . 20)' (530.7–531.9) at the bottom of
                   the facing right-hand page; a line across the notebook's
                   hinge connects 'week' and 'H. 95', indicating the intended
                   sequence]

530.7–12   ↑⟨61⟩63 . . . ⟨4[9]7⟩⟨427⟩441↓ | ↑⟨36 . . . 252⟩↓
                   ['⟨61⟩63 . . . day' *is written in the top margin of the*
                   page above 'Fellow-craft' (530.13); '7' and '⟨4[9]7⟩⟨427⟩
                   441' *extend downward to the left of 'Fellow-craft';*
                   '⟨36 . . . 252⟩' *is written in the margin to the right of*
                   'Fellow-craft . . . Nov. 16.']

530.7   ⟨61⟩63 ['3' *written over* '1']

530.9   ⟨4[9]7⟩⟨427⟩441 ['2' *written over what appears to be*
                   '9'; '41' *written over* '27']

530.13–14   Fellow-craft . . . 16. [*written in brownish black ink*]

530.15   Dec. ⟨7,⟩ ↑14↓

530.16   ↑Col. . . . Supt.↓

531.1   Miss . . . (Dean). [*written in brownish black ink*]

531.10–11   ↑Roberts Bros. Boston.↓

532.5   ⟨McEw[an]⟩McEwen ['en' *written over what may be*
                   'an']

533.5   Invite gov't printer[⟨.⟩]—thro' [*the dash may be written*
                   over a period; it is unclear whether a line below 'Invite
                   gov't printer' *was intended for emphasis or to conclude*
                   the entry at 'printer[.]'; the line was left standing when
                   the entry was continued]

533.7   2h 10m. [*the bottom fifth of the page is blank below this*
                   entry]

533.8–534.3   Proposition . . . carriage to [*written in brownish black*
                   ink]

533.12   anything. [*the bottom half of the page is blank below*
                   this entry]

533.13–534.2   Telephoned . . . none. [*written on the recto of a leaf that was torn out and may at some time have been removed from the notebook; the verso is blank*]

533.13–14   ⟨At . . . again;⟩ ↑Tele at 7.30↓

533.15   then ↑**X**↓ why ['**X**' *interlined without a caret above* 'then why']

533.16–17   ↑at 7.40 . . . 8.30.**X**↓

533.17–19   9.30; Telephoned . . . ago." ['Telephoned . . . ago.'' *written with a paragraph indentation below* 'bill.' (533.23); *a line connecting* 'Telephoned' *with a caret following* '9.30;' *indicates the intended placement*]

533.19–20   ⟨at . . . here.⟩ ↑Just . . . arrived.↓

534.3   ⟨6.[2]o⟩6.30 ['3' *written over what looks like* '2']

534.11   ↑7 hours per day↓

534.11–12   ↑50^c daily paper↓ [*interlined without a caret above* '$16.80 per day']

534.13   ⟨$5,[5-]o⟩$6,132 (6,132) ['6 132' *written over a partially illegible number; then* '(6,132)' *added, presumably for clarity*]

534.14   ↑say↓ $2.00

534.23   ⟨a⟩ ↑the ⟨sole⟩exclusive↓ right

534.23   MANUFACTURE ['manufacture' *underlined twice*]

534.24   ↑the further . . . right↓

535.9   ↑& sold↓

535.14–16   ⟨⟨May . . . but⟩ May . . . but . . . people.⟩ ['May . . . but' *canceled, then apparently restored with the instruction* 'STET.'; 'STET.' *may possibly have been intended to restore the entire paragraph, which is canceled with a large* X]

535.15–16   ⟨a slightly . . . than⟩ ↑as↓ cheap ↑a↓ rate ↑as to↓ [*originally* 'a slightly cheaper rate than'; 'a slightly' *canceled;*

'as' *interlined;* 'er' *of* 'cheaper' *canceled;* 'a' *interlined;*
'than' *canceled;* 'as to' *interlined*]

535.17   ↑as we say,↓

535.27   to it. [*the bottom two-fifths of the page is blank below
          this entry*]

536.1   ⟨his⟩their ['t' *added to* 'his' *and* 'eir' *written over* 'is']

536.2–3   ↑Both . . . anyway↓

536.6   Chatto & Windus. [*the bottom fifth of the page is blank
          below this entry*]

536.7–537.12   Hartford . . . $40. [*written in brownish black ink except
               for the entry at* 536.23 *written in black pencil*]

536.23   West Point ⟨Dec.⟩ ↑Jan↓ 11 [*written in black pencil*]

536.24   ⟨2⟩31 ['3' *written over* '2'; *possibly originally* '21']

537.16   ↑New England road.↓

537.18   ⟨Adelini⟩Adelina [*probably* 'a' *written over* 'i', *but pos-
          sibly* 'i' *written over* 'a']

538.2   ⟨advances⟩advantages ['tages' *written over* 'ces']

538.11–12   race↑.↓⟨—& . . . reward!⟩ ['—& . . . reward!' *heavily
            canceled*]

538.13   His aristocratic ['h' *of* 'his' *underlined three times*]

538.17   LANG . . . KURZ ['lang' *and* 'kurz' *underlined twice*]

538.19   GUT.— ['gut' *underlined twice; the period may have been
          canceled*]

539.1–2   BREI | VIELE ['Brei' *and* 'Viele' *underlined twice*]

539.3   ⟨ALS GUT⟩als gut ['als gut' *underlined twice; then the
          underlines apparently canceled*]

539.4–5   Title: | M o n a r c h y [*printed*]

539.11   ↑Gardiner's Elixir of↓

539.15   resting. [*the bottom third of the page is blank below this
          entry*]

539.17   ⟨a⟩ republiclican [*possibly originally 'a republic can'; 'li'*
                may have been added between 'republic' and 'can', pos-
                sibly when 'a' was canceled]

539.18   ↑liberty,↓

540.16   ↑Feb. 1890.↓ [*written in the top margin of the page*]

541.5   figures. [*the bottom quarter of the page is blank below*
                this entry]

541 *illustration*   [*illustration*] Rolfe's . . . 20,000 [*written in brownish*
−542.8   *black ink*]

541.16   ↑for Elsie Leslie.↓

542.8   20,000 [*the bottom third of the page is blank below this*
                entry]

542.9–545.12   Had . . . täglich. [*written on right-hand pages only, ex-*
                cept for entries at 545.1–5 written on a left-hand page]

542.15–16   permanent, ⟨[h]e cannot [co]⟩↑—↓ [*the dash interlined*
                below what appears to be canceled 'he']

543.1   B. ['B.' *underlined twice*]

543.4   ⟨his⟩ ↑Frohman's↓

543.7   (THIS . . . DO.) ['This is what I dearly want to do.' *under-*
                lined twice]

544.4   ⟨merit⟩Merit ['M' *written over* 'm']

544.4–5   ⟨& ⟨gol⟩god⟩ & ⟨godliness⟩Godliness ['d' *written over*
                'l'; 'G' *written over* 'g']

545.1–5   Can . . . damages? [*written on a left-hand page opposite*
                'me. I should . . . suit.' (544.1–9) *on the facing page;*
                since surrounding leaves are inscribed on right-hand pages
                only, it is likely that Clemens added these entries later
                than at least some of the entries on the facing page; the
                bottom third of the page is blank below 'damages?']

545.6   ↑täglich↓

546.9–10   ↑Optician↓ | ⟨↑Dʳ↓⟩

549.5	↑till↓
549.8	⟨[1]o⟩20 ['2' *may be written over* '1']
549.9	⟨Sck⟩ ↑Agt,↓
549.11–12	⟨10,000⟩20,000 . . . ⟨20,000⟩40,000 . . . ⟨30,000⟩60,000 . . . ⟨50,000⟩100,000 ['2' *written over* '1', '4' *over* '2', '6' *over* '3', *and* '10' *over* '5' *or possibly over* '15']
550.1	⟨33⅓⟩40 pc. ['40' *written over* '33'; 'pc.' *written over* '⅓']
550.2	6 m⟨.⟩—the [*the period mended to a dash; a line originally ending the entry at* '6 m.' *was disregarded when the entry was continued*]
550.5–13	3 Can't . . . ¼ h. [*probably the table was originally written without either the left-hand column of numbers or the line across the page above* '1. . . . ¼'"; *it appears likely that* '1.' *and* '2.' *were the first numbers entered in the left-hand column after the table was otherwise complete, that the preceding lines (mistakenly beginning with the second) were then numbered* '3.' *through* '8', *that the first line was then numbered* '3' *and the subsequent lines were renumbered* '4.' *through* '9', *and that the line was then drawn across the page to emphasize where the numbering system begins*]
550.6–10	⟨3.⟩4. . . . ⟨4.⟩5. . . . ⟨5.⟩6 . . . ⟨6.⟩7. . . . ⟨7.⟩8. ['4' *written over* '3', '5' *over* '4', '6' *over* '5.', '7' *over* '6', *and* '8' *over* '7'; *the periods left standing*]
550.11	⟨13,000⟩⟨14,000⟩28,000 ['4' *written over* '3', *then* '28' *written over* '14']
550.13	⟨5,000⟩2,000 ['2' *written over* '5']
550.16	Proof . . . REVISED . . . ↑or 3 times↓ ['revised' *underlined twice; the whole sentence underlined once; the single and double underlines overlap below* 'revised' *in such a way that it seems unlikely that triple underlining was intended for that word*]
550.18–24	⟨the time . . . proof, ⟨he⟩⟩ ⟨the lines . . . non-

existent⟩ the time . . . proof, he has then ['the time
. . . proof, he' *canceled;* 'the lines . . . non-existent'
written and canceled; 'the time . . . proof, he' *restored
with the instructions* 'stet' *written in the margin near the
beginning and* 'STET' *written across the end of the canceled passage;* 'he' *following* 'proof,' *canceled again, probably when the entry was continued with* 'he has then']

550.25   6,000⟨.⟩; [*the period mended to a semicolon*]

550.28   ↑Both . . . ⟨[men—]⟩apprentices.↓

550.30–551.2   watch. ↑Ignore . . . doubled.↓ . . . returned.⟩ [*apparently the bottom three-fifths of the page below* 'watch.'
was originally left blank; 'Ignore . . . doubled.' *is
squeezed into the narrow space between* 'watch.' *and the
line below* 'watch.' *that ends the entry there, as though to
leave the remainder of the page blank;* '⟨3¼⟩ All . . . returned.' *is written and canceled at the bottom of the
page;* 'It . . . capital', *written a short distance above*
'⟨⟨3¼⟩ All . . . returned.⟩', *was probably added when
that sentence was canceled; about two-fifths of the page
is now blank between* 'doubled.' *and* 'It is all', *and about
two lines of blank space stand between* 'capital' *and*
'⟨⟨3¼⟩ All']

551.1   ⟨3¼⟩ ↑All↓ of ⟨their⟩ ⟨↑our↓⟩ ↑their↓ stock

551.10   Turnips [*the bottom fifth of the page is blank below this
entry*]

552.2   come. [*the bottom third of the page is blank below this
entry*]

552.5   sogleich. [*Clemens drew a hand pointing across the hinge
of the notebook from* 'sogleich.' *on a left-hand page to*
'And . . . out.' (552.13–14) *on the facing page; he drew
an arrow pointing across the hinge from* 'sogleich.' *to*
'Oder . . . Conditions.' (553.1), *also on the facing page;
see notes 210 and 216*]

552.12   N. H. Ave. [*the bottom third of the page is blank below
this entry*]

553.4	↑⅕ oder ⅖ hier.↓
553.12	↑May 19↓
553.14	⟨24⟩25 ['5' *written over* '4']
553.18–19	↑52	$3,220 a year.↓ ['$3,220 a year' *is written following* '52' *on the same line because space is lacking on the next line below the rule*]
554.1	⟨a⟩2 page↑s↓
554.3–4	↑in 7 hours↓
554.4	would cost ['would' *is at the bottom of a left-hand page and* 'cost' *is at the top of the next surviving right-hand page; a leaf which originally stood between these pages has been torn out and is missing; the leaf beginning* 'cost', *which is the surviving conjugate half of the missing leaf, remains in the notebook but is not attached to it*]
554.4	⟨$1[4]⟩$12 ['2' *written over what looks like* '4']
554.5	⟨$7-wo⟩$7,000-worth [*the comma and the zeros written over* '-wo']
554.6	⟨$20⟩$18 ['18' *written over* '20']
555.3	⟨guide⟩ ↑courier↓ ↑£5 a day↓ ['£5 a day' *interlined without a caret above* 'Pouchere']
555.6	Typothetæ [*ligature indicated by a line above* 'ae']
555.10–12	Philip . . . Whittall. [*each of these three names is followed by about one line of blank space, as though addresses were to be supplied*]
555.13–15	Edw. Bettle, Jr. ↑2007 . . . Walnut↓ [*about two lines of space originally left blank below* 'Edw. Bettle, Jr.'; '2007 . . . Walnut' *written in part of that space*]
555.17	Mary McMurtry [*followed by about one line of blank space*]
556.6	day? [*the bottom third of the page is blank below this entry*]

556.9   Eine Grösse [*a faint line below 'Eine' may have been in-*
               tended to emphasize that word]

556.9   ⟨millione⟩Millione↑n↓ ['M' *written over* 'm']

556.10   Millionen [*originally* 'Million'; 'en' *added before the fol-*
               lowing word was written]

556.12   sagt; [*possibly originally* 'sagt.'; *if so, the comma may*
               have been intended either to cancel the period or to mend
               it to a semicolon]

557.8   (Fuller's friend) ↑Delamater↓

557.10   ⟨monatlick.⟩monatlich. ['h.' *written over* 'k.']

557.13   *Die . . . geriethen.* [*boxed*]

557.13   ⟨gereethen⟩geriethen ['i' *written between* 'e' *and* 'e',
               probably intended to replace the first; see Doubtful
               Readings]

558.2–23   Actien-Gesellschafft . . . Handel. [*originally the bottom*
               four-fifths of a left-hand page was left blank below 'revo-
               lutions.' (558.1); 'Actien-Gesellschafft . . . sei.' (558.2–
               14) *was written on the facing right-hand page, filling it; at*
               some time, '300,000.00' (558.15) *was written faintly in the*
               blank space below 'revolutions.'; 'Oder . . . Handel.' *was*
               written lengthwise in the blank space, filling it and cover-
               ing '300,000.00']

558.3 $⟨1[-],000,000⟩⟨1[5],000,000⟩ ↑$14,0,00⟨0⟩↓ [*appar-*
               ently originally '$1[-],000,000'; *the unrecovered second*
               digit was overwritten by what looks like '5' *and possibly*
               by other numbers as well; '1[5],000,000' *was canceled, the*
               dollar sign was left standing, and '$140,000' *was interlined*
               above the cancellation; probably the comma after '4' *was*
               added when the terminal 'o' *was canceled; a mark above*
               the superfluous comma may have been intended either
               to cancel the comma or to join the zeros on either side
               of it]

558.6   ⟨1[3]0,000⟩⟨1[7]0,000⟩140,000 [*order of revision uncer-*
               tain; the second digit overwritten several times; '4' *written*

heavily over what had apparently been '7' and '3' and possibly other numbers as well]

558.7   ⟨1[-]0,000⟩⟨180,000⟩ ⟨↑1[-]0,↓000⟩ ↑150,000↓ ['18' *written over '1' and an unrecovered digit, which may in turn have been written over something else; '180,' canceled and '1[-]0,' interlined above it, presumably to form a six-digit number in combination with the three zeros left standing on the line; '1[-]0,' and '000' canceled and '150,000' interlined*]

558.9   [--],000/↑10,000↓ [*the first two digits overwritten so heavily as to be illegible, presumably in an attempt to alter them; '10,000' interlined above '[--],000'*]

558.13   ⟨vollmacht⟩Vollmacht ['V' *written over 'v'*]

558.19   ⟨anstifften⟩angestifft ['an-' *written at the end of a line; 'stifften' written at the beginning of the next line, then canceled, and 'gestifft' written following the cancellation*]

559.1   ↑¼ inter⟨set⟩↓ [*written in the top margin of the page above '$2,000,000 zum'*]

559.10   15th & K. [*the bottom fifth of the page is blank below this entry*]

559.11   ⟨200,000 shs.⟩ [*written in purple pencil; canceled in black pencil*]

559.15   ⟨[$]⟩ 2,000 [*what appears to be a dollar sign canceled*]

560.8   100 ['100' *underlined twice*]

561.1   ↑& Carnegie↓

561.11–13 ⟨specifications now existing.⟩ ⟨↑the . . . made?↓⟩ ↑existing . . . 100).↓

562.4   ↑Palenville.↓ [*written in the top margin of the page and boxed*]

562.5   ⟨9.50⟩9.40 ['4' *written over '5'*]

562.6   ⟨1.37⟩1.40 ['40' *written over '37'*]

562.13   Jumping Frog. [*about three lines of blank space follow these words*]

563.5   ⟨87½ᶜ⟩ ↑$1.15↓

563.18   ↑This . . . *solid.*↓

563.21 $16.50⟨.⟩ of it ['o' *of* 'of' *written over the period*]

564.1–12   Leave . . . play. [*written in brownish black ink, except for the addition at 564.5–6 written in black pencil*]

564.1–4   Leave . . . 8.52 [*boxed*]

564.1   ⟨4.0[4]⟩4.05 ['5' *written over what may be* '4']

564.5–6   ↑Ask . . . 5000.↓ [*written in black pencil*]

564.11   POST JONES ['post Jones' *underlined twice*]

564.13–565.12   ⟨280 . . . 8,935 [*written at random on a left-hand page, the bottom fifth of which is blank; following this page, one leaf has been torn out; the next surviving right-hand page is blank*]

565.19–20   ↑Also . . . terms.↓

566.1–568.16   (Copy . . . boy⟩ [*written in brownish black ink, except for the entries at 567.12, 568.6, and 568.8–9 and the cancellation at 568.15 in black pencil*]

566.23   with you [*one leaf has been torn out following the page that ends here; the entry continues on the next surviving leaf*]

567.12   *X*-1. Remark [*written in black pencil at the top of an otherwise blank page; followed by five blank pages*]

567.13   ↑Fred.↓

567.19   ⟨4680⟩4584 ['584' *written over* '680']

568.6   Book . . . agent. [*written in black pencil*]

568.7   Buffalo [*the bottom half of the page is blank below this word*]

568.8–12   Sept . . . case. [*written at the top of an otherwise blank page*]

568.8–9   ↑Sept 30↓ . . . B'way. [*written in black pencil*]

568.15   ⟨Mrs. Custer⟩ [*written in brownish black ink; canceled in black pencil*]

568.17–569.2   ↑J. S. Quin . . . Falls.↓ [*written to the right of* 'Gen. Sherman . . . boy⟩' (568.13–16)]

569.3   TALK ['talk' *underlined twice*]

569.3   ↑(quadruple time)↓ [*interlined above* 'hands down' *with a line to* 'TALK' *indicating placement*]

569.3–4   Bon (right) APARTE ['parte' *underlined twice*]

569.4   TALK ↑(2)↓['talk' *underlined twice;* '2' *interlined within an irregular shape that serves as caret, parentheses, and enclosing circle*]

569.4   e-CARTE ['carte' *underlined twice*]

569.5–6   ⟨M. H. Anot, [E]⟩ . . . Buf. [*written in brownish black ink*]

569.5   ⟨M. H. Anot, [E]⟩ ↑M. H.↓ Arnot, Elmira. ['Arnot' *mis-written and partly corrected, then* 'M. H. Anot' *canceled;* 'Arnot' *written over a partially completed* 'E'; 'M. H.' *interlined*]

569.7   ⟨Dʳ⟩ [*the bottom half of the page is blank below this entry*]

569.8–570.4   3 . . . Library). [*written on the recto of the back flyleaf*]

569.8–21   3 . . . 28 [*written in the upper right part of the page and partially obscured when* '⟨[----]⟩ . . . Library).' (569.22–570.4) *was written in the same space;* '26' (569.9) *was probably canceled to avoid confusion because* 'Six . . . '28/89.' (569.23) *is written so that* '26' *appears immediately after* 'royalties' *and may have looked like part of the sentence; since* '⟨[----]⟩ . . . Library).' *is written in ink, while* '26' *is canceled in pencil, it is likely that the cancellation was made when* 'one hundred.' (570.1) *was canceled, also in pencil*]

569.22–570.4   ⟨[----]⟩ . . . Library). [*written in brownish black ink, except for the revision at 570.1 in black pencil*]

569.22   ↑⟨[- - - -]⟩ . . . 6↓

569.26   ⟨17th⟩12th ['2' *written over* '7']

570.1   ⟨one hundred.⟩ ↑50↓ ['one hundred.' *written in brownish
                black ink; revised in black pencil*]

570.4   Library). [*the bottom three-fifths of the page is blank
                below this entry*]

Notebook 30

Emendations and Doubtful Readings

	MTP READING	MS READING
578.12	MacKenzie	[*possibly* 'Mackenzie']
579.12	crowd,	[*possibly* 'crowd;']
580.17	Pinney	[*possibly* 'Pinny']
586.18	cot bed	[*possibly* 'cotbed' *or* 'cot-bed']
586.19	TO-DAY	[*possibly* 'TODAY']
586.21	Reutz	[*possibly* 'Rentz']
587.3	to-morrow	[*possibly* 'tomorrow']
*587.15	against us, possibly.	[*possibly* 'against us, possibly.' *or* 'AGAINST US, POSSIBLY.']
*588.4	⟨1[0]⟩14.	[*possibly* '⟨13⟩14.']
*589.10	**X**-2	[*possibly* '**X**2']
*589.19	whole	[*possibly* 'whole']
589.20	second-hand	second-|hand
*589.23	back in	['back' *possibly alternative to* 'in']
591.10	One	[*possibly* 'Our']
*591.23	⟨131,000⟩	[',ooo' *uncanceled*]
*592.4	⟨ems per hour⟩	[*overwritten ditto marks below preceding* 'ems per hour']
594.12	[&] royal	[*possibly* 'a royal']
*595.2	⟨[9]¹⁄₂₀⟩ ¹⁄₂₀	[*possibly* '⟨⁶⁄₂₀⟩ ¹⁄₂₀']

596.5	station	[*possibly* 'Station']
596.10	half dozenth	['half | dozenth'; *possibly* 'half-|dozenth']
*600.8–9	¼ down & ⟨ . . . ⟩in 6, & the rest in 12 mos.	[*possibly* '¼ down & ⟨ . . . ⟩the rest in in 6, & 12 mos.']
*600.9	12 mos.,	[*possibly* '12 mos.;']
601.10	wages.—	[*possibly* 'wages,—']
*602.5	(Copy).—in substance	[*possibly* '(Copy)⟨.⟩—in substance']
*606.8	securing impressing.	[*possibly* 'securing, impressing.']
607.8	approached,	[*possibly* 'approached.']
*608.10	[4.]56	[*page torn*]
608.21	Yarn	[*ditto marks below* 'Yarn' *at* 608.19]
612.7	cheap Huck	[*possibly* 'Cheap Huck']
613.4	And both	[*possibly* 'And both,']
615.13	out-go	[*possibly* 'outgo']
616.5	Expense	[*possibly* 'expense']
616.20	$32,000,	[*possibly* '$32,000.']
617.5	an immense mistake	[*possibly* '*an immense mistake*']
618.7	LaNeaugan	[*possibly* 'La Neaugan']
619.5	gunflints	[*possibly* 'gun flints' *or* 'gun-flints']
619.13	breast pocket	[*possibly* 'breast-pocket' *or* 'breastpocket']
621.9	Tappan	[*possibly* 'Teppan']
621.11	Feather-duster	Feather-|duster

622.1	in Havre	['Havre' *replaces ditto marks below preceding* 'Havre']
622.12	both or	[*possibly* 'both ar']
622.12	Mrs. S.'s	[*possibly* 'Mrs. S.',']
623.23	percent	[*possibly* 'per cent']
627.2	⟨Spit f[ire]⟩	[*possibly* 'Spitf[ire]']
*627.2–3	"Hellfire", aged 58,	"Hellfire" aged 58,,
630.1	church	[*possibly* 'Church']
630.21	plain-spoken	plain-|spoken
631.10	overcoat	[*possibly* 'over-coat']
631.11	servant girl	[*possibly* 'servant-girl']
631.15	some one's	[*possibly* 'someone's']
632.5	$1,000,⟨[o]oo⟩	[*possibly* '$1,000,⟨800⟩']
635.7	scrap-book	scrap-|book
637.9	watermelons	[*possibly* 'water-melons' *or* 'water melons']
639.4	overcoats	over-|coats
641.4	[Sl]	[*possibly* '86']
641.21	All-Knowing	[*possibly* 'All-knowing']
642.9	sea-boat	sea-|boat
643.11	foot-rope	foot-|rope
644.16	Sir	[*possibly* 'Sis']
647.3	non	[*ditto marks below preceding* 'non']

Details of Inscription

[Entries are in black pencil unless otherwise noted]

575.1–576.4	Send . . . failure.⟩	[*written on the verso of the front flyleaf*]

575.4–5   ↑John . . . E. D.↓ [*written in brownish black ink across the entry at 575.1–2 ('Send . . . Patrick.')*]

576.3   ⟨¹⁹/₂₀⟩⁹/₂₀ ['1' *canceled*]

576.5   ⟨5[000?]⟩ ↑12,000↓

577.3–4   ↑F. J. Hall, . . . 32ᵈ.↓ [*written lengthwise on the page across the six preceding paragraphs*]

577.6–10   Geo. . . . (Schweine) [*bracketed in the margin*]

577.7   ⟨National⟩ ↑American↓

577.10   (Schw↑e↓ine)

577.11–15   Geo. E. Spencer . . . Mail. [*written in brownish black ink*]

578.6   ↑(Paige)↓

578.10–15   Andrew . . . Bankers. [*written in brownish black ink*]

578.13   ↑Bismarck Dak.↓ [*squeezed into the left margin of the page beside 'Andrew Mellon,' (578.10), with a short line below 'Dak.' apparently pointing toward 'MacKenzie' (578.12)*]

578.14–15   ↑Thos. . . . Bankers.↓ [*written lengthwise in the left margin of the page beside 'Bohunkus. . . . MacKenzie' (578.9–12)*]

578.20   months. [*one fifth of the page is blank below this entry*]

579.1–5   P. . . . ⁴/₁₀. [*boxed on three sides*]

579.7   No ¼ gross. [*heavily underlined*]

580.1 $600,000,000. [*the bottom half of the page is blank below this entry*]

580.4   ⟨last⟩ ↑first↓

580.8   ⟨Bashaw⟩ ↑Begum↓

580.8–9   from ⟨Hong *Kong*,⟩Hong *Kong*,/↑Canton,↓ ['Hong *Kong*,' *canceled, then restored with the instruction* 'Stet.'; 'Canton,' *interlined without a caret above* 'from Hong']

580.11   **X**-1 [*circled*]

581.1   Conf. Agnostic [*a quarter of the page is blank below this entry*]

581.14–582.6   ['I] W . . . The C$^{s.}$ [*written in brownish black ink*]

581.15   Bryn Mawr [*the bottom quarter of the leaf has been torn out following these words on the recto and 'Phila' (582.10) on the verso*]

581.16   ⟨R. I.⟩ ↑Tramp Ab.↓ = Miss.

582.6   ↑have↓ miss↑ed↓

583.7   Kitson. [*the bottom half of the page is blank below this entry*]

584.5   ⟨s[ein]⟩sind ['ind' *written over what appears to be* 'ein']

584.8   Or ↑of↓ my proceeds

585.1   Hause. [*a quarter of the page is blank below this entry*]

585.2–586.13   ⅙ . . . cost. [*written on two facing pages; Clemens numbered the right-hand page '1' and the left-hand page, which begins at 'P. Comp.' (585.22), '2'; at the bottom of the right-hand page he drew a hand pointing left and upward along a line drawn across the hinge onto the left-hand page; the order of the printed text follows the apparent instructions of this drawing and of Clemens' page numbers*]

585.6   ⟨5[0,]⟩540,000 ['4' *written over what appears to be* '0,']

585.12   ⟨1725⟩1525 ['5' *written over* '7']

585.13   ⟨2[1]30⟩1830 ['1' *written over* '2'; '8' *written over what appears to be* '1']

586.10   ⟨20,8050⟩208↑,↓050 [*the original comma canceled and a comma added following* '8']

586.14   Ask [*preceded by one blank page*]

586.19   TO-DAY ['to-day' *underlined twice*]

586.25   Boy's Town" [*a quarter of the page is blank below this entry*]

587.8   ↑Hamilton Aïdé↓ [*written in the margin beside 'White-hall | London' (587.6–7)*]

587.15   against us, possibly. [*Clemens may have drawn one or both of two lines below these words for emphasis rather than simply to separate this from the following entry; see Doubtful Readings*]

588.3–7   ↑10↓ 10. . . . ↑$85↓ . . . ↑25↓ . . . ↑21↓ [*the added figures are written over lines that may have indicated blanks to be filled*]

588.4   ⟨1[0]⟩14. ['4' *written over what may be* 'o'; *see Doubtful Readings*]

588.11   ⟨[3 -]⟩8 [*what appears to be* '3' *canceled;* '8' *written over an unrecovered number*]

588.17   Perfect Wednesday ↑or Thursday.↓ Oct. ['or Thursday.' *interlined without a caret above* 'Wednesday']

589.1   ↑**X**1↓

589.7   This ↑noble↓ sacrifice

589.9   Write . . . Pauper [*preceded and followed by about three lines of blank space*]

589.10   ↑**X**-2↓

589.14   perfectly true. [*a fifth of the page is blank below this entry*]

589.19   man. ⟨↑[at]↓⟩ ⟨Paid⟩ ⟨↑Bt the whole State for↓⟩ Paid $40 [*originally* 'man. Paid $40'; 'Paid' *canceled;* 'Bt . . . for' *interlined, then canceled, and* 'Paid' *restored with the instruction* 'stet'; *what appears to be* 'at' *interlined and canceled below* 'Bt . . . for'; *it is unclear which is the earlier interlineation; see Doubtful Readings*]

589.20   ⟨army⟩ [*canceled in brownish black ink*]

589.23   ↑chin driven ↑back↓ in between shoulders↓ [*crowded into*

the top margin of the page; 'back' interlined without a
caret above 'driven in', possibly as an alternative to 'in']

590.1–2 ⟨↑or any other Bey↓⟩

590.10 any ⟨r[--]⟩reason ['ea' written over two unrecovered
letters]

590.19 character. [a third of the page is blank below this entry]

591.2 ⟨Into . . . nonp.⟩Into . . . nonp. ['Into . . . nonp.'
canceled, then restored with the instructions 'STET'
written lengthwise in the margin beside the entry and
'.stet.' written below the entry]

591.18–20 ↑57 . . . 52↓ [written in the top margin of the page;
'31' written to the right of '57' because space was lacking
below '26']

591.23 ⟨1[24],000⟩⟨13[2],000⟩⟨131,000⟩ ↑131,000↓ [order of
revision unclear; '3' written over what may be '2'; '1' written over what may be both '4' and '2', one of which apparently written over the other; '131' canceled and '131,000'
interlined, probably for clarity; ',000' of the original number inadvertently left standing; emended]

592.1 Ask . . . Hutchins [heavily boxed]

592.2 Forgot about Batterson. [boxed]

592.3 Forgot . . . brass. [boxed on three sides]

592.4–5 2,550 ⟨ems per hour⟩ ↑per hour.↓↑saves 2 men's wages.↓
[originally '2,550' followed by ditto marks below the preceding 'ems per hour'; 'saves 2 men's wages.' written over
the ditto marks, and 'per hour.' interlined with a caret
following '2,550']

594.5 East ⟨14th.⟩34th. ['3' written over '1']

594.8 days old. [a fifth of the page is blank below this entry]

594.13 ⟨Stratford Hotel⟩Hotel Stratford [altered by a line indicating transposition]

594.14–16 W. H. . . . Brooklyn [heavily circled]

595.1   ↑1↓ [*written in the top margin of the page*]

595.2   ⟨[9]⅟20⟩½20 ['1' *written over what appears to be* '9'; *see Doubtful Readings*]

595.9   Constantine. [*a quarter of the page is blank below this entry*]

595.19   ↑Dec. . . . Whitmore.↓ [*written lengthwise in the margin of the page beside* 'Dec. 13, '90. . . . affair.' (595.10–16)]

596.3   Dec. ⟨1[8]⟩19 ['9' *written over what may be* '8']

597.1   ↑Dec 22↓ [*written in the margin of the page near the end of the preceding paragraph and beside what was apparently the original position of the newspaper clipping pinned to the page; see note 82*]

597.18   ↑How many notes?↓ [*written diagonally in the available space to the right of the preceding entry and separated from it by a line*]

598.5   this-&-the-that↑ity↓

598.7   ↑1↓

599.8 $4. [*a line originally ending the entry here was canceled and the entry was continued*]

599.14–16   to me⟨.⟩, ↑under certain conditions.↓ S L Clemens [*the period altered to a comma;* 'under . . . conditions.' *interlined without a caret below* 'to me . . . Clemens']

599.17   James W. Paige. [*Paige's signature*]

600.3   ↑17 . . . 51st↓ [*interlined in brownish black ink without a caret between* 'Andrew Carnegie.' (600.2) *and* 'Thos. L. James.' (600.4)]

600.5–6   ↑W. J. Arkell↓ ↑Depew, Vander↓ [*written in purple pencil;* 'W. J. Arkell' *written in the margin of the page beside* 'Alex. Graham Bell.' (600.1); 'Depew, Vander' *interlined without a caret between* 'Bell.' *and* 'Carnegie.' (600.1 *and* 600.2)]

600.7–9   13, ↑½↓ cash . . . on delivery ↑& ½ in ⟨6⟩3 mos.↓; ⟨or⟩ $16, ¼ down & ⟨⟨¼⟩ ⟨↑the rest↓⟩ ⟨↑[¼]↓⟩⟩ in 6, 12 & 18

mos;⟩in 6, ↑&↓ ↑the rest in↓ 12 ↑mos.↓, [*originally* ' . . .
¼ *down &* ¼ *in* 6, 12 & 18 mos;'; *the second* '¼' *canceled,
and* 'the rest' *interlined without a caret above the cancellation;* 'the rest' *canceled, and what may be* '¼' *interlined following that cancellation; then* 'the rest in' *interlined with* 'the' *written over the interlineation that may
be* '¼'; *the intended position of* 'the rest in' *is uncertain;
in the present text, a caret following* '6,' *has been taken
to locate these words as well as the interlined* '&'; 'mos.'
interlined with a caret following '12'; '& 18 mos' *canceled,
and the semicolon apparently altered to a comma; see
Doubtful Readings*]

600.13   4↑½↓^c

600.15   ⟨[48]⟩56 ['56' *written over what may be* '48']

600.20–22   The Courting . . . 1000.) [*written in brownish black ink*]

600.23–601.12   Fresh-Air . . . locomotives [*written in purple pencil*]

601.6   ↑Hall see both↓ [*written diagonally to the right of* 'Tom
                  Donaldson. . . . address' (601.4–5)]

601.7   ⟨operators⟩ ↑force↓

601.13   ↑Saturday . . . o'clock↓ [*crowded into the top margin
                  of the page*]

601.15   seem↑ed↓

601.20   for ⟨to-night⟩ ↑Sunday↓ night ['to-' *canceled;* 'Sunday'
                  interlined]

602.5   (Copy).— [*the dash written above the period, possibly
                  intended to cancel it*]

602.16   him. [*a third of the page is blank below this entry*]

602.17–603.7   (Copy. . . . &c. [*written in brownish black ink*]

603.8   ↑D^r. . . . 19th.↓ [*written in black pencil in the top
                  margin of the page*]

603.9–10   Mary . . . 59th. [*written in brownish black ink*]

603.11   ↑Prest. J. R. Rhoads.↓ [*interlined without a caret above*
                  'Mawr, ⟨offered⟩ to']

603.11–12   ⟨Friday⟩ ↑Monday,↓ . . . ⟨Apl. 10.⟩ ↑March 23.↓

603.13   ↑McClane, Simsbury, 21.↓ [_squeezed in above_ 'Phono-graph . . . N. Eng.' _(604.1)_]

604.1   The Boylston . . . N. Eng. [_written in brownish black ink_]

604.2   Feb. ⟨24⟩20 ['o' _written over_ '4']

604.17   ⟨15⟩10 ['o' _written over_ '5']

604.19   Blue-jay⟨.⟩— [_the dash written over the period_]

605.9–11   "Impressions . . . hotel. [_boxed_]

605.10–11   ↑of a visiting Englishman↓

605.14   boy. [_a fifth of the page is blank below this entry_]

606.1   ⟨↑Sharpener↓⟩ [_interlined without a caret above_ 'Builder.' _and canceled_]

606.4   ↑& retaining↓

606.8   ↑securing impressing.↓ [_written in the top margin of the page_ 'Arabian . . . Becky &c.' _(605.15–606.11); see_ Doubtful Readings]

606.10   ⟨seeks⟩ ↑scans↓

606.12   ↑**X**3↓

606.16   ↑**X**4↓

607.9   says. [_a line originally ending the entry here was disregarded when the entry was continued_]

608.1   ↑the shabby↓

608.2   Link. [_the bottom half of the leaf has been torn out following this word on the recto and_ 'Arm . . . 5|61⟩' _(608.10–11) on the verso_]

608.5–10   ⟨↑4.↓ . . . ↑4.12↓ . . . ↑4.27↓ . . . ↑4.34↓ . . . ↑4.51↓ . . . ↑[4.]56↓⟩ [_apparently added before the bottom half of the leaf was torn out; see 608.2 and_ Emendations]

608.18   ⟨—⟩↑4.27↓ ['4.27' _written above the dash_]

608.19   ⟨—⟩↑4.34↓ ['4.34' *written above the dash*]

608.20   ↑Drilling . . . ↑4.49↓ . . . <u>4.49</u>↓

608.24–27   ↑Huck . . . to Hare-lip↓ [*written in purple pencil between the widely-spaced lines of* '⟨M. . . . 10⟩' *(608.12–15)*]

608.24   Huck & Hare-Lip. [*boxed*]

609.1–2   ↑Add ⟨German Lesson⟩ ↑Clive↓ ↑at Simsbury &↓ ⟨Gov. Gardiner.⟩ ↑CLIVE.↓↓ [*written lengthwise in the margin beside* '⟨M. . . . 10⟩' *(608.12–15); order of revision uncertain; probably originally* 'Add German Lesson | Gov. Gardiner.'; *'Clive' interlined with a caret following* 'Add'; *'at Simsbury &' interlined above* 'Gov. Gardiner.'; *'CLIVE.' written and boxed following* 'Gardiner.']

609.9   ⟨They⟩Their ['i' *written over* 'y']

609.18   22   "   " 5   " [*followed by about two blank lines*]

609.19   ↑200 . . . cylinder↓ [*written lengthwise in the margin beside the three preceding paragraphs*]

610.1   PAMPHLET PINACOTEK ['Pamphlet Pinacotek' *underlined twice*]

610.4–7   The book . . . Notes. [*Clemens drew two heavy lines in the left margin beside these entries*]

610.4   ⟨⟨[5]⟩2⟩ ↑3↓ ['2' *written over what appears to be* '5', *then canceled*]

610.7   SEE NEXT PAGE ['See next page' *underlined twice*]

610.10   ⟨should⟩would ['w' *written over* 'sh']

610.12   ⟨an asset⟩ ↑a liability↓

611.1   Otto Schlutter. [*followed by about two blank lines*]

611.2–5   under ⟨Section/↑Chapter↓ 44,368 Revised⟩ ↑the↓ Statute⟨s⟩ ↑Extra-hazardous↓ ⟨of the United States, which provide⟨s⟩ for the⟩ "protection [*originally* 'under Section 44,368 Revised Statutes of the United States, which provides for the "protection'; *'Chapter' interlined above*

'Section'; *then the sequence of revision is uncertain, but was possibly as follows: 's' of* 'provides' *canceled,* 'Section/Chapter . . . Revised' *canceled, and* 'the' *interlined; then* 'of the United . . . for the' *canceled (*'of the United . . . provide' *and* 'for the' *may have been canceled separately and not necessarily in that order);* 's' *of* 'Statutes' *canceled;* 'Extra-hazardous' *interlined without a caret above* 'of the United'; *the intended position of* 'Extra-hazardous' *is uncertain*]

611.5   arts." [*the bottom half of the page is blank below this entry*]

611.6   48 Park Ave. N.Y. [*the top half of the leaf has been torn out above these words on the recto and above* 'Readings.' *(611.13) on the verso; a line drawn in purple pencil along the torn edge of the recto probably marked the end of an entry written in purple pencil on the torn-out fragment*]

611.8   ⟨Thursday⟩Wed'sday, Apl. ⟨23.⟩22 ['Wed'' *written over* 'Thur'; '2' *written over* '3.']

611.10   (afternoon. ↑3. p.m.↓) ['3. p.m.' *interlined in brownish black ink with a caret centered below* '(afternoon.)']

611.11–12   Conditions: . . . 5̇. [*written in brownish black ink*]

611.14   Mary. [*a third of the page is blank below this entry*]

611.15   ↑Lev . . . 1.20.↓ [*written in the top margin of the page*]

611.16   SHAVE [*boxed*]

611.17   ⟨12.40⟩10.40 ['0' *written over* '2']

612.4   ⟨[--]⟩should ['sh' *written over two unrecovered letters*]

612.4 $95,000. [*a fifth of the page is blank below this entry*]

612.6–613.11 $10,000. . . . $10,000 . . . $10,000. . . . $5,000. . . . $10,000. [*these amounts are written somewhat more heavily than the entries they follow and are heavily underlined; the amounts, the underlines, or both may have been added later*]

614.7   ⟨is⟩ ↑are↓

616.5	⟨'8⟩'90 ['9' *written over* '8']
616.8	Chatto. [*a third of the page is blank below this entry*]
616.18	↑$50 . . . $1000.↓
617.6	Gen. . . . 71ˢᵗ [*boxed; the bottom half of the page is blank below this entry*]
617.7	↑Metcalf.↓ [*written in brownish black ink in the top margin of the page*]
617.15	↑**X**5↓
618.2–5	From . . . Archipelago." [*written in brownish black ink*]
618.7	↑Annette . . . Lannigan.)↓
618.10	↑DIARY.↓ [*written in the top margin of the page*]
618.14	↑chartered↓
618.24–620.2	"Lay . . . mine." [*written in purple pencil, with the exception of* '**X**6' (619.7) *added in black pencil*]
619.7	↑**X**6↓ [*written in black pencil*]
619.11	↑Phila↓ [*interlined without a caret above* '—Women's']
620.3	⟨THHITT⟩ [*canceled in brownish black ink, probably when the entries that follow were written in the same ink*]
620.4–10	Carry . . . gone. [*written in brownish black ink*]
620.13–14	Collections . . . Apl. '91. [*written in purple pencil*]
620.13	↑$5,500 before.↓ [*the intended position of this phrase is uncertain; interlined without a caret above* '$4,500 in 6 days,']
620.15	Don't . . . July 1. [*written in brownish black ink*]
621.1–15	Stop . . . Holsatia [*written in purple pencil*]
621.16–17	71 days. [*a quarter of the page is blank below this entry*]
622.10	↑**X**7↓
622.15	⟨[- -]⟩40 ['40' *written over two unrecovered figures*]
622.19	↑**X**8↓

623.2	↑*wax*↓
623.6	nearly ⟨↑nearly↓⟩ ['nearly' *interlined above somewhat miswritten* 'nearly'; *then canceled*]
623.13	⟨[$900.]⟩$1000. ['1' *written over what appears to be* '9'; *the final zero appears to be written over a period*]
623.14	↑9**X**↓ [*circled*]
623.20	↑10**X**↓
624.1	↑11**X**↓
624.8	Chic**A**go ['ca' *underlined twice*]
626.3	↑12**X**↓
627.2–3	⟨Spit f[ire]⟩ ↑"Soft Soap"↓ & ↑"↓Hellfire↑"↓, ↑aged 58,↓ ['aged 58,' *interlined with a caret inadvertently placed before the comma following* '"Hellfire"'; *emended*]
628.18	D^r· Burton [*followed by about two lines of blank space*]
629.1	Jo ⟨– – –⟩Lawrence ['Lawrence' *written above a broken line indicating a blank to be filled*]
630.1	Robbery . . . church [*written in brownish black ink; followed by about two lines of blank space*]
630.2	↑**X**13↓
630.2	↑(pets)↓
630.4	↑(↓including . . . ones⟨[)]⟩⟩ [*the closing parenthesis may have been canceled and restored; possibly the opening parenthesis was added when the closing parenthesis was restored*]
630.17	↑**X**14↓
630.21	↑consequence-scorning,↓
631.9	study. [*a fifth of the page is blank below this entry*]
631.13	↑15**X**↓

632.2   thing. [*a quarter of the page is blank below this entry*]

633.4–5   ⟨invest⟩ ⟨↑lend↓⟩ ↑invest↓

633.11   ticket. [*a quarter of the page is blank below this entry*]

633.18   Aquarius the Prohibitionist ['Prohibitionist' *possibly
                 added later in a space originally left blank*]

634.4   ↑Clark↓

634.5   ↑Shipman↓

634.6   ↑Warner↓

634.7   ↑Burton↓

634.9   ↑Perkins↓

634.10   ↑(I.)↓

634.12   ↑Hamersley↓

634.13   ↑**X**16↓

634.17–19   Telegram . . . Clemens [*written in brownish black ink;
                 a fifth of the page is blank below this entry*]

634.20   Hall—1. [*written in the top margin of the page; possibly
                 added later*]

634.24   How MANY ['How many' *underlined twice*]

635.6   ⟨2 copies⟩↑1↓ copy ['y' *written over* 'ie'; '2' *and* 's' *can-
                 celed*]

635.7   ⟨2⟩ ↑one↓

635.10–12   In . . . story. [*written in brownish black ink*]

636.6–8   John . . . days. [*bracketed in both margins of the page*]

636.9   ⟨street⟩Street ['S' *written over* 's']

636.12   ↑Spoke . . . morals.↓

636.14   ⟨that⟩ ↑a so↓ . . . ⟨honesty⟩ ↑morals↓ that'⟨ll⟩
                 ↑they'll↓

637.7   useful ↑only↓

637.19   ↑$8 or $8.50.↓

638.7   ↑Remarks Overheard.↓

638.11   ↑(diagram)↓

638.23   J[es] [*scrawled, and apparently extending off the edge of the page*]

639.6   ↑**X**17↓

640.6   ↑**X**18↓

640.15   on ↑these long↓ deck↑s↓

640.26   &c&c&c [*a fifth of the page is blank below this entry*]

641.1–7   ⟨[--] . . . [---]2⟩ [*this heavily canceled table of letters and numbers was apparently written before the entry* 'June . . . differently?' (641.8–18), *which is indented to fit around the canceled table on the same page*]

641.25   ⟨smoking-cavern⟩smoking-cabin ['cabin' *written following canceled* 'cavern']

642.17   ⟨Any idiot⟩A ↑sour↓ ['ny' *of* 'Any' *canceled;* 'sour' *written above canceled* 'idiot']

642.19   ↑*June . . . sea.*↓

643.22–26   Smith . . . back. [*bracketed in the margin*]

644.10–645.14   Amen . . . whistling. [*written in two columns,* 'Amen . . . embarrassed' (644.10–645.1) *and* '⟨H⟩O. . . . . whistling.' (645.2–14), *separated by a vertical line*]

644.10   ↑Amen!↓

645.2   ⟨H⟩O. ⟨Hostler⟩Ostler. ['O' *written over* 'H' *twice;* 'o' *of* 'Hostler' *canceled*]

645.19   painted. [*the bottom half of the page is blank below this entry*]

645.20   ↑**X**.↓1.

645.25   ↑**X**↓5.

646.2   ↑**X**-↓6.

646.3   ↑**X**↓7.

646.11   ↑**X**↓13.

646.15   ↑**X**↓15.

646.15–16   & | milk-route   horse.   [¶]⟨16.⟩   ↑**X**16↓   Robbing . . .
                 woman [*the exact order of inscription is unclear; '& milk-*
                 route horse.' may have been added; '16.' is written in the
                 left margin beside 'milk-route' *and above* 'Robbing'; *there*
                 is not space for '16.' *in the margin beside* 'Robbing', *and*
                 the number may have been added later; '16.' *may have*
                 been canceled so that it would not appear to refer to
                 'milk-route horse'; '**X**16' *is interlined above* 'woman' *in*
                 the only available space; '**X**' *may have been added later*]

646.17   ↑**X**↓17.

646.18   Batavia. [*the bottom half of the page is blank below this*
                 entry; following this page, ten pages are blank, then a leaf
                 has been torn out, and then five more pages are blank]

646.19–28   350 . . . 194 [*these two calculations on the last page of*
                 the notebook were apparently written, perhaps at differ-
                 ent times, before Clemens wrote 'World, 8 non . . .
                 48,400 World' *(647.3–21) on the same page;* 'Col—'
                 (647.15) is written across '350' *(646.19)*]

647.3   non ⟨ems⟩ ↑lines↓ . . . 200 ⟨lines⟩ ↑ems;↓

647.6   Herald, ⟨7⟩6 non   ″   ″   [*the first pair of ditto marks*
                 stands for 'lines', *which is interlined at 647.3 above can-*
                 celed 'ems'; *Clemens may have written the ditto marks*
                 before he canceled 'ems' *and added* 'lines']

647.6   ⟨189⟩162 ['62' *written over* '89']

647.6   World (11 ems) wider. ['World' *and* 'wider.' *possibly*
                 written later; 'World' *written above and* 'wider.' *below*
                 '(11 ems)']

647.18   ⟨[-]⟩25 ['2' *appears to be written over an unrecovered*
                 number]

Index

Webster's Biographical Dictionary is normally the authority for forms and spellings of names of prominent people. Contemporary newspapers, periodicals, and scholarly publications which appear merely as citations are not listed. Mark Twain's writings are indexed by title. Works by other authors are indexed by author and also, when necessary, by title. Letters by Mark Twain quoted in the footnotes are listed by recipient under Samuel Langhorne Clemens.

The text of this book is set in Illumna, a typeface adapted by the Harris Intertype Corporation for photocomposition from the Electra font designed by W. A. Dwiggins (1880–1956) for the Mergenthaler Linotype Company and first made available in 1935. Headings are set in Elegante, an adaptation of Palatino, and in Michelangelo. Palatino and Michelangelo are display faces designed by Hermann Zapf for Stempel Type Founders in 1950. The paper is P & S offset laid regular, an acid-free paper of assured longevity manufactured by P. H. Glatfelter Company, Spring Grove, Pennsylvania.

The book was composed by Typothetae Inc., Palo Alto, California, on the Harris Fototronic 4000. It was printed by Publisher's Press, Salt Lake City, Utah, and bound by Mountain States Bindery, Salt Lake City, Utah.